An Examin...

Edwi...

Copyright © 2012 Edwin A. Suominen

ISBN: 978-0-9851362-2-2

This work is licensed under the Creative Commons Attribution-NonCommercial-NoDerivs 3.0 Unported License. To view a copy of this license, visit **http://creativecommons.org/licenses/by-nc-nd/3.0/** or send a letter to Creative Commons, 444 Castro Street, Suite 900, Mountain View, California, 94041, USA.

Briefly, you may copy and distribute this ebook for non-commercial purposes, provided the book remains in its complete original form. You must attribute the author, but not in any way that suggests that he endorses you or your use of the work. You may not use this work for commercial purposes, nor alter, transform, or build upon this work, except that the author hereby waives the "no rights to make Adaptations" restriction of the license for the following adaptations: (1) an excerpt of the cover image by itself, unmodified in appearance; (2) one or more excerpts of the entire text found under each numbered heading, so long as the formatting (links, italics, etc.) and any accompanying footnotes are preserved; and (3) a faithful translation into a different language. In any case, a reference must be made to a source for the original, unmodified ebook. Of course, this author both relies upon and respects Fair Use in U.S. copyright law, and nothing in this license should be construed as infringing on your right to such use, including making appropriate quotations.

This book is being distributed for nonprofit educational purposes. Any net revenues from sales of non-free copies will be donated to **The Innocence Project** <http://www.innocenceproject.org/>, "a national litigation and public policy organization dedicated to exonerating wrongfully convicted individuals through DNA testing and reforming the criminal justice system to prevent future injustice."

Scripture references indicated by "NASB" taken from the NEW AMERICAN STANDARD BIBLE®, Copyright © 1960, 1962, 1963, 1968, 1971, 1972, 1973, 1975, 1977, and 1995 by The Lockman Foundation. Used by permission.

This book quotes extensively from sermons and publications of the OALC, SRK, AALC, and LLC under the Fair Use provisions of 17 U.S.C. §107: (1) "the purpose and character of the use" is not of a commercial nature; (2) the "nature of the copyrighted work" being quoted was public awareness of doctrinal positions rather than for profit; (3) "the amount and substantiality of the portion used" is fragmentary and extremely small "in relation to the copyrighted work as a whole"; and (4) "the effect of the use" will have no impact "upon the potential market for or value of the copyrighted work."

Cover design by Carol Selby Price. Thanks to Antti Kaunisto, Antti Samuli Kinnunen, Emerson Beishline, Maunu Holma, Mauri Kinnunen, Mikko Alasaarela, and some anonymous correspondents for translation assistance, and numerous other friends and correspondents inside and outside of Conservative Laestadianism for their insights, information, and inspiration. Special thanks to Robert M. Price–friend, counselor, and scholar extraordinaire.

AN EXAMINATION OF THE PEARL

To Sheila,

With all my love and admiration,

In prosperity and adversity alike.

An Examination of the Pearl

Table of Contents

1 Introduction..3
   1.1 Examination...8
      Uneasy in Eden...8
      Eating of the Tree of Knowledge..10
      Research...12
   1.2 Disputation...14
      The June 2010 Edition..14
      Alienation..16
      Off With the Muzzle...18
   1.3 Publication...19
      Whose Voice is the Chorus?...19
      Layout...20
      Language..22
      Sources...26
      An Appeal to Readers (and Non-Readers).........................27
2 Foreword to the June 2010 Edition 29
3 Introduction to the June 2010 Edition 33
4 Conservative Laestadianism 37
   4.1 Spiritual Heritage..37
      4.1.1 Luther 39
      4.1.2 Laestadius 41
      4.1.3 Raattamaa and His Contemporaries 45
      4.1.4 The Keys and Conversions 46
         Laestadius 46
         Raattamaa 48
         Other Early Conversions 50
         The Discovery of the Keys 51
      4.1.5 Mysticism..53
      4.1.6 Schisms..58

- The OALC 60
- The New Awakening 67
- The Apostolic Lutheran Federation 68
- The FALC 71
- The IALC..75

4.2 The Kingdom of God..79
4.2.1 The One True Church...79
- Development 80
- Implications 84
- Biblical Justification 87
- No Compromises 91

4.2.2 Which "True Church"?...93
- The Christian Convention Church 95
- The Churches of Christ 96
- The New Apostolic Church 97
- More Than Conquerors Faith Church 99

4.2.3 Inside vs. Outside..101
- Separation from the World 101
- Persecution Complex 107
- Caricature and Blame 109
- "Narrow-Minded" 113
- Outreach 114

4.2.4 The Call to the Kingdom 119
4.2.5 Conversion...128
- The Proclamation of Absolution 131
- Personal Experiences 134

4.2.6 Obedience and Humility 138
4.2.7 Servants of the Word 146

4.3 The Bible..151
4.3.1 Creation and the Fall of Man 151
- Adam and Eve 154
- Conflicts with Science 161

Evolving Doctrine	171
4.3.2 Noah and the Ark	173
4.3.3 The Old Testament	181
Atrocities	181
Ancient Israelite Laestadianism	184
Prophecy	189
The "Wilderness Journey"	192
Continuity with the New Testament	193
4.3.4 Inerrancy	195
4.3.5 Hermeneutics	203
Textual Issues	204
Allegory and Symbolism	207
4.3.6 Value and Limits	213
4.4 Spiritual Entities	218
4.4.1 The Father	218
Omnipotence	220
Omniscience	222
Unchanging and Eternal	224
Omnibenevolence	225
Hidden	229
4.4.2 The Son	231
4.4.3 The Holy Ghost	240
4.4.4 The Mother	243
4.4.5 Angels	250
4.4.6 The Enemy of Souls	252
4.4.7 False Spirits	258
4.5 Justification	261
4.5.1 The Law	262
4.5.2 Works	269
4.5.3 Faith	274
4.5.4 Reason	285
4.5.5 Doubt	291

4.6 Sin 299
   4.6.1 Specifics 299
      Primary Motives 301
      Authoritarianism 303
      Asceticism 306
      Appearance 309
      Entertainment 311
      Reading 317
      Sports 319
      Sex 320
      Intoxication 321
      Sins of the Right 324
      Sins Unto Death 328
      Thoughts and Words 330
      Life and Death 333
   4.6.2 Forgiveness of Sins 335
      The Proclamation of Personal Absolution 335
      The Sole Means of Grace 339
      Regular Usage 340
      From Faith to Faith 342
      Public Proclamations 346
      Getting it in Writing 351
   4.6.3 Confession 352
   4.6.4 Rebuke 362
4.7 The Life of a Believer 372
   4.7.1 Joys and Sorrows 372
   4.7.2 Prayer 381
   4.7.3 Sacraments 386
      The Lord's Supper 386
      Baptism 393
   4.7.4 Marriage 398
      Divorce 398

    Intermarriage 400
    Courtship..402
4.7.5 Children...403
    Contraception 403
    Christian Upbringing 410
4.7.6 Women..413
    Women's "God-given Lot" 413
    Role in the Church 417
    Obligatory Motherhood 420
    Human Rights Concerns 423
4.8 Time..428
    4.8.1 Unchanging Faith..428
    4.8.2 Eschatology 432
    4.8.3 Eternity..437
4.9 The Problem of Evil 443
    4.9.1 An Ancient Dilemma..443
    4.9.2 Soteriology 444
    4.9.3 Predestination...447
        Which is it? 449
        The Calvinist View 451
        Flirting with Free Will 453
    4.9.4 Human Suffering...456
4.10 Taking Responsibility..462
    4.10.1 Child Sexual Abuse...463
        The Whistleblower 464
        Out in the Open 466
        Fallout 468
        LLC Editorial 469
        Doctrinal Issues 473
    4.10.2 Rethinking the 1970s...475
5 Martin Luther 483

- 5.1 Predecessors 483
  - 5.1.1 Luther's View 485
  - 5.1.2 Problems 487
    - Absent Absolution 489
    - What They Said (and Didn't Say) 491
    - Confession 495
    - Rigorism 499
    - Duplicating the Keys 502
    - Hiddenness Again 505
- 5.2 The Church 506
- 5.3 Zwingli and the Real Presence 514
- 5.4 Conversion and The Forgiveness of Sins 515
  - 5.4.1 Voice of Zion Article 516
  - 5.4.2 Historical Context 518
  - 5.4.3 Shared Doctrine and Significance 522
  - 5.4.4 Thorns in the Rose Bed 527
  - 5.4.5 Lay Absolution 531
  - 5.4.6 Luther's Conversion 533

6 The Old Testament 537
- 6.1 Genesis 537
- 6.2 Exodus 542
- 6.3 Leviticus 545
- 6.4 Numbers 548
- 6.5 Deuteronomy 550
- 6.6 Joshua 552
- 6.7 Judges 555
- 6.8 First Samuel 556
- 6.9 Second Samuel 559
- 6.10 First Kings 562
- 6.11 Second Kings 563

- 6.12 First Chronicles..564
- 6.13 Second Chronicles...565
- 6.14 Ezra..566
- 6.15 Nehemiah..566
- 6.16 Esther..567
- 6.17 Job...567
- 6.18 Psalms...570
- 6.19 Proverbs..577
- 6.20 Ecclesiastes...578
- 6.21 Isaiah...580
- 6.22 Jeremiah..589
- 6.23 Lamentations..591
- 6.24 Ezekiel..591
- 6.25 Daniel..603
- 6.26 Hosea...605
- 6.27 Joel..607
- 6.28 Amos...607
- 6.29 Jonah...608
- 6.30 Micah..609
- 6.31 Nahum...611
- 6.32 Habakkuk..611
- 6.33 Zephaniah...611
- 6.34 Zechariah..612
- 6.35 Malachi...614
- 7 The New Testament 617
  - 7.1 The Gospels..617
  - 7.2 Acts..639
  - 7.3 Romans..641
  - 7.4 First Epistle to the Corinthians..644

7.5 Galatians 647
7.6 Colossians 649
7.7 Hebrews 650
7.8 First Epistle of John 651
7.9 Revelation 651
8 Epilogue 655
    No Cheating 655
    Pre-Publication Correspondence 656
    Conclusion 657
References 665
Index 681

There are many mistakes in your historical and theological knowledge—in fact, I think most of your quotes quite naive and one-sided. I think that is caused by a narrow sample of material. In many cases it can clearly be seen, that you don't know the theme very well, only superficially, and therefore you have made mistakes and misinterpretations—in some cases I think not understood the core of the question at all. Some of your observations may be correct in America, I don't know, but definitely not in Finland. For example, the question of evolution is such. It is also one of the themes where I think you haven't understood, which is the core of the question.

The content of your book is so wide and mistakes so many, that it would require much more time to discuss them in detail. In addition to that, I am not an expert of all those themes either. I know some of them, but not any of them very well. Still I can notice clear mistakes in your text. In many cases your supposed criticism of the conservative laestadianism is in fact a criticism of the Christian faith itself. It is evident that you don't know the Church history and the tradition of the Christian doctrine. Had I more time, it would be interesting to discuss more of the details with you.

Anyway, I think the biggest problem with your examination is that you don't understand that the Bible is not a book of natural sciences nor history—and definitely not can be taken as such. It is a book of faith, and for me its evident mistakes in scientific and historical respects don't diminish its worth as such.

—SRK pastor, Feb. 2012

God's children have no need to debate and to argue. We are at peace. We have our sins forgiven. Like the disciples said, "Lord, where [sic.] else would we go? For thou has the words of everlasting life." We don't need to debate.

—LLC pastor, Oct. 2012

1 Introduction

The kingdom of heaven is like unto a merchant man, seeking goodly pearls: Who, when he had found one pearl of great price, went and sold all that he had, and bought it.

—*The Gospel According to Matthew*

There must be the ability to encounter facts with openness and honesty, even when the facts are not pleasing to us.

—SRK, Päivämies *article concerning the 1970s*

There is a distinct sectarian group, primarily located in a single small country, that claims to be the only true Christian Church. It is only through this church "that man can receive redemption and the forgiveness of sins," as one writing from the group puts it, and Jesus invites man to enter his fold in order to be saved. According to God's plan of salvation, one must believe not just in Christ, but also in his church–they are inseparable. Others "say that to believe alone in Christ is enough to gain salvation," the group notes, but it claims they are wrong about that.

This group asserts that one must be given understanding, which only comes through those whom God has sent. It criticizes "false preachers" of our times who all say they are of God but have diverse and conflicting religious views, whom it claims simply do not have the God-given authority to preach the true gospel. It teaches, in the words of one outside commentator, "simple and straightforward religious principles, which together provide a secure and compelling spiritual anchor for the faithful." The members value these components of faith and righteous behavior as embodying eternal scriptural truths.

It originated from the revelation and work of a single founder, who reached what the outsider commenter called "a pivotal point in his personal religious odyssey." After that distinct event, which occurred well before the birth of even the oldest current members of the group, the founder began evangelism among the indigenous people of his isolated land and quickly gained converts. The group believes that its founder "was guided by the Holy Spirit," and that the same Spirit now guides its ministers in preaching the gospel. Many years after his death, the group remains profoundly influenced by the founder's theological ideas.

The group interprets the way that a single isolated Old Testament passage mentions one of the points on the compass to justify its claim that, during "these last days," the true church is now located (for the most part) in a distinct location thousands of miles away from ancient Israel. Fairly early in its history, however, members of the group emigrated to America and, with guidance from the leadership back home, established congregations there. Now there are numerous American congregations. But the movement has not attracted substantial interest outside the original ethnic group from the old country. The American adherents still represent only a fraction of the total membership.

One critic on the Internet claims that members "are not allowed to think for themselves when it comes to interpretation of the Bible," and disagreements are not tolerated. Ultimately, those who are in opposition to the church's teachings will be cast out and told that they are headed for hell. There is tremendous intimidation to stay in the church, he says, especially for "those who are second, third, and fourth generation," who are "convinced they are in the true Church." In the group's own words, what it offers is "encouragement" to the faithful to not allow anybody to destroy their faith: "Resist the devil and his tricks (many of them are on the Internet)." Writings from the group emphasize unity and make clear that submission and obedience are expected.

There are strict lifestyle rules against drinking, drug use, gambling in any form, adulterous relationships, foul language, and performing (again quoting the group's writings) "the kind of dances popularized in the world, characterized by provocative and sensuous behavior." Even "joining organizations or labor unions whose principles are in conflict with Bible teachings" is to be avoided. Members, to quote the outside commenter again, "cannot marry outside the faith and they are advised to live modestly as law-abiding citizens in a secular world. Recalcitrant individuals commonly endure shunning or even expulsion."

Those within Conservative Laestadianism will readily recognize this as a description of their exclusivist group of 100,000 or so in Finland (the *Suomen Rauhanyhdistysten Keskusyhdistys* or **SRK** <http://srk.fi>) with an associated *Laestadian Lutheran Church* (**LLC** <http://llchurch.org>) in North

America having another 7,000 or so adherents that are almost all descendants of Finnish immigrants. It fits completely, from the historical background to the statements by outside critics. But many believers will be surprised to learn that the description is actually of the *Iglesia ni Cristo*, a church based in the Philippines that condemns everybody outside what it has designated itself, the "Church of Christ."[1]

I doubt if many Conservative Laestadians reading this will be overly troubled by the knowledge that they are considered destined for hell by a group of some 5,000,000 Filipinos. But why not? Does it just seem too ridiculous to contemplate that God would condemn *you* for being outside a group you've never heard of until now, made up of people from a very different culture, none of whom you'll probably ever have a

---

1. Here are the supporting references with the same paragraph layout as the description itself:

"Certain that the Iglesia ni Cristo is the only 'true' Christian church, the ministers and members work in concert to implement a far-reaching programme of evangelism that has no national bounds" (Reed 2001, 564). "Salvation was promised by the Lord Jesus Christ to His Church–the Church of Christ . . . It is only through His dear Church that man can receive redemption and the forgiveness of sins . . . This explains why He invites people to enter His fold or join His Church to be saved" (Pasugo, 1/1997). "He who has faith and believes in our Lord Jesus Christ, must also believe in the existence of the Church of Christ"; "In God's scheme of salvation, Christ and the Church of Christ are inseparable" (Pasugo, 9/1988). "Do not let others deceive you when they say that to believe alone in Christ is enough to gain salvation" (**Manual for New Members** <http://incworld.faithweb.com/info.htm>).

"Without being given understanding or revelation, one can never know the mystery of God's words and can never come to know the truth"; "Those sent by God–His inspired messengers–of the ones exclusively given the understanding of His words: they speak God's words" (Pasugo, 10/1995). "In our times, we witness the burgeoning of preachers or evangelists professing that they are of God despite their diverse and conflicting religious views and precepts. Whether or not they are aware of it, these false preachers have to face the fact that they have no divine authority to preach the true gospel" (Pasugo, 10/1998). "Scholars interested in the Iglesia ni Cristo agree that its binding creed is an amalgam of simple and straightforward religious principles, which together provide a secure and compelling spiritual anchor for the faithful. Although these components of faith and righteous behavior are unequivocally dogmatic, and abhorrent to many Catholics and Protestants, the Church membership is convinced that they embody eternal scriptural truths" (Reed 2001, 574).

chance to meet? Surely it can't be their limited reach that allows you to so casually dismiss their claims–there are about fifty times more of them than there are Conservative Laestadians, after all. Is it their humble origins with a single founder? Their assertion that the Holy Spirit is now found only among the people of (almost entirely) a single ethnic group largely unknown in your culture or anybody else's? Or is it their obviously fabricated interpretation of an Old Testament passage to support the idea that God would conclude his salvation work with *them* of all people? Your ho-hum reaction to all of these aspects of *Iglesia ni*

"Felix Manalo reached a pivotal point in his personal religious odyssey during November 1913. . . . [H]e embarked on a programme of evening evangelism in Punta, Santa Ana (Manila), thereby launching the Iglesia ni Cristo. Within several months, Manalo had attracted a dozen people to his new indigenous Church . . . [B]y year's end it embraced around 100 converts" (Reed 2001, 568). "[W]ho are the capable guides/preachers of the Bible? The messengers of God because they are guided by the Holy Spirit. The Holy Spirit that guided the biblical writers is the same Holy Spirit that guides the true preachers . . . This is the primary reason why the Iglesia Ni Cristo consistently upholds the authority of Bro. Felix Manalo in preaching the pristine gospel since as a messenger of God, he was guided by the Holy Spirit . . . The same Holy Spirit is guiding now the ministers of the Iglesia Ni Cristo in preaching the gospel truth throughout the world" (**Introduction to the Iglesia Ni Cristo Part II** <http://incworld.faithweb.com/intro2.htm>). "Even today, some 37 years after the death of its prophet and organizational mastermind, the Iglesia ni Cristo remains profoundly influenced by the theological ideas and managerial legacy of Felix Y. Manalo" (Reed 2001, 565).

"The Church of Christ that appeared from the Philippines (in the Far East) during these last days is the fulfillment of the prophecies made by God and Christ. This is the third part of the Church founded by Christ. It arose in these last days after the Church built by Christ in the first century was completely led astray by the false prophets. This Church's later extension into the Far West is equally the realization of God's prophecies in the Bible" (**Manual for New Members** <http://incworld.faithweb.com/info.htm>). "The third group of people unto whom also is the promise of the Holy Ghost are those that God will bring from the Far East, whom He calls 'my sons' and 'my daughters' [Isa 43:5-6]" (Pasugo, 11/1995). Emigration to America: Reed 2001, 583-85. "Iglesia is not better known, despite its numbers, because the majority of Iglesia's members are Filipino. Virtually the only exceptions are a few non-Filipinos who have married into Iglesia families" (Anonymous commenter on **aboutiglesianicristo.blogspot.com**).

"Members of the Iglesia Ni Cristo, unlike the rest of us Filipinos, are not allowed to think for themselves when it comes to interpretation of the Bible. They must submit to the official interpretation of Scripture from the Central Administration

Cristo are exactly the reactions that most everybody outside Conservative Laestadianism (i.e., 99.998% of the people on this planet right now) has to the *very same aspects* of your own exclusivist group.

It is from the perspective of those outsiders that this book is presented. Such a viewpoint is far different from the simplistic, comforting reverence of the devotional writings provided by the church itself. And, depending on how much you have allowed yourself (or been allowed) to consider anything else, that might make the book quite a bracing read, with many more surprises and challenges ahead that may well be uncomfortable for you to encounter. But taking that objective stance–what John Loftus presents as *the outsider test for religious faith*–is the only honest way to evaluate any religion. The result of the test is that "the

---

of the Iglesia Ni Cristo. If any member disagrees with the interpretation of the Scriptures as taught by the Central Administration of the Iglesia Ni Cristo, they are cast out and told they are damned into the flames of hell"; "The force by which members of INC are intimidated to stay in the membership is tremendous, especially those who are second, third, and fourth generation. By now they are brainwashed in the cult's teachings and convinced they are in the true Church of Christ"
(**What about the INC Church** <http://jesus-messiah.com/html/is-jesus-god.html>). "A word of encouragement for the faithful brethren throughout the world who stood firm in their calling and election, let us continue the good work. Let us not allow anybody to destroy our genuine faith. Resist the devil and his tricks (many of them are on the Internet)"
(**Introduction to the Iglesia Ni Cristo Part II** <http://incworld.faithweb.com/intro2.htm>).
Unity valued, submission expected: see *Pasugo* quotes from **Salvation? By what way** <http://www.letusreason.org/Iglesia6.htm> Let Us Reason Ministries.
"If you used to get drunk or you used to drink liquor or take drugs, you must refrain from any of these acts now. God forbids them. If you used to gamble, you must know that all forms of gambling are prohibited in the Church of Christ, like: racing, lotteries, card or dice games, slot machines, etc. If you are involved in an adulterous relationship, you should stop this right away. God forbids adultery. If you are employed in a dishonest occupation, committing fraud or any illegal acts, this is not allowed. We should live decently and righteously. You must cease from any vice or sin in your life. Refrain from swearing or using foul language and do not perform the kind of dances popularized in the world, characterized by provocative and sensuous behavior"; "You are also commanded to avoid joining organizations or labor unions whose principles run in conflict with Bible teachings" (**Manual for New Members** <http://incworld.faithweb.com/info.htm>). Members "cannot marry . . . endure shunning or even expulsion" (Reed 2001, 575).

presumption of skepticism" becomes "the preferred stance when approaching any religious faith, especially one's own." It is "simply a challenge to test one's own religious faith with the presumption of skepticism, as an outsider. Test your beliefs as if you were an outsider to your faith" (2008, loc. 1052-54).

The remainder of this section tells the story of my personal struggle with Conservative Laestadian Christianity, why I wrote the book, how I wrote it, and things to keep in mind as you read it. If you want to get right to my examination of this pearl that Conservative Laestadianism puts on offer as the Kingdom of God, you can skip to **Section 4**. If there are specific issues you're wondering about, there is an extensive **Index** with over 1300 entries that you can consult. Those readers whose interest is more geared toward Christianity in general might want to begin with my discussion of various issues about the Bible in **4.3**, or even jump ahead to the specific discussion of the Old and New Testaments in **Section 6** and **Section 7**, respectively. In any event, I hope you will read the rest of this Introduction to better understand the context of the book, whether you proceed through it now or come back to it later.

1.1 Examination

> *Honest investigation is utterly impossible within the pale of any church, for the reason that if you think the church is right you will not investigate, and if you think it wrong, the church will investigate you.*
>
> —Robert G. Ingersoll, *Lecture on Individuality*

Uneasy in Eden

Ever since childhood when I wondered how there could have been no rainbows before Noah's Flood, given the refractive properties of water (**6.1**), I have lived with an uneasy combination of faith and doubt. My lifetime of fascination with science and engineering led to a rewarding professional life, but the problem-solving mental attributes that work well for designing a radio or writing a patent aren't particularly compatible with "childlike faith."

Engineers don't like to leave unsolved problems just laying around. They want to analyze the data, come up with a mathematical model or design that integrates the data in some sensible fashion, and produce a solution. I knew about only a few "unsolved problems" with Conservative Laestadianism for most of my life, and fewer still with Christianity in general. But they still bothered me, and I yearned for some kind of solution beyond the admonitions to just accept the gift of faith humbly and gratefully, and to regularly obtain forgiveness not just of sins but also of doubts.

Things went along uneasily but steadily for years. There were many moments of frustration and doubt but also joy and fellowship in the church. My family grew and grew until reaching 11 children, not at all an unusual size for Conservative Laestadianism. My work was a source of great fascination, and one day it led me to some research about an intriguing way of optimizing design parameters without the engineer having to explicitly specify those parameters: genetic algorithms.

This was amazing stuff! In computer software, you set up an artificial chromosome with each "gene" determining a design parameter. Then you run a simulation of your widget a few hundred different times, with different sets of parameters specified by random numbers in the genes of each chromosome. Each simulation produces a "fitness" metric, a value that shows how well the widget works in its simulated environment with the particular "DNA" that it was randomly assigned as a starting point.

Then the fun starts: The widgets mate with each other, crossing over their chromosomes just like parents do in real life. Each widget in the next generation has a randomly shuffled combination of the genes from two widgets in the first population, plus a few mutations sprinkled in. Things are set up so that only the "fittest" widgets from the first generation are likely to be parents of those in the next.

The result: evolution by a simulated form of natural selection. I had been raised believing that Adam and Eve were my ancestors and Darwin was of the devil, but now Darwin had come to my computer. What was happening on the screen before my eyes not only worked, but made a lot of sense. I could understand exactly what was happening, because it was computer code, and pretty simple code at that.

I decided that I should learn a little bit about this evolution business to help give me some perspective about how to use this new engineering tool. Not only that, but I found it fascinating. Could there really be something to this, after all? I started cautiously reading, initially feeling guilt and anxiety about leafing through evolution books as if I were over at the rack of porn magazines instead of the Natural Sciences section of the bookstore. But read I did, and after a few hundred hours of study, I came to the conclusion that evolution was true and Genesis 1-2 were not (**4.3.1, 6.1**). It was not an easy or welcome discovery for a fundamentalist Christian to make.

Eating of the Tree of Knowledge

The acceptance of evolution put me at odds with most of my fellow believers and everything I could recall the LLC ever saying about creation and original sin. I thought and thought, and could not stop thinking about the problem. Most every sermon and issue of the LLC's *Voice of Zion* monthly newspaper seemed to talk about Adam and Eve and how their transgression was the reason why Jesus had been sent as a sacrifice for "sin-fallen mankind." Yet what I had finally, reluctantly accepted as indisputable truth–that I am not the descendant of any first human pair but the product of millions of years of primate evolution–didn't match up with that story. How could I avoid the awful conclusion that Christianity–my troublesome but beloved Conservative Laestadian Christianity–was based on a false premise?

Soon a tragic and shocking death occurred before my eyes, which made the reality of my own mortality all too apparent. As a result, I was able to put my concerns back on the shelf for a while. But they didn't stay there more than a few months. When they intruded again, I was seized by the separate and conflicting drives to learn the truth about my religion and also to salvage my faith in it. I listened to podcasts about religion, including a very entertaining and informative one called **The Bible Geek** <http://www.robertmprice.mindvendor.com/biblegeek.php> by Robert M. Price. I started reading voraciously about the Bible and Christian history, which had always been interests of mine anyhow. (About 15 years ago I learned German for the express purpose of reading Luther in his own language.) Now I was learning with the blinders off, daring to ask the difficult questions not just about evolution but also about the Bible, the foundations of Christian doctrine, and the history of my own Conservative Laestadianism.

1 Introduction

What Luther called "the whore of reason" had been living in my head and fighting with my believing heart for a long time, fuming and grumbling under her closeted second-rate existence, as I put it in my Introduction to the June 2010 edition of this book. But at that point, her cries of resistance became almost intolerably shrill. Yet she, or some vaguely defined opposing faculty in my "heart" remained terrified of the horrific consequences that could accompany open rebellion. It was an unbearable situation, and I was receiving nothing but unsatisfying non-answers to my questions from my LLC brethren. Finally, I contacted Dr. Price and asked if he could act as a sort of theological therapist, a reasonable and sympathetic partner for intelligent discussion of these vexing issues. He graciously agreed, and I decided that the best way to proceed would be to write an email to him summarizing just what it is that I am expected to believe in this obscure little movement, which of course he had never heard of.

What began as a summary quickly turned into another full-blown research project. I had the time to spare, and my desk was soon covered by stacks of *Voice of Zion* issues and books from the LLC and its predecessors, their pages festooned with tabs that marked particular statements on a wide variety of topics. A love of things old and arcane was also expressing itself in some work I did transferring recordings of decades-old sermons from reel-to-reel tape to digital format. In the process I came across a few interesting statements that I transcribed into written quotes. Mapping out the many points of doctrine, which collectively form what is supposed to be a simple, childlike faith, was confirming my longtime suspicions that things weren't nearly so simple. There was some satisfaction in that even as absurdities and inconsistencies became more apparent and filled me with dread.

Finally, after compiling many pages of quotes from the pages I had flagged and recorded statements I had transcribed, I sent my "summary" (whose length had reached over a hundred pages) to Dr. Price. Perhaps I wasn't clear enough with him about my goal to find some way of remaining in the church, despite my nagging concerns, because within a few days he responded with his observation that

> it appears as if you are trapped (simply by irrational, childish, wakeup-in-the-night fear of going to hell) in an introverted, brain-dead cult whose tenets fundamentally contradict one another. It stresses, in Lutheran fashion, the finished work of the

> atonement yet makes everything depend upon the shifting mists of pious feeling. It claims salvation is by faith but adds onto it a degrading ritual of self-criticism and absolution (what a control mechanism!). It celebrates charismatic phenomena yet forbids them. It cultivates a sheltered plausibility structure in which it is impious to think for oneself or to hold onto one's convictions if the mass cannot affirm them (out of ignorance and fear, I might add). No movies? No TV? No sports? No novels? It's like eighteenth century revivalism, almost like the Amish, certainly like the Plymouth Brethren. I cannot imagine what keeps you desirous of sticking with this cult which is clearly making you suffer. Tillich: "Fundamentalism has demonic aspects in that it splits the conscience of its thoughtful adherents and makes them suppress aspects of the truth of which they are dimly aware." Only in your case, it's not "dimly."

I called up Dr. Price and said, "No, Bob, let me be clear: I want to *stay in* this church, not leave it. It means a lot to me, and I'd like to find a way to make it work somehow." He agreed to explore things with me, and we had some great discussions. With one doctorate in systematic theology and another in the New Testament, Price has tremendous respect and sympathy for religion (despite not adhering to any belief in God himself), and he offered many words of encouragement.

Research

Since pat answers were not doing the job for me anymore (and Dr. Price was certainly not giving any of those), I felt compelled to continue my research. In doing so, I met Carl Kulla, a member of the Apostolic Lutheran Federation (**4.1.6**) who is a historian and, at age 90, a living repository of Laestadian history. He helped broaden my inquiries beyond just what the LLC was saying about itself, to writings by (and about) other Laestadian groups and the movement as a whole.

I quickly expanded my summary with footnotes expressing various concerns about the compiled quotes. I wound up reading over those quotes and footnotes many times, comforting myself with the hope that somehow the issues might be frozen into the printed page and left there. Seeing it all laid out in the cold medium of print helped me to deal with the mental disconnect that I was continuing to experience every Sunday between the beliefs that were expected of me and what I was finding out from my studies.

I also decided to read the Bible–the entire thing starting with Genesis 1:1. After hearing Dr. Price praise the *New American Standard Bible* (NASB) as being the most faithful to the currently available manuscripts, I checked it out and found that it's not just well regarded among Bible scholars, but a highly readable result of careful and conservative scholarship:

> [T]he NASB translation team adhered to the principles of literal translation. This is the most exacting and demanding method of translation, requiring a word-for-word translation that is both accurate and readable. This method follows the word and sentence patterns of the original authors in order to enable the reader to study Scripture in its most literal format and to experience the individual personalities of those who penned the original manuscripts. [**www.lockman.org/nasb**]

The King James Version is a venerable translation that the LLC seems to esteem almost as the Holy Word itself–its website has a *How We Believe* page that begins, "The Holy Bible (KJV) and the Lutheran Confessions . . ." But the KJV is not the most accurate translation by any means, nor particularly understandable by today's reader. With a copy of the NASB in hand, along with the trusty old KJV and a newfound appreciation for a scholarly rather than merely devout approach to the ancient text, I began reading. I spent much of the Summer of 2009 doing so, learning the historical and theological context of each book and even subtexts within each book in an effort to appreciate what the Bible writers *actually meant to say* rather than what pious but ill-informed interpreters would like to have them mean.

All told, I think I've read most of what's been written in English about Laestadianism, most of what the LLC and its North American predecessors have written about themselves, and a fair amount of what's been written by and about the SRK. I've studied (not just read) the entire Bible. I've become intimately familiar with Luther's teachings and understandings. I've gone through the writings of earlier Christians, too, including most that are preserved from the first several centuries as well as some of Augustine's from the fifth.

I've come across expressions of simple, childlike faith, and criticisms of such faith. I've discussed my historical interests and concerns with some wonderful people who share them–in the SRK and LLC, in other branches of the Laestadian movement, and in other faiths or no faith at all. It's been a distressing but fascinating quest.

1.2 Disputation

> *People who are insecure in their religious beliefs may feel the impulse to silence and harass those who disagree with them, because their mere existence arouses the painful dissonance of doubt.*
>
> —Carol Tavris et al., Mistakes Were Made (But Not by Me)

The June 2010 Edition

By June 2010, I had a 200-page book on my hands, with nearly as much of it being footnoted comments as there was of the quotations being commented on. I decided to share the results of my research with a few carefully selected friends in the LLC and SRK. Before doing so, I asked Dr. Price to carefully review the book for consistency and accuracy, especially my comments about the Bible itself. He wrote a glowing foreword to it, which I toned down as much as I could to avoid charges of arrogance, high-mindedness, etc. It captures very well, I think, the motivations behind my research and writing, and is preserved here in the next section, **Foreword to the June 2010 Edition**. As he put so well, I was walking "the lonely, narrow path of great love for [my] faith community and simultaneous, painful alienation from it, because [I] cannot avoid asking the questions that [my] tradition fears." My own anguished introduction also explains those motivations and questions, and is in the next following section, **Introduction to the June 2010 Edition**.

About a dozen people read the June 2010 edition, but many more than that heard about it. And one of the people I shared it with, an elder of my local LLC congregation, was deeply troubled by what he was reading. Although our subsequent phone conversations seemed to go well, his concerns were not just about what I was writing, but about me for writing it. Marlene Winell makes an observation to troubled fundamentalist Christians that may have more truth about the situation than that elder or his fellow critics would care to admit: "In trying to make sense of your doubts and fears, you might try to get help from church leaders, only to find that they don't want to hear you; it triggers their own fears" (Winell 1993, 17).

In retrospect, the elder's reaction should not have been surprising to me. Our values are sacred "when they are so important to those who hold them that the very act of considering them is offensive" (Dennett 2006, 22). The word is *sacred*, not *scared*, though the typological similarity is perhaps telling. Seeing our cherished religion paraded naked before the world can be both frightening and awkward. Our first impulse is to rush in and restore modesty, to drape the faith's exposed beliefs and cultural peculiarities in a cloak of piety and escort it away from the gaping crowd.

In September 2010, the congregation's preachers and board of trustees called me to a meeting to discuss the book. It was stressful, coercive, and emotional–about a dozen somber men sitting around a conference table with one person whose faith and motives were being questioned. "Are you *really* believing? *Are you?*" Beyond some concern about how I could dispute what "God's Word" says regarding Adam and Eve and Noah's Ark, there wasn't much substantive discussion of what the book actually had to say. It was mostly about me for having said it.

They said the book was an expression of my doubts, which would have been best kept to myself or private conversations. (The messenger-shooting extended beyond just me; one board member brought printouts from Price's website, no doubt intending to impugn him as a bad influence.) It could be dangerous if it fell into the wrong hands, they said. It would leave the impression among outsiders that there are differences of opinion in "God's Kingdom." And it is certainly not something that believers should be reading. Indeed, one board member said he personally would not read the book because *he wouldn't be able to do so and still keep his faith*. I don't know whether to applaud his honesty or grimace at the hollowness of his purported faith.

After over two hours of this, the meeting concluded with the understanding that I was to retrieve copies of the book. Some of those present were unhappy about my unwillingness to cave in about Adam and Eve, but one board member (a longtime friend) put out his hands in resignation and said something to the effect of, "It is what it is." All their pressure about Noah's Ark did coerce me into saying, "I guess I can leave it open about the boat," though I can't imagine what I was thinking in saying that. After I did, some of the brothers proceeded to chuckle amongst themselves about aspects of the Noah story. I didn't find that amusing at all: "You sit here telling me I have to believe this story, and then you *laugh* about it? *It's not funny!*"

I went home and told my wife, "You are about to witness the intellectual disintegration of your husband." Then the years of doubt, fear, and frustration–culminating in being muzzled into silence by a church far more interested in rebuke than reality–boiled over. I collapsed into my wife's arms in tears, and went to bed for a fitful night.

A few days later, I called Dr. Price and said, "Well, Bob, I have examined the pearl and found it to be a cheap imitation." He cautioned me not to act rashly, and asked if I still found the preaching of absolution to be of value. I replied that yes, the forgiveness of my sins was the whole reason I went to church, and I didn't feel I could do without it. "So go, then," he said, "And take that." And go I did, sitting through sermon after sermon full of things I knew the preachers were wrong about, just to hear the comforting words of forgiveness. But I could never get over the blatant disregard for the truth that had revealed itself to me that evening. The pearl had a big crack in it, and would never appear whole again.

Alienation

There was a long process of alienation from my LLC brethren, even before the meeting. Even without actually leaving the faith, but merely raising questions about it, I understood what Price meant when he wrote, "When and if born-again Christians discover someone who has actually been where they are and left, it is a terrible threat to their faith" (2006b, 335). As one longtime friend told me, it isn't easy to have someone so close to you questioning the things you have held dear since childhood.

And I have to acknowledge that it wasn't just the discomfort of those friends with my questions that caused tension. Frankly, I think I just wore some of my friendships out. During Sunday afternoon visits with other couples, I would bring up various issues of concern and eagerly grab hold of our friends' sympathetic replies, which were full of support and understanding. Each time someone confessed sharing doubts or concerns with me about one issue or another, it was heartening to learn that I wasn't the only one struggling with my faith. But the relief and sense of solidarity was accompanied by the concern that a person thrashing around in the water alongside me might not be in the best position to pull me back into the boat.

Visits between Conservative Laestadian families are times for having the kids disappear into a boisterous cloud, enjoying a long-standing and strong sense of camaraderie (see **4.2.3**), and chatting about everyday life. Discussing "the way and the journey" is much less about theological questions than comparing notes about what is happening to whom in the church community and commiserating about challenges posed by the shared behavioral norms. I'm sure the questions I continued to raise soon became an unwelcome intrusion into that pattern of things. As was the case with William Bagely in the midst of born-again Christians, my "intense intellectual investigations were not always welcomed by those with whom I fellowshipped. Doubt was considered a sin or a door through which Satan could enter to confuse believers" (2003, 186).

As I learned and questioned more about church history, the Bible, and aspects of science that conflicted with important points of doctrine, the resulting frustrations undoubtedly must have showed, too. My behavior soon became much like what Rachel Held Evans admits to concerning her own difficult days:

> Publicly, I grew obstinate and incorrigible, ready to debate family and friends whose easy confidence baffled and frustrated me and gave me an excuse to be angry at someone besides God. It bothered me that other people weren't bothered. I couldn't understand why no one else was stressed out about the existence of hell or angered by all the suffering in the world. I feigned surprise when my friends got annoyed that I raised such topics at bridal showers and poker games. Wherever I sensed a calm sea, I sought to rock the boat; *I wanted others to share in my storm*. [2010, 113-14, emphasis added]

In the year following the September 2010 meeting, I just lost the energy to continue swimming against the current of the church's clannish, insular social scene (**4.2.3**). I found myself unwilling to engage in any more one-sided efforts toward social contact. In response to my own withdrawal, there was little but silence from most of my old friends.

The difficult thing about silence is that it's hard to interpret. Perhaps my silent friends were all very busy making a living in a bad economy.

Perhaps they felt the best thing to do was let me sort it out on my own. Perhaps they were angry, intimidated, or just plain disinterested. The most disturbing thing to me is how it affected the rest of my family, too. My wife and children were just as disregarded, despite having expressed no questions, no concerns, nothing at all. Finally, some months prior to this writing, the lack of interest *towards us* found itself accompanied by a lack of interest *by us* in the whole LLC social milieu.

There is something quite disturbing to me about conditional friendship. Most of the bonds that seemed so strong turned out to fray pretty quickly. Let the "earnest Christian start questioning the party line, and he will find a pink slip enclosed in the next handshake. He is henceforth a leper," (Price 2006b, 163) and apparently his family is, too.

Off With the Muzzle

Given all of that, with news about troubling responses to child sexual abuse, with various people close to me leaving the faith for reasons against which I had no arguments, I finally decided I was ready to shake off the muzzle and publish what I had learned and observed. Over the past several months leading up to this writing, I have put into print what has been swirling around my head and flagged in the pages of my library of books, more than doubling the size of the June 2010 edition. Given the outraged reaction I encountered to a very limited, private distribution of the book, which consisted mostly of church statements and relatively restrained footnotes about those statements, I have no illusions that this published edition will be well received. As Ken Daniels noted about his own book, "whether I take a gentle or harsh approach, I am sure to elicit criticism. The very act of confronting deeply cherished religious convictions is unforgivable to some, regardless of my tactics" (2010, 13).

So be it. About 18 centuries ago, Clement of Alexandria wrote, "If our faith is such that it is destroyed by force of argument, then let it be destroyed; for it will have been proved that we do not possess the truth" (*Stromata* 6.10.80, from MacDonald and Porter 2000, xv). Is the faith of that board member who refuses to read anything critical about what he supposedly believes really faith *in anything* other than the people around him who are repeating the old slogans? They, too, are ignoring the facts about their "faith," making the whole thing a self-sustaining doctrinal bubble that quivers unsteadily in the air, vulnerable to being poked by the slightest intrusion of fact.

1.3 Publication

> Christian groups are known for banning books and objecting to certain curricula, such as the teaching of evolution. Clearly there is a fear that too much outside information will threaten faith, so it should be controlled. Children grow up thinking that what they have been taught is all there is. If you control the information people receive, you restrict their ability to think.
>
> —Marlene Winell, Leaving the Fold

Whose Voice is the Chorus?

I often treat Conservative Laestadianism as a single system of belief and practice having a single unified standpoint at any given time. I will often say that Conservatives do this or believe that as a group, or did so at some particular point in the movement's history. That unanimity is certainly what I have perceived as the LLC's claimed and desired mode of operation in my own decades of life within it. Neither the LLC nor the SRK seem eager to acknowledge dissent, and they highly prize the idea of unity of the spirit, as attested to by many quotes about the "Kingdom of God" in **4.2.1** and **4.2.3**, the importance of unity in **4.2.6**, and the near-deity of the congregation "Mother" in **4.4.4**.

One correspondent observes that the appeal to unity is made by both individuals and the movement itself in public discussion as a last resort when no actual basis or argument is available to defend particular opinions. According to my correspondent, Conservative Laestadianism has never actually agreed that any stamp of doctrinal approval should be placed on everything written and said in the movement's name. Indeed, we will see in **4.1.6** that the Conservatives differentiated themselves early on from a rival movement that formed around the idea of the "firstborn," which established a strict hierarchical control over its doctrine from a group of exalted elders in Lapland. A consequence of rejecting the doctrine of the firstborn has been a century of aversion to allowing any single or central authority to speak for "God's Kingdom." Despite a succession of strong-willed preachers rising to prominence and sometimes going outside the bounds established by that principle in the last hundred years, it seems to remain in place.

I saw the "no central authority" principle in action myself during an hour-long discussion in 2011 with Matti Taskila, the second highest official of the SRK. I wanted to nail down what the SRK's current official position is on evolution after hearing nothing but ambiguous and contradictory answers. Taskila convinced me that even he really couldn't speak for the organization or even the SRK board on the matter. His statements were heartfelt and sincere admonitions to retain the faith of a child and trust in "God's Word," but seemed no more authoritative than the same statements I've heard time and again from preachers in the local congregation.

What does seem to be acknowledged is that there are differences in thought from one era of Conservative Laestadian history to another. For example, Väinö Havas made statements (many of which are quoted in this book) that were undeniably different from what was being said in the 1960s and 1970s (Palola 2011).

Layout

To capture that change in viewpoints over time, I present my quotes (really excerpts) of church writings and sermons in chronological order within each sub-section unless otherwise indicated. Those excerpts are denoted by a cross symbol ("✝"). Although they are indented like block quotes, they use quotation marks and inline citation format like regular text. For brevity and clarity, they sometimes include my own paraphrases to connect or introduce quoted language. Here's an example, copied from **4.2.1**:

> ✝ Often "members of other churches and groups" ask the question "Why is it then that only here in your church men are saved?" Several Bible passages are quoted in reply: Eph 4:4 ("one body, one spirit," etc.); Gal 1:8 ("though an angel preach any other gospel let him be accursed"); John 10:1 ("he that entereth not by the door into the sheepfold is a thief"); John 10:16 ("one fold and one shepherd") (VOZ, 6/1980).

The connecting language outside the quotation marks helps to concisely present a pretty lengthy original statement about biblical justification for the church's exclusivity doctrine. I trust it does so without detracting from what the original author had in mind.

These excerpts are the result of an effort to make a representative sample of statements from Conservative Laestadian writings and sermons for each of the various topics I came across during my research. Contrary to what critics have said both in the September 2010 board meeting as well as the most recent review by some prominent LLC preachers, the excerpts were emphatically not taken "out of context."

Nor are the excerpts the result of any attempt to find and focus on errors. Of course, I'm only human, and my attempt to fairly sample the myriad documents on my desk (and in my camera) wasn't perfect. When an outrageous statement by Peter Nevala or Heikki Saari catches one's eye, there is an inclination to include it no matter what. But I submit that you will find Nevala's gem about women and henpecked husbands in **4.7.6**, for example, not just because I found it too good to pass up but because *it was the kind of thing that was being written* thirty years ago.

When I felt that I had enough statements to represent the thinking for a particular era of the church's 150 years or so of history, I refrained from flagging any more of them. Similarly, I went to some trouble to find statements from times for which documents weren't so readily available. Carl Kulla's books were helpful in providing statements from the earliest days of the movement, as were Hepokoski's three historical documents. I spent about a day and a half of a vacation to Phoenix with 3-ring binders of old *Greetings of Peace* issues borrowed from the Phoenix LLC congregation, snapping away with my camera to include material from the 1940s through the early 1970s. Of all the accusations one might make against this book, I don't think a lack of thoroughness or fairness in collecting my samples of Conservative statements should be among them.

I also tried to avoid quoting articles or sermons from individuals who departed from Conservative Laestadianism even decades later. For example, I passed over many beautifully written articles in *The Greetings of Peace* by Walter Torola simply because of the possible charge that he was among those (the leader, in fact) who "went out from us, but they were not of us" (1 John 2:19) after the 1973 schism. For all articles quoted from the pre-1973 *Greetings of Peace*, I include the author's name in case others disagree with my selection of sheep versus goats.

Immediately after the 1973 schism, the Conservatives began another publication from which I quote thereafter, *The Voice of Zion*.

The book is divided up into sections under numbered headings and subheadings. Some large sections are further divided up by subheadings without numbering. Within each section (or subsection), the ("☦") church statements are generally presented in the order in which the Conservative authors and preachers wrote or said them.

I tried to relate topics in adjacent sections, but sometimes it may seem that they are just jammed together. For example, the sacraments (**4.7.3**) of Communion and baptism may not seem particularly related to marriage (**4.7.4**) and children (**4.7.5**). But they are all part of the "life of a believer" (**4.7**), and there seemed no better way to group them.

In some sections there may seem to be a tiresome redundancy of quotes. That again is simply a product of my effort to arrive at a fair sample of Conservative Laestadian statements. The movement emphasizes some topics far more than others, and I wanted to give a flavor of that variation in emphasis rather than just conveying what has ever been said about each topic. Also, the repetition serves to show subtle differences where they exist, and unanimity of thought where it exists.

The discussion of Luther (**Section 5**) and the Old (**Section 6**) and New Testaments (**Section 7**) designates new sub-topics with each section or subsection with a leading bullet point ("•"). My hope is that the bullets make it easier to see continuity within each sub-topic without going overboard with the subheadings.

The extensive **Index** may be helpful in cases where a topic of interest is not readily located within a particular section. It also reveals the level of emphasis on various topics, and just how detailed the various theological nuances are for certain issues.

Language

Referring to Conservative Laestadians by the third-person pronoun ("they," "them," etc.) is something I avoid because doing so implies that I am not one of "them." I've heard quite enough "us versus them" talk in my decades within the church, and do not intend to contribute to it any further. Despite finding many of its claims indefensible, I have been very hesitant to come out and repudiate my childhood faith.

I believe in a God who started everything with the Big Bang, who is the reason that there is something rather than nothing. But the seemingly endless problems with both the Bible and the opinions of its Conservative interpreters (including their naïve viewpoint that the Bible *has* no problems) leave me wondering what to think beyond that. My affection for this odd little sect persists, though, despite a diminished ability to tolerate the rants of its ill-informed preachers. This book is not the result of caring too little about the faith of my childhood, but sadly, of caring too much.

It may offend some people to see Conservative Laestadianism referred to as an "odd little sect." But that's what it is: undeniably "odd" in so many respects; "little" to an extreme, with its total membership (including children) that amounts to less than 0.002% of the world's present population; and a "sect" according to all four definitions of the term provided by **Dictionary.com**.

Nobody would have an issue with Conservative Laestadianism being a body of people "adhering to a particular religious faith," of course. The second definition of "sect" is "a group regarded as heretical or as deviating from a generally accepted religious tradition," and that may be more controversial. But that's actually what happened both with Luther *deviating from* medieval Catholicism, and Laestadius *deviating from* the Lutheranism of Sweden. The OALC would even argue that Heideman deviated from Laestadianism, as we will see in **4.1.6**. Indeed, Laestadius's successor Raattamaa (whom the Conservatives claim as one of their own, along with A.L. Heideman) criticized Heideman's followers as departing from the "firstborn" Laestadians and following "the dictates of a newborn sect" (Palola 2000, 50).

It also seems indisputable that Conservative Laestadianism meets Dictionary.com's third definition: It is certainly "a Christian denomination characterized by insistence on strict qualifications for membership, as distinguished from the more inclusive groups called churches." And, per the fourth definition, it is a group that puts great emphasis on being "united by a specific doctrine."

Conservative Laestadianism is also a *fundamentalist* religious movement. That's used as a term of disparagement by many. But those who put such stock in being "God's Kingdom," led by the Holy Spirit to preserve true Christian doctrine in the face of an evil world, should not find anything disagreeable about the label. According to Martin E. Marty and R. Scott Appleby, religious fundamentalism

> manifests itself as a strategy, or set of strategies, by which beleaguered believers attempt to preserve their distinctive identity as a people or group. Feeling this identity to be at risk in the contemporary era, these believers fortify it by a selective retrieval of doctrines, beliefs, and practices from a sacred past. These retrieved "fundamentals" are refined, modified, and sanctioned in a spirit of pragmatism: they are to serve as a bulwark against the encroachment of outsiders who threaten to draw the believers into a syncretistic, areligious, or irreligious cultural milieu. Moreover, fundamentalists present the retrieved fundamentals alongside unprecedented claims and doctrinal innovations. These innovations and supporting doctrines lend the retrieved and updated fundamentals an urgency and charismatic intensity reminiscent of the religious experiences that originally forged communal identity. [from Mercer 2009, xxi]

Mercer lists some tendencies of fundamentalists that have all been exhibited by Conservative Laestadians at various times. They "form dramatic eschatologies; name, dramatize, and mythologize the enemy; engage in missionary work with zeal; exhibit a crisis of identity; replace inherited structures with their comprehensive ideological system; and seek out charismatic and authoritarian male leaders" (2009, xxii).

I can't resist adding Robert M. Price's one sentence summary of the distinction between a fundamentalist Christian and an evangelical one: "An evangelical is a fundamentalist who'll let you go to the movies" (2006b, 45). We will see which category better fits Conservatives in **4.6.1**.

Another loaded term is *indoctrination*, which may raise images of high-pressure cults and mind control. However, I take the word simply to mean what its roots imply: *in*stilling **doctrine**. Doctrine is "a codification of beliefs or a body of teachings or instructions, taught principles or positions, as the body of teachings in a branch of knowledge or belief system" (**Wikipedia** <http://en.wikipedia.org/wiki/Doctrine>). Indoctrination "is the process of inculcating ideas, attitudes, cognitive strategies or a professional methodology." The more benign term "education" is much preferred by those tasked with teaching Conservative Laestadian doctrine, especially to impressionable children, but what they are doing is "distinguished from education by the fact that the indoctrinated person is expected not to question or critically examine the doctrine they have learned" (**Wikipedia** <http://en.wikipedia.org/wiki/Indoctrination>).

Finally, an important and inflammatory term must be mentioned that this book never uses to describe Conservative Laestadianism: *cult*. Critics of the movement haven't hesitated to label it that way, as evidenced by the alternative queries suggested by Google when searching for the term *Laestadian*. But the term is unfairly perjorative, and has never really applied to Conservative Laestadianism. At various times in its history, the movement has had many of the traits that appear on checklists of cults and cultlike groups, to be sure.[2] But two essential features are missing: a single individual, living or dead, whose

---

2. Diane Wilson lists 36 "Characteristics of Cults and Cultlike Groups," which seem to be tailored to her critique of the Jehovah's Witnesses. Nonetheless, there are undeniably a lot of traits in common with Conservative Laestadianism, especially before the moderation of recent decades.

Here are twenty of those characteristics in her checklist that seem applicable: (1) "Members of the group must believe the doctrines of the group are the one and only 'Truth'"; (2) "Members must follow the doctrines even if they do not understand them"; (4) "An 'Us-vs.-Them' belief that no outside group is recognized as godly"; (5) "No independent thinking by members is allowed"; (8) "Members are made to feel elite, chosen by God to lead humankind out of darkness"; (9) "The group looks down on other religious groups"; (12) "When members leave the group, the love that was formerly shown to them turns into anger, hatred, and ridicule"; (14) "Fear is a major motivator"; (16) "Many groups teach that 'The Apocalypse' is just around the corner, and have timetables for its occurrence with dates near enough to carry an emotional punch"; (18) "The future is a time when members will be rewarded because 'The Great Change' has come"; (19) "There is never a legitimate reason for leaving the group"; (20) "Members are indoctrinated with the belief that if they ever leave the group, terrible consequences will befall them"; (21) "Members are forbidden to think negative thoughts about the group"; (25) "There is no allowance for interpretation of or deviation from the group's doctrines"; (27) "The group causes members to become extremely dependent on its compliance-oriented expressions of love and support; dread of losing the group's support"; (30) "Members must believe the group is always right, even if it contradicts itself"; (31) "Members spend more and more time with and under the direction of the group"; (32) "Those who do not conform to the group's requirements will be expelled"; (33) "Disagreement with or doubts about the group's teaching are always the fault of the member, due to lack of faith or lack of understanding"; (34) "The group is superior to and different than all other groups" (Wilson 2002, 148-49).

leadership is so strong as to make him or her an object of veneration, and the invention of entirely novel doctrines or practices. Even when strong leaders like Juhani Raattamaa, A.L. Heideman, and Peter Nevala wielded a great deal of personal influence, it was clear that they were servants and not masters. And every single aspect of Conservative doctrine and practice has some basis in earlier forms of Christianity. It is indeed a *sect* of Swedish and Finnish Lutheranism, but that is a very different and less judgmental term.

Sources

My sources, about 180 in all, are listed in the **References** list at the end of the book. Yes, I quote extensively from "heretics" and "unbelievers," even from some books with disconcerting titles like *Biblical Nonsense* and *Leaving the Fold*. It would be impossible to undertake an objective examination of a religion without citing its critics as well as its devotees. In the middle of those two extremes are many honest historians (both amateur and professional) who try not to mix their personal faith with their impartial assessment of what has actually happened and is happening in the church.

I have the highest respect for those church historians and the tightrope of objectivity they must walk. I would like to single out Tuomas Palola and John Lehtola, ordained preachers within the SRK and LLC, respectively, for my appreciation. Their sincere and unfeigned faith has moved them to caution me about my plans for publication even as their intellectual honesty has prevented them from condemning me. This book is not their fault, not by a long shot. I hope they are not tarnished in any way by my citing their personal communication with me about various interesting and helpful facts from their vast awareness of church history.

Bible quotes are from the King James Version unless otherwise indicated. Usually, those exceptions are cases where the New American Standard Bible seemed to offer a clearer or more accurate reading. For some Old Testament texts with extant manuscript sources in the Dead Sea Scrolls (far older than the Septuagint or Masoretic Text), I refer to the *Dead Sea Scrolls Bible* (Abegg et al. 1999).

I cite a number of sources from the first five centuries after Christ, which are listed in **5.1** as part of my introduction to the question of Luther's Christian predecessors. Those early Christian writers are interesting for several reasons. First, they provide us with evidence–usually the only evidence we have–of early Christianity's doctrine and practices. Second, some of the earliest ones are authoritative in their own right. They were treated much the same as our canonical New Testament books by early Christians, as evidenced by the way they are referenced in other writings as well as the inclusion of their books in early copies of the New Testament. And at least one of them, Augustine, was viewed by Luther as a fellow believer and source of inspired wisdom.

Luther's own writings make frequent appearances, too. In many cases, I have checked the English translation of quoted materials against Luther's original German, or have provided my own translation. Also included is the *Apology of the Augsburg Confession* [1531], which was written by Philipp Melanchthon, Luther's co-worker in the Reformation. Its purpose was to defend *The Augsburg Confession*, which is the centerpiece of the Lutheran Confessions that Conservative Laestadianism prizes as one of its founding documents.[3] Conservatives might harbor suspicions about the authority of Melanchthon's writings, but Luther was involved with the writing of the *Apology* and approved of it. In a 1533 letter, Luther urged Leipzig Christians to adhere to both it and the original 1530 *Augsburg Confession* (McCain 2005, 70).

An Appeal to Readers (and Non-Readers)

Luther began his *95 Theses* by saying he was motivated to discuss the matters at Wittenberg "out of love for the truth and the desire to bring it to light." I take the risk of being presumptuous in making the comparison because that statement of his is really what this book is all about. The church claims to be the "pillar and ground of truth." If that's the case, why not engage the truth rather than seeking to suppress or ignore it? Would such a negative reaction have been appropriate to Luther's *95 Theses*, too, or do we simply deem *that* critique of the established Church laudable because, well, we're Lutherans?

This is a study of Conservative Laestadian doctrine and practice, and their historical and biblical foundations, by a lifelong and troubled member of the church who still believes in God. I have a great deal of

---

[3]. "The teachings of Laestadianism are based on the Bible and the Lutheran Confessions" (*Our History*, LLC Web site, llchurch.org/our-history.cfm).

affection for both the faith of my childhood and the many good and decent people in that faith. But after years of suppressing my concerns, and then being told to suppress them, I am not going to hold back from offering my honest, unapologetic commentary in the pages ahead. There's no getting around the fact that many of the statements and positions we will encounter from both Conservative Laestadianism and the Bible are–I'm afraid there's just no other way to put it–simply outrageous. I will not overly restrain my writing from raising its eyebrows, or smiling a bit here and there, in discussing them.

In the calm waters of a pool of reverence, even a drop of criticism creates disquieting ripples. No doubt my bluntness and, at times, even bemusement about sacred matters will cause discomfort for those who have never heard their faith discussed with anything but devotion, piety, and praise. I'm sorry about that, I really am. I wish there were a way to honestly share the knowledge I've acquired over these past years without some of those who have been my closest friends taking it as an act of betrayal. I have already lost many of those friends, and know that I am likely to lose more. Please don't think it hasn't weighed heavily on my mind.

Here's the only thing I really ask: *Please only talk about this book to the extent that you have read it.* I understand if you'd rather not read it at all. In fact, I sincerely think that it's not in some people's best interests to do so. If you are one of those people, I ask (through those who have dared to read at least this far) that you refrain from characterizing or condemning either this book or its author.

It's really just an issue of honesty–you *cannot* justifiably criticize that which you do not understand. That's why I spent over a year of full-time work researching the faith that had been causing me so much heartburn. *I take it too seriously to have done otherwise.* Only now do I dare to speak out about its problems, after having done everything possible to understand them.

The next two sections refer to the June 2010 edition. They're pretty short, but if you've grown impatient with all this prologue, you may choose to skip directly to **Section 4**.

2 Foreword to the June 2010 Edition

I have been mightily impressed with the penetrating acumen of Ed Suominen as he has fed me questions for my *Bible Geek* podcast, so when he approached me to sift the manuscript of the work you are about to read, I welcomed the opportunity. My main task was to scrutinize the accuracy of his many references, making sure nothing was taken out of its biblical context and that none of the literature he was critiquing had been misinterpreted as far as I could tell. I believe I found one single instance in the whole book where I suspected the original author had not intended a theological distinction Ed thought he had found in a quoted passage, and Ed changed it. So I am happy to add whatever credibility I may have to the soundness of Ed's arguments on theology and scripture.

But the book is much more than a survey of biblical teaching, as if in a vacuum. For one thing, I was delighted to receive a thorough introduction to the social and theological character of a branch of Lutheranism of which I had never heard, that set in motion by the nineteenth-century preacher Laestadius. Ed's comprehensive grasp of the history, beliefs, and theology of this movement, and of the rival opinions rampant throughout the group and all the documentary sources is just phenomenal. And as soon as one looks through the other end of the scope one sees a whole new work, equally interesting: a testament of tortured faith. Here is the case of a man who loves his religious tradition very much, loves it enough to want to know everything about it (and seemingly does know everything about it!). And such deep inquiry forbids him be satisfied with the apologetical sedatives that satisfy others whose goal is merely to "get along." No, Ed shows himself to be a prime example of what Paul Tillich calls "The Theologian" in a series of sermons bearing that title. He asks

> which one of us can call himself a theologian? Who can decide to become a theologian? And who can dare to remain a theologian? Do we really belong to the assembly of God? Can we seriously accept the paradox upon which the Church is built, the paradox that Jesus is the Christ? Are we grasped by the Divine Spirit, and have we received the word of knowledge as a gift? If somebody were to come and tell us that he certainly belongs to the Church, that he does not doubt that Jesus is the Christ any longer, that he

continually experiences the grip of the Divine Spirit and the gift of spiritual knowledge, what should be our answer to him? We certainly should tell him that he does not fulfill even the first condition of theological existence, which is the realization that one does not know whether he has experienced the Divine Spirit, or spirits which are not divine. We would not accept him as a theologian. On the other hand, if someone were to come and tell us that he is estranged from the Christian Church and its foundations, that he does not feel the presence of the power of the Spirit, that he is empty of spiritual knowledge, but that he asks again and again the theological question, the question of an ultimate concern and its manifestations in Jesus as the Christ, we would accept him as a theologian (in *The Shaking of the Foundations*, NY: Charles Scribner's Sons, 1948, 120-21.)

Ed Suominen is such a theologian. He walks the lonely, narrow path of great love for his faith community and simultaneous, painful alienation from it, because he cannot avoid asking the questions that his tradition fears. But so great is his love for Conservative Laestadianism as to cast out all fear. The questions he raises plague him perhaps much more than they would the common faithful (those whom I call generically, "pew potatoes").[4] Pulpit rhetoric easily condemns "doubts," and pious heads nod "Amen," but none can really see why anyone would raise the questions unless they were looking for excuses to leave the fold. Ed, by contrast, knows too well that his questions are hands extended for help. He wants to be drawn safely into the boat, not forced out. And the last thing he wants to do is to jump out.

Perhaps the one sin Jesus takes aim at more than any other in the gospels is hypocrisy. And Ed, too, hates this above all. He cannot abide the thought of being a hypocrite. He will not impose himself on a faith

---

4. One person who was part of the very limited distribution of my June 2010 edition took offense at the "pew potatoes" label. At least one other reader found it amusing, as did I, so I made no effort to censor it from Price's foreword. I leave it here with a question for the offended reader and any others having the same reaction. How does the label mischaracterize the vast majority of Conservative Laestadians whose sole exposure to theology and church history is to sit in the pews Sunday after Sunday passively accepting what they are told by preachers who have little to back up their statements except a bald claim of inspiration by the Holy Spirit and dire threats against disbelief or even honest doubts?

community that will not have someone like him, a "doubter," in its ranks. Thus this book. It is a forthright record of his deep and troubling questions, really a self-examination as much as an examination of his inherited theology. He asks the reader and his church: do you love our tradition, and do you love the Bible, enough to look at them unafraid, let the chips fall where they may? Because if we do not, then our professed loyalty to both Bible and Church will be hollow, pat, superficial, and not nearly so deeply rooted as we claim. If we love our faith we will not hesitate to question it. Otherwise we can never really understand it or appreciate it.

–Robert M. Price, June 5, 2010

Professor of Theology and Scriptural Studies, Colemon Theological Seminary; Host, *Point of Inquiry*; Founder and Editor, *The Journal of Higher Criticism*; Fellow, The Jesus Seminar; Fellow, The Committee for the Scientific Examination of Religion; Research Fellow, Center for Inquiry Institute; Host, *The Bible Geek Podcast*; Author, *Inerrant the Wind: The Evangelical Crisis of Biblical Authority*, *The Pre-Nicene New Testament*, and *The Reason-Driven Life*, among others.

3 Introduction to the June 2010 Edition

The Conservative Laestadian church resides in a tight-knit association between the SRK in Finland, the SFC in Sweden, the LLC in North America, and various congregations of new converts that they support via mission work in Russia, Togo, and Ecuador. This document, in **Section 4**, presents the teachings and history of the church largely as quotations, grouped in subsections and listed chronologically. Each subsection represents an attempt at a fair sample of what the church has taught on a particular topic over the decades via its doctrinal books, periodicals, and sermons. Some material is presented based on observations of the author and of historians from both inside and outside the church. Not every conceivable topic of interest is included, some of the topics overlap, and the sampling of quotations may understate or overstate the emphasis put on topics at particular times of the church's history.

But, for all those flaws, the collection aims to provide a uniquely accessible survey of church doctrine and its development across a range of subject matter and time. It both comforts and confronts the Conservative reader, with many teachings that are consistent and supportive of what is heard from the pulpit today, and some that are not. In some cases, the harshness and (even for Conservative Laestadianism) archaic content calling back from past decades can make the reader wonder just which faith is being discussed. The author's own difficulties with the material are laid bare in the footnotes that nip at the heels of almost every page, along with historical notes and references to Luther's teachings.[5]

The church claims Martin Luther as a spiritual father and brother in faith, and his teachings are discussed in **Section 5**. The Bible is held as "the highest authority and standard by which matters of soul and doctrines of salvation are judged" (VOZ, 3/2007), and its Old Testament and New Testament are discussed in **Section 6** and **Section 7**, respectively. Much of the discussion takes the traditional modes of biblical interpretation at their word. It then challenges the reader to

---

5. In the 2010 edition, the quotes from church writings and sermons formed the body of the text. I made my comments to the various quotes in footnotes to them.

maintain such interpretation in the face of many contradictions and Old Testament outrages that are almost never brought to light in sermons or discussions.

This work is entirely unofficial, the product of its author's longtime and ongoing struggle to remain a believing member of the Conservative Laestadian faith. The Gospel of Matthew records Jesus as comparing the Kingdom of God to a merchant who found a valuable pearl and sold all that he had in order to buy it. This author continues to desire to partake of a grace and love that some part of him finds as priceless and indispensable as that merchant's pearl. Yet no merchant of fine pearls would ever buy one that he had not examined carefully. To take the supreme leap of selling all for the price of one particular pearl would require that merchant to have either found it flawless after detailed examination, or to enter blindly into what might well turn out to be a bad bargain out of impulse, emotion, or deceit.

Questioning one's convictions is always a painful process, and never more so when the questions center on religious beliefs that have been held for a lifetime. No doubt many fellow believers would consider the whole exercise sinful and to be avoided at all costs; the pearl is to be accepted as flawless, without critical examination or doubt, based on the word of the Divine Supplier. Luther acknowledged that doubt will always accompany faith, but said that doubtful thoughts should never be allowed to make a nest in one's mind. What he called the "whore" of reason is an unseemly mistress who must be reluctantly tolerated for companionship in the daily existence of this profane world, but a most unwelcome guest in any spiritual discussion or contemplation.

The whore of reason kept in this author's own head has long fumed and grumbled under this closeted second-rate existence, but in recent years her cries of resistance have become almost intolerably shrill. Yet she, or some vaguely defined opposing faculty in "the heart" remains terrified of the horrific consequences that could accompany open rebellion. The infinite threat of eternal torment for apostasy or even feigned faith is impossible to disregard no matter how much reason tries to minimize its probability. And so, unable or perhaps even unwilling to leave her dismal little lodgings and servitude, she continues her passive-aggressive jeers and jabs. The questions remain open sores, their scabs painfully scratched off every time reason strikes out with yet another conflict between doctrine and undeniable facts about the natural world, the very words of the Bible itself, and obscure writings of predecessors in history whom the church counts as its own.

If you dare to read further, fellow believer, you will learn much about your faith: history and doctrinal teachings that are often comforting, consistent, and edifying, but that can also raise disturbing questions many would consider best never asked. Nothing here is intended to be mocking or frivolous, but neither are inconvenient facts dismissed or ignored. If there is error or mischaracterization with regard to those facts, correction is welcome.

Finally, this author would like to dedicate this work to Robert M. Price, whose friendship and scholarly insight has allowed him to remain believing without losing his mind, to numerous Conservative Laestadian brothers and sisters whose enduring friendship and preaching of grace in word and deed have allowed him to remain thinking without losing his faith, and to his beautiful and long-suffering wife, whose unconditional love has been a steady light shining in his darkest nights of the soul.

–EAS, June 2010

4 Conservative Laestadianism

> *Isn't it a little suspicious that the only true religion is the one with which we happened to grow up?*
>
> —Rachel Held Evans, *Evolving in Monkey Town*

4.1 Spiritual Heritage

> *Most fundamentalists naïvely think their form of Christianity was lifted intact from Jesus of the first century.*
>
> —Calvin Mercer, *Slaves to Faith*

Christianity "is a historic faith that relies on the credibility of its theological formulations and its Scriptures." Its "beliefs are founded on what is believed to be historical facts–not merely on myths or moral stories" (Tucker 2002, 118). "It asks the faithful to believe certain historical events took place, like the prophesied virgin birth of Jesus, his reputed miracles, his teachings as told to us by 'inspired historians,' his death on the cross, his resurrection from the dead, and his ascension into heaven" (Loftus 2008, loc. 3077-80). Conservative Laestadianism takes that historical dependence to an extreme degree with its claim to be the latest (and in the mind of many believers, the last) in an unbroken chain of incarnations of God's Kingdom on this earth. Each link in the chain depends on the personal transmission of the gospel via the proclamation of the forgiveness of sins "from faith to faith." Thus there is considerable pressure on the church to provide a plausible history of its spiritual heritage.

Typical believers tend not to concern themselves too much about the details of this history, seeming rather to take comfort in a widespread feeling that elders and historically minded individuals in the church have it all figured out. Decades ago, before undertaking my own historical investigations, I remember being fascinated and inspired by hearing gray-headed members of the flock refer to Laestadius's conversion in the presence of "Lappish Mary," to the spirit "burning as fire in the snow" during the early years of the Laestadian awakening, to some Pietist "readers" who had kept the candle of God's Kingdom burning dimly before then, and to Luther being a believer just like we were. Things got pretty vague further back than that, though. We all understood that the Holy Spirit had to have been carried in the hearts of believers from Luther to Laestadius, but nobody had the faintest idea how it happened.

And of the time before Luther nothing was known beyond a supposition that there were true believers hidden somewhere within the Catholic Church (see **5.1**) and some cautious optimism that John Huss had been one of God's Children. This lack of information and even interest in such information was made clear to me when I wrote an article about Luther and the Reformation for an issue of the *Voice of Zion* (**5.4.1**) and proposed a paragraph mentioning some possibilities for "believing" predecessors to Luther. One of the several editors of the article, a widely respected, historically-minded LLC preacher, rejected the paragraph, saying that such speculations were interesting material for discussions in the sauna but not appropriate for a church publication.

The same dim level of awareness is widespread in the church concerning the many Laestadian splinter groups that travel separately, rejecting each other but all claiming spiritual fellowship with the same founders of the movement. To the average Conservative Laestadian, they are all just "heretics," differentiated from each other and the true faith by a few mere sentences of caricatured summary about their beliefs. Most know about the "last heresy" of 1973 because they or their parents lived through it, but its cause is mostly chalked up to "leniency," which mostly involved a desire to accept television and organized sports for schoolchildren, and some obscure theological issues. Some are aware of the "Kirkkokunta" and "Esikoinens" but very few know anything about those groups or what precipitated the schisms between them and Conservative Laestadianism.[6]

Church history is an obscure and arcane topic. I certainly don't blame anybody for not taking the time to research it, or even have an interest in it. But without investigating it for myself, I personally was unwilling to claim myself as one of 100,000 or so of the only true Christians, the

---

6. The LLC has recently published a historical book, *Unto this Day the Lord has Helped*, based on a manuscript left by the deceased Peter Nevala and edited by Keith Waaraniemi. I have read the book and, while I have concerns about some things it says and many things it leaves unsaid, I applaud it as an earnest and well-intentioned step forward by the church to address its history.

sole heirs of Christianity's vast spiritual and cultural legacy over the course of 2,000 years. For those readers who have made that claim as current or former Laestadians, the following discussion about our spiritual heritage will be of interest and significance. Other readers with a more general interest in Christianity and the Bible might find their eyes glazing over from all the historical minutia, and may wish to skip ahead to **4.2**.

4.1.1 Luther

> *For Luther, the greatest good which the [Christian] community possesses is that forgiveness of sins is to be found in it.*
>
> —Paul Althaus, *The Theology of Martin Luther*

Three essential links in the chain of Conservative Laestadianism's spiritual heritage are the Apostle Paul, Luther, and Laestadius. Of those three doctrinal fathers, Martin Luther is the one who has left the most written evidence of his beliefs. His collected works occupy over 100 volumes, spanning subjects from Adam's creation to Zwingli's heresy. And yet Conservative Laestadianism, whose American denomination is called the "Laestadian *Lutheran* Church," pays almost no attention to what the man had to say. Indeed, there is some apprehension about delving too deeply into his writings, as exemplified by the following quote from the January 1980 *Voice of Zion*:

> ✝ "In some of the homes of the children of the kingdom are seen volumes of Luther's Works. These have been translated into English by what we may call modern scribes of a dead faith. Consequently, as edited versions, the living truths of the gospel of the kingdom have been sometimes diluted." These "translated versions have a significance to a child of God only as a reference, and are supplementary to the current publications of God's Zion. They are recognized to be of value only by those already in faith, unless they are influential in awakening lost souls. More often, many read Luther, Laestadius, or other reformers who were in faith and who wrote voluminously, only to find that their own preconceived notions of unbelief have been reinforced. The word as read does not benefit them, not being mixed with faith."

What the quoted writer had probably become aware from his own reading is a little known fact among Conservative Laestadian believers:

there are real and significant conflicts between important doctrinal positions of the church and the teachings of Luther. But those conflicts cannot be dismissed as the result of mistranslations. Having heard that excuse many times in decades past, I went to the trouble of becoming somewhat fluent in Luther's German for the express purpose of skipping the widely suspected step of relying on others' translations. The result was not learning penetrating insights that were unavailable to English readers of Luther, or uncovering deceit by "modern scribes of a dead faith," but a realization that the translations faithfully convey Luther's teachings, and those teachings must be reckoned with.

Another way that some have attempted to deal with inconvenient Luther writings is to assert that they were written before Luther's conversion, or altered after his death. Neither assertion is tenable. Almost all of Luther's writings are from *after* his revelatory "Tower Experience" in the Wittenberg monastery around 1518, which was itself several years after his conversion experience in the Augustinian monastery at Erfurt. And the charge of changes in his writings is easily dismissed by that fact that those writings were widely circulated and scrutinized immediately upon publication. Luther's forceful personal presence and the diligence of his wide circle of supporters would have made short work of any attempt at forgery. (Ironically, the theological writings whose authenticity and accuracy are most suspect from a purely historical and scholarly basis are found not in the works of Luther or Laestadius, but in the New Testament.)

In my studies, I have also found some amazing commonalities with Luther. Despite the passage of nearly five hundred years, Conservative Laestadians follow Luther's teachings about personal absolution to a degree that is remarkable, especially considering how little attention has been paid to his writings within the movement. I will always remember one day some fifteen years ago when I read the words *Vergebung der Sünde* (forgiveness of sins) in a musty old book containing some of Luther's sermons in their original German and realized that the personal preaching of such forgiveness was not just a Laestadian invention after all. (It may well be a *Lutheran* invention to a great extent, but that is a topic for later, in **5.1.2**)

What links of the chain connect Luther back to the Apostle Paul? In the words of Paul Althaus, Luther himself thought that

God has always preserved his church, even under a church organization such as the papacy which erred in many ways. He has done this by marvelously preserving the text of the gospel and the sacraments; and through these many have lived and died in true faith. This remains true even though they were only a weak and hidden minority within the official church. [1963, 343]

The *Voice of Zion* made a similar claim in its July 2008 issue:

> ✝ "During Luther's time the main message of the Bible was lost in the teachings of the Catholic Church, which taught that salvation was attained by a combination of faith and good works. After his conversion, Luther finally understood that a merciful God is to be found without one's own merits and that the central message of the Bible was salvation alone by grace, alone by faith, alone through the merits of Christ. We agree with Luther's telling statement: 'Christ is the Lord and King of the Bible.'"

But the Conservative Laestadian teaching is that the Holy Spirit and its power of the forgiveness of sins must have been passed on *directly* from believer to believer since Christ gave it to the assembled disciples. To me, that makes the question a vexing one. Just where were those true believers before Luther's conversion, even in the years immediately prior to that pivotal event? I discuss this, along with the various conflicts and commonalities I've found with Luther, in Section 5.

4.1.2 Laestadius

> *We have strange difficulties to meet in Lapland, and one of them is a sect called "Loestadians," who believe that they are the only people who are going to heaven.*
>
> —Andrew Wangberg, *Bible Pioneer Work in Norwegian Lapland*

The third link is Lars Levi Laestadius, whose importance to the movement bearing his name is summarized on the *About Us* page of the LLC website:

> ✝ "The Laestadian Lutheran Church takes its name from Martin Luther and Lars Levi Laestadius. The name of the reformer Martin Luther and his teachings are well known around the world. The name of Laestadius is less familiar. Lars Levi Laestadius was a Lutheran pastor who served in northern

> Sweden from 1825-1861. In 1844, after nineteen years in the ministry, Laestadius was helped into living faith by a woman named Milla Clementsdotter, a member of a group known as 'Readers.' Following his conversion, Laestadius' sermons were instilled with a new power, the power of the Holy Spirit. . . . The teachings of Laestadianism are based on the Bible and the Lutheran Confessions."

Despite his significance to Conservative Laestadianism, the vast majority of its adherents know nothing about what Laestadius actually preached and taught. He is almost never quoted or discussed beyond brief historical summaries of his conversion and the early Laestadian awakening. There's probably a good reason for that; the harsh and crude tone, unrelenting legalism, pagan superstition, and sexual imagery and content found throughout Laestadius' sermons are shocking and deeply disturbing, at least to me. And the sermons in question are almost all post-1844, authored by the post-conversion Laestadius who is considered to be a brother in the same living faith.

Just imagine the following passages being read in church today:

> [T]he merciful Lord Jesus who is the true Father of all poor orphan children lift up these helpless naked wretches from the cold floor of the world; He will wash them clean with the water of life; He will take them into His lap and teach them to suckle at His breasts of flowing grace, yet not so fast that the milk of grace should cause them to choke, but only as fast as the wretched ones are able to swallow. [Farewell to Karesuando Congregation, 1849]

> God laments through the prophet Ezekiel that Israel is one spiritual whore, who committed adultery with many idols and allowed the Egyptian whorebucks to squeeze her breasts. So also the devil's whore has allowed the devil to squeeze her breasts and has lain in the bosom of the devil for many years, and has committed adultery with many idols. She has committed adultery with so many that she has finally become unfruitful or an inappeasable harlot. Such an inappeasable harlot does not become fruitful, although she would lie near the Holy Spirit every night. And how could tribulation of birth come to such a one who is unfruitful? And such unfruitful ones and inappeasable harlots are first the wise of the world, who look at the effects of the Holy Spirit as the effects of the devil's spirit. The devil has squeezed

their breasts so long, that they have hardened. [Third Sunday after Easter, 1850]

We know that not one woman will become fruitful without a seed. So also God's congregation, which in the Scriptures is compared to the bride of the Saviour, cannot become fruitful without seed. The bride of the Saviour becomes fruitful when she lies near the Holy Spirit or in the Saviour's lap; He then pours the incorruptible seed into the heart of the bride. And if that person, into whose heart this incorruptible seed is poured, is a pure virgin, she would immediately become fruitful. But there is no other pure virgin than the virgin Mary. All others are the devil's whores and some have committed adultery with so many, that they have become unfruitful. . . . Are you, devil's whore, worthy to bear the crown of glory? . . . When you have no longer been acceptable to the devil for a whore, the Saviour took the devil's whore for His bride. The devil's angels spit upon her and said, "Is that the kind the bride of the Son of God is, who now shamelessly barks at honorable people?" One naked, scabby, and old whore, full of smelly wounds from which the pus of deviltry runs, is no longer acceptable to the devil for a whore, what then for a bride for the Saviour. [Third Sunday after Easter, 1850]

[W]hen a naked whore wants to live very meekly, she removes her sack-cloth shirt from herself and in place puts on a cambric shirt, through which the moon and the sun shine. On top of the cambric shirt she puts on a crinoline skirt, and so beautifully decked she goes to dance with the whore bucks, so that they would see her beauty. Both breasts she leaves uncovered for pleasure for the eyes of all those who desire to look upon her, but the moon and the sun shine through her clothes, and when she comes into the sunlight or before a candle, all the shameful places are seen, although she has meekly covered those shameful places with finery. . . . If she was so wise that she would wear clothes of skins, which God made for Eve, the shameful places would be covered better. [Twentieth Sunday after Trinity, 1850]

Woe, woe! Children, take heed that the blood which is in your heart and in your veins has come from the Parent's heart. Should you mock the Parent's tears anymore, you who have received blood from the Parent's heart, which sustains your life? And the heavenly Parent must still suckle you, He must allow you to suckle His grace flowing breasts so that the weak life which is in you would remain with you. Remember now, children, these tears of the Parent, which today have flowed from His eyes because of you and all ungodly children. [Tenth Sunday after Trinity, 1851]

What living beings are they who love darkness? All those people who live under the earth, as elves and earthlings and bastards who screech in the dusk and frighten the living and those people who live upon the earth. So also the magpies and forest devils who laugh at and curse the light.... Have you not heard how elves steal the children of men before they are baptized, and even afterwards they exchange the children of men on whose breast a cross has not been placed? For elves cannot bear a cross to be placed upon the breast of their children; elves surely swaddle their children, but it is not allowed in the kingdom of the elves that the swaddling bands would be put to cross upon the child's breast. It is well known from that, that elves are enemies of Jesus' cross, and how could the elves carry the cross, who eat devil's dung and the manure of old adam. After that drinking they are so filthy and drowsy, as if they would have eaten dung, but just the same they consider devil's dung sweet although it stinks as poison a quarter of a mile away. [Second Pentecost Day, 1854]

[W]hen the groom tarried, when death did not come quit then after the first sign of grace, then the first zeal began to end, carrying the cross became troublesome, that female devil, the world, began to show its beauty to them, as the world's whores bare their breasts to the whore bucks, so this female devil the world, bares its breasts of fornication to the Christians and entices them with its beauty. [Twenty-Seventh Sunday after Trinity, 1856]

The proclamation of the forgiveness of sins in Jesus' name and blood is central to Conservative Laestadian preaching. Yet it is a little-known fact in the movement that Laestadius himself was reluctant to accept the use of that proclamation. He "feared dead faith so much that he did not dare to comfort very much" (Kulla 2010, 129). Jussila claims that Laestadius and Raattamaa "were united with the closest of bonds in the same doctrine and spirit, although with different gifts" (1948, 28). But he admits that it

> † "has been known to us and to all the people of the Lord that Laestadius was so eagerly chasing the wolves that he would forget to feed the sheep. It is also known that at first he was [so] aghast over Raattamaa's preaching of the remission of sins that he said: 'Now all the scoundrels are accepted into the Kingdom of God.' But he found it easy to believe and comprehend the words of the Lord Jesus: 'Whosoever sins ye remit; they are remitted unto them.' And when he noted that this is the office of the Holy Spirit, which it exercised through those people who have received its gift, then he also rejoiced over this discovery" (p. 29).

I have found one early sermon of Laestadius that does contain an absolution proclamation of sorts: "So believe now, you palsied one, that your sins are forgiven" (Nineteenth Sunday after Trinity sermon, 1847). See the full quote in **4.6.2**. It is such a rare find in his law-oriented writings, especially given the early date, that one might be excused for wondering about the authenticity of the passage. Another bit of absolution language "in the name and blood of Jesus" is contained in an 1849 Laestadius sermon whose manuscript authenticity is suspect (Hepokoski 2002a, 38; Leivo 2005, 129).

4.1.3 Raattamaa and His Contemporaries

> *As long as Raattamaa lived the Laestadian revival was outwardly one unit in Europe. Although there were undercurrents of differences, Raattamaa was a respected and well beloved elder to whom all submitted.*

—Carl A. Kulla, *Journey of an Immigrant Awakening Movement in America*

Juhani Raattamaa was "the most notable of Laestadius' disciples. He had been presented with the lofty gifts of the Holy Spirit" according to Heikki Jussila, a Conservative preacher [1863-1955]. In his 1948 autobiographical book *The Grace of the Caller*, he quoted approvingly the following summary of Raattamaa originally written in 1873:

> † "He has been gifted with that spirit of wisdom and knowledge which, free of bias, understands how to preach all of the doctrine of salvation fully, and correctly divide the word of truth–he has

during the entire time of this Christianity [preached] with greatest exactness both freedom from the law of Moses and the law of Christ in the congregations" (p. 39).

Jussila also lists other "messengers of Laestadius and preachers of Finland," including Juhani Raattamaa's brother Peter, Erkki Antti Juhonpieti, and Pietari Nuutti, who was better known as "Antin Pieti" (pp. 39-41).

Raattamaa is in some respects even more significant to the movement than Laestadius himself. As discussed below, it was he who "discovered the keys" with the proclamation of the forgiveness of sins and made use of it despite Laestadius's reluctance. And he was heavily involved with the early days of Laestadianism in North America. But he seems to have received even less attention than Laestadius.

Here are the two quotes mentioning him that made it into my sample. The first is from a historical sermon published in 1963 by Pauli Korteniemi, and the other is from the *History* page of SRK's website:

> ✝ "Juhani Raattamaa then came after Laestadius in the North Country as the father of Christianity and to direct Christianity, or as a great prophet of the Lord, or worker in the Lord's vineyard."

> ✝ "The most effective spreader of the Laestadianism was the missionary school organisation led by the school master... Juhani Raattamaa."

4.1.4 The Keys and Conversions

> *The penitent ... is led into the midst of the gathering, whereupon, the preacher, putting his hands round the penitent's neck, in a solemn tone pronounces the forgiveness of sins to the sinner.*
>
> —Andrew Wangberg, *Bible Pioneer Work in Norwegian Lapland*

Laestadius

Laestadius wrote of his **1844** meeting with a Lapp girl "Maria" or "Mary" in an autobiographical article "Concerning the First Causes of the Awakenings" that appeared in *The Voice of One Crying in the*

Wilderness, which I will abbreviate as *VCW* from this point on.⁷ That winter, he

> came to Åsele Lapland to conduct examinations. Here I met some Readers, who were of the more moderate kind. Among them was a certain Lapp girl named Mary who, upon having heard my communion sermon, opened up her entire heart to me. This simple girl had experiences in the order of grace which I have never heard before. She had traveled long distances in her search for light in the darkness. In her travels she had finally come to Pastor Brandell in Nora, and when the girl opened up her heart to him, Brandell freed her of doubt; through him, the girl was led to living faith. And I thought: "Here is another Mary who sits at Jesus' feet. And only now"–I thought–"now I see the way which leads to life; it had been hid from me, until I had opportunity to converse with Mary." Her simple story of her wanderings and experiences made such a deep impression in my heart that the light dawned for me also; I was able to feel that evening, which I spent in Mary's company, a foretaste of heavenly joy. But the pastors in Åsele did not understand Mary's heart, and Mary also felt that they were not of this sheepfold. I shall remember poor Mary as long as I live, and hope to meet her in a brighter world on the other side of the grave. [*VCW*, 36]

This was certainly a definitive conversion experience for Laestadius, but it is remarkable that he declines to mention anything about Mary proclaiming the forgiveness of his sins when he writes of the event, sometime after 1853. Rather, he attributes his "dawning of the light" to the impression made in his heart by the "simple story of her wanderings and experiences." *In Lars Levi Laestadius and the Revival in Lapland*, Hepokoski writes:

> Although it is assumed by some who consider themselves followers of Laestadius that he confessed his sins to Maria and that she freed him by proclaiming absolution, he nowhere indicates that anything like this took place. His focus is not on his own experiences–which he may indeed have shared with her–but

---

7. The "girl" has been identified with some certainty as Milla Clementsdotter. She would have been 30 years old at the time of her visit with Laestadius in Åsele (Hepokoski 2002a, 11 & 16-17).

on hers, and by hearing her story he saw the light. Furthermore, individual absolution was not practiced by laymen during the first six years of the revival, and if the Pastor himself had been absolved from his sins by a "simple" Lapp on that day in 1844, there could have been no subsequent discovery of the keys. [p. 9]

In 1872, Raattamaa wrote of the event with an added detail that at least hints at personal absolution. He said that Laestadius became contrite and sought for salvation, but "did not understand it until the Lapp maid Mary told him that he, in the condition in which he now was, must believe his sins forgiven. He then comprehended peace by faith, and began to preach with the power of the Spirit" (from Kulla 1993, 72).

Raattamaa

In his description of Laestadius' conversion, Raattamaa wrote that he himself "also became awakened at about the same time" (Kulla 1993, 72). In his compilation of *Background Writings and Testimonies* from the Laestadian movement, Warren Hepokoski states that Raattamaa's conversion occurred in early **1846** and translates a biographical article on Raattamaa, originally published in two issues of the early periodical *Kristillinen Kuukauslehti*, Dec. 1881 and Jan. 1882. The article describes Raattamaa's battle between an awakened conscience and recurring sin, especially drunkenness, over a period of some six years. Then, the article quotes Raattamaa as saying,

> It made a vivid and deep impression on me when Pastor Laestadius spoke with me in a gentle and loving manner and recalled how a certain Lapp girl had set him straight. He also said that it is self-righteousness that prevents the penitent from receiving the grace of God in Christ. This tender speech aroused in me a hope that God might be graceful even to me for the sake of the name of his only begotten Son. From that moment, like the prodigal son, I came to myself, and I felt the love of God the Father, that my immortal spirit wouldn't perish. [p. 33]

Raattamaa still felt, though, that his "sins weighed heavily on the Son of God and are the iron nails that the soldiers drove into his hands and feet on the mount of Golgotha. This was followed by deep sorrow in my soul over my sins, and the awful sin of unbelief revealed itself. I also feared that I had committed the sin against the Holy Spirit. However, I didn't despair, as I had at 16 years of age, but I clung firmly to the intercession of the Lord Jesus, who prayed: 'Father, forgive them, for they know not what they do.'" He promised God "during moments of prayer and devotion, night and day" that he "would teach transgressors his ways so that sinners would repent, for general impenitence and drunkenness had overcome the men and women of Lapland" (p. 33). He was

> in this condition nearly two years. Occasionally I was comforted by the gospel. Otherwise I would not have had the strength to live and preach repentance to others.
>
> But when, in faith and spirit, I was allowed to view the blood-red, thorn-crowned King, power issued from Him, and Christ's suffering effected a living power in my soul. I believed my sins forgiven in the shed and sprinkled blood, and this was followed by a knowledge of the risen and living Lord Jesus. That which I had sought afar was indeed near and effected joy and peace in my soul. I had thought even previously that I believed Jesus had died and risen from the dead, but now I was ashamed of my unbelief and realized that previously I hadn't believed from my heart after all. [pp. 33-34]

Raattamaa mentions being "comforted by the gospel," which in current Conservative Laestadian parlance equates to the proclamation of absolution. But he seems to connect believing his "sins forgiven in the shed and sprinkled blood" with a vision of Christ crucified in "faith and spirit." In another account, Raattamaa described great joy coming to him when Laestadius "conducted services in the church, and there within was sung" a hymn, "In my great distress I cry up to the Lord." Then, he writes, "when I felt joy and Jesus appeared to me with His love, I had to believe, even if I had not wanted to" (*Father's Voice II*, 238). In neither place does Raattamaa mention any proclamation of absolution from Laestadius or anyone else.[8]

---

8. When recalling his "discovery of the keys," Raattamaa writes that he often "personally needed to hear the audible affirmations of my brothers and sisters of the cross, and beg for the forgiveness of my sins in Jesus' name and blood" (Laitinen, 34). But I think it is clear that he was referring to his spiritual practices at the time of his writing, well after the discovery. See **4.6.2**.

Other Early Conversions

Juhani Raattamaa's brother Peter experienced "the day of redemption" in March **1846**, as Laestadius wrote of it several years later:

> He was outdoors and paced back and forth along the river, for he lacked the strength to do any particular work. In the midst of his walking, a few words of grace struck his heart like lightning, and in the same twinkling-of-an-eye he felt an inexplicable joy streaming through his entire inner being. [*VCW*, 79]

In an 1882 autobiography, Erkki Antti Juhonpieti recalled his conversion as an event that began with five years of struggle with an awakened conscience, a visit with a "repentant man" who came to visit him around **1849**, and subsequent reflection and reading. The 1849 date is based on Juhonpieti's recollection that he was 35 years old at the time, and that he was born in 1814 (Kulla 1993, 79 and 81). He and his visitor

> talked together of what we understood of the way of salvation. That evening after he went home, death and judgment stood before me and I had great sorrow over my condition. I then beheld the Savior nailed to the cross, from which sight my conscience became greatly distressed, and I wondered if God would still accept me and if there still was time to be saved, before death cut the thin cord which held me from falling into hell, which was burning with fire and brimstone. . . . In that time of distress I read and prayed that God would help, if God could still find a place in me. [from Kulla 1993, 81]

He read a book entitled "The Order of Grace," and "the promises of grace and the gospel opened to me, that if you believe on the Lord Jesus Christ you are saved." But then

> came unworthiness, that how is it fitting for me to believe when I haven't yet had true penitence or repentance? I will become a hypocrite. But the spirit of God, who is the Beginner and Finisher of faith, went internally through that Word that had been read, saying that if you don't believe you will go to hell, no matter how penitent you might be. Fear was great, but there was also hope. Then I took firm hold of the promises of grace, and in the proportion that I believed, I felt peace and rest. I also felt joy, and I was allowed to see Jesus in the glory of victory for the first time, when I was able to believe that I was saved. [p. 81]

Again, there is no mention of any proclamation of absolution. Indeed, Juhonpieti makes it quite clear that he was not "allowed to see Jesus in the glory of victory" or "able to believe that he was saved" until well after his visitor had departed.

The Discovery of the Keys

Things changed dramatically sometime around **1851-1853**, when Raattamaa found himself confronted with a girl who remained in distress of conscience even after his evangelical teaching. On that occasion, he made a "discovery" of the "keys of the kingdom of heaven" that would change the experience of conversion and form a fundamental doctrine of the Laestadian faith. After its 1846-1847 beginnings, the Laestadian "spiritual movement had spread for six years already before I really understood the freedom," Raattamaa recalled in 1881, confirming the date.[9] "Since then, I and some brothers and sisters have put the keys of the kingdom of heaven into use, by which troubled souls began to be freed and prisoners of unbelief began to lose their chains, and they rejoiced in spirit" (Hepokoski 2000, 9-10).

As recalled by Erik Johnsen, who claimed Raattamaa told him about the event in 1894, Raattamaa

> was just leaving to go home. The reindeer was harnessed and standing before the door. Many people had gathered at the house. Some were already in living faith. But one girl was moaning due to a troubled conscience. Raattamaa and others preached to her about faith and the gospel, but she could not appropriate faith and was not comforted. Raattamaa put his coat on, bade farewell to the people, and went out the door; but then he turned, went back into the house, and asked the girl, "Do you believe that we are God's people?" The girl answered boldly, "I believe with all

---

9. The dating of this event at 1853 is also supported by Hepokoski, who, it should be said, is hardly an unbiased observer on this point, having something of a theological ax to grind against the idea of personal absolution. He says that the date is confirmed by "Martti Miettinen, on the basis of impressive research" (Hepokoski 2002a, p. 38). He also cites two letters of Raattamaa, one in 1881 recalling that "the preaching of the gospel and the forgiveness of sins have been preached purely only 30 years in Tornio Lapland and on the banks of the Tornio River," i.e., since 1851, and another in 1891 recalling that the keys have "been in use over 40 years," i.e., by 1851 (p. 39).

> my heart that you are God's people." Again Raattamaa said, "Then you believe what we say to you in behalf of God." She responded, "I believe." Then Raattamaa went to her and placed his hand on her. When he had declared the forgiveness of sins to her, the girl was so overcome with joy that she began praising God. (Leivo 2005, 126-7)

Raattamaa wondered "whether he had done the right thing," but was reassured when he arrived home and consulted his New Testament. It opened to John 20, "which tells about how Jesus blew on his disciples and said, 'Receive ye the Holy Ghost: whosoever sins ye remit, they are remitted unto them; and whosoever sins ye retain, they are retained.'" Then Raattamaa "finally realized that this is indeed the command of Jesus" (p. 127).

This belated realization by Raattamaa, the timing of his "discovery of the keys" and Laestadius' initial misgivings to it, and the lack of first-hand accounts of the keys being used in conversion before the discovery makes it seem that the early awakenings did not involve the proclamation of the forgiveness of sins from a believer to a penitent one. But that is completely contrary to the Conservative Laestadian doctrine that such a personal proclamation is the only way for one to receive forgiveness of his sins, including the "greatest sin" of unbelief (see **4.2.5** and **4.6.2**). It seems like a vexing problem indeed for a church to teach that its doctrine never changes and yet have its founders entering into "living faith" without the benefit of the very proclamation of the forgiveness of sins that is one of its distinguishing characteristics and central doctrines.

Aatu Laitinen, a prominent early Laestadian preacher who eventually became estranged from the Conservatives, provided another description of the event in a 1917 writing:

> There was once at services an awakened servant, whose time to return home had come. The hour of departure approached, and her sorrow grew because she had to leave with her load of sin. Raattamaa then asked her whether she believed they were the people of God. She said that she believed. He then asked whether she believed it to be the grace of God if they, on behalf of God, testify the forgiveness of sins to her in the name and blood of Jesus. She promised to believe that too. Then Raattamaa laid his hands on her and declared to this sorrowing soul the most

precious testimony that can be uttered on earth, and the effect was immediately evident in the servant's great joy and rejoicing. So she, praising God, left for home rejoicing in the manner of the royal chamberlain of Ethiopia [Acts 8:39]. From that time on, Raattamaa said, he was convinced that the keys of the Kingdom of Heaven are to be kept in use in the congregation of God for the salvation of men and that repentance and forgiveness of sins are to be preached boldly among all the people. [from Hepokoski 2002a, 37]

In **1884**, with the doctrine of the keys firmly in place, we finally see a conversion experience in which they are used, as Heikki Jussila recalls that event in his own life some 50 years after the fact in *The Grace of the Caller* (1948). He had spent months in distress over his sins and experienced only temporary relief through confession at his local parsonage (pp. 22-23). Then he encountered "a believing seminarian" who "had the gifts and light of the Holy Spirit to explain false righteousness" and "went immediately to ask him for advice. He had the keys of the Kingdom of Heaven. Then happened simultaneously in Heaven that pardon which was given here upon Earth." Jussila "was able to come in from the outside, into the Kingdom of God" (p. 25).

4.1.5 Mysticism

> *Penitents are said to be true when, in confession before the people and the preachers, they make a loud weeping noise, with strange and wild gesticulations, and in general behave like people bereft of reason.*
>
> —Andrew Wangberg, *Bible Pioneer Work in Norwegian Lapland*

Laestadius wrote of many mystical experiences, his own and those of his contemporaries. As a child, he experienced sensations of an "oft-smelled odor of death" and dreams in which he struggled with the dead, both of which he looked back on as being "without doubt a reminder or foreboding of spiritual and eternal death" (*VCW*, 26).

Following his 1844 conversion, his sermons "took on a more strident coloring" and bore "a strange mysticism," with his parishioners' hearts beginning "to feel tender, hard, or swollen" in spiritual distress (pp. 36-37). After a year of such preaching, "the first 'signs of grace'" began to appear. An earthquake was felt "in the same instant" as a "certain Lapp woman, who had long been under the law, became reconciled or graced," something he connected with trembling of "the underground powers" (p. 43). He considered the "sign of grace" experienced first by the Lapp woman to be "a holy goal for all the awakened but not yet graced souls–an infinitely great and high goal, toward which all who have a troubled spirit should strive" (p. 44). In the following years, he would report,

> it has happened, even though somewhat rarely, that men have smelled the foul odor of brimstone, when someone has wailed under hard pain of conscience; they have even seen vapor rising from the mouths of those from whom the odor of brimstone has come. Sometimes light-colored streaks have been seen hovering over those who have been intensely moved or joyous. I myself have seen these light-colored streaks, lightnings, and flashes many times, yet without the ability to decide with certainty whether this has happened outside of myself or within myself; however, it appears to be most believable that the lightnings and flashes, which I have seen, have been in my own heart. On Christmas Eve in 1847, as I was going to church–when I saw the church road full of people–I was struck in my heart by an inner lightning or flash, which I have felt many times in circumstances such as these. The sight of the crowd of people streaming into church, namely, awakened a momentary feeling, which like lightning flashed through my heart, and which was followed just as quickly by an awakening thought: 'Is it wretched I that must be the leader of these blind ones into eternity?' A few seconds afterwards, I saw a great, bright flame rising from the roof of the Karesuando church, in a southerly direction. [pp. 49-50]

Forces of evil were believed to have made visible appearances, "as small black specters flying and flapping around the lighted candles in the chandelier" in the Karesuando church, "as a bear, which lay under my bed and tried to lift up the bed," and a "great dragon showing me his teeth" (p. 50).

Laestadius defended the "Christians' visions and revelations" against "rationalist theologians" who considered them to be "superstition, imagination, and delusion," noting that the Bible told of spirits crawling into a herd of swine and casting a youth into the fire and the waters (p. 50). Most of his awakened hearers of the word have seen the Savior, whether on the cross, or in the garden, or as risen from the dead. And even though the insensitive intellectual can consider visions such as these to be the consequences of highly-agitated imagination, the believer must nevertheless hold them to be real; for reality and religion is precisely in this, that the doctrine of reconciliation becomes alive and clear to the doubting one, even as the disciples had to receive the visible and feelable assurance of the reality of this living Word. [p. 51]

He was impressed by the fact that "the objects appear so clearly and brightly, in definite order and time sequence. Children who have never read the Bible can quote some Bible passages by chapter and verse while experiencing a vision," and a few "have had the ability to speak in tongues" (p. 55). Vividly describing a woman's dream visions of Jesus, heaven, hell, and people on the road to both, he marveled "at the clarity of comprehension, the orderliness and clarity of thoughts" (pp. 56-60).

In addition to visions, the mystical "manifestations of living Christianity" (p. 47) around Laestadius included overwhelming emotions experienced by parishioners during services, who filled the church with ecstatic outbursts of movement and utterance that came to be known as *liikutuksia*. Due to these "high feelings," which Laestadius held to be "the essence of living Christianity" (p. 46), without which there is only "dead faith" (p. 83), people "shrieked and screamed, rose and embraced one another, swung their arms, jumped, spun in circles, danced and fell in heaps on the floor or even in snowbanks" (Hepokoski 2000, 12).

It's worth asking whether Laestadius was aware of very similar manifestations and "high feelings" in the "great awakenings," religious revivals that had been occurring in America, off and on, for 100 years (Mercer 2009, 11-13). At the Cane Ridge, Kentucky camp meeting (see **caneridge.org** <http://www.caneridge.org/>), Peter Cartwright preached over 14,000 sermons and baptized 12,000 people, and would recall in his 1857 autobiography that the "heavenly fire spread in almost every direction. It was said, by truthful witnesses, that at times more than one thousand persons broke out into loud shouting all at once." In the presence of "a warm song or sermon, "people were "seized with a convulsive jerking all over, which they could not by any possibility avoid," and would usually "rise up and dance" (from Mercer 2009, 13). I have not come across any indication that Laestadius knew of these events, but if so, he would have needed to either accept the thousands of new converts in America as being in "living faith" (which seems unlikely), or back down from his view that such ecstatic experiences were essential indications of living faith.

Raattamaa was also a participant in the early mysticism, writing an 1873 letter about a trance he had experienced about a year earlier, in which he

> saw a brown dragon driving through the air on a brown horse from the south to the north with a great sound and rumbling, so that people were terrified, and brown scales fell to the earth. This is a new reminder to us that the dragon is not a fly, but a roaring lion. After that I saw a great brightness on the western side of the heavens which suddenly spread itself. There was a new heaven and no sun, for all was just as bright; and a great multitude sang sweet hallelujah with a loud voice. [from Kulla 1985, 390]

In a sermon published in 1898, Antin Pieti described "a certain vision, which appeared to an awakened soul." The visionary "saw hell burning as a foaming rapids, where the condemned heathens were swimming. On the flames of hell was set a great kettle with a lock, which the evil spirit guarded. Then another evil spirit was brought to hell," which the visionary "said was a soul which once was a Christian, but had not followed the footsteps of Jesus. This soul was put into the flaming kettle, when the evil one opened the cover. Hot fiery flames shot up, and as people endeavored to cling to the sides the evil spirits swiped at them with a great saber, and then closed the lid (*Sanomia Siionista*, from Kulla 1993, 84).

Also in 1898, after a contentious meeting with doctrinal opponents, Heikki Jussila "fell into a trance and a voice from Heaven said: 'Jussila, keep what thou hast, that none may take away thy crown.' Then it opened to me that God's way to grace is that to which God had helped me from the way of self-righteousness and on which he had also preserved me" (Jussila 1948, 72).

The Conservative historian Mauri Kinnunen has supplied me with a translation of an interesting set of recollections about Laestadianism in the 1860s and 1870s. They were recorded in 1883 by the preacher Erik Stock, based on what his father had told him. They include a vivid description of the deep Pietism and mysticism that was expected at the time:

> When Laestadius was still alive, a burning sense of sin was required, one that made you scream for mercy from God. The Elders named a couple things that you had to know as a testimony of receiving the grace. Firstly, you had to know the time and place of the resurrection. Secondly, you had had to have seen Jesus in spirit, suffering, death and resurrected. To those who could figure these out with their experience (even without meaning) was given the testimony of a child of God. Then the power of law was stronger than the power of grace. [from Kinnunen 2012]

After Laestadius's death in 1861, however, it was felt "that enough law had been preached and that the number of believers had not became as great as they had hoped it would." The Laestadians felt that the awakenings had concluded, especially among the young, and that excessive sensitivity about the law's demands left people with a sense that they had no strength to follow suit. So "they started to use grace and forgiveness of sins to make people admit that Jesus is in their hearts and that all the sins have been forgiven for them." But that

> didn't work too well either, because some were reluctant to say such things. After that, they began to preach forgiveness of sins at services, without asking whether they [the audience] wanted or needed it. Consequently, it looked like it worked well, and that the congregation started spreading at a great pace. However, this effect was like morning dew that disappears before noon. Namely, this was like patching an old garment instead of getting a new one. Also, there was neither knowledge, enlightenment [of the Holy Spirit], unanimity nor vigilance ... [from Kinnunen 2012]

By 1978, an article in *Päivämies* would speak quite disparagingly of "signs and wonders":

> † "Into the picture of false prophets, particularly in the last times, belongs not only the performing of small tricks, but great wonders and signs. For this reason, if someone declares unto us that a certain such wonder happened at one of these meetings, and on this basis assures us that the great power of God was in

effect there, we can answer, "Whether or not such wonders took place is not conclusive. According to the teachings of Jesus, such wonders will still, and especially in the last times, be associated with the works of false prophets" (from VOZ, 6/1978).

The mysticism that Laestadius valued so highly had fallen by the wayside. It only remained in the form of vocal outbursts of "rejoicing" that occurred during services, a "voice of praise to the Lord Jesus heard from the House of God" that was, in Erkki Reinikainen's 1969 observation, "a continual object of ridicule" (p. 42). And even that mild vestige of the *liikutuksia* from a hundred years earlier became less and less frequent until it completely disappeared in the 1990s.

4.1.6 Schisms

> *Protestants are still an unsettled bunch. To this day they continue to fight theological battles among themselves; battles that result in increasing numbers of official denominations.*
>
> —Calvin Mercer, *Slaves to Faith*

The Laestadian movement has split into numerous separate factions in the past hundred years. This diagram, reprinted with permission from *A Godly Heritage* (Foltz and Yliniemi 2005), illustrates the timeline of the divisions with approximate size of the resulting groups. (Not shown is a very small schism that took place in the OALC, and two in the SRK, some decades ago.)

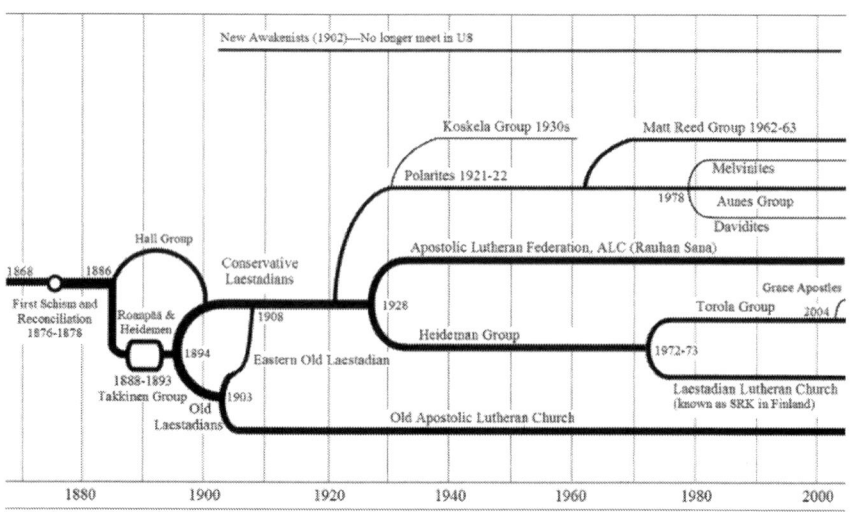

The Conservative ordained pastor John Lehtola discusses the history of the various schisms in his 2007 Master's Thesis, the first of which occurred at "the turn of the century," when "Laestadianism in Scandinavia splintered into three major groups in three different geographical locations in Finland and Sweden. Until the death of Raattamaa [in 1899], there was formal unity among the different groups, even though differences in doctrine existed. Time and again, Raattamaa was able to reconcile the differences between the groups, but after his death the schisms became a reality. The Eastern Laestadians who lived in the Tornio River valley were known as the Conservative Laestadians" (p. 9). The other two groups were the "Firstborn," Laestadians west of the Tornio River who claimed (with considerable justification) to follow in the footsteps of the original Laestadian elders, and the "New Awakening."

"After 1908," Lehtola continues, "American Laestadianism, or the Apostolic Lutheran church, was divided in three main groups." The Conservative Laestadians organized as the SRK and were called "the Heideman Group, after their leader," Arthur Leopold (A.L.) Heideman, and were in spiritual communion with the Tornio River valley Laestadians. The other groups were "the Old Apostolic Lutheran Church, or the First Born," led by John Takkinen and in communion with the Firstborn west of the Tornio River, and "the 'Large Meeting Group'" who would later become the Apostolic Lutheran Federation (pp. 23-24). The divisions between the three groups were not entirely complete until the 1930s, and there were even residual affiliations between the Conservatives and the Federation later than that in the Wolf Lake, MN area, with the final division between the two taking place in 1956 (Palola 2010). Until the 1950s, in some remote locations of the Dakotas and Alberta, the Apostolic Lutheran settlements were so small in size that all of the Apostolic Lutherans would join together for services whenever a preacher came from any of the three groups (Palola 2011).

The Conservatives would suffer four other schisms in the 20th century. Although each was mostly confined to one side of the Atlantic, there were connections between the various offshoot groups. In North America, a group of "extreme evangelicals" led by John Pollari, "who did not believe in the need of reproofs and instruction" withdrew and built their own church buildings and congregations, forming the Independent Apostolic Lutheran Church (Kulla 2004, 63). That occurred over the course of a few years around 1920, when the Conservatives still had some ties with the Federation (pp. 63 and 75-76). A 1973 split cost the North American Conservatives most of their preachers and about half of the total membership, who formed the First Apostolic Lutheran Church (FALC) under the dominant leadership of Walter Torola.

In 1934, some Finnish preachers "who had gone to America without approval" were "expelled from the SRK," and formed the "Small Firstborn," which now has ties with the Federation (p. 86). A "minister's heresy" resulted in the departure of most of the SRK's ordained clergy from 1959 to 1961, forming the "Word of Life," but that schism had limited impact on total membership. At issue was whether the Lutheran confessions take priority when they conflict with Laestadian ideas. One Finnish pastor with a Conservative Laestadian background told me, "The heresy of pappis [ordained pastors] was that they could not join the heresy formed by lay preachers" in allowing the Lutheran confessions to yield in such cases. In an ironic twist, those "who were in the forefront of expelling" the ordained pastors from the SRK found themselves considered heretics by the SRK and, in 1977, formed their own group that became associated with the FALC in America (Kulla 2004, 86).

Today the SRK is a dominant voice of Laestadianism in Finland, with highly visible spokesmen, publications, and widely attended Summer Services. It has two main rival groups there, whose total membership is only a fraction of the SRK's. In North America, the situation is quite different–the remainder of the SRK's remaining counterpart (now organized as the LLC) has four rival Laestadian groups, three of comparable size as the LLC. They are the Old Apostolic Lutheran Church (OALC), the Apostolic Lutheran Church or "Federation" (or ALC), the First Apostolic Lutheran Church (FALC), and the Independent Apostolic Lutheran Church (IALC).

The OALC

The Firstborn is known in America as the Old Apostolic Lutheran Church (OALC). It is the most conservative of the Laestadian factions. Kulla's estimate is that the OALC has about 8,000 members and "is possibly the largest group of Laestadians in America (Kulla 2004, 102).

When comparing the different groups, labeling the SRK and LLC as "Conservative Laestadianism" can be misleading, because the OALC is far more conservative in its adherence to the teachings, social outlook, and even language patterns of Laestadius himself. It also adheres to stricter behavioral norms and practices confession as part of absolution much more consistently.

If you want to see 19th century Laestadianism preserved like an insect in a chunk of amber, just attend an OALC service. I have done so twice, at two different localities, and found it a fascinating experience both times. The services begin with slow, mournful singing unaccompanied by any musical instruments and then proceed to a reading of one of Laestadius's sermons. I sat in the pews surrounded by men in long sleeve western or dress shirts (no ties) and women wearing headscarves and dresses, listening to the harsh, archaic rantings of Laestadius about whores and grace thieves and wondered if I had stepped into a time machine. Things didn't lighten up much from that point, either.

The sermon reading was followed by a long pause as the congregation's entire cohort of preachers–all sitting in chairs several feet behind the pulpit and facing the congregation–awaited the inspiration for one of them to take the helm for a live sermon. Finally, one stepped forward with a great show of reluctance, sat down, and asked for a text to be read by another who joined him at the pulpit. Then began a full ten minutes of drama as the preacher mournfully lamented his unworthiness to expound on the great words already provided by the elder Laestadius. Perhaps some words might still be given, he at last allowed, and sure enough, I sat through another 40 minutes or so of traditional, repetitive exposition of the text, line by tedious line.

If the Book of Mormon is "chloroform in print," as Mark Twain put it, then those two sermons were the audio version. Most of those under the age of about 15 seemed oblivious to what was being said. (They had tuned out the Laestadius reading entirely.) I remained awake mostly because of how interesting I found the parallels to be between the sermon and those I had grown up listening to in the late 1970s. I noticed a number of phrases that are still used in LLC sermons, e.g., "living faith," "a new day of grace," "we want to be obedient." Interjections like "I believe," "even," and "we could say" were scattered throughout the sermons as a sort of verbal curtseying before God who was, after all, the one providing the words. The public proclamation of forgiveness–the "general blessing" to the assembled congregation–was present, too.

Like the sermons of my childhood, the delivery had a sing-song cadence that is almost hypnotic. As the preacher grows more and more emotional, the high notes get louder and the cadence quickens. Everybody knows what is coming–subconsciously or otherwise, they start feeling the spirit as well. Finally, the preacher tearfully confesses his own sinfulness and the congregation preaches absolution to him, as he did to them a few moments earlier. (In the OALC sermons, the preacher also turned to his pulpit companion for absolution.)

It seemed to me that the emotionalism was a bit forced in the OALC sermons. I would not be surprised if the OALC's devotion to tradition is motivating both its preachers and its members to produce the appearance of a pietism that isn't always genuinely felt. Still, the next thing that happened in the OALC services was a genuine spiritual experience for at least a significant part of the congregation. Immediately after the congregation preached the words of absolution to the preacher, perhaps a third of the congregants confessed and preached absolution to each other in the pews and aisles. For 10-20 minutes, the sanctuary was filled with the sound of confessions–in voices that often took on a plaintive, wailing sound–and the preaching of forgiveness in response. The keening sound of women rejoicing could also be heard, and I saw a lot of people wiping away tears, men and women alike. During all of this, the preachers remained at the front of the sanctuary behind the pulpit, standing to receive the 5-10% or so of the congregants who felt the need to go to one of them for absolution.

During these encounters, women embraced and men stood with one hand on each other's shoulders. The amount of time they spent indicated to me that there was always some sort of a confession, not just the general request for "a blessing" that occurs among Conservatives. (In the LLC, that now consists mostly of turning to your spouse or friend at the communion rail and–if you are not too young or bashful–occasionally raising your hand during a particularly emotional part of a sermon.)

In none of this can I find cause for Conservative Laestadianism to condemn the OALC. Perhaps one might charge that the OALC lapses into idolatry with its zealous esteem of "the dear precious elders of Swedish Lapland" who all reside in Gällivare, Sweden, and in its belief that Laestadius is the seventh angel of Revelation, a prophet it refers to as the "firstborn" (not to be confused with the name of their movement).

He is set apart even from the Gällivare elders, who themselves are above the lay members, congregation elders, preachers, and missionary preachers of the OALC's strict hierarchy. But as a Conservative correspondent remarked to me, "They have their elders, and we have the Mother congregation" (see 4.4.4).

The condemnation between the OALC and the Conservatives is a mutual feeling. They consider each other heretics, bound for hell just like everybody else in the "dead faiths" of the world. The introduction to the OALC's *History of Living Christianity in America* (1974) provides a glimpse of its view of itself in opposition to everyone else:

> Throughout North America the true Laestadian or living Christianity is flourishing. All those who have sought and found the truth have entered into the one Sheepfold through the door, Lord Jesus. There, under the care of the one Shepherd in the Church of the Firstborn, have they found peace and rest for their immortal souls. There they have received the indwelling Holy Spirit and the love of Christ, and there they stand united in one-mindedness and love, in the bosom of the true Mother.
>
> Let the winds of false doctrine below, let the waves of ungodliness roar, they stand firm and secure for they have a sure place of shelter and refuge. They need not fear nor be in great distress as so many of those who grope about in blindness in the various factions, not knowing which way to turn nor what to hold onto.

The book makes an oblique reference to Conservative Laestadianism when discussing the history of the OALC in Brainerd, Minnesota and recalling "some of the terrible trials that beset the living Christianity":

> When another spirit began to work in man, which was opposed to the spirit of God, great harm was done to God's work in the hearts of many innocent ones. So it was in Brainerd also, that the spirit of opposition to the truth lead the greater number away, leaving only a few clinging to the original doctrine with full trust upon the Elders of Swedish Lapland. [p. 7]

Brainerd was probably the last place where fellowship continued between members of the OALC and the Conservatives. It was actually a three-way relationship of lingering Laestadian ties that included members of the Federation as well. Two of those Federation members are Carl and Martha Kulla, who were born in the area in 1920 and 1927, respectively. They both recall the common fellowship. "We were all just Christians," Carl told me in one of my visits to their Brush Prairie, WA home. Martha sadly told a story of her little friends in the Conservative group finally coming to her one day and saying they had needed "to repent of considering her a Christian."

Another OALC reference to the other Laestadian groups is found in a 1953 article by William Eriksson:

> For those, who have completely separated themselves from the truth of the original doctrine, even though they labor in the name of Laestadius, labor not within that doctrine or follow it in faith, doctrine, and striving, but labor together with dead Christendom. They have by name dispersed into many different groups and factions, yet all have the same spirit with the world and permissibility to commit sins, such as finery, friendship with the world, greed, fleshly freedom and lordly Christianity, against which they have not dared to preach severely, because the world and dead Christianity would be offended. . . . However, there is still one flock which wants to follow the original truth of the doctrine in life, in walk and in faith . . . [*The Father's Voice*, 324]

Eriksson's comment about "the original truth" leads to an uncomfortable issue for Conservative Laestadians: Raattamaa, the successor to Laestadius, was firmly in support of the OALC and their first leader, John Takkinen. While the Conservatives and the OALC consider each other heretics, both claim Raattamaa as their own. Though he is himself a Conservative, Tuomas Palola presents a history that appears quite unfavorable to the Conservative position in his 2000 Master's thesis:

> Raattamaa wrote already in January 1889 to Takkinen, who had been removed from the pastor's office, and stated that he still had the support of the Scandinavian Laestadian leadership. During spring in 1889, the Scandinavian Laestadian leadership took a stand repeatedly in their letters to North America supporting Takkinen: Takkinen "has been sent by God," and, although "he may be driven out of the Calumet parsonage, he will not depart from the firstborn congregation," which will protect him. . . . When he received a description of the events in Calumet from Takkinen, Raattamaa especially criticized Hietanen, Juola, and

Jacob Vuollet for opposing Takkinen. Raattamaa and Juhonpieti admonished the Apostolic Lutherans toward reconciliation. [Palola 2000, 48]

During the summer of 1889, Raattamaa continued his defense of Takkinen, writing

> to Takkinen and Henrik Koller (1859-1935) in Calumet. According [to] Raattamaa, the "persecution" of Takkinen was caused by the fact that Takkinen was the "real preacher of the gospel." Takkinen was not to give in because he lost the keys to the Calumet Church, for "the keys to the Kingdom of Heaven are more important than the church keys, which the official clergymen can keep." At the same time, Juhani Raattamaa marveled in a letter that he sent to his son, Peter Raattamaa, how he could be against Takkinen. Juhani Raattamaa admonished his son toward reconciliation with Takkinen[,] ... emphasized the firstborn congregation[,] ... and stated that "they who are in fellowship with it will not follow the dictates of a newborn sect." ... In Raattamaa's opinion, those who had struggled against Takkinen were not appropriate to be sent to America. [pp. 49-50]

When A.L. Heideman (who would lead the Conservative group after 1908) stated his intention to go to America during these doctrinal disputes, Raattamaa

> said to Heideman that the Apostolic Lutherans did not want an ordained clergyman, especially those who were in agreement with the firstborn congregation. Heideman had stated to Raattamaa that he would go to America as a secretary, and not as a clergyman. Raattamaa reported to America that he had not sent Heideman even as a secretary and thus avoided giving support to Heideman. In addition, Raattamaa stated that only Lumijarvi and Takkinen had been sent by the firstborn congregation, and Daniels, Starkka and Koller were "approved otherwise." Raattamaa reported that he trusted the supporters of Takkinen the most. Only a few days later, Raattamaa clarified his impression of Heideman: Heideman was a true Christian, but young and had recently repented, and for that reason the firstborn congregation had not wanted to send him to North America as a representative of the firstborn congregation. [p. 52]

Raattamaa didn't condemn Heideman; he did declare him "competent to preach to the 'sorrowless'" (p. 52) and, when Heideman and his traveling companion had arrived in Calumet, "admonished them to be considered as 'precious' brothers" even though they "had not been sent by the firstborn congregation" (p. 54). Even so, he

> used strong language regarding the opponents and wrote that "piggish animals want to destroy the wall of the vineyard which Takkinen has built and cared for over a decade." He admonished his son, Peter Raattamaa, to repent before Takkinen. Raattamaa could not understand how such men could rise from Laestadianism who did not approve of Takkinen. [p. 54]

In March 1891, after Takkinen's group had lost ownership of the Calumet church to Heideman's group (Lehtola 2007, 13-14), Raattamaa still "encouraged the supporters of Takkinen to continue their work: although the church was gone, the true preachers have not gone. In April, Raattamaa repeated the thought: 'We do not obey sects nor sectors, but we remain in the bosom of the firstborn congregation'" (Palola 2000, 57). Later that year, Raattamaa wrote to Takkinen rejoicing of his retaining many supporters, "although 'the clergy prepared in colleges' had started to break up the congregation" (p. 59), and marveling at how the Americans could have been offended in the name, 'firstborn congregation'" (p. 60).

Takkinen died unexpectedly in February 1892. "Raattamaa admonished both parties involved toward reconciliation when he reported Takkinen's death" and "wrote as his own viewpoint that the [Calumet Firstborn] congregation should elect a pastor from among the supporters of Takkinen" (p. 63). In an 1892 letter following Takkinen's death, Raattamaa made his conclusions clear about Takkinen's eternal fate: "Yet we remember our beloved brother and fellow laborer, John Takkinen, with sorrow and joy, even though his body is resting in the bosom of his Fatherland, but his glorified soul is rejoicing in the Paradise of God" (from Kulla 1985, 393).

In 1898, less than a year before his own death, Raattamaa addressed a letter to a number of Takkinen supporters, calling them "beloved brothers and faithful workers in the Lord's Vineyard" (from Kulla 1985, 395). They included Matoniemi and Ojala, two Firstborn pastors who had succeeded the deceased Takkinen (Palola 2000, 82) and Koller, who five years hence had begun using "the paper *Siionin Sanomat* that he published to assist him more clearly in his attack against the congregation led by Heideman" (p. 68). In the letter, Raattamaa sent "greetings of love" to Heideman and his preaching companion, Rajaniemi, and said, "Yet I remind, preach the sermon of reconciliation. Forgive and believe the sins of controversy forgiven. Don't judge one another for all kinds of faults" (from Kulla 1985, 396).

Today, Conservatives consider Takkinen and his Firstborn group (now the OALC) to be heretical, *but Raattamaa never held that view*. As Palola concludes, albeit with some caveats about potentially incomplete information to or from Raattamaa, "[b]ased on preserved letters it appears that in the 'crisis of two churches,' Raattamaa clearly placed himself in support of Takkinen and the Old Apostolic Lutherans" (Palola 2000, 71).

During my first visit to an OALC service, I wound up discussing some of this history during the dinner they provide afterwards. It was an odd feeling to be surrounded by *Laestadians* gently prodding me about my unsaved status, considering *my* group one of the heretics who had left the original Christianity. The nerve of them, when of course it is *they* who are the heretics! We had an interesting and cordial time, though, talking about arcane topics like the Heidemans booting the OALC out of the Pine Street church in Calumet, Michigan a hundred years ago like it was yesterday's news. (*Me, with a smile:* Yep, we sure did.) And, despite their understated manner, they seemed surprised at my willingness to concede that the OALC is the group following in the footsteps of the original elders. As I have found throughout my research for this book, facts are facts whether we like them or not.

The New Awakening

Heikki Jussila spent a considerable part of his preaching career battling the New Awakening. He compared it to a storm that, in 1896 "had burst throughout the land even to the outermost areas.... It tried the foundations severely, wishing to rob faith and hope from everyone. It sought to examine and condemn everyone. Because it had a different spirit and doctrine, it did not recognize the work of the Holy Spirit nor consider it correct. It prohibited the forgiveness of sins in the name and blood of Jesus. It ridiculed the doctrine of absolution in justification and elevated inner imaginations in its place" (Jussila 1948, 71). "The most sorrowful matter of all," Jussila writes, "was that in the New Awakening it was taught to reject the former Christianity by repentance and that they spoke mockingly of the blood of Jesus in absolution" (p. 78).

Jussila was given to hyperbole, but the New Awakening was certainly a soul-searing, pietistic movement that did have a legalistic inclination, as acknowledged by one defender quoted in a 1973 lecture: "We have been warning against hypocrisy and dead faith for so long that we don't dare to believe at all" (from Kulla 2010, 128). One can get an idea of how emotionally demanding it was to the penitent from the following passage by one of its founders, Mikko Saarenpää, written in 1912:

> Preciously redeemed souls cannot be freed from these bonds of the devil in any other way than by awakening from sin, and, as in the time of John the Baptist, confessing their sins, becoming naked, open, and honorless. Let it be known, wretched men, that you cannot go to heaven with your honor; you must be shamed, despised, and persecuted by the world. You cannot go from a joyful world to a joyful heaven. You must weep and cry for yourself and your children, as Jesus said on Good Friday to the women and to His disciples. [from Kulla 2010, 50]

Consider, though, that Conservative Laestadianism in decades past has used much the same type of pietistic language, as did Laestadius. See the quotes from earlier years in **4.2.6**.

There was an effort at reconciliation in 1911. "The New Awakened were accused of withholding forgiveness from people, but when they did ask forgiveness, for statements and harshness of words, forgiveness was withheld from them" by the conservatives (Kulla 2004, 93). As of 2000, they had membership of about 3,000 in Finland (p. 95). "It is no longer an awakening movement," having "been almost entirely assimilated into the national Lutheran Church of Finland" and with none remaining in America (Kulla 2010, 5).

The Apostolic Lutheran Federation

The schism with the "Large Meeting Group" slowly erupted among the Eastern or Conservative Laestadians from the 1920s into the 1930s. According to Lehtola, the

> main doctrinal difference between the Heideman Group and the Apostolic Lutheran Federation concerned the "doctrine of the church." The Federation wanted to grant all Laestadians freedom

to attend the services of any Laestadian group they desired, and were dissatisfied with a "narrow party spirit." They urged all Laestadian groups to show more love to one another, for God had children in all groups who must someday get along in the same heaven, they claimed. In heaven there will be no party boundaries, they stated. All God's children will be united there. The Federation adherents greeted the Heideman Group members with "God's peace" and kept them as spiritual brethren, but the Heideman Group members refused to reciprocate. The Heideman Group did not consider them as spiritual brethren, for God had children in only one outwardly determinable group." [2007, 24]

The same positions remain held by the three groups to this day. The Conservatives and the First Born consider each other and the Federation heretical, while the Federation offers its unrequited acceptance to them both.

I have had the privilege of becoming friends with a wonderful old couple in the Federation, Carl and Martha Kulla. In four visits to their home, I have been able to learn some of the facts of church history that Carl holds in such amazing depth and accessibility in his 90-year old brain. But I also learned something that my history books about Laestadianism failed to fully convey: The fruit of the spirit ("love, joy, peace, longsuffering, gentleness, goodness, faith, meekness, temperance," Galatians 5:22-23) is to be found among other Laestadians as well. As I sat at the Kullas' little kitchen table and in their living room, hearing their stories and testimony of unfeigned faith, being greeted with "God's Peace" by some of their many grandchildren who stopped by the house, my already waning belief in the exclusivity of my own particular group flailed about in search of support that I could no longer find.

Carl has reached out to the LLC in the same way he has to the other Laestadian groups. Copies of *The Voice of Zion* arrive at his home along with the FALC's *Greetings of Peace* and his own group's *Christian Monthly*. He has attended the LLC summer services as well as local services in Longview, WA. He has visited and written to the LLC offices, telling of his struggle in writing a letter to an LLC preacher in October 1997 "because I accept you as a brother in faith, but I realize that for you this is impossible." Yet he would "not ask you to do otherwise than your conscience allows."

Responding in a November 1997 letter, the LLC preacher acknowledged that his "conscience will not allow me to accept you as a brother in faith." He declined to cite any reason for that judgment (and let's call it what it is), admitting that he had "not lived through nor witnessed firsthand any of the heresies that have torn living Christianity." But, he was "nonetheless certain that they have been caused by true differences in spirit and doctrine. Surely, you must recognize this as well." Why was he so certain that the schisms were not caused by something else, e.g., the divisive leaders of the era, misunderstandings, and prejudices? Because the LLC's view of its history and exclusivity (**4.2.1**) had fixed his conclusion firmly in place. His unspecified spiritual and doctrinal differences are the roads that all lead to Rome, and, unsurprisingly, he does "not believe that these can be dismissed as insignificant nor that unity can be purchased at the expense of doctrine."

What the LLC preacher does dismiss as insignificant are all of the fruits of faith present in Carl's life along with the signs by which Luther said a "Christian, holy people" could be identified (*WA* 50, 628). Unlike Luther, the preacher is not at all "certain that where the Gospel is preached, there must be Christians" (*PE* 4, 75). Instead, he is certain of his own superficial observations during a brief visit Carl had made to the LLC office, where the preacher "was left with the impression that you were a man who recognized his sinfulness and despaired of it, but who was not confident of his salvation and did not possess the peace that Christ gives His own." As someone who has taken the time to get to know Carl, to sit down with him for hours and hear him speak of a humble and heartfelt faith, I shake my head in disgust at the arrogance of this statement. Unfortunately, we will encounter many more like it in **4.2.3**.

The LLC preacher continues: "Knowledge of Christ and His redemption work is not at all the same thing as faith in Him and His work." You might well ask, what's the difference? It is the preacher's encoding of "faith" to mean a manifestation of the Holy Spirit that is only in the LLC (see **4.5.3**). "It would be my great joy to someday receive you as a brother in Christ," the preacher concludes, "but I am convinced and firmly believe that it can only happen if you repent from the heresy in which you are presently entangled."

That kind of "repentance" seems more like an oath of loyalty to a new allegiance than a turning away from actual sin and unbelief. It's not a unique demand of Conservative Laestadianism. In the Christian Convention Church, for example, converts are required to "renounce any previous 'born-again' experience while in another 'Christian' church, saying that it was an emotional experience of Satan" (Lewis 2004, 10-11). Anyone wanting to join "who has believed in Jesus before he heard the True ministry is not allowed Fellowship until he admits that he had not received Jesus before he met the workers. They want to hear the new member declare that all his previous Christian faith was wrong. That is their view of 'repentance'" (p. 11).

One of my visits with Carl and Martha was in the company of two other LLC preachers, whom I brought along in hopes that some sort of acceptance could be had. But those preachers, who went there more to speak than to listen, soon found themselves being preached back to on every point. During the drive to and from the Kulla home, we had discussions of Carl's spiritual state that seemed to me to quickly devolve into circularity. "Why is Carl not 'believing,' when he accepts the preached proclamation of forgiveness, including when he hears it at LLC services and when I preached it to him?", I asked. The answer: "Because he does not 'comprehend the doctrine of the Kingdom.'" To which I said, "I don't 'comprehend' that doctrine either, so why I am I 'believing'?" There was no satisfactory answer. When confronted by the awkward case of a person who accepts the forgiveness of his sins as preached from "God's Kingdom" but not the need to forsake his existing non-LLC Christian fellowship, the LLC exclusivist resorts to the tautology that one is not "in the Kingdom" simply because he is not "in the Kingdom."

I would also inquire about the spiritual state of the LLC's "doctrinal father" Luther, who quoted Jesus the same way Carl answered the LLC preachers ("The kingdom of God is within you," and "cometh not with observation"), and who asked how he could "deny Christ, Who clearly says here that there is no locality, place or anything external in the kingdom of God." See **5.2** for the full quote and many others like it. If one must acknowledge the walls as well as reside within them, as discussed in **4.2.1** ("No Compromises"), the Laestadian Lutheran Church must condemn the man whose name is part of its own.

The FALC

The First Apostolic Lutheran Church (FALC) was formed by Walter Torola and his followers as a result of a 1973 schism with the

Conservatives. (Torola had a very forceful presence, as did his son Peter, and I don't think it's unfair to characterize the group as comprised of a leader and followers.) The split occurred after several years in which

> the life and conduct of many was at variance with the norm of Conservative Laestadianism in America and Finland. Marriages with out-group members occurred and were often tolerated, televisions were brought into some homes and defended as acceptable, greeting members of past schisms with "God's peace" and keeping them as spiritual brethren became somewhat common and defensible. [Lehtola 2007, 42]

Those adopting and accepting these practices would coalesce into a group surrounding "Walter Torola, the long-time revered pastor of Calumet Apostolic Lutheran Church." The "Torola Group" also propounded two points of doctrine that the Conservatives would not accept. "The first concerned the doctrine of the congregation," which held that "every local membership church is its own 'mother,' a spiritually independent congregation" (p. 42). The second point

> concerned spiritual leniency. A fear of admonishment and words of teaching about conduct by Torola and his supporters existed. They also taught that apostle Peter, even after his outright denial of Christ, did not fall from faith. Some even maintained that drunkenness, adultery, fornication, and so forth, were not causes for falling from faith and inflicting spiritual death. [p. 43]

Of course, there is another side of the story. In a 1987 pamphlet, Walter Torola refers to a "strong spirit of vehement legalism" that began to be apparent in the late 60s. He mentions the "caretaking meetings" and the excommunication of those who "were not able to respond in repentance according to their examiners' requirements" (1987, 1). During a 1972 trip to Finland, he found himself and other American visitors at such a meeting "arranged by the SRK board, and [we] were greeted with a harsh accusation, that you are of a false doctrine and spirit–heretics!" (p. 2). He claims that the SRK board had "plans for a new central organization for Christianity in America," and were only "waiting for a suitable time to put into function!" (p. 4).

He and his son Peter were called to a meeting in Minneapolis in the fall of 1972, where he claims that the prominent SRK preacher Heikki Saari "had such a 'timely' understanding that if a Christian falls into any kind of a fault, he at the same time loses his faith also. He was supporting his understanding with apostle Peter's falling ... on Good Friday eve, saying, that *he surely lost his faith too at that very moment!*" (p. 5, emphasis in original). Torola's view–a main point of doctrinal contention–was that "Jesus had no doubt about His Father's help to keep even His disciple Peter in faith, although He knew, that he was going to fall into a fault." Citing Mt 26:31 and Mk 14:50, Torola continues, "He also was sure that he, the poor and faulty Peter through faith receives strength to convert (repent) from his own fault and that he also will gladly strengthen his brothers, who also were going to fall into faults in the same evening" (p. 7).

It all might seem pretty arcane to today's readers. But in the judgmental atmosphere of the time, which I believe Torola accurately portrays, those sheep who thought they smelled goats in their midst wouldn't need much of a doctrinal distinction to force a separation. Peter Herriot writes in his textbook *Religious Fundamentalism* that

> fundamentalisms are in general absolutist movements, that is, they believe that there is only one truth (their own). Hence, there is major scope for dissent when a theological or moral dispute occurs, as, by definition, only one of the parties can be right. Leaders may trigger such disputes by over-ambitious re-interpretations of doctrine to legitimate their strategic plans." [2009, 93]

With both the "Peter's denial" question and moral disagreements over television and school sports available as triggers, the contentious, strong-willed leaders on both sides had the opportunity they needed to be rid of each other. They both claim the spiritual high ground, of course. But the two sides are preaching nearly identical Laestadian theology three decades later while condemning each other as heretics, something that should give the objective observer pause before accepting the claim of either.

Another claim made by both the Torola group and the Conservatives is for Paul Heideman's name. But he had advanced dementia by 1973 and there's no basis for saying he had picked one side or the other. His wife went with the Torolas, and Paul was at least physically among them when he died (Palola 2010).

The FALC is one of the Laestadian splinter groups that I know the least about in its present day teaching and practice. That's ironic, since my parents spent some time there after the split. But the FALC publishes nothing that the general public can easily access, and indeed they seem to take a perverse sort of pride in that. So, during my latest visit with Carl Kulla (who has collected seemingly everything ever written by any Laestadian group), I spent some time reading through back issues of the *Greetings of Peace* from 2010.

Despite the charge of "spiritual leniency" that the Conservatives make against the Torola group, there was nothing in the articles that I could see a Conservative preacher finding objectionable. The articles strongly emphasize the forgiveness of sins, with no more than a few paragraphs seeming to go by without a reference to it somehow. They contain the same type of direct proclamation of absolution to the reader that went out of style in the *Voice of Zion* around the mid 1990s, as well as some of the requests for forgiveness by the author and the response by the editor that disappeared by the 1980s (**4.6.2**).

I came across one reference to Peter's denial of Christ, which indicated that it is still something that arises in their thinking somewhat, but not a major issue. However, I was surprised to see that there wasn't any overt defense of him being still "in faith" after his sin, just a statement to the effect that Peter was a sinner like the rest of us and needed forgiveness. It seemed like the kind of writing that is often used to present an issue to the younger generation in a way that conforms with the teachings of the older generation, but doesn't raise unnecessary questions on the part of the younger generation.

Overall, the issues have the same look and feel as the *Greetings of Peace* just before the 1973 split, a look that remained in the *Voice of Zion* for some years thereafter. And the articles are all theology, with the same language patterns and unrelentingly pious tone of the LLC's older publications. There is none of the "current events" and "human interest" flavor of today's *Voice of Zion*. I found that ironic, given that the Torola group was seen as the more liberal of the two at the time of the split.

Walter's son Peter Torola died in 2010, and as I expected, he was given a lengthy, somewhat worshipful obituary. But it wasn't really any more devotional to him than what I've seen in the *Voice of Zion* about prominent LLC preachers such as Elmer Alajoki and Peter Nevala. I found it amusing that they refer to their youth gatherings as "the kyds," just like the Conservatives did at the time of the split and for a while thereafter, right down to the funky spelling.

The Torola group is also exclusivist, rejecting the Conservatives along with everybody else (Kulla 2004, 103). One correspondent who recently left the FALC told me that "everything that is preached on or written in the *Greetings of Peace* is taken very literally by the members. I feel that it's getting worse the older I get, or maybe the older I get the more I see ... the FALC does preach that their church is the only way to heaven. That they are in fact the 'one true faith.'" A statement by a prominent FALC preacher, Richard Eskola, appearing in the May 2011 *Greetings of Peace*, makes that clear:

> Many sad separations have taken place in our visitation time because high minded people have no longer been content with the simple grace gospel. Many of these groups would now want to entice us to their fellowship with words like "we believe the same." This is not so. Those very words betray them. They believe there is living faith in more than one fellowship. All children of God believe there is one, and only one, kingdom of God. The body of Christ is not divided.

Kulla estimated that the FALC has 4,000-5,000 members (2004, 103). Based on the list of names in their "Christmas Greetings" in the December 2010 *Greetings of Peace* issue, I would guess that the FALC has about the same number of members as the LLC.

The IALC

Earlier, I briefly introduced John Pollari's breakaway group with Kulla's assessment of them as "extreme evangelicals" (2004, 63). Jouko Talonen has the same view, writing that Pollari reinforced "an extreme evangelical trend" that had developed in the late 1800s among North American Laestadianism, which "shunned the preaching of counsel, admonition, and repentance to Laestadian believers" (2005, 205-206).

By Warren Hepokoski's reckoning, the separation of the "Pollarites" manifested itself as a single incident between Pollari and the young Paul Heideman sometime in 1917-1918. (Hepokoski's sympathies lie much more with the Pollarite side than the Heideman one, but he is a reputable historian and the source he cites for the story is from what he calls the "legalist" side.) In Astoria, Oregon, as Hepokoski tells it,

> a young woman asked whether it was sufficient to settle a certain quarrel she had with someone privately or if it had to also be confessed before the congregation. Pollari took the position that a private settlement was sufficient, but Heideman demanded public confession. It is said that Heideman and Pollari separated as a result of this dispute and never preached together again. [2002b, 82]

There have been many further schisms within the Pollarites. The largest remaining faction is the Independent Apostolic Lutheran Church (IALC), with membership of about 3,000 (Talonen 2005, 206). An anonymous commenter on the **extoots site** <http://extoots.blogspot.com/2006/06/from-taboo-to-wahoo_7682.html> provides a summary of the current situation and a slightly higher estimate of IALC membership:

> The IALC is the Independent or Pollarite branch of the Apostolic Lutheran/Laestadian religion. There are two groups in this branch. One is small, maybe 400 or so members, and seems to be dying out. It's been referred to as the "auneslaiset." The other, the "riitimattilaiset" has probably 4-5,000 members. The smallest branch of the two is probably the LEAST restrictive of all LLL faiths in terms of lifestyle, and is also not a very shaming church at all. They preach that their God is a loving God. They do, however, seem to be in rapid decline as far as their population goes, and there are few young families in their church. The larger IALC group seems to be growing and has a tolerance for wearing modern clothes, televisions, secular music, smaller families, college educations, etc. but tends toward a more exclusivist doctrine. Both groups are known to still practice outward emotional manifestations in their religious services, so in that way, they resemble the OALC. Both groups also shun musical accompaniment (except for weddings) in their services like the OALC. However, you would not be able to pick out an IALC member on the street as they look pretty much like anyone else.

Though it imposes less lifestyle restrictions than the other Laestadian groups, "the exclusivity, shunning, and legalism is the same," according to an ex-IALC member "Mr. Smith" posting a comment **elsewhere**

<http://extoots.blogspot.com/2007/02/unbearable-loneliness-no-more_14.html> on the extoots site. He clarifies that in **another comment** <http://extoots.blogspot.com/2007/03/juletomte-to-rescue_03.html>, saying that "shunning is probably too harsh of a word." But he remembers "other people who were leaving or borderline and how some people in the congregation would purposefully ignore them in order to make the person feel ostracized, almost to force them into staying." He says, "I was overtly told that I was not welcome with my friends if I did not toe the line." **Another commenter** <http://extoots.blogspot.com/2005/08/lurkers-please-post_3989.html>, "a current member" of a "Pollari group" notes the lack of lifestyle restrictions: "My church is not conservative in dress and women are free to limit their families and to get an education. We can go to the movies, watch TV and secular music, listen to the radio and go on the [Internet]." But, it is still "exclusive in doctrine for the most part." Regarding shunning, the commenter says,

> We don't shun people who have left us, they remain dear in our hearts and in our families. Maybe that is why nothing negative (so far) has been posted about us. I believe I am believing in the right way and every morning I know I must wake up and believe anew. However, I reserve the right for judging to Jesus, who sitteth on the right hand of God and who will come to judge the quick and the dead. I believe I am following the right doctrine. When I came to this realization I felt free. Before, I felt burdened. I feel free to love others outside of my faith.

The Pollarites have a "long-standing tension between law and gospel" (Talonen 2005, 207). Confession "has always been minimized," which Talonen attributes at least partly to Pollari's background as a convert from Finland's Evangelical Movement (pp. 206-207). An IALC commenter **writes** <http://extoots.blogspot.com/2008/05/good-night-sweet-prince_8756.html> that

> there is no such "asking for forgiveness" part of the church service. Confessing your sins to another is considered optional and private. I've never seen anyone do this at a church service. Though I've seen a lot of rejoicing and crying, but most often [it's] a joyous sort of rejoicing. I've always been told not to look back at sin, lest you turn into a pillar of salt like Lot's wife. In other words, have your private conversation with God, or a trusted

> believer if its still bothering you, go to communion, and go and sin no more.

The "rejoicing and crying" to which the commenter refers is something of a Pollarite trademark, a vestige of the *liikutuksia* that was an important part of church life in Laestadianism's early days (**4.1.5**). A "member of a Pollari group where 'jumping, weeping, and wailing' frequently occur, but not always with every service," **describes it** <http://extoots.blogspot.com/2005/08/lutherans-do-vary_158.html> as a sincere expression of rejoicing, with it usually

> hitting me before I ever knew what had happened to me. Rarely my heart warms through movement or [visibly] with tears, more often my insides feel like warm though my outward demeanor is unchanged, and sometimes I feel stone cold. At those times I feel a bit cold is when I find another's rejoicing a bit ridiculous, and I can understand why those who have not experienced it might feel like it is not real. I don't rejoice out of sadness for my sins, I rejoice out of gladness that those sins that I do have can be washed clean with the blood of the Lord Jesus Christ and that God loves even me.

Others are not so charitable. "Mr. Smith" **provides** <http://extoots.blogspot.com/2007/02/unbearable-loneliness-no-more_14.html> his childhood recollections:

> What is so scary about rejoicing? Well first off as a child, watching a woman (sometimes a man, rarely) burst out of the pew wailing and violently jumping and [waving their] hands, throwing song books, swinging chairs, with tears streaming down their face. Spooky stuff. Top that off with the chain reaction that would start off and you would have multiple people doing this "kooky" behavior. I distinctly remember sometimes somebody would kind of start and there would be no other reaction from the congregation and they would die down pretty quickly. I would think to myself when a rejoicer would go off (and they always seemed to be the same rotation of people, I guess some feel the spirit more then others) "is there going to be a chain reaction this time?" If there was a chain reaction they seemed to feed off each other and push each other to fevered heights.

He says he personally watched 13 year old girls practicing their "style" when away from church. They exhibited the same "style" when he "saw them rejoicing in church for real later on."

4.2 The Kingdom of God

> *And when he was demanded of the Pharisees, when the kingdom of God should come, he answered them and said, The kingdom of God cometh not with observation: Neither shall they say, Lo here! or, lo there! for, behold, the kingdom of God is within you.*
>
> —*The Gospel According to Luke*

4.2.1 The One True Church

> *According to some fundamentalist groups, only they are true Christians, and only they are going to heaven, while the rest of the world's "so-called" Christians, including those in other fundamentalist groups, are going to hell.*
>
> —Edward T. Babinski, *Leaving the Fold*

Conservative Laestadianism has about 100,000 adherents in Finland, although estimates vary from 80,000 to 120,000. There are some 33,000 formal members of the SRK, a status that can be obtained at age fifteen (Hallamaa and Parry 2009). About 40,000 Finnish Conservatives are adults (Hurtig 2011). Another 7,000 or so Conservatives are in North America, with the same demographic of less than half being adults (3,000 formal members). Sweden, Togo, and Ghana each have congregations of several hundred. Finally, there are some very small isolated congregations in a few other places, together accounting for perhaps a few hundred more.

The movement equates itself with "God's Kingdom," and claims to be the only true church, the exclusive repository of grace on this earth after 2,000 years of Christianity. All of the billions of mentally competent individuals over the age of accountability who now occupy this planet, other than the approximately 60,000 fortunate enough to have been "born into a Christian home" or the fewer than a thousand converted "from the world," are headed for an eternity of unthinkable torture. And, unless the world finally ends after two thousand years of failed expectations, that same horrible fate will be shared by almost all of the billion or so of the world's children as they reach the age of accountability without any clue about how to be saved.

It is a claim that cannot be viewed by an outsider as anything but outrageous. The Conservative believers with whom I have had many private discussions about the topic will rarely venture to defend it, resorting to a form of **Pascal's Wager** <http://en.wikipedia.org/wiki/Pascal's_Wager> and saying that it's enough for them to be part of a group that surely won't be condemned itself. Even the website of the LLC tiptoes around the issue, dropping hints about the kingdom of God (It "is to be found on earth according to the teachings of Jesus. It is a kingdom of grace on earth and a kingdom of glory in heaven. The kingdom of God is one-minded in faith, doctrine, and love") but never coming out and saying that you, the stranger who has come across the site, are going to *fry forever in hell* if you don't join up. I asked a member of the LLC board about that, and he said that they didn't want to scare people off. So much for the preaching of the law to the unsaved (**4.5.1**).

But the exclusivity doctrine is a significant point of the church's teaching, and as we will see from the quotes below, it is what the organization professes even if its individual members and public relations efforts are more hesitant to do so.

Development

With its claimed doctrinal and historical ties to Luther, it is natural that Conservative Laestadianism would seek support for its exclusivity doctrine in Luther's writings. What it has found, and frequently cites, is his explanation of the Third Article of the Creed. For example, a 1979 article in *Siionin Lähetyslehti* quotes Luther's explanation more or less accurately as follows:

> † "The Holy Spirit first leads us to the communion of saints and within the pale of the congregation, under whose caretaking He exhorts us and takes us to Christ–the Holy Spirit having a special congregation on this Earth. This is the mother who gives birth to and sustains all Christians with the word of God. I believe that there is on Earth a small holy flock and congregation, under one head, Christ, called together by the Holy Spirit, in one faith, one mind, and one understanding. They possess various gifts, but are

of one mind in love, without factions or divisions. I also am a part and member of this flock and a sharer in its blessings. To this flock the Holy Spirit has led me and joined me because I have heard and continue to hear the Word of God. This then is the first step toward entrance (from VOZ, 1/1980).

This is, however, hardly the end of the matter. Luther's teachings on the scope and extent of the Church will come as a surprise to most Conservatives (**5.2**). An early quote by Raattamaa is quite in accord with Luther's assessment that Christianity is scattered "under the Pope, Turks, Persians, Tartars, and everywhere," but "spiritually gathered in one gospel and faith" (*Confession Concerning Christ's Supper*):

> † The power to forgive sins "has not been given to the pope, but to the flock in living faith which is scattered around the whole world of all peoples and tongues. The sermon of repentance and forgiveness of sins is established with them" (Raattamaa, sermon given 1894, from Kulla 1985, 181).

But it would not be long before the Laestadian movement would undergo its first major fragmentation and the factions on opposite sides of the Tornio river would associate "living faith" with "one living congregation." The Firstborn and the Conservatives were closer to each other doctrinally than they were to any other religious body on Earth. Thus their spiritual rejection of each other could not help but entail a rejection of everybody else as well. The sermons of Väinö Havas attest to how firmly in place the exclusivity doctrine was by the early 20th century:

> † "The Holy Ghost is always a gathering power. It melts believing men to a living fellowship. It does not beget isolated Christians, one into one corner, and another to the next, but it forms one flock around the Good Shepherd" (Havas [1935], 18).

> † "There is but one Congregation of Christ. It is according to the Bible the Fellowship of believers that the Holy Spirit has called, gathered, enlightened and by the true Faith protected in Christ. It is the Savior's Body and, therefore, one and indivisible here on Earth. Outside of this Congregation no one can be saved" (Havas [1938], 16).

> † "This foundation of the living Church stands, for this holy temple is not built upon great earthly property of church

organizations or high civilization, nor broad knowledge of the doctrine of Divinity, neither upon the support granted by the stately power, as important factors as they may be when looked through the natural point of view. Every member of the family of God is built upon the unwavering rock foundation of God's Word, the holy writings of the prophets and the apostles" (Havas [1940], 14).

In 1948, Jussila claimed that Raattamaa himself had been of an exclusivist viewpoint. He considered the claim that

> † "Conservative Laestadian Christianity has moved from the early Raattamaa line to the line of a single congregation" to be false in every respect. "I had been believing over 15 years during Raattamaa's lifetime and had traveled at services in the north, in the south, in the east, and in the west, and the congregational doctrine has not changed at all since that time. No one would have been believed that Raattamaa would have had a line or two of several congregations" (Jussila 1948, 119).

But it is hard to see what Raattamaa could have meant by "the flock in living faith" being "scattered around the whole world of all peoples and tongues" if he taught a "single congregation" doctrine so exclusive that even different Laestadian factions were not of the same flock. And, if he held that just one Laestadian group was correct, that would leave the Conservatives unable to claim him as a spiritual brother, as he never repudiated the Firstborn (**4.1.6**).

The exclusivity doctrine has never softened. Conservative Laestadian preachers provide the flock with reminders of their special status in just about every sermon, by expressing praise and thanksgiving to God for allowing them the incredible good fortune to be one of "God's children," to have the "precious gift of living faith," or even (in an acknowledgment of how almost everybody comes to be a Laestadian) to be "born into a Christian home." And it is equally emphasized by references to the world and how lost and sadly ignorant it is of "God's Kingdom."

> † "There are not many spirits by which we have access to the Father through Jesus Christ. There is only one, the Holy Spirit, which is of God. Neither are there many kingdoms, as the world would believe. There is only one kingdom that has the foundation

of the faith and doctrine of the prophets and the apostles with Jesus Christ the chief cornerstone" (VOZ, 9/1979).

† "There have always been, and are today, peddlers of false doctrines who try to open the narrow gate so wide that everyone can enter no matter how they believe. They attempt to pave a road to heaven, to have a wide gate, saying that the best of every religion will be saved through good works. Some even use the comparison that there are many highways in this world to get from one place to another; so also, there are many roads to heaven. They say you just need to commit yourself to Christ and choose a road with which you are comfortable, and where you can find friends that have the same interests as you. These people have not themselves entered through the narrow gate. How, then, can they save others? Jesus called this doctrine, the blind leading the blind (Mt 15:14)" (VOZ, 7/1999).

† "We have witnessed how God has led seeking ones from many lands" to the gate of his kingdom, which "does not consist of one country or nationality, but dwells among believers.... The unbelieving world has tried to create many gates to the kingdom. They teach that you can enter through prayer, or by changing your behavior. But Jesus made it clear when he said, 'I am the door: by me if any man enter in, he shall be saved, and shall go in and out (VOZ, 8/2003).

That last quote refers to mission activity taking place in the past two decades. I recall a lot of inspiring stories about conversions in Russia in the early 1990s, with talk about more believers being there than in North America. Then, suddenly, not much more was said about it. The attention shifted to conversions in Ecuador, Togo, and Ghana. I was finally able to learn that the vast majority of the Russian converts had drifted away, as have most in Ecuador. However, it appears that Laestadianism still has a vibrant, active presence in Africa, with several indigenous preachers and well-organized congregations.

Actually, it's not just *Conservative* Laestadianism that is active in Africa. The Apostolic Lutheran Federation has been conducting mission work there for years, and is also working in Russia, India, and the Philippines. For someone maintaining the belief that the Federation is a heresy lacking the Holy Spirit (4.1.6), the stories and photos at **foreignmissionnewsblog.blogspot.com** will be as disturbing as they are intended to be inspiring. Somehow God's grace is being denied to these people who are believing in the proclamation of the forgiveness of their sins in Jesus' name. One page even shows some of them preaching the forgiveness of sins to each other. But their experiences of love and piety are supposedly just a cruel joke being played on them by a God who has entrusted his offer of salvation only to those other Laestadians operating in Togo and Ghana who are saying similar things and having similar experiences.

Implications

The need to deny any value in the Federation's mission work is just one example of the exclusivity doctrine's troubling implications. It is an extreme aspect of the "soteriological problem of evil" (Myers 2003) that is posed by Christian exclusivity in general (**4.9.2**). The problem had already troubled me for years by 2009, when I learned of Bible passages and teachings of Luther that really brought my doubts about Conservative Laestadian exclusivity to a head.

The following are some thoughts I wrote down in December of that year after attending the Christmas program of my younger children's elementary school. The scene I describe is of a group of kids around 7-8 years old on stage. Ours is a rural, simple, and fairly religious community, but of course, nobody there or most anywhere else in the U.S. has ever heard of Conservative Laestadianism.

The Christmas Program

Children stand on stage singing Christmas carols, twirling their curled hair and smiling shyly out at the faces of their parents. They have learned words that tell of Wishing us a Merry Christmas, of a little Town named Bethlehem, of a jolly old man named Santa Claus. In their classes they are also learning about one plus one and the alphabet, and even about bugs and plants.

But something they will never learn is that they are damned. Neither they nor their beaming parents will ever hear about a small, nondescript church 20 miles away that is attended by a few hundred children and their parents who look exactly like them and their parents, but who are (largely) not damned. They will grow up to embrace various beliefs. Most will confess a belief in the saving powers of the Jesus they are singing about (more or less) in their caroling. Some will be more enthusiastic about that belief than others, and some of them will come to reject the whole notion entirely. But all of them are damned, every single now-innocent one of them, because they will never enter that small, nondescript church and accept its particular doctrine of salvation.

Perhaps as their adult forms are writhing in unspeakable, eternal agony someday, many of them will ask, what about the Jesus we believed in? Didn't we accept him as our personal savior? Didn't we read the Bible that spoke of him, which said that God loved the whole world so much that he gave his only begotten Son, that all men might have eternal life?

Perhaps one of them, surprised that the particular Jesus doctrine he so piously confessed and taught was to no avail, will scream in his agony, "Why? Why? Why? **Now** *I find out that there were just a few hundred people for hundreds of miles around me who made it to adulthood and then to heaven? And because none of these people ever had occasion to speak to me (including two parents who were apparently in the audience at my first grade Christmas program but never could or did say anything to me), I am going to be tortured forever? How could I have believed in a doctrine I'd never even heard of? If you are a loving God, why did you hide it from me? Why did you give me instead a lifetime of false consolation about Jesus that would prove utterly worthless to the fate of my soul?"*

The extremity of this scenario, but not its horrible nature, is apparent in Gus Wisuri's observation:

> † "There are cities of millions and millions of people without a Christian in them. I have just returned last evening from a city of over a half million people where to the best of my knowledge there is not a Christian. There is one little girl there who believes the gospel message, but she is a little too young to go out and preach it to the other people. That city is surrounded by religious faiths that make a thorough study of the Scripture and lay down strict rules of beliefs for the members of their congregations but they have no peace of God" (sermon published in *Greetings of Peace*, 12/1953).

But when something sounds crazy, you can count on theologians to call it a mystery that can only be understood by divine revelation:

> † "The spiritual body has and will always remain a mystery to man, because he has sought salvation through spiritual leaders and has not recognized that true salvation is found in the

communion or fellowship of the body of Christ, where He himself dwells" (VOZ, 6/2006).

† "Throughout the Bible, various names are used for the congregation of God's people on earth: the Kingdom of God, the kingdom of heaven, New Jerusalem, kingdom of our Lord and Savior Jesus Christ, etc. the Psalm writer uses the term 'Zion.' Regardless of the name however, one key characteristic is that God's people are a united flock or group and are spiritually separate from all other religious groups. It remains God's will that His people are spiritually separate from other groups, as He said to Moses and the wilderness travelers: 'I am the Lord your God which have separated you from other people' . . . the Kingdom of God is always a mystery to man's own mind. Sometimes man has imagined the kingdom to be strictly an earthly or political entity. Other times man has expected a utopia or perfect outward kingdom" (VOZ, 7/2007).

† "With the human mind one may appear to see signs of right faith in many churches. Nevertheless, the Holy Spirit reveals one faith and one fellowship of believers" (VOZ, 12/2008).

In a 2010 sermon, Jim Frantti makes a frank admission of the difficulties with the exclusivity doctrine. He tells of Naaman the Syrian taking offense that he had to wash in the lowly Jordan when there were mightier rivers in Syria (2 Ki 5):

† "Isn't that the same kind of reaction we sometimes hear today when we speak about God's Kingdom? 'You really think this is the only place where forgiveness is found? Do you really think that you are the only group that is traveling to heaven, the only group of believers? Do you really believe that?' And of course, to the rational mind it does seem like an awfully simple way to believe, doesn't it? When we look around us in this world and we see the people and the churches and the deeds that people do and all of these outward things, certainly we can understand that to the carnal mind our faith is so foolish. That's what Paul found too, when he preached. He said we preach Jesus Christ and him crucified, and to the Jews it's a stumbling block, and to the Greeks it's foolishness."

Frantti attempts to defend the doctrine in the face of its incredible implications by invoking Paul's statement in 1 Cor 1:18-23 about the preaching of the cross being foolishness to them that perish. But that is an entirely different subject than sectarian exclusivity. One wonders what Paul, who in the same chapter exhorted the Corinthians to all agree and have no divisions among them, would have thought about the claim that Christ's suffering and death would become utterly ineffectual in all but one of the tens of thousands of Christian denominations that would emerge over the next 2,000 years.

Biblical Justification

Jesus' statement to the disciples, "Fear not, little flock; for it is your Father's good pleasure to give you the kingdom" (Lk 12:32) is one of the texts used to justify the claim that there is one group of true believers, and that it is a small one:

> † Jesus "is the Good Shepherd who has a flock, a precious flock of sheep, a sheepfold here on earth, a kingdom of grace, His living church and congregation to which He brings converted souls, to which He has brought each of us when we were gone astray" (Paul Heideman, *Greetings of Peace*, 6/1954).

In an article entitled with the question, "Can a man be saved outside of God's Kingdom?", the SRK preacher Eino Rimpiläinen began by expressing some impatience with the matter: "One might think that in the midst of God's Kingdom [one] should have so clear [a] conception in this matter that there would be no room for doubts. But Satan is always tempting and leading the child of God to doubt, even in this matter." His biblical support for the answer began with a general reference to the Old Testament, stating "that no one was saved unless he remained in that flock and believed as they did, where they had God and His saving word." Then,

> † "at the beginning of the New Testament[,] God shows the scribes and pharisees that God's Kingdom has approached them. Even they now had the opportunity to repent and believe the Gospel," but Christ's "doctrine and His church became an offence, foolishness, [a] stumbling stone to those who did not believe. And so they were not saved." In our time, by "the office of the Spirit" and "a foolish preaching in the eyes of men", "it has pleased God to save those who believe. Salvation is attained

through this, and nowhere else. Thus believing according to the will of God, the eyes of the soul are opened, that there is salvation nowhere else, no faith, no true fruits of faith. You realize that God can not be found anywhere else as a merciful and forgiving and healing God than in Israel (2 Ki 5:15). That is in the Kingdom of God (Lk 15:17). Be there questions of churches, denominations, revivals, or any other. Christ is not divided (1 Cor 1:13)." We teach, Rimpiläinen concludes, "that everyone who has broken his covenant of baptism and has fallen into unbelief, must repent and the congregation of the Holy Ghost declares absolution to him" (*Greetings of Peace*, 3/1957).

Another justification is Paul's statement that the righteousness of God is revealed in the gospel of Christ "from faith to faith" (Rom 1:17). The gospel

† "moves from one believer to another and it must move from a believer to the unbeliever to be received. Never can an unbeliever bring this gospel to another unbeliever but it is revealed as we heard 'from faith to faith.' This also supports and strengthens the teachings of all scripture that the Kingdom of God is a single unity of Spirit and faith, from which fellowship the gospel is proclaimed unto all nations. First there must be a believing and living member of the believing and living fellowship to bring this gospel" (Peter Nevala, *Greetings of Peace*, 3/1971).

Conservatives usually refer to the "gospel" only in the limited sense of the proclamation of the forgiveness of sins, rather than the general good news of Jesus as the resurrected savior. With that limited viewpoint, this passage could indeed be considered relevant to the idea of one coming into faith only via the proclamation of forgiveness from one who is already in it (**4.2.5**). But even then, the only way it supports the idea of a "single unity of Spirit and faith" is by limiting "the believing and living fellowship" just to those who experience or at least teach the "faith to faith" preaching.

What destroys that argument is the existence of the OALC and FALC. The fact that those "heretics" use pretty much the exact same absolution formula would not persuade Nevala that they are part of the "Kingdom of God." Thus it has no evidentiary value on that point. If you condemn someone as lost and misguided even though they are practicing some important point of your doctrine, you cannot rely on that point of doctrine as a way to distinguish yourself from the lost and misguided world.

There are some favorite passages that refer to a single spiritual body:

> † Often "members of other churches and groups" ask the question "Why is it then that only here in your church men are saved?" Several Bible passages are quoted in reply: Eph 4:4 ("one body, one spirit," etc.); Gal 1:8 ("though an angel preach any other gospel let him be accursed"); John 10:1 ("he that entereth not by the door into the sheepfold is a thief"); John 10:16 ("one fold and one shepherd") (VOZ, 6/1980).

First Clement, dated at around 95 A.D., makes a statement that sounds similar:

> Why are there strifes, and tumults, and divisions, and schisms, and wars among you? Have we not [all] one God and one Christ? Is there not one spirit of grace poured out upon us? And have we not one calling in Christ? Why do we divide and tear to pieces the members of Christ, and raise up strife against our own body, and have reached such a height of madness as to forget that "we are members one of another?" [Ch. 46]

Besides having this modicum of scriptural support, the idea of a single true church makes some logical sense. If the "Spirit of truth" Jesus promised to his followers will guide them "into all truth" (John 16:13), it is reasonable to expect that those so guided will not be found in different groups with significantly different teachings. But as my research for this book has made clear, to me at least, there is not particularly impressive consistency even within Conservative Laestadianism, for all its exclusivism and separation from worldly influences. Preachers cannot decide whether God wants everyone to be saved or not, yet speak confidently of both contradictory ideas (**4.9.3**), certain activities are sinful at one point and widely accepted a few decades later (**4.6.1**), one of the doctrinal foundations of the church is a mode of conversion that was not employed by its earliest founders (**4.1.4**), and significant deviations are found from the teachings of one of the most historically prominent members of the church (**5.2**, **5.4.4**). And the bare idea of a single saved group doesn't give any of the many groups competing for that designation any indication that *they* are the ones being saved. Also, see the discussion of Romans 10:8-9 in **7.3**.

John 6:68 is also a favorite text. When Peter said,

> † "Lord, to whom shall we go? Thou has the words of eternal life," he "knew that there is no one else to go to, and no other place to go. The only place one can go to find the Lord Jesus is in His kingdom. We also want to remain like the disciples of Christ, keeping faith and a good conscience" (VOZ, 5/2000).

As in so many other quotes throughout this collection, the quoted writer is injecting words into a Bible passage to narrow its plain meaning into a sectarian interpretation. Peter is talking about his decision to continue following Christ himself ("to *whom* shall we go"), not any particular group of Christians. Indeed, at the time of Peter's statement, there was not yet a single group of people calling itself "Christians," just followers of Christ himself.

The "where else would we go" sentiment, often accompanied by a shrugging of the shoulders, strikes me as a theological version of Winston Churchill's statement that democracy is the worst form of government, except for all others. I find it interesting to see it used in other religious groups in the same way. During Diane Wilson's time in the Watchtower Society of Jehovah's Witnesses, for example,

> the Society continually impressed on everyone's mind that "There is nowhere else to go." Although complaining is forbidden, still many times during my long association with the organization I had heard small groups of Witnesses murmuring their disagreements with the Society; these conversations always had the same ending–frustrated voices would sigh, "But there is nowhere else to go." So thoroughly indoctrinated were the congregation members with this mindset that no other options existed, that rare was the person who challenged it. [2002, 273]

The writer of the next quote, from the October 2002 *Voice of Zion*, takes a text that would seem to oppose sectarian exclusivity (Rom 10:13-17) and attempts to qualify its plain meaning:

> † "The first sentence 'For whoever shall call upon the name of the Lord shall be saved' is often quoted by those in self-righteousness. It is certainly appealing to the mind of man to stop at this point in Paul's letter. However, the invitation [by Philip to the skeptic of anything good coming out of Nazareth in Jn 1:46] to

'come and see,' is essential. As Paul writes [in verse 14], 'how shall they believe in him of whom they have not heard?'"

You don't need to be in "self-righteousness" to see that people cannot believe in something that they've never heard of. There's nothing surprising or spiritual about the "good news" of Jesus being spread by "the feet of them that preach the gospel of peace, and bring glad tidings of good things" (Rom 10:15). Paul's was an era when words could only be conveyed in the minds of messengers or the few bits of writing they could carry–writing that almost nobody could read. That has nothing to do with the verbal proclamation of forgiveness that the quoted writer has in mind.

During my study of the Bible from cover to cover, which occupied several months of 2009, I came across some passages that seem to extend the scope of God's attention well beyond just a single sect: **Mark 9:38-40, Romans 10:8-9, 10:10-17, 1 John 4:2, 4:15, 5:1**. Even the Old Testament with all its focus on God's chosen people has a universalist passage of sorts, **Psalms 145:18-20**.

No Compromises

The exclusivist writings of the 1970s were particularly shrill. There was an emphasis not just on being personally within the walls of Zion, but on fully accepting their dimensions as well. Perhaps it was a reaction to the aftermath of the 1973 schism, when most Conservative believers had friends or relatives whom, according to official doctrine, they could no longer consider spiritual brethren.

> † "The office of the Holy Spirit is only entrusted to those who are in this one and only congregation of Christ here on Earth." The Apostle Paul describes the church as "one body, and one Spirit even as ye are called in one hope of your calling; one Lord one faith one baptism, one God and Father of all [Eph 4:4-6]," the "house of God which is the Church of the living God, the pillar and ground of truth [1 Tim 3:15], "the temple of God [1 Cor 3:16-17]." "God in His word does not ever teach that there are many churches where men are saved." "[I]f any man desire to be saved, he must acknowledge and believe this truth, that the doctrine of the congregation of Christ is one; and that the Lord Jesus has his own children on Earth to whom he has entrusted the word of reconciliation. . . . In this true church of Christ we dear brothers

and sisters have been called through God's grace and love" (VOZ, 5/1974).

† "In God's kingdom there is no 'beating around the bush' so to speak. One is either inside of the kingdom or outside of the kingdom. If one has not received the love of the Christians regardless of whatever excuses or alibis, that person is lost and must come unto repentance" (Quentin Ruonavaara, sermon given 1975).

† "But if someone in the kingdom of God begins to waver in the doctrine of this one congregation and begins to greet those who are in other churches in the world or in heresies which have left from the living churches of God, and begins to say that there are other churches where men are saved, his condition is also serious. He is not in an acceptable state before God. He needs to come unto repentance of this false and wrong spirit and doctrine into which he has fallen. This is living in spiritual fornication, and no one in this condition shall inherit the kingdom of heaven" (VOZ, 6/1978).

That seems like a local emergency room refusing admission to a dying man until he makes a statement that none of the other hospitals around would be suitable for his treatment. And, to continue the analogy, he is sternly discouraged from investigating the merits of those other hospitals!

It reminds me of the Mormon "testimony" that faithful members bear to each other Sunday after Sunday, which includes the assertion, "I know that the Church is True." They *must*, according to one ex-Mormon, "believe that God has one, and only one, true church, which is The Church of Jesus Christ of Latter-day Saints" (Worthy 2008, 33). And he had his investigations likewise limited, having "been taught early on that the only reliable evidence about the Church–in fact the only evidence at all worth looking at–comes from the Church itself. This evidence can be undeniably confirmed, not through logical, deductive reasoning, but by the emotional feelings we were taught from early childhood to recognize as being from the Holy Ghost" (p. 54).

Thirty years later, even though the writings had toned down somewhat, one's private thoughts on the topic would remain the subject of concern:

† "It is no small matter when an individual or group, either secretly or openly, begins to believe that the house of God is not necessarily 'the pillar and ground of truth' in all matters of soul and conscience or that there is more than one saving faith" (Walt Lampi, presentation given 2007).

On several occasions, I personally proclaimed the forgiveness of sins to Carl Kulla, a member of the Apostolic Lutheran Federation who became a dear friend. Yet as discussed in **4.1.6**, he is officially not to be considered a "believer" because of his failure to "comprehend the doctrine of the kingdom." His acceptance of the forgiveness of sins, preached from one of the Conservatives, is not enough without repenting of his "heresy" as a member of the Federation.

Privately, a few Conservative friends whom I told of my interactions with Carl said they accept him as a believer based on his acceptance of the preached gospel. They dare not say it too publicly, however. Kathleen Lewis also found that not all of her fellow members of the Christian Convention Church were

> convinced of the righteousness or exclusiveness of salvation to this church. They are careful to keep this idea to themselves, however, for they know it isn't safe to express it to others. Anyone who verbally makes an unacceptable statement like that is immediately suspected of not having "the right Spirit" and they are shunned or avoided and people are encouraged not to spend time with them. [2004, 201]

In private discussions, Conservatives seem similarly unconvinced. To paraphrase one friend who has gotten to know too many "worldly" friends and attended too many of their funerals to remain believing they are all going to hell: *We are better individually than our doctrine makes us collectively.* But there is the same motivation Lewis noted to keep one's opinions to oneself.

4.2.2 Which "True Church"?

> *Does not each religion claim to be the only one? And does not the priest of every religion, with infinite impudence, consign the disciples of all others to eternal fire?*
>
> —Robert G. Ingersoll, *Lecture on "Which Way?"*

Lewis's former Christian Convention Church also calls itself "the Kingdom of God" (2004, 242), with their main belief being "that their church is the only true church, the only way to heaven, the body of Christ" (p. 1). But it is only one of many contenders for that title. "Tragically, each sect, cult, and denomination seems convinced that it alone is 'The Truth' in its entirety. All others are heretics" (Harpur 2003, 99).

It's as old a phenomenon as Christianity itself. Ehrman says that "believers attacked other believers for their false beliefs" in every early Christian community (Ehrman 2011, 182). "Nothing generated more literary forgeries in the names of the apostles than the internal conflicts among competing Christian groups" (p. 183). Given the simplistic and idealized picture I had from childhood about "the early Church," it was surprising to me just how ancient and extensive the problem was. The Christians around Clement of Alexandria [c. 200 A.D.], for example, had to field the objection of unbelievers "that they ought not to believe on account of the discord of the sects. For [they say] the truth is warped when some teach one set of dogmas, others another" (*Stromata*, Book 7, Ch. 15)

No religion wants to be characterized as just one of many, "because that way of understanding any particular faith logically relativizes it" (Price 2006b, 218). The Conservative Laestadian who looks out at the billions of people above the age of accountability on this Earth and condemns all of them but himself and perhaps 60,000 others in "God's Kingdom" may find it unsettling that millions of others are believing similar things, and condemning *him* in the process. Jesus' warning to the self-satisfied in response to the question "Lord, are there few that be saved?" seems appropriate: "There shall be weeping and gnashing of teeth, when ye shall see Abraham, and Isaac, and Jacob, and all the prophets, in the kingdom of God, and you yourselves thrust out" (Lk 13:28). If *any* of these groups are correct—and Conservative Laestadianism *is* in fact just one of many—everybody else is going to be in for a rude surprise. Don't be too quick to automatically exempt yourself.

We were confronted by the *Iglesia ni Cristo* group in the **Introduction**, and then in **4.1.6** by three Laestadian factions (the **OALC**, **FALC**, and **IALC**) that all believe anyone outside their small boundaries is headed for hell. Some others rendering the same judgment, either officially or by common consent in the pews, are the Churches of Christ, the New

Apostolic Church, and an interesting group of Charismatics in the American South. Let's take a brief look at some similarities between these groups and Conservative Laestadianism before proceeding with the latter's view of itself versus everybody else. Of course there are many differences, too, but a comprehensive description of each group is not the point of the brief, admittedly one-sided comparison of religions I am doing in this section. Rather, my goal here is to show how Conservative Laestadians have some interesting things in common with other groups who nonetheless are pointing their own bony fingers of condemnation right back.

The Christian Convention Church

Lewis estimates that the Christian Convention Church has about 450,000 people in the United States, with another couple hundred thousand in other parts of the world (2004, 5). Her name for the group is an unofficial one, as it refuses to take a public name. Instead, the church members informally refer to it as "The Truth" or "The Way" (p. 13). Outsiders often call them the "Two by Twos," referring to the way that the "workers," a distinct group of lay ministers, would go out preaching in pairs.

The main belief of the Christian Conventionists "is that their church is the only true church, the only way to heaven, the body of Christ" (p. 1). "They believe that only those with the right Spirit can understand the scripture. The right Spirit is only obtained through the workers" (p. 3). "People raised in this church have been taught that this is the only 'Way,' that they are the only ones on earth with an understanding of God's Word" (p. 85).

The workers of the Christian Convention Church "don't like 'Christian' activities," accusing "those who do charitable works of being in bondage and trying to work their way into heaven" (p. 25). They "encourage people to criticize other church practices, doctrine, histories or failures" (p. 58). On the other hand, the "workers build enthusiasm with effusive glamorizing of the fellowship" (p. 61) within their group.

As with all of these high-demand groups, submission is important. "Anyone who exercises his own viewpoints or logic will be rebuked or looked down on if he verbalizes it" (p. 68).

The Churches of Christ

The Churches of Christ also have an aversion to being designated by a particular name, or even being considered a mere "denomination" of Christianity. Using the plural form when referring to them is appropriate because there is no single organization under which the various congregations operate. Rather, each is a "*Church* of Christ." Collectively, they have over a million adherents in the U.S. and at least three times as many worldwide.

Like Conservative Laestadianism, the Churches of Christ have had a "strict emphasis on 'correct' Biblical doctrine and disagreements," with the same result: numerous schisms. Yet "their core group still has the audacity to claim to be the 'one true church'" (Simpson 2009, 42). Condemning all "mainstream denominational congregations" as unscriptural, the Churches of Christ likewise "do not join in ecumenical events for charitable, educational, counseling, or religious service activities" (p. 6). Simpson found that members

> cannot carry on a legitimate conversation about religious matters with members of other faiths because they enter those conversations automatically assuming that the other person is wrong and going to hell. From a religious perspective, theirs is a different kind of friendship with people of other faiths. It's not about developing a close personal relationship based on mutual interest but rather about exhibiting patience and tolerance until a lost soul can be saved. [p. 87]

The comments on this thread <dead link> of an ex-Church of Christ discussion forum show there isn't much "patience and tolerance" for questioning from the inside:

> Fear was evident all around us at church. Real questions were usually met with hostility even if the person asking was new to the CoC. Forget about it if you were a lifer. People that questioned the party line were usually kicked/pushed out eventually. It was because of people's fears of being wrong that so much anger was in all of us. If your whole salvation paradigm revolves around being completely accurate in doing church and in interpreting what God meant . . . , then any inkling that one could be wrong is emotionally devastating. [Toeing] the party line was like a defense mechanism I think.

Another defense is when a church "discourages any exposure to other faiths and allows for no interpretation of Scripture other than the one arbitrarily claimed by it as if it were God's direct revelation," which Simpson implies is the case with the "closed society" of the Churches of Christ. Then, he says, it is especially true that anyone "attending church regularly will come to accept the doctrines and beliefs being taught by that church" (2009, 7).

The New Apostolic Church

The New Apostolic Church (no relation to Apostolic Lutherans) has, according to a **fact sheet**
<http://www.nak.org/fileadmin/download/pdf/ZDF/ZDF_010110__engl_.pdf>
it publishes, over 10 million members. The vast majority are in Africa. There are over 300,000 in America and over 400,000 in Europe. In 2003, ex-member David Stamos gave a considerably lower estimate of its total membership at 1-2 million (Stamos 2003, 338).

According to Stamos, the New Apostolic Church "believes it is the only true and valid church of God today," which he considers unsurprising, given his belief that the same stance is taken by "most Christian denominations." (I'm not so sure that such exclusivity is really so commonplace, though of course no denomination feels that it is *not* "true and valid.") The NAC holds that "salvation is only open to New Apostolics," Stamos claims (p. 338), which is in accord with this statement from a paper entitled "The New Apostolic Church":

> It is the belief of the NAC that the true church of Jesus cannot exist apart from the Apostles to whom Jesus gave his authority. Often it is likened to someone having a key to a door. You cannot go through the door unless someone unlocks it, and the Apostles have been entrusted with the keys to God's Kingdom. In fact, much like the Roman Catholic Church justifies the office of Pope, so does the NAC justify the modern office of Chief Apostle by appealing to Matthew 16:18.[10]

---

10. A PDF file of the article is available at **acfar.org/pdflibrary/AJET_article_on_New_Apostolic_Church.pdf**. It says the article "originally appeared in the Africa Journal of Evangelical Theology (AJET), Volume 24.1, 2005, pp. 63-79."

It also fits with this description from the NAC's **Wikipedia** <http://en.wikipedia.org/wiki/New_Apostolic_Church> page:

> The Apostles of the New Apostolic Church consider themselves as successors of the first Apostles during Early Christianity, who had been sent by Jesus Christ. In their tradition, they act as missionaries, who go to all men to preach the Gospel of Jesus Christ, and to prepare them for the Second Coming of Christ and eternal life. According to the NAC, the apostles are the only ones on earth who have the mission to forgive sins and baptise with the Holy Spirit.

However, the Wikipedia page also adds a nuance to this: "Because the Holy Spirit acts in other churches as well, God alone forgives sins, and may find His 'Children' without Holy Sealing," which is the conveyance of the Holy Spirit via prayer and laying on of hands from one of the NAC's several hundred apostles. Thus the NAC "considers the affiliation of non-members to the Second Coming of Christ to be possible."

That wasn't the impression Stamos and his peers were given as children. They were taught to consider themselves "a different species from the rest of this world, that only New Apostolics are children of God, the rest are children of Satan." He writes of a constant struggle ever since leaving the church "to purge myself from the vestiges of this psychology, the feeling of distance from my fellow man" (p. 341). There was also no shortage of "church taboos" to make that distinction clear: "No long hair on males . . . and no short skirts on females. No jeans, at least at church functions like picnics and gatherings. No going dancing, no going to moves, no going to bars or worldly parties, no premarital sex, no drugs . . . , no joining organized sports or clubs" (p. 340).

After some troubling Bible studies on his own, Stamos started asking questions. He found inconsistencies in church history, which made him suspicious about "why the church was so selective in what it told us of its origin" (p. 339). He challenged some NAC clergy, "since they supposedly had a monopoly on truth, being official bearers of the Holy Spirit, to answer my questions" (p. 343). The few replies he received "ignored my arguments and only tried to make me feel foolish and stupid," with one lamenting that "they've lost me to the world's philosophies" (p. 344).

More Than Conquerors Faith Church

Price mentions "fringe Pentecostals who claim that anyone who fails to speak in tongues is no real Christian and is headed for the Inferno" (2006b, 88). One such group is the **More Than Conquerors Faith Church** <http://mtcfc.org> of Birmingham, Alabama. I had some fascinating correspondence with one of the 3,000 members of the group who is now quite disillusioned with it and no longer attends. Regarding the claim about speaking in tongues, she told me,

> Yes, you must show outward signs of emotion during worship. We were taught that Lutheran churches and others like that were Dead, and God does not reside in Death. The Glory of God's Gift of life and Breath is enough to make any true christian exult and shout to the heavens with praise. Also Holy tongues is the language spoken in heaven. How can you go to heaven if you don't know the language?

There is a delicious irony in knowing that Conservative Laestadians, with no shortage of racist attitudes (until recently, at least) and readiness to call other religions "dead faith," are condemned as "dead" by an obscure Black church in the Deep South.

Conservative Laestadians do not just fall short in the area of charismatic worship, either. To be saved in my correspondent's old church, one must

> have a full immersion Baptism usually around [age] 7-9 or so unless an adult is renewing his faith. Baby baptisms don't work because a baby cannot understand and confirm its faith. You have to be able to speak the fact that you are a christian and believe in the trinity (we went to a class the Saturday before and they told us what to say) before you can become baptized and also before you become a full member of the church.

There are actually a lot of Christians in the United States who have the same "full immersion" requirement for salvation, including the Churches of Christ discussed above. It seems incredible that a failure to be completely dunked during the sacrament rather than merely sprinkled would result in one's eternal damnation. But we will see it asserted in **4.2.5** and **4.6.2** that the failure to hear somebody with the right sectarian affiliation proclaiming, "You can believe all your sins forgiven in Jesus' name and blood" has the same dire consequences.

The exclusivity is as strong as the theology is weak, according to my correspondent. As "in all charismatic nondenominational churches," the weak theology allows More Than Conquerors

> to say "We are special and divine." If they had real doctrines they would have to choose between pentecostal or evangelical etc. and give up the special relationship and exclusiveness. As long as it's not written down they can still claim to be new and unique while flip-flopping through a long list of beliefs. The congregation doesn't care; they just want the feeling that God knows them more closely and is more protective of them than the other 7 billion people on the planet. It's a shame that they have to send everyone else to hell for that.

And there's quite a list of people who are going there:

> Mormons, Catholics, Jehovah's witnesses, Universalists, atheist/agnostics, anyone who didn't believe that the bible (only the KJV) was the literal word of god, evolutionists, Jews, people who believe in dinosaurs, people who didn't believe in the healing power of god, people who didn't believe in the preacher's healing/prophetic word, people who had ill will towards an individual in church or the church as a whole, people who had ill will toward people the church associated with, people who didn't believe Jesus was born in the 25th of December, killed and raised on Easter, Masons, ... I must include people possessed by demons.

Although "the rhetoric has been toned down" in the past few years, she remembers that in her time at the church, it "was always us versus someone, or rather everyone, else." The exclusivity applied to everyday life, too. When my correspondent attended a church-affiliated school, she said "you only hung around other church members." She added that one of her friends "who recently left the church for a white church" has been shunned as a result.

4.2.3 Inside vs. Outside

> *Fundamentalists believe that their religion is under mortal threat from the secularism of the modern world, and they are fighting back. They may resist in different ways, but they are all essentially oppositional; they have to have an enemy.*
>
> —Peter Herriot, *Religious Fundamentalism*

When your doctrine makes you reject almost everybody on the planet as hellbound "unbelievers," it is only natural that you will attempt to separate yourself from those unbelievers both mentally and in your everyday life. It is not just to avoid the influence of their contrary viewpoints, but to protect your worldview from the bare fact of their existence as happy, functioning human beings.

The separation is not just social, but mental. The evil (or at best, misguided) outsiders are labeled and caricatured in church writings, sermons, and everyday conversation among believers. "As soon as people have created a category called *us*," write the social psychologists Carol Tavris and Eliot Aronson, "they invariably perceive everybody else as *not-us*" (2008, 58). And once that categorization has been made, attitudes and actions follow: "The very act of thinking that *they* are not as smart or reasonable as we are makes us feel closer to others who are like us. But, just as crucially, it allows us to justify how we treat *them*" (p. 59).

Robert M. Price writes about a moment when the "them" and "us" distinction collapsed for him:

> I found myself in a Cambridge café having supper with some friends.... As I looked at the secular students gathered there, I suddenly thought, "Listen, is there really that much difference between 'them' and 'us'?" I had always accepted the qualitative difference between the 'saved' and the 'unsaved.' Until that moment, it was as if I and my fellow seminarians had been sitting in a "no damnation" section of an otherwise "unsaved" restaurant. Then, in a flash, we were all just people. [2003a, 148]

Separation from the World

Mercer describes isolation of members from "worldly influences" as a characteristic of "many fundamentalist churches." The ideal of such churches is that "the fundamentalist Christian can live his or her life inside a protected cocoon constructed in a form consistent with fundamentalist ideology" (2009, 152). That kind of separation is not unbiblical–we are told not to have friendship with the world (James 4:4), and Jesus speaks approvingly about those who leave their house, brethren, sisters, etc. (Mk 10:29). Paul Heideman refers to Jesus' statement in a 1938 sermon:

> † "There are many who at conversion have literally had to give up homes, give up brothers and sisters, fathers and mothers, wives and children." He told of a "beloved old Christian brother" who said he had been "cast out of his home, and his father forbade him to ever return again." Jesus' words "are true for everyone who comes to a true conversion and a living faith." At that time there "comes a parting of the ways with the former, unbelieving friends of the world. Also a parting of the way with unbelieving relatives in this respect that the Christian, the converted and believing soul, when he steps upon the pathway of light to follow in the bloody footsteps of the Good Shepherd, turns his back to the world and to the former sinful ways of the world." Heideman concluded the sermon with the advice "to young Christians ... that they might seek the company of Christian people, that they might also find fathers and mothers and brothers and sisters according to the promise of Christ" (from *Greetings of Peace*, 4/1959).

Nowadays, Conservative Laestadians are more integrated into society (especially in Finland), with careers that entail exposure to a lot of people from the outside. For all the aversion to liberalism and social change, Conservatives have benefited from society's increased level of tolerance for all different types of people, including members of what can easily be seen as an oddball little sect. The shunning and being shunned by "unbelieving" friends and relatives that Heideman describes doesn't happen so overtly anymore. Nor does the near-monasticism that Heikki Jussila seems to advocate:

> † The "Great Teacher" admonishes "His disciples to shun the cares of the world as a sin of the heathens. When He has chosen them so that they might go out to work for the growth of the kingdom of God, He thus shows that to be the highest and noblest goal in the life of man. They do not have time to linger in

small matters, when the great building of God's kingdom is to be prepared. It is a sacrifice of love, to which only the true appreciation of the value of God's Kingdom can induce. This goal for the life of a man is unknown to the worldly-minded people. They receive their good in this life, and do not think that they need the kingdom of God. But to us, let it be the highest goal of our life. Let us shun the cares of life, the delusion of riches, and the lusts of the world, which have caused the fall of many. It is worth while even for the young to sacrifice their whole life to God and to the service of His kingdom" (*Greetings of Peace*, 11/1943).

One should make a "confession of faith" by one's words and actions. "Almost every Evangelical will say they live by example, following their understanding of the Bible's life instructions, hoping that unsaved neighbors will notice their happiness, remember their faith, infer causation, and come down to the altar" (Welch 2010, 128). But considering how infrequent it is for the unsaved neighbors of Conservative Laestadians to "repent," I don't think the confession of faith is really done because of any realistic expectation of that outcome. Even in "worldly" Evangelicalism, with its far greater numbers of conversions, Kevin Henke "saw little interest in fundamentalist Christianity by non-Christians." That was contrary to what he and his companions at a Christian fellowship on his college campus had been told: Non-Christians, it was claimed, would be curious about their faith, watch their Christian behavior and be drawn towards their peaceful relationship with God (Henke 2003, 249).

Instead, the Conservative believer seems to confess his or her faith more as a matter of conscience (confess Jesus before men so he confesses you before the Father), to avoid self-blame for condemning acquaintances whom one has grown to like and respect ("You can't say I didn't warn you!"), and to maintain the desired separation with the world:

> † "You young people, children of God, do not be ashamed to confess yourselves as believers before the children of this world; you are asked, then there will pour forth the strength of heaven into your souls. Through this confession you become blessed. That is honest before the face of God. . . . Nothing is harder for the believer than when at home, he wishes to speak of faith and grace to an unbeliever and the necessity of conversion. That is very

difficult. You often measure yourself, 'What is the reason I do not know how to speak? I do not have strength, I do not have words.' That is very noticeable but from this no one is left out. But when God with his love gives words to speak, then you have a thankful prayer to God that He gave you utterance" (Ville Suutari, *Greetings of Peace*, 9/1954).

✝ "It is hard to remain as a light unto our unbelieving friends, but having to talk to them honestly and openly has perhaps made it easier. When we discuss faith matters with them it puts a space or wall between us and them. When we are not in such close contact with them it is not such a great temptation to join some of their sinful activities" (VOZ, 8/1974).

The separation not only shields one from worldly influences, but provides a "plausibility structure" to reinforce one's beliefs. "Why is it better for the health of one's faith to remain within the Camp of the Saints? Because you will be much less inclined to doubt your beliefs while surrounded by others who are constantly affirming them" (Price 2006b, 169). The Jehovah's Witnesses have a "prohibition of socializing with anyone outside the organization," which is viewed "as a form of protection for the group. It was a deterrent to being influenced by others; thus, it helped to ensure that the Witnesses would stay within the safe confines of the organization" (Wilson 2002, 29). Conservative Laestadianism doesn't prohibit outside socializing, but it certainly doesn't encourage it. And the effect is the same–from childhood on, relationships are primarily within the church:

✝ "In school, at work, or wherever we are, we gladly seek out the fellowship of other children of God. We receive support from each other. The unbelieving wonder at this segregation, but still they cannot for long tolerate the company of the children of God, especially then, if God grants the strength to speak to them of the necessity of repentance" (*By Faith*, 104-105).

The results of that lifetime of insularity are viewed with awe by Peter Nevala in a 1981 sermon:

✝ "This is one of the peculiar mysteries and gifts of God's true kingdom, that those who are in this kingdom know one another. We can sense, we can feel the spirit of children in one another. It unites, it blesses."

It would seem surprising to me if there were *not* some special bond felt between members of a small group of people who have associated almost exclusively with each other from childhood, refrain from any exposure to the religious experiences of others, and have deeply enmeshed family relations and common ethnicity. And it's actually not something that is only felt by Conservative Laestadians:

> Who, indeed, can describe the pleasure with which the members of Christ's flock do meet each other face to face? They may have been strangers before; they may have lived apart, and never been in company—but it is wonderful to observe how soon they seem to understand each other, there seems a thorough oneness of opinion, and taste and judgment, so that a man would think they had known each other for years; they seem, indeed, to feel they are servants of one and the same Master, members of the same family, and have been converted by one and the same Spirit; they have one Lord, one faith, one baptism; they have the same trials, the same fears, the same doubts, the same temptations, the same faintings of heart, the same dread of sin, the same sense of unworthiness, the same love of their Savior. Oh—but there is a mystical union between true believers, which they only know who have experienced it; the world cannot understand it—it is all foolishness to them. ["The Character of the True Christian," by J.C. Ryle (1816-1900), Anglican bishop]

I have made many beloved friends within Conservative Laestadianism after spending some four decades within its narrow boundaries. There have been wonderful times of fellowship, visits between families and weekend camping trips where Ryle's "mystical union between true believers" was clearly and joyously present. It is a sense of acceptance and belonging that fills a deep social need, one not easily met in the isolation of today's suburban, technology-driven society. Winell observes that fundamentalist Christians

> constitute a full-blown subculture with a common language, belief system, and behavioral code. As with other subcultures, but even more so, it can be very comforting for members to find safety and understanding so widely. Within a denomination particularly, believers can travel to new places and fit into a church community immediately. Evangelicals worldwide share a purpose that unites them. In addition, every church or Bible

group can be a social group with all the benefits of a community" (1993, 53).

But there has also been much frustration from a lifetime of wedging myself (and my family) into the insular mini-society of the LLC. Almost all of my peers were raised in happy, loving homes with 8-12 siblings who grew up and have had large families of their own. Their parents themselves have many siblings and have long supplied our peers with truckloads of cousins for their earliest friendships. All those relatives constitute a body of comfortable and familiar companions who share many attitudes–not just about religion but also politics, leisure activities, and education. They are there for Sunday afternoon visiting, holidays, celebrations, employment, babysitting, and weekend outings.

My family doesn't have such a family social network, unfortunately. To get the attention of our peers beyond just visits over the snack table after services, we needed to compete with the extensive social networks that they have inherited. It gets tiresome. And the claim I've so often heard that I have a "true family" in the church convinces me no more than "the ostentatious claim that 'The brothers and sisters are there for you'" did Diane Wilson when she heard it as a Jehovah's Witness. To both of us–with a few happy exceptions–it is "really just a fantasy" (2002, 138).

The last time I heard that claim was in the meeting between myself and the local congregation's Board of Trustees concerning this book's June 2010 edition. My response was, "I have family in the church! Great! I'll see you on Thanksgiving, at Christmas, on Easter." But in the year following that meeting, the number of invitations my wife and I received to socialize with the families of those board members or anyone else in the local LLC congregation can be counted on a single hand.

Most of my friendships within the church are now strained due to my inability to keep my mouth shut about religious matters, a story told in **1.2**. Those who still seem comfortable with me personally either don't know of my questions about the faith (not much chance of that continuing, once this is published) or are not overly intimidated by them. Some just don't seem to take any of it too seriously or personally, while others are veterans of their own struggles and have learned to live with the difficulties one way or another.

Persecution Complex

There's a fair amount of persecution against the "believers" by "the world," at least according to some preachers and writers. Since Christians are no longer being fed to lions or burned like torches to light the streets of Rome, the acts of persecution are limited to the realms of thought and word. That was mostly true even in 1855 when Laestadius delivered his Second Rogation Day Morning sermon lamenting the hatred and persecution that the few elect had to suffer:

> † "In the text of the morning sermon we read: *The Lord is nigh unto them that are of a broken heart.* But how many such ones are there who have a broken heart? Perhaps one in a hundred or a thousand. The seven thousand in Israel who had not borne hatred, were scarcely one in a hundred, and the three thousand souls who were converted on Pentecost, were hardly one in a hundred, when compared to the great sorrowless flock. From this we can observe that the elect of God have at all times been only a few, and these few have been despised, hated and persecuted by the world. Do you think that any true Christian can live in the world without being ridiculed? Positively not! For that reason there are only a few who can truly claim some comfort to themselves from today's text" (*Fourth Postilla*, 96).

Two sermons by Uno Makela paint a grim picture of believers suffering the hatred and intolerance of "the world":

> † "We are here in this world for a short while; we are not of the world but we are in the world. We are those peculiar people which the world ridicules and hates. We are the ones that are pointed out as the narrowminded, we are persecuted by the world. We know if we did not receive this persecution and ridicule the world would accept us. For that reason, Jesus Christ, Himself, said, 'Do not marvel if the world hates you,' for it hated Him more. So we understand that as long as the world ridicules us, we are still in the kingdom of God. The dangers begin when the world starts accepting us" (1979).

> † "When we think how many people are upon earth, we are but a few and strangers and hated of all people. It is not a wonder that the world hates us, says Jesus; and they first hated him. We experience daily that the world has nothing to do with us. If we

speak of the salvation of our soul, the man of the world does not want to hear it but wants to separate themselves from us. As long as we speak of other matters people can be friendly but they cannot stand it when we speak of the salvation of the soul. In this way, they have hatred towards us, for it disturbs their life and reminds them of the condition of their souls" (1985).

The same kind of paranoia can be seen in the OALC today. When an OALC member posted one judgmental comment after another on the **extoots** site <http://extoots.blogspot.com/2007/02/unbearable-loneliness-no-more_14.html> and didn't like the pushback it generated, he responded with a lament about how "the world hates us." I like the way that claim was addressed by several respondents: "The vast majority of the world doesn't know that the OALC even exists"; "Why do you think 'the World' even *cares* about the OALC? You sound like egocentric children, who think the sun rises and sets on your concerns"; "You condemn people to hell. None of us do to the best of my knowledge. How does that make you the persecuted one, and not the reverse?"

In an interesting twist, Peter Herriot posits that the self-esteem of fundamentalists is actually *enhanced* by the disapproval of "the world":

> [N]on-believers' criticisms of fundamentalist beliefs or actions indicate to the believers that they must be doing God's will. Such criticisms simply confirm fundamentalists in their belief that they are right, since if the Devil assaults us, we must be doing God's will. Conversely, if they start to be accepted or valued by "the world," then they must be going against the will of God. Their self-esteem is therefore enhanced, both by the approval of like-minded believers and by the disapproval of "the world." [2009, 177-78]

Still, two points must be acknowledged. First, there *has* been some criticism of Conservative Laestadianism that takes on a mocking tone, especially by those who were once in the faith and have left it, and in Finland. There the movement attracts a fair amount of media attention, with nearly as many Conservative Laestadians per capita as there are Mormons per capita in the U.S.[11] Second, those leaving their religion are

---

11. Based on an estimate of 40,000 adult SRK members (Hurtig 2011), Finland's population at around 5,200,000 in 2000, about 2,700,000 adult Mormons in the U.S., and a U.S. population of about 271,000,000 in 2000.

not immune to seeking self-vindication by imagining or exaggerating persecution themselves:

> Ironically, I have now carried the persecution complex with me; as an unbeliever, I am in an even smaller minority than I was as an evangelical. This provides the potential to differentiate myself from those around me, especially in the predominantly Christian Dallas, Texas suburb I now call home. I must guard against this tendency to cherish the persecution complex or to consider myself a cut above those who have not "seen the light." [Daniels 2010, 90-91]

Caricature and Blame

Stereotyping outsiders and blaming them for their unsaved condition began early on in Laestadianism:

> † "Some have believed and endured in patience, others have been choked by the thorns or by the sorrows of this world's riches. The blackbirds have pecked the Word of God from the hearts of some. Some have not received the dew or moisture from heaven. But the drought of this world of unbelief has scorched and slain them. Truly God gives the moisture of Heaven to all those who pray, but it is their own fault if they have not receive moisture, when they have not prayed for moisture from the God of Heaven" (Raattamaa, sermon given 1896, from Kulla 1993, 67).

Matti Suo [1861-1927] wrote of the hiddenness of the kingdom, and the various ways the unfortunate outsiders were deluded:

> † "Much indeed is spoken of God and Jesus, but few know and, it even seems, care to know, how and where God is to be found. The kingdom of God, which should be sought for first (Mt 6:33), is therefore unknown and hidden. But as long as the kingdom of God is secret, it is impossible to know its King. The people grope for the wall like the blind, Isa 59:10. Here is one who in his imagination hovers in the heavens, hoping to receive something

---

There is a significant issue with the usual estimate of 100,000 Conservative Laestadians in Finland, a figure that I cite elsewhere in this book myself. Most of those are children who have not even reached the age of accountability for their own religious beliefs. If we were to count innocent children as being part of one particular sect, its membership numbers would skyrocket to over a billion.

therefrom; here one in his chamber with his private prayers; here one at the root of a tree in the wilderness; here one says he bases all in baptism; another in his good works and deep devotion; another who boasts that he looks only to the word, and says he does not believe any man and explains that God does not need or use any middle hands to save the sinner. Thus outside of the kingdom of God there are in respect to the things of salvation 'as many minds as men.' The third article of the creed: I believe in the Holy Ghost, etc. is altogether an unknown secret" (from *Greetings of Peace*, 8/1950).

Whose fault is it that the kingdom is so "unknown and hidden" if God is using "His congregation to assist Him in seeking man," and "speaks to the unbelieving world" through his children, wishing "that those in the darkness of unbelief could come to the light, repent, and believe the gospel," as asserted in various quotes in **4.2.4** and **4.9.3**?

The religious activities of other Christians have even been attributed to Satan:

> † "In these last times there are increasingly many who go about crying 'Lord, Lord,' professing that they have accepted [Jesus] as their personal Savior. They gather especially on the college campuses to distribute their literature, preach their doctrine and be seen of men. Beware of these people, especially you fellow Christian college students. They are hypocrites and false prophets in sheep's clothing, inwardly ravening wolves who work iniquity and have their reward. Taking the name of Christ as a banner they have united with Satan in the work of deceit" (VOZ, 10/1974).

Charles Simpson writes about similar statements in the exclusivist Churches of Christ and gives those who talk that way a warning:

> If blasphemy is defined as attributing to Satan the works of God through the power of the Holy Spirit, and if the Holy Spirit does indeed manifest Himself in the lives of the [outsiders], some within the Churches of Christ are treading on very dangerous ground in their tirades against these men of God. "Truly I tell you, people will be forgiven all their sins and all the blasphemies they utter. But whosoever blessings against the Holy Spirit will never be forgiven, but is guilty of an eternal sin" (Mk 3:28-29). To

deny the Holy Spirit's indwelling of God's anointed is to repeat the sin of the Pharisees in Christ's time. [2009, 116]

In a 1985 sermon, Jon Bloomquist summarized the motives and insecurities of those in the "dead faiths" of this world:

> † "Those who are in the dead faiths of this world seek to establish their own righteousness. They are unsure of their righteousness and have no security. They have the spirit of fear, but God's children do not have the spirit of fear, but of power. We can hear and feel the difference between the sermons of those who are in the dead faiths of man and the living Word of God which is not of men but of God."

As a former Catholic, Bloomquist is one of the rare converts to Conservative Laestadianism, so he has seen at least some of what happens in other religions. But his blanket statements about the "dead faiths of man" still annoy me on several levels. As the following two quotes illustrate, they are unfortunately still representative of what one reads and hears in sermons today:

> † "Living faith is a precious gift from God. It is a childlike faith. As it was in Jesus' time, many in this world today also have blinded eyes and hardened hearts. They do not see God's kingdom through eyes of faith. With their own understanding they examine God's Word, which may appear too simple, for it disregards their good works" (VOZ, 2/2008).

> † "People seek for happiness and peace with their own means, only taking them further away from God. A lack of roots and hopelessness increase with those things that numb the mind and from which people try to build their happiness" (VOZ, 4/2008).

First, the charge of self-righteousness and reliance on good works is just another stereotype (also see **4.5.2**) from people who choose not to know much about the actual lives and beliefs of outsiders. The fact is that many if not most Christians look to the work of Jesus Christ rather than themselves for their salvation. The statement of Ken Daniels about that aspect of his former Christianity is not at all unusual: "I understood from Paul's epistles that God's acceptance of me was based entirely on his love for me, his sacrifice on my behalf, and not at all on any of my personal accomplishments or righteousness" (2010, 19). One of the most compassionate and caring Christians I know is my friend and family physician. His motivation for the work he does–a level of community outreach that few Laestadians will ever bother to undertake–is a simple desire to live out what he sees as a Christian life.

And what about their insecurities and doubts? Does Bloomquist think they are any different than the doubts and intellectual discomfort that are so apparent from the statements in **4.5.4** and **4.5.5**? Had Bloomquist ever actually listened to any "dead faith" sermons–beyond the Catholic homilies of his upbringing–to get an accurate assessment of differences between them and "the living Word of God"? Since attending other services has always been nearly unheard of, I doubt it.

Herriot discusses the small-group nature of "fundamentalist movements and organizations" and how they

> have been unremitting in their hostility to their out-groups. They have therefore used their small groups to tie adherents in to the [beliefs, values, and norms of behavior] of the movement and to strengthen their social identities as movement members. Movements can then become more differentiated from their out-groups, thereby more effectively providing the self-esteem and certainty that motivate their adherents. The in-group will seek to make itself as different as possible from the out-group. To do so, it will create a stereotype of the out-group. . . . The stereotype is the belief that the out-group consists of people who all share certain characteristics, characteristics that firmly differentiate the out-group from the in-group. [2009, 143]

It's not just something Conservatives do. Jerry Falwell was often "inventing a cabal of secularists where there was none, providing his congregation with something to define itself and unite against" (Welch 2009, 123). Once a group has differentiated itself from others, real or imagined, "[i]n-group conformity and cohesion, and stereotyping and discrimination against perceived out-groups, often follow. Oneself and others are depersonalised: perceived primarily as prototypical or stereotypical exemplars of categories rather than as individuals" (Herriot 2009, 282).

Ed Babinski offers another explanation for the bad-mouthing of outsiders. The believer is psychologically projecting what he knows is worst about himself onto them while blinding himself to the existence of genuine goodness in them. Because those outsiders are all going to hell, "there must be something essentially wrong with 'them' (otherwise they would not be 'eternally damned,' which they 'obviously' are–just look at what they believe)" (2003, 49).

"Narrow-Minded"

For a church that writes off the 99.998% of the world's people who are outside its boundaries as being destined to hell, Conservative Laestadianism seems ironically sensitive to the label of narrow-mindedness. And as we've seen, it certainly hasn't hesitated to apply labels to those outsiders. Matti Suo did so in a defensive-sounding writing that indirectly addressed the church's black-and-white thinking:

> † "[I]f a christian should mention something of wrong doctrine, it is considered horror to some ears. Wrong doctrine, self-righteousness etc. should not be mentioned. It is stamped partiality, unjust, and a christian should not be partial. But if spiritual things are thus understood, then the Holy Bible can be a discarded book. What then can be the background for preaching if the Bible is forsaken which mostly teaches of right and wrong doctrine. Wrong doctrine, with other sins causes its followers condemnation. Christ's doctrine brings its followers to the joys of Paradise. . . . But some have begun to broaden in their conception. God has become so merciful that all divisionals, be their trend of opinion anything, as long as some form of godliness is pursued, are suitable to be in the same stall. They should not be called divisionals, for fear that tender feelings of love are severed. Showing partiality is evidence of uncivilness, etc." (Matti Suo [1861-1927], from *Greetings of Peace*, 9/1954).

Two more recent writings deal with the "narrow-mindedness" label directly, again seeming a bit touchy about it:

> † "Like the disciples, we also often doubt whether we truly believe in Him correctly, or wonder about the destination of faith. The world wishes to cast doubt, saying Laestadian believers are so narrow-minded to think they are the only ones who are believing correctly" (VOZ, 5/2004).

> † "There has always been a division in this world between God's kingdom and those outside of its walls. Throughout history, this division has been apparent. A continual warfare between Satan

and God's children has been taking place. Today Satan is combining the forces of various faiths into one ecumenical group. The 'broad-minded' ones see believers to be narrow-minded and judgmental" (VOZ, 11/2004).

I wonder if those writers would consider Luther one of the "broad-minded" ones, given his criticism of "every judgment which attempts to establish who are Christians and the people of God and who are not" (from Althaus 1963, 292). Still, despite having a broader view of the church and more reluctance to define its boundaries than Conservative Laestadians, Luther was by no means a champion of ecumenism and tolerance. Even though he wrote that "the Holy Church is not bound to Rome, but is as wide as the world, the assembly of those of one faith" (*PE* 1, 361), it was still his belief "that no one can be saved who is not part of this community and does not live in harmony with it in one faith, word, sacrament, hope, and love" (from Althaus 1936, 291).

Unfortunately, whether the boundaries are drawn around one particular sect or not, there is no way for Christianity to avoid Sam Harris's observation that "'respect' for other faiths, or for the views of unbelievers, is not an attitude that God endorses." He continues, "While all faiths have been touched, here and there, by the spirit of ecumenicalism, the central tenet of every religious tradition is that all others are mere repositories of error or, at best, dangerously incomplete. Intolerance is thus intrinsic to every creed" (Harris 2005, 13).

Outreach

"In the fundamentalist view," Winell writes, "unbelievers have only two relevant attributes. They are potential converts and sources of temptation" (1993, 76). Similarly, Welch criticizes "the simple-minded attitude that the only redemptive quality in others was their ability to become more like her," referring to an evangelical Christian she spent time with (2010, 145). The following quote reflects that attitude, though at least it leaves open the possibility of outside friendships:

> † "Can a believer then have an unbelieving friend? Even an unbeliever needs a person to whom he can speak about his troubles. I think this kind of friendship does not need to be terminated. Many times school and work friends can even become close friends so that discussion can be trusting and open. It can be so that we are the only trustworthy person to that

unbeliever. Maybe he or she will come to comprehend the grace of repentance when we tell about it to the person" (*Siionin Kevat* [1988], from VOZ, 3/1990).

At this point, it will not come as a surprise that the church has done little outreach toward the society in which it resides. The following is an exception to that, a welcome one in my view:

> † "[A]ll we have is from God and God has certainly blessed believers. Even in today's prosperous economy, however, there are those who suffer from want and are in great need, greater than our own. We frequently think only of our own wants and forget others to whom we could give so much. For what we do for others we are also doing for God. . . . There are many ways in which we can serve the poor in our own communities. There are soup kitchens, food and clothing drives, giving money or time to charity, or various other community services" (VOZ, 7/2000).

In a 2002 presentation during his pastorate at an LLC congregation, Matti Kontkanen allowed that there is sometimes "room for criticism" about Conservative Laestadianism's approach to "the people of the world":

> † "For the most part, we see how the congregation approaches unbelievers only with the word of God. We really have not become accustomed to the idea that the congregation would direct its activity toward the unbelievers in any other manner, for example: by taking collections for unbelievers, for founding hospitals or schools for them, or by taking stands on political issues. But individual Christians need not look at this restraint by the congregation as a whole as an example for their personal involvement. Even so, it may be that this example is duplicated to some degree in our individual lives as well."

That presentation was given a year after the 9/11 attacks. It was on the Sunday after those attacks that I saw the only instance of outside charity during my lifetime in the church before or since, a collection for the Red Cross.

One explanation for the lack of outreach, besides the movement's insular nature, is provided by Welch's observations about her evangelical companions: "There wasn't much point in helping the needy if they were just going to end up in hell anyway. Focusing on corporeal problems made as much sense to Christians as offering people pool floaties in the middle of the ocean; getting them saved would allow them to live underwater" (2009, 140).

The following quote at least acknowledges the tragic nature of a nearly empty heaven, and that God has some purpose for the existence of the unbeliever:

> † "It seems tragic to think that only we will get to heaven. But we haven't come here to judge. We can always hope and pray. [An unbelieving brother] is not here in vain. Surely God has given him a purpose" (VOZ, 6/2004).

But the vicious beast of predestination lurks in the tall grass of that seemingly kind sentiment. Jason Long, as usual, does not mince words in his critique of the God he no longer believes in:

> God brings people into this world without a choice in the matter and expects us to do certain things, otherwise he'll punish us severely without rest for an eternity. God's omniscience must necessarily allow him to know which names will not be included in his book of life. Therefore, we can only conclude that *he purposely brings people into the world with zero chance of avoiding Hell.* Any deviation from this predetermined course would make God wrong, but since God cannot possibly be wrong, it's impossible for us to deviate from the absolutely unalterable plan that he has already envisioned. Thus, Christians can only logically claim that we are exclusively involuntary pawns at the mercy of God's whimsical decisions as to where we will spend our ultimate eternal destinations. This heartless exercise of brutality can only be the single most hateful crime any being could ever commit. [2005, 105, emphasis added]

Recently, the church has encountered an unexpected and unwanted form of "outreach" in the form of discussions and criticism on social networking sites, blogs, and discussion forums. Having some of its members airing their grievances and doubts to each other and outsiders is an uncomfortable new reality for both the SRK and the LLC. "According to [SRK chairman Olavi] Voittonen, it is natural that young people want to question, but he would like to restrain the discussion taking place via blogs and social media." Rather, "the right place for discussion is a local [SRK meeting house]. There the writers of confusing texts can be also guided to repent" (Pulkkinen 2011).

The church is very sensitive to having itself discussed in anything but an officially sanctioned, devotional manner, on the Internet or otherwise. As I experienced from the hysterical reaction to my limited distribution of this book's June 2010 edition–which had far less commentary than is present here–the consequences of individual, public critique are severe enough to make it practically unheard of. Thus the Internet discussions are mostly found in private, restricted groups or on blogs and forums where both the postings and comments can be made anonymously. That hasn't found favor officially, either, with the SRK's previous secretary-general Aimo Hautamäki concluding that "anonymous discussion is worthless discussion and worthless knowledge" (Ijäs 2010).

It turns out that even utterly orthodox, devotional writing on the part of individual believers has been a source of concern. If you draw from your experience and education to publish Sunday school lesson plans on your own, for example, you can expect to be the subject of inquiry. And, on a social networking website,

> ✝ it "is good to consider that our messages and comments can be viewed by all who have access to the site. A personal, loving message, even one calling to God's kingdom, reaches beyond the intended recipient. The love for the undying soul expressed in such messages is understood by believers, but may seem insensitive or harsh to some. A personal card, letter, e-mail, conversation, or thoughts relayed through a close family member may be more appropriate" (VOZ, 7/2009).

Here is a good example of such a "personal, loving message" e-mailed to a friend of mine who left the LLC:

> You have said it [has] always been your desire to believe. If so then by all means you can. It requires one to acknowledge [you're] in the wrong. It requires penitence over sin and even wrong understanding and unbelief. I would sincerely say to you that the mercy of the heavenly father is immeasurable and if it is your desire to believe then you can [be] free [to] do so and put away your unbelief. I would also like to add that there is nothing humble about denouncing the existence of god. I know it is

fashionable in many universities to call ones self an atheist. Many people find a sense of broad understanding and a high intellect by having this view that athiesm [sic] is the new and modern type of intellect. The devil doesn't need to attack you any longer. The uneasiness and lack of peace in your heart is put there by god. Your conscience is telling you that something isn't right with you. It isn't the devil who is tormenting you. It is your knowledge that you are not currently a child of god. I am not "preaching" to serve myself . . . but because I care about your undying soul and would like to call you a brother in faith. I did not want to continue this conversation because of the evil research and beliefs you presented me and your attempt to dissuade me of my faith. If you would like to continue to speak about matters of faith I would be happy to continue. But I will not delve into works of evil men and look at articles referring to the bible being evil. It is your desire to believe . . . and I would encourage you to put away your doubts and unbelief. It is a joy being a child of god and it is said that when a lost sheep is found and gathered back to the flock that even the angels in heaven rejoice. You don't need to continue on the path to destruction but your time of visitation is open yet and you can believe.

It is completely in accord with Conservative Laestadian doctrine and was no doubt motivated by genuine concern. But even clean underwear is an awkward thing to see out in public.

The issue of social networking was addressed at the July 2011 annual meeting of the LLC, but from the perspective of danger to the believer's faith rather than as a turn-off to outsiders. Item 10.3 of the meeting minutes states, "Concern was expressed about the use of social media websites. It is dangerous to our faith to seek answers about religion and faith from this type of media. These sites answer to our flesh and mind, but not our faith." Whoever said that would agree with Ingersoll's conclusion, though certainly not his sentiment: "The church never doubts–never inquires. To doubt is heresy–to inquire is to admit that you do not know–the church does neither" (*Lecture on Thomas Paine* [1880]).

4.2.4 The Call to the Kingdom

> *All fundamentalists believed in spreading the good news of Jesus Christ, but the old guard had put so much energy into doctrinal and ethical purity that it left little time and room for effective evangelistic efforts.*
>
> –Calvin Mercer, *Slaves to Faith*

Conservative Laestadianism has traditionally been quite hesitant to undertake any missionary activities. The LLC's ongoing efforts in Ecuador and West Africa are the result of people in those places coming into contact with individual believers, being converted, and then spreading the word. Other conversions followed, and the new believers expressed a desire for services to be held in their localities. At that point, it was felt that a sufficient call was being heard from God to send preachers, perhaps for the first time in the history of the LLC or its predecessors going back to Laestadius, to places where most of the listeners would not be already in the fold.

The work is driven by a genuine spiritual hunger by those out in remote areas who want to hear the preaching for themselves or share it with their friends and loved ones. Conservative Laestadianism is too restrained to impose itself much on disinterested strangers. That makes the mission work it does carry out genuine and unforced, welcomed by those receiving it. But it also limits the reach of the message.

For the past 20 years or so, there have also been broadcasts of sermons on local radio stations, especially during large, national service events. More recently, live and archived recordings of sermons have been made available on the Internet. In all of these cases, the forum for evangelism is the service led by a preacher. His words, once enclosed within the sanctifying wrapping of an opening prayer and a closing prayer (preferably also with some singing by the assembled listeners) become God's Word.

Back when the following two statements were made in sermons, any outsider hearing them would have physically made his way into the church by invitation or accident:

> † "God desires to enlighten to you that without the preaching of the gospel from God's kingdom you will perish. Here God offers this grace gospel, and you need not perish in your sins. This is the

greatest love for you, that you would be free from a bad conscience and receive your sins forgiven in the name and blood of the Lord Jesus" (Alajoki [1981], 141).

✝ "[I]f one would have come to the services here who feels he is not part of this living kingdom of God, God is calling you, dear friend, this afternoon. We can even say this that through your own power you have not been able to come to the services. God in His love has called and led you here and desires also to make known unto you His love" (Wesley Hillukka, sermon given 1985).

It was, and remains, a pretty limited and haphazard call. Yet, nearly invisible and devoid of results though it seems to be, it is how God chooses to do what surely should be the most important work imaginable, given the supposedly eternal stakes:

✝ "The work of the Spirit is to call sinners to repentance. Through the children of God, the Spirit speaks to the unbelieving world. God wishes that those in the darkness of unbelief could come to the light, repent, and believe the gospel. However, Jesus himself has revealed . . . 'that men loved darkness rather than light, because their deeds were evil' [John 3:19] . . . We understand that the Holy Spirit of God continues to function here on Earth until the work day is ended and it is no longer possible to proclaim the gospel of the kingdom" (VOZ, 7/1998).

✝ "God uses His congregation to assist Him in seeking man" (Uljas 2000, 13).

One attempt to explain the undeniable and disturbing limitations of God's call has been that there are "times of visitation" in which God supposedly favors certain localities with the presence of his Kingdom. I've often heard Luther's warning *To the Councilmen of All Cities in Germany* cited: "God's word and grace is like a passing shower of rain which does not return where it has once been" (Lull 2005, 463). It was with the Jews, and in Greece, and in Rome, and then in Luther's Germany. And then, apparently, the "elect people of God" wound up being found in a few hundred congregations scattered across Finland and a few locations in North America:

✝ "The time of visitation is not a matter that affects only one person, but an entire nation or community. Scriptures recount how the elect people of God had a time of visitation during the

Old Covenant and even at the beginning of the New Covenant. The living congregation of God was in their midst.... History indicates that God has given different nations a time of visitation at different times" (Uljas 2000, 15).

† "[W]hen the children of Israel, for the most part, rejected the grace of the caller the invitation was then directed to the Gentile nations. In our time of visitation the same invitation is extended to those on the outside through the servants of God, His children. The same kinds of excuses are heard today as in Jesus' time. One co-worker said to me that he could not 'join our church' because he would have to give up too many things that he enjoys in his life. In North America we have noted that few from the outside accept the invitation to come and hear the Word of God, even though God's children, in many localities across this continent, have preached repentance for many generations. The fault has not been with the caller, but those who have been invited 'began to make excuses' (Luke 14:18)" (VOZ, 10/2002).

Luke 14:16-24 is, as the quote indicates, a parable about the Jews being invited to the "great supper" but making excuses not to attend, at which point the Gentiles were invited. The quoted writer extends that parable in an effort to address the fact that so few of those invited to the Conservative Laestadian version of the "great supper" feel any inclination to attend. It's bad enough that only a tiny fraction of the world ever gets the invitation. How do we explain the overwhelming lack of interest on the part of those who do?

Usually, a person's decision to remain outside (or leave) Conservative Laestadianism is attributed to an unwillingness to give up "worldly pleasures," which avoids the need to acknowledge that the *doctrine* might have been found flawed, untrue, or unconvincing. But what sane person could possibly reject the faith for long–no matter *what* the cost– while maintaining a sincere belief that doing so is going to send him or her to eternal, unimaginable torment?

The reality is that, in all but a few cases, people who haven't grown up in the church just aren't interested in what it is offering. Daniel Everett encountered this "challenge of the missionary" in his own efforts at Christian evangelism in the Amazon jungle. (Conservatives would consider his work nothing more than sadly misguided peddling of "dead faith," but try telling that to Everett or the people he worked with.) The goal of his dedicated efforts over many years with the Pirahã Indians of Brazil was "to convince a happy, satisfied people that they are lost and need Jesus as their personal savior" (2008, 266).

What he found, after undertaking the formidable task of learning their very different language and culture, was that his two-thousand year old story about Jesus had absolutely no impact on the Pirahã people. After listening, unimpressed, to an audio recording of a fellow Pirahã reading the Gospel of Mark in their language, they said, "Well, he has never seen Jesus. He told us that he doesn't know Jesus and that he doesn't want Jesus." And with that simple observation, the Pirahãs signaled that Everett's recordings of Bible readings "would have little or no spiritual influence" (p. 269).

Instead of Everett converting these "primitive" Amazonians, they wound up de-converting him. He lost "confidence in the universal appeal of the spiritual message" he was bringing. "The Pirahãs were not in the market for a new worldview. And they could defend their own just fine" (p. 269). He came to greatly admire the Pirahãs, including their hard-headed skepticism:

> They were a sovereign people. And they were in effect telling me to peddle my goods elsewhere. They were telling me that my message had no purchase among them. All the doctrines and faith I had held dear were a glaring irrelevancy in this culture. They were superstition to the Pirahãs. And they began to seem more and more like superstition to me. [p. 270]

In the 1990s, with much fanfare, conversions to Conservative Laestadianism finally began taking place in some numbers. There was a wave of interest in Russia after the fall of Gorbachev, then in Togo and Ecuador:

> † "God has given us a precious time of visitation. For over 100 years in many localities in the United States and Canada, God has been with us. Scripture says that if God be for us, who can be against us. In our time, God has given a special time of visitation to the people of Togo, Ecuador, Russia, and other countries. . . . In times of visitation, God especially offers His grace" (VOZ, 8/2004).

The "other countries" mostly refers to places where Finns have wound up going for work and have formed congregations, with a few conversions from the surrounding community. Even the Swedish association of Conservative Laestadians, the SFC, is made up primarily of expatriate Finns. There have been some conversions in Estonia, but only a few dozen of the converts remain (Palola 2010).

I remember being fascinated along with everybody else in church by the stories about African and South American Laestadians. And it was captivating to hear some of the new converts from Togo talking about their newfound faith, as two of them did during a tour of North American congregations. In addition to the novelty of an inward-looking bunch of Finns being exposed to an entirely different culture, there was a genuine feeling of joy at the salvation of souls. The presence of Laestadians in faraway places provided an emotional comfort–certainly not a rational one, given the tiny numbers involved–that God's call was not quite so provincial and limited as we had thought. And, as Dennis MacDonald notes, conversions to one's worldview provide a way of proving it correct: "We can't be wrong if so many believe what we do. Never mind that so many who once found now have lost it" (2003, 114).

The reality of MacDonald's "never mind" comment is evident, too, in how the LLC publicly discusses its mission work. As discussed in **4.2.1**, the attention quickly fades about things that aren't going well. Russians, what about them? There are believers in *Turkey* now! The *Voice of Zion* continues to feature articles about mission work in Ecuador–it is visited by LLC preachers several times per year–but makes no mention of how significantly the numbers there have dwindled. The sunny, upbeat nature of its reporting is understandable for a devotional newspaper, but it doesn't provide an accurate view of the situation. One example is best illustrated with a photo appearing on the front page of the March 2011 issue:

The accompanying article stated that "many young people and a number of adults from the Quito, Riobamba, and La Merced areas gathered at the Hacienda la Merced for a weekend of instruction, fellowship, and fun ..." I count ten Ecuadorian young people in that picture.

During my research for this book, I was surprised to come across a letter from Oswald Koivisto in the March 1949 *Greetings of Peace* that told of an attempt at mission work in China during the aftermath of World War II. The letter, addressed to Paul and Eva Heideman from "Lutheran Mission, Pakhoi, Kwangtung, China," told of difficulties encountered in attempting to "be the 'voice shouting' in this dark wilderness of heathenism":

> It is true, that even the Chinese will learn something of Christianity. But if it is difficult for every one to confess his sins and humble himself to repentance for his sins, yet this is especially difficult for the Chinese. For he is very careful to not "loose [sic.] face." And the confessing of sins and begging forgiveness, means the loss of honor to the Chinese. And this he dreads more than death. And because of this attitude on the matter of confessing sins, which is so important in true and living Christianity, the work for God's kingdom is extremely difficult. We have spoken of this matter with our Chinese pastor, but even he does not seem to understand anything about it. Other missionaries here have complained about the same matter. But

we still can not leave the work where it seems difficult for the work is the Lord's. And He is powerful to break down even the hard heart.

Koivisto's activities never enjoyed the approval of the Conservative Laestadian leadership in either America or Finland. Uljas acknowledges that forty years before his writing (i.e., in the 1960s) foreign mission work had risen as a topic of dissension." The problem was the ecumenical nature of the effort (Uljas 2000, 117). Conservatives are in the same position as the similarly exclusivist Churches of Christ–they "are taught that they are right and that all other Christians are wrong, [so] they simply do not have the ability to understand, accept, or interact with other Christian faiths on spiritual matters" (Simpson 2009, 9). And so,

> Conservative Laestadians turned down the offer for mutual work, but agreed on the importance of mission work and remained waiting for the time when God would provide opportunity for their own mission work. This position was held in spite of accusations and criticism. God's time came thirty years later. [Uljas 2000, 117]

It's certainly convenient to be able to refer to "God's time" whenever there is an otherwise unexplainable resistance to taking action. For some reason, God decided to let the "dead faith" Christians of Finland go off and preach supposedly empty words in foreign countries for several decades. Meanwhile his true believers sat around preaching to each other and awaiting some sort of divine inspiration to undertake any missionary efforts of their own.

The movement was so allergic to either change or outreach that most of the sermons in the United States were delivered in Finnish until the 1960s. There was a hide-bound tradition of retaining what had become almost a sacred language in this second- and third-generation immigrant community. When the youth finally started learning English as their first language, that tradition was, for about a decade, more important than ensuring that those young people were able to fully understand what was being said in their parents' own churches. In that environment, the problem of outsiders failing to adequately comprehend "the call to the Kingdom" could not have been the subject of much concern.

The following quote about offering the gift of faith is entirely sensible and biblical, but it does not begin to describe the massive responsibility for evangelism that rests on the shoulders of each Conservative Laestadian:

> † "The gift of faith should be offered to all. It cannot be given if it is not offered. We should preach the word in season and out of season" (VOZ, 11/2004).

If you believe that your contact with someone at your workplace, school, gym, barbershop, etc. is likely to be the only means by which God offers him or her the gift of eternal life, of avoiding perpetual, unimaginable torment in hell, one would think that you would indeed feel compelled to "preach the word in season and out of season," using every opportunity to convince that person to accept this incredibly valuable offer. Yet how much does this actually happen? How many worldly acquaintances are even invited to services?

Let me be blunt: You certainly wouldn't hesitate to interrupt some activity or risk being considered rude if you thought your worldly acquaintance was just about to eat some food tainted with *E. coli*, or even had an untied shoelace. So what does your reluctance to "offer the gift of faith" say about your belief that you are indeed the only means by which such a priceless gift can be offered? A certain quote, repeated in various forms and difficult to attribute, comes to mind: "Don't tell me what you believe. Show me what you do, and I'll tell you what you believe."

The responsibility is evaded by appealing to God's sovereignty:

> † "[M]an, on his own, cannot find God. He cannot consciously decide that he would like to have God in his life. We do not have the wisdom or means to bring ourselves to Him. Rather, it is God who reveals himself to us. He instills in us a troubled conscience and a desire to find peace. . . . God controls the search for peace. He leads a searching person to His kingdom where His word is found. . . . God has chosen to reveal His kingdom unto babes–those who feel unworthy to come to God. Their feelings of unworthiness cause shame and leave one begging for mercy from the Father" (VOZ, 6/2005).

> † "Man cannot approach God or come to the Lord Jesus unless God calls him. . . . One cannot be self-invited. Through God's

kingdom the message of salvation is made known through the preaching and teaching of pardoned sinners. . . . The invitation to come into God's kingdom is still being made through His servants around the world. The search continues for those individuals who seek a gracious God. 'Yet there is room' in God's house for the sin weary, the conscience stricken, and those who labor under sin burdens. One day, however, the invitation will end. Enough guests will have been found to fill God's house" (VOZ, 6/2005).

† "Each person has a day of visitation in his or her life. The most important matter is that one would not reject that opportunity to make repentance and believe the gospel when God's kingdom approaches" (VOZ, 12/2005).

Again, we are back to the problem of predestination (**4.9.3**). Conservative Laestadianism considers its own congregations to be the only place where God's kingdom has been present for the past century and a half. In that time, there have been perhaps 200,000 members of those congregations, the vast majority of them in Finland. *Almost all* of humanity has lived and died, and will die, *without ever even hearing* about Conservative Laestadianism, much less having any "opportunity to make repentance" into it. It might seem nice and fair to assert that "each person has a day of visitation in his or her life," but it is manifestly untrue.

Some anxiety about that is evident in the following quote from the June 2008 *Voice of Zion*:

† "It's not unusual that we, with our own minds, can wonder why God's kingdom is not presently offered to certain cultures or peoples. We might wonder why we don't start mission work in this place or that, or perhaps with those people or that culture. These thoughts can be prayerful and with hope. We've marveled, however, how God in His remarkable way has opened the door in His time. The work of the kingdom does not progress with man's efforts and aims, but with God's."

But man's efforts are obviously required, since people cannot find the kingdom on their own. So we have the most important matter in the life of any person alive being dependent on the highly unlikely possibility of personal contact with a Conservative Laestadian. And not just any contact, but the rare case where it is spelled out for the unbeliever just what is at stake and what must be done:

> ✝ "You who are not a partaker of grace, hurry and take care of your matters with the living God! Pray that He would have mercy on you by sending a believer to you. They bear with them the words of grace and forgiveness. God likes to hear such a prayer" (VOZ, 7/2009).

What about all the sincere prayers for salvation that are said by people who have no clue about any of this? You must feel a need to depart from the spiritual (or atheist) worldview that you inherited from your parents, something never done by the vast majority of people in the thousands of varieties of religion and culture around the world. Somehow, that dissatisfaction must lead you to pray for an encounter whose nature is entirely foreign to your current beliefs, with a person from a tiny sect you've never heard of. Then, that encounter must convince you–which it almost never does–that you need to renounce your previous self as a damned sinner and accept the "words of grace and forgiveness" along with the requirement for membership in this sect. *This* is how God carries out his desire for all men to be saved?

4.2.5 Conversion

> *The evidence of conversion existed in the various and immediate physical and emotional expressions of the converted. Fast conversions, accompanied with vivid evidence, led to an emotionally charged form of religiosity with almost no intellectual or deep theological content.*
>
> —Calvin Mercer, *Slaves to Faith*

An article in the December 2005 *Voice of Zion* provides a good introduction to the Conservative Laestadian view of conversion, which is also often referred to as "repentance":

> ✝ "By faith we understand that true repentance contains three interrelated parts. First is sorrow over sin, the second is forgiveness for sins or absolution, and the third is a change of heart and mind, which is sometimes referred to as the 'amendment of life.' The depth of the feelings of sorrow is not the basis for repentance. It is sufficient to know that one is a sinner

and is in need of God's grace in order to be saved. In true repentance, righteousness or amendment of life is the result of the righteousness of faith. It does not precede the righteousness that comes by faith."

The article downplays the importance of feelings of sorrow, but Laestadius greatly emphasized the need for sorrow over sin. Indeed one of his favorite terms for unbelievers was "the sorrowless." For them to convert, a "great change must come ... not only that they must first walk in hell and be in tribulation of conscience as was David, but they must cry from the depths unto the heights even as David has cried" (Fourth Rogation Day sermon [1856]; *Fourth Postilla*, 227).

It's understandable that there might be a difference in emphasis about personal feelings associated with conversion. Claims about "unchanging faith" aside, there is a vast difference between the deep and fiery Pietism of Laestadius's time and the subdued Christianity of current-day Conservative Laestadianism. And Luther was a bit confused about the role of human emotion–specifically the sense of humility–in his early writings, with contradictory statements about whether humility preceded or followed conversion (Harran 1983, 57-59).

What Conservative Laestadianism has always shared with Laestadius (and Luther) is the importance of the great change of conversion. It's not a surprising attitude for what is referred to in Finland as a *revival movement* (*herätysliike*). Conversion is closely linked with the forgiveness of sins, which is also of great importance and a prominent topic of discussion (**4.6.2**). The forgiveness of sins not only begins a new believer's life of faith, but sustains it.

In view of all that, I found the following a very disturbing fact to learn about the Bible: With one possible exception that I will discuss shortly (2 Cor 2:10), it contains no teaching or examples of people being converted to or sustained in Christianity by hearing the proclamation of the forgiveness of their sins. Even in the case where such an example would seem most instructive–Peter's denial of Christ–there is no description of conversion or repentance at all. In Mt 26:69-75, the

> † "words and actions of Peter were a complete denial of his faith. The Bible does not record the actual account of Peter's repentance, but the words of [John 21:15-19, 'feed my sheep']

assuredly testify that Peter did receive grace to repent and return to God's kingdom" (VOZ, 4/2008).

The Gospels tell us about a wilting fig tree and a coin in a fish's mouth, but nothing at all about the repentance of Jesus' primary disciple from a complete denial of his faith?

An important conversion that *is* described—in Acts, a continuation of the gospel of Luke—is the conversion of Paul. That is a favorite text for explaining how one needs to interact with another believer in order to be converted. When Paul (or, to use his pre-conversion name Saul of Tarsus) had been struck down by a light from heaven and asked what he should do,

> † "Jesus told Saul to go into the city and it would be told to him what he must do. Saul needed to be led into Damascus, as he had lost his sight. God then sent a believing man, Ananias, to Saul. Ananias laid his hands on Saul and preached the gospel, and Saul was immediately filled with the Holy Ghost and received his sight. Not only did Saul receive his physical sight, but he also received spiritual sight" (VOZ, 1/2009).

But there are issues here, too. As discussed in **7.2**, none of the accounts of the event in Acts say that Ananias "preached the gospel." In the letters attributed to him, Paul denies that the gospel is something he received from man or was taught.

Paul does make one intriguing statement about forgiveness in 2 Corinthians concerning an unnamed offender who had been duly punished for some unspecified offense. Paul expressed concern that his readers "should rather forgive and comfort" the offender, "otherwise such a one might be overwhelmed by excessive sorrow" (2:7, NASB). He urges them to reaffirm their love for him, and says, "[O]ne whom you forgive anything, I forgive also; for indeed what I have forgiven, if I have forgiven anything, I did it for your sakes in the presence of Christ" (2:10, NASB). Robert M. Price, skeptical of the book's Pauline authorship as he is about most all of the epistles, says "that the writer is using Paul's persona to tell them how to deal with offenders in their own time" (Price 2006a, 385).

In his apologetic history of confession and absolution, the Catholic theologian Thomas J. Capel does not hesitate to read Paul's statement as evidence of "an agency of reconciliation" (Capel 1884, 13). In his view, a "clearer case of retaining and remitting is unnecessary" (p. 16). Price is certainly no apologist for absolution or indeed Christianity in general, but he also notes a connection to the "keys of the kingdom" passages of Mt 16:19; 18:18, and Jn 20:23: "Here Paul is made to bequeath judicial authority to his successors. He is the vicar of Christ and, more to the point, so are they" (Price 2006a, 385).

The Proclamation of Absolution

The idea that conversion can only take place by hearing the forgiveness of sins–as proclaimed by someone who is already a believer–is a central point of Conservative Laestadian doctrine. Here is one of a very few passages I have found in Laestadius's teachings suggesting it:

> † "If Thomas abides alone and seeks Christ in solitude, will Christ come to seek him there? I think, Thomas, that you must first come to the Christians' meetings before Christ will come to show His wounds. You will not, in any case, become a partaker of the grace of resurrection before you come into the congregation. No matter how you would read the Book in solitude and keep prayers at home, you will surely not become a Christian there. But come first to the Christian meetings and seek first the congregation before you will find Christ" (Laestadius, Fourth Sunday after Easter sermon, 1859).

Laestadius's near-silence on the topic is troubling, as is his description of the solitary conversion of John Raattamaa's brother Peter, discussed in 4.1.4. And John Raattamaa was less than clear about it, too. In a sermon printed in the May 1897 *Sanomia Siionista*, he said,

> There has been a dispute in Finland about whether the written word has the effect that one can be led to living faith through it; and this we have answered, that both the written and preached word bring one unto salvation. Peter's words had the effect that those who heard them received the Holy Spirit. [p. 83][12]

---

12. Author translation after a draft provided by Antti Kaunisto. The original is as follows: "On Suomessa ollut tinka sen päältä, vaikuttaako luettu sana, että ihminen voi sen kautta tulla elävään uskoon saatetuksi, ja siihen olemme vastanneet, että sekä luetun että saarnatun sanan kautta autuaaksi tullaan. Pietarin sanat vaikuttivat, että ne, jotka sen kuulivat, saivat Pyhän Hengen." A facsimile of the article was obtained from **digi.kansalliskirjasto.fi/index.html**.

That quote came to my attention recently, and wasn't part of my sample of Conservative writings and sermons. Neither was an early story of conversion by personal absolution from a 1912 issue of *Siionin Lähetyslehti* that I feel must also be mentioned.

A resident of Atlantic Mine, Michigan accompanied his wife to the Conservative services instead of staying home as he usually did. He arrived to the sound of rejoicing, and asked "if grace really belonged to such a great sinner as he was, and if so, he was ready to accept it. The Christians blessed him, and his own Christian wife was the first to bless him with the forgiveness of sins in the name and blood of Jesus, and so he was added to the number of newly converted that evening" (from Kulla 2004, 58). It is a remarkable testament to the endurance of the doctrine of conversion by personal absolution. There's nothing about the story that would be any different for a conversion to Conservative Laestadianism today, a century later.

The earliest quote from my actual sample that provides a real articulation of that conversion process is from a January 1950 *Greetings of Peace* article by Arvi Hintsala:

> † "[W]here God is given to begin His work, to effect awakening, there sin begins to cause grief and trouble. The love and enjoyment of sin ceases. And the only question comes up[, ']What must I do that I might be saved? God, help, I perish!'. . . In [the] awakened state, man is helpless. It is not God's intention to only awaken man, and then let him wait [for] what God does in heaven. No, but God is near to the awakened, is near in the word of the gospel. To the awakened the gospel brings the very heart of God, the love which He has shown when He gave His only son, the Lord Jesus, to repair the poor matters of the prodigal son, who had lost everything. . . . The consoling sweet word of the gospel releases the awakened soul from his feeling of worthlessness and leads him to behold the Sacrifice and to see the Father's heart and the precious redemption-blood of the Lamb, how it is sprinkled in the gospel word. And what wonderful power there is in the sprinkling of the blood to the distressed sinner. It cleanses the soul, heals the wounds and brings about the miracle of life, which is called the new birth. The awakened soul experiences the great miracle of forgiveness, and God testifies to it by pouring the Holy Ghost into the heart."

There's never been any change in the position that conversion occurs by personal absolution and nothing else:

> † "The fires of living faith can kindle only where recipients of the Holy Ghost, God's own, have preached to a penitent sinner, by the command of Christ, all sins forgiven in His name and atonement blood." Jesus did not forgive Saul's "sins straight from heaven, even though He spoke to the man" because "the authority to forgive sins was already left upon the earth and God would not change His grace-order even toward the highly learned Saul. God surely took care of his matters and sent an ambassador of His kingdom to the blind and praying man, and by his proclaimed gospel the scales fell from the eyes of Saul and he regained his sight and was filled with the Holy Ghost" (Taskila 1961, 19-20).

> † "True repentance is not possible without God's kingdom and its preaching of remission coming from hearing distance" (Uljas 2000, 47).

Despite the doctrinal focus on repentance and conversion, the fact is that very few Conservative Laestadians are converts. The overwhelming majority were "born into a Christian home," with ties to the faith going back several generations in most cases. Inheritance of religion is actually a common phenomenon, as Richard Dawkins notes with some disdain:

> Out of all of the sects in the world, we notice an uncanny coincidence: the overwhelming majority just happens to choose the one that their parents belong to. Not the sect that has the best evidence in its favour, the best miracles, the best moral code, the best cathedral, the best stained glass, the best music: when it comes to choosing from the smorgasbord of available religions, their potential virtues seem to count for nothing, compared to the matter of heredity. This is an unmistakable fact; nobody could seriously deny it. Yet people with full knowledge of the arbitrary nature of this heredity, somehow manage to go on believing in their religion, often with such fanaticism that they are prepared to murder people who follow a different one. . . . The religion we adopt is a matter of an accident of geography. [from Loftus 2008, loc. 1070-75]

According to Schimmel, most people acquire their religious beliefs "through a process of socialization that begins at birth, in one's family and in the religious community into which one is born. The individual embodies the ideas, beliefs, values, sights, sounds, touches, and fragrances of the religion, and one practices its rituals for many years, long before he has sufficient cognitive ability to think about them critically" (2008, 168).

What sustains Conservative Laestadianism is not persuasion, but reproduction. The SRK historian Seppo Lohi acknowledged as much, saying that a change in the movement's position regarding contraception (**4.7.5**) would result in its slow death.[13] As it stands, the large families in the movement have provided it with an ample supply of new members, indoctrinated from earliest childhood. This has freed Conservative Laestadianism from much emphasis on recruiting outsiders and promotes a sort of social evolution that helps preserve its fundamentalist nature.

Personal Experiences

By relating their own conversion experiences, numerous preachers and lay members have attested to the "personal proclamation" doctrine in a very personal and emotionally powerful way. Sometime in the 1950s, Gust Wisuri gave a sermon in which he described his own conversion by hearing the preaching of forgiveness:

> † "God showed his mercy to me. And led by two men, I sat down at the end of a table where they were just finishing their meal. And when the gospel was preached to me, the forgiveness of sins in the name and blood of Jesus, by the power of the Holy Spirit, a weight was lifted off of me like a ton rock. I shall never forget that moment."

My grandmother Sophia Suominen had a conversion experience of her own, probably sometime around 1910. She recalls it in an article in the January 1968 *Greetings of Peace*:

---

13. Lohi's statement was reported in a Finnish local newspaper *Kalajokilaakso*: "Seppo Lohen mukaan ketään ei asiassa painosteta eikä makuuhuoneisiin kurkistella, mutta hän pitää ehkäisykantaa koko liikkeen kannalta olennaisen tärkeänä. –Jos tässä asiassa kanta muuttuu, kuolema on lestadiolaisen liikkeen padassa, ja liike sammuu."

☩ "I spent my childhood and the days of my youth in an environment where there was spiritual darkness. They were two of us schoolgirls who had an inward restlessness, and a longing to find peace for our souls, and the hope of salvation, but we didn't know how. We went to the pastor and asked his advice; it was evening, and the shades of night were falling. The pastor was reclining on the sofa, when we came into the parsonage. When we said we wanted to talk with him, he received us very cordially. We related to him of our inward restlessness, and a longing to find peace for our souls, and the hope of salvation. Not knowing where these feelings came about, he asked a few questions, and together with us read the Lord's Prayer, and that was all. We returned to our homes just as empty as when we left, and just as forlorn with our burdened conscience. We then began to partake of sinful pleasures, but even that was difficult to do with our awakened conscience. Then at 19 years of age, I came to America [from Finland], and God miraculously brought me into contact with His children. It was through them that I found what my soul was longing for. They preached the forgiveness of sins to me, and how blessed I was, then, and am still blessed now, even though in myself I have not become any better. Even yet all I have is through His grace, and I need to be blest again and again by the children of God."

Another example was given by Hannes Kamula in a 1978 sermon:

☩ "I remember that marvelous day in my life when I stood before this mercy seat. One child of God was the spokesman there. I knew that the Lord Jesus was speaking through his mouth and for that reason I pledged on the knees of my heart before this altar to hear what is said unto a big sinner. And what did he say? 'Your sins are forgiven unto you in Jesus' name and blood for the peace and freedom of your soul.'"

In a "Personal Experiences" article in the October 2000 *Voice of Zion*, a convert from Catholicism wrote a detailed account of his conversion experience. He said he had distress of conscience already in his youth, when he would receive absolution from a priest and feel better,

☩ "but only for a little while. Shortly after doing my penance, my conscience would again start pointing out things until I felt I needed absolution every minute of the day." He wrote of despairing of ever reaching heaven and knowing that the works of his hands would never earn him salvation. Then he "met a believer. After visiting some time, this believer made a comment that struck a chord within me. She told me, 'I wish I could tell you how I believe.' I asked her to tell me and in the next couple of weeks, she proceeded, along with other believers, to explain living faith." After overcoming two remaining issues he found hard to accept–the thought that it was "belittling to God that even a child could be God's mouthpiece in speaking the words of absolution" and how much his conversion would hurt his father–the "grace fountain flowed and I was reassured that I was now in living faith, that my unbelief and all my sins from that unbelief were forgiven in the name and blood of Jesus. The understanding of a child of God came quietly over the next few days. Many things that I used to think, say, and do, I no longer wanted. I had found a treasure in a field–living faith in God's kingdom."

The emotional impact of these conversion experiences is undeniable, but before allowing them to draw us to any conclusions about the unique validity of Conservative Laestadianism, we should consider how widespread and profound such experiences are in the religious realm generally. Consider the following testimonials, all by different people in different religious settings, from *The Varieties of Religious Experience* by William James:

> I halted but a moment, and then, with a breaking heart, I said, "Dear Jesus, can you help me?" Never with mortal tongue can I describe that moment. Although up to that moment my soul had been filled with indescribable gloom, I felt the glorious brightness of the noonday sun shine into my heart. I felt I was a free man. Oh, the precious feeling of safety, of freedom, of resting on Jesus! I felt that Christ with all his brightness and power had come into my life; that, indeed, old things had passed away and all things had become new. [Lecture 9]

> I felt myself in a new world, and everything about me appeared with a different aspect from what it was wont to do. At this time, the way of salvation opened to me with such infinite wisdom, suitableness, and excellency, that I wondered I should ever think of any other way of salvation; was amazed that I had not dropped my own contrivances, and complied with this lovely, blessed, and

excellent way before. If I could have been saved by my own duties or any other way that I had formerly contrived, my whole soul would now have refused it. I wondered that all the world did not see and comply with this way of salvation, entirely by the righteousness of Christ. [Lecture 9]

At that instant of time when I gave all up to him to do with me as he pleased, and was willing that God should rule over me at his pleasure, redeeming love broke into my soul with repeated scriptures, with such power that my whole soul seemed to be melted down with love, the burden of guilt and condemnation was gone, darkness was expelled, my heart humbled and filled with gratitude, and my whole soul, that was a few minutes ago groaning under mountains of death, and crying to an unknown God for help, was now filled with immortal love, soaring on the wings of faith, freed from the chains of death and darkness, and crying out, My Lord and my God; thou art my rock and my fortress, my shield and my high tower, my life, my joy, my present and my everlasting portion. [Lecture 10]

I felt something solemn and sacred within me which made me ask for a priest. I was led to one; and there alone, after he had given me the positive order, I spoke as best I could, kneeling, and with my heart still trembling. I could give no account to myself of the truth of which I had acquired a knowledge and a faith. All that I can say is that in an instant the bandage had fallen from my eyes, and not one bandage only, but the whole manifold of bandages in which I had been brought up. One after another they rapidly disappeared, even as the mud and ice disappear under the rays of the burning sun. I came out as from a sepulchre, from an abyss of darkness; and I was living, perfectly living. [Lecture 10]

So I made one final struggle to call on God for mercy, with the same choking and strangling, determined to finish the sentence of prayer for Mercy, if I did strangle and die, and the last I remember that time was falling back on the ground with the same unseen hand on my throat. I don't know how long I lay there or what was going on. None of my folks were present. When I came to myself, there were a crowd around me praising God. The very heavens seemed to open and pour down rays of light and glory.

> Not for a moment only, but all day and night, floods of light and glory seemed to pour through my soul, and oh, how I was changed, and everything became new. [Lecture 10]

> I had attended a series of revival services for about two weeks off and on. Had been invited to the altar several times, all the time becoming more deeply impressed, when finally I decided I must do this, or I should be lost. Realization of conversion was very vivid, like a ton's weight being lifted from my heart; a strange light which seemed to light up the whole room (for it was dark); a conscious supreme bliss which caused me to repeat "Glory to God" for a long time. [Lecture 10]

Even the everyday absolution of the already converted has emotional impact for the "worldly" and Conservative Laestadian Christian alike. Here's the effusive testimony of Cardinal Newman in that well-known religion condemned by Luther and Laestadians:

> If there is a heavenly idea in the Catholic Church, looking at it simply as an idea–surely, next after the Blessed Sacrament, confession is such. . . . Oh, what a soothing charm is there which the world can neither give nor take away! Oh, what piercing heart-subduing tranquility, provoking tears of joy, is poured almost substantially and physically upon the soul–the oil of gladness, as Scripture calls it–when the penitent at length rises, his God reconciled to him, his sins rolled away forever! [from Capel 1884, 40]

4.2.6 Obedience and Humility

> *The highly authoritarian individual is submissive to authority, aggressive towards out-groups, and holds tight to conventional values and norms of behaviour. Psychometric measures of authoritarianism are found to be highly correlated with measures of religious fundamentalism.*
>
> —Peter Herriot, *Religious Fundamentalism*

From early on, there has been an emphasis on "childlike faith," a simple and submissive acceptance that one's own thoughts and ideas are to be subjugated to those of the group:

✝ "What then is the reason, why so many salvation seekers, do not accept the Kingdom of Heaven? The reason is, because he does not desire to lower himself to become a child, to forsake his own wisdom, and to become foolish before God and His Kingdom. He does not want to forsake his own righteousness, and become naked. And the gate is so narrow, that one cannot enter it as rich and great into the Kingdom of Heaven. Into this Kingdom one does not enter as great, and as a wise adviser, but as a small child, who is in need of aid and advice" (Leonard Typpö [1868-1922], from *Greetings of Peace*, 9/1956).

The scriptural basis for that is Jesus' statement that one must become as a little child (Mt 18:3). There's also support in Eph 5:1, "Be ye therefore followers of God, as dear children." But as Rachel Held Evans writes, "Those who say that having childlike faith means not asking questions haven't met too many children. Anyone who has kids or loves kids or has spent more than five minutes with kids knows that kids ask a lot of questions" (Evans 2010, 225). And, as with so many topics, the Bible contains contradictory passages: Heb 6:1, 1 Cor 13:11 and 14:20.

The submissive attitude is not just for the spiritual well-being of the individual, but for the unity of the flock:

✝ "Different mindedness scatters the flock, but unity strengthens. Godly love builds up. Therefore harmony and unity in this wearisome land is strength, namely, when by faith we are struggling in united love against evil" (Matti Suo, *Siionin Lähetyslehti* [1923], from Kulla 1993, 151-52).

✝ "God's grace-work has been great and wonderful in our behalf, but we have been disobedient children. We have rewarded the Heavenly Father's patience and mercy with our unthankfulness and disobedience. We cannot boastfully expand our chest above others. With reluctance we must admit contrary to our proud nature that, 'I am the greatest of the world's sinners'" (Havas [1938], 72).

✝ "Harmony and like-mindedness brings joy, over which the weak rejoice and become strengthened. Strife and dissension bring grievous temptations. When those who are weak in faith come to meetings to receive consolation, and the like-minded with psalms and hymns of praise teach and admonish one another, the weak are given to rise up from beneath temptations with new power and new resolutions, even with one mouth to praise the Father and the Lamb (Rom 15:6). When the weak one has been taken care of with the love of Christ, this does not make him dissentious, but unites him with the bond of love. In the knowledge of the love of Christ he sees his own preciousness and the preciousness of all other [of] God's children and he has a thankful mind for the care he has received" (Heikki Jussila, *Greetings of Peace*, 2/1950).

A defender of the New Awakening (**4.1.6**) said its "sacred heritage . . . is that the sacrifice of Jesus becomes a living reality" (from Kulla 2010, 132). It was important to have "a deeper awakening and a closer communion with the Redeemer and the walking in the light" (p. 129). Consider how much these two quotes from Conservatives–who reject the New Awakening as a legalistic heresy–put an emphasis on lowering oneself, even to the point of taking part in Jesus' humiliation:

† "Be of good cheer, you who do not yet see your own fruits of faith nor the merits of your life, but find yourself in the position of the unworthy servant. From just that position, you can still believe your sins forgiven in the name and holy blood of the Lord Jesus. And you whose merits have grown so great, so that you find yourself a laborer who has worked since morning and you have been wronged in the payment of wages, pray that a lean year might come and a longing for the children's kingdom to receive gold tried in fire. Pray that you might become rich and receive the white robes that your nakedness might not be seen. Come to get some eye-salve to anoint your blind eyes, that you might still see the beautiful dwelling place of God, which shall never be taken away" (Lauri Taskila, *Greetings of Peace*, 5/1963).

† "We must become partakers of [Jesus'] humiliation if we desire to get to heaven. For this way of heaven is the way of humiliation and the way of the cross. The Apostle says . . . 'Humble yourselves beneath the mighty hand of God, that He might exalt you.' There are slaves and prisoners of unbelief, who feel pain and distress in their soul because they are slaves of the Prince of this world. They feel that they should start out on that way of humility so that they would become participants of eternal life, but the enemy of the soul preaches on the other hand: How could

you, who are a person who is considered honorable, so lower yourself, so that you begin to confess before God and men, that I am altogether without honor and glory of God" (Lauri Hakso, *Greetings of Peace*, 5/1965).

Statements from the tumultuous 1970s emphasized the importance of obedience as much as self-abnegation:

> † "Certainly, we would not willfully be in contempt of the Spirit and love of the Christians, for again our humble prayer to God in all meekness is that His will be done and not our own. In no way would we want to hinder the work of God in His church or cause the Holy Spirit in us or in the hearts of other Christians to be grieved" (Alajoki [1970], 173-74).
>
> † "But if the trumpet has a foreign sound, that is of the flesh. Brothers and sisters, it's time for the congregation and its saints to take heed. And that is exactly what has happened, and let it continue in this way. We are told to hear what the spirit has to say unto the congregation. And that spirit does not lie. It's God speaking, that is his mouth. We can believe this" (Peter Nordstrom, sermon given 1972).
>
> † "We do not live like the world lives or participate in ungodly activities. If we strive to remain in faith and to keep a good conscience, we try to be obedient to the word of God. Even if we do not always understand the reason why something is preached as sin, we still strive to live in obedience. The word of God and the voice of the Holy Spirit in the congregation are above our consciences. God's word is correct even then when it testifies other than what our consciences tell us" (VOZ, 11/1974).

All that would sound familiar to someone asking questions among the Jehovah's Witnesses, where

> the questioner is all too often told that he or she is to accept whatever the Society teaches and is not to "reason" about it, but must blindly and dogmatically fully accept whatever is taught. The individual's reason, they stress, is "human reasoning," but the Watchtower's reasoning is "God's reasoning." If one does not blindly accept all that is taught–however foolish–often their spirituality is impugned, even for sincere and honest questions.

> One then learns that questions are not to be voiced. [Wilson 2002, 293]

Terrible things have been done throughout history when the individual's sense of right and wrong is subjugated to that of a group. And it is very difficult to resist in the face of a group claiming such imposing authority as God's Kingdom on this earth. During the "caretaking meetings" I witnessed in the early 80s, I often heard not a single voice dare to call out of the collective silence to proclaim forgiveness to individuals requesting it. If you took the initiative and did so (and I certainly never did), and the right people did not join you or lead the way, you might be the one sitting up there behind the examination table at the next meeting.

Some church members in a wrong soul-condition and under rebuke failed to

> † "discern that the Bridegroom of their soul, through His own disciples, has come to care for the fallen. The love of God constrains the believers to urge, that, make repentance dear brother or sister, of that error. The reproached have no thought even, that the power of the Lord is in those people. They just want to claim that such and such pointing out as being sin is the decision of only a certain few babbling old men. To anyone in that sort of condition there is a danger of becoming a blasphemer of the Holy Spirit. That is sin which is not forgiven in this or the coming life, since the grace of repentance does not come to one who has blasphemed the Spirit of Grace. The eyes are once and for all blinded from seeing that man without the Holy Spirit in the 'old portion' is altogether wretched and miserable, poor, blind and naked [Rev 3:17]. Such a man's lot is truly among the hypocrites. The door is closed. The Lord no longer knows him as His own" (VOZ, 6/1979).

Well, I will go on the record and call it "the decision of only a certain few babbling old men" to condemn as sin the reading of novels and the use of "instructional films in any form in elementary school teaching functions," as was done thirty years ago (**4.6.1**). And I will also call it arrogant to label your voice as that of the Holy Spirit to make yourself immune from criticism when you say such things.

A healthy dose of humility was expected of preachers in one sense, at least:

> † "[M]uch evil has resulted when believers–preachers or others–have become puffed up in themselves and have begun to seek carnally a state of preeminence in the Kingdom, in the congregation" (Peter Nevala, sermon given 1981).

Preachers and elders do not accumulate any of the outward trappings of privilege and power that so many leaders of religious movements seem to covet. But in the mind of some at least, it was

> † "very important for all of us to show obedience, respect and honor to the servants that God has chosen to serve in the administration of the house and church of God [1 Tim 3:15, Heb 13:17-18 cited]. If someone in the living church of God rises against the teachings, instruction and decisions of the Holy Spirit that God has spoken in the church through the mouths of His children, then that person has fallen into disobedience in his life of faith to the word and spirit of God" (Elmer Alajoki, presentation given 1995).

For the most part, the emphasis was and remains on obedience to the congregation rather than elders or preachers. For example, regarding the Internet, video, and video games,

> † "We want to journey in obedience to God's Word. If we have a different understanding of these issues than another family, we need to ask ourselves if we understand this matter as the Holy Spirit teaches in God's congregation. There are not two different understandings of matters in God's kingdom" (VOZ, 12/2005).

Everything is sacrificed on the altar of unity, as one friend put it. The individual conscience is entirely subjugated:

> † "Someone may think that some matter is not sin to him, since his own conscience does not consider it wrong. Where, then, can the love between believers be seen?" (VOZ, 3/2006)

> † "Through faith we understand to abandon individual understanding and reason when it does not agree with the Holy Spirit in God's kingdom. In God's kingdom we have one understanding and one spirit as it must be in the living congregation of God" (VOZ, 8/2007).

The mindset at work here, on the part of both leaders and follows, is *authoritarianism*. It is discussed in **4.6.1** as one of the motives behind Conservative Laestadianism's seemingly endless behavioral norms.

Calling it "a great pity," Karen Armstrong notes the irony that "religious institutions often insist on this type of conformity, which is far from the spirit of their founders, who all, in one way or another, rebelled against the status quo." Luther and Laestadius were certainly not exceptions. "Blind obedience and unthinking acceptance of authority figures may make an institution work more smoothly, but the people who live under such a regime will remain in an infantile, dependent state" (2007, 271). It's hard not to when we are told that doing otherwise is "falling into traps of the devil":

> † "Human reasoning can begin to prevail and accuse those who faithfully serve with their God-given gifts. One might begin to criticize those who have served in the role of caretaking, saying that the caretaking methods were not conducted correctly. We want to pray that we don't fall into these various traps of the devil and instead, place our gifts to be used where God desires to use them. God promises to care for those who travel as obedient grace beggars in His kingdom" (VOZ, 7/2008).

Now, just a few years after that statement was published, the SRK has apologized for the way those "God-given gifts" were used. It has finally acknowledged that the caretaking methods were *not* in fact conducted correctly (**4.10.2**). Neither the 1970s caretakers nor those who continue to advocate obedience and acceptance today has "perfect understanding," and in that respect the following quote is ironically correct:

> † "It is very important that we gather with the children of God at services and in our homes. We are a level-headed flock, where there is no person with perfect understanding. We all live by the merits of Jesus Christ, the Son of God, who atoned for our sins. We all need to hear, again and again, the reassuring words of the gospel" (VOZ, 5/2008).

When I was being grilled by the local board about the June 2010 edition of this book (**1.2**), one of the board members waved off my research into the conflicts between some of Luther's teachings and those of "God's Kingdom" by saying that Luther "was just a man." My reply: "Yes, and so are we, right here, right now, in this room." *None* of us has perfect understanding. Those who claim to speak on behalf of the Kingdom of God in all its supposed "unity" should keep that in mind.

I'm just a nobody who has relentlessly investigated the difficult questions that have troubled me. But it seems to me that God might take better care in giving understanding to those whom he has chosen as leaders of his church throughout history. The fact is that, *even at the highest levels of the church today*, there has been and continues to be division about some important issues.

The theological education of my fellow nobodies who sat across the table from me at that board meeting consists largely of a lifetime of church indoctrination and dogmatically blinkered, selective Bible reading. Armed with that and a reluctant perusal of a book they wanted to ban, they casually passed judgment on the single most prominent member of "God's Kingdom" in post-medieval history, the doctor of theology at Wittenberg whose writings encompass over a hundred volumes. Sorry, but it strikes me as laughable arrogance. I criticize Luther, too. But I don't claim to have the *true* doctrine that Luther sadly failed to comprehend in significant respects while somehow maintaining that he was still a chosen leader of the church out of the darkness of 16th century Catholicism.

One aspect of the "level-headed flock" attitude that I find positive is the way preachers are included along with everybody else. At least in the LLC, nobody stands above the congregation–not preachers, local board members, or even officers of the national organization. A longtime friendship with one preacher who is a member of the LLC board has made that abundantly clear to me. He approaches his duties with genuine humility and feels the need for grace as much as anybody else in the church. As the author of *First Clement* wrote around the turn of the second century, "Christ is of those who are humble-minded, and not of those who exalt themselves over His flock" (Ch. 16).

4.2.7 Servants of the Word

> *And I, brethren, when I came to you, came not with excellency of speech or of wisdom, declaring unto you the testimony of God. For I determined not to know any thing among you, save Jesus Christ, and him crucified. And I was with you in weakness, and in fear, and in much trembling. And my speech and my preaching was not with enticing words of man's wisdom, but in demonstration of the Spirit and of power: That your faith should not stand in the wisdom of men, but in the power of God.*
>
> —*The First Epistle to the Corinthians*

The sermons have long been delivered extemporaneously, with the prayer that God would offer his "service blessing" and provide words to the preacher:

> † "In interpreting the word, preachers and Christianity have usually sat behind a table. One has read the text and the other has spoken of that text, as the Lord has seen expedient to reveal at that time to the hearers as well as to the preacher himself. The main principle in proclaiming the word, is this, that every preacher speak the pure word of God; that is, solidly stay in the Bible. He who speaketh, let him speak the words of God! In this portion, the servants of the Congregation of Christ have always had humble timidity. They have not dared to open the mouth to preach without the Holy Scripture" (Havas [1933], 35).

I remember being somewhat awestruck in my youth at how the preachers could just go up to the pulpit and start talking without any notes. It was often touted as evidence that the Holy Spirit was working in them. (In the last decade or so, however, they have been encouraged to do some study and mental preparation beforehand.) The problem is that other preachers who supposedly lack the Holy Spirit do the same thing, with the same claim:

> In some mountain churches not only was education regarded with disdain, but also the practice of the preacher was not to prepare his sermons. Instead, he stepped up to the pulpit, opened the Bible, read aloud whatever passage his eyes landed on, and preached from that text, relying on the Holy Spirit to tell him what to say. [Teeple 2003, 352]

> [S]ermons aren't supposed to be "prepared" or eloquent. They are supposed to be spoken by the Spirit on the spot. At least that is what the older workers used to claim. [Lewis 2004, 259-60]

> No notes are allowed to be used. No sermons are written in advance. For three hours the [Swartzentruber Amish] minister preaches from memory and out of devotion. [Mackall 2007, 115]

The two OALC sermons I've observed certainly involved a lot of sighing about lack of words and reaching up for God's inspiration. An anonymous poster at the **extoots site** <http://extoots.blogspot.com/2005/01/i-have-dream_4662.html> was told by the OALC preachers each Sunday morning "that nothing had been prepared ahead of time so that 'the intellect' would not interfere with God's words."

There has long been an aversion–a healthy one, I think–to selecting those who have particular ambitions for the office:

> † "Always the goal in the work of the Lord is the glory of God, the salvation of the souls of men and building the Congregation of Christ. From all effectiveness of the word, the Lord alone receives praise. It is sickening to hear someone of us preachers, as if boasting, relate of large crowds of listeners who have come to his services; tens of converts whom he has blessed; and songs of praise which that in that minister has given of his sermons, etc." (Havas [1933], 36).

> † The usual custom is "that no congregation puts to preach such a one who especially desires this responsible office" (Havas [1939], 42).

> † It "is always most necessary, in the matter of feeding the sheep, that the shepherd has a feeling of his own sinfulness. 'Good' shepherds, those who themselves never feel that they have also stumbled neither in doctrine or life, but who boast of their good Christianity, such shepherds do not feed the sheep. They preach more of their own selves than of Jesus Christ. . . . But the poor shepherds, who together with the sheep weep over their own sinfulness, are themselves hungry and gladly lead the sheep, faulty and sinful, even those who are in need of special guidance, to the green pasture, where the good-speaking blood drops of Jesus feed the hungry soul with the forgiveness of all sins" (Arvi Hintsala, *Greetings of Peace*, 11/1949).

† "There is yet a certain danger of the sin of pride of which we should be reminded. It is the swelling of the heart by pride over spiritual gifts. God grant that He would protect the workers of Zion from this sin, for it can bring about much offense" (Reinikainen 1969, 50).

Jon Bloomquist, who has been entrusted with positions of considerable trust and prominence in the LLC for most of his life, put the matter into memorable words that I haven't forgotten in the more than ten years since hearing them: *God's Kingdom is not a forum for the fulfillment of personal ambition.* Luther would have agreed: "Ambition is the rankest poison to the church, when it possesses preachers. It is a consuming fire" (*Table Talk* §414).

Luther also diminished the role of clergy with the doctrine of the priesthood of all believers. "Since forgiveness rests on faith, not on the powers of the priest in his special office, it is not surprising to find Luther advocating that in times of need one Christian may absolve another of his sins" (Harran 1983, 168). As Ronald Rittgers says in his exhaustive book about the use of the keys at the time of the Reformation, "The priest no longer possessed divine authority by virtue of his office to remit sins. Authority resided in God's Word, not in a human being" (2004, 55). In Conservative Laestadianism, the priest has become a "servant of the word" or preacher, which follows Luther's thinking (Althaus 1963, 328) and reflects the emphasis on proclaiming the word to the faithful rather than interceding for them:

† "Every Christian, whether man or woman, who is a partaker of the Holy Spirit, is this kind of a royal priest who can proclaim the gospel, absolution from sin in Jesus' name and atonement blood [John 20:21-23]. . . . Although every Christian, in this sense, is a priest, yet God has especially called and installed specific persons to perform the preaching office in His congregation" (*Päivämies* No. 42, 1978).

The selection of preachers is done very carefully, since it is usually a lifetime position:

† The congregation's board discusses a potential new preacher when the brother "is not present. When the board unanimously discerns the matter to be so, that he can be recommended to the congregation, then the matter can be presented to the

congregation ... It has always been considered embarrassing and strange in the kingdom of God if some have much eagerness to be preaching. It is often so, that it is with difficult persuasion and much encouragement with God's Word, that the one who is weak in himself has been escorted to the place of speaking" (*Päivämies* No. 42, 1978).

† "We hope that there would always be a feeling of poorness and also the mind of a child so that one would only, as a weak servant, serve the Lord Jesus, that there would truly be this purpose, the feeding and tending of the Lord's Zion, the children of God" (Alajoki [1983], 134).

The desire for a sense of reluctance and humility on the part of the selected preacher is consistent with Luther's teaching that, "When the Christian is in a place where there are Christians, who have the same power and right as he, he should not thrust himself forward, but should rather let himself be called and drawn forth to preach and teach in the stead and by the commission of the rest" (*Right and Power of a Christian Congregation* [1523]; PE 4, 80-81). "God very wonderfully entrusts his highest office to preachers that are themselves poor sinners who, while teaching it, very weakly follow it" (*Table Talk* §73). I also find it a refreshing contrast with the naked ambition shown by so many Evangelical preachers of prominence today, and well in accord with Paul's own sentiment expressed in 1 Cor 2:1-2 and quoted in the epigraph to this section.

† "It is marvelous when in openness and unity of Spirit the matter of calling servants [preachers] is pondered in the congregation among its members and board of trustees with prayerful hearts that God's will would be done" (VOZ, 9/2009).

The selection entails a good deal of drama, and it is felt especially keenly among men who are whispered about as candidates. They are generally not overjoyed at the prospect of being thrust in front of the congregation as both "ensamples to the flock" (1 Pet 5:3) and mouthpieces for its doctrine. To struggle with doubts as just another member of the flock is one thing, but to do so as a preacher is another: "But now I've got to preach this stuff!" The time commitments add up, too, especially when they start getting sent on preaching trips. Their wives (all preachers are men), wind up sacrificing a great deal as well.

All in all, there is a lot of similarity to what Mackall saw happening with his unlikely Amish friend:

> Unlike non-Amish ministers, who choose their calling, most Amish men–at least the Amish men I know best–hope beyond hope they will not be called, that the lot will not fall on them. If it does, the minister is a minister for life. The job comes without pay but with many responsibilities, serious ones. All the preparation that goes into the position is done on top of farming and family. The last thing Samuel wanted was to become minister, but he was chosen, so he has to serve. [2007, 115]

The preacher's role in the service is by far the most prominent one, but there are other aspects of Conservative Laestadian worship that should also be mentioned. The basic format, instituted by John Takkinen at the turn of the 20th century, is as follows. There is congregational singing, an opening prayer, reading of the text, and the preacher's extemporaneous sermon based on the text. The service closes with another prayer and more congregational singing. The words of the songs are viewed as instructional and edifying in themselves, which I find ironic since about half of them were written by "unbelieving" outsiders.[14] The group singing is also part of what Winell calls a "ritualized group process" of church services:

> Music, prayers, and a mesmerizing preaching style can create a state of relaxation and suggestibility. When a congregation proceeds to sing and pray aloud together with enthusiasm and speaking in tongues, an individual can easily conform. The aroused emotions and the group consensus about reality are convincing enough to inspire a response to get saved, "rededicated," or "filled with the Spirit." [1993, 72]

There is indeed something warm and comforting about sitting in the pews with your voice joining the singing of your "brothers and sisters in faith." You see the familiar faces, old friends whose children are

---

14. For any fellow detail-obsessed math lovers reading this, I base the "about half of them" statement on a sample of 20 random selections from the 604 songs found in the LLC's *Hymns and Songs of Zion*, 2008 edition. Eleven of those were written by people who were not associated with Laestadianism at all. The 95% confidence interval for the proportion of songs written by "unbelievers" is 33-77%.

sometimes sitting intermingled with yours, in a safe and trusted environment that you have known since you were one of those children yourself. You see your spouse sitting there beside you, singing away and–to all appearances–fully part of the unquestioning throng. It all makes you desperately want to just believe and accept whatever is about to be said.

4.3 The Bible

> *For those who believe that they already know what the Bible teaches and consequently do not need to wrestle with its interpretation, their job is a relatively simple one, however uninformed.*
>
> —Lee Martin McDonald et al.,
> Early Christianity and its Sacred Literature

4.3.1 Creation and the Fall of Man

> *It is not an easy thing for a soul, under the influence of error, to be persuaded of the contrary opinion.*
>
> —Irenaeus, Fragments

The realization that evolution might possibly have some truth to it was the most disturbing event in my life of faith. It took me quite a while to really understand the scientific issues, and to accept their profound implications both theologically and for my own place in the universe as a conscious, self-aware organism. What I saw right away, however, was that an *unguided, natural* process of evolution threatened to remove the strongest intellectual prop that had been shoring up my weak faith. It provided a simple, elegant, and tangible answer to the question for which the *guided, supernatural* process of creation was previously my only answer: "How could all of these amazing forms of life, myself included, have just happened to arise?"

There is a mental roadblock that seems to stand in the way of many thoughtful, educated people accepting that, as Darwin famously put it, "from so simple a beginning endless forms most beautiful and most wonderful have been, and are being, evolved" (1859, 428). How could such complexity *just happen to* arise from a single first fragment of life, not yet even a complete cell? But my electrical engineering work in signal processing allowed me to quickly bypass that roadblock. I understood that filtering out random noise is the key to selecting weak bits of intelligence from noisy communication channels. It didn't take me long to appreciate how evolution uses its own type of filtering to select those few useful and beneficial mutations that occasionally appear in the midst of the noise of random genetic mutation. Eventually, the complexity and *apparent* design of cells, organs, organisms, and ecosystems emerges much like the faint tones of Morse code signals became perceptible–with appropriate audio filtering–amidst the static of my ham radio receivers decades ago.

And those mutations are very few indeed. We each carry about 50 mutations in the approximately 3 billion base pairs of our DNA–complete novelties not found in the DNA of either parent (Wells 2006, 16). They are infrequent random accidents in an otherwise amazingly accurate DNA replication process.

Yet the variations resulting from genetic mutations are the raw material of evolution. It is an unguided process that results in the "preservation of favourable variations and the rejection of injurious variations," a phenomenon that Darwin called natural selection (1859, 81). The randomness of the mutations is the noise, and natural selection is the filter. Every "slight modification" that the mutations cause, "which in the course of ages chanced to arise, and which in any way favoured the individuals of any of the species, by better adapting them to their altered conditions, would tend to be preserved; and natural selection would thus have free scope for the work of improvement" (p. 81). Natural selection "is just differential reproduction. Some organisms because of their features do better at reproduction than others. That is all there is to it. Nothing more" (Ruse 2010, 164).

Putting a micromanaging creator God out of business is only one of the theological problems posed by evolution. I don't think anyone is better at summarizing those problems than John F. Haught, though I find his proposed theological solutions utterly unconvincing. In the introduction to his book *Making Sense of Evolution*, he invites the reader to just ponder, for a moment, "Darwin's claim that all life on earth has descended from a single common ancestor that lived ages ago, an idea not original with him but one that is fundamental to his science." He then summarizes most of the major issues raised by that idea, so succinctly that I have taken the liberty of inserting a numeric label before his mention of each one:

> What does [Darwin's] idea of common ancestry mean for **(1)** our understanding of life, **(2)** of who we are, and of what our relationship with the rest of nature should be? Or consider Darwin's idea of "natural selection," the impersonal winnowing mechanism responsible for the emergence of new species over an unimaginably immense span of time. **(3)** If all the diverse species arose gradually by way of a blind natural process, in what sense can God still be called the author of life, if at all? And **(4)** if our own species is a product of natural selection, can Christian theologians still responsibly pass on the news that we are created in the "image" and "likeness" of God (Gen. 1:26)? Since human beings apparently evolved as one species among others, what does this imply for our ideas about the **(5)** soul, **(6)** original sin, and **(7)** salvation? And **(8)** what does "Christ" mean if Jesus also is a product of evolution? [Haught 2010, xii]

In addition, there is what the SRK preacher and writer Erkki Reinikainen called "a profound contradiction [that] exists between the biblical account of creation and the generally accepted theory of evolution in the natural sciences" (1986, 17). As we will see below, the conflict is real and disturbing, enough so to send me on a research quest that would occupy hundreds of hours and a shelf full of books on the subject.[15] My study began with a hope that I might confirm the truth of the biblical creation account, or at least the possibility for it to be true. But it was not to be.

---

15. Here are some of those books, listed roughly in the order I would recommend them to those interested in pursuing the subject for themselves: *Why Evolution is True* by Jerry Coyne; *The Selfish Gene* and *The Greatest Show on Earth* by Richard Dawkins; *Finding Darwin's God* by Kenneth Miller; *The Language of God* by Francis Collins; *Evolution: What the Fossils Say and Why it Matters* by Donald Prothero; *On the Origin of Species* by Charles Darwin; *Evolution: The Triumph of an Idea* by Carl Zimmer; *Before the Dawn: Recovering the Lost History of Our Ancestors* by Nicholas Wade; *The Origin of Humankind* by Richard Leakey; *Human Natures: Genes, Cultures, and the Human Prospect* by Paul Ehrlich; *Mapping Human History* by Steve Olson; *Endless Forms Most Beautiful* by Sean Carroll; *The Third Chimpanzee* by Jared Diamond; *The Mating Mind* by Geoffrey Miller; *Quantum Evolution* by Johnjoe McFadden.

I've had some stressful and heated discussions about evolution with people whose opinions are far stronger than their knowledge. I am all too aware of how unlikely it is for my few words of explanation here to change the minds of those who reject it because "they have been solemnly told that the theory of evolution is false (or at least unproven) by people they trust more than they trust scientists" (Dennett 2006, 60). So I will now conclude this brief introduction with the words of Kenneth R. Miller, who is both a Christian (Roman Catholic) and professor of biology. What saddens him about the creationists who stubbornly refuse to acknowledge the evidence he spends page after page presenting in *Finding Darwin's God*

> is the view of the Creator that their intellectual contortions force them to hold. In order to defend God against the challenge they see from evolution, they have had to make Him into a schemer, a trickster, even a charlatan. Their version of God is one who intentionally plants misleading clues beneath our feet and in the heavens themselves. Their version of God is one who has filled the universe with so much bogus evidence that the tools of science can give us nothing more than a phony version of reality. In other words, their God has negated science by rigging the universe with fiction and deception. To embrace that God, we must reject science and worship deception itself. [2007, 80]

Worshiping or even defending deception is something I must decline to do.

Adam and Eve

A specific aspect of creationism is the belief that there were two actual people, Adam and Eve, who were formed either after vegetation (Gen. 1) or before (Gen. 2), wandered around some of it in the Middle East thousands of years ago, listened to some unfortunate (though ultimately accurate) advice from a talking snake, and ate a forbidden piece of fruit. Consequently, they noticed their nakedness and became the originators not just of the "R" movie rating, but the entire human race.

They also became the source of all our problems, at least according to Apostle Paul in Romans 5:12-19:

> Wherefore, as by one man sin entered into the world, and death by sin; and so death passed upon all men, for that all have sinned:

(For until the law sin was in the world: but sin is not imputed when there is no law. Nevertheless death reigned from Adam to Moses, even over them that had not sinned after the similitude of Adam's transgression, who is the figure of him that was to come. But not as the offence, so also is the free gift. For if through the offence of one many be dead, much more the grace of God, and the gift by grace, which is by one man, Jesus Christ, hath abounded unto many.... For if by one man's offence death reigned by one; much more they which receive abundance of grace and of the gift of righteousness shall reign in life by one, Jesus Christ.) Therefore as by the offence of one judgment came upon all men to condemnation; even so by the righteousness of one the free gift came upon all men unto justification of life. For as by one man's disobedience many were made sinners, so by the obedience of one shall many be made righteous.

He makes the same basic point in 1 Corinthians 15:21: "For since by man came death, by man came also the resurrection of the dead. For as in Adam all die, even so in Christ shall all be made alive."

It's hard to avoid the conclusion that the very purpose of Pauline Christianity is to solve a supposed problem that is rooted in myth rather than fact. The dilemma this presents is eloquently addressed on the website <http://biologos.org/blog/pauls-adam-part-i> of the BioLogos foundation, which advocates a form of theistic evolution:

> A strictly literal reading of the Adam story does not fit with what we know of the past. Some choose to ignore the data altogether. Others marginalize or interpret the data idiosyncratically to salvage some type of literal/historical reading. But, by and large, everyone—even including this latter group—has to do some creative thinking about how to handle the Adam story. A "just read it literally" mentality is not an available option. "What do I do with the Adam story?" is a real and pressing question for most people of faith.
>
> In my experience, a lot of Christians—I might even guess most—have come to some peace with all of this. They may handle it in different ways, and some may not have arrived at a conclusion, but they at least recognize that something has to be done. They sense that a simple literal reading of the Adam story won't work

without creating a lot of cognitive dissonance, and so they are open to ideas.

But, sooner or later, another issue comes up that is hard to get around and for some simply ends the discussion entirely.

Paul.

One commentator on that page asked, "[I]f Paul is mistaken about sin's origin, does that lessen the reality of sin or our need for a Savior?" Another commentator replied, with evident anguish, "Frankly, if Paul couldn't get the origin of sin right, it would tend to make me wonder why I should trust that he got the 'solution' any more right. If I am to base my understanding of God, sin, salvation, heaven and hell on the writing of a guy who lived 2000 years ago I would like to know he's reliable. How am I to trust Paul now?"

I don't think it's overstating the case to say that this is a foundational point of Christian theology. That's what an LLC preacher told me–with concern about my spiritual condition–after reviewing the portions of my June 2010 edition that dealt with evolution. I certainly don't fault him for saying what is clearly the state of the church's theology, well summarized by this quote from Uljas's 2000 book *A Treasure Hidden in a Field*:

> † "God created man in His own image. He made man to be an eternal being and responsible for his deeds. The man created by God was righteous, so that in that aspect, too, he was the image of God. These characteristics separate man from the rest of creation. Only man can be righteous or lack righteousness, the remainder of creation does not have this gift. When God looked at His creation, He saw that it was very good (Gen 1:31). Thus, man also was good. But man fell into sin when he was not obedient to, but rather transgressed the will of his Creator. As a result of the Fall, man was separated from God and lost his righteousness. The trusting relationship of the child to the Father disappeared, and in its place, came fear and a need to flee from God. We all bear this poor heritage of the Fall of the first people, which is called inherited sin." [pp. 27-28]

The theological significance wasn't lost on Luther, either: "[T]he Son of God had to become a sacrifice to achieve these things for us, to take away sin, to swallow up death, and to restore the lost obedience. These treasures we possess in Christ, but in hope. In this way Adam, Eve, and all who believe until the Last Day live and conquer by that hope" (*Lectures on Genesis*, Ch. 3, §15). It's a legitimate concern to note, as does the president of the Southern Baptist Theological Seminary, that the "denial of an historical Adam and Eve as the first parents of all humanity and the solitary first human pair severs the link between Adam and Christ which is so crucial to the Gospel," and to ask, "How are we to understand the Bible's story, if we can have no confidence that we know how it even begins?" (Mohler 2011).

But *theological imperative does not equal truth*. It couldn't do so even when the Church had the rack and the stake at its disposal. The facts just sit there, mute, uncaring about how vehemently people deny their existence. Genetic evidence now makes clear that there have never been fewer than about a thousand members of *Homo sapiens* throughout the more than 100,000 years of its existence (**Coyne 2011** <http://whyevolutionistrue.wordpress.com/2011/09/18/how-big-was-the-human-population-bottleneck-not-anything-close-to-2/>), which began in Africa, not Mesopotamia. Actually, that was well understood before scientists started looking into DNA: The "paleontological record thoroughly establishes that one population is always preceded by another, making the idea of a single pair of humans procreating an entire species unthinkable" (Ronald Youngblood, quoted in Loftus 2008, loc. 4838-39). Even the Bible indicates that there was more than just Adam and Eve and their two kids: Cain takes a wife, worries about being killed by passers-by, and goes off to build a city.

The only alternative to accepting the overwhelming evidence of man's non-Adamic, evolutionary origins is to say that the evidence is false and was planted by God in fossils, vestigial body parts, patterns of speciation, ongoing and directly observed evolutionary changes, and a newly discovered treasure trove of information in our own DNA that matches up remarkably with all the observations that had been made beforehand. There is absolutely *nothing* contradicting that evidence except some ancient Hebrew writings (which themselves contradict each other) and the mountain of theology that has piled up on top of those writings over the centuries.

The remainder of my sample of quotes I now present in the usual chronological order, beginning with two early ones:

† "When man fell into sin, the Heavenly Parent received a deep wound in His heart. As earthly parents, when a child wounds himself with a knife, take away the sharp tool and throw it into the fire, so also God took this sharp knife of sin with which His youngest child pierced himself to death and threw it into hell fire and began to heal those poisonous wounds with the oil of grace when He, Himself, had to suffer the agony and pain of hell because of this unfortunate child" (Laestadius, Mary's Day sermon [1848]; *Fourth Postilla*, 189).

† Jesus "has given his life, in fact forfeited everything through love for the fallen sons and daughters of Adam and Eve, to open the gates of Paradise, which were closed through disobedience and sin" (O.H. Jussila, *Siionin Lähetyslehti*, 9/1919, from *Greetings of Peace*, 8/1949).

As we will see from the rest of the quotes, Conservative Laestadianism has firmly maintained that theological emphasis, and does so with an utterly credulous, unwavering acceptance of Adam and Eve as historical figures. It has been over *one hundred and twenty years* since Ingersoll asked the largest audience ever assembled at the Tabor Grand Opera House in Denver, "Is there an intelligent man or woman now in the world who believes in the Garden of Eden story? If there is, strike here," he said, tapping his forehead, "and you will hear an echo. Something is for rent" (*Lecture on Orthodoxy*, 1884). Yet, despite all of the astounding scientific progress that has been disproving the story ever since, Conservative preachers are churning out references to Adam and Eve seemingly more than ever:

† "After God had created the earth and everything in it, He finally created man and a suitable 'help-mate' for him. He gave them Paradise as their dwelling place. The life of the first human pair was happy. They passed amidst beautiful trees and ate of their good fruit" (*By Faith*, 21).

† "God knew that man, whom He created in His own image and nature, would fall into sin and come under the dominion of the prince of darkness. God drew up, together with His Son in eternity, a plan of salvation for man" (Lepistö 1985, 119).

† "In the Fall into sin, man lost his connection with God. He had gone astray, although he probably didn't notice it right away.

God, however, noticed and went out to seek His children who had strayed. This shows the deepest essence of God, love. He could have turned His back forever on the disobedient ones and left them under the power of death. They, themselves, had chosen their portion. But God did not act in this fashion, but went to seek them" (Uljas 2000, 12).

✝ "As a result of the Fall, man was separated from God and lost his righteousness. The trusting relationship of the child to the Father disappeared, and in its place, came fear and a need to flee from God. We all bear this poor heritage of the Fall of the first people, which is called inherited sin. Man became incapable of doing that which is right before God" (Uljas 2000, 28).

✝ "In an attempt to be acceptable before God, Adam and Eve clothed themselves to cover their nakedness. This work, which arose from the unbelieving mind, was an attempt to be acceptable before the Heavenly Father. The initial disobedience to God in the attempt to hide their sin kindled the Heavenly Father's wrath. God punished the first human pair by inflicting trials upon them and their offspring. However, God's anger was directed towards the works of the flesh which are filthy rags before Him. Nevertheless, in His great love and compassion He clothed Adam and Eve with the garment of righteousness" (VOZ, 9/1998).

✝ "The original inherited desire to sin still remains in the flesh of all people, descendents of Adam and Eve. All humans experience the same types of temptations in various degrees and forms. The Devil has gained much experience and practice since the garden of Eden" (VOZ, 10/2000).

✝ "Jesus watched His Father blow the spirit of life into Adam's nostril on the morning of creation; He created man in His own image" (VOZ, 6/2001).

✝ "In the beginning God created the heavens and earth. He formed a man from the dust of the ground and breathed into him the breath of life, and man became a living soul. And so it was that God created man in His own image. God put him into the garden of Eden to keep it. Further, he took a rib from the man and made a woman to be a helpmate for him. He created man and woman to be male and female. He blessed them and told them to be fruitful and multiply and to replenish the earth and to subdue it and have dominion over it. Their purpose was to live in the garden and to dress it and keep it. In all this, God saw everything He had made and it was good. However, a fall came into the lives of this first human pair. They were tempted into sin by the serpent in the garden of Eden. They were not able to withstand the enemy of souls' temptations, but fell with the first onslaught of the serpent. With the fall into sin, the Scriptures reveal that corruption fell upon all mankind" (VOZ, 4/2004).

† "The Creator especially blessed mankind, having breathed the breath of life into Adam's nostrils so that he became a living soul. God provided all life's necessities for man in the Garden of Eden, and put man there to dress it and keep it. Through deceit by the enemy of souls, however, Adam and Eve fell into sin, and the shadow of fear and death descended on mankind" (VOZ, 12/2008).

† God's work of creation, including man, was good, but God's good work was "corrupted in the Fall. It corrupted God's image in man. As a consequence Man's will and nature are now inclined to evil. . . . Man is not tempted to do evil because of his genetic composition, but because of his sin-corrupted will and nature" (VOZ, 7/2009).

† "There in the Garden of Eden after the first human pair fell into sin, God spoke to the serpent: 'And I will put enmity between thee and the woman, and between thy seed and her seed: it shall bruise thy head, and thou shalt bruise his heel' [Gen 3:15]. God in His great love did not leave Adam and Eve and all people to die in their sins, but promised a Savior who would be the sacrificial Lamb of God, who would take away the sins of the world. The Old Testament believers journeyed in faith, believing on this promise" (VOZ, 12/2009).

It is all taken quite literally, with none of the allegorizing and theological hand-waving to which "worldly" theologians are increasingly retreating as they slowly come to accept the realities of science. The discussions are nearly as matter-of-fact and unquestioning about the Eden story as Luther was 500 years ago. "On the sixth day [Adam] was created; Eve likewise was created toward evening or near the end of the sixth day, while Adam was sleeping," he blandly reports to us in his *Lectures on Genesis* (Ch. 2, §3). The events in Paradise "are all historical facts. This is something to which I carefully call attention, lest the unwary reader be led astray by the authority of the fathers." Apparently, those church fathers were doing the same thing as the worldly theologians are now, as they "give up the idea that this is history and look for allegories" (§9). Luther at least acknowledges, "To our reason it appears very ludicrous for one fruit to be so injurious that the entire human race, in an almost infinite series, perished and died an eternal death." But "the true cause of the evil" was "that Adam sins against God, disregards His order, and obeys Satan" (§9). Regarding Eve's creation from Adam's rib, Luther also admits that,

> so far as this account is concerned, what, I ask you, could sound more like a fairy tale if you were to follow your reason? Would anyone believe this account about the creation of Eve if it were not so clearly told? This is a reversal of the pattern of the entire creation. Whatever is born alive, is born of the male and the female in such a manner that it is brought forth into the world by the female. Here the woman herself is created from the man by a creation no less wonderful than that of Adam, who was made out of a clod of earth into a living soul. This is extravagant fiction and the silliest kind of nonsense if you set aside the authority of Scripture and follow the judgment of reason. [§21]

Overwhelming scientific evidence that Luther could not have possibly imagined has shown the story to be "extravagant fiction" indeed.

Conflicts with Science

Despite Luther's warning about the danger of following "the judgment of reason" and all the claims about faith being contrary to reason that we will encounter in 4.5.4, nobody really likes to profess belief in things they feel, deep down, are indefensible. In a technological age, we rely on the benefits and insights of science, including evolutionary biology. I suspect that many Conservatives have at least some nagging awareness of the contradiction between all that science and the Adam and Eve story. It makes for an uncomfortable situation, because "to hold two ideas that contradict each other is to flirt with absurdity and, as Albert Camus observed, we humans are creatures who spend our lives trying to convince ourselves that our existence is not absurd" (Tavris and Aronson 2008, 13-14).

So perhaps it's not surprising to see some defensiveness accompanying the literalism. My sample of quotes making that sort of response begins with a sermon given by Gust Wisuri in the 1950s:

> † "The schoolbooks in this day and age teach a theory that man came from an animal. But that is the theory of those people who have never feared God and never have accepted the word of God as the only truth on this Earth." God "created man after his own image and breathed his spirit into the man, and gave him a companion after none of the other creatures on Earth were suitable companions for man.... After God had all the animals that had been created passed in review before Adam, the first created man on this Earth, and Adam had named them according to what came to his mind at that time–a descriptive word–it was found that none of them were suitable companions for man. Therefore, a woman was created, as God says that it was not well for man to live alone."

Writing in 1961, Lauri Taskila shows why theologians should resist the urge to argue science with the scientists:

> † "In this present world not all men believe that they have been created and made by God, but that they are descendents of an ape, or have evolved from some lizard. They believe that man has during the time of billions of years developed into what he is now; but the wise ones of the world are seeking for that missing link which is still lost. What is the reason for advanced and educated man to put his ancestry so low, when men generally wish to be of some noble family and are proud of it that they know that they are of one? The reason may be that man would want to be freed from the sense of responsibility, which he has in life as a man created in the image of God, as a crown and lord of all creation. However, the true fact is that man was created from the very beginning as man, for if man had developed from an ape, why does he not even yet develop from apes? Why doesn't man yet come from apes, so that there would be half finished and almost finished ape-men? What could have stopped the wheel of evolution now?" (p. 38).

Those arguments are silly grade school stuff, and were easily dismissed even when they were written almost fifty years ago. Now we have many transitional fossils and have witnessed real-time cases of evolution in action; that's why penicillin doesn't work for most infections anymore.

In a 1973 sermon, Peter Nordstrom did not even attempt to deal with any specifics, sticking with six day creationism and a "childlike faith" acceptance of things:

> † "We are told from God's word, that when our Heavenly father created all things, we are told that it took him six days. Not five, not ten, but it took six days. I've often heard, and especially from my confirmation children, they've often asked me, well why couldn't God, if he was almighty, why couldn't he have created all things in one day? And I said, yes, I'm sure he could have. But it says that it took him six days. That's what he tells us from his word. And in childlike faith we're going to believe that and accept that. But our mind, our sin-corrupt mind that is of the flesh, wants to tamper with God's word and wants to change it and wants us to say this and say that which is of us."

But preachers could not resist trying to make it all seem sensible:

> † "Once in the 'beginning' came that time when God with His word through His Son created the visible heaven, that is, the wide reaches of space and the Earth. In all this God paid close attention to detail. The stars, Earth and Sun stay in precise orbit and in the correct time unto this day. God is a God of order. Before this wonderful system, even modern astronomers consider the denial of God utter foolishness" (*Päivämies*, 1974).

The quoted writer makes quite a claim about the theistic conclusions of "modern astronomers." Members of the National Academy of Scientists were surveyed about their religious beliefs in 1998, and of the physicists and astronomers in the survey, just 7.5% expressed a personal belief in God. The overall result among all the scientists surveyed was a 7.0% personal belief. Already in 1933 just 15% of scientists in a comparable survey had expressed belief in God (*Nature* 1998, 313). That might all have come as a surprise to the writer of the quote, whose comment about the orderliness of the orbits of celestial bodies goes back to the pious "natural theology" of Isaac Newton's day.

By the late 1970s, the devil of Darwin was being addressed specifically:

† "Our children are being taught Darwin's theory of evolution as fact! We do not object if our children are taught that a man named Darwin once lived; that he expounded a *theory*, and only a theory, which claimed that all life evolved spontaneously from nothing. But they should also be told that the so-called scientific community itself *has never accepted* Darwin's theory entirely. They should be told the truth!" (VOZ, 1/1977).

The quoted writer calls for truth, but the truth is that the "so-called" scientific community had largely accepted Darwin's theory by the end of his life in the 1800s; he was buried in Westminster Abbey alongside Newton as a national hero. The myth that there is some undercurrent of scientific objection to evolution is a persistent one, which Alan Almquist and John Cronin addressed twenty years ago. Regarding the "notion that agreement among scientists about the factual support for evolution is wavering," they write:

> Nothing could be farther from the truth. In Endler's [1986] *Natural Selection in the Wild* we find a clear demonstration that evolution and natural selection are alive and thriving in the scientific community [Cooke 1986]. In fact, the vast majority of scientists generally favor evolution over other explanations for life. The recent signing by 72 Nobel laureates of a brief urging the U.S. Supreme Court to declare unconstitutional a Louisiana law requiring the so-called balanced treatment of evolution and its primary opponent, creationism, in state schools (see Palca 1986, Norman 1986) is the clearest statement by scientists in support of evolution yet produced. That this was the largest group of Nobel laureates ever to sign a single document (Norman 1986) clearly indicates that if there is still confusion in the public mind concerning the validity of evolution the scientific community does not share it. [Almquist and Cronin 1988, 520]

I was initially sympathetic to objections about evolutionary "theory" (a scientific term for a testable explanation of observed phenomena, like the equally well-established "theories" of gravitation and relativity) and studied many of them in hopes that they would allow me to retain a creationist worldview. But it soon became apparent that, without exception, those objections were motivated by religion rather than science and fact. Here is an example:

† In Darwin's theory of evolution, "it is taught that man evolved from apes. This is contrary to the Word of God. Genesis 2:7 states, 'And the Lord God formed man of the dust of the ground, and breathed into his nostrils the breath of life; and man became a living soul.' No other creature was created with a living soul. This clearly makes man different from all other of God's creations. It is not possible, then, that man evolved as Darwin states. However, if this theory is presented to the young Christian child, it can cause heavy doubts to weigh in the mind and heart [of] the child. This should not be allowed to pass by uncorrected" (VOZ, 6/1977).

In Erkki Reinikainen's 1986 book *Näin on Kirjoitettu*, the SRK propounded day-age creationism and condemned theistic evolution. The book acknowledges research in the natural sciences to the extent that it shows "that the origin of the earth, just as the origin of the total universe, dates back billions of years." The biblical "account of creation states that the formation of the Earth and the origin of all forms of life happened in six days, although all the evidence found in nature shows the timeframe of the origin of creation to be very long." But the creation account does not have the Sun, along with day and night, being created until the fourth day, so one is entitled "without arbitrarily interpreting the Bible . . . to the conclusion that the days of creation were eras, God's days, in His creation work" (p. 14).

Reinikainen was one of a long line of creationists retreating from young-earth literalism to the "day-age" idea. Already at the time of Robert G. Ingersoll's 1884 interview with *The Detroit News*, "they had been saying "that 'days' did not mean days. Of these 'six days' they make a kind of telescope, which you can push in or draw out at pleasure. If the geologists find that more time was necessary they will stretch them out. Should it turn out that the world is not quite as old as some think, they will push them up. The 'six days' can now be made to suit any period of time," which didn't impress Ingersoll in the least.

That was certainly not the case with Luther. Right in the beginning of his *Lectures on Genesis*, he confidently stated, "We know from Moses that the world was not in existence before 6,000 years ago." He asserted "that Moses spoke in the literal sense, not allegorically or figuratively, i.e., that the world, with all its creatures, was created within six days, as the words read. If we do not comprehend the reason for this, let us remain pupils and leave the job of teacher to the Holy Spirit."

But the 6,000 year figure was erroneous, Reinikainen asserts with equal confidence, being based on "written genealogies, which are clearly incomplete" (1986, 16). Instead, "[w]e see, as a natural phenomenon, that people have been children of their time, interpreting these things in the Bible from their own presumptions, without contradiction. At this time we know more about natural science and history, as well as other things" (p. 17). Now, in our newfound enlightenment, we can see that "the listing of ancestors from Adam to Abraham [in Genesis 5 and 11] is not complete, but many generations in between are missing." Otherwise, "no more than about 100 generations would have lived on the earth up to this time."

Rather than admit any biblical error, he concludes that it "has clearly been quite common for biblical authors to shorten the genealogies, leaving out those generations which they thought were not important [Mt 1:8 vs. 1 Ch. 6:7-9 cited]" (p. 16). Based on Deut 7:9, Reinikainen proposes an alternate calculation, in which "the Bible verifies that from Adam until the second coming of Christ there are about 1,000 generations." Thus, able to acknowledge "about 10 times more than the amount verified earlier" of human existence, a "Christian believes that the Bible speaks the truth" (p. 16).

Unfortunately, we are still left wondering how Adam's descendants, i.e., tool-making, anatomically modern *Homo sapiens*, could have been leaving their bones and artifacts strewn across the Mideast, Southern Europe and Asia, and Australia by 40,000 B.C., after having already occupied parts of Africa for over 100,000 years. Then there are those inconvenient *Homo erectus* fossils in Africa and parts of Asia dating back hundreds of thousands of years, which are accompanied by evidence of "human" activities; their own stone tools, fire usage, and even seafaring (130,000 year-old stone tools have been found on the island of Crete). And, going millions of years further back, there are *Homo habilis* and the Australopithicenes. All of those extinct predecessors look a lot like *Homo sapiens* but have features that gradually evolve toward our own as time moves forward: receding brow ridges, increasing brain capacity, improving bipedalism, emerging vocalism.

According to Reinikainen, though, none of those earlier hominids could have been ancestors. Despite his willingness to "draw out the telescope" of the biblical six days in view of overwhelming evidence, he reaches his limit when it comes to scientific research showing the evolutionary origins of life. No such accommodation is given there:

> † [A] profound contradiction exists between the biblical account of creation and the generally accepted theory of evolution in the natural sciences. An attempt to remove this contradiction has been made in this way that the biblical account of creation is interpreted to mean that God's creation work occurred through evolution, the conclusion being "the birth" of man. Such an interpretation is *an outrage to the word of God*, for God created all living things, each according to its own kind. . . . The opposing line of thought to the theory of evolution is certainly not fundamentalism, or the literal interpretation of the Bible, but the interpretation of the Bible according to the spirit and doctrine of the word of God. [p. 17, emphasis added]

The book goes on for several pages with practical objections to evolutionary theory and concludes that a "Christian can examine the achievements of science, securely accepting that which is true, and rejecting that which does not verify the truth," seeing through faith "that positive scientific results are not contradictory to the proclamations of the Bible" (p. 21).

All of Reinikainen's practical objections, which include and do not go much beyond the "why aren't we still evolving" tripe, have been long refuted in the scientific literature. Like Haught, "I confess to a certain impatience with such groundless objections to Darwin's carefully constructed theory" (2010, xiii). Haught is frank with his fellow theists, saying that

> dismissing evolution offhand after two centuries of reliable research by sciences ranging from geology to genetics smacks of ignorance and arrogance unbecoming to people of faith. I am not a scientist, but I am fully aware that knowledgeable people now almost universally accept Darwin's version of evolution as updated by the discovery of the units of heredity known as genes. Like all scientific ideas, the theory is open to improvement or even falsification if the evidence leads in that direction, but so far it has withstood every test. [pp. xiii-xiv]

Whether it is "an outrage to the word of God" or not, I now accept that I am the product of evolution by (apparently) random mutation and natural selection. Like it or not, we are descendants not of any first human pair but of now-extinct hominids originating in Africa, who themselves have common ancestry with other apes, most closely the chimpanzee.

However, Reinikainen is not wrong in asserting a conflict between the Bible and evolutionary theory. As we've seen, the theological imperative to deny evolution is strong for a number of reasons. I completely understand why the SRK still felt compelled to say in September 2006,

> † "In Laestadian teaching we hold fast to the truth of traditional creation doctrine, that God has created man in his image and we are not descended from other species" (Aimo Hautamäki, SRK Secretary-General).

But the cold, unyielding scientific fact is that "traditional creation doctrine" is not the truth at all, and holding fast to it means going down with a sinking ship. It is a slow but inexorable demise, and those still on deck assuring each other that the Titanic is unsinkable are going to find themselves needing to change their story sooner or later. "About a century and a half ago Charles Darwin surprised the world with his remarkable new theory of evolution. Theology has yet to come to grips with it" (Haught 2000, 1). As discussed in the sub-section below, there are indications that the SRK is finally starting to do so, at long last.

Evolutionary theory has no unexplainable "gaps" or "holes" other than man's own "sense of hesitancy and even dread" at being merely biological and evolved by Darwinian natural selection, and at the thought that "genetic chance and environmental necessity, not God, made the species" (from Ruse 2010, 107).[16] Of course, that's not what

---

16. Though Ruse is an agnostic, he is quite sympathetic to the theistic view, subtitling his 2010 book "Making Room for Faith in the Age of Science." The point of the quote, I think, is that we do not *see* any evidence for God making the species, rather than just the natural forces of "genetic chance and environmental necessity." The result looks exactly the same as it would if there were no God working in the background pulling the strings. But the significant question remains open of how *nature* got here with its well-ordered laws, stunningly well-proportioned forces, and fortituous raw materials of life. That keeps me thinking (not just "believing") that there is a God behind it all

Juhani Alaranta wanted to hear in 2006 from his *opisto* students fresh out of elementary school:

> † "Each year, we discuss this matter" of faith and reason "with the youth in the religion class of the 'opisto,'" a folk college run in association with the SRK. "As the students typically come to the folk college after elementary school, many have a fresh memory of the instruction they received in school about man's development of a theory about the earth's origin. Its basis is materialistic, so it is against the biblical concept of creation. Often in this evolutionary theory is spoken of the so-called "Big Bang," with the origin of all life as a result. When one asks young people whether there are any holes in this theory, they reply that such a hole is the lack of a subject or operator, one who acts. This answer is one good example of the impact of the congregation's Bible class work and of this, that children and youth are brought to services and the hearing of God's word. 'So then faith cometh by hearing, and hearing by the word of God' (Rom 10:17)."

One aspect of the Eden-based theology that I find disturbing is how, as this November 2008 *Voice of Zion* article states, it "invites us to see man as a sin-fallen and sin-corrupted being." Calling "the basic goodness of man" a "humanistic illusion" that "has replaced the biblical truth" about our wretchedness, the article takes a subtle jab at evolution without coming out and saying it's not true:

> † Modern man's concept of man also favors the evolutionary explanation of man's origin. This theory is often interpreted with a view that sees man's creation taking place autonomously, without the hand of the Creator of heaven and earth. The book of Genesis expresses the simple belief of a Christian that God has created everything by His Word."

Well, the book of Genesis also "expresses the simple belief" that there was a "firmament" (NASB, *expanse*) of heaven into which God placed two great lights, the sun and the moon, to give light on the earth during the day and night, respectively. Speaking of this firmament and one of those lights in his exegesis on Gen. 1:6, Luther attributed it to "a work of the Divine Majesty" that "the sun follows its course so exactly and in a most precise manner without deviating a fingerbreadth from the

---

somehow, despite some good arguments by the atheists.

straightest possible line in any part of the heaven. Moreover, it maintains this course in the most tenuous atmosphere without any support by solid masses; but it is borne along like a leaf in the air." This firmament has waters below it–the seas–but also waters *above* it. Amazing, huh? But let's not dare doubt it, warns Luther: "Moses says in plain words that the waters were above and below the firmament. Here I, therefore, take my reason captive and subscribe to the Word even though I do not understand it" (*Lectures on Genesis*, Ch. 1, §6).

I doubt if it would offend many people today to call the firmament the misconception of ancient cosmology that it so obviously is. But I will go further and criticize an equally inaccurate view of man's origins and the fear, loathing, and disgust that it forces pious humans to direct into themselves. Psychologist Marlene Winell tells us what we are doing to ourselves with this kind of thinking:

> The key is that you are considered fundamentally wrong and inept, beginning with the doctrine of original sin. Everything about you is flawed, and you desperately need to be salvaged by God. The damage to self is more than hurt self-esteem. Your confidence in your own judgment is destroyed. As an empty shell, you are then open and vulnerable to indoctrination because you cannot trust your own thinking. Your thoughts are inadequate, your feelings are irrelevant or misleading, and your basic drives are selfish and destructive. [1993, 74]

The slander is not just against ourselves as creatures, but against the creator. Genesis 1 tells us that God created "man in his own image," male and female, and saw that everything that he had made, including man, "was very good." Yet he was helpless to prevent the serpent–one of *his* creatures–from corrupting man, the supposed crown of creation. The entire human race would become so utterly depraved from a single act of its ancestors as to be worthy only of an eternity of unthinkable torture at the wrathful hands of its creator.[17] Ingersoll pitied "any man or woman who, in this nineteenth century, believes in that childish fable." He dryly observed, "A god that cannot make a soul that is not totally depraved, I respectfully suggest, should retire from the business. And if a god has made us, knowing that we would be totally depraved,

---

17. Or at the hands of Satan and his minions. It's the same thing either way, since almighty God is the one allowing it to happen.

why should we go to the same being for repairs?" (*Lecture on Orthodoxy*).

The last quote of my sample acknowledges that there has been some increase in knowledge about creation. But God gets the credit for revealing it to us:

> † "God has blessed humankind by slowly revealing the wonders of His full creation. As man discovers what God has created (Gen 1), his knowledge increases" (VOZ, 11/2009).

Really? God is the one who has been telling us about our DNA with its near-identical similarity to that of chimpanzees, evidence of our existence as *Homo sapiens* over 100,000 years ago in Africa, and "fossil genes" that once coded for things like egg yolk and vitamin C production in our distant ancestors? God has been developing vaccines and antibiotics to deal with the problem of microorganisms evolving resistance? It seems that it is rather the (mostly) atheist scientists who have been doing all that while God's Conservative Laestadian spokesmen have droned on about Adam and Eve and childlike faith. "The practical track record of naturalistic science is available for all to evaluate, while supernatural science comes up empty handed. Indeed, the enterprise of science is to turn unknowns into knowns, while the business of supernaturalism is to make pronouncements concerning what cannot be known and which therefore requires magic" (Daniels 2010, 141). I think it is a fair question to ask, as Ingersoll did over a hundred years ago in his *Lecture on Ghosts*, "Is science indebted to the Church for a single fact? Let us know what it is."

Evolving Doctrine

Though the LLC has never said anything that is the least bit accepting of evolution, the SRK recently has made some intriguing and science-friendly statements. In a 2008 article, the SRK ordained pastor Jorma Kiviranta said the "stamp of fundamentalist creationism fits us very poorly." He referred to fundamentalists, "especially in the United States," who

> demand that the teaching of Darwinian evolution (the idea of species steadily developing or evolving) be removed as heretical from all schools. By every means possible, they seek strong scientific evidence for creationism, modeled as the "intelligent

design" theory of the Universe. Not even once have we needed an explanation for the birth of the universe and evolution. We just simply believe in God, the Father, the Almighty, Creator of heaven and earth. [Kiviranta 2008]

That same year, another SRK ordained pastor, Pauli Rentola, gave a presentation that seemed to seek an accommodation with evolution. Though he clung to a few whisps of mystery about transformation from one species to another, and attributed everything to "God's wise creation work," he had no criticism of modern science, which

> has evolved the theory of evolution quite extensively from just a simple thought. Rentola made it known that species continually change in small ways constantly, which science tries to and has explained. Science also tries to explain some of the bigger changes between species, but explaining how a species transforms itself into another is still difficult. As believers we understand that all of the changes that happen in Nature are a testament to God's wise creation work, Rentola said. [Junes 2008]

Rentola concluded with the hesitancy that all religious responses to evolution must have if they want to hold out for *any* sense of the divine in nature: "We do not understand God's creation work very well. In its light we quieten [ourselves] with that secure thought that, above all, through faith we receive a desire for 'the eternal.'" One speech given after the presentation "acknowledged that we could study God's creation of Nature and its evolution" (Junes 2008).

Remarkably, a *Päivämies* article has just appeared as of this writing that goes so far as to criticize creationism as something *foreign* to faith. It is something I think LLC members need to hear, though I suspect many of them would find it disturbing:

> Extremist thinking has not been a part of the believers' worldview. The doctrine of rationalism that submits the Bible to reason, as well as religious fundamentalism that requires literal interpretation of scripture, are both alien to living faith. The understanding of science and the origins of the universe and belief in God's creation has not given rise to party lines that would break the love [between believers, *rakkautta rikkovia rintamalinjoja*]. Creationism is a foreign [*vieras*: strange,

unfamiliar] attempt to reconcile man's limited intelligence and God's great, still ongoing work of creation. [Hintikka 2012]

I'm stunned but happy to see the "literal interpretation of scripture" being called "alien to living faith" in a Conservative Laestadian publication.[18] But let's not forget why this change is happening. "The doors leading out of scriptural literalism do not open from the inside. The moderation we see among nonfundamentalists is not some sign that faith itself has evolved; it is, rather, the product of the many hammer blows of modernity that have exposed certain tenets of faith to doubt" (Harris 2005, 18-19).

4.3.2 Noah and the Ark

> *Why is Ed worried about Noah's Ark? None of us believe it, either.*
>
> —LLC Preacher [2009]

I am no more capable of dismissing the abundant evidence against Noah's Flood than I am of believing in Adam and Eve popping into a world littered with hominid fossils and artifacts, or the real presence of Christ's body in the Communion wafer. The image that will always be associated with the topic of Noah in my mind is of Kangaroos hopping from Australia to Turkey and back again, leaving not a trace on the way. Of course, there is much more to it than that; the impossible quantity of water required, the miraculous survival (or recovery) of delicate marine life, the geological record, the millions of species involved, the logistics of feeding (many carnivores, remember) and sanitation, the incredibly rapid evolution of humans into their varied characteristics from three breeding pairs. *It just didn't happen.*

But the story remains told literally and unapologetically in Conservative Laestadianism. Unlike Adam and Eve and the Fall, though, this myth seems to have no real theological consequence beyond God's "be fruitful and multiply" directive and comparisons of the Ark to God's One True Church. Perhaps familiarity and an unwillingness to

---

18. Meanwhile, seemingly oblivious to these developments, the January 2012 *Voice of Zion* devotes several paragraphs to "the first human pair" tending the garden of Eden, living "a life of perfection" before being tempted by "the enemy of souls."

acknowledge errancy or myth in the Bible forces us to let it hang around like an old uncle who tells bad jokes.

Both literalism and symbolism are evident from the very beginning of this sample of quotes:

> ✝ "Who is able to comprehend the amount and power of the waters of Noah? They covered even the greatest mountains and the highest hills. Their power raised the ark from the deepest bottom, held it up and safely carried it to the new land where the vine-tree is blooming. When the grace of God that is through the redemption work of our Lord Jesus is compared to the waters of Noah, who is able to comprehend its amount and power? The great flock of unbelievers was not able to comprehend where so much water could come from, which could cover the great mountains and the hills. How difficult it was also even to our consciences to open up to receive the gospel and to believe that its grace as the waters of Noah suffice to cover the greatness of our sins. . . . Where have the great mountains of our sins gone, and where the high hills of our proudness and vain glory? What changed the sight of our eyes to see this old ark as so beautiful a dwelling place, although it is tarred inside and out . . . ?" (Heikki Jussila [1915], from *Greetings of Peace*, 8/1970).

> ✝ "Noah himself believed the word of God and built the ark of salvation. The moment came finally, when men saw how all that Noah had prophecied, was fulfilled. When Noah stepped into the ark, it began to rain, and all perished. Surely the word of God would have then been acceptable, if it only had been [available] to be heard. But it was not heard, no matter how men prayed and begged for mercy. The waters only rose higher, finally covered all. How horrible it was to perish knowing that the reason for this terrible calamity was that they had not believed the truth God had proclaimed through His servant, the preaching of that gray-headed old man, who so lovingly and patiently had spoken of truth and grace?" (Arvi Hintsala, *Greetings of Peace*, 11/1949)

Noah was a loving, patient gray-headed old man speaking about truth and grace? Those writers were just making that up. Hebrews 11:7 tells us that Noah prepared the ark "to the saving of his house, by the which he condemned the world." That doesn't sound very evangelical to me.

All we hear about his supposed preaching career is that he was "a preacher of righteousness" (2 Pet 2:5).

If we want some biblical biography about Noah, he "was at first cast as the inventor of wine, the means by which he brought the human race 'relief from out of the ground' for the toil to which God had consigned us after Eden (Genesis 5:29 and 9:20-21). After a hard day's work, they'd lift a few, saying 'It's Noah time!'" (Price 2006b, 103), joined by Noah himself (Gen 8:21). The following quote seems ironic coming from a preacher of what began as a temperance movement and rejects alcohol consumption to this day:

> † "It is very noteworthy that scientific examination reveals that the source of wine growing was in the regions of Ararat where the ark of Noah once rested" (Saari 1968, 13).

In the years leading up to the 1973 schism, those who ultimately departed were warned and rebuked many times by the Conservatives. It seems clear to me that the writers of the following two quotes had those events fresh in mind in their portrayals of Noah:

> † "Before the first world was destroyed by the flood, the consciences of men hardened in horrible sins and acts contrary to nature. Not one repentant one could be found in the entire world, although Noah warned, admonished and reproached long. Only Noah with his family in the ark were rescued from destruction" (SRK speaker's meeting presentation, 1973).

> † "[E]vil corrupted people and made them fall to serve the filthy lusts of the flesh, even so deep that when God looked down He saw that the sons of God had seen the daughters of men that they were fair and they had taken them to [be] their wives. (James 6:2). This was sin before God that His children so mixed themselves with the world ... Finally came the moment when people could see that what Noah had prophesied came true. When Noah entered the ark and God closed the door of the ark there was such a flood that all people and everything were drowned. Then they would have accepted the word of the Lord if they had been able to hear. But it was not preached, no matter how much they prayed and cried for grace. The waters just rose and finally covered everything. Oh, how terrible it was to be drowned and know that the reason for this terrible calamity was that one had

not believed the truth, which God had let be preached by His servant, the sermon of that grayhaired old man who had looked so mild and suffering and had spoken grace and truth. So unbelief brought the people of that time to eternal calamity. Only Noah and his family were saved from this terrible fate. They were saved in the tarred ark through faith, for they were partakers through faith of the righteousness that is acceptable to God" (VOZ, 10/1974).

Sometime around 1979 I heard about the sons of Noah being the progenitors of three major races of humanity. I was surprised to come across that racist, non-scriptural, and unscientific teaching in print:

† "The sons of Noah were Shem, Ham and Japeth. Shem's skin was white, Ham's skin was black and Japeth's skin was yellow" (VOZ, 5/1975).

I was even more surprised that it was taught to one of my children at a confirmation school in 2006.

The following quotations show how the Ark is portrayed as the Kingdom of God in which all of the saved will be found on the last day:

† In the first world, the "disobedience and ungodliness of man became so great that God regretted that He had made man. In His love, God, nevertheless, called man unto repentance. Noah preached 120 years concerning the opportunities of salvation. He built an ark in which he and the animals were saved from the destructive flood. Only eight people were saved. All others drowned. After the flood, God made a covenant in which He promised never again to destroy the earth by water. He placed the rainbow into the clouds for a sign of this covenant. The faith of Noah, the preaching of faith and the saving ark signify today's Kingdom of God. Outside the ark of the Kingdom of God there is no salvation from the destruction of the second world" (*By Faith*, 25).

† "When Noah preached the destruction of his world, people thought him foolish and simple-minded. They did not heed his warnings, considering them irrational. Noah's words were not accepted as God's Words.... In our time the warnings of God's children appear similar to Noah's" (VOZ, 11/2004).

† "Today, as during the time of Noah, God's kingdom is likened to a saving ark. Think how foolish Noah might have felt at times when building the ark in an arid place, and how foolish he would have appeared to the world. The ark was built of wood, pitched on the inside and out, with one door, and one window said to have opened towards heaven. There was little outward beauty to the ark, yet it was seaworthy enough so that it carried God's children through the difficult times of the flood. One can only imagine the anguish of the people as they sought the highest ground when the waters rose, and then were left to perish as the children of God were safely protected against the flood. God's kingdom today remains a place for the child of God to be protected against the storms of our day" (VOZ, 7/2008).

There is, of course, only one Ark and the few people in it all know each other. Luther also made a comparison between the Ark and the Christian Church:

> [A]s it happened when Noah was preparing the ark, so it takes place now. As he took refuge in the ark which swam upon the waters, so, it is to be observed, must you also be saved in baptism. Just as that water swallowed up all that was then living, of man and beast, — so baptism also swallows up all that is of the flesh and corrupt nature, and makes spiritual men. But we rest in the ark, which means the Lord Christ, or the Christian Church, or the Gospel that Christ preached, or the body of Christ, on which we rest by faith, and are saved as Noah in the ark. You also perceive how the image comprises in brief what belongs to faith and to the cross, to life and death. Where there are only those that follow Christ, there is surely a Christian Church, where all that springs from Adam, and whatever is evil, is removed. [*The Epistles of St. Peter and St. Jude Preached and Explained*, "The First Epistle General of St. Peter," Ch. 3]

But note the difference in emphasis between his comparison and the sectarian interpretation of the *Voice of Zion* quotation. Rather than just being "God's Kingdom," i.e., Conservative Laestadianism, the Ark is a picture of the Lord Christ, the Christian Church, the Gospel, and the body of Christ, and taking refuge in it amidst the rising waters constituted salvation in baptism.

Despite what we know about telomeres and the impossibility of humans living much beyond 100 years, the unthinking literalism continues to this day:

† "Noah was six hundred years old when the flood came and drowned everyone except Noah and his family. God saved Noah and his family for their faith" (*Päivämies* No. 46, 2009).

Those who reject evolution and hold to this story so literally should explain how the world's population went from "Noah and his family" drying out their laundry somewhere on a mountain in Turkey a few thousand years ago to 7 billion people on six continents in all their amazing racial and cultural variations:

How did these people get to look so different, with adaptations to their specific locations, if there is no such thing as evolution? According to creationists, "microevolution" (a distinction from "macroevolution" that is cited far more by creationists than scientists) was enough to get the job done in a few thousand years. So why is it so hard for them to imagine the scientific reality that we have a common ancestor with these guys in the next picture that lived about *5-7 million* years ago?

4 Conservative Laestadianism

Simply put, the story of the Flood is impossible to reconcile with reality. It had three floors of some 34,000 square feet each (Gen 6:15-16), totaling about the square footage of the average Wal-Mart, but held all the beasts, creeping things, and birds, literally millions of species. Thousands of different specimens made the trip from (and back home, after the flood) far-flung locales over hostile terrain, including polar bears and wolves from the arctic, penguins from the antarctic, African fauna such as lions, elephants, and giraffes, Australian kangaroos, Asian Koala bears, tigers, and monkeys, innumerable birds of paradise and prey, anacondas, gazelles, bison, tropical insects, ground-dwelling varmints, etc. The ark also held all the food supplies for everybody for a year, including live food for carnivores, various exotic plants, particular fish species, etc. All the waste was shoveled out somehow with a tiny crew, and ventilation provided through the single window (Gen 6:16), when it was open.

There is absolutely no evidence for such a worldwide deluge, and it is impossible to dismiss all of the practical problems, just a few of which are listed here. Basic geology and the fossil record provide no evidence for, and plenty of evidence against, any global flood. There are in fact no "fountains of the great deep" (7:11), and the amount of rainfall needed is far beyond what would completely saturate the air.

And this is only a brief and incomplete summary of all the problems with the Flood story. Jason Long provides a much better and more thorough description in his book under the heading "101 Reasons Why

Noah's Story Doesn't Float" (2005, 46-60). The text of his devastating critique is also freely available at http://biblicalnonsense.com/chapter6.html, a link I think is definitely worth taking the time to visit before reading further here. Go ahead, I'll wait.

If you are finding all this disturbing enough to just close this text right now and then try to forget or dismiss it, welcome to *cognitive dissonance*. It "is a state of tension that occurs whenever a person holds two cognitions (ideas, attitudes, beliefs, opinions) that are psychologically inconsistent." It "produces mental discomfort, ranging from minor pangs to deep anguish; people don't rest easy until they find a way to reduce it" (Tavris and Aronson 2008, 13). "The more committed we are to a belief, the harder it is to relinquish, even in the face of overwhelming contradictory evidence. Instead of acknowledging an error in judgment and abandoning the opinion, we tend to develop a new attitude or belief that will justify retaining it" (Burton 2008, loc. 149-51).

I've heard people attempt to reduce their dissonance about the Noah's Ark story in some interesting ways. Perhaps all of the animals were miniaturized and teleported to the Ark. Perhaps their DNA was kept in test tubes on the Ark. All cultures have flood stories so that proves a worldwide flood. (Actually, it seems to indicate the likelihood that the Genesis account is just another instance of a common mythic theme.) The most frequent and conversation-stopping response however, is that nothing is too difficult for God. And just like that, God becomes a stage magician, waving his wand and poofing absurdity into reality for the sole purpose of conforming it to the words of an ancient text that can't even get its stories straight. (Seven pairs of ritually clean animals, or one? Forty days of flooding, or 150?)

As Long concludes about the "utter ridiculousness" of the Noah story:

> Sure, one can easily explain the whole fiasco by use of miracles: God made all the water appear and disappear; God prevented all the water from becoming too hot; God put the animals into hibernation; God kept the ark afloat; God repopulated the earth with life; and God erased all evidence of the flood. By invoking the miracle clause, however, Christians are using unverifiable

events that *any* person can insert into *any* scenario in order to maintain the legitimacy of *any* religion. [2005, 60]

It seems to me that answers purporting to address any conceivable problem really turn out to be answers to nothing.

4.3.3 The Old Testament

> *Why does the Old Testament incessantly violate my idea of right and wrong? Why does it regard women in such a poor light? Why are the people of Yahweh supposed to wipe out men, women and children but are allowed to take the virgins for themselves?*
>
> –Ken Daniels, Why I Believed

Atrocities

My sample contains just three quotes about the atrocities of the Old Testament. That reflects the lack of attention they receive in church; during the months of 2009 I spent reading the Bible from cover to cover, I was repeatedly shocked at the awful stuff I was encountering for the first time. Just as disturbing to me were the excuses I heard when mentioning it to Conservative friends. One memorable line I remember hearing, after complaining about the conquest narratives of Joshua: "You're talking about human life. This life means nothing to God!" So much for a pro-life God, then.

Not only were the explanations utterly unconvincing, but the

> attempt to explain it away only lowered my respect for the apologists doing the explaining. Why would anyone, particularly mothers who love their daughters and daughters who value their dignity, even want to try to defend passages like these? The very inclination to justify such barbarism revealed to me the unyielding grip of an absolute faith upon its adherents. [Daniels 2010, 46]

Price asks the apologist for these texts how dangerous it would be if Christians nowadays were to actually heed and obey the commands of God that they read in them. "Can we really believe the true and existing God told the ancient shaman and his client warlord to exterminate every single Amalekite baby? Hold on! Wait a minute, my friend, before you begin to defend the gruesome act as an act of God, lest you utter some cold-blooded enormity you otherwise would never entertain" (2006b, 128).

Even without the subject coming up, just knowing how readily my Conservative companions would offer such excuses and defenses made it difficult for me to spend time in conversation with them. One evening as I sat across the coffee table from a preacher, listening to him talk about some everyday matter, I couldn't get the thought out of my mind: *This man defends as God's Holy Word a book that refers to slaves as mere property and excuses beating them to within an inch of their lives* (Exodus 21).

In church, almost nothing is said about the Old Testament, much less these horrible texts. Robert Wright calls that "selective retention":

> You can just conveniently forget certain parts of your scriptural heritage. During the Crusades, when Christians were in the mood to slaughter infidels, they were very cognizant of God's sanctioning faith-based mass murder in parts of the Bible. During the Cold War, when the United States was part of an international multifaith alliance that included Muslim and Buddhist nations, this motif was played down; whole generations of American Christians were weaned on a misleadingly sunny selection of Bible stories. [2009, 192]

The first of my sampled quotes is from the April 1938 *Siionin Lähetyslehti*. There O.H. Jussila spiritualizes God's tormenting of innocent Egyptians for their leader's stubborness. He also provides an example of a phenomenon I've noticed far too much–someone who considers himself saved praising God as being "merciful" for saving his lousy hide while damning everybody else:

> † "When God announced to His people Israel in Egypt His merciful and saving plans for them and his instructions, He said, 'And the blood shall be to you for a token upon the houses where ye are: and when I see the blood I will pass over you', Exod. 12:13. On the terrible night when Israel slaughtered the Passover lamb, from the Egyptians' houses were heard cries of anguish and wailing because the angel of death did not spare one home, but spread death from house to house. There was only one means which saved. God had not given this saving means to any but His own people. . . . Do you who read this have this blood for your protection? Or do you live in 'Egyptian' that is, in the perilous

abodes of this world's children without protection from the wrath of God...?" (from *Greetings of Peace*, 3/1955).

There is a key difference between the passover story and Jussila's call to unsaved readers; none of the grieving Egyptian parents were ever even offered the opportunity to save their firstborn children. It was just one of many cases of the tribal God of the Old Testament inflicting terror and death on innocent members of a population because they didn't happen to be his chosen people.

Next we come to Lot's offering his two daughters to the men of Sodom, which

> † "is quite incomprehensible to the mind, but we should examine it through faith. Then we will see the firm trust that Lot had in the protection of God" (Saari 1968, 52).

Oh, come on. He told the men to do with his daughters whatever they wanted, and what they had on their minds was very clear to all concerned. It was a case of the rules of hospitality taking priority over the value of mere women in the ancient setting of the story. And we never hear about Lot getting drunk and impregnating those same two daughters:

> And Lot... dwelt in a cave, he and his two daughters. And the firstborn said unto the younger, Our father is old, and there is not a man in the earth to come in unto us after the manner of all the earth: Come, let us make our father drink wine, and we will lie with him, that we may preserve seed of our father. And they made their father drink wine that night: and the firstborn went in, and lay with her father; and he perceived not when she lay down, nor when she arose. And it came to pass on the morrow, that the firstborn said unto the younger, Behold, I lay yesternight with my father: let us make him drink wine this night also; and go thou in, and lie with him, that we may preserve seed of our father. And they made their father drink wine that night also: and the younger arose, and lay with him; and he perceived not when she lay down, nor when she arose. [Gen 19:30-35]

In the final quote of this small sample, we have a reluctant acknowledgment of Joshua's campaigns of genocide against the Canaanites, which are some of the most horrible atrocities of the Old Testament. Biblical inerrantists insist that they "were not only wholly justified, but good. Although every genocidal regime claims to have the sanction of some deity, inerrantists insist that in ancient Israel's case, it was true. It had to be true, because it's in the Bible" (Stark 2011, 101). This article in the June 1990 *Voice of Zion* offers a few creative justifications:

> ✝ "The enormous number of casualties may raise questions even in the mind of a believer. Let us consider the terrible sins which the Canaanites wantonly practiced: snake worship, religious prostitution, and even more horrendous, children were sacrificed on altars to appease false gods. Does this horror have a parallel even in today's society (abortion)? The measure of the sins of the Canaanites was full, invoking the wrath of God upon these people who had rejected Him from their forefathers onward; hence, total darkness and ungodliness. When we consider this suffering through the light of the Holy Spirit, how insignificant this is compared to the eternal torments of hell."

Invoking hell only compounds the atrocity, though. Joshua abruptly ended the lives and thus any possibility of grace for thousands of hell-bound adult Canaanites. Of course, grace is largely a New Testament concept; the book of Joshua is a narrative of tribal conquest and records no efforts toward or even opportunities for Canaanite conversion.

Ancient Israelite Laestadianism

The Old Testament unfolds over the course of about 1500 years, and the religion it describes underwent significant changes during that time. It begins in the Bronze Age just one step away from polytheism (Wright 2009, 103-106) with God making regular appearances, smiting people left and right, and receiving ritual sacrifice as a major part of his worship. It concludes with books that emphasize wisdom and prophetic vision, which treat sacrifice with disdain and God as being somewhat above it all. At no point in that history did the religion of the ancient Israelites look *anything* like Christianity, much less the Pauline grace-and-forgiveness version of it practiced by Conservative Laestadians.

But that hasn't stopped the theologians from coming up with some pretty creative attempts to make it seem otherwise, beginning right in the earliest books of the New Testament. One of many examples is 1 Cor 10:2-4:

> [A]ll our fathers were under the cloud, and all passed through the sea; And were all baptized unto Moses in the cloud and in the sea; And did all eat the same spiritual meat; And did all drink the same spiritual drink: for they drank of that spiritual Rock that followed them: and that Rock was Christ.

My sample of Conservative Laestadian quotes typecasting the Israelites as proto-Christians "just like us" begins, appropriately enough, with one from that theological innovator of the 1960s, Heikki Saari:

> † "When Daniel explained Nebuchadnezzar's dream, reciting to him his sins, he preached repentance to the king and offered the forgiveness of sins to him. Daniel entreated lovingly and tenderly 'O King, let my counsel be acceptable to thee, and break off thy sins.' But that loving gospel fell on deaf ears" (1968, 35).

The story of Nathan rebuking David of his sin and then pronouncing that he was forgiven of it (2 Sam 12) strikes me as the only plausible example in the Bible of the Laestadian-style absolution being employed:

> † "Nathan was sent by the Lord to speak to David and to reveal his transgressions to him. This is how God has always done. He has spoken to all sinners through His servants. When David comprehended that he had sinned against the Lord, the servant was ready to pronounce forgiveness, and said to David; 'the Lord also hath put away thy sin; thou shalt not die.' It is no wonder, after receiving forgiveness, that David was rejoicing in his heart" (VOZ, 10/1976).

The *Apology of the Augsburg Confession* uses this same example as one of its biblical arguments for repentance being comprised of contrition and faith. It asserts that "the Power of the Keys administers and presents the Gospel through Absolution, which is the true voice of the Gospel" and "can properly be called a Sacrament of repentance" (Article 12a; McCain 2005, 162). After several pages of discussion that conforms remarkably with Conservative Laestadian doctrine on the topic, the *Apology* mentions Nathan's encounter with David along with two other Bible stories. (Those are God's rebuke and promise of grace to Adam, and Jesus' proclamation "Thy sins are forgiven" to the sinful woman who anointed his feet with her hair in Luke 7:48.) David's terrified statement, "I have sinned against the LORD" (2 Sam 12:13) was an act of contrition. "Afterward, he hears the Absolution, 'The LORD also has put away your sin; you shall not die.' This voice encourages David, and through faith it sustains, justifies, and enlivens him. A punishment was also added, but the punishment does not merit the forgiveness of sins. Nor are special punishments always added" (p. 165).

Of course, one must recognize that there was not even a remote mention of Jesus during the encounter. Imagine the noise that Christian apologists would have made of such a thing if it were there, seeing how they scour the Old Testament for the vaguest of statements that might be considered messianic prophecies! No, it was the time of the "Old Covenant," when the forgiveness of sins supposedly was facilitated through animal sacrifices:

> † "The Old Testament is the evidence and document of the way revealed by God. The children of God in the Old Covenant believed the prophecies and promises concerning the coming Savior of the world," who "was seen through faith in the sacrificial animals of sacrificial worship." Salvation was "through faith upon the word of promise regarding Christ" (*By Faith*, 13-14).

> † "The Hebrew congregation was of the Jewish people. They observed the Old Testament Tabernacle worship of God. They performed those sacrifices and offerings which God had spoken of through Moses when He established the Levitical priesthood. The priests of the tribe of Levi performed these duties every day, offering sacrifices for sin. This sacrificing directed the people to that one great priest, the Lord Jesus" (Alajoki [1985], 91-92).

So why was nothing written about such sacrifices for David, one of the highest-profile sinners of the Bible? Instead, he simply had his sins pronounced forgiven. If you want to consider the encounter one of confession and absolution, you have to abandon the idea that the animal sacrifices were what did the job before Jesus made the ultimate sacrifice. Think about it.

Naaman the Syrian merely had to wash in the River Jordan:

> † "Through Elisha, the Spirit of God humbled Naaman to repentance. This repentance is portrayed by the washing in the River Jordan" (VOZ, 7/1998).

No animal sacrifices were involved there, either. Perhaps the answer is that the 'old believers' merely had to believe "on the promise" of the coming Savior. We see that along with some references to the animal sacrifices in the remaining quotes of my sample:

† "The transition between the Old and the New Testament times was difficult. The time of sacrificial worship and faith in the promised Messiah was ending, and faith in the fulfillment, Jesus Christ the perfect sacrifice, was beginning. God in his infinite wisdom provided a precursor to Jesus, someone to help with the transitional time. This was Jesus' cousin, John the Baptist" (VOZ, 12/1999).

† "The Son, Christ, existed for a long time among men only as the Word of the Promise. They, who believed the Promise, awaited its fulfillment. They probably thought that God tarried long. However, He did not tarry, not even to try the faith of the children of God of the Old Covenant. His time had not yet come" (Uljas 2000, 116).

† "In the worship service of the first covenant, the high priest offered the blood of animals for himself and the errors of the people.... Yet, in those sacrifices, it was revealed through the Holy Ghost, of the day of Christ, the Lamb of God, who would offer himself as a perfect atonement for sins" (VOZ, 12/2004).

† "Throughout Old Testament times, God spoke to the people through prophets. God revealed through them very specific details about the coming birth, life, and death of Jesus. These prophecies were fulfilled hundreds of years later. God gave His Words of the prophets and they spoke to the people, exhorting them to put their sins away through believing in the promise of the Savior. Many heard God's call. The Bible testifies of their lives. They were sinners, but they believed their sins forgiven. They were acceptable to God" (VOZ, 12/2007).

† The living water that Jesus gives "is found in the gospel, and Jesus invites all who are thirsty to come to Him and drink. Scriptures [1 Cor 10:4, Isa 55:1 cited] show that the Old Testament travelers also believed upon this water of life and the promise of the coming Messiah" (VOZ, 5/2008).

Accurate or not, viewing the characters in the Old Testament through a Christian lens as "believers in the promise" was something Luther also did, and with ample precedent from the New Testament writers themselves. The following is from a sermon of his for the third Sunday before Lent, from *Epistle Sermons: Epiphany, Easter and Pentecost* (Lenker 1909):

> Adam was saved by the word of promise (Gen 3:15): The seed of the woman shall bruise the serpent's head; that is, Christ shall come to conquer sin, death and Satan for us. To this promise God added the sign of sacrifice, sacrifice kindled with fire from heaven, as in Abel's case (Gen 4:4), and in other cases mentioned in the Scriptures. The word of promise was Adam's Gospel until the time of Noah and of Abraham. In this promise all the saints down to Abraham believed, and were redeemed; as we are redeemed by the word of the Gospel which we believe. The fire from heaven served them as a sign, as baptism does us, which is added to the word of God.
>
> Such signs were repeated again and again at various times, the last sign being given by Christ in his own person–the Gospel with baptism, granted to all nations. For instance, God gave Noah the promise that he should survive the flood, and granted him a sign in the ship, or ark, he built. And by faith in the promise and sign Noah was justified and saved, with his family. Afterward God gave him another promise, and for a sign the rainbow. Again, he gave Abraham a promise, with the sign of circumcision. Circumcision was Abraham's baptism, just as the ark and the flood were that of Noah. So also our baptism is to us circumcision, ark and flood, according to Peter's explanation. 1 Pet 3:21. Everywhere we meet the Word and the Sign of God, in which we must believe in order to be saved through faith from sin and death.
>
> Thus the children of Israel had God's word that they should inherit the promised land. In addition to that word they were given many signs, in particular those Paul here names—the sea, the cloud, the bread from heaven, the water from the rock. These he calls their baptism; just as our baptism might be called our sea and cloud. Faith and the Spirit are the same everywhere, though the signs and the words vary. Signs and words indeed change

from time to time, but faith in the one and same God continues. Through various signs and revelations, God at different times bestows the same faith and the same Spirit, effecting through these in all saints remission of sins, redemption from death, and salvation, whether they lived in the beginning or at the end of time, or while time progressed.

Prophecy

All the exposition from Conservatives about "believers in the promise" is enough to make one expect to find the Old Testament filled with stories of people gathered around forgiving each other's sins in the name of a Messiah whom God would be sending someday to serve as the ultimate sacrifice. It's not too far from what this next quote describes, which I'm not surprised to see is from a December (Christmas) issue of the *Voice of Zion*, in 2008:

> † After the Fall, God "promised a redeemer, a savior who would overthrow the power of the devil and offer complete atonement for sin-fallen man. Thus the 'Old Covenant' or promise was born, and those 'old believers' from antiquity by God's grace, were saved by living faith in those promises. As the ages passed and biblical epochs unfolded, God repeated His promise again and again. In the life of Abraham and the other patriarchs God reconfirmed His covenant.... The Old Testament prophets were later able to behold, by faith, a distant but approaching moment when the Creator would send the promised savior. God then began to further open the mysteries and reveal through these prophets that great miracles and wonders, and incomprehensible to the human mind, would mark the arrival and life of the coming Redeemer."

I spent several months of 2009 carefully reading the entire Old Testament. It was surprising and, yes, disappointing, to see how much Christian wishful thinking and recontextualization has been applied to its supposedly messianic character and prophecies. Time after time, I would come across a passage that had been touted as a prophecy of Jesus, and recognize it only because the words of the supposed prophecy were so familiar from hearing them recited in church. But in their proper context–which one can best appreciate by reading each book of the Bible in turn, starting at the beginning–those passages didn't seem impressive at all. I had to confront the realization that what had been "repeated again and again" were not God's promises that he would incarnate himself as the savior of mankind from its sins, but assurances of Christianity to itself that it is really the religion of Abraham, Isaac, and Jacob after all.

Those self-assurances began right in the pages of the New Testament and have continued to this day. After turning from reading the Old Testament to the New, it became sadly evident to me as it did to Charles Francis Potter that the author of Matthew "stood out as a Christian writer, so anxious to prove to the Jews that Jesus was the Messiah they had long been looking for, that he lost all sense of proportion and accuracy, twisted quotations to serve his purpose, and revealed himself as an earnest but unscrupulous propagandizer" (1951, 392). A prominent example is Matthew's use of Isaiah 7 (**6.21**), out of context and based on an important translation error of which Hebrew speakers could hardly have been ignorant, as support for the virgin birth. According to Stark, the religious community that promoted the Gospel of Matthew was "not interested in the text for its historical meaning," but only "in using the text to elucidate their own present-day experiences and to reinforce their sense of identity" (2011, 29).

I know this may be difficult for some to read. It was an even more difficult thing to learn from reading the conflicting words themselves. I am not making this stuff up–I didn't want it to be true any more than I wanted evolution to be true. But it *is* true, as Potter's fellow students learned in "a two-term course on messianic prophecy, a thorough study of the Hebrew text of all passages alleged to be prophecies of the coming of Jesus or even reference to him." The majority of those students went in "believing at least to some extent in messianic prophecy, and several of them fought strenuously to find foundation for that faith." But he and they "were unanimous at the end in agreeing that the so-called Old Testament predictions of Jesus were better accounted for by the events of the period during which the prophets themselves lived" (Potter 1951, 392).

It is just one more reason why the most difficult and heart-wrenching reading I've ever done was of the Old Testament. My notes from that study make up **Section 6**.

Another Old Testament passage was once widely discussed in Conservative Laestadianism as a prophecy not of Jesus, but of Laestadianism itself. It was a prominent topic of a historical sermon given by Pauli Korteniemi and published in the *Greetings of Peace* in 1963:

> ☦ "Look at these white horses which had left on their journey [Zech 6:6]. They knew their destination, where they had to go. For it is said here, that behold, these that go toward the North Country have quieted my spirit in the North Country. How surprising this is. How surprising that this is verified by the geographies, although afterwards this has been tried to be changed a little so that it would not be this clear, according to the geographies and maps. So in the new edition it says 'in a Northern Country.' But here it says 'in the North Country.' And if this is not acceptable to us that it is thus and that in it is no changing. And so it happened that living Christianity was preserved in the North Country, in Sweden."

Zechariah has a vision of four horses with different colored horses pulling them in various directions. An angel tells him that they are the "four spirits of heaven, going forth after standing before the Lord of all the earth" (NASB, 6:5). Of a chariot pulled northward by white horses he is told, "See, those who are going to the land of the north have caused my spirit to rest in the land of the north" (NASB, 6:8, literal translation), or as the KJV puts it, "the north country." Much has been made of this in Laestadianism, due to its roots in the northernmost reaches of Europe.

But the words were not written by anyone who had the slightest idea that a place like Lapland even existed. Rather, they were written in Judah by someone who had returned from exile in Babylon. His journey homeward had taken him along the fertile crescent, through the lands of Assyria and Israel that lay to the north of Judah along the Mediterranean coast. When Zechariah looked northward, what he saw was the route from which many of his country's enemies had come, and a hostile land from which he himself had returned.

The supposed "North Country" prophecy is not emphasized much anymore in Laestadian Christianity. The change is evident in a 2008 revision to a song verse originally written in 1973: "The Spirit now rests in the earth's northern land, The words of the prophet how clearly they stand." Now, "The Spirit sends servants to preach through the lands." The shift is probably more due to the emergence of Laestadian churches in Africa and South America than any newfound reluctance to impose modern geographical knowledge on ancient writers.

The "Wilderness Journey"

The life of a believer is often compared to a journey, and often more specifically to the Exodus:

> † When the wandering Israelites "finally came to a spring, the water was too bitter to drink. God instructed Moses to throw a tree, which God showed him, into the water. Moses did this and the water became sweet. When a child of God has murmured, as these Israelites had murmured before finding the spring, the water would at first be bitter and unsuitable. When one is in faith and obedience and submits oneself to follow God's instructions, then God makes the water sweet. Jesus is 'the branch,' and by and through Him we receive the water of life. Once the travelers' thirst had been relieved, they suffered from hunger. They suffered from hunger although they had plenty of cattle with them. The people murmured. Moses prayed. God sent swarms of quail and manna which fell like dew to feed them. It was not fitting for them to eat of their own cattle; neither can today's journeyer on the way to Heaven seek nourishment from that which he has brought. One has to be content with that which God provides as food" (VOZ, 5/1990).

> † "God did not forget His chosen people as they fled from Egypt. He shielded them from being seen by the army through the night, as He caused the wind to create dry land through the sea. The angel of God and the pillar of cloud went behind the people 'so that the one came not near the other all the night.' When the way was dry across the sea the Israelites were able to cross with a wall of water on both sides. When the Egyptians tried to follow in the way that was prepared for the Israelites, God did not allow this to happen. He allowed the waters to return upon the Egyptians so that His people could go free" (VOZ, 7/2006).

There are some truly astounding things being described here. More than a million people (and their livestock) marched across soggy sea bottom one morning with walls of water on both sides. Then they spent forty years wandering around one of the world's most inhospitable deserts, receiving sustenance out of nowhere and leaving not a single trace for diligent archeologists to find (see 6.2). The quoted Conservative writers give a matter-of-fact report on those things like they are yesterday's news–incredulity is not expected. As Ingersoll dryly noted in his 1885 interview with the *Cincinnati Plain Dealer*, "Most people are willing to believe that wonderful things happened long ago and will happen again in the far future; with them the present is the only time in which nature behaves herself with becoming sobriety."

> † "We find comfort in knowing that God is always with us just as He was with Moses. He is not with us in a visible pillar of cloud or fire, but in the Holy Spirit that resides in His kingdom" (VOZ, 6/2008).
>
> † "The journey of God's children is the same kind of journey in the wilderness as the Israelites' journey was. The enemy wishes to plant the seed of bondage, permissiveness of sin, and the love of the world into our hearts so that we would be exhausted by the obstacles he places before us and return to the dark Egypt of sin. We should always use the gospel in the midst of temptations. We should use this rod to strike the rock of Christ from which flows pure water that quenches our thirst" (VOZ, 1/2009).
>
> † Lot's wife "was instructed not to look back to her former life in Sodom. She was disobedient, looked back, and was turned into a pillar of salt. Likewise many of the travelers on the Wilderness Journey remembered Egypt's fleshpots and longed for them. They died in the wilderness before the sojourning flock reached the Promised Land" (VOZ, 6/2009).

Most of that is pure allegory, quite a ways from letting "the words retain their natural force, just as they read," as Luther advocated. One should "give no other interpretation unless a clear article of faith compels otherwise" (from Althaus 1963, 386), unless of course you are trying to explain away Scriptural praise for the bashing of babies' heads against rocks (**Psalms 137:9**), as Luther stooped to doing.

Continuity with the New Testament

The difficulties with the Old Testament have been recognized since the beginning of the New. Marcion, a controversial theologian of the early second century, "believed the God of the Old Testament was a morally atrocious deity, a God of violence and vengeance, far removed from the

New Testament's God of love. Thus Marcion and his followers cut the Old Testament out of their canon and were branded by other Christian factions as 'heretics.'" (Stark 2011, 33). The church father Tertullian devoted an entire book of his writings to refuting Marcion, and the Old Testament has remained in the Christian Bible ever since. Naturally, it must have a reason for being there:

> † "The stories of the Old Testament are often symbolic. They have an inseparable connection with the happenings of the New Testament" (*By Faith*, 23).

> † "The Old Testament is a good teacher; it has many lessons for us about the importance of faith from the beginning of time" (VOZ, 9/2008).

In an undated presentation <http://www.llchurch.org/gods-word-unchanging-eternal.cfm> entitled "God's Word is Unchanging and Eternal," Walt Lampi claims continuity between the Old and New Testaments, and the God of both:

> † "Since the beginning of time God has not changed His will, nor the Word by which He communicates His will, toward mankind. He revealed to the prophet Malachi: 'I am the Lord, I change not,' and James described Him as 'the Father of lights, with whom is no variableness, neither shadow of turning.' . . . The God of the Old Testament is the same God as He of the New Testament. The Old Testament reveals God's promise of a Savior to sin-fallen man and the New Testament is the fulfillment of that promise. The Old Testament is more than a historical account of ancient Israel or just an ancient literary work of the kind found in other nations of that time. Rather, the Old Testament is the revelation of God's salvation plan through the history of His chosen people."

I invite you to read the Old Testament (or at least my notes on it in **Section 6**) and see if you can still persuade yourself that "the God of the Old Testament is the same God as He of the New Testament" or the same loving, gracious, omniscient God that Conservatives like to talk about. Even within the Old Testament itself, "the Bible's depictions of a vivid, dramatically interventionist Yahweh decline in frequency as the biblical narrative unfolds. It is near the beginning of the story that Yahweh is most likely to appear to people or speak to them or do widely witnessed wonders" (Wright 2009, 128).

4.3.4 Inerrancy

> *All it takes is one miniscule disagreement with the Bible for the whole house of cards to come tumbling down. And eventually, if they allow themselves to be pressed, it will happen to every honest would-be inerrantist. There is no such thing as an inerrantist. Inerrantists just haven't realized it yet.*
>
> —Thom Stark, *The Human Faces of God*

The modest size of my sample of quotes on biblical inerrancy surprised me, considering how seriously the Bible is taken as "God's Word." But I have come across other topics that are so well settled in the minds of Conservatives that they appear not to require much discussion in writings and sermons. (Examples are the rejections of extramarital sex, **4.6.1**, and intermarriage with unbelievers, **4.7.4**.) The idea of the Bible as the inerrant word of God is likewise very deeply ingrained.

The subject didn't even seem to come up for most of the movement's history. My first quote is from 1980, an attribution of the Bible to the Holy Spirit and a claim that it is "one completeness":

> † "The common characteristic of all the writers of the Bible is that they had the Holy Spirit. The Bible has been written according to the revelation of the Holy Spirit. . . . Even though the Bible has been written with different gifts and in different languages and even though it contains many books, it is nevertheless one completeness" (*By Faith*, 11).

In a July 1990 sermon, Quentin Ruonavaara makes the first clear statement of inerrancy of my sample:

> † "Surely we must say the Scriptures have never erred. We believe in Jesus Christ according to the law and the prophets."

I once accepted that simple, dogmatic statement. Though there were nagging questions about a few Old Testament stories I'd come across in Sunday school or my cursory Bible readings, "The Bible was, after all, the verbally inspired word of God, so if I had found problems in it, there had to be solutions to them," as Farrell Till thought (2003, 294). But the longer he studied the Bible critically, the more he realized that he would never find solutions to the problems I had identified, because there were no solutions. The Bible is not the verbally inspired, inerrant word of God; it was just a collection of contradictory, discrepant books that had been written by superstitious ethnocentrics who thought that the hand of God was directing the destiny of the Hebrew people. [p. 294]

No doubt many readers will find that a shocking statement for me to quote. But my own studies of the Bible, its manuscripts, and the history surrounding its writing and canonization have, unfortunately, left me not far from Till's conclusion. Uljas even shows some anxiety about the Bible's "human side":

> † "Due to the manner of its birth, the Bible also has a human side. The saints of God, who spoke and wrote the Word of God, were bound to the image of the world and the culture of their time. This is seen also in the writings of the Scriptures. However, the divine and the human aspects are so intertwined in the Scriptures, that there is no reason to ponder what is divine and what is human in them. The Bible is the Word of God in human words.... Some people say that the Bible does not need to be interpreted so literally, nor do its teachings hold any longer, for it has originated within the sphere of the old Semitic and Hellenistic cultures. We cannot agree with these statements, if we consider the Bible to be God's Word" (2000, 22-23).

The second part of that statement contradicts the first. You cannot attempt to excuse the Bible's undeniable errors and contradictions as the result of humans being "bound to the image of the world and the culture of their time" while denying that those humble origins limit its applicability today. (**John 21:4-13** is one striking example of a Bible story that seems to have Hellenistic origins.)

The fact is that the vast majority of biblical scholars–academics who are not bound to some particular dogmatic commitment–have been calling the Bible's claims of divine revelation into question for over a hundred years. These next quotes acknowledge that, not as a positive development of course:

> † "An instruction for concord from one of the Lutheran church's confessional books affirms: 'The Old and New Testaments' prophetical and apostolic books are the only rule and guide

through which all doctrine and teaching is to be examined and evaluated.' Nowadays, even in Finland, some church workers call into question the Bible's revelation of God" (*Päivämies* No. 17, 2006).

† "We live in a time in which the authority, holiness, and inerrancy of the Holy Bible has been placed under doubt and suspicion by those who challenge it as a divine revelation of God's will toward men. This position is in direct opposition to that held by the believer, that the Holy Scriptures are the highest authority and standard by which matters of soul and doctrines of salvation are judged. . . . By faith we accept the Holy Scriptures, both Old and New Testaments, as the divinely inspired and revealed Word of God" (VOZ, 3/2007).

One of those who has expressed "doubt and suspicion" about parts of the Bible is none other than Luther himself. In his 1522 preface to the Epistle to the Hebrews, he wrote that he "could not put it on the same level with the apostolic epistles," noting that some of its teachings (**7.7**) seem "to be against all the Gospels and St. Paul's epistles" (*PE* 6, 476-77). He criticized the Epistle of James, who "does nothing more than drive to the law and its works; and he mixes the two up in such disorderly fashion that it seems to me he must have been some good, pious man, who took some sayings of the apostles' disciples and threw them thus on paper; or perhaps they were written down by someone else from his preaching" (*Preface to James and Jude* [1522]; *PE* 6, 478). Concerning the authenticity of Jude, he wrote that "no one can deny that it is an extract or copy from Saint Peter's second epistle, so very like it are all the words" (p. 479). He wished that the book of Esther "had not come to us at all" (*Table Talk* §24).

In my experience, it is far easier to believe in the inerrancy of the Bible when you haven't really ever read the whole thing. Undeniable deviations from historical evidence and internal contradictions are numerous and well known, many cases of which are discussed in the **Old Testament** and **New Testament** sections below. To claim, as this next writer does, that the Bible is "one book, one doctrine, and one plan of salvation" is to reveal a state of denial or just plain ignorance about the many different threads of thought and authorship even within individual books, and the significant conflicts and the varying ways that are presented for reconciliation with God.

† "The Bible itself has been written by over forty authors, who wrote sixty-six books over a period of approximately 1,500 years: yet it is one book, one doctrine, and one plan of salvation. Our faith is according to the one correct doctrine that is found in Scriptures. This same doctrine is heard in the preaching of God's kingdom" (VOZ, 5/2007)

And, guess what! That "one doctrine" is just what *we* are preaching! Never mind all that Old Testament stuff, passages that contradict sectarian exclusivity, the lack of examples of Laestadian-style absolution, or the admonitions to take care of the needy even at the expense of one's own wealth. While in the New Apostolic Church (no relation to Laestadianism), David Stamos encountered the same shock that I did from extracurricular studying. He also had relied on what he was taught in church, but then discovered many

> problems connected with the New Testament, not only internal contradictions but also major external ones, contradictions between what my church had always taught me and what was taught in the Bible. And here my church was teaching as it always had, not only that the Bible is God's true and holy Word, but also that only the New Apostolic Church is truly based on the Bible! [2003, 343]

The claim will sound very familiar to Conservatives, it is just one example of how hundreds–probably thousands–of disagreeing and disagreeable Christian denominations and sects each find their own image reflected in the pages of the Bible. It seems to me, as it did to Robert M. Price and Ernst Käsemann whom he cites, that "the diversity of thought and conviction among the New Testament writers is surely responsible for the analogous diversity among the churches who appeal to the New Testament" (2006b, 199).

Here are just a few of the issues no longer even disputed in biblical scholarship that come to my mind as I contemplate the claim of "one book, one doctrine, and one plan of salvation":

- Multiple authors of Genesis with different theological agendas, who provide conflicting accounts of both the creation and flood stories;
- Significant evolution of God from a talkative, blundering, temperamental warrior deity to a distant "Father" who limits his

human interactions to the occasional dove or earthquake and is approachable only through the loving, caring image of his Son;

- Edicts and actions made under God's command that reflect the cruel, misogynist, scientifically ignorant, and genocidal nature of the Old Testament writers and that are completely dismissed by the New Testament writers of a (slightly) more enlightened age;

- Conflicting claims about the existence of any place of eternal torment, or indeed any afterlife at all;

- Detailed and exacting demands for sacrifice followed by the claim that God does not desire sacrifice, which is then followed by the claim that the old sacrifices were really about Jesus all along;

- Significant evolution of Jesus from a servant–submitting to John's baptism of repentance and showing anger, limited powers of healing and prophecy, and uncomprehending anguish about his fate–to the mystical, divine Son of God;

- Non-apostolic authorship of many New Testament epistles.[19]

The faith that is required to gloss over these and many other issues is not a faith in God or the Son of God, but faith in the book that sits on the pulpit, and in the preacher who reverently thumbs through its gold-leaf pages in search of safe, comfortable passages on which to expound. "[M]any Christians don't even know *what* they believe because they never take the time to read the whole Bible" (Long 2005, 3), and indeed they can be discouraged from doing so lest their human reasoning about what is written lead them astray. Among Orthodox Jews, too,

---

19. Bart Ehrman recent published an entire book about this issue, *Forged: Writing in the Name of God–Why the Bible's Authors Are Not Who We Think They Are* (2011). Peter probably didn't write 1 Peter and almost certainly not 2 Peter (pp. 68-77). Paul didn't write the Epistles to Timothy and Titus (pp. 93-102). Nor is Paul likely to be the writer of 2 Thessalonians (pp. 105-108), Ephesians (pp. 108-112), or Colossians (pp. 112-14).

L. Michael White writes of Ephesians that it "is not typical of Paul's letters in form, style, or theological language" (2005, 266). It "seems to be based in large measure on Colossians," and the "weight of the evidence points to" both books being written by someone other than Paul (pp. 264-65). Difficulties with 2 Peter are well known, but White says the authenticity of 1 Peter also "is now doubted by almost all modern scholars" for numerous reasons (p. 272).

there is awareness that exposure to the evidence and arguments of critical biblical scholarship "might generate doubt." Because "the consequences of doubt can be dangerous and painful, it is better to remain ignorant of the counterevidence and competing theories" (Schimmel 2008, 63).

So what is left is the kind of "biblicist" faith reflected in this next quote:

> † "Exactly how the historical facts concerning the life and work of our Lord and Savior were collected and how they were transmitted to others and by whom, we don't know, but we trust to faith in its accuracy and purposefulness" (VOZ, 7/2007).

Another bit of unwelcome information I learned is that we have access to *no* "historical facts concerning the life and work of Jesus" from anything recorded until several decades after his death at the earliest. Those earliest records are found only in the Gospels, which were written by Christians–clearly not eyewitnesses themselves–who wanted to promote particular, often conflicting, viewpoints of who Jesus was. It would be more decades still before any objective historian would finally mention Jesus, and then mostly just in reference to the movement that had begun in his name (**4.4.2**). The earliest references to anything about Jesus in the Bible are from Paul: a brief statement of second-hand information to be accepted on faith and three paraphrases of things Paul believed Jesus had said but could not have known first-hand (**7.4**).

But historical difficulties are far from the minds of these Conservative writers. Even the realities discovered by scientific investigation must yield, somehow:

> † "In following the paths of science, we may sometimes mistakenly believe that which can not stand in the light of the Bible" (*Päivämies* No. 44, 2009).

For the fundamentalist, God "has revealed Himself clearly in His Word, and, as God cannot be in error, neither can His Word. Hence any apparent contradictions within the book have some theological explanation that God has not yet revealed." That includes any "contradiction with external sources of knowledge, for example, science," which "must by definition be resolved in favour of the holy book, since it, and it alone, is the ultimate criterion of truth" (Herriot 2009, 198).

This next statement summarizes hundreds of years of retreat from a time when questioning the Bible's teachings about the natural world was heretical and dangerous (**4.8.1**):

> ☩ "It is not the purpose of the Bible to answer questions about genetics, medicine, or natural sciences. God has given us His Word for another, nobler purpose. By His Word God shows us how He saves mankind from sin" (VOZ, 7/2009).

The very proposition that mankind *needs* to be saved from sin is inextricably linked to the Bible's narrative about Adam and Eve and the Fall (**4.3.1, 7.3**). So that dodge won't work.

At times, it seems to me that the Bible itself becomes an object of worship:

> ☩ "We believe that the Bible is God's Word. While men have written the Scripture, they have not done so as an expression of their own will, but God has moved them by His Spirit to express His own will. God's Word is not to be treated or regarded in the same manner as man's Word but rather granted our highest esteem.... We believe that God's word is Christian faith's highest authority, and thus Christian faith's guiding principles and doctrine must be examined and evaluated in the light of God's Word" (LLC, *The Bible, God's Word*).

Tom Harpur says that most Protestant Christians "have mistakenly elevated the Bible into an infallible 'paper pope.' Taking a view of the New Testament that would have astonished its authors–whose only Bible was what we call the Old Testament–they have to an alarming degree become Bible worshipers. The Bible has become an idol, assuming the place reserved for God alone" (2003, 100).

The following quote refers to "eyewitness accounts," which is an appeal to history:

> ☩ "Jesus Christ suffered and died and after three days He rose from the dead. The prophets of the Old Testament, like Isaiah in the words above, foretold and described Christ's suffering, death, and resurrection hundreds of years before it happened. Jesus' disciples have left us eyewitness accounts that confirm His fulfillment of those prophecies. Their accounts, recorded in the Bible, are not fabricated tales, as some said then and some say

now, but the disciples sincerely declared what they had heard, seen, and also touched" (LLC, *Christ, the Ransom for Our Sins*).

Actually, there are no eyewitness accounts of Jesus in the Bible. What we find in the Gospels is a great deal of copying from one source, Mark [c. 70 A.D.], which is quite spare in its details and paints a very human picture of Jesus, and another now-missing source "Q" that Matthew and Luke appear to have both used to recount Jesus' sayings. Added onto that are conflicting details in important stories, mistakes about history, geography, and customs of the time, and differing views about the nature of Jesus himself.

The Gospels do not even provide consistent reports of the most important single story of Christianity, the resurrection. It is a miraculous event that carries a heavy burden of proof. So even if the Gospel accounts *were* consistent, it would be hard to consider them anything other than "fabricated tales." Even the Christian authors of the encyclopedic *Early Christianity and its Sacred Literature* acknowledge that it may be very difficult to find any modern historians who would accept the resurrection of Jesus as an attested historical fact (MacDonald and Porter 2000, 7). They quote one historian's critique of the common, theologically motivated assessment that the resurrection was probably historical. How could a critical historian say such a thing "when dealing with an event so initially improbable as the resurrection of a dead man, the two-thousand-year-old narratives of which are limited to the community dedicated to propagating the belief and admittedly full of 'legendary features, contradictions, absurdities, and discrepancies' . . . ?"

MacDonald and Porter ask, as they must to preserve their faith, "Is there a reality of the past that is beyond the scope of the historian's inquiry?" The historian cannot, as a historian, "answer reasonably about the origins of Christian faith, but what of Christians? Is it possible to arrive at some other approach that accounts for Christian origins and is, at the same time, historically responsible?" This they term a "historical-theological approach" (p. 15), and take recourse in the role of faith: "If the historian could prove the unique actions of God in history, there would indeed be no need for faith at all." Yet, it is also true that "even though one cannot prove it historically, to deny the resurrection of Jesus is to deny the very heart of the Christian proclamation" (p. 16).

It is clear that there is a dilemma here. We have professed belief in these astounding events, along with many other things that seem crazy to any objective observer, not because we were convinced by any evidence but because *there is no other choice*. Such faith is not so much an intellectual assent as it is an act of will, as Karen Armstrong was once told by a Jesuit priest. "Christians could accept their essentially incredible tradition only by making a deliberate choice to believe. You could not prove or disprove these doctrines, but you could consciously decide to take them on trust. They might even turn out to be true" (2007, 118). It's an honest statement, at least, but certainly not the kind of thing that would persuade those not already convinced to make drastic changes in their lives and adopt this "essentially incredible tradition" of Christianity. And the "act of will" that is required of those who have already made the "deliberate choice to believe" turns faith into what Price calls "a cognitive work, a matter of managing to believe things that you know and can see are not true in the public reality, the reality *out there*." It is not something one can do "without cheating, suppressing the truth, denying your better judgment with the excuse of 'faith'" (Price 2006b, 137).

4.3.5 Hermeneutics

> *The fundamentalist hears his own voice magnified through the Bible and mistakes it for the word of God.*
>
> —Robert M. Price, *The Reason-Driven Life*

Arch Taylor provides an important conclusion about inerrancy that also leads us into the topic of hermeneutics, the study of how biblical texts are assigned meaning by those who expound upon them. What the "champions of inerrancy" really seem to be defending with their often strained and awkward hermeneutics

> is not the authentic Word of God, but a system of belief and practice of their own devising. Then they search the Scriptures to find proof texts that support their particular view. They make the leap directly from the Bible to their current debate, without considering what the Bible really says. Is the translation they are using an accurate one? Is the original text on which the translation is based dependable? What did those words mean in the time and context in which they were first spoken or written?

How do those words fit into the total context of the biblical canon, including both Old Testament and New? What is the meaning of those words in the light of the full revelation of God in Jesus Christ? When they pull a prooftext out of context and say: "The Bible says ..." they may not be teaching what the Bible–the whole canonical Bible–says, but only what they are forcing one small bit of the Bible to say. [Taylor 2003, 167]

Textual Issues

Luke 17:20-21 is a passage that has great significance for Conservative Laestadianism's claim to be the place where the Kingdom of God is now found:

> And when he was demanded of the Pharisees, when the Kingdom of God should come, he answered them and said, The Kingdom of God cometh not with observation: Neither shall they say, Lo here! or, lo there! for behold, the Kingdom of God is within (ἐντός) you.

The word *entos* (ἐντός) can be translated as either "within" or "among," and the choice has been a point of controversy in Christian theology. "The correct location of the Kingdom of God would seem to be an issue central to Christian theology–so central, in fact, that a resolution of the ἐντός question is imperative, if Christians are truly to be one body of believers" (Marcin 2008, 2).

After doing an initial analysis on the word ἐντός, Marcin says that "it does seem at this point in our analysis that the Kingdom of God is more *within* us than *among* us." But, he continues, "to give a semantic answer– even a tentative one–is not necessarily to capture the full meaning of a word, especially its meaning in the context of so important a scriptural passage" (p. 6). So he continues his analysis, and then concludes as follows:

> Theological preference aside, analyses of the simple meanings of the preposition ἐντός, its adverbial counterparts, its antonym, and its Septuagint usages in the Old Testament leave little doubt but that the Kingdom of God is "within" us, and provide scant support for the notion that the Kingdom is to be understood as being "among" us. [pp. 8-9]

That is certainly the meaning that Origen took from the passage: "The Savior does not say to everyone, 'The Kingdom of God is within you.' For, in sinners, the kingdom of sin exists. Without any ambiguity, either the Kingdom of God reigns in our hearts, or the kingdom of sin" (*Homilies on Luke*, No. 36; Lienhard 1996, 197). The original Greek was Origen's mother tongue, so his interpretation is hard to disregard.

So is the fact that both Luther and Laestadius followed that interpretation. As discussed in **5.2**, Luther referred to this passage in defense of his position that "there is no locality, place or anything external in the kingdom of God; it is not here or there, but the spirit *within us*" (PE 3, 395, emphasis added). Similarly, Laestadius explained the mystical experiences of his contemporaries as being a result of the kingdom of heaven being "within man" [Luke 17:21]:

> ✝ The Savior says: the kingdom of heaven is within you. If now a man's eyes are open to see this kingdom of heaven, he has in truth begun to enjoy the salvation which this viewing brings with it. And to the extent that the philosopher cannot prove that the kingdom of heaven is in someplace outside of man, it must be *within man*. (*VCW*, 47)

Laestadius referred to the "within you" interpretation of Luke 17:21 in an 1850 sermon:

> ✝ If now the kingdom of God is within us, then we should strive after this, that the kingdom of God would come into our heart, that we would come to feel the power of the kingdom of God in our hearts, which is to be the temple of God and God's dwelling place. And how else could this come into our hearts, if not in that way, that we strive after it, that we first become Christians and children of God, so the kingdom of God would come to us and we would become a partaker of the greatest power and honor of the kingdom of God. When now the Saviour tells His disciples to seek the kingdom of God and His righteousness, it signifies that they must strive after Christianity, or be diligent to beg, to hasten, to strive, to cry out and to knock upon the door of heaven, and to pray to God that he, through true penitence, repentance, and living faith, could receive his sins forgiven, would become a partaker of God's grace, and thus would find the kingdom of God in his own heart. [Sermon for 15th Sunday after Trinity]

Later, however, Conservatives found themselves having to defend the doctrine that God's chosen are found in an identifiable group on Earth. The less preferred "among you" translation was what the 1776 Finnish Bible chose ("Jumalan valtakunta on *teidän keskellänne*"), and it became one of their tools for doing so. For example, Heikki Jussila argued with an ecumenically minded opponent about the Luke 17:21 passage and claimed that even a seven year-old child in "living Christianity" would understand that the Pharisees Jesus was addressing did not have "the kingdom of God inwardly in" them. Rather, "All the preachers in Christianity have explained the words of Jesus according to the old translation" (Jussila 1948, 127).

Recently I heard an LLC preacher read the KJV text with its more accurate but less doctrinally convenient "within you" translation and then go on to build his sermon around the "among you" alternative as if *that* is what the book in front of him actually said. If you are going to base your theology on a particular interpretation of a word–one that contrasts with what your two most prominent spiritual predecessors expounded with very different views of things–shouldn't you at least let your audience know what's going on?

How can it ever be the case that erroneous biblical scholarship is propounded by God's Kingdom, the "pillar and ground of truth," as it is often called? Yet that is what Conservative Laestadian preachers do all too often. One example that I find particularly vexing is the continued sermonizing on the *Pericope Adulterae*, the story of the woman caught in adultery (John 8:3-11), by preachers who ought to know better. This passage didn't appear in manuscripts until the 5th century, and is notoriously inauthentic. Yet it remains a favorite text, treated as God's Holy Word with no distinction from any other part of the supposedly inerrant Bible resting on the pulpit. Another example is this exposition on the Trinity:

> † "The leading theologians of [Finland] and princes of the church do not believe in the trinity of God as is the Jehovah Witnesses' fashion. Therefore, they have left out of their Bibles the verse: 'For there are three that bear record in heaven, the Father, the Word, and the Holy Ghost: and these three are one' [1 John 5:7]" (VOZ, 6/1979).

There is actually a very good reason why others "have left out of their Bibles" this verse: it is simply not authentic. The *Comma Johanneum*, as it is called, does not appear in any manuscripts until the 7th century. It's one of the more notorious of several cases where scribes made additions to the text of the New Testament. I find it especially tiresome to see evil motives assigned to the viewpoints and actions of those in "the world" when they turn out to have a sound factual basis.

Allegory and Symbolism

"To play with allegories in Christian doctrine, is dangerous," Luther warns in his *Table Talk* (§765). "The words, now and then, sound well and smoothly, but they are to no purpose. They serve well for such preachers that have not studied much, who know not rightly how to expound the histories and texts, whose leather is too short, and will not stretch." Despite his urging that "we should accustom ourselves to remain by the clear and pure text," Luther could not resist making use of allegory himself. Ironically, he provides one immediately after his *Table Talk* warning in response to a question by Melanchthon about the theological significance of an eagle's nesting behavior.

It's been going on for a long time. Philo of Alexandria [20 B.C.-50 A.D.] "employed the allegorical method to explain away the more unsavory aspects of the Hebrew scriptures in order to make them palatable to Hellenistic sensibilities" (Stark 2011, 32-33). Origen's homilies on Leviticus are awash in quotation marks that he uses to wrap his Old Testament text in the gloss of his New Testament understanding. Here's an example: "When it says that [the bullock] is burned up 'with the dung and the intestines' [Lev 4:11], see if perhaps this body of human nature is not figuratively called dung in comparison to the heavenly body" (Homily 2, §3; from Barkley 1990, 65).

Apostle Paul did his share of allegorizing right in the New Testament. An example is where he treated Abraham's fathering of a bastard son by a slave woman as part of an allegory about the old and new covenants. Instead of being the powerless sexual pawn of a barren old woman desperate to appease her husband's patriarchal need for an heir, the slave woman becomes "mount Sinai in Arabia, and answereth to Jerusalem which now is, and is in bondage with her children" (Gal 4:25). And just like that, the profane becomes sacred, the sordid becomes spiritual.

In the hands of a creative expositor, there is seemingly no limit to what can be accomplished by allegory. The sacred text is just brimming with symbolism if you look closely enough. Stark cites Paul's treatment of Deut 25:4 ("Thou shalt not muzzle the ox when he treadeth out the corn," right after a bit of instruction about beating the loser of an adjudicated civil dispute "before his face" with no more than forty lashes). That, it turns out, was just what Paul needed to show that those preaching the gospel are entitled to get their living by it. He concludes that the ancient agricultural advice was really written for the sake of his brethren, "that he that ploweth should plow in hope; and that he that thresheth in hope should be partaker of his hope" (1 Cor 9:10). Stark calls that an astounding claim: "God does not care about oxen; the historical-grammatical meaning of the text is of no concern to God or to us–that is not its usefulness as scripture. The real reason that passage is in the text is that it was intended for the last days, a message to the Pauline churches" (2011, 31).

There's been no shortage of creativity among Conservative expositors, either:

> ✝ In Rev 12, John is "looking into the future at how living Christianity would be born. Indeed, you have heard awakened souls crying in remorse over their sins, as here the woman, or the Lord's congregation, cried as she travailed in birth. The congregation is a travailing woman through which Jesus brings forth a manchild, or a new man. The old man becomes ill when the new man must be born. The woman's crown of twelve stars signifies the light of the gospel, the doctrine of the apostles. Man's wisdom is the moon which is dark of itself, and thus is to be put under the feet, if the gospel is to enter the heart by faith and a new man is to be born. As the woman is clothed with the sun, so the church is clothed with the Sun of Righteousness, Jesus Christ" (Raattamaa, [1897], from Kulla 1993, 68).

> ✝ The greater meaning in the covenant of the rainbow "was the grace covenant of God which He renewed to His believers. The rainbow in the clouds was a sign of this covenant," and that "cloud is a picture of the grace cloud which rains drops of grace to moisten the dry hearts of believers" (Saari 1968, 11).

> ✝ "The burning of the bricks of Babel portrays nothing else than a strange fire or a false doctrine. It burns the clay brittle, hard, and durable. The false doctrine with a false spirit also burns man's conscience into a hardened condition" (Saari 1968, 22).

† "As God took one rib of Adam and of it made Eve, likewise the Church of God is taken of Christ" (VOZ, 5/1974).

Stark notes that it "is much easier to be an 'inerrantist' when the intended meaning of the original author can be disregarded." When you use "allegorical interpretations which have the effect of ascribing some meaning to a text other than the meaning intended by the author" (2011, 32), your "carnal mind" can readily dispense with problems like Jacob's impersonation and defrauding of his brother Esau:

† "It may seem to the carnal mind that Jacob did wrong by taking the blessing. But before God, the blessings of God always belong to the Christians, the people of God. It is that spiritual Church of God here on earth, the Mother Rebecca, who prepares and makes ready the savory meat for her son Jacob. She also does the clothing of her son. The goodly raiment of her firstborn son was with her in the house (in God's kingdom)" (VOZ, 7/1975).

Here we see some of that allegorical interpretation sanitizing the story in Acts 5:1-11. God kills a married couple for not coming clean about holding back some of their wealth from the church. Can anybody imagine a preacher threatening such an outrage to reluctant dues-payers today? But we learn from this article published in the midst of the "caretaking" hysteria of the 1970s that it was really all about being honest and obedient to the congregation of God:

† "Ananias and Sapphira had sold a possession and decided to give part of the price to the apostles to be used for common needs. They did not tell the apostles that they had hidden a portion of it for their own needs," and were struck dead. The "congregation of God cannot be deceived even if an individual is. Ananias and Saphhira had fallen into the sin of greed of which the Word of God says that it is the root of all evil (1 Tim 6:9-10). The temporal possessions had formed into a true god for them. With the help of these goods, in form of gift giving, they could even care for the needs of undying souls. The Giver of all gifts, the blessing God, was forgotten." They "began to see the fellowship of the believers in a different light than before. They did not see God's kingdom as the foundation and pillar of truth anymore. They did not believe that the Spirit of truth guides the congregation and the decisions thereof. Human failings in the congregation became apparent to them and when this happened

they did not find it important to be obedient to the voice of the congregation. It was not hard to deceive the congregation anymore even to the point of telling lies" (*Siionin Lähetyslehti*, 2/1976).

Similarly, Jacob was really thinking about Laestadian heresies when he came up with a scheme for getting some of what was coming to him from his recalcitrant boss:

> † "[W]hen the flocks of Laban and Jacob were divided, as divisions have often been made, the 'spotted sheep' and those which were a little white were left in Jacob's flock. And such still is the flock of God's children. Not all the sheep are pure white and spotless" (VOZ, 11/1976).

Even in a crowded field of highly imaginative allegory, this one stands out:

> † "Spiritually, we understand the heavens [that 'declare the glory of God,' Psa 19:1] represent God's children. "Heavens" here is plural. We could say that the heavens represent the local congregations, all of which are united. That same sun of God's grace which is mentioned later in this text goes through its circuits." The person who serves in whatever capacity is "serving in the firmament," which "shows the handiwork of God" (Quentin Ruonavaara, sermon given 1978).

The following quote casts the deafness and dumbness healed by Jesus in Mark 7:31-37 as the enemy's work in preventing the sinner of first century Palestine from engaging in the act of confession. Besides being far-fetched, the comparison suffers from the fact that confession was not destined to become part of Christian practice for quite some time yet (**5.1.2**).

> † "When we look specifically at these sicknesses of deafness and dumbness" healed by Jesus "in a spiritual sense, we see the effects of the work of the enemy of our souls. He, who has been a liar from the beginning, is always attempting to close the mouth so that a person would not be able to speak of the sins that he has fallen into" (VOZ, 9/1990).

In explaining Isaiah 38:8, when God made a shadow go back ten steps on a stairway, Uljas focuses on a spiritual interpretation. That allows him to avoid dealing with the overwhelming scientific and historical evidence that the actual event never could have occurred:

> ✝ "Hezekiah, himself, had experienced that time was not in man's control. It was just as difficult for him to understand, as it is for us, that time and the laws of nature are ruled by God. It is a blessed and marvelous thing that the Sun of Grace moves counterclockwise and wipes away previously committed sins" (2000, 118).

That understated story is possibly the most astounding one of the entire Bible when you know, unlike the ancient author, that the Earth is round and spins on its axis to make the Sun appear to be moving across the sky. See the discussion of the passage in **6.21**, and of Joshua 10:13 with a similar miracle, in **6.6**.

It is common to hear the Gospels' healing narratives being linked with the forgiveness of sins, as in the following two quotes:

> ✝ "Jesus proclaimed the gospel message of the kingdom of God to the sick: 'Your sins are forgiven unto you.' It was a common understanding at that time that physical sicknesses were caused by sin or evil spirits. The scribes held that only God can forgive man's sins. To them, therefore, Jesus' proclamation of the forgiveness of sins was blasphemy. It is because of unbelief that people are unable to overcome the powers of sin. They are tied to the bed of sin which is sinful life" (VOZ, 10/2002).

> ✝ "Unbelief was the greatest sickness during the time of Jesus' life on this earth, and it is still the greatest today. When unforgiven sin weighs on the heart of man, it can cause the same deafness and dumbness that plagued the man in our text [Mk 7:31-37]. Ears do not hear the call of the Father, and the tongue becomes halting and made of clay" (VOZ, 8/2007).

The first quote reveals some ambivalence about literalism. By acknowledging that it "was a common understanding that physical sicknesses were caused by sin or evil spirits," isn't the quoted writer also recognizing that we no longer really share that understanding? (See the discussion of Mark 9:17-29 in **7.1**.)

Luke 18:9-14 tells us that the publican in his self-abnegation at the temple was "justified," which is contrary to the Conservative belief that the publican still had to go find someone to proclaim absolution to him:

> † "It is related [in Luke 18:9-14] that the publican went to his house 'justified' rather than the Pharisee, implying that he was justifiable. Jesus does not say that he was saved or that he was made righteous by humbling his heart. With a humbled heart, the publican still needed to 'seek the kingdom of God,' as Jesus teaches" (VOZ, 8/2007).

But how can saying someone is "justified" imply that they really aren't yet? Finding that the plain words of a text conflict with its present-day doctrine doesn't give the church a warrant to just go and read all those additional caveats into it. At least not if Luther's *sola scriptura* is to mean anything.[20]

"The Holy Spirit is the plainest writer and speaker in heaven and earth," Luther wrote in his 1521 *Answer to Emser of Leipzig*, "and therefore His words cannot have more than one, and that the very simplest, sense, which we call the literal, ordinary, natural sense." Even though "all of God's works and creatures are living signs and words of God, . . . we are not on that account to say that the Scriptures or the Word of God have more than one meaning." He cautioned that it "is much surer and safer to abide by the words in their simple sense" (*PE* 3, 350). In 1524, he famously criticized those expositors who "very frequently miss the sense of their text and twist it like a nose of wax to suit their fancy" (*To the Councilmen of All Cities in Germany*, from *PE* 4,

---

20. Regarding a similar issue of justification without absolution, Luther in his *Smalcald Articles* [1537] says that Cornelius, "living among the Jews, had heard long before about the coming Messiah, through whom he was righteous before God (Acts 10:1-2). In such faith, his prayers and alms were acceptable to God (since Luke calls him devout and God-fearing)." This was due to the Word about Jesus having come to him and him believing it. When Peter finally came to him, Luther says, Cornelius "must now know that he is saved by the present Messiah and must not, with the Jewish people, deny or persecute him" (Article 8; McCain 2005, 281). It's an imaginative way to reconcile the Bible's designation of Cornelius as righteous without diminishing the role of Christ as redeemer. But it doesn't begin to account for Conservative Laestadianism's additional requirement of a personal proclamation from a believer.

116). But, it must be said, he was not immune to Scripture-twisting, as when he glossed over the brutality of Psalm 137:9.

Price criticizes all this as "plumbing the depths of the Bible." What an irony it is, he notes, that "the fundamentalist champions of the Bible seem to care nothing for the text, but only for those doctrines and devotional 'promises' they pry out of it." (2006b, 348). We see yet another example of such plumbing with a quote concerning the staff that Moses held above his head–a token of individual power and leadership in the ancient world. It is a case where, as Price notes generally, the "Bible does not actually deal the requisite slogans and the desired devotional idiom," and the quoted writer "rewrite[s] the text so that it does" (p. 348). That gives us "the staff of God's Word," i.e., a symbol of conformity to particular interpretations of carefully selected biblical texts:

> † "Moses knew that God was faithful and that He would deliver them from [the battle against Amelek, Exodus 17:9-13]. In order for them to win, however, he needed to remain watchful and needed to hold the staff above his head. It is the same in the battle that we face in God's kingdom today. We need to remain watchful in faith and hold the staff of God's Word higher than anything else" (VOZ, 5/2008).

4.3.6 Value and Limits

> *Consider, too, the fact that Jehovah's organization alone, in all the Earth, is directed by God's holy spirit or active force . . . To it alone God's Sacred Word, the Bible, is not a sealed book.*

— *The Watchtower*, from Diane Wilson, *Awakening of a Jehovah's Witness*

The Bible sits somewhat uneasily on a pedestal in Conservative Laestadianism. It is revered as the Word of God, yet the reader cannot really depend on its words for instruction. Instead, God expects obedience to whatever "faith" and "God's Children" say that it says:

> † "The Bible does not ask us what we consider to be the most important or what we would regard as foremost in our life. The Word of God shows us that, and God expects all of us to follow the Lord Jesus in the obedience of faith and in the flock of His children" (*By Faith*, 8).

Herriot identifies five distinctive features of fundamentalist movements, one of which is the belief of fundamentalists "that their *holy book*, through its interpreters or read directly, has supreme authority over what to believe and how to act. It reveals God's will for mankind." One of the other distinctive features, however, is that "fundamentalists' interpretation of the holy book is *selective*. They choose specific ideas from it and emphasise them, often changing their traditional meaning when they do so. Such selective adaptation of the holy book provides justification for resistance strategies and tactics" (2009, 2).[21]

That "selective adaptation" is not done so much in the mind of an individual believer reading the text on his own and wondering what to make of it. Rather, it is the task of the preacher behind the pulpit, who begins with the words of the text and then uses his sermon, under the imprimatur of divine revelation, to lead those words toward doctrinal conclusions that have been firmly fixed in place already. Two quotes of my sample, one quite early and one very recent, illustrate the viewpoint that the Bible is "closed" and "locked" without such divine revelation:

> † "The Bible is a closed book, if the Lord, himself, in His grace does not open it" (Havas [1933], 37).

> † "[T]he real author of Scripture is the Holy Spirit who worked through the holy men of God to produce a written declaration of God's relationship to, and plan for the salvation of man. As a consequence it cannot be understood or interpreted in the way that God intends without the key of the Holy Spirit to unlock the otherwise mysterious and locked book of the Bible" (VOZ, 3/2007).

It is just like the claim made by the Christian Convention Church that the Bible is "a dead history book if one is without the Spirit" (Lewis

---

21. The other three distinctive features of fundamentalism (Herriot 2009, 2) are *reactivity*—"their religion is under mortal threat from the secularism of the modern world, and they are fighting back. They may resist in different ways, but they are all essentially oppositional; they have to have an enemy"; *dualism*—"they conceive of the world in binary opposites: God and the Devil, good and evil, truth and falsehood, etc."; and *millenialism*—"expecting God to fully establish His rule over the world at some future time." Clearly, Conservative Laestadianism has all of these features as well as the two discussed in the main text: reliance on a holy book and selective interpretation of it.

2004, 80), that it only comes alive if "it is revealed through a worker because the seed is not living until spoken by a true minister who is carrying out Jesus' command for the apostles" (p. 4). Like Conservative Laestadians, that group likes to use the scriptural phrase "faith cometh by hearing." The Christian Conventionists "don't believe that anyone could be born again simply by reading the Scripture nor through a heart felt prayer to Jesus Christ to receive salvation" (p. 4). Uljas says much the same thing, of course with a very different idea of just who it is one must be hearing:

> † "The reading of God's Word is a good thing. However, the Bible teaches that faith comes by hearing and accepting the gospel. Study and knowledge of the written Word of God is necessary for us, because it leads us to seek Christ and His grace kingdom. It also teaches a child of God to grow in the knowledge of God and the Savior, Jesus Christ" (Uljas 2000, 25-26).

Luther showed his confidence in the Bible's value to the individual Christian reader by translating it into simple, clear German that everyday people could read, men and women alike. (I find it easier to read than a modern German novel, but perhaps that's due to my focus in learning the language.) He also criticized the idea of Scripture being obscure or ambiguous: "Are we not obscure and ambiguous enough in ourselves, without an increase of it by obscurity, ambiguity, and darkness being sent down unto us from heaven?" (*The Bondage of the Will*, §36).

The remaining quotes of my sample, presented chronologically as usual, emphasize the value of the holy book without too much concern about divine revelation of it:

> † "Dear brothers and sisters, how could we despise God's holy book wherein has been revealed to us such great treasures. From the Bible we have learned that God in His righteousness punishes sinners with everlasting death. When He by His word made Himself known to us, we began to despair and fear. It was grace to us to comprehend our wretched state in the reflection of the law. But what would we have drawn for a cover for our wretchedness if God had not through His word revealed to us our Lord Jesus as a Savior.... God's holy book, the Bible, is an invitation to the wedding of the King's son where the bridegroom, Jesus, shows and reveals His love towards His bride.

. . With heartfelt desire and full confidence we study the Bible at home and at services which testifies God's good will to men's salvation, testifies of our bridegroom Jesus and of the reward that awaits us at the end of the journey" (Matti Suo [1895], from *Greetings of Peace*, 7/1952).

Indeed, this quote directly criticizes the understanding that the Bible is a "dead letter":

† "In the understanding of some, the word of the Bible is a dead letter and it comes alive only when persons who have received the Holy Spirit explain it. For if the word of the Bible were living, they would have received life by reading it. But since they have not received peace or life from it by reading, they have drawn the conclusion that it is a dead letter. And even Paul says, 'The letter killeth, but the spirit giveth life' (2 Cor 3:6). But if the word of the Bible were a dead letter, how then could there be a power to kill in it, as the words say, 'The letter killeth'? It does not say that the letter is dead but that in the letter itself there is that killing power" (Matti Suo, *Siionin Lähetyslehti* [1919], from Hepokoski 2002b, 13).

These next authors offer the refreshing view that reading of the Bible is important for its own sake. The first quote even notes that scriptural knowledge can help guard against "misleading word phrases and explanations" that one might hear from an erring preacher:

† "We should not discontinue reading the Bible even though we do not understand it and it does not remain in our memory. We have often experienced how God through His Holy Spirit reminds and reveals His word when He sees necessary. . . . With what would the Christian, God's child, war against the onslaughts of Satan, if there did not exist the word of the Lord, that two edged sword, Eph. 6:17. Satan attacks from all sides and in all places. With false spiritualism and freedom of the flesh. There are former separations and new ones will come, Matt. 24:5, Acts 20:30. A preacher, in whom we have confidence and whom we love, can get lost and if we did not have the written word of God in our memory, and did not read it, then with misleading word phrases and explanations, we can be brought easily astray. We take modes and manners that are not in accord with God's

word. For that reason let us keep the Lord's word dear. Let us read it!" (Eino Rimpiläinen, *Greetings of Peace*, 3/1955)

† "All scripture has been written by the holy influence of God. God has in His great love and grace given gifts to His followers, to put down His word, which is there for our instruction and study. We should be diligent in reading and following the Scriptures, for that is our source of strength in this wicked world. If this cultivation of the word of God, reading and hearing should end, the strength in our soul would also cease.... Our doctrine is grounded in the Holy Word of God. All that is necessary for the salvation of our souls is contained in this book" (VOZ, 1/1975).

† "Dear brothers and sisters, it is so important for us to know the Scriptures, for the devil is as a roaring lion walking about, seeking whom he may devour (1 Pet 5:8). God's Word is the voice of God from heaven" (Elmer Alajoki, presentation given 1994).

† "Dear young believers, do not forget what a treasure you have in your home when you have the word of God there. Many of you have your own Bibles. Do not let them sit neglected on the bookshelf. When we examine how we spend our time, we find that we have the time to do those things that we really want to do and to read those books and other materials that we enjoy reading. Let's find time to read and to study the word of God" (Jim Frantti, presentation given 1999).

he reality, however, is that few believers read much of the Bible at all. When I did so and raised questions about what I was finding, it resulted in concerns that I was not "asking God to help me" in my reading, whatever that is supposed to mean. "Fundamentalists do not typically read and interpret the Bible on their own, leading private Christian lives. Rather the church group is considered vital and the minister or Bible group leader essential for correct interpretation of 'God's word'" (Winell 1993, 78).

4.4 Spiritual Entities

> *Everywhere in the history of revelation God embodies himself for us. His spirit came in the form of a dove and of the fiery tongues of Pentecost. And God still embodies himself for us. The Holy Spirit comes to us and brings Christ to us through the external, physical, sensible means of the word, of the human voice, and of the sacraments. All these words and sacraments are his veils and clothing, his masks and disguises with which he covers himself so that we may bear and comprehend him.*
>
> —Paul Althaus, The Theology of Martin Luther

4.4.1 The Father

> *Theology winds up with a God who thunders in his petty irritation against helpless, hapless mortals, reducing them to masochistic servitude if they hope to escape the ultimate doom of eternal torture.*
>
> —Robert M. Price, The Reason-Driven Life

For many centuries, Christians have been saying, "I believe in God the Father almighty, creator of heaven and earth." But that brief summation is just the merest hint of all the myriad ways humans have described and characterized their vision of the Deity since they first started leaving records of him, or them.

At first, the Old Testament God was *Elohim*, one member of a pantheon ("Let us make man in our image, after our likeness," Gen 1:26) who rested after a hard week's work (Gen 2:2). Soon the Genesis account begins to use *Yahweh Elohim*, "the LORD God," but vestiges of early anthropomorphism and polytheism remain: The LORD God strolls around Eden in the cool of the day (Gen 3:8), worries about man's godlike status and potential immortality after the Fall ("the man is become as one of us, to know good and evil: and now, lest he put forth his hand, and take also of the tree of life, and eat, and live for ever," Gen 3:22), chats with Cain (Gen 3:6-15), and has sons who intermarry with human women (Gen 6:2). He watches the humans' efforts to reach heaven with concern and finally says (to whom, if not one or more fellow gods?), "Come, let Us go down and there confuse their language"

(Gen 11:2-7; biblical scholars have plausibly argued that this was done to prevent the humans from reaching the divine realm). He has extensive discussions with Abram (Gen 13-15). In Gen 18, Yahweh appears to Abram personally as one of three men and stands beside him to haggle about how many righteous there must be in Sodom in order for it to be spared.

In these first Old Testament conceptions, Yahweh was remarkably like the "'primitive' gods of hunter-gatherer societies and chiefdoms" that preceded him: "strikingly human—with supernatural power, to be sure, but not with infinite power" (Wright 2009, 103). "Early affirmations of devotion to Yahweh don't single him out for being the only god, just for being the best god for the Israelites, the one you should worship" (p. 104).

As ancient Israelite religion matured and moved away from its polytheistic roots, the God of Israel became so exhalted that his holy name could not even be uttered. When he introduced himself to Moses in the burning bush, centuries after the events of Genesis, he did so with the enigmatic and all-encompassing statement, "I am that I am," and commanded Moses to describe him to the children of Israel as "the LORD God of your fathers, the God of Abraham, the God of Isaac, and the God of Jacob, hath sent me unto you: this is my name for ever, and this is my memorial unto all generations" (Exodus 3:14-15). Later still, it was understood that God knows and sees all, an idea that for the writer of Psalm 139:1-6 was "too wonderful for me; it is high, I cannot attain unto it."

Now we have a God who is unfathomable, beyond human comprehension. In the lofty (and late) words of John 4:24, "God is a Spirit: and they that worship him must worship him in spirit and in truth." But "we're pretty sure He's against birth control" (Price 2011), and we still seem quite certain about many other aspects of God's views and personality. An article in the September 1998 *Voice of Zion* informs us that,

> † "above all, God is a gracious, good, and loving God" (VOZ, 9/1998).

A 1999 presentation given by John Lehtola summarizes the various other attributes that God is supposed to have:

† "God is a spirit, who is eternal. He is the first and last. He is all-knowing, all-seeing, and everywhere. God is all-mighty, righteous, holy, and not to be ridiculed."

As we will see, however, it is not possible for any creator of the "heaven and earth" we know about to have all of these attributes, any more than it is possible for a circle to have corners. Theologians often resort to the claim that such combinations–like an omnipotent and omnibenevolent God creating a world full of evil–are *possible* for God but beyond our understanding. But then *what they are saying* is likewise beyond understanding, their words having no useful content (Price 2011). Yet, as we will see in this section, there is little reluctance to offer such words, characterizing God in all sorts of all-too human ways.

Many readers who are unused to hearing sacred matters discussed with anything but gauzy reverence will find it offensive, even arrogant for me to offer an analysis of the Almighty. But what I am really scrutinizing is not God but the all-too human attempts that his spokesmen and apologists have made to characterize the Creator of the Universe. And that, I submit, is bound to fail as much as a dog's speculations on the mind of Newton, as Darwin famously put it.

Omnipotence

In a slim, apparently self-published book that is rough around the edges but full of profundity, Matthew Taylor explains a fundamental problem with the idea of omnipotence:

> Absolute omnipotence is absolute autonomy and completely self satisfied. It needs nothing and is mutually exclusive to the notion of adding anything to its existence. The notion of absolute omnipotence is mutually exclusive to terms such as "need," "want" or "desire" and adjectives such as "offended" or "jealous," which imply needs indicative of impotence, not omnipotence, and weakness, not power. [Taylor 2005, 33]

If God has any of those needy attributes–which the Bible does not hesitate to assign to him even in the New Testament–he simply cannot be omnipotent. Taylor also restates the ancient Epicurean problem of evil (**4.9.1**) to show the impossibility of an omnipotent creator: "A perfect and omnipotent being (is one) that creates perfect things. The universe has imperfect things. As a consequence, a perfect and omnipotent being did not create the universe" (p. 41, emphasis omitted).

How can perfection yield imperfection without being imperfect itself? The "heretics" with whom Clement of Alexandria argued in his *Stromata* artfully posed the question with regard to whether "Adam was created perfect or imperfect." If "imperfect, how could the work of a perfect God–above all, that work being man–be imperfect? And if perfect, how did [Adam] transgress the commandments?" (Book 6, Ch. 12).

Taylor anticipates the argument that "an omnipotent God can perform as a weak God if he *wants* to," but calls that "a tribute to man's own mental inability to grasp what he at first proposes, i.e., the consequences of omnipotence and its mutual exclusions" (pp. 41-42). "Omnipotence can never be unsatisfied," but "creation is the fulfillment of desire" (pp. 33-34). In addition, being omniscient about the future means that you are helpless to change it. If you did change it, you wouldn't have correctly forseen the outcome! The omnipotent ability to choose whether to make a change in course defeats the omniscient ability to know *whether it ultimately gets changed* or not.

It would also be deceptive for a perfect creator to make himself look bad and then demand that people worship him as perfect. And the suffering produced by the universe's imperfections make it impossible (not merely difficult to understand) for an omnipotent God to also be omnibenevolent.

These questions are not imposing human limits on an omnipotent God. Rather, they ask whether the *very idea* of an omnipotent God is supportable, as a basic logical premise or in combination with other postulated characteristics of the Deity.

Judges 1 provides an example right from the Bible of how God's omnipotence has been limited to human imagination. Yahweh commands Judah to go fight the Caananites, and Judah does so in fine fashion. He slays 10,000 men whom Yahweh "delivered into their hand." He and his troops slay Sheshai, and Ahiman, and Talmai, and then the inhabitants of Debir. They utterly destroy Zephath, and take Gaza, Askelon, and Ekron along with their coastal areas. "And the LORD [Yahweh] was with Judah, and he drave out the inhabitants of the mountain; but *could not drive out the inhabitants of the valley, because they had chariots of iron*" (Judges 1:19). God was with Judah for all that slaughter and conquest of tens of thousands, but the divinely directed power could not overcome a lousy bunch of iron chariots.

Here is a statement that is not just implausible, but simply impossible to reconcile with the view that God desires for all men to seek him (**4.9.3**):

> † "God's power is much greater than any other, and [it] can humiliate the powers of man and of Satan. . . . In the world there is denial of the power of God, and there is also denial of the powers of Satan" (VOZ, 3/2010).

If God's power is greater than any other, including man in his unbelief and Satan in his constant efforts to thwart God's work, then *nothing* can stand in the way of his wishes or efforts. And it certainly seems odd for an omnipotent God who is jealous and demands preeminence over all other gods (Exod 34:14) to be permitting a denial of his power to pervade the world. If he is "not to be ridiculed," as Lehtola asserted **above**, then why does God put up with so much impiety, unbelief, and downright mockery in today's society?

It's no answer to claim that the impious mockers have it coming to them in eternity. Those unbelievers just don't believe the threat–that's their whole point in many cases. And an infinite punishment that is dished out to the jeering and praying alike is so broad and incomprehensible as to be meaningless. Christopher Hitchens is supposedly going to roast in hell for writing books like *God is Not Great*, but so are Anne Frank, Mohandas Ghandi, and Mother Teresa.

Omniscience

Closely related to being able to *do* everything is the ability to *know* everything. What good is Superman's ability to lift the sinking ship out of the water if he can't use his telescopic vision to spot the faraway crisis in the first place? And so, even before God called out to Adam and Eve as they cowered guiltily behind some bushes in Eden, he had the whole plan of what to do about the situation figured out:

> † "Before the beginning of this world, God decided on a specific time when a savior would be born in the form of man, and when He would begin His ministry" (VOZ, 12/1999).

The whole drama of the Fall played out with nobody watching but the actors, and to no more purpose than an author reading his own book.

Omniscience is not a property of God that we see in the Old Testament. God learned of events and changed course based on them: "When God saw their deeds, that they turned from their wicked way, then God relented concerning the calamity which He had declared He would bring upon them" (Jonah 3:10, NASB). He had regrets: "The LORD was sorry that He had made man on the earth, and He was grieved in His heart" (Gen 6:6, NASB). He felt the need to inflict trials on Abraham (Gen 22) and Job to determine their faithfulness. He is still doing so, according to this writer:

> † "God tries our faith to see if we really love Him but does not tempt us as James writes, 'Let no man say when he is tempted, I am tempted of God . . .'" (VOZ, 2/2002).

But, according to this next writer,

> † "God sees into the heart of man and knows even the most secret deeds, even though no other person knows of them. God knows a person's sins and requires that he answers for them before Him one day. In that hearing, one can neither cover his deeds, nor transfer the blame to someone else. Only those whose sins have been forgiven in the gospel of God's kingdom will receive a sentence of freedom" (VOZ, 9/2002).

Guys, you need to do a better job of staying "on message" here. If God knows *everything*, it doesn't take much contemplation or "wordly philosophy" to see that he does not need "to see if" *anything* is true. He certainly doesn't need to inflict trials on man to see what happens, like a rat in some lab experiment, if he "sees into the heart of man and knows even the most secret deeds."

The idea of an omniscient creator is also incompatible with the "blind, mechanical, foresightless sifting-and-duplicating process that has produced the exquisite design of organisms by natural selection" (Dennett 2007, 79-80). Haught, as always, is ready to admit this theological difficulty of evolutionary theory, even as he struggles to find ways to reconcile with the undeniable reality of it:

> [I]n order for natural selection to bring about so many new species, an enormous period of time has to pass, indeed, many

millions of years. Thus, at least according to human calendrical standards, by taking so much time, evolution looks inefficient and wasteful. Wouldn't an infinite wisdom, if it exists, do a more efficient job of engineering life's diversity? Furthermore, even with all the delay, death, and bloodshed that evolution entails, the varieties that survive are never impeccably engineered anyway. Adaptation is never perfect. So, isn't evolution proof that ultimately nature rests not on divine providence, but on an abyss of absurdity? How can one expect to make any theological sense of it at all? [Haught 2010, 33]

Unchanging and Eternal

Uljas describes God as timeless and eternal:

> † "God has always existed. He has neither beginning nor end, and time does not bind Him. Even the fourth dimension is freely in His use. He is also unchanging, for change belongs to time. God has His own time. It is not the same as man's time. It cannot be measured with our clocks or calendars" (2000, 115).

I have the same criticism of that statement as I did of one by Lampi (**4.3.3**) about God being the same in the Old Testament as in the New. I have already noted in this section that the Old Testament God had an all-too-human personality, and will discuss that at some length in the chapter-by-chapter details of **Section 6**. Besides the human appearances, emotions, and actions already mentioned, here are some more: God hardened Pharaoh's heart so that he would have an excuse to rain plagues onto innocent Egyptians and give Moses some good stories to tell his son and grandson (Exodus 10:1-2). He gets so angry at the Israelites' making a golden calf that he asks to be left alone and threatens to destroy them all, but Moses convinces God to change his mind about the harm which he said he would do to his people (Exodus 32:10-14). He smells soothing aromas of burnt offerings (Genesis 8:21, Numbers 15:3).

Jason Long observed "that God was consistently angry and vengeful for what appear to be petty reasons. He even threatened to kill people for excuses most of us would consider insane if offered by an ordinary earthly individual" (2005, 7). Seeing that for myself over the course of months of Old Testament study was not a pleasant experience. On many days I would get up from my desk in disgust and think that there's just no way I could worship a God who carried out the kinds of atrocities I was reading about. But the next day, I would sit back down again and search among the ancient words for the loving, caring God I thought I knew from my Sunday School days. He didn't show up much. Instead, what I found, to my continual disappointment, were mostly descriptions of a Deity who

> exhibits immature rage when no one pays attention to him; he makes people suffer for what others have done; he has no regard for human life; and he tortures decent people for such reasons as winning bets with Satan. If we were to extract this behavior into human terms, we would most likely draw a comparison with that of a spoiled child. Because of an obvious state of fear and panic over similar reports heard by authors of the ancient Hebrew scriptures, they wrote and sang praises to this terrible creature thinking that such measures might assist in helping them escape his unconscionable wrath. [Long 2005, 106]

By the time we get to the later Old Testament books (e.g., Jonah) and then the New Testament, God seems to have been rehabilitated somewhat. Long finds it suspicious that "God conveniently ceased his murdering and slave driving when modern philosophers, enlightened thinking, and accurate historical records began to appear" (p. 106). It was enough to make the second-century theologian Marcion deny that the Christian God was even the same entity as Yahweh of the Old Testament. Ignatius condemned him as a heretic, of course: "If any one confesses Christ Jesus the Lord, but denies the God of the law and of the prophets, saying that the Father of Christ is not the Maker of heaven and earth, he has not continued in the truth any more than his father the devil" (*Epistle to the Philadelphians*, Ch. 6).

Omnibenevolence

God is supposedly "omnibenevolent," or all-loving. This is the gracious Father who has showered us (in the relatively prosperous developed world) with blessings. Most importantly,

> ✝ "God in His immeasurable, and incomprehensible grace took our sins and placed them on His pure Son" (Havas [1938], 71).

That quote summarizes one of the "fundamentals" of Christianity, substitutionary atonement.[22] "The view here is that the death of Christ was designed to propitiate God, that is, to regain the favor of God by having Christ bear the penalty for human sin. This view . . . echoes the Old Testament notion of sacrifice as a substitution" (Mercer 2009, 78). Winell says that "once a convert has wrapped his or her mind around this story, anything can be accepted as truth":

> First the believer is to suspend familiar notions of justice, such as punishment of the guilty as opposed to an innocent party. You are then expected to accept the necessity of blood sacrifice for sin; that wrongdoing must be paid for, and not necessarily in proportion to the crime. A father's sacrifice of his innocent son is supposed to be not only just but generous and wonderful. Then the temporary three-day death of this one person is supposed to wipe out all the wrongdoing and ineptitude of the species. And finally, you should believe that all you need do to erase responsibility for your actions and enter a haven of eternal reward is to believe. [Winell 1993, 75]

What really makes it "incomprehensible grace" to me is why the omnipotent God couldn't exhibit enough of it to just forgive the sins of mankind–*everyone's* sins– by divine fiat and be done with it. Now that would be grace! Instead, we have what Evans calls "pond-scum theology," where "human beings have no intrinsic value or claim to salvation because their sin nature makes them so thoroughly disgusting and offensive to God that he is under no obligation to pay them any mind" (2010, 116). Uljas claims "God is so upright that He *can* never accept anything wrongful. He *cannot* turn a blind eye to our sins, thinking as people do, 'Oh, it's not such a big deal'" (2000, 27, emphasis added). *Says who?* A theologian who seeks to impose limits on the Deity

---

22. The name "fundamentalist" comes from the title of a series of booklets called *The Fundamentals*, published in 1910. There were five "core 'fundamentals' [that] constituted the non-negotiable beliefs one must absolutely hold to in order to be a Christian." They were "the divine inspiration and total inerrancy of the Bible," "the Virgin Birth of Christ as a testimony to his divinity," "the 'substitutionary atonement' of Christ on the cross for the sins of the world, and his bodily resurrection from the dead," and "the imminent second coming of Christ 'in glory'" (Cox 2009, 147-48).

in an attempt to defend his otherwise indefensible theology. Uljas thinks his view exhalts God above humanity, but it does precisely the opposite.

As Daryl Domning notes in his 2001 **article** <http://www.americamagazine.org/content/article.cfm?article_id=1205> "Evolution, Evil and Original Sin," none of the supposed sins arising from the fallen nature of man are actually unique to our species. "From ants to apes, the animal world is awash in [intraspecies] aggression, deceit, theft, exploitation, infanticide and cannibalism. Our cousins the great apes are adept at political intrigue and quite capable of serial murder and lethal warfare." Those other creations are off the hook, though, as "they are simply doing things that would be sinful if done by morally reflective human beings."

The only "morally reflective human beings" who are beneficiaries of this grace and love are those few winners of what Evans calls "the cosmic lottery" (2010, 98), with whom God shares the good news of Christianity. The problem is much worse when you shrink the scope of "Christianity" down to the merest sliver of humanity. Not just any old Christianity will do, certainly not the compassionate, nonjudgmental version that Evans struggles to retain, but a very specific form of it unknown to her or most anybody else.

In the case of the animals, there was no putative common ancestor, no temptation, and no Fall behind it all. However, the Fall is neither factual (**4.3.1**) nor needed as an explanation for sin. In humans and non-humans alike, "these behaviors exist *because they promote the survival and reproduction of those individuals that perform them*. Having once originated (ultimately through mutation), they persist because they are favored by natural selection for survival in the organisms' natural environments" (Domning 2001, emphasis added).

To Domning's list of "natural but sinful if humans do it" behaviors I would add another that obviously promotes reproduction: the drive for sex, especially in males whose genes can propagate almost without limitation from promiscuity with little of the cost incurred by females. You are inclined to do those things–including wanting to have sex early and often–not because some mythic first human couple ate a piece of fruit, but because your ancestors had what it takes to *be* your ancestor in a harsh and competitive world. And they passed those traits on to you.

But God is not about to excuse anything as the inevitable consequence of evolutionary biology, at least not according to O.H. Jussila in a 1949 issue of *Siionin Lähetyslehti*. He has "condemned sin in the flesh" and punished his son "with sickness for the sake of our sins":

> † "The Lord of Heaven and Earth is a righteous judge. He condemned sin in the flesh, the sharp pricks of His holy law pierced the only begotten Son nailed on the cross, who had taken upon Himself to carry the sins of the world. Nowhere is the judgment of sin so terrifyingly revealed, than before the altar of that God who did not spare His only begotten son, but punished Him with sickness for the sake of our sins. How terrible to those, unto whose heart the knowledge of God's judgment has not been impressed in the time of grace. They will meet judgment at the coming of that Righteous Judge when He comes to judge the quick and the dead. But then no more will be heard the voice of redeeming blood from the altar" (from *Greetings of Peace*, 1/1950).

Following Trinitarian doctrine to its full conclusions, here's what we have to believe, somehow: God the creator and righteous judge made a blood sacrifice *of himself* in human form to appease his own displeasure with what he had created. The posited relationship between these two forms of God was a father and son, the latter proceeding from yet somehow co-eternal with the former. The son was around before even the unauthorized fruit consumption that made his sacrificial role necessary. Thousands of years after that event, a third part of God finally impregnated a virgin so that this second part would be made man, spending some 30-40 years in that state before his blood sacrifice and return to heaven.[23]

Finally, I have to ask what it even means to call God "gracious" and "loving" in view of the long-recognized "problem of evil" (**4.9**). God many times ordered the conquest and slaughter of hundreds of thousands in the Old Testament (see, e.g., **6.4**, **6.6**), including innocent women and children, and has allowed untold billions of people to die of starvation, disaster, war, and disease (**4.9.4**). Worse yet, he condemns billions of people to eternal torture in hell (**4.9.2**), perhaps even as part

---

23. According to the fourth-century Nicene Creed (Lutheran version from **Wikipedia**), there is

of his divine plan (4.9.3). We might as well call God "purple" or "rectangular."

Hidden

All this gives Uljas good reason to say that God is incomprehensible and "remains hidden." But, there's good news! God has revealed himself *to us*:

> † "God is a hidden God. The Almighty God, the Creator of heaven and earth, does not fit into our comprehension, but remains hidden. However, He has revealed himself to us, so that we would come to know Him" (Uljas 2000, 19).

How does he go about doing that? Through a Bible that is filled with factual errors and contradictions including, for example, "a series of very different ideas about death and the afterlife" (Price 2006b, 53). Your eternal fate is certainly no trifling matter, yet God failed to really express his viewpoints on the matter until Jesus came along and started threatening eternal consequences for those who wouldn't follow him. (See 4.8.3, 6.8, 6.17, 6.18, 6.20, and 6.25.) If God inspired or dictated the Bible, "he has a funny way of making himself clear. I don't see how an inspired but ambiguous book is any more helpful than an uninspired book" (p. 53). The end result is the same: Those same people who claim that God has revealed himself to *them* are the ones saying just what it is that God has supposedly revealed.

---

one Lord, Jesus Christ,
the only-begotten Son of God,
begotten of His Father before all worlds,
God of God, Light of Light,
very God of very God,
begotten, not made,
being of one substance with the Father,
by whom all things were made;
who for us men and for our salvation came down from heaven
and was incarnate by the Holy Spirit of the virgin Mary
and was made man;
and was crucified also for us under Pontius Pilate.
He suffered and was buried.
And the third day He rose again according to the Scriptures
and ascended into heaven
and sits at the right hand of the Father.

To everyone else, including the writer of Isaiah 45:15 ("thou art a God that hidest thyself, O God of Israel"), God remains hidden. In most cases, he permits people the erroneous belief that they have experienced some sort of correct understanding or revelation of him, and *allows them to go to their graves damned by that false consolation*. Think about it: God does not just hide himself and the sole means of avoiding his eternal wrath from the vast majority of mankind. No, he also lets most of the damned spend their entire lives thinking that they actually *have* been reconciled–usually with whatever religious system they inherited–and need do nothing else.

That horror is the implication of Conservative Laestadianism's unprovable exclusivity claims (4.2.1), but what about real-world cases where God's silence seems like a repudiation of his very existence? A vivid example was the martrydom of Japanese Christians by drowning in the seventeeth century:

> What a miserable and painful business it was! The rain falls unceasingly on the sea. And the sea which killed them surges on uncannily–in silence. . . . Behind the depressing silence of this sea, the silence of God. . . . the feeling that while men raised their voices in anguish God remains with folded arms, silent. [from Tucker 2002, 152]

God's refusal to intervene or even make his presence known was enough to make two priests apostasize, one of them "to save Japanese Christians from torture." The other said to him, "Listen! I was put in here and heard the voices of those people for whom God did nothing. God did not do a single thing. I prayed with all my strength; but God did nothing" (from Tucker 2002, 153).

Again, Ingersoll offers his unflinching clarity, from a harsh 19th century:

> If you see a man in prison with the chains eating into his flesh simply for loving God, you've got to ask why does not a just God interfere? You've got to meet this; it won't do to say that it will all come out for the best. That may do very well for God, but it's awful hard on the man. [*Lecture on Religious Tolerance*]

4.4.2 The Son

> *Are we supposed to believe that 5 seconds after Jesus rose from the dead, everyone on earth was responsible for that information? How is a guy living in . . . Outer Mongolia in 15 A.D. supposed to figure out that Jesus died on the cross for his sins, was buried, and rose again on the third day?*
>
> —Rachel Held Evans, *Evolving in Monkey Town*

My sample of quotes about Jesus begins with one by Laestadius in his 1857 Reading Examination Sermon:

† "May all the penitent who do not yet believe, now read that their debt is paid; read the receipt that has been confirmed at the place of the skull and sealed with a bloody seal on Good Friday, where the great reconciliation was fulfilled and the debt-book of the penitent torn asunder, which the Father nailed on the cross. And these tokens of love, the bloody wounds, testify that your debt is paid and the mouth of the accuser has been closed" (*Fourth Postilla*, 118).

In these early years, a great deal of emphasis was put on Jesus' persona as both a fighting and a suffering redeemer:

† Jesus' "bloody love has been revealed to us when He endured the death of the cross. When the iron nails were driven into His hands and feet, He did not become angry, but sighed, 'Father, forgive them, for they know not what they do!'" (Raattamaa, sermon given 1894, from Kulla 1985, 184).

† "The Lord Jesus calls the poor child of Adam as He crawls in the pit of hell where it is so hot that His head and His locks are wet with the drops of the night. He cannot stand, but falls to His knees. He cannot stay upon His knees, but falls upon His face on the ground. There He lies drenched with the stream of His blood which pours forth from His holy body to the accursed Earth. His every pore is opened as a fount of bloody tears" (Matti Suo, *Siionin Lähetyslehti* [1917], from Kulla 1985, 206).

† "If the Great Warrior would not be fighting in behalf of us we would have long ago become tired and weary under the cross. But we children of God have a great helper who is the King of

Kings and the Lord of Lords, who still go as before his flock, smiting the enemy with the two-edged sword of his mouth" (*Siionin Lähetyslehti*, 1920).

Heikki Jussila's 1923 quote (especially in the last sentence) addresses a doctrinal dispute of his day about the emphasis to be put on Christ's suffering and death versus his resurrection:

> ☦ Paul "received Christ as a gift in the gospel. This Christ then was the center of his preaching. Not a cross, neither a nailing to the cross, but Christ as crucified and risen from the dead. The doctrine of redemption as a whole is: Christ has died and risen from the dead. It was the gospel that Paul himself had received, and the same he had delivered unto others. He assures that he and all Christians who are converted into faith by this gospel are saved.... They which have avoided the preaching of the victory of resurrection in fear that it leads to a light manner of Christianity, have gone astray from the biblical gospel" (from *Greetings of Peace*, 4/1971).

Nowadays one hears very little mention of gory crucifixion details. The events of Golgatha are mostly recounted in songs during the Communion service. But the shift in focus from suffering to redemption would take some time yet:

> ☦ "The disciples saw from afar off how He carried His cross, came to the place of the Skull, Golgotha. They heard the sound of the hammer that drove the nails into the precious hands. The cross was lifted up between two thieves. He was suspended between heaven and earth and there He hanged–He, who was so dear to their hearts. They heard His agonizing cry, heard Him call to the heart of God in heaven and then He died" (O.H. Jussila, notes taken from sermon given 1936, *Greetings of Peace*, 6/1949).

> ☦ "The Lamb of God of Golgotha's middle cross took away your sins, and from His wounds flowed the blood of reconciliation to settle your heart's confused account book. You may thus own a full forgiveness in the blood of the Son of God" (Havas [1940], 75-76).

Writing to soldiers in battle during WWII, Paul Heideman told them to remember that

✝ "it is for such miserable sinners that God, in His wonderful love, gave His beloved Son to make a perfect and complete sacrifice for us. When Jesus died upon the cross, He shouted, 'It is finished!' Our sin debt was completely paid. Jesus has become our righteousness before God. We have no other reason for being acceptable to God and Heaven than Jesus. Neither do we need any other reason. For He is sufficient reason, Who is our Righteousness at the right hand of God" (from Kulla 1993, 224).

The portrayal of Jesus as God's "beloved Son" does not start to appear until fairly late in the Gospels. The four books show what Loftus calls a "process of deification of Jesus" that took place over the many decades from the earliest (Mark, c. 70 A.D.) to the latest (John, after 100 A.D.):

> In Mark's gospel . . . a man comes to Jesus saying, "Good teacher what must I do to inherit eternal life," and Jesus says to the man, "Why do you call me good? No one is good but God alone" (10:17-18). According to James Barr, "This only makes sense if Jesus is not claiming to be God," because "it fits with the fact that Jesus fully accepted Jewish monotheism." But by the time Matthew's gospel was written, the church had developed a higher, more glorified view of Jesus, so this same conversation is amended to read, "'Teacher, what good deed must I do to have eternal life?' And he (Jesus) said to him, 'Why do you ask me about what is good? There is only one who is good'" (19:16). Gone is the description of Jesus as a "good teacher," so that Jesus' rhetorical question can be deleted and his statement revised. Jesus now merely asks him, "Why do you call me good?" Noticeably absent is where Jesus said, "No one is good but God alone." By contrast, John's gospel . . . reveals a very exalted view of Christ. [Loftus 2008, loc. 5637-44]

Karen Armstrong came across this difficult reality when she "stumbled unawares into the minefield of New Testament scholarship":

> A disturbing number of eminent scholars agreed that Jesus had no intention of founding a new religion. He had preached only to his fellow Jews, and there was nothing strikingly original about his teaching, which was in line with other strands of first-century Judaism. Jesus certainly never claimed to be God, but preferred the title "Son of Man," which emphasized his humanity. After the scandal of his crucifixion, his traumatized disciples had had

> visions of him risen from the tomb and concluded that he was the long-awaited Jewish Messiah, who would shortly return to inaugurate the kingdom of God on earth. But the early Christians still regarded themselves as forming an exclusively Jewish sect. It was Saint Paul, who had never known the historical Jesus, who had first marketed the faith for the non-Jewish world of the Roman Empire. But even Paul had not seen Jesus as divine in any simplistic way. [2007, 231-32]

I doubt if the writers of these remaining quotes knew about any of those complexities, though, nor that they would have given them the slightest weight if they had. They stick with the biblical accounts with a bit of devotional elaboration thrown in, personalizing Jesus as lowly and humble, our best friend, the Good Shepherd, a perfect sacrifice suffering under the weight of our sins, and the Author and Finisher of our salvation:

> ✝ Jesus "is lowly, and with the merit of His humbleness, He makes the daughter of Zion rich and the heir of Heaven. The King brings to the poor of His Kingdom His treasures. He Himself sits upon the back of a borrowed ass, when He goes out to draw the prisoners of Zion out of the waterless pit. He bears shackles and is bound, scourged and crowned with thorns. He opens the barred door, when the gates of Paradise are opened to the thief. The precious myrrh drips from His holy and blessing hands" (Heikki Jussila, *Greetings of Peace*, 3/1943).
>
> ✝ "[T]he Good Shepherd permitted all of our sins to be cast on His innocent shoulders. It was under their load that He groaned and wept in the garden of Gethsemane. Our sins were the nails that pierced His hands, our unbelief pierced His loving heart and caused His precious blood to be shed not to bring curse upon us, but to bring blessing and life eternal" (Paul Heideman, *Greetings of Peace*, 6/1954).
>
> ✝ Jesus "is the best friend among all friends. On the cross on Good Friday, Jesus, out of love for us, has given His heart which was pierced with the spear" (Alajoki [1966], 110).
>
> ✝ "Hasten to turn and to open your ears again to that beautiful heavenly voice, come you weary and tired traveler, rest in the bosom of your Good Shepherd. Believe your sins and temptations

forgiven in Jesus' Name and precious Blood. You will again receive strength to journey, rejoicing in faith. If temptations easily beset you the voice of the Shepherd will give you strength to resist them. What a precious Shepherd. He left the sheepfold for us, that are still in this world, where He still cares for us through the power of the Holy Spirit. He shed His Holy Blood as a perfect sacrifice before the throne of God, that even we though great sinners, washed and cleansed in His Blood, can stand before that throne clean and spotless, acceptable to God" (Art Forstie, *Greetings of Peace*, 2/1968).

† "Raise your head and look in faith and spirit and count the wounds of the innocent Sacrifice lamb of God from which the blood of forgiveness was shed for the cleansing of your sins" (VOZ, 10/1974).

The *Epistle of Barnabus* has similar language to these quotes about the shedding of the blood and its purpose: "For to this end the Lord endured to deliver up His flesh to corruption, that we might be sanctified through the remission of sins, which is effected by His blood of sprinkling" (Ch. 5).

† "God gave his son to be nailed on the cross, shed his blood for the remission of sins. . . . This was a great moment when Jesus took the sins of the world upon himself to reconcile lost sinners unto God" (VOZ, 4/1974)

† "It is wonderful in our eyes that even such wretched ones as you and I are still permitted to raise our gaze to the Author and Finisher of our salvation, Jesus Christ, who is the Alpha and the Omega of our salvation. We do not need to be ashamed, our nakedness and shame has been taken away. We are clothed in the beautiful garment of righteousness which the Lord Jesus knitted on Golgatha's cross" (Alajoki [1981], 235-36).

† "The Prophet Isaiah describes Jesus as despised and rejected of men. He was wounded for our transgressions and bruised for our iniquities" (VOZ, 3/1999).

† "Jesus hung for six hours on the cross and the final three hours he hung in total darkness as all of God's creation bowed to the death of the Savior, God's Son" (VOZ, 6/2001).

✝ "We live of faith where the Lord Jesus is the foundation, and that work that was done on Good Friday's cross was done on our behalf. The Heavenly Father's love was so great he sent His Son to the cross for your sins and mine, indeed the sins of the entire world" (VOZ, 10/2005).

✝ "The sermon of the gospel always takes us to behold Golgatha's cross and the morning of resurrection. From Christ's cross shines the love of God, and in the Resurrection is the power of God, which crushed the power of sin, death, and God's adversaries" (*Päivämies*, 2006).

✝ "By God's grace, the gospel is preached in the name of Jesus and through the same drops of blood He shed on Golgatha's cross" (VOZ, 6/2008).

As discussed in 7.4, the earliest information about the historical Jesus is found in Paul's letters, and those references are very scant. There would be another 20-30 years until the first of the Gospels, Mark, which probably didn't appear until after 70 A.D. Bart Ehrman notes, "This means that our earliest surviving written accounts of Jesus' life come from thirty-five to sixty-five years after his death" (2010, 145). Christianity spread from person to person, he wrote, "year after year, decade after decade, until eventually someone wrote down the stories" about Jesus and the apostles. He asks, "What do you suppose happened to the stories over the years, as they were told and retold, not as disinterested news stories reported by eyewitnesses but as propaganda meant to convert people to faith, told by people who have themselves heard them fifth- or sixth- or nineteenth-hand?" (pp. 146-47).[24] Ehrman then discusses what information exists outside the Gospels "that can be thrown into the mix," and asks rhetorically, "[I]f Jesus lived and died in the first century (death around 30 C.E. [A.D.]), what do the Greek and

---

24. *Propaganda* is a loaded term that evokes a strong reaction in people, but its first definition is merely "The systematic propagation of a doctrine or cause or of information reflecting the views and interests of those advocating such a doctrine or cause" (thefreedictionary.com). And the Gospels surely did that, as John explicity notes toward its end: "[M]any other signs truly did Jesus in the presence of his disciples, which are not written in this book: but these are written, that ye might believe that Jesus is the Christ, the Son of God; and that believing ye might have life through his name" (Jn 20:30).

Roman sources from his own day through the end of the century (say, the year 100) have to say about him?" The answer, he says,

> is breathtaking. They have absolutely nothing to say about him. He is never discussed, challenged, attacked, maligned, or talked about in any way in any surviving pagan source of the period. There are no birth records, accounts of his trial and death, reflections on his significance, or disputes about his teachings. In fact, his name is never mentioned once in any pagan source. And we have a lot of Greek and Roman sources from the period: religious scholars, historians, philosophers, poets, natural scientists; we have thousands of private letters; we have inscriptions placed on buildings in public places. In no first-century Greek or Roman (pagan) source is Jesus mentioned. [p. 148]

Jason Long notes two prominent Jewish authors of the first century who were well situated to provide us with something to break that deafening silence, but did not. The first is Philo of Alexandria, who died in 50 A.D. and was

> a devotedly religious Jewish philosopher with a volume of work sizable enough to fill a modern publication of nearly one thousand pages with small print. Even though he was adamant about the legitimacy of the Hebrew scripture, not once does he indicate that he knew the first thing about an earthly Jesus. However, Philo did choose to refer to the son of God in the form of Logos, which is to say a spiritual medium between God and man. As it stands in the biblical world, the supernatural son of the universe's almighty creator was supposedly performing unprecedented miracles and fulfilling prophecies that this philosopher spent his life analyzing, yet Philo, living well before Jesus' birth and well after the crucifixion, never mentions such occurrences! [Long 2005, 186]

The second is the Galilean-born Justus of Tiberias [*c.* 35-100 A.D.], "who never offered Jesus one line of notation in his works. Justus made extensive historical writings on the Jewish war for independence and other contemporaneous events of local interest, but he never mentioned the name of Jesus once" (p. 187).

We have to wait until the second century to get some mention of Jesus, and they are indirect and problematic. One is from 112 A.D. where Pliny the Younger inquires about how to handle a group of people called Christians, who "worship Christ as a God," and another in 115 A.D. by the Roman historian Tacitus:

> Tacitus explains that the Christians get their name from "Christus [some writers say *Chrestus*] . . . who was executed at the hands of the procurator Pontius Pilate in the reign of Tiberius" (*Annals* 15.44). He goes on to say that the "superstition" of Christianity first appeared in Judea before spreading to Rome. . . . If we cast our net over all surviving Greek and Roman (pagan) sources for the first hundred years after Jesus' death (30-130 C.E.), these two brief references are all we find. [Ehrman 2010, 149]

Then there is Josephus, a Jewish historian whose voluminous writings of around 90 A.D. contain just two mentions of Jesus. The more detailed of the two, the *Testimonium Flavianum*, has been discredited as being at least partially fraudulent. The other "simply identifies a man named James as 'the brother of Jesus, who is called the messiah'" (p. 149). The account that Josephus gives of John the Baptist, however, suggests that it was *he* who "was the more 'popular voice' of the period" (White 2005, 103).[25]

Ehrman summarizes the matter as follows:

> [I]f we want to know about the life of the historical Jesus, we are more or less restricted to using the four Gospels of Matthew, Mark, Luke, and John. These are not disinterested accounts by eyewitnesses, however. They are books written decades after the fact by authors who had heard stories about Jesus from the oral tradition, stories that had been altered and even made up over time. There were lots of discrepancies in these stories, and the Gospel writers themselves changed them as they saw fit. [p. 151]

---

25. Even the Gospels show some tension about the Baptist's role. The earliest one (Mark) has Jesus submit to John's "baptism for the remission of sins" seemingly as a matter of course. The later Synoptics, having greater emphasis on Jesus' divinity, strain to apologize for the awkwardness of the Son of God showing up to be washed in the baptismal waters by the preacher of repentance. John, the latest of the Gospels by far and with the highest "Christology," ignores Jesus' baptism entirely (Price 2003).

Francis Potter writes about a friend who confronted those discrepancies at Newton Theological Seminary and labored for many weeks over a "huge cardboard chart on which he was trying to reconcile Matthew, Mark, Luke, and John." He finally became "exhausted and disgusted" by the effort and quit the ministry. He said to Potter

> rather ruefully and with a sigh that night as we stood looking at the tangled lines of the chart: "Well, Pottie, if Matthew, Mark, Luke and John didn't know what Jesus said and did, well enough to agree on it, I'm sure I don't, and I'm not going to fake it, not to please anybody." [1951, 391]

What I find just as remarkable as the historical silence about Jesus is the utter lack of any mention outside the Gospels of the astounding events attested by those books. Long notes that "Paul was the first known individual to write about Jesus," and I agree that "it seems quite peculiar that he chooses to abstain from mentioning any of the astounding miracles accomplished by his subject" (2005, 184).

Those miracles include raising a girl from the dead, and the fame of that act "went abroad into all that land" (Mt 9:25-26). The "multitudes marvelled" about Jesus casting out a devil and restoring speech to a man (Mt 9:32-33). "Jesus went about all the cities and villages, teaching in their synagogues, and preaching the gospel of the kingdom, and healing every sickness and every disease among the people" (Mt 9:35). He fed nine thousand people from a mere armful of food (Mt 16:9-10). On Good Friday afternoon, there "was darkness over the whole land" for three hours (Mk 15:33). Upon Jesus' death, "the earth did quake, and the rocks rent; and the graves were opened; and many bodies of the saints which slept arose, and came out of the graves after his resurrection, and went into the holy city, and appeared unto many" (Mt 27:51-53).

Yet *none* of the authors and observers of the day–Paul, Pliny the Elder, Josephus, the hundreds of anonymous writers whose personal letters and mundane records have been preserved–had *any* of these events brought to their attention and thought them worth recording?

4.4.3 The Holy Ghost

> *Try the man who has the Divine Spirit by his life. First, he who has the Divine Spirit proceeding from above is meek, and peaceable, and humble, and refrains from all iniquity and the vain desire of this world, and contents himself with fewer wants than those of other men, and when asked he makes no reply; nor does he speak privately, nor when man wishes the spirit to speak does the Holy Spirit speak, but it speaks only when God wishes it to speak. When, then, a man having the Divine Spirit comes into an assembly of righteous men who have faith in the Divine Spirit, and this assembly of men offers up prayer to God, then the angel of the prophetic Spirit, who is destined for him, fills the man; and the man being filled with the Holy Spirit, speaks to the multitude as the Lord wishes. Thus, then, will the Spirit of Divinity become manifest.*
>
> —*The Shephard of Hermas* [*c.* 140 A.D.]

Earlier we saw how God has made a blood sacrifice of a second part or "person" of himself in human form, which proceeded from God (the first part, that is) but was somehow always present. There is a third part of God, too, a holy "spirit" or "ghost" having no tangible form at all. The Nicene Creed <http://en.wikipedia.org/wiki/English_versions_of_the_Nicene_Creed_in_current_use> asserts that this third part of God "proceeds from" the first two parts. It also states, oddly enough, that this third part is what made the second part "incarnate," by impregnating the virgin Mary. If it isn't weird enough for the monotheistic God of Israel ("Hear, O Israel: The LORD our God is one LORD," Deut 6:4) to have three "persons," you can ponder the idea of the third part proceeding from the first and second parts while the second part is incarnated into a man by the third part that the second part helped produce. The Trinity is one of those "seriously perplexing nuggets of incomprehensibility" that Dennett says religion gives our brains "to gnaw on, like an unresolved musical cadence, and hence something to rehearse, and rehearse again, and baffle themselves deliciously about" (2007, 230).

Anyhow, after the second part of God rejoined the first in heaven, the Holy Spirit (part #3) was sent to earth. Here it inspires a small, hidden group of people to speak and write about, and believe in, the work done by the Son (part #2) to appease the Father (part #1):

> † "The preaching [of the word] today is not your own. It is brought forth from God and through the Spirit has been ordained to do that duty" of reproof, rebuke, and exhortation. Children should not "be ashamed to confess yourselves before the children of this world," for from "God pours forth blessed strength and protection." It is difficult to "speak of faith and grace to an unbeliever and the necessity of conversion," but "when God with his love gives words to speak, then you have a thankful prayer to God that He gave you utterance" (Ville Suutari, *Greetings of Peace*, 9/1954).

Justin Martyr's student Tatian [110-172 A.D.] envisioned a similar teaching role for the Holy Spirit, as well as its being limited only to the righteous: "But the Spirit of God is not with all, but, taking up its abode with those who live justly, and intimately combining with the soul, by prophecies it announced hidden things to other souls" (*Address to the Greeks*, Ch. 13). Assuming that this third part of the Trinity is what John 14:26 means by the *Paraclete* (KJV: *Comforter*; NASB: *Helper*)–an assumption that has been questioned by a number of biblical scholars– its job was to teach the disciples (and presumably everyone else through them) all things, and to bring all things to their remembrance that Jesus had said unto them.

Other references both ancient and modern say that the Holy Spirit is not just supposed to inspire its hosts to speak about righteousness, but to live righteously. The writer of *First Clement* praises the Corinthians for humility, obedience, "a profound and abundant peace," and "an insatiable desire for doing good, while a full outpouring of the Holy Spirit was upon you all" (Ch. 2). Paul writes in Galatians 5 about the "fruits of the spirit," making a sharp distinction between the expected behavior of those who have the spirit and those who don't. Unfortunately, as the discussion of that passage in **7.5** makes clear, it is not actually possible to see much evidence of any such distinction.

There is not much of a distinction when it comes to certain critical aspects of *ecclesiastical* teaching and practice, either. As discussed in **4.1.6**, the OALC and FALC both place great importance on the forgiveness of sins by personal absolution. In their churches, thousands of those "heretics" are sincerely and emotionally preaching forgiveness and accepting it. Yet they are supposedly without the Spirit that teaches and guides in all truth. I wonder how many Conservative Laestadians realize how much the church's exclusivity backs itself into a theological corner in this regard. If there is no distinction between how those with the Spirit and those without are understanding and practicing the single most significant aspect of "God's Kingdom," then the Spirit is *making absolutely no difference* where it matters most. The result is what Robert M. Price and Emil Durkheim say happens in evangelical Christianity: The "God evangelical Christians worship so fervently is evangelicalism itself, externalized and made into a totem" (Price 2006b, 89).

O.H. Jussila [1888-1955] describes the Holy Ghost as a gift and agent of God's love:

> ☦ "The love of God then is the miracle-power, through which the Holy Ghost creates new life in the soul of man. Love has its home in heaven, for God is love. From heaven the Holy Ghost brings love down into this loveless world and directs its power streams of new life into the heart of man. . . . The Holy Ghost is the gift of the heavenly Father. And so also the new life which the Holy Ghost creates and its fruit are the gift of God. A gift is given, it is not forcibly taken. In receiving it there is not the slightest amount of compulsion. But God-given salvation with all its blessings is a grace gift" (from *Greetings of Peace*, 10/1961).

It sounds pretty nice, until you recall that the consequence for not accepting this gift is the loss of one's closest relationships in this lifetime and an eternity of the most horrible torment imaginable thereafter. (The implications of this will be discussed further in **4.5.3** with respect to the gift of faith.) And God's love is sadly limited in scope, when you consider what a tiny sliver of humanity is being offered this gift.

Jussila wrote those words at least half a century ago, and his overlooking the implications of what he was saying might be excused then, especially considering how insular Conservative Laestadianism has always been. But when a sect of a hundred thousand members maintains a doctrine of exclusivity in a world of seven billion, it is chaining itself to a rotting corpse. No amount of literary perfume can disguise the stench of the horror it drags along with it everywhere it goes.

Many attempts have been made to explain the mystery of the Trinity. Tertullian provided one succinct explanation that "the connection of the Father in the Son, and of the Son in the Paraclete, produces three coherent Persons, *who are yet distinct* One from Another. These Three are one *essence*, not one *Person*, as it is said, 'I and my Father are One,' in respect of unity of substance not singularity of number" (*Against Praxeas*, Ch. 25).[26] These last quotes in my sample about the Holy Spirit describe the separate duties of the three "persons" in the trinity, which nonetheless "is still one indivisible unity":

> † "Each person of the Godhead has His own duty: God the Father has created, the Son Jesus has redeemed, and the Holy Ghost takes care of the sanctification but this He does through those in whose hearts He dwells" (VOZ, 4/1974).

> † "Although there are three forms or persons in God, He is still one indivisible unity. For salvation, a person must believe upon the complete Triune God. If any of the Articles of faith are rejected by unbelief, then faith and hope of salvation is without foundation" (*By Faith*, 60).

> † "The Holy Spirit continues the work of the Father, through His Son, until the end of time. This Comforter assures us of God's love and the forgiveness of all of our sins through His Son, Jesus Christ. This same Holy Spirit also continues to call sinners from the darkness of unbelief . . ." (VOZ, 5/2008).

4.4.4 The Mother

> *It was a sad and disillusioning lesson to learn. Why wasn't he told that in the first grade? Or the first day at the university? That all institutions, every last one of them—no matter the claim, no matter the purpose, no matter the stated goals—exist sooner or later for their own selves, are self-loving, self-concerned, self-regarding, self-preserving, and are lusting for the soul of all who come near them.*
>
> —Will Campbell

---

26. According to Wikipedia <http://en.wikipedia.org/wiki/Tertullian>, Tertullian's views on the trinity were rejected as heretical at first but then accepted as Christian orthodoxy. That's ironic, since Tertullian was a zealous heresy-hunter himself.

Such emphasis has been put on the congregation "mother" that it sometimes seems to be viewed as a fourth member of the Godhead. It is also an entity recognized by the Jehovah's Witnesses, who say, "If we are to walk in the light of truth we must recognize not only Jehovah God as our Father but his organization as our mother" (from Wilson 2002, 43).

The only supporting Scripture appears to be a single passage in the New Testament, Gal 4:26, which refers to "Jerusalem which is above" (NASB: *the Jerusalem above*). Much has been made of the wording *"from above,"* which is how it appears in the 1776 Finnish translation favored by the SRK, as indicating that the kingdom or mother is right here with us, having come down from above. Though Luther translates the phrase as *"is* above," as does every other translation of which I'm aware, he did caution not to "mistake this one word 'above' to refer to the triumphant Church in heaven, but to the militant Church on earth," saying that "Jerusalem here means the universal Christian Church on earth" (*Commentary on Galatians* [1535], from Graebner, Ch. 4). He also counseled honor and obedience to "the spiritual mother, the holy Christian Church, the spiritual power, so that we conform to what she commands, forbids, appoints, orders, binds and looses" (*Treatise on Good Works* [1520]; *PE* 1, 257).

An early quote shows a reasonable reference to the "heavenly Jerusalem" without any anthropromorphizing (i.e., making it into a human-like entity):

> † "[W]e have been lead to Mount Zion, the city of the living God, the heavenly Jerusalem, and to an innumerable company of angels, to the general assembly and church of the first-born, which are written in heaven, and to God the Judge of all, and to the spirits of just men made perfect, and to Jesus, the mediator of the new covenant, and to the blood of sprinkling, that speaketh better things than the blood of Abel (Heb 12). In this company to which we have been led, we lack nothing. It is no wonder then, that we here are content and that from all our hearts we have fallen in love with those who have led us here. Through the gospel-word preached in the Lord's congregation, we have become free, and fully enjoy our freedom, to live still a brief time here in mutual love, begging forgiveness and forgiving one another and once to die in good cheer as heirs of life and

salvation" (A.L. Heideman, sermon given 1886, from *Greetings of Peace*, 4/1952).[27]

The first "mother" reference in my sample of Conservative statements is from a 1926 issue of *Siionin Lähetyslehti*:

✝ "Our spiritual mother is the Kingdom of God. Therefore, it is not at all appropriate for a child to oppose his mother or object to the precious truths of God's Word taught by her. The unity and love of the Spirit are precious and are also a uniting bond. Whether a disagreement is of a temporal or spiritual nature, when it spoils fraternal and common love, it is required as a condition of salvation that one submit in humility to the common understanding of the Kingdom of God and publicly repent" (from Hepokoski 2002b, 50).

In 1948, Jussila distinguished the Mother (now with divine capitalization) from the Holy Spirit. There are *two* separate divine entities at work here, separate from the Father and the Son! As with his discussion of Raattamaa (4.2.1), he attempts to cast his view backward in history:

✝ "In early Christianity until this day, it has been believed and taught that the Congregation of God is the Mother which both gives birth and nourishes with the Word that the Holy Spirit causes to be preached" (Jussila 1948, 185).

Elmer Alajoki wrote glowingly of the kingdom in 1966. He doesn't personify it, leaving it to the Heavenly Father to occupy:

✝ "It is a beautiful kingdom in which the children of God dwell. It is a kingdom where the good speaking blood of Jesus always flows, washes, and cleanses from all sin. None of us will be saved except there where the blood of Jesus can always freely flow,

---

27. Paul Heideman prefaced the article in which that appeared with an editor's note that is worth reproducing just for the affection he shows there for his father, both of them being major figures in the history of Laestadianism: "As I have been translating this conclusion of a sermon held by my father, Arthur L. Heideman, in Finland in 1886, shortly after his own conversion, my heart has rejoiced. I have remembered the countless many of us, to whom God in His unmeasurable love and mercy, gave truly converted, believing fathers and mothers, and through them, let His Kingdom come to us. . ."

> there where we as poor sinners can gather the blood drops of Jesus to our sinful hearts. There joy is always kindled. There is peace. There is rest. There we comprehend the beauty and preciousness of the kingdom of God. There is such a rich Heavenly Father here. All the riches are hidden in the congregation of God; outside there is no salvation or life" (Alajoki, 125).

With the 1973 schism and its renewed emphasis on childlike obedience, the mother took on a position of prominence that would remain pretty extreme for about a decade:

> † In the mutual congregation, not "one is left in his wounds to languish or die, but the 'Mother' cares for her children. The congregation could not even be a Mother, unless it experiences sorrow and concern especially for those who have soiled and hurt themselves. All the children are dear to the 'Mother,' even the soiled and those literally covered with filth! Have we not seen how many times even the natural Mothers scold and exhort the children who have soiled themselves, but immediately begin to wash and cleanse them! . . . The kingdom of God attempts to the last possible moment to care for the one who has come to fault" (*Päivämies*, 1973).

Here, the translator went so far as to use divine capitalization in the pronoun "Her" in addition to the proper name "Mother":

> † "We show obedience to God when we listen to that voice, what the Spirit saith unto the congregation (Rev 2:29). We have the Mother who instructs. Let us listen to the Mother, the living congregation of God. Through Her the Spirit of God speaks. Thus even then when we are defeated in battle. The Mother instructs to put the sin defeats away as they have happened. Oh, how good the Mother's instruction is. Here in Zion are open fountains against sin and defilement. We have a God to whom ungodliness is not acceptable, but who still loves the penitent faulty child of man" (*Päivämies*, 1975).

The Mother's "holiness and office in the matters of faith" was not to be questioned:

> † "It is a very significant fact, that no matter which kind of spiritual error or carnal religion men may err into, this spiritual

'Mother' becomes a dimmed doctrine. Her holiness and office in the matters of faith is questioned, doubted, and disputed with undisguised arrogance. The one in the 'leaven of hypocrisy,' the Laestadian Pharisee, sees the kingdom as a fault infested, scruffy lot who walk in undisciplined slackness who rant of grace and forgiveness so tiresomely. On the other hand, the humble hypocrite whose faith is so staunch and durable he cannot rid himself of it even by denying it, sees the kingdom, the 'Mother,' as a demanding but fallible teacher, whose instructions 'one lone defender' can dispute and ignore! The disobedient, who is hidden under the guise of 'self-chosen worship and humility' defends all manner of doctrinal and carnal error with the argument that the 'Mother' is erring" (VOZ, 1/1975).

In an effort to explain how "individual members, even member congregations can err in all manner of things," the quoted writer defines the infallible Mother as "the church universal, the total fellowship of all believers present in the entire world." It is distinct from "[i]ndividual Christians, the local congregations, [who] are members of the 'body' the 'Mother,' and are not the 'Mother.'" He makes a reasonable point when he concludes, "There is only one body (1 Cor 12:12). But the body is not one member but many! (1 Cor 12:14). How can such clear words be twisted? The body is not one member, it is the total of the members."

> † "The kingdom of heaven is the pillar of truth and the foundation of truth. By that we mean it cannot err, it is our spiritual mother. It is this mother that gives life and new birth," that "wants to take care of us when we are disobedient children" (Peter Nordstrom, sermon given 1978).

Meanwhile, having been separated from and entirely out of contact with Conservative Laestadianism for three quarters of a century, the OALC was urging "that we wouldn't begin to form our own opinions, but rather place our understandings, no matter how right they seem to us, before the right judges: Christians having the Holy Spirit. This lowliness, humility, and obedience to the rule of the congregation is the secret of strength. We must place our trust in God and His congregation that has the Holy Spirit. Man can err but the Holy Spirit does not err" (*History of Living Christianity*, 34). Here is an observation from another authoritarian religious group that may sound all too familiar:

> The Watchtower Society wants its members to stay as children in relation to its authority, referring to the organization as "Mother"; thus, Jehovah's Witnesses spend most of their time in the "child" mode, looking to the organization as their "parent." When a Witness voices any disagreement with this "parent," the organization disrespectfully views that disagreement as tantamount to a child throwing a tantrum. [Wilson 2002, 226]

It is the same kind of thing that was being said about the relationship of the "Child of God" to the "Mother":

> ✝ "Sometimes when a child gets older he can be more disobedient and not listen to his temporal mother and what sorrow that causes her. How the congregation of God sorrows when spiritually a child is disobedient and does not heed its admonitions, because he has grown too big in himself. How happy a Christian mother is when the blood of Christ can flow between her and her child, because she herself can err by going into the flesh when her child is disobedient. The spiritual mother rejoices when a wayward child repents, but differs from the natural mother in this way–the spiritual mother cannot err even though her child does" (VOZ, 11/1980).

While this attitude is still common, a couple of Finnish correspondents have told me that it is not universally held within the SRK now. And one of those correspondents, Antti Kaunisto, notes a 1909 annual meeting of the SRK that indicates some organizational humility early on. There a prominent lay preacher, Juho Kanniainen is recorded as saying, "God's word is the only strong and infallible foundation upon which the congregation is built.[28] The congregation can err sometimes. We don't give the due respect to God's word if we put any other foundation beside it." Kanniainen concluded that the Bible was enough for Jesus and we should let it be enough for us, too, and the other brothers agreed (Kaunisto 2011).

---

28. Hepokoski says that there were "cliques" among the Conservatives in Finland a few years later. In 1917, Kanniainen was in one group with Heikki Jussila, whom I quote extensively in this book. Another leading voice of Conservative Laestadianism, Matti Suo, whom I also quote extensively, but at the time he was in another group (Hepokoski 2002b, 55). Regardless of those tensions, Jussila and Suo are both considered Conservative Laestadians, and I know of no formal split between the cliques that Hepokoski describes.

Kaunisto says this presents "an embarrassing contradiction to the inerrant Mother doctrine so widely preached in the 1970s–what's the use of an inerrant congregation that has made the mistake to proclaim itself fallible sometimes?" There is also "the problem of who has the authority to speak *ex cathedra* on behalf of the Holy Congregation, if no organization or a group of people is qualified for the task." An inerrant Mother who is somehow hidden among fallible believers becomes invisible and of no practical consequence (Kaunisto 2011).

Though Luther recognized the analogy of the church as a mother, he didn't emphasize it much in his writings. Here is one case where he referred to it, in his 1520 *Treatise Concerning the Ban*: "When an earthly mother rebukes and chastises her erring son, she does not give him over to the hangman or to the wolves, nor make a knave of him, but she restrains him and shows him by her chastisement that he is in danger of the hangman, and thus keeps him at home in his father's house. In the same way, when the spiritual power puts anyone under the ban [with the key of binding], it should be in this spirit," to put one "outwardly under the ban in the sight of men" until he comes to himself and brings back his soul (*PE* 2, 40-41).

After this next quote from 1980, my sample shows no discussion about the Mother for almost three decades. (It should be noted, however, that the quote is from a book that has been passed out to confirmation students during that entire time.)

> † "The mother feeds and cares for her children. So also does the Kingdom of God, the spiritual Mother, which Rebekah-mother in the Old Testament portrays" (*By Faith*, 31).

Then, in 2008, as some dissident voices began to be heard in the SRK, the "congregation mother" got some fresh attention, along with warnings about the 1970s, her last heyday:

> † "People of our time see faith as a personal matter, with which no one should interfere. But through the example of the Good Samaritan, Jesus taught that we are to care for those wounded by sin and wearied in their faith. God's congregation is like a mother who wants to hold her child in her arms. Discussions about doctrine and soul care especially rise in importance during times of battle in Christianity. This was also experienced in the 1970s, when a schism separated from Conservative Laestadianism. Even

during difficult times, God does His work in the Holy Spirit through His children who, in themselves, are lacking. It is important that through all times our trust in the grace-care of God's kingdom would be preserved" (*Päivämies* No. 2, 2008).

† "The believer in God's kingdom has a Father in heaven and a spiritual mother here on this Earth. Our mother cares for us and guides us on his way to heaven. . . . There is reason for concern if one has a different understanding of spiritual matters than the congregation mother." In the schism of the 1970s, the "people who went astray had lost the correct doctrine of the congregation mother. They no longer kept it as an unerring kingdom" (VOZ, 8/2008).

Now it seems that the mother is enjoying something of a comeback. Obedience to her will was mentioned frequently during a 2010 youth discussion in Minneapolis, and Ray Waaraniemi's 2011 presentation says, "It is vital to personal faith that we understand the role of the congregation mother. We always want to be obedient to the congregation of God. It is a beautiful matter that we can entrust our endeavor into the care of the congregation of God, our spiritual mother."

At least he didn't capitalize her name.

4.4.5 Angels

> *An angel is a spiritual creature created by God without a body, for the service of Christendom and of the church.*
>
> —Martin Luther

There is little mention of angels in the last century of writings and sermons. The topic is mostly for children, and the presence of angels in the everyday life of an adult believer does not seem to be taken too seriously.

† "It feels so secure to be in faith, when each of us has a guardian angel, even for such a weak one who thinks that God hardly looks down so low. Let us not even then tremble in the waves of doubt, or when the anger and envy of Babylon beat over us. God sends His Angels to protect us, like he did to the den of lions to

rescue Daniel, and to the furnace to save Shadrach, Meshach, and Abednego" (Saari 1968, 32).

✝ "There are so many of these [spiritual] angels [Heb 1:14], that there are enough for each child of God to have his very own. Remember, children, that angels accompany you, and they see the face of the heavenly father. When the time comes for us to leave the world, these angels will come and carry a child of God to his rest" (*Lasten Siioni* [1978], from VOZ, 12/1979).

✝ "Jesus indicates that His children have angels in heaven. The Arch-angel Michael and his angels cast the devil and his angels from heaven (Rev 12:7-9). In this, we see a picture of how Jesus Christ is the victor over the enemy of souls [Rev 12:10 cited]. There are angels on earth also; the Bible refers to servants of the word as angels. The servants of the seven churches in Asia were called angels (Rev 1:20). A child of God often feels that the other children of God are angels sent to minister in time of need" (VOZ, 10/2000).

✝ "Scriptures relate of angels many times. Angels were created by God to protect us, to be messengers, and to guide us on the road to heaven. Some angels in the Bible even have names" (VOZ, 10/2009).

✝ "One can only imagine what it would be like to be visited by an Angel. God has created Angels to serve Him, although they belong to the invisible world. The Bible, however, relates of several occasions when Angels have visited man. Sometimes they have come as messengers from God, and other times they have come to protect and deliver God's children from danger" (VOZ, 3/2010).

The scarcity of angels, demons, or other personal manifestations of religious experience in everyday life (e.g., feeling the presence of God, being "filled with the Spirit") is in accordance with a fairly low-key and pragmatic role of religion in the everyday lives of Conservative Laestadians today. That may come as a surprise to outsiders, given the uncompromising belief structure, extensive behavioral norms, and mystical roots of the movement.

Any personal expressions of evangelical piety such as ecstatic worship or outwardly visible individual prayer would be viewed as awkward and inauthentic. The visitor to worship services will find no one standing in the pews, hands outstretched, swaying with the tempo of some ecstatic praise song. Everyday conversations, whether in the church foyer or in private homes, are not overly focused on the spiritual realm or peppered with pious epithets like "praise the Lord" and "God willing." Public prayer is almost entirely reserved for the opening and closing of services (**4.7.2**).

4.4.6 The Enemy of Souls

> *When Luther wants to designate the power to which every man is subject in his sinfulness, he speaks of "flesh," of "the world," and of "the devil." He repeatedly places these three concepts together. Each of the three powers seduces men to sin and holds them captive in it; all three are opposed to God, to his word, and to faith.*
>
> —Paul Althaus, *The Theology of Martin Luther*

One spiritual entity that does hold a prominent and personal place in Conservative Laestadian theology is the "Enemy of Souls." Early on in Laestadianism, the devil had more of an individual character, but in later decades developed into an antithesis to the Trinity, the "three-fold enemy" consisting of Satan, the world, and one's own sin-fallen flesh.

† "When the Holy Spirit which speaks through the mouth of the Christians makes the devil that lives in the hearts of the unbelievers restless he becomes fierce. Now he comes out of their mouth with hide and hair. He puts them to gnash their teeth because of hate. He becomes so wroth that he thirsts after the blood of Christians" (Laestadius, Pentecost Morning sermon [1852]; *Fourth Postilla*, 121).

† "But now the devil of unbelief has launched an attack against us, for he knows that the blood of the Lamb of God is falling upon the hearts of the believers, and that is a deadly poison to him. So the devil strengthens the unrepentant and the enemies of the cross of Christ in the faith that God is merciful if they are penitent. But the devil prevents the awakened who should believe, from believing" (Raattamaa, letter written 1854, from Kulla 1985, 179).

† "We have often heard the enemy whisper: 'It is better that you give up your faith. If you in this state cling to what the Savior has done, you will fall into the sin of hypocrisy.' Thus we have become involved in the very marrow of the matter. We have come to see that if we now relinquish Jesus Christ we are lost. We have been compelled to answer the enemy: 'Everything else you may take, but do not estrange me from Jesus Christ'" (Havas [1940], 73).

† "When the God of this world opened his enticing bosom where he showed all of the allurements of sin and the flesh, then the unwary soul [became] careless with respect to the warnings of the word of God and gradually grew cold towards the companionship of Christians. The devil began in a refined manner to offer pride of life–finery. The victim began to beautify the old Adam. It became allowable to read romances and filthy literature written by this world's children; the eye began to search in the world for 'nice' friends and other good and 'innocent' companionship" (Eino Rimpiläinen, *Greetings of Peace*, 2/1944).

† "[L]et us not leave this Kingdom, although the enemy entices us through the world and the love of sin. At another time he oppresses [us] through our own corruption. And if he does not succeed with this, he comes to entice us through self-righteousness or through a preacher of false doctrine to lead us astray from God's Kingdom" (Kalle Timonen, *Greetings of Peace*, 8/1961).

† "The indwelling sin and corruption, which is the inheritance of our forefathers, together with the unbelieving world with its friends, and the sly enemy of the soul, work to steal all that which is heavenly from the hearts of children. With sorrow, many Christian parents see how powerfully the triune enemy attacks against their sons and daughters. The world is evil. If ever before, now in our day the enemy of the soul invents new snares with which to entangle the souls of the young people" (Paul Heideman, from *Greetings of Peace*, 5/1963).

† "The enemy of souls seeks to lead one astray in many ways. Also the young children of God feel how the enemy goes about as a roaring lion seeking whom he can devour" (Alajoki [1966], 125).

Throughout the writings and sermons, we find interesting descriptions of the enemy's actions and motives. In a 1974 *Päivämies* article, we also enounter an imaginative expansion of Rev 12:7-9 to explain the origin of the enemy:

> ✝ "Once in eternity God made plans to create a visible heaven and earth with all its hosts. But before His plans were carried out, a sad thing happened in the glory of heaven: one of the chief angels began to envy the omnipotence of God and together with some other angels made a secret plot against God to overthrow Him from His throne. But the works of darkness came to light then, even though they were done by glorious creatures. God cast out this chief angel from heaven, he who is called the devil and Satan, with all his multitudes, into outer darkness without any promise of redemption, without any grace and forgiveness. This angel became the satanic majesty of darkness who resolved to destroy the very crowning work of God's creation, man."

The actual passage on which this story is based merely states that there was war in heaven and Satan "was cast out into the earth, and his angels were cast out with him." Remember, the book of Revelation also testifies "unto every man that heareth the words of the prophecy of this book, if any man shall add unto these things, God shall add unto him the plagues that are written in this book" (22:18).

Returning to the enemy's motives, we read:

> ✝ "The enemy of the soul does everything possible to corrupt the work of God" (VOZ, 5/1974).

> ✝ "In these last times there are so many evil forces afoot with which we must do battle and the author of them all is Satan," who wants "confusion and doubts" among the believers (VOZ, 10/1978).

Well, for a condemned fallen angel who lost a war in heaven, he's doing a pretty good job of it, isn't he? Out of the seven billion people on earth, all he hasn't managed to grab are the children (who most everyone claims are innocent or saved somehow), the mentally incompetent, and a hundred thousand or so Conservative Laestadians. And he's actively working on them, too, as the other quotes in this section attest.

† "Already before the creation of the earth, the spiritual powers of darkness existed. The angels which rejected God had been placed into darkness with eternal shackles [Jude 1:6]. Adam and Eve were tempted by the powers of darkness" (*By Faith*, 21).

† "We know that the enemy of our souls always tries to break the love of the brothers and sisters and lead us into wrong watchings. We experience this warfare and have felt the wounds of sin. There isn't a single traveler on the way of faith that has not experienced the power and cunning of the threefold enemy–our flesh, the world, and Satan. The enemy surrounds us with temptations" (Alajoki [1989], 220).

† "We all feel the weakness of our flesh and the lusts which arise from within. However, there is no better place to be, when faced with such evil and temptations, than in the household of the living God as His child. Here we find comfort, support and encouragement in fighting 'the good fight of faith.' Our ability to battle against the evils of the world, Satan and our own flesh comes not of ourselves, but through faith" (Lawrence Byman, presentation given 1997).

† "James wrote that we are drawn by lust into sin, 'and sin when it is finished, brings forth death.' In both battles, Satan attacks God's Word first; his strategy is to raise doubts: 'Yea, hath God said?' even though he clearly understood what God said. When our thoughts are thus corrupted by our doubts concerning our lustful desires, we can then give ourselves permission to sin" (VOZ, 10/2000).

† "Our ever present three-fold enemy is forever trying to get us to fall into sin. Satan is at the forefront of this endeavor and wants us to serve him and his evil kingdom. He is a master of a thousand lies and is very subtle, persuasive, and crafty at his full-time occupation of trying to turn man away from God" (VOZ, 2/2002).

It all paints quite an impressive portrait of the enemy. And I wonder if those who are writing this stuff are really aware of what they are doing. As Price notes,

> Theologically, to posit such attendance of Satan upon every detail of every Christian life in the world today is to make Satan into an

evil God with an all-embracing negative providence. It is to say, virtually, that not a hair of your head will perish without his consent. In short, fundamentalism has, apparently without realizing it, gone the whole way with Zoroastrianism, making Satan into the opposite-but-equal God. Do you really mean to ascribe such all-embracing knowledge and activity to Satan? [2006b, 254]

Apparently so, because the fervor with which the topic is treated continues unabated to the present day:

> † "There is a daily battle between the Spirit of God within us and our sin-corrupt flesh. We also must deal with the influences of the world, which is in continuous turmoil around us. Satan is so close to us. He knows he does not have much time and is 'seeking whom he may devour.' . . . Satan desires to devour the believer. That is his work. He tries to sow confusion in our midst around various matters" (George Koivukangas, presentation given 2004).
>
> † "There has always been a division in this world between God's kingdom and those outside of its walls. Throughout history, this division has been apparent. A continual warfare between Satan and God's children has been taking place. Today Satan is combining the forces of various faiths into one ecumenical group" (VOZ, 11/2004).
>
> † "Wearing the helmet of the hope of salvation helps to ward off the enemy's attacks. It helps fight against this world's vain philosophies and wisdom. It reminds us to keep the wisdom of this world from mixing with the wisdom of the Spirit" (VOZ, 9/2006).
>
> † "[T]he things of this world may entice and tempt the child of God. The enemy of souls will whisper that a little fun and enjoyment with sinful life is acceptable. We remember that the enemy of souls is a liar and that those things that tempt a believer can be dangerous and lead one away from God's precious kingdom" (VOZ, 10/2007).
>
> † "We battle an enemy that does not show himself as easily as the army of Amelek did on the battlefield [Exodus 17:9-13]. There are many temptations that face God's children today. The enemy is

always devising clever schemes to trick God's children into sin and break the love between brothers and sisters" (VOZ, 5/2008).

† "Satan would want us to forget that there is power over sin. He is the master of lies and has practiced them from the beginning of time" (VOZ, 9/2009).

† "Satan is very resourceful and deceiving. He knows our weaknesses and is not shy about exploiting them. Recall how cunning Satan was in tempting Eve in the Garden of Eden. Satan questioned Eve whether God truly said they shouldn't eat of every tree in the Garden. He then tempted her and caused her to fall," knowing that "created man valued knowledge" and "how to cause a person to doubt" (VOZ, 10/2009).

† "When we put sin away, we're given the strength to battle against the three-fold enemy–the devil, the world, and our own flesh" (VOZ, 10/2009).

† "We are in a battle against an enemy coming from three directions. The enemy of souls tries to entice us to live by our corrupt flesh and blood and according to its desires. The enemy also tempts us with the enticements of the sins of the world. The enemy of souls continues to preach a sermon of lies, trying to thwart the counsel and instructions of God's Word and deny the consequences of disobeying God's Word" (*Christmas in Zion*, 2009).

The last two quotes show how the demonic antithesis to the Trinity is alive and well. Its three forces of evil are discussed separately at various points in the New Testament, but where is the Scriptural support for emphasizing this "threefold enemy" as much as it is in sermons and writings? Judas' treachery was not attributed to his own inherently evil "flesh." Rather, Satan "entered into" Judas (Luke 22:3, John 13:27), though Jesus did refer to Judas as a devil (John 6:70). Peter asked Ananias why Satan had "filled his heart" to lie to the Holy Ghost, rather than labeling his sin-corrupt heart as a source of evil itself (Acts 5:3). Certainly the "threefold enemy" as a concept is not new or unique to Laestadianism or even Lutheranism (see the epigraph to this section), but the level of emphasis it receives seems to be.

4.4.7 False Spirits

> *In fundamentalist groups . . . the movement, organisation, and group nested social identity is usually so strong that deviants . . . are likely to be treated as being in error. One of the several reasons for this intolerance of deviants is that any example of deviance decreases the group's homogeneity, and hence its distinctiveness from its out-groups. We all need to be absolutely clear where we stand, particularly where the deviant "heresy" is actually a part of the out-group's social identity. Moreover, we will all feel much purer and more virtuous if we have rooted out sinful error from our midst. Alternatively, if the deviant repents and requests re-acceptance, we will feel better for our act of forgiveness.*
>
> —Peter Herriot, *Religious Fundamentalism*

The 1960s, 1970s, and 1980s were times of doctrinal strife in which "false spirits" were deemed to be present in many church members. There was a "spirit of leniency," a "dry spirit," and a "spirit of the freedom of the flesh." There was also a "Kososlainen spirit" named after Juho Kosonen, who preached decades earlier from 1914 to the late 1930s and came to be considered a heretic. A 1964 issue of *Päivämies* published a written repentance from "Kosonenism":

> † The issue of the so-called Kosonenism and my involvement in it, which was taken up at the Joensuu meeting of preachers and elders, came as a great surprise to me, and so I couldn't even immediately recall all the points involved in the matter though I understood that repentance from Kosonenism was expected of me. I couldn't directly repent because, in my opinion, I have never approved of false doctrine. Therefore, my repentance turned out as clumsy as it did. . . . Now I indeed recall that in some 'discussions' I found myself defending Kosonenians because I have considered them believers. I haven't understood this matter previously as I do now since they have been confronted. And since I have thus found myself implicated in Kosonenism, I ask forgiveness for it from God's congregation. [from Hepokoski 2002b, 74]

In the 1980s, I was encouraged, along with many of my young peers, to repent of the "spirit of the freedom of the flesh" as a root cause of wayward behavior. My mother repented of the "Kososlainen spirit" without ever figuring out what it was. The spirits had been amply described in their fascinating variety:

> † "One of the first fruits of false spirit is that it immediately begins to undermine the authority of" the Christian church, as represented in Mt 18:23. "All who have fallen into bondage, whether of the spirit of self righteousness, or the spirit of leniency, or of ecumenism, or whatever, immediately begin to admire like Hagar their own fruitfulness and despise the unfruitful Sarah" (VOZ, 3/1974).
>
> † The birth of the "dry spirit" is often concealed, "and when it begins to come we do not often notice this. But its signs are very clear. When one repents of dryness, it does not take long when one is in the same dryness, in the same matters, in the same circles, in the same fault-findings as concerns other Christians. Then when the congregation of God counsels repentance for this and repentance is made, yet it is not long when one is back in the same dryness. Thus, little by little, as if unnoticed, false spirit has come into the heart" (VOZ, 5/1975).
>
> † "The same scriptural Word which effects life in the Christian by the Holy Spirit, works death when used by those who are governed by a foreign spirit. This spirit may be any of several kinds: lawful, lenient, dry, or any other, which if unchecked by the caretaking of the kingdom, will surely result in a final separation from the love of the good Shepherd" (VOZ, 8/1975).
>
> † "When a false spirit has taken the place of the Holy Spirit one begins to feed oneself with the faults of others and sees the instructions of God's kingdom as the sermon of the law. Those in the wrong can also join and feel strong unity of spirit–unity of a false spirit" (*Päivämies* No. 33, 1978).

A *Päivämies* article about "The Battle of Spirits" describes symptoms of the "dry spirit" and "lenient spirit" and states that one

> † must receive grace to repentance of false spirit, so that one can be delivered from under the power of the spirit of darkness to subjection of the Holy Spirit. In other words, "the tree has to be made good." It does not help at all, however diligently one would

amend or correct the fruits, for this does not change the spirit. [from VOZ, 6/1978]

A "false spirit" seeks "support and comfort" from like-minded individuals, which just sounds like simple human nature to me:

> † "The simplest formula for discerning the false spirit from the true and Holy Spirit is given by John: 'we are of God: he that knoweth God heareth us; he that is not of God heareth not us. Hereby know we the spirit of truth and the spirit of error.' . . . Whenever a false spirit of carnality or self-righteousness attacks and confuses a Christian, he begins to seek support and comfort from and among those who are in the same condition of error. Thus are the seeds and foundations of heresy established" (VOZ, 10/1978).

Einari Lepistö provided a detailed description of the "Kososlainen spirit" in a 1979 issue of *Päivämies* (from VOZ, 9/1979). Although the "manifestations and fruits of the Kososlainen spirit are varied," a common feature is that it, "in one way or another, quarrels against the Holy Spirit of God. . . . It speaks of the preciousness of God's congregation, but at the same time criticizing in a fault-finding way, sometimes an individual Christian, speaker-brothers, or persons who are in positions of trust in the activities of Christianity." Rather than depart as a heresy, the "Kososlainen false spirit hangs on with Christianity."

It is a "spirit of freedom of the flesh," yet is "a doctrine of works." One with the Kososlainen spirit "uses confession but has no intention of giving up the sin," often engages in "carnal rejoicing" (ecstatic outbursts) when instructed to repent, though "those rejoicings are not inspired by the Holy Spirit." To the Kososlainen spirit belong "false Bible prophecy" and "visions and dreams." It "prophesizes of upcoming events or times and also of the end of the world," and dreams "go before God's Word. One believes in dreams more than in the word of God." (It is surprising to see "prophesying the end of the world" and experiencing "visions and dreams" associated with a "false spirit." Conservative writings and sermons of the period were full of "end times" sentiment, **4.8.2**. And doesn't the writer realize how important "visions and dreams" were to Laestadius and his contemporaries, **4.1.5?**)

The article attributes some interesting behaviors to the Kososlainen spirit. It "can hide itself underground. It goes into hiding for long spells. In a suitable time it raises its head. Often it happens so, that a Kososlainen will repent when reprimanded, is still for a while, and then again rises to the surface, the same and unchanged." Often, it "can be clearly seen," but at "other times, Kososlaisuus can hide so, that it is very difficult to recognize the false spirit." It can even "fight the same Kososlainen spirit in another person."

Amazing stuff. The next quote is more restrained in its description, but not in its variety of spirits:

> ✝ "[I]f a permissive frame of mind becomes one's attitude toward life, and a permissive stand on all matters is prevalent, then a wrong spirit rules the heart–a permissive spirit. . . . If, on the other hand, the enemy of our soul has succeeded in causing a dry spirit in us, the fruits are apparent in overzealousness and in furthering the development of divisions. The one in the dry spirit feels he is in the right and does not readily agree to counsel or guidance" (VOZ, 5/1980).

My sampling yielded just two more references to spirits. Here is one:

> ✝ "Throughout time, believers have battled false doctrines and heretical spirits. Apostle Paul spoke openly to the Corinthians saying, there must be heresies among you so that those who are tried in your midst shall be made known (1 Cor 11:19). Recognizing this evil time, we need to be watchful on our journey of faith" (VOZ, 7/1999).

The other is a brief reference to the "lenient spirit" in 2009 (**4.6.4**). Sometime not long after this point, the whole legion of false spirits galloped over the Gadarene cliffs. The younger generation has never heard of them, and the older generation recalls them privately with bemusement.

4.5 Justification

> *Pure religion and undefiled before God and the Father is this, To visit the fatherless and widows in their affliction, and to keep himself unspotted from the world.*
>
> *—The Epistle of James*

4.5.1 The Law

> *The law was our schoolmaster to bring us unto Christ, that we might be justified by faith.*
>
> —*The Epistle to the Galatians*

The earliest Christians were all Jews bound to the law, which had been set forth in the Torah (the first five books of the Bible) and then subjected to over a thousand years of interpretation, augmentation, and watering down. By the time Jesus came along, boys were no longer being stoned to death for lipping off to their fathers, nor were girls for failing to produce evidence of virginity on their wedding night. But the law was still very much an ideal to be preached if not fully practiced. As Matthew 5:17-19 tells it, Jesus did not change that, either:

> Think not that I am come to destroy the law, or the prophets: I am not come to destroy, but to fulfil. For verily I say unto you, Till heaven and earth pass, one jot or one tittle shall in no wise pass from the law, till all be fulfilled. Whosoever therefore shall break one of these least commandments, and shall teach men so, he shall be called the least in the kingdom of heaven: but whosoever shall do and teach them, the same shall be called great in the kingdom of heaven.

It was Peter's zealous interpretation of the law—still of great importance to him even after Jesus' resurrection supposedly fulfilled it—that made him so reluctant to visit the house of Cornelius.[29] Only after Peter did so, having been persuaded by a divine vision, does Acts 10:44-48 tell of the first Gentiles being accepted into the new sect of Jesus followers. A few

---

29. Deuteronomy 7:2-6 is an example of how the Old Testament was not exactly a textbook for tolerance and warm community relations: "[T]hou shalt smite them, and utterly destroy them; thou shalt make no covenant with them, nor shew mercy unto them: Neither shalt thou make marriages with them; thy daughter thou shalt not give unto his son, nor his daughter shalt thou take unto thy son. For they will turn away thy son from following me, that they may serve other gods: so will the anger of the LORD be kindled against you, and destroy thee suddenly. But thus shall ye deal with them; ye shall destroy their altars, and break down their images, and cut down their groves, and burn their graven images with fire. For thou art an holy people unto the LORD thy God: the LORD thy God hath chosen thee to be a special people unto himself, above all people that are upon the face of the earth."

chapters later, we read about Paul and Barnabus shifting their preaching efforts to the Gentiles (13:45-46). The Gentile conversions marked the beginning of the end of Jewish influence in Christianity. "Christianity generally ceased to be a part of what survived as mainstream Judaism well before the end of the first century A.D." (McDonald and Porter 2000, 245).

Right away there was a squabble about the new converts' observance of the Jewish law. Before Jesus, there had been Gentile "God fearers" who respected and worshiped the Jewish God but were not full converts. Those who took the full step into Judaism had to promise adherence to the law. That included circumcision for the male converts, not exactly a pleasant prospect. So when some of the Jewish Christians expected the same treatment of their new Gentile brethren, there was "no small dissension and disputation" (Acts 15:2). A meeting of "the apostles and elders" was convened (v. 5). "And when there had been much disputing," Peter–who had been so scrupulous as to not even want to meet with a Gentile god-fearer–gave a rousing little speech about the law being "a yoke upon the neck of the disciples, which neither our fathers nor we were able to bear." Rather, he and the Jewish Christians deliberating with him now believed "that through the grace of the LORD Jesus Christ we shall be saved, even as" the new Gentile converts (vv. 7-11).[30]

Ever since, the general idea has been that Christians are under grace, and not the law:[31]

> † "We are not rejecters of the law as some believe us to be. The law is spiritual, and we are carnal; therefore we cannot fulfill the law, but we must flee unto the Mediator of the new covenant, in whose wounds we are healed of those wounds which sin has

---

30. This is all, of course, from the perspective of the writer of Luke/Acts. Had the writer(s) of Matthew been telling the story, we might be reading a very different account with a lot more deference to the Law.

31. Clement of Alexandria makes an interesting point that would seem to oppose any such distinction: The "law is not at variance with the Gospel, but agrees with it. How should it be otherwise, one Lord being the author of both?" (*Stromata*, Book 2, Ch. 23). He veers far afield from Pauline Christianity, though, when he asserts that "there are two paths of reaching the perfection of salvation, works and knowledge" (*Stromata*, Book 4, Ch. 6).

made in our consciences, which the law makes clearly apparent" (Raattamaa, sermon given 1894, from Kulla 1985, 185).

> † "The question has sometimes risen, does the grace of God alone suffice to give power and to teach the child of God against the temptations of sin. . . . Nowhere does the word of God place any other rule or guide of life for the believer at any time. In God's wholesome grace it is alone. Every one, whom the law has awakened to the conviction of sin and compelled him to flee to Christ, remembers, how bottomless was the grace of God in Jesus Christ" (Eino Rimpiläinen, *Siionin Lähetyslehti*, 12/1948, from *Greetings of Peace*, 3/1949).

The purpose of the law is to preach damnation to unbelievers:

> † "The law cannot take man any farther than to the knowledge of sin. It cannot pardon and justify a transgressor, for the purpose of the law is to preach of death and damnation" (Taskila 1961, 14).

You won't find much of that preaching in the writings and statements of the SRK and LLC that are directed to the unsaved public, though. Apparently, "death and damnation" don't make for good PR. And "the knowledge of sin" with all its seemingly endless, mostly unwritten specifics (**4.6.1**) is stressed not to outsiders, but to those within the fold, particularly the youth.

> † A person only understands that he cannot fulfill the law when it opens up to him "that the law demands from him unconditional obedience and perfection in everything, not only in external deeds, but also in a spiritual mind. . . . Thus the law shows a person his sinfulness and undresses him of his self-righteousness. When the law rebukes of sin it awakens bitterness towards the commands of law and God, and so a person under the curse of the law is made to realize even this other true matter, that he hates God, whom he should love with all his heart, all his soul, all his mind and all his strength. Thus the duty of the law through the letter killeth, for through the law comes a consciousness of sin. . . . Every awakened person, who has felt the fear and distress over one's sins and trespasses, has also been able to experience how God has through the gospel in His kingdom comforted him" (*Päivämies*, 1974).

Supposedly God has written the law into the hearts of all mankind, and they are thus "without excuse" (Rom 1:18):

> † "God gave His Holy Law through His servant Moses on Mount Sinai. God wrote them on tables of stone in the form of the Ten Commandments. They were delivered in the midst of thunder, lightning, and quaking and brought terror and fear into the hearts of those present.... Could we say then, that if one had no knowledge of the law that he is excused from it? The answer is no. The Apostle explains . . . that it has been written into the hearts of all mankind [Rom 2:12-15]" (Dan Rintamaki, presentation given 1994).

What about the Pirahã Indians that Daniel Everett tried converting in the Amazon jungle (**4.2.4**)? "There was no sense of sin among" them, "no need to 'fix' mankind or even themselves. There was acceptance for things the way they are, by and large. No fear of death. Their faith was in themselves" (Everett 2008, 271). Are they "without excuse," because somehow, in some hidden way that Everett could not detect in all his vain efforts to get them to appreciate Christianity, "the wrath of God is revealed from heaven against all ungodliness and unrighteousness of men" (Rom 1:18)? Paul's assertion that "the invisible things of [God] from the creation of the world are clearly seen" (Rom 1:20) is no more true of the Pirahãs than it is of the "childhood atheists" who dominate Sweden and Vietnam.

The reality is that the law is neither preached nor effective. It comprises a set of harsh and often baffling commandments (not just the ten that everybody talks about, but page after page of rules strewn throughout the Pentateuch) to a tribe of Bronze Age desert nomads. They have so little applicability to today's society that they are largely unknown, not least to the Conservatives who claim them to be God's divine edict.

It won't do to say that Jesus dispensed with the need for us to concern ourselves with the specifics of the Old Testament rules. What exactly is "the law," then? It certainly wasn't about watching movies and wearing fingernail polish. And let's not forget what Jesus himself said, at least according to the legalistic writer of Matthew 5:17-19:

> Think not that I am come to destroy the law, or the prophets: I am not come to destroy, but to fulfil. For verily I say unto you, Till heaven and earth pass, one jot or one tittle shall in no wise pass

from the law, till all be fulfilled. Whosoever therefore shall break one of these least commandments, and shall teach men so, he shall be called the least in the kingdom of heaven: but whosoever shall do and teach them, the same shall be called great in the kingdom of heaven.

One example of how Christians routinely violate the law without having any idea they are doing so is discussed in **6.2**. And it's part of the Ten Commandments!

The idea that the law writes anything like directions for contacting Conservative Laestadians (the only knowledge that really matters, after all) into the hearts of all mankind is simply ludicrous. Only a few million out of the seven billion people throughout the world are even aware of this sect claiming to be "God's Kingdom." Of those, only a tiny fraction show any interest in converting to it. And, from the experience of recent years anyway, most of those few converts wind up leaving sooner or later. If "God gave His Holy Law" to awaken people to the knowledge of sin and ultimately lead them to "His Kingdom," it's hard to imagine how he could have failed more spectacularly.

Perhaps due to the movement's Pietist nature, some also considered the law applicable as an instruction book for the believer who was living by grace in Christ. Uljas notes that this so-called "third use of the law"

> was a central subject of contention in the discussions at the end of the 1800s and beginning of the 1900s, when the New Awakened and Firstborn [OALC] separated from the original Laestadianism. Conservativism retained the original understanding of Laestadianism: the Law does not belong to a Christian. [2000, 53]

"During the schism of the 1930s" with those who formed the Apostolic Lutheran Federation, "the third function of the Law was one of the reasons for disagreement, though more covertly." Then he tries to have it both ways:

> † "The Law does not belong to a Christian," but the rejection of "the third function of the Law has not led the children of God to permissiveness of sin. We have received another teacher in place of the law, for God has given us His Spirit to be our home tutor. . . . The wholesome grace of God that brings salvation does not teach one to commit sin but give strength to fight against it.

Grace does not teach differently than the Ten Commandment Law" (p. 53).

Uljas plays a word game to have "grace" function as some sort of active agent that "teaches" a believer just like the law does to an unbeliever. It is not just a game, though, when you condemn a whole group of people based in large part on a distinction without a difference. I wonder what Uljas would have thought of my conversation with Carl Kulla in 2010, where I asked Carl to say just what he believes (as a Federation member) about the role of the law in his life. After considerable discussion, neither I nor the Conservative preacher who was with me could find anything doctrinally problematic about Carl's viewpoint. It is the love of Christ that motivates him to live the life of a Christian; his actions arise from his faith just like the Conservatives say it should.

This next quote describes the first use of the law, to drive a person to Christ:

> † "The purpose of the preaching of repentance is to awaken the unbeliever to the hopelessness of his sin-fallen condition. The condition of one in unbelief is hopeless, because without faith one is under the law, and the righteous law of God demands perfection. If one sins he comes unto death. Unless he is awakened from the sleep of sin, he will die in his sins and suffer eternal death. But if he can be awakened, he will seek refuge from his burden of sin" (VOZ, 1/2000).

This quote one hints at the second use, as God's instruction book for the good of mankind:

> † "God has proclaimed his will in the Ten-Commandment Law. Its outward observance has a positive affect on man's life, even though the Christian is not under the Law" (*Päivämies* No. 11, 2004).

But those instructions are impossible to follow:

> † "Jesus shows how futile it is to attempt to fulfill God's Law. He explains that not only does the Law condemn one who actually commits an act such as murder or adultery, but it also condemns one who even thinks these things in their mind. . . . because we are all so thoroughly corrupt, we are not able to fulfill the demands of the Law; we are under its condemnation. That is

exactly why Jesus came to earth and suffered and died on our behalf. By believing upon Him, we are acceptable to God. We are no longer under the curse of the Law, but under the free grace of God" (VOZ, 7/2007).

† The rich man of Mark 10:17-27 showed "the fruits of his self-righteousness. He thought he had fulfilled the commandment, but still lacked the assurance of being heaven acceptable. This is one of the primary results of attempting to make oneself heaven acceptable. No matter how much is done, it is never enough. The Law demands perfection. No mortal can fulfill such demands and, thus, this man was left questioning what more was required of him. He hoped to hear Jesus say that he had done all that was necessary to inherit heaven" (VOZ, 6/2008).

Here is something for Conservative Laestadian men to consider after an outing at the water park, the mall, or the beach. You probably lusted after a woman in your heart at least once, more likely several times. As the first of the above two quotes indicates, Jesus said that doing so is the same as committing adultery (Mt 5:28). And adultery is a "sin unto death"; adulterers shall not inherit the Kingdom of God (1 Cor 6:9). Do you really believe you will go to hell if you get in an accident and die on the way home?

In the last quote of this sample, we read that God has given everyone a conscience, and a basic knowledge of right and wrong. Unfortunately, though, we can't rely on it:

† "Even before God gave the Law through Moses, He had given every person a conscience and 'written into his heart' the natural law which is a basic knowledge of right and wrong. . . . Through the conscience God 'speaks' to the individual. Sin, however, causes one to become spiritually hard of hearing and God's voice to seem faint and distant. For that reason one cannot depend solely on his conscience as the only guide for making spiritual decisions. In order to remain spiritually alive and heaven-acceptable one's conscience must be bound to the Word of God, which is unchanging and eternal" (VOZ, 12/2008).

What the quoted writer really means by "God's Word" is, of course, "What we say that God says." Hearing that business about God's Word being "unchanging and eternal" from people who neither know much about nor particularly follow the Bible's multitude of edicts never ceases to annoy me. Does the quoted writer keep kosher? Would he have his son stoned to death for speaking disrespectfully to him, or his daughter for being raped without crying out loudly enough? Would he kill his wife if she decided to worship a different God? Would he condone the beating of a slave to the brink of his life because he is mere property? Would he check the family history of a new convert to make sure the prospective member was not born out of wedlock, nor his ancestors out to ten generations? Does he object when a woman sits in church with no head covering, speaks up during Bible class or a congregational discussion, or teaches Sunday School? See **6.2**, **6.3**, **6.4**, **6.5.**, and **7.4**.

4.5.2 Works

> *What doth it profit, my brethren, though a man say he hath faith, and have not works? Can faith save him?*
>
> —*The Epistle of James*

Conservative Laestadianism follows Luther's lead in siding with Paul's "salvation by grace, without works of the law" theology. The "faith without works is dead" counterargument of James gets little attention. Laestadius went so far as to consider works "done in faith" good no matter what:

> † "Christians will be judged, not according to those works they had done in sorrowlessness before their conversion, but according to the works done after their conversion which are accounted as good works, for they have been done in faith. For if God judged the Christians according to their former works which were done in sorrowlessness they would be condemned to hell. But Christians will be judged according to the works which they have done in faith, which are considered good even though they are not good" (Twenty-sixth Sunday after Trinity sermon [1848]; *Fourth Postilla*, 179).

Leonard Typpö framed the matter precisely in Lutheran and Pauline fashion:

> † "[T]he merits of the Lord Jesus by the grace of God are the only means by which we are acceptable to God" (*Siionin Lähetyslehti*, 1915).

Writing around the same time, Matti Suo [1861-1927] relates the matter to the "fruits of faith," warning those who confess faith through their words but not their actions:

> † "I am amazed, when in the world so much is spoken of faith and still it does not bear the fruit which it should. Can we call that faith by which nothing is won? Life is as ungodly and sinful as can be, and as I already mentioned with sorrow, in the form of christianity, there are preachers and advocaters of liberty and provision for the flesh. I would like to say a few words in warning, be whom you are, do not allow, mortal man, the enemy to deceive you into believing that you will be saved by just saying that you believe, though your life and works in your every step testifies that your confession of faith only speeds you to destruction and hell" (from *Greetings of Peace*, 1/1953).

A couple of decades later, Havas had much the same criticism, and referred to the pardoned sinner's "persistent combat" against sin:

> † "Whoever confesses salvation by faith through grace and allows his members freedom to indulge in the servitude of sin, is a loathsome liar, a swine that dishonors the blood of Jesus" (Havas [1937], 66-67).

> † "[T]raveling in the Light is a pardoned sinner's submission in repentance before God and man, a persistent combat against the intrigues of sin" (Havas [1939], 81-82).

Paul Heideman, with the gentle pastoral manner that comes through in his writings and sermons, allowed readers some comfort about their failings:

> † "We feel and find ourselves so sinful, so poor even in our profession of faith. Dear young brothers and sisters, do not think for a moment that the fact we have confessed faith for 30 or 40 years that it has made us in ourselves meriting before God and thus claiming heaven. No, but on the contrary, we feel in ourselves we have become poor Christians, weaker Christians, colder Christians . . ." (*Greetings of Peace*, 6/1954).

Works were to follow faith, not the other way around, consistent with Luther's expectation that the certainty of God's forgiving mercy would work joyful obedience to God's will (Althaus 1963, 235):

† "When the grace of God reaches the bottom of the tortured and fearful heart, a desire also comes to walk in truth. It does not happen, as the world fears, that when free grace is preached and all sins are forgiven without any conditions, the result will be a loose Christianity, but there awakens the will to fight against all evil" (Taskila 1961, 15).

† "The question about faith and works has always caused a conflict between the Spirit and the flesh. Even many an awakened person being aware of his own ungodliness may think, that if he first be able to correct the manners of his life, become holier and more ardent, then it would be more possible for him to be converted. Yet, the apostle proclaims altogether differently: 'To him that believed on him that justifieth the ungodly, his faith is counted for righteousness.' ... [A] man who works for his salvation praises himself, which is despising Jesus' work of redemption" (Lauri Hakso, *Greetings of Peace*, 4/1971).

† "The righteousness of life follows the righteousness of faith. It is the fruit of the righteousness of faith. It is never before faith or goes before it" (VOZ, 2/1979).

Those phrases "righteousness of life" and "righteousness of faith" took on a life of their own during the early 1980s of my youth. I suspect it had something to do with the demands for spiritual purity associated with the caretaking meetings (**4.6.4**). It really didn't matter how well you spoke or acted if it had been "revealed" that a false spirit (**4.4.7**) was present and the "righteousness of faith" was not the driving force.

In the next several quotes (except for one by Uljas), the timeworn caricature of the "world" being in "self-righteousness" and relying on works for salvation makes yet another appearance. Besides trying to distinguish "them" from "us" (**4.2.3**), I wonder if these statements conceal some embarrassment about how little Conservative Laestadianism actually accomplishes as a force of tangible, temporal good in society. The question arose for Dennis McDonald when he saw the "apostate" Catholics and Episcopalians, but not his fellow church members, working with the poor in the migrant community of Salinas, California. "Why was it that we fundamentalists, who claim the Bible as our ultimate authority and Christ as Lord, were doing so little to live out the gospel? Something was wrong, terribly wrong" (2003, 111).

† In Rom 10:1-8, "Paul writes of two kinds of righteousness–the righteousness of God and the self-motivated righteousness which is called self-righteousness. Although according to the Bible, self-righteousness is not acceptable to God, nevertheless, it has been widely supported through the ages. What is the basis of self-righteousness? It is a product of man's own thoughts and mentality.... The righteousness acceptable to God is that we humble ourselves to believe according to the Word of God" (*Siionin Lähetyslehti*, 1980).

† "Many people are counted as 'good and honorable' human beings in life. Many churches teach listeners to give to the poor, live a clean life, refrain from drinking, pray to God, attend church on a regular basis, and be nice to people, to name a few good works. False religions and the carnal mind teach that this is the road that leads to everlasting life. Even to the carnal mind of a child of God, these teachings can sound reasonable. In spite of our carnal thinking, it is through the grace of God, that the child of God is enlightened by the power of the Holy Spirit to comprehend the righteousness of faith" (VOZ, 9/1998).

† "The believer does not become perfect; he commits sin every day in thought, word, and deed. We are both sinful and righteous at the same time. However, the direction of life changes. The first sign of this is love. The relationship to God changes to one between a child and a loving Father. The children of God, brothers and sisters, become dear. The heart begins to be ruled by the wholesome grace of God, obedience of faith, and the correct fear of God" (Uljas 2000, 48).

Matthew emphasized the importance of works and Jewish law. That's not how it comes out in this exegesis of Mt 25:31-46, though:

† "The people of the world live thinking, they do works to justify salvation: they build huge churches, they give money, they listen to the speeches of their blind guides. Believers, on the other hand, feel weak and poor, and that they have done nothing worthy of such a great reward. But Jesus answers them that you have fed me with the living word spoken from one believer to another. You have offered my peace and safety to strangers looking for a home and the promise of life. You have clothed seeking ones with my robe of righteousness through the proclamation of the Gospel.

Those sick in sin, you forgave, and those bound in the shackles of death and unbelief, you freed through proclaiming that they can believe all sins forgiven in Jesus' name and precious shed blood. In this way God's children have served the Lord of Life" (VOZ, 11/2002).

Matthew says absolutely nothing about any "living word spoken from one believer to another," "promise of life," "robe of righteousness through the proclamation of the Gospel," "sickness of sin," etc. This interpolation of Pauline and Lutheran "grace and forgiveness" meaning into Bible passages about works is commonly heard in sermons, but isn't it a bit dishonest? (See 4.3.5.) Imagine the reaction if the words "you, Peter, and your successor popes and their priests" were explained as being an implicit part of Jesus' giving the Holy Spirit to the disciples for the remittance and retaining of sins. (As discussed in 7.1, that Roman Catholic interpretation of Mt 16:18-20 is not nearly so far-fetched.)

† "There is nothing a person can do in his own behalf in order to be acceptable to God and merit salvation. It is alone by God's grace that one can believe. When a person feels distress over sin in his heart and hears and believes the gospel of Christ, he is made heaven acceptable" (VOZ, 9/2003).

† "Cain offered as sacrifice the works of his own hands–which he felt would be good and acceptable. His own works were rejected by God. Abel offered the unblemished lamb, which represented the Lord Jesus. Abel's sacrifice was acceptable by faith . . . [N]othing man does on his own can be pleasing to God" (VOZ, 7/2007).

Note the emphasis in the following quote on *not* doing things:

† "Believers are sometimes asked, 'What is it about you that makes you different?' or 'Why don't you do these things that everyone else does?' There may be other similar questions and observations that reveal God's light that shines forth from His children. We, God's children, are as Moses–small and helpless in ourselves. The light emanates not from our mortal flesh and blood, but from the Holy Spirit of God" (VOZ, 6/2008).

There are no visible efforts by Conservative Laestadians to perform works of charity on behalf of those outside the group; even the humanitarian aid work of recent years is directed specifically to the new believers in West Africa and Ecuador. There are no Conservative Laestadian soup kitchens or shelters for the homeless or battered women, nor is there any real encouragement for individuals to work with "worldly Christians" at such efforts, at least not in North America. This situation has been publicly addressed a couple of times; see a quote from the July 2000 *Voice of Zion* and one in 2002 by Matti Kontkanen in 4.2.3.

In the U.S. at least, the political mindset of almost all individual Conservatives is, well, conservative, and not given to much sympathy for the poor and downtrodden. I disagree with but can respect an honest political stance that it is not the place of government to do charitable work. But those who take that position and yet do nothing as individuals or a church to care for their neighbors have reason to consider just what they stand for, I think.

The New Testament is quite a socially liberal collection of writings in many ways, with Jesus' admonitions to care for the least of his brethren (Mt 25:34-40), the sharing of all things in common and parting to all needy men in Acts 2:44-45, and the criticism of the selfish rich by James, who raised Luther's ire by saying "faith without works is dead" (2:20). James offered the specific example of a brother or sister who is "naked, and destitute of daily food." If one says unto them, "Depart in peace, be ye warmed and filled; notwithstanding ye give them not those things which are needful to the body; what doth it profit?" (James 2:15-16). Perhaps the words of Irenaeus in the fourth of the *Fragments* attributed to him would be worth remembering as well: "As long as any one has the means of doing good to his neighbours, and does not do so, he shall be reckoned a stranger to the love of the Lord."

4.5.3 Faith

> *Faith is a thing in the heart, having its being and substance by itself, given of God as his proper work, not a corporal thing, that may be seen, felt, or touched.*
>
> —Martin Luther, *Table Talk*

Going back to Laestadius with his many references to "dead faith," Conservative Laestadianism presents faith less as an act or viewpoint of piety or belief, "the substance of things hoped for, the evidence of things not seen" (Heb 11:1) than as a spiritual possession, essentially equivalent to the Holy Spirit itself. It is actually quite rare to define faith as a belief *in* anything. Rather, as the SRK website states on its *Thus We Believe* page, "Faith is a gift from God," which he "has given to each child born into this world." (Unfortunately, it is a gift that stops working as soon as the person reaches the age of accountability.)

There is some scriptural support for treating faith as an object apart from belief:

- 2 Cor 4:13 (gifts of the Spirit include words of wisdom and knowledge, faith, gifts of healing, etc.);
- Gal 5:6 (faith works through love);
- Eph 2:8 ("For by grace are ye saved through faith; and that not of yourselves: it is the gift of God");
- 1 Tim 1:19 ("Holding faith, and a good conscience");
- 2 Pet 1:1 (addressing "them that have obtained like precious faith with us through the righteousness of God and our Saviour Jesus Christ").

More often, however, the New Testament refers to faith in the context of belief. In Jesus' references to faith as an object, it is clearly an act of belief in God's power:

- Mt 17:20 (mustard seed);
- Mt 21:21 (move mountains);
- Mk 10:51-52 ("thy faith hath made thee whole");
- Lk 7:7-9 (the centurion's plea for his servant);
- Lk 18:8-9 (criticism of those trusting in their own righteousness).
- Acts 11:24 says that Barnabus was "full of the Holy Ghost and of faith," but that implies that the two are not equivalent, and one can be "full of faith" in the same way one can be "full of doubt."
- Rom 10:17 is often cited for the proposition that "faith cometh by hearing, and hearing by the word of God," but the previous verse makes it clear that the writer is referring to an act of belief: "[T]hey have not all obeyed the gospel. For Esaias saith, Lord, who hath believed our report?"

- Rom 12:3 encourages every man "to think soberly, according as God hath dealt to every man the measure of faith," indicating faith to be a gift but intertwined with thought and a "renewing of your mind" (Rom 12:2).

- Gal 3:22-23 talks about the promise by faith and the coming of faith, but as a gift "to them that believe."

- What Gal 5:22 refers to as "faith" in the KJV is faithfulness (NASB) or fidelity (Price 2006a), one of several fruits of the spirit.

- Eph 3:16-18 encourages the reader to have Christ "dwell in your hearts by faith" for comprehension of the breadth, length, etc.

- Hebrews 11 describes the faith of various Old Testament figures in terms of their trust in God.

Conservatives also often refer to faith as something that a person is "in," with a believing church member being "in faith" and an ex-member having "left faith." This essentially uses "faith" as a synonym for the true church, which also has scriptural support:

- Acts 6:7 ("a great company of the priests were obedient to the faith");

- Acts 13:8 (a sorcerer sought "to turn away the deputy from the faith");

- Acts 14:22 ("continue in the faith");

- Rom 1:5 ("obedience to the faith");

- 2 Cor 13:5 ("Examine yourselves, whether ye be in the faith");

- Gal 6:10 (those "of the household of faith");

- Eph 4:5 ("One Lord, one faith, one baptism");

- 1 Tim 1:1, 4:1 ("Timothy, my own son in the faith," "some shall depart from the faith");

- Titus 1:13 ("rebuke them sharply, that they may be sound in the faith").

Note, however, that the last references–from Ephesians, 1 Timothy, and Titus–were probably written not by Paul, but others in Paul's name. It is a significant distinction. For the later author of the Pastorals (including 1 Timothy and Titus), faith "means the body of teaching that makes up the Christian religion," which had coalesced into a hierarchical church by that time. But for Paul, faith "refers to the trust a person has in Christ to bring about salvation through his death" (Ehrman 2011, 99).

My sampling seems to indicate a slight difference in how faith was viewed at different intervals in Conservative Laestadian history, too. I don't see why that would be the case, and am not convinced it is significant. In any event, my review of the sample is without subgroupings, with all the quotes here in a single chronological sequence. The first of them is by Leonard Typpö [1868-1922]:

> † "The sinner is not justified only by having the doctrine with all its truth nor the works that are ordered by it, but the sinner is justified according to the doctrine of Christ by faith in the core of the doctrine which is the Christ. One should not stop to an outward crust, for there is no power of life, but he should be able to go through the crust to the open fountain, the forgiveness of sins which is in the blood of Jesus. There God pours out the innocent righteousness of his Son into sinners' believing hearts. This is the righteousness by which one is acceptable to enter into the kingdom of heaven, and he is becoming a partaker of all goods of the house of the Father. Then the poor sinner has righteousness, peace and joy in the Holy Ghost" (from *Greetings of Peace*, 8/1970).

The believer is to have faith not just in Christ, but "in the core of the doctrine which is the Christ." Is God in his three persons being forced to share the stage with "doctrine" as an object of worship? Contrast this with:

- Mk 11:22 ("Have faith in God");
- Acts 3:16 ("faith in his name");
- Acts 20:21 ("faith toward our Lord Jesus Christ");
- Acts 24:24 ("the faith in Christ");
- Rom 3:22 (righteousness of God "is by faith of Jesus Christ");
- Rom 3:25 ("faith in his blood");
- Rom 4:20 (Abraham "staggered not at the promise of God through unbelief, but was strong in faith");
- Eph 1:15 ("your faith in the Lord Jesus");

- Col 2:5 ("your faith in Christ").

The following quotes taking us up to 1984 all have what seems to me like an appropriate emphasis on the object of Christian faith:

> † "A living faith in Christ is the power by which the fleshly desires are suppressed, and obedience to God's will obtained. 'Who is he that overcometh the world but he that believeth.' By faith, then, we conquer the world both inward and outward. Faith is not an empty saying, but believing the gospel brings also God's power" (Matti Suo [1861-1927], from *Greetings of Peace*, 1/1953).

> † "It is impossible for a believer to continue in faith, without every moment looking unto Jesus. . . . If you ask what is meant by looking to Jesus, the answer is, the exercise of faith in our Lord Jesus Christ. Faith unites us with God, we walk by faith and live by faith, depending every hour on Jesus to feed us, clothe us, lead and guard us" (John Nelson, *Greetings of Peace*, 8/1950).[32]

> † "God's Holy Spirit, with the word, gives us strength, comforts us and testifies of the blessed faith, the teachings of the truth, and the faith of Jesus Christ, in whose faith we are going forward and through strength derived from faith we are believing" (Ville Suutari, *Greetings of Peace*, 9/1954).

> † The letter to the Hebrews says "how faith is the substance of things hoped for: the evidence of things not seen. Jesus says, blessed is he who has not seen, yet believes; Believes what? Believes that God, the Creator of all things, has given His only

---

32. The Nelson family has had remarkable exposure to the various factions of North American Laestadianism. John Nelson was originally with the Federation but joined the Conservatives in the 1930s after his move to the Midwest from the West Coast (Kulla, personal communication 2010). He remained a Conservative until his death in the early 1960s (Lehtola 2010), but his three sons, who all became preachers, went with the group surrounding Walter Torola in the schism of 1973. Then, decades later, two of the sons found themselves alienated from Walter's son Peter Torola and one of them wound up in the Federation (Pieti, *Reconciliation*).

Oddly enough, it appears that John Nelson switched sides from the Federation to the Conservatives without making any public repentance from his association with that "heresy" (Palola 2010).

begotten Son for payment of our sin debt. Believes these promises of God, that [Jesus] is the propitiation of our sins. That it is He who on that final day of judgment will claim His own and bring His own before the Father" (VOZ, 3/1975).

✝ Despite our longing to have "warm spiritual feelings," we "know that we are not saved by feelings but by faith. Our faith is not based on our feelings but upon that rock which is the Lord Jesus Christ" (Jon Bloomquist, sermon given 1984).

Remember, though, how important "high and living feelings" were to Laestadius, who considered them "the essence and subjective foundation of living faith," and wrote that "if faith is only in the understanding without corresponding blessed feelings, it is dead faith–faith without sufficient foundation" (*VCW*, 83). Man will not become saved by "just knowledge in understandings alone," he preached in his Third Rogation Day Morning sermon of 1853, "but man becomes saved by feelings of living faith in the heart" (*Fourth Postilla*, 218). There is some similarity to Luther's view that a man's faith is not just a belief in Christ being sent to act on behalf of sinful men, but an affirmation that he is one of those men, with confidence about his own personal salvation (Harran 1983, 119).

These quotes from 1986-2000 treat faith as an object, something that is received as a gift:

✝ "We would continue this walk in faith even though this faith is so small and so weak. Yet as even the former Saints have often said, a little faith will be sufficient to heaven, why would we desire much. We are taught in Scripture to be content with that which God has given us and to walk in this precious faith. . . . We cannot learn faith. We cannot find it as some people in the churches of this world say. But how does one receives faith? It is given as a grace-gift of God to the seeking one who seeks the kingdom of God and that righteousness. Then faith is established into the heart. Not by man but by the Lord God. Then begins the travel as a child of God to preserve that faith which God has given into the heart by and through His Son our Lord and Savior. This faith is so important that without it, we can do nothing" (Reino Kuoppala, sermon given 1986).

† "Coldness and dryness are very familiar feelings, along with better times of good and fervent feelings. Faith is never founded on how it feels or seems. The foundation of faith is always the same: Jesus Christ and that which He has done for us. Faith is a gift of God from the beginning to the end. Salvation is never to be measured with an amount of good feelings" (*Päivämies*, 1989).

† Faith is a gift that "dwells in the heart of a childlike believer. No merits or works of man, no thoughts or works of the mind can open and gain this gift from God. It is by the love of God, as He has first loved, called, gathered, and enlightened by His Word, that one receives such a precious gift in the heart–the gift of living faith" (VOZ, 2/1990).

† "Faith is not a deed of man, but it is a gift of God. Therefore, faith is not a merit, on the basis of which we are declared righteous, but man owns the perfect righteousness of Christ through faith. The righteousness of faith is righteousness that has come from outside of us" (Uljas 2000, 29).

To praise and treasure faith as a "gift of God" may seem an entirely appropriate expression of gratitude for someone who views it as a ticket to heaven, and an incredibly rare one at that. But I see a couple of troubling aspects to that viewpoint. First, it diminishes the view of faith as an aspect of belief or trust. Rather than having faith *in* God, we just *have* faith in the same way we might have a birthday present. I think the mindset of being the passive recipient of the gift of faith is much the same as "defining ourselves as slaves to God" that Price criticizes evangelical Christianity for emphasizing:

> It is a holdover from the ancient societies that gave birth to our religions. In them, the mass of people were slaves and serfs, and power lay in the hands of tyrants and monarchs whom one hoped might be feeling benevolent on any particular day. God's grace was not much different from Nero's–sometimes he gave the "thumbs-up" sign, and you praised him for his gratuitous magnanimity. [2006b, 278]

This leads to the second issue I have with the gift of faith: *You cannot turn it down*. One LLC preacher who is particularly effusive in expressing gratitude for "this most precious gift of living faith" has made some pretty inflammatory statements about those who would dare to reject it. I sat in the pews stunned one Sunday morning as he said that doing so is the worst possible thing imaginable, that the act of leaving the faith is worse than anything else a person could ever do. The next time he spoke, he repeated that assertion, adding for emphasis that yes, it was *even worse than murder* to give up one's faith.

We see that kind of talk for what it is when spoken by an outsider. Consider your reaction to Charles Simpson being told by a Church of Christ preacher that attending a Baptist church made him "no different in the eyes of God than a child molester or rapist" (2009, 31-32). A hundred years ago, Ingersoll observed that the "denunciations that once blanched the faces of a race, excite in us only derision and disgust" (*Lecture on Gods*). It may still be a long time before that happens in certain congregations of the LLC.

Although I wonder what kind of a father he could possibly be to any children who might decide to leave the faith ("Hey murderer, thanks for the father's day present. Why don't you come to church with us today?"), I suppose the preacher is just crudely expressing the implications of some pretty harsh theology. You are faced with a pile of unresolvable dilemmas (most of which the average believer doesn't even know about) and told to profess belief no matter what. Too bad if "the cogs of your poor brain simply lock," as Rupert Hughes lamented about his failure to understand the theory of vicarious atonement (1924).[33] If those parts of your brain that make decisions based on the weight of evidence *in every other aspect of your life* behave the same way when it comes to religion, if after hours of research and desperate soul-searching you simply cannot leave a check in the box marked "faith" in your mind, then the creator of that brain and mind has an eternal torture chamber waiting for you. You have offended the divine benefactor by rejecting his "gift." For making the honest choice

---

33. "Whatever my fault may be, the cogs of my poor brain simply lock when I try to understand the central theme of Christianity: the theory of vicarious atonement. I can't even understand the beginning of it. God created a man, then a woman, and forbade them the fruit of a certain tree, which when his children ate with childish curiosity and at the suggestion of a snake (which God never warned them against) eternal damnation was apportioned to them and to all their descendants for thousands of years. I could not tolerate such a god and his revolting sense of persecution. I could not understand his logic: because Adam sinned, we are all born in sin and as Cotton Mather says, 'man's best works are a stench in God's nostrils'" (Hughes 1924).

guaranteed you by the Constitution of a free nation and an enlightened age, you are condemned as being worse than a murderer. In the face of this, all those words of praise in the quotes above seem less like genuine gratitude than the symptoms of **Stockholm Syndrome** <http://en.wikipedia.org/wiki/Stockholm_syndrome>, "the pathetic transfer of affection to one's captors and tormentors (Price 2006b, 279).

The next quotes ascribe all kinds of characteristics to "faith," which seems to become a devotional luggage cart that believers wheel around, onto which preachers can pile every conceivable aspect of Christian piety. "Faith" has blessings, is something "we are left to live by," is "not of every man," is owned and has priority over other matters, and "comes through the realization" of one's own unworthiness:

> † "The first and most precious blessing of faith is the forgiveness of sins, whereby we receive the Holy Spirit and the righteousness, or holiness of Christ" (VOZ, 2/2000).

> † "Our day-to-day human feelings are not a measure of our love toward God, the Lord Jesus, or the children of God. At times the darkness of human reason makes us fearful of Jesus' question, 'Lovest thou me?' (John 21:15-17). When grace feelings have fled we are left to live by faith. Man's love toward God falters or fails because of the effect of original and actual sin" (VOZ, 6/2001).

> † "Faith is not of every man. Not everyone in this world has the gift of faith. Even though they once owned it when they were born, most lose it because of unforgiven sin and transgressions" (VOZ, 10/2001).

> † "If the only justification before God is by faith, then shouldn't faith be the most important matter to us? The believer owns faith as a gift of God, but also carries this old portion which would put other matters ahead of faith." For the "nourishment of their undying souls," believers "hear words of instruction and exhortation from God's kingdom as God himself reveals through the Holy Spirit." Those "outside of God's kingdom" also need to hear because "faith cometh by hearing and hearing by the Word of God." And because "there is no justification without faith, they also need faith to be saved" (VOZ, 11/2002).

> † "A person does not receive faith and God's blessings in life through his position or power, no matter how great he is. Rather,

faith comes through the realization of his own unworthiness, of how his sin separates him from God, followed by believing the gospel of the forgiveness of sins" (VOZ, 1/2007).

Luther characterized faith as "a divine work in us. It changes us and makes us to be born anew of God (John 1); it kills the old Adam and makes altogether different men, in heart and spirit and mind and powers, and it brings with it the Holy Ghost. O, it is a living, busy, active, mighty thing, this faith; and so it is impossible for it not to do good works incessantly" (*Preface to the Epistle to the Romans* [1522]; *PE* 6, 451). Similarly,

> † "Faith is not some separate entity, but it gives direction to a person's whole life" (VOZ, 4/2008).

Note what a significant distinction that characterization creates between those who supposedly have faith (and, consequently, the Holy Ghost) and those who don't, which is discussed further in **7.5**.

Here "faith is a mystery," somehow coming before even doctrine or understanding:

> † "Correct doctrine is a necessary fruit but is not in itself sufficient for salvation. Faith is the salvative factor, and thus it needs to come first; doctrine, understanding and life then follow. ... Faith is a mystery, a matter not opened to our understanding. Yet, we know something about faith [Heb 11:1; Mt 7:15-20; Gal 5:22; 1 John 5:1; 1 John 4:7-10 cited]" (VOZ, 9/2008).

In other words, you have to "believe" even without understanding what it is you're supposed to believe! Clement of Alexandria thought of faith in much the same way: "[F]aith is discovered, by us, to be the first movement towards salvation; after which fear, and hope, and repentance, advancing in company with temperance and patience, lead us to love and knowledge" (*Stromata*, Book 2, Ch. 6).

This is what Dennett calls "belief in belief." It is the nodding of the head that is valued, not what might be going on inside the head. Dennett notes that scientific experts understand their methods and can explain "the amazingly accurate results" of those methods. "In religion, however, the experts are not exaggerating for effect when they say they don't understand what they are talking about. The fundamental incomprehensibility of God is insisted upon as a central tenet of faith, and the propositions in question are themselves declared to be systematically elusive to everybody." Theologians "insist that *they themselves* cannot use their expertise to prove–even to one another–that they know what they are talking about. These matters are mysterious *to everybody*, experts and laypeople alike" (Dennett 2006, 220).

What Dennett offers is the hard-headed critical observation of a philosopher and atheist. But theologically speaking, the idea of faith as a mystery seems problematic, too. It shares an element of "secret knowledge" with Gnosticism, which was rejected as heretical by what eventually claimed itself as orthodox Christianity. "The Gnostic religions taught that some of us have a spark of the divine trapped in our bodies. Salvation will come to the spark only when it learns the truth of where it came from and who it really is. In other words, the inner element of the divine within us *needs to acquire the true and secret 'knowledge' that can set it free*" (Ehrman 2011, 96, emphasis added). There was much more to it, but initially, the secret knowledge or *gnosis* was identified with faith, "closely connected with the reception of the Spirit, illumination, deification and the beatific vision" (Kirk 1966, 211). "The spirit of gnosticism was always esoteric, always mysterious and secretive" (p. 212).

In the last quote of my sample concerning faith, it is associated with belief rather than being treated as an object. Unlike the earlier quotes, the emphasis is not on belief and faith in God or Jesus per se, but in God's "word," e.g., doctrine:

> † "All that is required of us is to simply believe–faith and trust upon his word, into a heart of a child. Living faith is so simple . . . We don't have to have great wisdom and understanding. All we need to have, dear brother and sister, is to believe the gospel. And even at this time, dear brothers and sisters, be assured, and be encouraged: all sins and doubts are forgiven in Jesus' name and precious blood" (George Koivukangas, sermon given 2010).

That also provides a reliable point of distinction from all the thousands of other Christian faiths in the world. They of course do not believe in what they probably have not even heard of, and which excludes them in any case.

4.5.4 Reason

> *Mental slavery is mental death, and every man who has given up his intellectual freedom is the living coffin of his dead soul.*
>
> —Robert G. Ingersoll, *Lecture on Individuality*

In the ironic tone he so often used, Laestadius spoke of "theological science" and of man who feels that he "need not be responsible to anyone, other than to his own divine intellect, for his deeds." Making a prediction of near-atheist liberal clergy like Bishop John Shelby Spong, he continued,

† "The science of theology may yet advance to such a degree that there is no God, only nature and natural forces" (*VCW*, 164).

Intellect and wisdom "of the world" have been unwelcome from the movement's earliest days:

† "According to our Lutheran doctrine, God's Word must be the only guideline for man in doctrine and life. Thus, the light of the intellect is not acceptable here. The wisdom of the world is not acceptable here. He who thinks that man can be saved without the Scripture and God's word, but only needs to follow his intellect, travels in darkness" (Laestadius, Third Rogation Day Morning sermon [1859]; *Fourth Postilla*, 223).

† "[T]he nearer we are to the sun of grace, the darker we find ourselves. We observe there, how dark we are in ourselves and how sinful in ourselves and how little we comprehend. Our own wisdom appears foolishness and we are ashamed, that, I dust and ashes have thought I am something on myself, although I am nothing. When our own blackness is evident, we cannot get too wise in our own mind, and holiness cannot accumulate, since our sinfulness is apparent in the light of the Sun" (Matti Suo [1861-1927], from *Greetings of Peace*, 9/1961).

† "The human mind cannot understand those things which are of God. The wisdom which has become darkened because of sin cannot see the wisdom of God nor explain it, for the prophetical word has always been revealed through the Holy Spirit. Also, it can only be explained with the help of the Holy Spirit, with that

> wisdom which God gives from above" (Erkki Reinikainen, sermon given 1959, from *The Storms Will Cease*, 107).
>
> † [T]he kingdom of God, at all times has been strange upon this Earth. The human brain will not accept it" (Ahti Korkala, sermon given 1975, from VOZ, 3/1979).
>
> † "It is truly so that when man tries to reason matters of salvation with his own mind, he cannot understand the mysteries of God" (VOZ, 12/1979).

In a 1984 sermon, Jon Bloomquist cited Noah's "foolish preaching" as part of the apparent foolishness of spiritual things that the world has always ignored. As I've said unhesitatingly in 4.3.2 and will say again in 6.1, the Noah story is a myth. Treating the story as an event of actual history is what seems foolish to me:

> † "Certainly, to the carnal mind, this preaching of the gospel is foolishness; but it was so also in the time of the apostle Paul and he has written of this to the Corinthians. It was so also in the time of Noah. They [the world] did not hear this foolish preaching of Noah. When Christ was here upon this Earth, they thought also that he was a fool. The carnal mind cannot understand or accept this but it is only by faith that we are able to believe."

The Methodist Bishop Mouzon's 1923 statement about biblical inerrancy comes to mind: "We make unbelievers out of intelligent people by saying things about the Bible which are not true" (from Babinski 2003, 40). It certainly doesn't help matters to disparage a "carnal mind" that is just recognizing provably false statements for what they are. "If you do not let people think within the church they will think without it" (p. 40).

"The persistent enemy of fundamentalism is education," writes the professor of philosophy and religion studies Joe Barnhart. "Today fundamentalist preachers regularly denounce the seminaries for undermining the faith of students, but the ultimate enemy of fundamentalism is still *literacy in an open environment*, one in which people are at liberty to think without fear of intimidation" (2003, 235). It certainly seems to be a concern in the following quote from the January 1990 *Voice of Zion*:

> † "Philosophical discussions about the creation of the world, the existence of God and the problem of the suffering, etc. may lead a

child of God into great temptations. Young people who are studying come in contact with such many-faceted trends. In this way speaking about matters of faith may decrease and become an attempt, with the help of 'philosophizing,' to reach false depths. Then can appear the aspiration for uniqueness, harshness, superficiality from which the obedience to God's Word is lacking."

Human reason is not just warned against, but disdained as "ignorant, blind, and perverse":

† "Although man's reason or natural intellect still has a dim spark of knowledge that there is a God, as well as of the teaching of the law, nevertheless, it is so ignorant, blind, and perverse that when even the most gifted and most educated people on earth read or hear the gospel of the Son of God and the promise of eternal salvation, they cannot by their own powers perceive this, comprehend or understand it, or believe and accept it as the truth. On the contrary, the more zealously and diligently they want to comprehend spiritual things with their reason, the less they understand or believe, and until the Holy Ghost enlightens and teaches them they consider it all mere foolishness and fables" (John Lehtola, presentation given 1995).

That certainly fits with Luther's viewpoint. In his sermon "The Twofold Use of the Law and Gospel," he wrote that,

when it comes to the knowledge of how one may stand before God and attain to eternal life, that is truly not to be achieved by our work or power, nor to originate in our brain. In other things, those pertaining to this temporal life, you may glory in what you know, you may advance the teachings of reason, you may invent ideas of your own; for example: how to make shoes or clothes, how to govern a household, how to manage a herd. In such things exercise your mind to the best of your ability. Cloth or leather of this sort will permit itself to be stretched and cut according to the good pleasure of the tailor or shoemaker. But in spiritual matters, human reasoning certainly is not in order; other intelligence, other skill and power, are requisite here–something to be granted by God himself and revealed through his Word. [*The Sermons of Martin Luther*, Vol. 8, 228]

The problem is that nobody really discards reason when considering matters of faith. They just fail to realize that they are using it and create artificial distinctions between "reason that supports faith" and "reason that questions faith":

> People of faith naturally recognize the primacy of reasons and resort to reasoning whenever they possibly can. Faith is simply the license they give themselves to *keep believing when reasons fail*. When rational inquiry supports the creed it is championed; when it poses a threat, it is derided; sometimes in the same sentence. Faith is the mortar that fills the cracks in the evidence and the gaps in the logic . . . [Harris 2005, 233]

Luther's own use of reason is attested by the volumes of discourse he wrote over his theological career, in which he argues his points by reasoning out the scriptures and even appealing to common sense and knowledge of his day, much of which the modern reader can find quite amusing. His *Lectures on Genesis*, for example, has page after page of details about the creation of the world in six literal days, right down to Eve being made during the evening of the sixth day, while Adam was asleep, and the Fall occurring the next morning (Vol. 1, Ch. 2, §3). And he has the gall to criticize some ideas about astronomy that didn't match his conception of what Genesis taught by calling them "rather silly and rationalistic ideas," and "stupid thinking" (Ch. 1, §6). It's not much different than the uninformed attempts to argue against evolution by Taskila and Reinikainen in **4.3.1**.

Christians of all types argue their various points of doctrine based on their interpretations of selected proof texts and what they have read and heard from their predecessors. As the quotes collected in this book make plain, Conservative Laestadianism is no exception to that. But what theologians do with reason is to slam a gate in front of it whenever a doctrinal problem comes up that cannot be dealt with any other way than to assert a reason-versus-faith paradox. The rough edges of unreasonable beliefs can thus remain obscured in what the philosopher Daniel Dennett has eloquently called a "pious fog of modest incomprehension" (2006, 10).

"A dogmatic religion," according to Winell, "is one that does not truly honor the thoughts and feelings of the individual" (1993, 5). There's not even an attempt to do so here:

† "No human ability or knowledge brings us to know God. We lack the means of thought, feeling, or will requisite for association with God. We can learn to know God, because He himself has made known His essence and will in His wondrous works, His mastery of the world, His Word, and above all in His Son Jesus Christ" (VOZ, 9/1998).

† "Because the natural mind or carnal wisdom belongs to our earthly part, it cannot be used to comprehend faith" (VOZ, 2/2000).

† "The Gospel of repentance and forgiveness of sins as preached by the believers is difficult for a man's mind to comprehend. It is too simple.... The Gospel message cannot be understood with carnal reason. It can only be understood by faith" (VOZ, 6/2006).

Here the paradox is stated with bald simplicity:

† In Romans 8:7, "Paul describes the battle between the rational mind and the Spirit of God. He shows that faith is not rational. When faith becomes rational, it is no longer faith" (VOZ, 9/2006).

Try maintaining that position and telling the Mormon how unreasonable his beliefs are that Native Americans are descendants of a lost tribe of Israel, contrary to archeology and DNA evidence, or that Joseph Smith translated what turned out to be mundane Egyptian funerary texts into a book of Mormon doctrine by sticking his face into a hat containing a seer stone. Without rationality, there is no reason for them to disregard the "burning in the bosom" of emotion they feel, against all evidence, when affirming their "testimony" that Joseph Smith was God's prophet. Indeed the irrationality of those beliefs would be, according to that last *Voice of Zion* quote, grounds for considering them to be based on faith.

Paul himself made ample use of this reason that is supposed to be the antithesis of faith, at least according to the Book of Acts. He went to a synagogue of the Jews "and three sabbath days reasoned with them out of the scriptures" (17:2). "He reasoned in the synagogue every sabbath, and persuaded the Jews and the Greeks" (18:4). He "came to Ephesus, and left them there: but he himself entered into the synagogue, and reasoned with the Jews" (18:19). Before Felix, "he reasoned of righteousness, temperance, and judgment to come" (24:25).

An article from the May 2008 *Voice of Zion* repeats the point that "Faith and reason contradict each other." Then it states something whose opposite formulation I think is equally valid:

> † "He who trusts in his own reason will quickly find himself traveling away from the living God" (VOZ, 5/2008).

He who trusts in the living God—or more precisely, what he has been told about God by people who avoid thinking too deeply about God and advise doing the same—will quickly find himself traveling away from his own reason. Many believers claim that's just fine with them. Reason won't get you to heaven, after all, even if you are expected to use it for everything but your religion. I've always found it somewhat maddening to be part of a subculture that looks down on someone who pays too much for a used car yet expects complete credulity when it comes to the most important question of one's life.

One friend calls that prevalent attitude in the LLC a "burka for the brain." Harris writes, "Ignorance is the true coinage of this realm—'Blessed are those who have not seen and have believed' (John 20:29)—and every child is instructed that it is, at the very least, an option, if not a sacred duty, to disregard the facts of this world out of deference to the God who lurks in his mother's and father's imaginations" (Harris 2005, 65). Even disregarding Harris's atheist crack about God being imaginary, he makes a valid point about the nature of religious faith, which he says "obscures uncertainty where uncertainty manifestly exists, allowing the unknown, the implausible, and the patently false to achieve primacy over the facts" (p. 165).

My sample for this section concludes with an article from the April 2008 *Voice of Zion*. There an SRK minister writes of his discussion with a confirmation student, who

> † "pointed out that knowledge has increased immensely, and that has changed people's view of the world. The teachings of the Bible are questioned, and the mind of man and knowledge is put above all else. In our time, a believer's childlike faith and trust in God dumbfounds our contemporaries and is even ridiculed." The minister "related how the thoughts of this young person spoke to him powerfully, especially when the student concluded by saying, 'regardless of all this, I believe.'"

According to the pagan critic Celsus, who wrote around 180 A.D., that sort of intellectual surrender is actually nothing new. Origen quotes him as saying of Christians that "some do not even want to give or to receive a reason for what they believe, and use such expressions as 'Do not ask questions; just believe,' and 'Thy faith will save thee'" (*Contra Celsus*, Book 1, Ch. 9, from McDonald and Porter 2000, 260).

Celsus also addressed the sentiment that the Truth is hidden "from the wise and prudent," and revealed "unto babes" (Lk 10:21), that God is to destroy "the wisdom of the wise, and will bring to nothing the understanding of the prudent" (1 Cor 1:19). As Luther would put it over a thousand years later in his exposition on Psalm 8, the invisible "Christ was magnified in the fall of all visible pomp; and that, not by giants, by men of fame, of learning, of wealth, or of nobility, but by fishermen, by fools, infants and without any appearance of power or wisdom" (Lenker, *Standard Edition of Luther's Works*, Vol. 1, 433). Celsus characterized the Christian injunctions as being "like this. 'Let no one educated, no one wise, no one sensible draw near. For those abilities are thought by us to be evils. But as for anyone ignorant, anyone stupid, anyone uneducated, anyone who is a child, let him come boldly.'" In a withering fashion, Celsus then states the unflattering but inevitable logical consequence: "By the fact that they themselves admit that these people are worthy of their God, they show that they want and are able to convince only the foolish, dishonorable and stupid, and only slaves, women, and little children" (*Contra Celsus*, Book 3, Ch. 59, from McDonald and Porter 2000, 260).

Harsh words, certainly. But they should be kept in mind by those who denigrate human wisdom and yet take offense when the wisdom of what they say is questioned.

4.5.5 Doubt

> *I also know how much effort it requires to be a fundamentalist. It can get tiring. You must constantly fight not only the skepticism of those around you, but the doubts that arise within yourself.*
>
> —Harvey Cox, *The Future of Faith*

Here is my definition of spiritual doubt: the disconnect between what you are supposed to believe and what you suspect might actually be true.[34] It is the sinking feeling, the hollow in the stomach, the noise that grates in the mind when, time after time, weighty doctrinal assertions grind and scrape against the rough edges of inconvenient facts. And in so many cases, they *are* facts–undisputed by anyone who does not labor under the weight of theological imperative. Evolution *is* true, for all its troubling theological implications. The Bible *does* contain errors and contradictions–lots of them, and about important things. Jesus *did* expect to return within the lifetime of those standing there with him, and was in some sense a false prophet. Luther *did* teach things that are in serious conflict with important points of Conservative Laestadian doctrine. The proclamation of absolution was *not* the means by which the founders of the movement entered into what it calls "living faith."

Although she is no doubt completely unaware of Conservative Laestadianism, Ruth A. Tucker certainly understands Christian doubt: "I understand the unbelief. I read the stories, and I say, 'Me too.' But unlike these who have abandoned the faith, I will not–if for no other reason than the mysterious fact that God has a grip on me" (2002, 25). She comforts herself with the thought that her salvation does not depend on the strength of her faith, but only on God's grace. Still, it is a difficult road to walk:

> I sometimes envy those who have an unwavering faith–people who, in many cases, are a lot smarter than I am. I desperately wish I did not have to fight and struggle for every little bit of faith I have. I wish the big question was not, at least unconsciously, ever before me: Is there really a God out there, or is my faith tradition a concoction of men, as the sociologists of religion would say? But I accept the conflicts and questions as part of my psychological and spiritual makeup, which allows me to humbly reach out to those with similar struggles. [p. 26]

Tucker concludes that "God knows and understands my often-wavering faith. God can handle the honest confession of my heart" (p. 28). Laestadius, as usual, was not so understanding:

> † When "Jesus dies in the hearts of the Christians[, they] fall into unbelief and doubt. They remain behind locked doors. They have not the strength to speak to anyone. But Jesus' true disciples do

---

34. Probably inspired by Mark Twain's cynical comment that "Faith is believing what you know ain't so."

not go along with the flock of the world to blaspheme the Crucified One" (Confirmation Sermon [1852]; *Fourth Postilla*, 251)

In an 1898 sermon, Antin Pieti takes a very different stance that sounds a lot like what Paul Tillich said about the true theologian (quoted by Robert M. Price in his foreword to this book):

> ✝ "[I]f you ask of the person who truly has the Holy Spirit, 'Have you the Holy Spirit?' He will reply, 'I do not know, dear friend, for my heart feels so wretched. But my soul yearns and longs for the peace of the Holy Spirit.' Such a person has the Holy Spirit, for he answers with truth and fear according to the Word of God" (*Sanomia Siionista*, from Kulla 1993, 84).

I can certainly relate to the feelings of yearning and longing that Pieti describes. But I think he risks overgeneralizing believers just as Laestadius did (though in the opposite way) when he implied in the earlier quote that doubt is something experienced by Christians in whose hearts Jesus has died. There *are* believers who are genuinely untroubled by doubt, perhaps a good deal more of them than might be apparent from reading this book. Some of them have managed to remain blissfully unaware of the issues that cast doubt on Conservative Laestadianism, or even Christian faith in general. Some of those who have learned about the issues have never taken them too seriously, assuming that they are the complaints of bitter apostates or defensive atheists who really just want to feel better about the *real* reason they don't believe, the desire to live a life of sin. Or, the "unbelievers also must secretly believe," but "are bitter against God or God's people and are merely taking out their frustration by denying God" (Daniels 2010, 81).

Most difficult of all for me to understand are those Conservatives, including friends of mine, who acknowledge the issues honestly and fairly but somehow remain untroubled by them. One friend points to the blessings of his Conservative faith and, despite some problems of his own with the church's clannish social scene, has not the slightest inclination to leave or even really question it. He is quite happy to let himself be carried along with the tide of tradition, a lifetime of church upbringing, and the fact that so many others in church are believing these things. (The sincerity of *those* professed beliefs is of course another question, but not one he is inclined to ask.) The issues that exact such a toll on other believers, from nagging doubt to complete loss of faith, are only amusing theological distractions to him. Frankly, I'm jealous.

Generally, doubt is acknowledged as part of a believer's life, albeit an unwelcome one and more about the believer's own shortcomings than any of the religion itself:

> † "When we view our feelings, many times we carry sorrow and painful burdens of doubts. We find ourselves so very lonely, strange and foreign in this world. This results from that, that we stray to gaze into ourselves and forget that we are holy members of the body of Christ" (Havas [1938], 17).

> † "[Y]ou felt yourself so dry, so black, that you could scarcely believe for yourself. Even though in the name and blood of Jesus sins were preached forgiven, we asked, 'Is it true?' It happened to many that the Bible was plodded through, the Book of the Blood was opened and they were shown that it is true. Many times along the way the heart has seemed to be so dry and chilled that we have asked, 'Have I any faith? Can I still own the gospel?' But we have experienced that when the grace of God has kept us humble and empty, that God has always to such beggars preached the gospel and broken the bread of grace" (Veikko Pentikäinen, *Greetings of Peace*, 4/1951).[35]

> † "There are those who are struggling on this narrow way who perhaps have come here besieged by many doubts and who are fearful and timid because of their weakness. Remember, through faith we have life! The just shall live by faith. Therefore, dear brothers and sisters, it is a blessed privilege that even today we may believe the gospel" (Kalle Timonen, sermon given 1951, from *Greetings of Peace*, 9/1956).

> † "Many times doubts can come very heavy–you might feel that you can't go any further; feelings of oppression, sin, corruption and your own poorness press your heart very low–to you echoes

---

35. As often occurs to this day in Conservative Laestadian sermons, the preacher felt his own shortcomings and touchingly asked the congregation, "I, too, at this place feel myself so hungry and thirsty that I beg would the children of God still bless me"? It is not a show, but a sincerely felt and welcome expression of the preacher's position as just another sinful member of the flock who has been entrusted with the responsibility of his office (**4.2.7**).

the joyous tidings of the Passover, 'He is not here, for he is risen'" (VOZ, 3/1975).

Although doubts are clearly viewed as common and understandable, there is still the viewpoint that they are sin that must be "taken care of" like any other. For example, a children's story appearing in a 1976 issue of *Päivämies* has a boy's mother scolding him, saying,

> ✝ "Listen Peter, we don't have permission to doubt God, that would He hear us or not, since He has asked us to call [upon him in prayer]. Doubting has always been preached as sin." The story continues, "In the evening there were services, and at them even doubts were preached forgiven. When they arrived home, Peter asked mother to go into the kitchen with him, and explained his doubts of the day, and begged to have them forgiven."

When preachers proclaim the general absolution in sermons, they often say, "You can believe your sins *and doubts* forgiven." When I have had a particularly bad time of it with what the preacher has just said in his sermon, noticing one problem after another as I often do with the quotes in this book, I must admit to being less than receptive to the offer of having my doubts "forgiven."

> ✝ "If there is yet even one who has sat through these services still doubting of his faith, perhaps feeling coldness and emptiness, remember our faith is not based on these feelings" (Eric Jurmu, sermon given 1990).

> ✝ "In times of uncertainty and doubt, it's important to ask for 'the old paths.' Visit with the believing elders in the congregations, ask board members or ministers for advice, seek instruction at camps and congregational discussions, or visit with a trusted brother or sister in faith. Pray for understanding. If God doesn't give understanding, be obedient and trust the advice of the Spirit in the congregation as God's Word encourages.... God will reveal all things in His time; if not in our time, then in eternity" (VOZ, 11/2009).

> ✝ "There has not been doubt, that is this vast multitude that we're in the midst of [at the annual LLC Winter Services], that is this the kingdom of God. No, we believe as a child that we are here in the midst of Zion, the living kingdom of God upon the earth. We don't doubt that. What do we doubt? What do we fear? We fear,

'Will I get to heaven?' That is the doubt and the fear that arises in your heart and mine" (George Koivukangas, sermon given 2010).

That last quote emphasizes the "sanitized doubt" that centers around personal failings rather than doctrinal incredulity. We can't begin to entertain the thought that *the religion* is subject to scrutiny–that part or all of it *might not actually be true*–so we shift the blame for our mental distress onto ourselves. It is a defense of the church at the expense of our own psyche, and MacDonald says that defensiveness is "the curse of credulity." At the fundamentalist university he attended,

> it was clear that nothing must be allowed to challenge the system. Its world was too fragile and had to be protected at any cost. No theological domino so carefully stood on end could be allowed to fall. All of life had to fit into place; no ambiguity could be tolerated; mystery was outlawed; doubt exiled. [2003, 114]

The cognitive dissonance takes its toll, something I know all too well after years of being a Christian "who suppressed similar misgivings" like Karen Armstrong in her struggle with Catholicism. We have "stamped on [our] rebellious thoughts, and felt all the while a sinking loss of intellectual and personal integrity" (2007, 230). Diane Wilson is another person who suffered "internal anguish," the "result of years of ignoring my feelings and thoughts" as a Jehovah's Witness. It finally "had become too great to ignore, yet it was difficult for me to see beyond the immediate pain that leaving the organization would cause. Thinking about breaking away from the organization struck terror in my heart" (2002, 123). Jack Worthy writes that his questions about Mormonism "made me miserable because I couldn't reconcile my beliefs with reality. There was a huge mismatch, and that depressed me" (2008, 114).

In recent years, I have heard quite a bit about this hidden, internal anguish from a number of Conservative Laestadians, both longtime friends and new acquaintances. There are people sitting in the pews–perhaps even some behind the pulpit–whose doubts venture all the way into unbelief. Yet they are–like Wilson was for many years–frozen in place by the terror of leaving, with its threatened eternal consequences and all too real social ones. "Rather than take a life-threatening chance, believers take pains to remain faithful and suppress unorthodox thinking. To do so, however, can require a highly developed 'tunnel vision'–forcing all outside information to fit the framework or be denied" (Winell 1993, 66).

Usually the dilemma is addressed not by drastic action or even publicly expressing doubt, but by rationalizing it somehow. The motivations and reinforcements for doing so can be nearly irresistible:

> When people are socialized in a relatively isolated or self-contained religious community and are not directly exposed to alternative lifestyles or worldviews ... there is little reason for them to, or little chance that they will, examine their religion critically. Everyone they know, respect, and love and who loves and cares for them, accepts the religious worldview, so why should it be questioned or challenged? Even if they begin to note certain discrepancies between some of what their religion teaches and the reality that they experience, the religion usually has ways of explaining these discrepancies from within the system itself. [Schimmel 2008, 169-70]

Just as strong a force for rationalizing doubt or ignoring facts that trigger it is the stubborn nature of our brains. "[C]ognitive dissonance tends to be resolved in favor of feeling over reason. Internal bias and a misplaced *feeling of knowing* routinely overpower and outsmart the intellect" (Burton 2008, loc. 1383-84). Tavris and Aronson point out neuroimaging studies showing that

> the reasoning areas of the brain virtually shut down when participants were confronted with dissonant information, and the emotion circuits of the brain lit up happily when consonance was restored. These mechanisms provide a neurological basis for the observation that once our minds are made up, it is hard to change them. [2008, 19]

Solomon Schimmel observes the phenomenon from the perspective of a non-believing Orthodox Jew: "When someone's religious beliefs and values are threatened, he will go to great lengths to protect and preserve them, allowing his emotions to overcome or distort his reason–no matter how rational and logical that person might be in his other pursuits including scientific ones" (2008, 72). When all else fails, one can resort to the "claim that 'simple, innocent faith' or 'the incomprehensible mysteries of the divine' or 'leaps into the absurd' trump reason, and that they can live with the irrational if their faith is incompatible with reason" (p. 29).

As discussed in my **Introduction to the June 2010 Edition**, my personal standby has long been to compartmentalize my thinking using the figure of Luther's "whore of reason," who will never accept the mysteries and contradictions of faith. Lately, however, it seems that she has moved out of her closet and demanded quite a bit more more respect. As difficult as it has been for me to maintain this sort of compartmentalization in my head anymore, I have a lot of understanding for those who can make it work for them. One who does so is this "devout and extremely intelligent Christian woman" with whom Schimmel corresponded:

> The doubts of the intellect are real, but the part of me that God has touched–which I call my spirit–has to allow these doubts a voice ... [F]aith and reason sometimes battle, but my being assents to one above the other. If I try to reverse their order, I am overwhelmed with loss, and in the end run back to my Father whose face was obscured by my experiments with thoughts that do not place everything in the context of Him. I can no longer live without Him, and have lost the desire to do so. From the point of view of the intellectual, I have sold out. Reason is not the ruling principle in my soul. But I would not have it any other way. [from Schimmel 2008, 26]

But I also can relate to how Bart Ehrman felt "compelled to leave Christianity altogether," though "kicking and screaming, wanting desperately to hold on to the faith I had known since childhood and had come to know intimately from my teenaged years onward." He finally came to a point where he simply could not believe: "I realized that I could no longer reconcile the claims of faith with the facts of life" (2008, 3). He felt there was no other choice but to "deconvert":

> What can *you*, or anyone else, do when you're confronted with facts (or, at least, with what you take to be facts) that contradict your faith? I suppose you could discount the facts, say they don't exist, or do your best to ignore them. But what if you are absolutely committed to being true to yourself and to your understanding of the truth? What if you want to approach your belief with intellectual honesty and to act with personal integrity? [p. 126]

If I had an easy answer to that, I wouldn't have spent over a year of my life writing this book.

4.6 Sin

> *The inescapable fact is that there is virtually no known human behavior that we call "sin" that is not also found among nonhuman animals. Even pride, proverbially the deadliest sin of all, is not absent.*
>
> —Daryl P. Domning, *Evolution, Evil and Original Sin*

4.6.1 Specifics

> *Let love, and intoxication, and senseless passions, be removed from our choir. Burlesque singing is the boon companion of drunkenness. A night spent over drink invites drunkenness, rouses lust, and is audacious in deeds of shame. For if people occupy their time with pipes, and psalteries, and choirs, and dances, and Egyptian clapping of hands, and such disorderly frivolities, they become quite immodest and intractable, beat on cymbals and drums, and make a noise on instruments of delusion; for plainly such a banquet, as seems to me, is a theatre of drunkenness.*
>
> —Clement of Alexandria, *The Instructor* [c. 200 A.D.]

Conservative Laestadianism is all about the forgiveness of sins, and there are a lot of potential sins to be concerned about. It is claimed that there are "no dos and don'ts," but in reality there are plenty of them, mostly unwritten prohibitions of things a believer "would not want" to do. Some disgruntled Finns have compiled a **wiki page** <http://scratchpad.wikia.com/wiki/Synnit> describing the situation, and helpfully include a categorized list of specific sins. Here is a summarized compilation of the list: membership in other religious movements; questioning or criticizing Conservative Laestadian practices, sermons, and publications; any sexual activity other than procreative sex within marriage (no contraception, masturbation, homosexuality, etc.); divorce or remarriage after being divorced; obscene materials and dirty jokes; abortion; alcoholic beverages (including going to bars whether alcohol is consumed or not); drugs; cosmetics, hair coloring, earrings and piercings; overly revealing dress; cosmetic surgery; profane and worldly speech; support of Finnish political parties other than the Center and National Coalition parties (the Democrats are similarly suspect in the LLC); being a player or spectator in organized competitive sports; participation in online discussion forums about religion; insufficient church attendance; gambling; playing cards; fishing, berry picking, and hunting on Sunday.

To this I would add the following from my years of observation in the LLC: reading about or believing in evolution; celebrating Halloween; watching videos that aren't documentaries, including cartoons and "G" rated movies; listening to most music other than church songs, patriotic or Christmas songs (as long as it isn't too "jazzy"), or classical (though not even all classical music is acceptable); attending live performances of most any kind other than (Republican) political rallies; attending a "worldly" church service except for a wedding or funeral; flirting and dating without serious thought of marriage; any physical contact between a "courting" couple other than handholding; even seriously considering marriage with an "unbeliever"; publicly or even privately doubting what is taught in "God's Kingdom"; declining to accept one's appointment by the congregation (or its board of trustees) to a particular position or task; violation of any laws (underage smoking is a particular source of concern, local ordinances and everyday speeding are not); leaving the impression with "unbelievers" that they are "heaven acceptable," e.g., by greeting "heretics" with "God's Peace"; spending more time with "unbelieving" friends than fellow LLC members.

In many cases, these are seen as symptoms of spiritual sickness or deviations from being "in the center of the flock" rather than particular infractions. Why would a believer *want* to be involved with unbelieving friends, when there are like-minded believers to have fellowship with instead? When you hear music with a beat, shouldn't that automatically seem uncomfortable and "foreign" to you? Why would a courting couple want to inflame lusts with physical contact when sex is unavailable until marriage? How *could* a believer vote for a Democrat who supports abortion and gays?

Primary Motives

From the devotional perspective, there isn't really much to say regarding motives for the various rules because they *are not recognized* as rules. Rather, as is commonly stated in Conservative Laestadianism, believers simply "do not want to" do things that are recognized in the movement as sinful. Individuals with viewpoints contrary to the supposed consensus tend to keep quiet about their disagreements, which preserves the illusion that the behavioral norms are self-evident and unquestioned.

For some issues, even the standard-bearers realize that it isn't enough to rely on a miraculous unanimity of desires among believers or "what God's Kingdom says." Then recourse will be made to "what the Bible says." Yet almost inevitably, the appeal to Scripture winds up being a highly selective, almost token observance of the edicts in the Jewish law. That law is supposed to be the basis for it all and of great importance in the grand scheme of salvation (**4.5.1**), but is really of surprisingly little relevance to any of the rules. The main one based on it is sabbath observance:

> † "Theaters, concerts are frequented, time is spent by a beer glass in bars, Sundays are spent in fishing and hunting [and] the day of rest is otherwise used in everyday toil, auto repairs, or laundry, so that one does not have time to remember this is a holy day" (VOZ, 8/1976).

Avoiding hunting and fishing on Sunday hearkens back, I think, to the very real work that those activities entailed for the Finnish grandparents of most Conservative Laestadians. However, they never put food on the table playing golf, so how about a round after church today?

Two other behavioral norms in the movement that I see arising from direct biblical statements are the prohibitions on extramarital sex and drinking to the point of drunkenness. For the rest, I propose the following primary motives. This is, of course, looking at things from the attempted objectivity of the outsider's perspective. The devotional viewpoint has stopped its inquiry by this point, saying, "The Bible (or 'God's Kingdom') said it. I believe it. That settles it."

Few of these proposed motives are consciously recognized, or would even be acknowledged, within the movement:

(1) authoritarianism;

(2) Christian asceticism;

(3) societal differentiation;

(4) keeping people within the fold;

(5) selective adherence to biblical edicts; and

(6) maintaining ample material for the forgiveness of sins to work with.

The first and second of those I will discuss at some length in their own subsections below. The third is all about maintaining the boundaries between the inside and the outside, which was discussed in **4.2.3**. Herriot sums it up:

> If you are the only true believers, then everyone else is the outgroup. However, if you do actually treat the whole of the rest of the world as your out-group you have a problem, because inevitably there are some out there who are quite like you. The rest of the world is, after all, a fairly inclusive category! The only way to ensure that you are different is to become uniquely extreme. [2009, 288]

We are obviously different from *them*. Why? Because we are so different! Motive #3 is to maintain the distinction between *them* and *us*, while trying to prevent any of *us* from becoming *them* is what motive #4 is all about.

My proposed **motive #6** is really pretty obvious when you think about it. What is the point of so much stress about the forgiveness of sins–the centerpiece of Conservative Laestadian doctrine–if there isn't an adequate supply of sins to *have* forgiven? Few believers (or anyone else, for that matter) engage in rape, murder, theft, and adultery on a regular basis. But take another look at those two long lists of unapproved activities above. There is no shortage of lesser ailments for Dietrich Bonhoeffer's "spiritual pharmacist" to treat. With plenty of rules, including ones that people almost cannot help but violate on a regular basis, he remains on the job "working to produce acute guilt, and then in effect saying: 'We just happen to have the remedy for your guilt here in our pocket'" (Harpur 2003, 99).

Authoritarianism

"The highly authoritarian individual is submissive to authority, aggressive towards out-groups, and holds tight to conventional values and norms of behaviour. Psychometric measures of authoritarianism are found to be highly correlated with measures of religious fundamentalism" Its first feature, as the name implies, is "submission to authority" (Herriot 2009, 149), which we've seen in **4.2.6**.

One authority on authoritarianism (I couldn't resist saying that) is Bob Altemeyer of the University of Manitoba. In a comprehensive book on the topic that he offers for **free online** <http://members.shaw.ca/jeanaltemeyer/drbob/TheAuthoritarians.pdf>, he writes about both authoritarian followers *and* leaders, and the significant correlation with religious fundamentalism that is noted by Herriot. Authoritarianism, Altemeyer says, is something authoritarian followers and leaders "cook up between themselves. It happens when the followers submit too much to the leaders, trust them too much, and give them too much leeway to do whatever they want" (2006, 2).

It has a two-way connection to religious fundamentalism. A submissive upbringing in a religiously conservative family is prone to produce it. Conversely, fundamentalism promotes "authoritarianism with its emphases on submission to religious authority, dislike of out-groups, sticking to the straight and narrow" (p. 112).

The connection between the two is evident in Altemeyer's psychometric scale, "Authoritarian Followers and Religious Fundamentalism" (p. 106). Altemeyer says the students in his introductory psychology classes average about 50. The highest group score he has ever seen was 93, from a "nationwide sample of some 300 members of an unnamed fundamentalist Protestant church in the United States" (p. 108).

I took the liberty of answering his questions in the manner I would expect of the LLC peers with whom I've locked horns the most and came up with a score of **94**. That's with answers moderated a bit by common sense. Answering completely in accord with Conservative Laestadian doctrine would raise the score by about ten points.

The respondent is to indicate level of agreement with the following 12 items, responding to each with anything from a -4 to a +4 (Altemeyer 2006, 106-107).

My proposed LLC dogmatist's answers are indicated in the parentheses for each item.

> 1. God has given humanity a complete, unfailing guide to happiness and salvation, which must be totally followed (+2).
>
> 2. No single book of religious teachings contains all the intrinsic, fundamental truths about life (+1).
>
> 3. The basic cause of evil in this world is Satan, who is still constantly and ferociously fighting against God (+4).
>
> 4. It is more important to be a good person than to believe in God and the right religion (-4).
>
> 5. There is a particular set of religious teachings in this world that are so true, you can't go any "deeper" because they are the basic, bedrock message that God has given humanity (+3).
>
> 6. When you get right down to it, there are basically only two kinds of people in the world: the Righteous, who will be rewarded by God, and the rest, who will not (+4).
>
> 7. Scriptures may contain general truths, but they should NOT be considered completely, literally true from beginning to end (-2).
>
> 8. To lead the best, most meaningful life, one must belong to the one, fundamentally true religion (+3).
>
> 9. "Satan" is just the name people give to their own bad impulses. There really is no such thing as a diabolical "Prince of Darkness" who tempts us (-3).
>
> 10. Whenever science and sacred scripture conflict, science is probably right (-3).
>
> 11. The fundamentals of God's religion should never be tampered with, or compromised with others' beliefs (+4).
>
> 12. All of the religions in the world have flaws and wrong teachings. There is no perfectly true, right religion (-3).

For items 1, 3, 5, 6, 8, and 11, the scoring maps from {-4,-3,-2,-1,0,+1,+2,+3,+4} to {1,2,3,4,5,6,7,8,9}. For items 2, 4, 7, 9, 10 and 12, it's inverted, mapping to {9,8,7,6,5,4,3,2,1}.

So how does this function as a motive for establishing and maintaining Conservative Laestadianism's many behavioral norms? In a number of ways, I think. First is the reflexive support for the established authorities of society, "such as government officials and traditional religious leaders," the "time-honored, entitled, customary leaders" (Altemeyer 2006, 9). Guess which side of the labor vs. management divide authoritarian followers will tend to take, even if they like earning high union wages?

> † We can belong to a labor union, "for we know that in many cases we must belong to a union to work. But this does not give us the right to support that which is wrong according to God's Word. If a man votes for a strike, then he is supporting the union, and is rejecting the Word of God. We know that not all employers are honest. If you feel that your employer has done you wrong, go to him to discuss the matter. If it cannot be resolved, and you cannot bear it, you are free to leave. One should not fight evil with evil" (VOZ, 4/1978).

The Bible of course does not prohibit workers from declining to show up for work after a labor contract expires. But an authoritarian mindset looks on the union rabble with scorn.

According to Tuomas Palola, the predominant employment of Conservatives in Michigan's copper mines initally kept the issue from being too clear-cut. Many belonged to unions there during the first decades of the 1900's. In some "Big Meetings" of the day, the issue started to be brought up and the idea of supporting unions looked on more negatively. The Copper Country strike of 1913 <http://en.wikipedia.org/wiki/Copper_Country_Strike_of_1913%E21914> and its aftermath greatly soured the movement's general attitude towards the union question (Palola 2011).

The anti-union mentality didn't stop A.L. Heideman and his son Paul from effectively going on strike from their preaching duties in Michigan's Copper Country. Apparently, it is a matter of historical record that they demanded to be paid more per sermon and stopped preaching until the congregation coughed up the extra funds (Palola 2010).

Second, authoritarians seem to have an almost instinctive aversion to anything that might disrupt the established social order. Consider not just the content, but the underlying thought process behind these next three statements:

† "In the world today there is all manner of sinfulness. There is drinking, drugs, greediness, lying, cursing, filthy books, cheating, riots, marchings, strife, anger, heresies, worship of idols, teaching of evolution and atheistic doctrines. Television is one instrument which the devil, the prince of this world, uses to tempt and entice even the Christian into sin" (VOZ, 6/1977).

† "[E]ven the speed laws of our respective countries are the laws of the land. We as God's children have a Christian responsibility to respect the laws of the land. These kinds of laws are not contrary to God's Word. Sometimes we may question these laws, but even in these, a childlike obedience is required" (Art Simonson, sermon given July 1990).

† "Some of the darts of the enemy in our time are ecumenism, humanism, atheism, abortion, evolution and homosexuality. The broad acceptance of such things in today's world poses a great danger to the child of God of becoming complacent" (VOZ, 11/1990).

Then there is the way that the authoritarian mindset works to preserve rules that have been established for other reasons. One LLC preacher fondly tells a story about his mother's reply to his defense of some type of edgy music as a youth. Her response was, "But what do the Christians say about this?" It's an appeal to authority, plain and simple. And, as the many quotes have made clear in **4.2.6** ("Obedience and Humility") and **4.4.4** ("The Mother"), it's done a lot.

Asceticism

Christian asceticism (**motive #2**) was partly rooted in a desire to emulate Christ's sufferings. Protestants who favor faith over works may object to that, but Paul made himself an example of it. Referring to himself in the plural (I'm still not sure why he sometimes did), he says that, "just as the sufferings of Christ are ours in abundance, so also our comfort is abundant through Christ. But if we are afflicted, it is for your comfort and salvation . . ." (2 Cor 1:5-6). To the Colossians, Paul (or perhaps someone else putting words in Paul's mouth) went so far as to say, "I rejoice in my sufferings for your sake, and in my flesh I do my share on behalf of His body, which is the church, *in filling up what is lacking in Christ's afflictions*" (Col 1:24, NASB, emphasis added). That last part is quite explosive; see the discussion of it in **7.6**.

Another aspect of Christian asceticism is a detachment from the world, which arose in part from the expectation of the earliest Christians that Jesus would be coming back any day (**4.8.2**). It would make sense to avoid too much attachment to a world one would soon be leaving. Whoever wrote Ephesians in Paul's name listed a number of immoralities to avoid and then urged his readers to "be careful how you walk, not as unwise men but as wise, making the most of your time, because the days are evil" (Eph 5:15-16, NASB). Paul viewed his time as being one of "distress" and "shortened" (1 Cor 7:26, 29), and for that reason thought it "good for a man to remain as he is," not released from his wife if bound to one, not to seek a wife if single. And if married, to be *as if without one*, i.e., celibate (7:26-29). For, he said, "the form of this world is passing away" (1 Cor 7:31, NASB). In Romans, Paul warned his readers: "[I]f yet live after the flesh, ye shall die: but if ye through the Spirit do mortify the deeds of the body, ye shall live" (8:13). Again, he looked beyond his present time, whose (partially self-imposed) sufferings he reckoned "are not worthy to be compared with the glory which shall be revealed in us" (8:18).

Clement of Alexandria raised Christian asceticism to grotesque extremes when he wrote against bathing for pleasure and seemingly every other possible joy of living in *The Instructor*. "[U]nblushing pleasure must be cut out by the roots; and the bath is to be taken by women for cleanliness and health, by men for health alone" (Book 3, Ch. 9). "[E]ven laughter must be kept in check; for when given vent to in the right manner it indicates orderliness, but when it issues differently it shows a want of restraint." "Smiling even requires to be made the subject of discipline" (Book 2, Ch. 5).

Laestadius was much the same:

> † Those in whom God dwells "cannot sit there, where the mockers sit. Neither can they find joy in the vain pleasures of the world. The world can find pleasures in drinking parties, drunkenness, lewdness, dancing, music, etc., but they who have a contrite spirit, can find no joy from the sinful pleasures of this world" (Laestadius, Examination sermon [1856]; *Fourth Postilla*, 262).

Eino Rimpiläinen, writing in the December 1948 *Siionin Lähetyslehti*, gave a list of things one should avoid in order to go about "mortifying and crucifying the flesh":

† "[T]he saving grace, through the word of God, illuminated by the Holy Ghost, taught us to give up the worldly lusts and to live godly and soberly. So even a young person could give up the theatre, the dance, the worldly fashions, curling of hair. And likewise the older person, liquor, cards, cursing, dishonesty, lying, indecent life, as well as all the world's sin-life and to begin to live an entirely new life, mortifying and crucifying the flesh with its desires and passions" (from *Greetings of Peace*, 3/1949).

With this mentality, there is seemingly no end of things to be concerned about:

† "On the part of auto trips and outings we are instructed to avoid dangers where the undying soul can receive wounds. Even driving to the neighboring community for services and the fellowship after the services, should not become too important" (VOZ, 7/1979).

The asceticism of denying oneself harmless pleasures is often justified as an effort to remain "in the center of the flock" or avoid the danger of wanting to move on to other, less innocent things (**motive #4**). Start painting your toenails, and the next thing you know, you'll be punching a time clock in a brothel.

† "The hardening of heart and conscience can begin with something that to one who has fallen may seem relatively small and innocent, for example, a little lie, the occasional use of make up, watching a ball game on television, listening to worldly music, watching unsuitable videos, or visiting offensive sites on the internet" (Don Lahti, presentation given 1997).

That oblique reference to "the occasional use of make up" is the tip of an iceberg of concerns about personal appearance, as we will see shortly.

Now video games and the Internet are providing plenty more things to be avoided for little apparent reason:

† "[T]emptations come into our homes in the form of the Internet, videos, and video games. We need to be ever vigilant in this area. A recent technology article stated that the area between video games and movies is going to blur. The videogame is going to look like a movie that the player directs, or tries to direct to an outcome. Certainly the content of the games is becoming

increasingly dangerous for a believer's faith life. The old saying that 'it is good to walk in the middle of God's kingdom' is still true. Why bring things into our homes that are such a danger to us and our children?" (VOZ, 12/2005)

† "Will I allow [my children] to play fast games in which they do not control their vehicle but drive through the city being thrown against the walls of the buildings, sometimes rolling into ditches at the side of the highway? Will I let them shoot, punch, fall and destroy illustrated symbols like living beings? Is the background music reminiscent of rock music?" (VOZ, 3/2006).

To the writer of that last statement and the writers of many others in this section, I would offer this line from *First Clement*, written around 95 A.D.: "Ye are fond of contention, brethren, and full of zeal about things which do not pertain to salvation" (Ch. 45).

Appearance

Clement of Alexandria (a different man with very different views from the writer of *First Clement*) thought it not "becoming for any part of a woman to be exposed," and he really meant *any* part. The virtuous woman's "arm is beautiful; yes, but it is not for the public gaze." Her "thighs are beautiful" and her "face is comely," but "for her husband alone." It was "prohibited to expose the ankle" and had "also been enjoined that the head should be veiled and the face covered; for it is a wicked thing for beauty to be a snare to men. Nor is it seemly for a woman to wish to make herself conspicuous, by using a purple veil" (*The Instructor*, Book 2, Ch. 11).

In his view, clothes were "for nothing else than the covering of the body, for defence against excess of cold and intensity of heat, lest the inclemency of the air injure us." Since the use of colors was "of no service against cold," dyeing of clothes was also to be rejected. Indeed, he considered pretty much everything beyond covering up to be unnecessary superfluity, rejecting the

> love of ornament, and dyeing of wool, and variety of colours, and fastidiousness about gems, and exquisite working of gold, and still more, of artificial hair and wreathed curls; and furthermore, of staining the eyes, and plucking out hairs, and painting with

rouge and white lead, and dyeing of the hair, and the wicked arts that are employed in such deceptions." [Ch. 11]

Poor old Clement would not have approved of Spandex, either. "For luxurious clothing, which cannot conceal the shape of the body, is no more a covering. For such clothing, falling close to the body, takes its form more easily, and adhering as it were to the flesh, receives its shape, and marks out the woman's figure, so that the whole make of the body is visible to spectators, though not seeing the body itself" (Ch. 11).

It's enough to make Antin Pieti's concern about women's wearing of hats seem quite reasonable:

> † "It is not becoming for a woman to wear a hat, but rather a scarf, for a hat is an unnecessary and worldly vanity. Both men and women should put away worldly styles, even as the conscience teaches a Christian" (sermon published 1898 in *Sanomia Siionista*, from Kulla 1993, 84).

Nowadays, Conservative Laestadian women daringly show their faces and ankles, and have little interest in hats. But there is still a complicated system of unwritten expectations for their appearance, mapped out and refined during private conversations, youth gatherings, and camps. A bit of hair styling is fine for females, as long as the color doesn't change. Jewelry is generally acceptable except for earrings or body piercings of any type. Clement would have agreed on that point: Women should "let not their ears be pierced, contrary to nature, in order to attach to them ear-rings and ear-drops. For it is not right to force nature against her wishes" (Ch. 13). A source of some consternation now is that women and girls in Africa, as well as those few remaining in Ecuador, Russia, and Estonia, have continued to wear their earrings despite predictions years ago that they would come to understand the matter and no longer do so.

Boys seem to have much more limited fashion interests, and consequently, few restrictions. Mostly the concern is about long hair, which is frowned upon in males due to 1 Cor 11:14. Depictions of Jesus in church publications alternate between the classic long-haired look and collar-length hair.

Although girls routinely test the boundaries with unpigmented lip gloss and clear nail polish, cosmetics have long been unacceptable:

✝ "When people have followed the course of this world, they are even painted from the toenails to cheeks. It is not enough that their lips are red, but their toenails must also be red. The worldly people believe that when God created man according to his image his work of creation was otherwise complete, but it is lacking paint, and man must now finish it by using it. We don't need to paint ourselves. As long as our conscience is washed in Jesus' blood we certainly are acceptable and follow the creation of God. Paul speaks to the children of God that they should not follow the course of this world and fashion themselves according to this world so that they would drift from the love of God" (Lauri Taskila, *Greetings of Peace*, 8/1956).

✝ "The worldly styles and modes change but we cannot imitate them. Hippie-styled clothing, bikinis, etc. are not suitable for a child of God" (VOZ, 8/1974).

Entertainment

Sometime around 180 A.D., Theophilus of Antioch wrote about how early Christians rejected the entertainment of their day. His reasoning is quite specific:

> [W]e are forbidden so much as to witness shows of gladiators, lest we become partakers and abettors of murders. But neither may we see the other spectacles, lest our eyes and ears be defiled, participating in the utterances there sung. For if one should speak of cannibalism, in these spectacles the children of Thyestes and Tereus are eaten; and as for adultery, both in the case of men and of gods, whom they celebrate in elegant language for honours and prizes, this is made the subject of their dramas. But far be it from Christians to conceive any such deeds; for with them temperance dwells, self-restraint is practiced, monogamy is observed, chastity is guarded, iniquity exterminated, sin extirpated, righteousness exercised, law administered, worship performed, God acknowledged: truth governs, grace guards, peace screens them; the holy word guides, wisdom teaches, life directs, God reigns. [*To Autolycus*, Book 3, Ch. 15]

It seems reasonable enough to refrain from watching people fighting each other to the death as a form of entertainment. Watching dramas that celebrate paganism, cannibalism, and adultery might not be such a good idea for Christians, either. But where does the Conservative writer of this next quote–and many after him–get the idea that attending "entertainment shows" constitutes "walking in the counsel of the ungodly," "standing in the way of sinners," and "sitting in the seat of the scornful" (**motive #4**)?

> † "To my sorrow I have occasion to see that when the God of this world has prepared entertainment shows for his slaves, even those who profess Christianity have attended. . . . Blessed is the man that walketh not in the council of the ungodly, nor standeth in the way of sinners, nor sitteth in the seat of the scornful. Dear friend, the seed of the word has remained too shallow in your heart: if the services of God's children can be passed by and you can go with the ungodly to dance after the pipes of those whom Satan leads in the frenzy of whoredom toward the lake of fire. How much difference is there between you and the ungodly, how can you be recognized as a Christian from the midst of the ungodly?" (*Siionin Lähetyslehti*, 1923).

Well, that appeal to Psalm 1:1 turns out to be almost as old as Christianity itself. Tertullian acknowledged that "we never find it expressed with the same precision, 'Thou shalt not enter circus or theatre, thou shalt not look on combat or show;' as it is plainly laid down, 'Thou shalt not kill; thou shalt not worship an idol; thou shalt not commit adultery or fraud.' But

> we find that that first word of David bears on this very sort of thing: "Blessed," he says, "is the man who has not gone into the assembly of the impious, nor stood in the way of sinners, nor sat in the seat of scorners." Though he seems to have predicted beforehand of that just man, that he took no part in the meetings and deliberations of the Jews, taking counsel about the slaying of our Lord, yet divine Scripture has ever far-reaching applications: after the immediate sense has been exhausted, in all directions it fortifies the practice of the religious life, so that here also you have an utterance which is not far from a plain interdicting of the shows. If he called those few Jews an assembly of the wicked, how much more will he so designate so vast a gathering of heathens! [*Apologetic*, The Shows, Ch. 3]

It's been a way of keeping the faithful away from public entertainment ever since, however innocent the actual content might be. The next verse of Psalm 1 says that the blessed man who has separated himself from the world (the writer means *entirely*, not just at entertainment venues) will have his delight in God's law and meditate on it day and night. Somehow, I don't think that part gets much attention.

This 1980 writing (one of two that I quote out of chronological sequence in this sub-section) shows how Psalm 1:1 continued to be stressed in the same fashion many decades later:

> † "We do not desire to be where people are 'living it up.' We do not want to sit where the scorners sit" (*By Faith*, 109).

Members of one LLC congregation in the swing state of Minnesota ignored the "seat of the scornful" admonition when they attended political rallies *en masse* for the Bush/Cheney presidential ticket in 2004. And it seems to me that you will find "scornful" in the seats of an IMAX theater (good) just as you will in any other (bad).

What really seems to be going on here is that entertainment was rejected due to Christian asceticism (**motive #2**) and societal differentiation (**motive #3**). Those motives are not recognized within the movement, and appeal was made to Psalm 1:1 (motive #5). Now the rejection of so many forms of entertainment is an integral part of Conservative Laestadianism's behavioral norms and provides an abundance of sin for people to get forgiven (motive #6), especially young people. Even things that nobody can find any actual problems with, like kids' cartoons and classical music concerts, are viewed as the first step on the slippery slope to hell (motive #4). And underlying it all is the authoritarian mindset (**motive #1**) that we must be obedient even if none of it makes sense.

Here some other creative *ad hoc* arguments are offered as well:

> † "Many unnatural lifestyles have worn modern man to physical weakness. The human soul is sick and weary. Sensual excitement and the numbing of minds have become a fashionable panacea against disease among all nations, especially since World War I. The effects of this are felt in all areas of life. Authors write as if they were hallucinating; music throbs; visual arts betray mad imagination" (O.H. Jussila, devotional article originally published 1929, from VOZ, 3/2007).

> † "It is a pitiful matter that even in our own land television is being developed with great haste. In this way a theater is obtained into the home, which can transmit all the evil that the world can offer to be absorbed. By its transmitting, everything is presented to the people: how crimes are committed, all drinking advertisements are presented and a craving for drink is aroused in a drunkard. Then it is considered startling when juvenile delinquency is increasing and 10 to 12-year-old boys are already full-fledged gangsters committing crimes and burglaries. Children lie before the television and ruin their eyes and health, and have no time for the pure and beautiful nature of God, nor time to do their schoolwork" (Taskila 1961, 40-41).

The "theater in the home" has now become a fixture in Conservative Laestadian households in the form of DVD players, personal computers, tablets, and smart phones. Despite this recent restatement of how TV is to be rejected (presented out of chronological order), the reality is that "Satan" has gotten his job done quite well without even needing a cable or dish hookup:

> † "Satan might say that there are many wholesome programs on television, so what can it hurt if you purchase a television for your home and only watch those kinds of programs?" (VOZ, 10/2009).

Ubiquitous Internet access has made unimaginable filth readily available at the press of a few keys or mouse clicks, and watching online videos is popular. The "slippery slope" of allowing some programming to be available has been turned into a cliff. Set up an Internet connection, and it's all there at your fingertips.

The gradual acceptance of video has been accompanied by its own unwritten and complex system of rules, which seem to be followed to a greater extent in the LLC than the SRK. No "entertainment style" videos involving drama or actors (real or animated), except documentaries, and those are preferably of a historical or "National Geographic" nature. No sporting events because they are not watched on television or in person, though listening to audio play-by-play is acceptable on the radio (and, presumably, online as well).

Another type of seating in which the scornful are prone to sit is in classical music concert halls. Don't let their fancy dress and quiet demeanor fool you; they are a seething mass of ungodly sinners that you don't want to be caught dead sitting with. The prohibition (largely unwritten, as in so many cases) against attending concerts applies despite the music itself not being considered sinful. This caused some consternation in Finland when some Conservatives embarked on musical careers within the state church; their official duties had them doing public performances that their fellow Conservatives were discouraged from attending! So it seems quite understandable that those condemning public performance regardless of its content would be labeled as "enemies of culture and enlightenment":

> † "A mighty shower of accusations and ridicule comes upon Zion these days because television with its brainwashing programs is not accepted as furniture for a Christian home. The Christians have been labeled as enemies of culture and enlightenment because they do not approve for their nourishment that which kills the spirit" (Reinikainen 1969, 42).

Around 2008, I had an amusing experience with the question of whether to allow my grade-school daughters to participate in a field trip to a classical music concert, something that would have been rejected out of hand during my childhood. Finally, after my wife and I made a private parental decision that depriving the girls of a beautiful and innocent cultural experience made no sense at all, they went, and returned to tell that all of their peers from church were present, too.

The aversion to seemingly *anything* entertaining has gone to extremes that even many Conservatives will find a bit nonsensical nowadays, especially those more culturally minded in the SRK. Decades ago, "instructional films in any form," going to a place "where music is played," and "too free, unlimited radio listening" were problematic:

> † "Using the shelter provided in the statutes of the elementary schools, a believing teacher does not use television or instructional films in any form in elementary school teaching functions. This practice is also observed according to the spirit of Christianity in other educational institutions" (Position Paper of 1978 Teachers and Speakers Meeting, Finland, from VOZ, 11/1980).

> † "Even roller skating or ice skating at a rink where music is played is not a place for a Christian, whether it is a school class

party or otherwise. One may try and justify the music by saying: music is played to drown out the loud noise of the skates, but this is not so. This is the voice of the devil speaking. The music here, too, gets under the feet and in the body. Before one is even aware of it, one is listening to the music and unconsciously moving with the music. When one finally becomes aware of the effect of what the music has done to the feet and body, it is easier to ignore the conscience and enjoy the music" (VOZ, 2/1978).

† "Too free, unlimited radio listening can defile the conscience little by little. When the desire is born, it is like a parasite, it has to be fed. Judgment of what is proper disappears. Radio programs can be compared to television and theater on the part of sound. A certain kind of radio program of this kind can become so important it can even keep [one] from going to services. Even in this matter it is important to take heed of oneself first and then of the children. Radio music, as background music, when doing lessons, is not necessary. The effectiveness of studying will suffer one part of the attention is on the music. It is good to remember that the enemy is afraid of silence" (VOZ, 7/1979).

† "In school one must sometimes refuse to participate in those teachings which are not fitting for a believer. In the name of learning, even such material is brought into schooling that does nothing but nourish the lusts and desires of the corrupted part of our nature. Such are, for example, theatrical presentations, many motion picture presentations and television courses, dances and concerts" (*By Faith*, 104).

A more recent quote seems to indicate that loud volume is part of the problem:

† "The world screams and shouts with its loud music and modes of entertainment, but the Good Shepherd speaks quietly and with meekness in our hearts warning of the dangers that are ever near. We want to keep that quiet voice and shut out the worldly temptations, so that the good seed would have good soil in our heart to grow" (VOZ, 5/2005).

Perhaps attending a nice quiet Chopin piano performance would be better? Nope. Despite the lack of recent writings on the subject, and some very nice classical music performances offered occasionally at church in a few LLC congregations, those scornful concert hall seats are still widely considered off-limits.

Music in general is a continuous source of pastoral hand-wringing:

> † "As the tool of the enemy of souls music can awaken the lowest and most shameful human instincts. God's children have always rejected the music of this world which embodies ungodly life. It's clear to see that rock, heavy metal, hip-hop, rap, and country music war against faith and good conscience and for that reason are rejected by believers. Performers of such music with the aid of synchronized lighting and other technology have enraptured and made huge crowds of people wild over their music. Their followers emulate their behavior, hair and clothing styles, morals, and values. . . . In recent years, performers and music producers have released products which combine different forms of music together: serious and light, religious and secular, patriotic and country, children's music and rock, classical and rock, etc. The danger in such music is more difficult to see, because the enemy disguises it at times with good words or in other cases with an innocent or familiar melody. But when one considers such music more carefully, we see that it draws us closer to the world and away from the path to heaven" (VOZ, 8/2008).

During the LLC's 2009 Summer Services, there was a congregational discussion (focused on the youth) about music that began with a **presentation** <http://www.llchurch.org/topics/09ssmusic1.pdf> sounding much the same. We will encounter the reactions of two young people to that discussion **below** in this section.

Reading

A "weak sister in the kingdom and tribulation" wrote of her greatest temptation having been

> † "the reading of the fiction books of this world, especially mystery and historical novels. I kept lolling myself into the spirit of permissiveness by saying it wasn't such a big sin. Slyly Satan's web was pulling me to live more and more in the world of unreality, the imaginations these stories effected. The truth is that the novels of this world are as garbage cans, even the little good in them is tainted, all just food to tickle the flesh. If in the early

days of Christianity, the elect saw fit to make a bonfire and burn their books [Acts 19:9], how much more reason have we to shun the fictional publications of these last times" (VOZ, 4/1975).

I recall being the subject of concern in my youth regarding my *Archie* (kissing and dating) and *Sgt. Fury's Howling Commandos* (war violence) comic books. One LLC friend recalls being told not to read Louis L'Amour in the late 1970s, but another–the son of a preacher–said there was never any concern about that. (Those innocuous little Westerns were certainly popular with the kids I grew up with.) There has always been concern about foul language and explicit sex scenes in books, but it seems to have little impact on what many people actually wind up reading nowadays.

The above quote seems to indicate a blanket rejection of "the fiction books of this world," which seems pretty extreme even for the time. Still, it appeared in the official church paper, as did this bracing tirade against bestsellers:

> † "In our homes as well as in school, we want to avoid reading the 'best-seller' types of paperbacks you usually see offered for sale in drug stores, supermarkets, and discount houses. I would venture to say, that almost 100% of those titles are 'trashy,' if not altogether pornographic. My guess is that many of these books would qualify for that famous fire that the Christians once kindled at Ephesus! . . . The 'best-seller' book industry is a shameful and shameless racket! It will sink to any level in its search for profits, it is just like the 'Pop Music' industry today–riddled with graft, corruption, and drug abuse. The 'bosses' of the industry promote what will sell millions of books, therefore, the authors, so-called, pour out volume after volume of the vilest drivel, copy that appeals to the lowest and most prurient instincts of man. The typical 'best-seller' usually contains violence, bestiality, brutality, and perverted sex, all described in the most lurid detail. In short, what these books represent is simply another form of pornography. As Christians, we cannot buy and read these in good conscience. They war violently against everything we believe in, and hold dear and precious in this life. And not only this, but in purchasing this trash we support the very people who are with this industry destroying the very fabric of decency in our land" (VOZ, 3/1982).

Sports

This next quote touches on the Conservative Laestadian prohibition against team sports at school, which is all about maintaining separation from the world (**4.2.3**, and **motive #3**). For some reason, watching people tossing a ball or whacking a hockey puck is considered sinful, too, even if you maintain a safe distance from the scornful by doing your viewing at home:

> † "We as Christians don't join worldly teams in any sport in school or after school. Sports of this kind with all their heroes and honor have truly become a false god in our day. Who can describe it? Also as Christians we don't listen to worldly games (hockey, baseball, football, etc.) on the radio. Surely we should not go over to our unbelieving neighbors to watch sports on TV or anything else on TV. And further, we don't want to be spectators watching worldly teams play" (VOZ, 7/1975).

From several different sources I've learned that it has become common for Conservative Laestadians in Finland to attend professional hockey games. Soccer is popular there, too. During the 2010 World Cup, one visitor to Finland apparently found that every SRK household on the itinerary was following the action via some form of video.

The only reason I've heard for prohibiting the watching of professional sports is that we might wind up worshipping the players:

> † "We want to keep our feet clean of the world's false teachings of self-righteousness and idol worship. We do not want to worship false idols such as worldly musicians or movie stars, sports stars, the wealthy business-world icons, or the religious stars of self-righteousness, who gather man's praise to themselves, as hundreds of thousands of people gather to cheer and praise them" (VOZ, 7/2006).

Attending political rallies to cheer (Republican) politicians is OK, though. At the risk of getting political here, I will simply nod my head over towards **motive #1**, authoritarianism.

Contrary to the viewpoint expressed in the 1975 *Voice of Zion* quote above, listening to sports broadcasts on the radio has been accepted since at least the early 1980s. So *listening* to these sports stars playing their games (and talking excitedly about the results over coffee next

Wednesday night) is not a problem, just watching them. Apparently the eyes have a special idol worshipping tendency that the ears do not. After all, we are warned "not to lift up [our] eyes to heaven and see the sun and the moon and the stars, all the host of heaven, and be drawn away and worship them and serve them" (Deut 4:19, NASB).

Sex

Here is an area where the prohibitions are mostly well-grounded in the Bible (**motive #5**):

> † "Only in marriage should an intimate physical relationship, expressly intended for man and wife, begin. Sexual activities of any kind not just intercourse, outside of marriage are sin; and such sin that the Bible clearly states that fornicators and adulterers will not inherit the kingdom of heaven, 1 Cor 6:9., but rather will fall into perdition, where there shall be 'weeping and gnashing of teeth.' Adultery and fornication are what we refer to as 'sins unto death.' We do not equivocate or leave unclear our position on these kinds of matters, but simply state the understanding in Christianity" (Tomm Stewart, presentation given 1996).

> † "There are many temptations that are familiar to God's children. Masturbation, fantasy, pornography, and provocative dress are all things that can move the conscience. . . . [I]t is not appropriate to touch oneself to arouse sexual desire. This is sin. A reference from Gen 38:8-10 [Onan] makes this point very clear" (VOZ, 8/2006).

It should be noted that what Onan–the bane of teenage boys for a thousand years–was actually guilty of was disobedience to God's command to raise up children with his late brother's wife. He didn't want to, and so he practiced *coitus interruptus*, the only means of contraception available to him. Regardless of its lack of biblical foundation, the prohibition of masturbation has provided an abundant supply of guilt for young people and thus works great for **motive #6**.

As might be expected, the recent and rapid trend toward acceptance of homosexuality has not gone unnoticed:

> † "The rise of open homosexuality and broader acceptance of it in our time has been preceded by a decline of moral and godly life

in our society. The sexual revolution of the 1960s, made possible by the development of effective birth control methods and their acceptance and widespread use, led to the loosening of norms governing heterosexual behavior in our society," which homosexuals have also sought. "In this environment, God's children truly feel discouraged and vexed like Lot, who dwelt in the wicked city of Sodom on the eve of its destruction. God did not forget Lot but delivered him from temptation and from the destruction that fell upon the ungodly. He will also protect and deliver His children in these evil times" (VOZ, 7/2009).

Remember how Lot then allowed his daughters to get him drunk and commit incest with him (4.3.3)? I really wish that part of the story would get some attention, too, along with the fact that this man who was so "discouraged and vexed" about the lustful mob offered up those daughters to it in order to spare his guests.

I suspect that any vexation felt by individual Conservatives about the moral decline of the world is mixed with a heightened sense of being special and enduring. "The perceived moral failings of modern societies are useful targets because they point up the authority of the holy book and the purity of its teachings, and enable fundamentalists to feel separate from, and superior to, the sinful world that surrounds them" (Herriot 2009, 44). And asserting that there is a trend of moral failure is nothing new: "The idle chatterer is the sort who says that people nowadays are much more wicked than they used to be" (Theophrastus [*c.* 300 B.C.], from Babinski 2003, 25).

Intoxication

Unconditional abstention arose from Laestadius's bad experiences with the whiskey-sodden Lapps. Their sobering up and consequent reparations of misdeeds was one of the external signs of the awakening. In an 1857 sermon, Laestadius called liquor

> ✝ "the drunkard's favorite god" and "the devil's shit, for the devil teaches people to ruin God's grain and to make it harmful to body and soul. The people who drink it become animals" (from Hepokoski 2002a, 25).

Then there is dancing, which is something drunk and ungodly people do:

† "Everyone knows that dancing is more than exercise. In dancing the ungodly satisfies worldly lusts and desires. Often the dancers are drunk. Also often the music is as the shrieking of the devil" (VOZ, 4/1974).

During one sermon I heard years ago, the preacher came across a description of dancing by God's people while reading from some Old Testament text. The preacher hastily added that what had been going on was surely good, wholesome dancing. I wonder what that would have looked like, since I had to be excused from even square dancing lessons in grade school. (Not that I minded!)

As Heikki Saari notes, the blanket rejection of alcohol began with Laestadius:

† "[T]he preaching of God's kingdom is a teaching of unconditional temperance. Beginning with Laestadius, not even moderate drinking has been accepted" (1968, 18).

The spiritual consequences of drinking and being drunk are severe:

† "Drunkenness seals entry to God's Kingdom . . . The standard of living Christianity has always been unconditional abstention. The enemy of the soul has always tried to widen the door to permissiveness of sin. Currently a specially tempting beer (lower alcoholic content) is available in every village shop. Many have weakened in this respect and given the enemy the little finger, thinking; one bottle won't hurt. Nevertheless it hurts insomuch that it is a beginning to disobedience, the consequence of which is spiritual death" (Einari Lepistö, presentation given at Nivala, Finland, 1973).

Conservatives are overwhelmingly of Finnish descent and, considering Finland's problems with alcohol, no doubt greatly benefit from the complete avoidance of it. But there is a tendency to retroject this abstention policy backward in history. Thus it comes as a surprise to many that Luther was an avid drinker. And the wine spoken of in the Bible really wasn't grape juice, a commonly held but mistaken belief that must have been shared by the writer of the following:

† Statements from Scriptures "clearly state that drinking, drunkenness and defending of drinking is sin before God! . . . Let us be frankly and adamantly opposed to drinking in any form or

circumstance! It is a shameful sin which has corrupted too many people already" (VOZ, 1/1978).

Here are some "statements from Scriptures" to ponder in view of that quote: "And thou shalt bestow that money for whatsoever thy soul lusteth after, for oxen, or for sheep, or for wine, or for strong drink, or for whatsoever thy soul desireth: and thou shalt eat there before the Lord thy God" (Deut 14:26); "Go thy way, eat thy bread with joy, and drink thy wine with a merry heart" (Eccl. 9:7); "He causeth the grass to grow for the cattle, and herb for the service of man: that he may bring forth food out of the earth; and wine that maketh glad the heart of man" (Psa 104:14-15); "Drink no longer water, but use a little wine for thy stomach's sake and thine often infirmities" (1 Tim 5:23). The appeal to the Bible, motive #5, to oppose drinking just doesn't work.

Drinking to the point of drunkenness, however, is indeed contrary to some Bible passages. Ephesians 5:18 warns its readers to "not get drunk with wine, for that is dissipation" (NASB). Galatians 5:21 includes drunkenness and revelings among its list of the works of the flesh that will bar you from the kingdom of God. That is the fate of drunkards along with fornicators, idolators, etc. according to 1 Cor 6:9-10. So Tomm Stewart is on to something in this 2000 presentation:

> † "It remains well understood among us that alcohol, marijuana, and other drugs are poisons to the body but even greater poisons to the undying soul. The seriousness of these sins cannot be overstated. Alcoholic and drug induced intoxications remove faith, and if one should die in that condition, the testimony would be sorrowful as only everlasting destruction awaits."

Again, though, the Bible is not entirely consistent. Proverbs 31 has a certain King Lemuel advising that princes and kings should not drink. But then he says, "Give strong drink unto him that is ready to perish, and wine unto those that be of heavy hearts. Let him drink, and forget his poverty, and remember his misery no more" (Proverbs 31:6-7).

Personally, I'm happy to have never drunk anything stronger than a thimbleful at a time of Communion wine, back when the LLC was serving the real thing instead of grape juice. But I like the practical, common-sense nature of Clement of Alexandria's advice about the acceptable use of wine "towards evening, about supper-time," when we are no longer engaged in more serious readings. Then also the air becomes colder than it is during the day; so that the failing natural warmth requires to be nourished by the introduction of heat. But even then it must only be a little wine that is to be used; for we must not go on to intemperate potations. Those who are already advanced in life may partake more cheerfully of the draught, to warm by the harmless medicine of the vine the chill of age, which the decay of time has produced. For old men's passions are not, for the most part, stirred to such agitation as to drive them to the shipwreck of drunkenness. [*The Instructor*, Book 2, Ch. 2]

Sins of the Right

Much of what we are seeing in this section are "sins of the flesh" or "the left." There are also sins of "the right" to be concerned about, especially for the older believer who isn't as tempted by wine, women, and song (or, in my generation, sex, drugs, and rock 'n roll). Thus the "narrow way" is defined on both sides, and there is plenty of guilt available for everyone:

> † "Narrow is the way, dangers are so great on both sides that there is a possibility of perishing. It is grace of grace that the heavenly Father has posted the road to heaven on both sides, even to the very end. Along the way there comes not a single situation where the Holy Spirit does not give counsel. In God's kingdom there is in operation continually words of gospel and reproof unless the heavenly Father leads me to His counsel I, wretched one, would soon stray. There are admonitions against these dangers on the left and on the right. . . . The left hand signs show the dangers of the liberty of the flesh. There the sign reads: 'For if ye live after the flesh ye must die.'. . . In the same manner is posted the right: 'Beware and take heed of the leaven of the Pharisees. Beware of false godliness, be it of whatever nature. Beware of spiritual filth.' . . . The signs are so close together that they form a narrow alley for us to proceed along. The Lord Jesus has trod it with unblemished steps, and although the way is narrow, its destination is an open heaven" (Havas [1936], 59).

One of these sins of the right (these are theological designations, not political ones) is hypocrisy:

† "What is most sorrowful is when even a Christian, although struggling, falls also into the sin of hypocrisy. This may become evident in the disappearance of open brotherly relations. Good is spoken to the face, evil behind the back" (Reinikainen 1969, 78).

There is no shortage of hypocrisy going on within the church. Altemeyer proposes that "fundamentalist Protestantism may directly promote hypocrisy among its members through one of its major theological principles: that if one accepts Jesus as a personal savior and *asks for the forgiveness of one's sins*, one will be saved" (2006, 133, emphasis added). Sunday after Sunday, Conservative preachers ask their congregations to forgive them for failing to do good for their neighbors or confess their faith, but their behavior remains unchanged. In one LLC congregation where I have numerous contacts (and probably others where I don't), a sizable percentage of the young people maintain worldly lifestyles while sitting piously in church every Sunday. The love of Christ is preached and lofty claims are made about the closeness of the brothers and sisters in faith, but I have found the reality to be quite different.

With few exceptions, nobody in the church has made any effort to socialize with or even keep in touch with me *or any members of my family* since I decided a year ago that I was sick of swimming against the LLC social tide (1.2). The last time a family in my local congregation came to visit our home, several months before this writing, my kids were delighted. Friends to play with! What a novelty! Yet it soon became apparent that the reason for the visit was for the father of the family to have a private chat with me about my perceived spiritual failings and get information from me about dissension in the church.

During the congregational discussion meetings that are still a regular occurrence (focused on topics rather than individuals) in the LLC, there is plenty of opportunity for people to express concerns and disagreement. But there is strong societal pressure to conform (4.2.6), and few people dare to express contrary views through the microphone. Instead, dissenters complain afterwards in private conversations or simply ignore what has been said.

Ingersoll observed, "You cannot change the conclusion of the brain by force, but I will tell you what you can do by force, and what you have done by force. You can make hypocrites by the million. You can make a man say that he has changed his mind, but he remains of the same opinion still" (*Lecture on Liberty of Man, Woman, and Child*). It is true even of talk within one's own mind. Altemeyer has used a "Hidden Observer" technique to determine that most highly authoritarian experimental subjects will indirectly acknowledge doubts about *the very existence of God*, something they would be far more reluctant to admit while "taking full responsibility for admitting it," even to themselves (2006, 139).

An unrecognized function of the LLC's congregational "discussions" seems to be providing an airing of the most pious and conservative viewpoints so that the party line is maintained. A young person wondering what on earth could be wrong with listening to some particular bit of "worldly" but seemingly innocuous music, for example, is not likely to raise the point. In all likelihood, the result of doing so would just be a series of platitudes about remaining in the center of the flock and being obedient to the voice of the Mother (**motive #1**). Not only are such responses unsatisfying, but they put unwanted attention on the questioner.

One young person who left the LLC described a discussion on music during the LLC's 2009 Summer Services as an environment "created so that there was an implicit understanding among attendees that participants in the discussion could not go against the groupthink and the church's norm without facing social ostracization in some form." She doesn't mince words about her reaction: "I found this alarming and the ridiculousness of the whole evening reconfirmed my disbelief in the church and its teachings. It was all a farce."

Another young LLC defector noted that the point is "to maintain and reinforce levels of indoctrination." With a large enough group, a sense of "group values," and a "sense of fear and consequences for going against the group values," the "group values shift more and more towards the extreme and people become radicalized." Thus, the group can make its own expectation clear that one shouldn't be listening to anything beyond church songs or "safe" types of patriotic or classical music. The discussion leaders don't even need to present any specific rules. Rather, the result appears to come from the assembled congregation itself rather than any heavy-handed authorities. The more devout young people can feel comforted that these matters have been divinely revealed to them, too. The elders can go home satisfied that all is well. And the disillusioned ones like my two correspondents either keep quiet or become marginalized as simply wanting to sin regardless of what the congregation has decided.

Greed and its frustrated companion, covetousness or envy, are also "sins of the right." Concerns about materialism were expressed, appropriately I think, during the prosperous 1990s:

> † "The sin of covetousness is very prevalent in the world today. Man strives for and seeks great possessions. This craving is never satisfied" (VOZ, 7/1999).

The writer of the following chalks up the failure to "relate of matters in a positive light" as being due to our "innate sin and evil." Apparently he failed to notice how the church has treated the religious views and motives of outsiders (**4.2.3**):

> † "The danger of gossip is bearing false witness of a near one, of which the eighth Commandment warns us. ... If our conversation is such that we relate of matters in a positive light, then we do not fall into sin. What makes us not relate of matters in a positive light? It is the sin and evil that resides in us" (VOZ, 2/2002).

The prohibition of gambling is another old standby of fundamentalist Christianity. It goes a long ways back: "The game of dice is to be prohibited, and the pursuit of gain, especially by dicing, which many keenly follow. Such things the prodigality of luxury invents for the idle" (Clement of Alexandria, *The Instructor*, Book 2, Ch. 11). Except for church raffles,

> † "In our Christianity, we think that gambling games in any form are not suitable for the believer" (*Päivämies* No. 4, 2007).

Now, of all things, an LLC preacher in Minnesota has recently gotten himself worked up about young people playing Rook, a card game that was introduced in 1906 "to provide an alternative to standard playing cards for those in the Puritan tradition or Mennonite culture" (**Wikipedia** <http://en.wikipedia.org/wiki/Rook_(card_game)>). Some of these guys just don't know when to stop. How about if we ban "Old Maid," too, since it violates the Old Testament edict against making graven images (**Exodus 20:4**) and disparages dear Christian sisters for whom God hasn't seen fit to provide a spouse?

Sins Unto Death

The phrase "sins unto death" probably has its roots in the Catholic term "mortal sin" (*mortus* meaning death or deadly), which is distinguished from "venial sin" (*venia* meaning pardon). Conservative Laestadianism uses it as follows:

> † "Sins unto death" are "sins which, when one falls into them, remove faith and the person goes out of the kingdom of God" (*By Faith*, 57).

The idea of mortal sins is based on the "sin unto death" of 1 John 1:16-17: "If any man see his brother sin a sin which is not unto death, he shall ask, and he shall give him life for them that sin not unto death. There is a sin unto death: I do not say that he shall pray for it. All unrighteousness is sin: and there is a sin not unto death." I can't recall ever hearing any mention or explanation of that passage in the church. Rather, the Scriptural support is the listing of "the works of the flesh" in Gal 5:19-21: "Adultery, fornication, uncleanness, lasciviousness, idolatry, witchcraft, hatred, variance, emulations, wrath, strife, seditions, heresies, envyings, murders, drunkenness, revellings, and such like: of the which I tell you before, as I have also told you in time past, that they which do such things shall not inherit the kingdom of God."

In his 1520 *Discussion of Confession*, Luther listed adultery, homicide, fornication, theft, robbery, usury, and slander as "open, mortal sins" (*PE* 1, 85). His 1537 *Smalcald Articles* state that "faith and the Holy Spirit" have left people who "happen to fall into manifest sins" such as David's sins of "adultery, murder, and blasphemy" (McCain 2005, 277-78). But, as discussed in **4.6.3**, he also downplayed and criticized the distinction between mortal and venial sins.

Tomm Stewart's **1996 presentation** lists adultery and fornication as faith-removing "sins unto death." In his **2000 presentation**, he also cites "alcoholic and drug induced intoxications" as removing faith. I have to wonder, though, where the bright line between salvation and damnation is drawn when one is in the "drug induced intoxications" produced by some prescription painkillers and sleep medications. Does a doctor's prescription serve as a modern-day writ of indulgence? What if you are entering the fuzzy narcotic fog for a legitimate medical reason but are finding it quite to your liking? Does that count?

Denial of one's "faith" is likewise considered a sin unto death. During the 1973 schism with the Torola group (**4.1.6**), there was a dispute about whether Peter's denial of Christ put him into a condemned state. The Conservative position was that it did, which seems sensible enough, given Jesus' statement that "whosoever shall deny me before men, him will I also deny before my Father which is in heaven" (Mt 10:33). But Walter Torola maintained that Peter simply fell "into a fault" that he creatively imagines was forgiven by the other disciples after Easter as they sat around "recalling their heavy trials during the bygone days" (Torola 1987, 7).

Paul's list of kingdom-disinheriting sins extends beyond what are usually considered "sins unto death," though. It includes the all-too-human emotions of hatred, wrath, and envy. They are certainly viewed as sinful, but no one would dream of arguing that experiencing them would "remove faith." If that were the case, or if there were any such imminent danger from variance, strife, and seditions (NASB: *strife*, *disputes*, and *dissensions*), it's hard to see how many LLC members could walk away from their car radios tuned to political talk shows with their faith intact.

One theologically oriented correspondent with an SRK background has offered me an interesting perspective on this topic of "sins unto death." He says that "those sins mentioned by Paul will doctrinally cause spiritual death, no doubt. As does any other sin. This true teaching of Paul and the Bible will became a problem if sin is considered only as an act (deed, thought, word)." But, he continues, neither Paul nor the Bible teaches sin to be an act but rather a governing power of a human's spiritual part, the "heart." As long as a Christian is governed by Christ who lives in his (or her) heart, the victory over sin gained by Christ overcomes the sin that exists in the very same Christian due to his sin-fallen humanity. Elsewhere in his writings, Paul portrays Christ as a counter-power for the sin in the battle of human hearts, a battle in which there is no stalemate but only one who winds up in favor. At the same time, Paul notes that even the best Christian may not get rid of his sinfulness, because all Christians are human, too. A human creature is always a sinner.

So, my correspondent concludes, removing faith from a Christian always requires one's own personal decision. To give up his faith, he must state that he no longer has any need for salvation and reconciliation, which is in Christ alone. Thinking that salvation and reconciliation is only 99% up to Christ and leaving 1% up to himself will remove faith. The Christian's heart or spiritual status has to rely on Christ even amid temptations. Keeping faith and good conscience (through faith) is always an act of God, which is expressed as a sincere will of the person to put the ultimate trust in Christ for his salvation.

It's a heartfelt testament to my correspondent's own Christian faith, and based on sound Lutheran theology. But I wonder how much of these nuances are really shared by everyday Conservatives. What does the distinction between an "act" and a "governing power of the heart" mean to an LLC parent talking with his child about the danger of going to hell for having had a few beers with high school friends, especially if they were "believing" friends? The understanding in the LLC, at least from my years of growing up in it, is that faith would have left the heart of the believer with the first onset of an alcoholic buzz, perhaps with the first sip of the drink, perhaps even with the decision to go buy the beer. There is no allowance (that I know of, at least) for theological niceties like whether one had fallen out of weakness rather than an overt act of rebellion.

Thoughts and Words

Some of Clement's less ridiculous mandates in *The Instructor* concern Christian speech. "From filthy speaking we ourselves must entirely abstain, and stop the mouths of those who practice it by stern looks and averting the face, and by what we call making a mock of one: often also by a harsher mode of speech" (Book 2, Ch. 6). "Let us keep away from us jibing, the originator of insult, from which strifes and contentions and enmities burst forth. Insult, we have said, is the servant of drunkenness" (Ch. 7).[36]

Vulgar talk is understandably to be rejected, but so is talking (and thinking), in however refined a manner, about the wrong topics. The biblical admonition to "avoid foolish questions," i.e., inconvenient and troubling questions, is alive and well, as evident in this next statement

---

36. Clement's description sounds a lot like AM talk radio with all its anger, hatred, and vitriol, which is nonetheless very popular among the political conservatives in the LLC. I agree with the sentiment of one friend in the SRK who wondered why listening to that is deemed acceptable while listening to Bluegrass music is not.

by Eino Rimpiläinen. Writing in response to a question to the editor of *Siionin Lähetyslehti*, "May the Christian divorce?", he replied in the December 1949 issue that he was

> ✝ "given occasion to ponder, are there in living Christianity so uncomprehending, not to say, so ignorant of the Word of God, that such a question can be raised." He concluded his article by saying, "May even the one who asked such a question believe even such thoughts forgiven in the holy name and precious blood of Jesus" (from *Greetings of Peace*, 2/1950).

Even asking an honest question required forgiveness! To keep their flocks from such temptation, many authoritarian religions have encouraged what Henke calls an "'ignorance is bliss' attitude." He tells of a woman who "even suggested that I would be better off not reading 'certain' books and magazines," a warning I've heard myself, including about my reading of the Bible. It makes me ask, as Henke does, "What good is a faith that cannot stand up to simple questions and criticisms?" (2003, 250).

My books on the Jehovah's Witnesses, Churches of Christ, Christian Convention Church, and Mormons are full of descriptions of the "ignorance is bliss" attitude. Here are some quotes from disaffected members of each of those high-demand groups, in the order I've just listed them:

> The Society claims that it has done all the research about various religions for us, so that we should not waste our valuable time doing research on our own. Especially forbidden was any literature that was critical of the Watchtower Society. [Wilson 2002, 106]

> The Churches of Christ have no idea what other churches teach, and they have no interest in finding out. With an attitude of being the "one true church," there is no need to know what anyone else might be doing. As a rule, their children do not participate in non-CoC vacation Bible schools, and their adults shun any community revival or ecumenical outreach efforts offered by other faiths. It is as if they feel that an open dialogue with other faiths might cause the discovery of error, and any admission of error is completely alien to a Pharisee. [Simpson 2009, 82]

> [The workers] warn people against Christian books and publications saying they are published by the "Enemy" [Lewis 2004, 229]

> Mormon culture makes a very conscious effort to teach children to believe in a specific version of reality, and it warns them about the dangers of contrary beliefs and ideas. All cultures with beliefs and practices that differ greatly from Mormon culture are said to be wrong and misguided at best, and inspired by Satan at worst. [Worthy 2008, 13]

Avoiding dangerous thoughts often entails avoiding the company of dangerous thinkers. Ignatius [c. 100 A.D.] warned his readers about "vain talkers and deceivers, not Christians, but Christ-betrayers, bearing about the name of Christ in deceit, and 'corrupting the word' of the Gospel; while they intermix the poison of their deceit with their persuasive talk" (*Epistle to the Trallians*, Ch. 6). He urged them, "Stop your ears, therefore, when any one speaks to you at variance with Jesus Christ" (Ch. 9). The warnings against exposing oneself to contrary ideas have never ceased:

> † "In these times there are inventions of clubs or clubs and hobbies for all ages. For children day clubs, young people have the clubs for their age group, and the elderly have silver clubs. If believers are leaders and the spirit in the club is preserved in a healthy foundation, then the Christian can be a partaker. But so often these type of clubs are occasions to sit where the scorners sit. There is always the danger that the corruption of wrong doctrines and the secret filth of self-righteousness slowly corrupts and the conscience becomes dimmed. The advice of the word of God is to avoid that which corrupts" (VOZ, 8/1978).

Be a light unto the world, but don't spend too much time with the people in it, is the basic idea (**4.2.3**):

> † "The dangers inherent in sports are found both in participation as a team member and attendance at games. In the past some have thought it possible to keep faith and good conscience and still participate in sports. They sought justification in thinking a believer could be a light to unbelieving teammates. However, there are many dangers in this thinking" (VOZ, 10/1999).

† "[W]hen a person makes repentance from unbelief . . . they forsake everything to be a believer." That may mean needing "to choose faith over their family, relatives, and friends," "changing an inappropriate career," or "giving up an unbelieving boyfriend or girlfriend" (VOZ, 2/2000).

A presentation directed to the youth taught that sin is always

† "the cause of falling away from faith. It often begins with hanging out with the wrong crowd and a need to fit in. It may be a time of testing borders, both with unbelieving and believing friends, and can involve sins such as inappropriate music, movies, [underage] smoking, and even drinking" (VOZ, 6/2008).

Life and Death

In his *Plea to the Christians* [c. 180 A.D.], the philosopher and early Christian writer Athenagoras defended himself and his fellow believers against the charge of murder and cannibalism, a slander that was common at the time due to people taking a bit too seriously the statements about eating Jesus' body and drinking his blood. "[W]e cannot endure even to see a man put to death, though justly," he wrote, so who "can accuse us of murder or cannibalism?" He explained how the Christians refused to even look on the spectacles that were of such great interest in that society, "the contests of gladiators and wild beasts," "deeming that to see a man put to death is much the same as killing him." Then he gave an eloquent explanation for the Christian rejection of abortion:

> And when we say that those women who use drugs to bring on abortion commit murder, and will have to give an account to God for the abortion, on what principle should we commit murder? For it does not belong to the same person to regard the very fœtus in the womb as a created being, and therefore an object of God's care, and when it has passed into life, to kill it; and not to expose an infant, because those who expose them are chargeable with child-murder, and on the other hand, when it has been reared to destroy it. [Ch. 35]

Writing around the same time, perhaps a few decades later, Tertullian made a similar argument:

> In our case, murder being once for all forbidden, we may not destroy even the fœtus in the womb, while as yet the human being derives blood from other parts of the body for its sustenance. To hinder a birth is merely a speedier man-killing; nor does it matter whether you take away a life that is born, or destroy one that is coming to the birth. That is a man which is going to be one; you have the fruit already in its seed. [*Apologetic*, Apology, Ch. 9]

Tertullian appreciated the ethical nuances of medical issues, however. Despite condemning abortion in the above quote, he provides the following gruesome description of late-term abortion as being undertaken "sometimes by a cruel necessity":

> [W]hilst yet in the womb, an infant is put to death, when lying awry in the orifice of the womb he impedes parturition, and kills his mother, if he is not to die himself. Accordingly, among surgeons' tools there is a certain instrument, which is formed with a nicely-adjusted flexible frame for opening the uterus first of all, and keeping it open; it is further furnished with an annular blade, by means of which the limbs within the womb are dissected with anxious but unfaltering care; its last appendage being a blunted or covered hook, wherewith the entire fœtus is extracted by a violent delivery. [*Apologetic*, The Soul's Testimony, Ch. 25]

Tertullian's acknowledgment of "cruel necessity" seems to value the life of the mother *over* that of the fetus. Caesarean sections were performed in ancient times, starting hundreds of years before Tertullian, but to save the life of the child with the understanding that the mother would face certain death.

Clearly, the reverence for human life has some long-established precedent in Christianity. (Except for the lives of Muslims during the Crusades, Jews and "heretics" during the Inquisition, rebellious peasants during Luther's political entanglements, and women suspected of witchcraft in 17th century New England.) In Conservative Laestadianism, that translates to a "hands off God's business" attitude:

> † "[A]ssisted suicide is contrary to God's Word. It breaks the fifth commandment; it is murder. . . . [E]ven in an extreme case, when a person lives but is left in a vegetative state, God has a reason for

this, though we may not understand. Many have experienced that God doesn't give us greater trials that we can handle, and He give strength to bear the trials we receive. Truly, it is God's decision when our lives are to end" (VOZ, 8/2000).

✝ "People have forgotten that God is the Creator and upholder of all, Lord over life and death. God alone has the power to create life and take it away. Man, in his pride, can begin to think that he is in control of his own life. Man attempts to take these matters of life and death into his own hands. This includes decisions regarding life and death themselves. This manifests itself, for example, in the prevention of conception, the termination of pregnancy, some kinds of gene manipulation, efforts to clone humans, and euthanasia. . . . God has not given authority to man to control life. Even in our time of great scientific and medical advances, God is the Lord over life and death" (VOZ, 1/2009).

It turns out, though, that there have been quite a few cases where God's sole "power to create life and take it away" has encountered limits in difficult situations. That will be discussed in **4.7.5** with regard to the Conservative position against contraception.

4.6.2 Forgiveness of Sins

> *For the forgiveness of sins begins in baptism and remains with us all the way to death, until we arise from the dead, and leads us into life eternal. So we live continually under the remission of sins.*
>
> —Martin Luther, from Paul Althaus, *The Theology of Martin Luther*

The Proclamation of Personal Absolution

Raattamaa wrote about using the "keys of loosing" in an 1854 letter:

✝ "After the law has been fully explained and preached, we must then preach the gospel and faith powerfully. If we do not use the keys of loosing, as well as the keys of binding, prisoners cannot be freed. And are we not to preach redemption to prisoners, freedom to the oppressed, and restoring of sight to the blind?" (from Kulla 1985, 177)

Laestadius mentioned forgiveness, but without any of Raattamaa's direct, evangelical approach:

> † "God is not as merciful as the sorrowless and grace-thieves think. God requires true penitence and repentance before He opens up His merciful heart. God requires living faith before he can forgive sins" (Laestadius, First Rogation Day sermon [1859]; *Fourth Postilla*, 85).

In his preface to the 1877 *Laestadius Church Postilla*, Raattamaa explains the distinction between Laestadius's legalistic approach and his own. There Raattamaa also shows that the formula of "forgiveness of sins through Jesus' name and blood" was clearly established at that point:

> † "In the beginning of the awakening the most part of people in the Churches of the parishes of Karesuando and Pajala were sorrowless. That is why Laestadius had to preach more law than at the present time. Now the most part of people who come to the meeting places and prayerhouses are believers and through law awakened ones. The preachers and those who declare the word of God must preach gospel and testify the forgiveness of sins through Jesus' name and blood, so that they may be able to by faith receive the grace of the Lord" (**laestadiustexter.se**).

And he sought such forgiveness in his own life, as he states when recalling his "discovery of the keys" (**4.1.4**):

> [B]ad thoughts, wicked lusts and desires have often wounded my conscience. I have often been incapable of self denial, and freeing myself of oppressing doubts. For this reason I have often personally needed to hear the audible affirmations of my brothers and sisters of the cross, and beg for the forgiveness of my sins in Jesus' name and blood. A weak traveler I have been. [Laitinen, 34]

Some seventy years later, Väinö Havas provided a beautiful summary and proclamation of the forgiveness of sins. It shows how this important point of doctrine had been remarkably preserved to that point, and for another 70 years to come:

> † "The matter is so unspeakably simple. You who sit in the church pew carrying a restless conscience listen to the sermon which is intended especially for you, and I authorized by my Lord as an ambassador of the Kingdom of God preach to you

forgiveness. I assure you, with the power of the Holy Ghost, that Jesus the Savior of the world, is your savior. In His name and blood, are your sins, especially your terrible sins, forgiven. The preacher of this truth is the Lord himself. Although at this moment, He has borrowed my weak tongue as His intermediate. I am only the crying voice of Heaven. That is why you can own this forgiveness of sins as the unyielding Word of God. Thus, that which is forgiven upon this earth, according to the testimony of our Master, is also forgiven in Heaven" (Havas [1940], 13).[37]

In a sermon published in the December 1953 *Greetings of Peace*, Gust Wisuri referred to what is perhaps the single favorite Bible text in Conservative Laestadianism, John 20:22. There Jesus breathed on the disciples and said "unto them, receive ye the Holy Ghost: whose soever sins ye remit, they are remitted unto them; and whose soever sins ye retain, they are retained":

✝ "There are a lot of people in this world who say they believe in God. There are a lot of people in this world who study the Bible daily. But when you bring up this very portion of the Scripture that we have read this evening to their attention, they very vehemently deny that this means that the preaching of the gospel was left in the hands of man." Why, he challenged, "did Jesus then tell these first disciples after He had given them the Holy

---

37. I wish the matter were truly "so unspeakably simple," that my youth hadn't been filled with demands for confession and battle against a pantheon of "false spirits" no longer recognized; that I weren't asked to sign on to the atrocities, hatred, misogyny, and superstition of the Old Testament or pretend it contains prophecies that just aren't there; that I didn't have to contend with being condemned by Luther for not believing in the Real Presence, by Laestadius for not having "high and living feelings of faith," by the Firstborn who follow in the footsteps of the church founder Raattamaa and were favored by him, and by Reinikainen for not denying the reality of evolution; that I wouldn't need to recoil with internal protests of "haven't you read . . ." and "how can you possibly say that when . . ." every time I listen to a sermon or open a new issue of the *Voice of Zion*, that I wouldn't be asked to view almost all of the people on this earth around me as being damned to eternal torture, including some who believe this very same "unspeakably simple" proclamation; that I hadn't needed to repeatedly walk away from heated discussions at church with critical voices still ringing in my ears about my impudent questions which were deemed to neither deserve nor require any answers.

Spirit that 'whosoever sins you remit they are remitted.' If there is one such person in our midst who doesn't believe, I would like to have you get up and answer that question now based on scriptures that what backing do you have for not believing the truth of God?"

Robert M. Price, a scholar of both the Bible and evangelical Christianity, has told me that modern evangelicals completely disregard this passage, finding it contrary to their widely held belief that one is saved through a "personal relationship with Jesus Christ." He finds such a belief ill-founded, and has some regard for the Conservative view about personal absolution. But he also thinks that Wisuri "is overstating the case: few if any evangelicals anymore deny that God has left the preaching of the gospel in the hands of man. (Some old Calvinists did, opposing missions for that reason.)" Where Wisuri has a point, Dr. Price believes, is that those same evangelists "take this passage to mean merely that Christ has given us the job of preaching the gospel, and that if we do, and someone accepts it, their sins will be remitted, not by the evangelist but by God." He calls that "a side-stepping of the force of the verse, which seems to intend that the apostles and their successors shall absolve sins as they see fit."

> † "God's mission command goes forth from generation to generation. At its core, for we who live and believe in New Testament times, is the forgiveness of sins in the name and blood of Jesus. This is the most important teaching and learning, the most important giving and receiving. It is the greatest blessing we, and our children, can own" (VOZ, 2/2001).

A presentation at the SRK's 2006 Summer Services discusses John 20:20-23:

> † "God's kingdom is a kingdom of grace and forgiveness. Jesus left the authority to forgive sins to his own disciples. . . . The children of God still forgive sins today with the authority of God and with the power of the Holy Spirit. God joins in this forgiveness in heaven. From this we too have received peace for our conscience, the hope of heaven and the joy of life."[38]

---

38. Accessed 2010 (but apparently no longer available) from suviseurat.fi/2006.

The Sole Means of Grace

There is no way to obtain forgiveness of sins in Conservative Laestadianism other than via the proclamation of absolution:

> † "Many people believe that they can confess their sins privately to God through prayer and that God, himself, will forgive their sins. . . . But God does not justify sinners privately, rather He sends the owners of the office of remission to preach the gospel of forgiveness to the penitent sinner" (Uljas 2000, 74).

> † "In many churches of this world, it is proclaimed that man can pray to God and be forgiven his sins and become saved. This is not according to God's Word. Man needs to become humble as a little child and believe his sins forgiven in the gospel preached in the name and blood of Jesus and take up the cross and follow Him. Many times Jesus preached this saving word and there were many who were offended, saying that 'who can forgive sin but God?' In Matthew is recorded, 'But that ye may know that the Son of Man hath power on earth to forgive sins'" (VOZ, 8/2004).

Those "many people" and "many churches" actually go back to the earliest days of Christianity. As discussed in **4.7.3** and **5.1.2**, I have found almost nothing in early church writings that is in accord with the Laestadian idea of personal absolution, but a fair number of references to forgiveness through baptism and prayer.

The Bible offers no examples of absolution, but it *does* discuss the forgiveness of sins via prayer. In the Old Testament, Solomon dedicated the temple he built with a prayer that talks about God forgiving sins through prayer, both inside the temple (1 Ki 8:33-34) and outside, but directed toward it (8:35-50). In the New Testament, James asked, "Is there any sick among you?" If so, the sick one should "call for the elders of the church; and let them pray over him, anointing him with oil in the name of the Lord. And the prayer of faith shall save the sick, and the Lord shall raise him up; and *if he has committed sins, they shall be forgiven him*" (James 5:14-15, emphasis added). No proclamation of forgiveness is mentioned, just the "prayer of faith." James confirms that in the next verse: "Confess your faults one to another, and *pray one for another, that ye may be healed*. The effectual fervent prayer of a righteous man availeth much" (v. 16, emphasis added). Confession was part of the picture, but Laestadian-style absolution was not.

Regular Usage

Believers always remain "repenting of their sins and faults" and desire, throughout life, "to walk leaning upon the pilgrim-staff" of the the forgiveness of sins:

> † "Only childhood christians, who have remained in the covenant of baptism repenting of their sins and faults, they have not forsaken the Kingdom of God through unbelief, they have always remained in the Father's home. But not as the older brother (Luke 15:29-30) who felt he had never broken the Father's command and therefore did not need forgiveness, of the Father he only demands payment for the faithfulness and work. But the right children of the Father live in the knowledge of their sinfulness and failings, and for that reason need the forgiveness of sins, even though they have not walked on the paths of sin together with the ungodly world. From childhood, they have had life in the Father's home through the grace of forgiveness in Jesus' blood. And they live in the same experiences and in the same grace as they who have returned as prodigal sons from the journey in the world through the narrow gate into the Kingdom of God, to the Father's home" (Leonard Typpö [1868-1922], from *Greetings of Peace*, 9/1956).

> † "Jesus alone, do you not perceive, fellow-pilgrim, Jesus alone is our salvation. And for that reason we desire to walk leaning upon the pilgrim-staff, the forgiveness of sins, that we might not soil our raiment in the cesspools of the world. I bid you farewell my friends in America and everywhere, with these words: Sins are forgiven us in Jesus blood through faith" (Matti Suo [1861-1927], from *Greetings of Peace*, 8/1950).

In a sermon given sometime in the 1950s, Paul Heideman makes Paul's statement to Timothy (2 Tim 1:1-9) as his "dearly beloved son," of whom he had remembrance in his "prayers night and day," into a full-blown Laestadian encounter complete with references to doubts, confession, absolution, and God's Kingdom:

> † Christian parents and children "have this consolation that there they have this altar of grace in their midst to which they can gather. And when each one needs, they can come and ask for blessing and forgiveness and they can forgive each other their

sins. Now in our read text, we have an example of this. When the Apostle Paul had come again to visit at Timothy's home and he had greeted young Timothy with God's Peace, the young Christian boy had been timid to confess his faith. And the apostle Paul had said, 'Well, what's the trouble, Timothy? Why do you hesitate to confess your faith?' Timothy broke into tears, and he said, 'I don't know whether I have the right to call myself a Christian anymore because I have committed sin and I have a bad conscience.' And the old apostle ... began to talk to him and say, 'Well, Timothy, confess your sin, there is forgiveness in God's Kingdom.' And when Timothy opened his heart and conscience to speak the trouble that had wounded his conscience, we read of how the Apostle Paul extended his hand in blessing upon Timothy to bless him in Jesus' name and to forgive him in Jesus' blood, so that Timothy's tears changed to joy, and again this young boy felt happy, that now again I have a good conscience cleansed in the blood of Jesus. My sins are forgiven and I am a child of God'"

With the possible exception of David and Nathan (4.3.3), there are no examples of such encounters in the Bible. That became clear to me from my reading of the entire thing in 2009, but it is certainly not a new discovery. The shoemaker and Luther admirer Hans Sachs was a vocal critic of auricular confession to a priest, the traditional–and until his time, the only–means by which a Christian would confess his sin and obtain forgiveness. His 1524 pamphlet *A Disputation between a Canon and a Shoemaker* responded to the question of why Lutherans never confessed their sins to a priest by noting that neither the old nor the New Testament contains any mention of it. "If auricular confession were such a necessary and holy thing," he says to his questioner, "then it certainly should be more clearly defined in the Scriptures" (from Rittgers 2004, 69). Luther himself, despite extolling the "secret confession which is now practised" as being "highly satisfactory, and useful or even necessary," and despite his assertion that "Christ has manifestly bestowed the power of absolution on every believer in Him," acknowledged that it "cannot be proved from Scripture" (from Kirk 1966, 421).

Nevertheless, hearing the absolution preached from another believer–preacher or not, and with or without confession of particular sins–is a regular part of a Conservative Laestadian's life:

† "It is not enough when at one time a person has been helped into faith, for salvation. We need to be preserved in faith until the end of our journey. We still need men and women like Barnabas [Acts 11:23] who preach faith in our surroundings" (Siionin Lähetyslehti, 1979).

† "Once believing, daily repentance is also needful, though it is different from the repentance from unbelief. It is daily recognizing the need for and care of the Gospel. Admitting before God that I am but filthy rags, and accepting the rich love and care of the Heavenly Father, through His kingdom here on earth. Daily one can believe that sins are forgiven in Jesus' name and precious blood" (VOZ, 12/1999).

† "God's Word reveals to us that we are weak and faulty travelers in our endeavor of faith. So often we find ourselves falling into sin and doubts, and we need the assurance of the gospel of the forgiveness of sins to uplift us. Through believing the preached gospel, a weak and faulty traveler receives strength from heaven to continue to journey. God has given believing companions to help us get to heaven. We can speak of our joys and sorrows and confess our sins one to another" (VOZ, 7/2009).

From Faith to Faith

A critical point about the Conservative doctrine of personal absolution is that forgiveness must be proclaimed by a believer. O.H. Jussila explained that in 1929 by reference to Jesus' gift of

† "the keys of the Kingdom of Heaven to his disciples. All believers in Jesus, who have received the Holy Spirit, now have power and authority to remit and retain sins in the name of Jesus, that is, in accordance with his command on his behalf. He knew man and realized that the human wretch, stripped naked by the fall into sin, no longer retained any ability to free himself from his bonds by his own efforts. This recognition of helplessness becomes evident even to man himself when his conscience awakens. Until then, a person may imagine that he can free himself from the bonds of sin in some way other than through the keys of remission. Whoever thinks thus reveals that he has not yet become sufficiently pressured in his conscience after all, for he rejects the aid offered by Heaven and also remains so bold as to

demand of God that aid be given in another way, determined by man himself. The keys of the Kingdom of Heaven have been lost many times, but the Holy Spirit of God has always fetched them anew from their hiding place for the use of Christ's congregation, for the Lord of the congregation himself has promised that the gates of hell would not prevail against his congregation" (from Hepokoski 2002b, 5).

The words have no power unless they are spoken by someone with the Holy Spirit:

† The proclamation of the forgiveness of sins by "an unbeliever, or [by] anyone without the Holy Spirit, will not open heaven for anyone, regardless of how piously and verbatim it is proclaimed even as in God's congregation" (Taskila 1961, 10).

† "There is much gospel in our time which does not free anyone from sin nor does it bring about anything but misguidance. When the Spirit of God is lacking from the proclaimer, then the proclamation is a mere jingle of words that does not heal anyone" (VOZ, 4/1974).

I have searched Luther's writings in vain for anything about what is such an important distinction to Conservative Laestadians. (Luther's discussions and writings usually assume that person to be a priest carrying out the duties of his office, despite his allowance for lay confessors.) It seems to me that he and his Reformation colleagues *did not even think to question* whether the absolution was dependent on the spiritual state of the person proclaiming it. The one possible exception of which I'm aware is Luther's advice "not to confess anything privately to a priest because he is a priest but only because he is a brother and a Christian" (from Althaus 1963, 317, n. 105).

Two separate propositions in the *Apology of the Augsburg Confession* seem to indicate that the reformers would not have been concerned about the proclaimer's spiritual state. One proposition is that absolution is a sacrament: "[M]ost people in our churches frequently use the Sacraments (Absolution and the Lord's Supper) during the year" (Article 11; McCain 2005, 156); "Baptism, the Lord's Supper, and Absolution (which is the Sacrament of Repentance) are truly Sacraments" (Article 13; McCain 2005, 184). The other is that the Sacraments [being] administered by the unworthy does not detract from the Sacraments' power. Because of the call of the Church, the unworthy still represent the person of Christ and do not represent their own persons, as Christ testifies, "The one who hears you hears Me" (Luke 10:16). (Even Judas was sent to preach.) When they offer God's Word, when they offer the Sacraments, they offer them in the stead and place of Christ. Those words of Christ teach us not to be offended by the unworthiness of the ministers. [Articles 7 & 8; McCain 2005, 148]

Luther debated his troublesome colleague Andreas Osiander about public absolution (the *Offene Schuld*) versus private absolution. During that debate, Osiander maintained that the faith of the penitent one is immaterial to the efficacy of the absolution (Rittgers 2004, 153-55; see **5.4.2**). In one joint reply to Osiander, Luther and Melanchthon wrote that (in Rittgers's words) "forgiveness could be obtained by believing hearts through either private absolution or a sermon. Both owed their authority to God's promise to be present with his Word, and both required faith" (p. 164). The only concern about "believing hearts," and an arguable one at that, was on the part of those *obtaining* forgiveness. God's promise was "with his Word," which doesn't make it seem important who was doing the preaching of it.[39]

---

39. According to Rittgers, Luther sometimes seemed to support the idea "that penitents could be bound or loosed apart from faith," that is, the faith of the recipient. Luther argued against those who, in Rittgers's words, "believed that the Spirit forgave sins directly," insisting "that forgiveness was always conveyed through the spoken word alone; *not even faith* affected the efficacy of the keys" (2004, 154, emphasis added). But Rittgers paints a picture of Luther having an "unclear, even inconsistent" viewpoint on the matter, and attempts to pull the loose ends together as follows: "Despite what Luther asserted about a person being bound or loosed apart from faith, here he clearly maintained that the keys gave nothing to the person who lacked faith. His point was that the objective working of the keys was in no way dependent on faith, or any other subjective foundation, but the actual appropriation by an individual Christian of what the keys offered absolutely required faith (p. 155).

The *Apology of the Augsburg Confession* makes clear what the Lutheran position was in 1531: "[T]hat Absolution is received only through faith is proven from Paul, who teaches that the promise cannot be received except by faith (Romans 4:16). Absolution is the promise of the forgiveness of sins. Therefore, it necessarily requires faith" (Article 12a; McCain 2005, 165-66).

Osiander had a stormy relationship with Luther, and I doubt Conservatives would find much fruitful about trying to decide whether Osiander was a "believer" or not. Regardless, he is important to this study because he "forced issues surrounding confession and absolution out into the open that otherwise would have remained concealed" (p. 217). The important questions Osiander raised included:

> Was absolution a sacrament or not? If it was, as most of Osiander's colleagues believed, what did this mean for its proper use? Could it be applied with equal validity and efficacy to crowds and to individuals? Given that most believed the individual encounter between pastor and confessant was to be preferred, how could one compel attendance at private confession if forgiveness could also be obtained through general absolution, a sermon, or a simple word of encouragement from a fellow Christian? Were the latter two also in some way sacramental? If so, what was unique about private absolution? Finally, what was the relationship between divine and human agency in confession, between God's Word and the confessor's words, between God's Word and the confessant's faith? [Rittgers 2004, 217]

For Conservative Laestadians, though, those questions mostly disappear behind the simple assertion that the disciples received the "office and the authority to preach the forgiveness of sins" from Jesus in his post-resurrection appearance, John 20:19-23:

> † "This office was not received only by those disciples of Jesus to whom He gave it himself; it has been received by all who have themselves believed the sermon of the forgiveness of sins. Man is truly unfit for this duty, but God has made His child fit for it" (Uljas 2000, 39).

From those disciples–somehow, over the course of 2,000 years of inconsistent church history–the true believers received it in turn. So,

---

It doesn't make sense to me that the keys could do anything for someone without faith, and I'm not convinced that Luther was ever willing to seriously embrace the idea, either. My point in raising the issue is this: If it was a question of debate whether the *recipient* of absolution had to have faith in order for it to work, it seems that the faith of the *proclaimer* was considered unimportant, not even worth discussing.

when Jesus said, "I will give unto you the keys of the kingdom of heaven," he

> † "speaks to Peter and the disciples, but includes all believers, even up to this day. Even though Jesus has physically left this Earth, the power of the forgiveness of sins is still here among the believers" (VOZ, 9/2008).

It seems clear to me that the "faith to faith" idea is a doctrinal cousin to the claims of apostolic succession that are made by many Christian groups. *We* got this (with a hundred intervening generations) *from the apostles*, so you need to come to us:

> [U]nder the surface, it did not take long for succeeding generations... to devise the idea of an inherited "apostolic authority," even though the apostles themselves had never claimed to hand on any such authority. Nevertheless, these would-be leaders claimed that they themselves were the true successors of these first apostles and therefore should exercise the same authority they declared that those apostles had exercised. [Cox 2009, 88]

Public Proclamations

The direct proclamation of forgiveness, practiced in Finland as the *yleinen saarna* and having roots in the *Offene Schuld* that preceded even Luther (**5.4.2**), occurs in nearly every Conservative Laestadian sermon. I have found only one written sermon from Laestadius containing any assurance of forgiveness to the listener:

> † "And you palsied one, who yourself have not been able to travel the road of Christianity from that time when this sickness of the palsy came upon you, take up now your old bedding of self-righteousness and carry it out, and remember! That you have received sins forgiven just then, when you got to hear these sweet words of grace from the mouth of Jesus: 'Thy sins be forgiven thee,' and do not henceforth go to commit sin, that something worse would not befall you, Thou palsied man! When the Son of Man has said to you: 'Thy sins be forgiven thee,' then you do not need to doubt anymore of the forgiveness of sins, although the Pharisees doubt, because at that moment that you believe, you receive that power to arise and walk the road of Christianity, but

only to the palsied ones He has said: Thy sins be forgiven thee. So believe now, you palsied one, that your sins are forgiven" (Laestadius, Nineteenth Sunday after Trinity sermon, 1847).

It is possible that Laestadius made such proclamations that are not reflected in the record of his *Postilla* (Palola 2010). He had a more expansive view of the essence of the gospel than just the proclamation of absolution, and when he urged listeners to lift up their eyes to the cruficied Christ, it had what he felt was the same effect (Palola 2011). I still find it a remarkable omission. Perhaps the Bible text for the 19th Sunday after Trinity inspired Laestadius to write out and deliver those words of assurance. It is the same text that Luther expounded upon when he explains the forgiveness of sins through personal absolution in a way remarkably similar to that understood by Conservatives (5.4.3).

For as long as I can remember, it has been said that it is a poor sermon that does not include this proclamation. It is a venerable practice; Havas proclaimed it in a 1940 sermon quoted **above**, as did Kalle Timonen in a 1951 sermon:

> † "There are many of you here who have asked in your heart, do I have the right to believe. The heavenly message assures us: all sins are forgiven in Jesus' holy name and precious redeeming blood! Lift your eyes in faith to behold our Lord Jesus Christ who has liberated us from the curse of the law ... Dear fellow pilgrims, let us travel the remainder of our sojourn here as participants in this blessedness. This blessing accompanies you each step of the way; at home, here at the services, and also at your place of work. It is for that reason you have come here, to hear whether this gospel of blessing is still extended to you. And because you have nothing but the longing to believe, it is just for such visitors here–dearly beloved, preciously redeemed souls, you especially should hear and claim our gracious Father's message" (from *Greetings of Peace*, 9/1956).

In most cases, the preacher feels the need to also ask for the assembled congregation to proclaim forgiveness of his own sins. It is also heard and requested during Bible class and discussions.

This quote refers to "the children of God in one accord" proclaiming the absolution to someone:

> ✝ "In the Kingdom of God, that blessed family of God, even you children have experienced this truth" that in Jesus' name and blood there is forgiveness of sin. "It is not strange to you when at the services of God's children, the speaker brothers preach the Gospel word" that sins are forgiven. "And someone whose heart longs and yearns for the gospel receives the strength to ask: 'May I believe my sins forgiven,' and the children of God in one accord pronounce: 'Sister, or Brother, believe your sins forgiven in the name and blood of Jesus'" (Ruben Alajoki, sermon given 1973).

Alajoki is referring to a variant of public absolution that happened on a regular basis during the highly emotional congregational meetings of the time. One after another, people in the pews would feel moved to raise their hands and ask for forgiveness from the assembled congregation, often adding a few words of confession about falling short in whatever area had just been discussed. Even during the "caretaking" meetings (**4.6.4**), focused as they were on particular individuals sitting at tables in front of the congregation, these requests from the pews would be heard. (I suspect many of those asking in that situation just wanted the relief of knowing that *they* were not going to be denied forgiveness that night.) Each request was dutifully answered by the chorus, "Believe all sins forgiven in Jesus' name and precious blood," accompanied by a flurry of hands being waved in the general direction of the penitent one. Often this would go on until seemingly everybody in the church had personally blessed everybody else.

In a sermon published in the May 1965 *Greetings of Peace*, Lauri Hakso addressed any unbelievers who may have been in the audience. He told them they were "welcome to come for a personal conversation," but warned,

> ✝ "although you respect Christianity, yet as long as you are outside of the Kingdom of God, in your unbelief, you are the enemy of the Lord Jesus." Later, he said: "[P]erhaps you are one who practices religion, but who have never been blessed from the Kingdom of God. You have never been blessed for the forgiveness of your sins in the name and blood of Jesus by men who have the Holy Ghost. And therefore you have never felt how sweet the Lord is to the sinner. He forgives him all his blood-red sins. If you are not [a partaker] of this blessing, beg to become [a] partaker. You did well when you came to these services. We

> rejoice already of this, for the word of God is powerful to open even your understanding and awaken your conscience. And we would have a great desire to bless you with this blessing in Jesus' name. You are welcome to come for a personal conversation with us concerning these matters pertaining to the salvation of your soul, of your very personal and perhaps very smarting matters. And you have leave to begin to complain over your troubles from the bench [where] you are sitting. Here around you is a flock of witnesses, of whom the Apostle writes, that when it is near, then it is a good time to put away sin and burden, repent of sin. The whole flock will proclaim your sins all forgiven to you. You will be blessed with this everlasting gospel. And even you will become a new creature in Christ."

I recall most of the sermons preached up until the 1990s containing both a proclamation *to believers* of the forgiveness of sins and an urging of repentance to any unbelieving audience members, with the implication that the general blessing would not effect their conversion. That has largely been replaced by the preacher simply making the proclamation that the unbeliever can also, if he desires to accept it, believe in the forgiveness of his sins. Although the quoted portion of Hakso's sermon makes it appear that he is following the older practice, he actually goes on to tell his unbelieving hearer to "permit yourself to be blessed with this gospel. Even I as a weak servant of Christ desire in this sermon intended for all, [to] preach your sins forgiven to you." But he follows that up by expressing certainty that the convert will feel the desire to ask for absolution personally:

> Our doctrine-father Luther says that we are allowed to believe the gospel from the general preachings. But we know that if someone receives power to believe from the general preaching, he does not remain a Christian who does not confess his faith. But he will certainly begin to say to others, what [a] miracle occurred to me, when even I [a] wretched sinner had my blood-red sins forgiven. He begins to confess his faith. And brothers and sisters, we have experienced, that when God is given to awaken the conscience, you feel the desire to ask personally, is it true that so great a sinner as I am, can believe my sins forgiven? And still, as in the days of the Apostolic church and congregation, the children of God laid their hands upon the repentant sinner and proclaimed the forgiveness of sins personally. And in this way we receive

power to believe that the gospel means just me. And this is not a doctrine discovered by the Laestadians. But as the Apostle writes of the doctrine of the Lord Jesus, he says that it also includes the laying on of hands.

The old preachers usually meant Paul when they referred to "the Apostle." The only thing about the laying on of hands that appears in the epistles attributed to him is in 1 Tim 4:14, which Paul probably didn't even write: "Neglect not the gift that is in thee, which was given thee by prophecy, with the laying on of the hands of the presbytery." The book of Hebrews– sometimes misattributed to Paul–mentions the laying on of hands, but see the discussion of Heb 6:1-2 in **7.7**.

The book of Acts describes multiple occurrences of the laying on of hands, but *never* associates it with any proclamation of the forgiveness of sins. (Paul's experience with Ananias is significant in this regard, see **7.2**.) Instead, the gift of the Holy Ghost was given as a transfer of spiritual force or power *through physical contact*, a practice well established in the Old Testament and Jesus' ministry. Note Jacob's patriarchal blessing of his sons (Gen 48:12-20), Aaron's putting the sins of the children of Israel onto the head of the scapegoat (Lev 16:21-22), Moses' anointing of Joshua as his successor (Num 27:22-23, Deut 34:9), Elisha's raising a child from the dead (2 Ki 4:32-35), and various healing miracles by Jesus (Mk 1:31, 1:41-42, 5:30, 5:41-42, 6:5, 7:32-35, 8:23-25, 9:27, 20:34). Jesus laid his hands on the little children who were brought to him (Mt 19:13-15), and his physical touch in breaking the bread was an important part of the miracles of the loaves and fishes (Mt 6:41) and the institution of Communion (Mt 14:22).

It was in the ninth century, as "the Church gradually asserted the power of the keys and reconciliation began to assume the character of absolution," that the laying on of hands became associated with the forgiveness of sins. The physical act was "accompanied by the invocation of the Holy Ghost and the prayers of the bishop, or the priest to whom he delegated the function" (Lea 1896, 52). A few centuries later, the "imposition of hands became a mere unimportant adjunct in the ceremony" of absolution, and by Luther's day it had been largely replaced by the sign of the cross (p. 53).

My last quote in this sample of public proclamations is from a sermon given in 1971 by Art Forstie:

> † "Believe through the strength of this gospel of blood yet even this morning, just as you are if you feel weak and weary, many doubts and lackings, that they are all forgiven in Jesus' name and precious blood."

But, despite the lack of any later quotes, the practice certainly has not stopped. Far from it. Preachers are careful to always assure the assembled congregation with the public absolution in their sermons, even at special service events where several sermons occur in a single day. After a while, one can start to wonder what sins really need absolving since the last proclamation was heard forty minutes ago.

It is a far cry from what was practiced when Luther came on the scene. The "monastic ideal" then was only "several confessions per year." Most people confessed during Holy Week, perhaps on a few other occasions throughout the year, before being married, and "whenever they were facing the possibility of death owing to sickness, childbirth, or dangerous travel" (Rittgers 2004, 26-27).

Getting it in Writing

At one time, church writings also assured readers of the forgiveness of their sins:

> † "I would greet you, dear fellow traveler on Life's Way with the word of encouragement. Do not give up your most precious faith. Believe still, as a sinner, that in the name and precious blood of the Friend of sinners, even your sins are all forgiven" (Paul Heideman, *Greetings of Peace*, 10/1942).

> † "Proclaim yet for awhile, you angels of the Lord of Hosts, the gospel, whose very core is the forgiveness of sins! You people of the Lord who suffer from your sinfulness, believe even now your sins forgiven in Jesus' name and holy blood!" (Taskila 1961, 4).

In the early days of the *Voice of Zion*, there were many such direct proclamations of absolution to the reader:

> † "Dear Reader! You may even now believe all your sins, your failings, your fears, forgiven in Jesus' name and shed blood. 'Behold the Lamb of God which taketh away the sins of the world!' Even your sins are taken away, they are cleansed and removed as far as the east is from the west" (VOZ, 1/1980).

From what I recall, these written proclamations were not understood as applying to outsiders. Certainly nobody expected someone to show up in church and be treated as a "believer" by virtue of having read the church newspaper.

It was even common for authors to lament their sinfulness and ask for forgiveness in their articles. A response would appear below each such article reading something like this: "You can believe your sins forgiven in Jesus' name and blood. –The editors." It surely stretches the credulity of even the most pious reader to imagine an author spending months awaiting the issue of the *Voice of Zion* to arrive that contains the response to his request and the assurance that, yes, his sins are indeed forgiven.

4.6.3 Confession

> *Thou shalt confess thy sins. Thou shalt not go to prayer with an evil conscience. This is the way of light.*
>
> —*The Epistle of Barnabus* [c. 100 A.D.]

According to Laestadius, a form of confession that "had come into practice among the awakened" was when

> † "the severe pains of conscience compel a sinner, who is penitent and willing to repent, to make an open confession of sins in the presence of some Christians, who may be many or few in number; and this open confession of sins is made to ease a burdened conscience" (*VCW*, 89).

He wrote that it

> † would be "pure nonsense" for a Communion participant not to be "obliged to confess his willful sins, which he actually has committed, but only in a general way to confess himself to be sinful. . . . What is so hard about becoming saved? The minister testifies sins forgiven every Sunday to shameless sinners, who continue to love their bosom sins. The minister does not require that everyone who signs up for Communion must make known his condition of soul. He requires no true confession of sin, but only the general, hypocritical confession of sin." In such case, "only a few Communion participants will make their confession of sin for the whole congregation" (*VCW*, 125).

Such "pure nonsense" is the norm now; it would surprise most Conservatives to hear that there ever was such a thing as a pre-sacramental examination, which goes back to Luther's time ("No one is admitted to the Sacrament without first being examined," *Augsburg Confession*, Article 24; McCain 2005, 47). As discussed below, general absolution is now proclaimed to all before Communion, usually multiple times.

One imagines that, if Laestadius ever read Luther's *Discussion of Confession*, he would have been horrified at the suggestion that the communicant go now and then "without confession, even if he has been immoderate in drinking, talking, or sleeping, or has done something else that is wrong . . . in order that a man may learn to trust more in the mercy of God than in his own confession or in his own diligence" (*PE* 1, 95).[40]

The usage of the keys to loose one from sins was associated with confession from the very beginning by Raattamaa, the (re)discoverer of those keys (**4.1**):

> ✝ "Private confession is allowed in the Word of God, and so we must often bring forth the great love of our Savior in reproof and counsel privately between one another. Nor is it fitting to condemn one another for all manner of faults, for the Lord Jesus is not rejecting His Bride for all manner of faults, as He has said of temporal marriage." In Mt 18:16-17, 20, "the key to loose and bind has now been given to the Christians" (Raattamaa, sermon given 1894, from Kulla 1985, 181).

During the 1920s, confession was a point of contention between the Conservatives and the Pollarites, whom the Conservatives "accused of rejecting confession and of having a spirit of carnality" according to Hepokoski (2002b, 83). Hepokoski also asserts that two prominent Conservative preachers of the day, O.H. Jussila and Matti Suo emphasized the need for confession, with Jussila "equating the foot washing of John 13:14 with confession" and Suo making "it clear that he does not believe that faith, without confession, is sufficient for salvation" (p. 83). Despite Hepokoski's obvious sympathies for the

---

40. The fact that Luther treats immoderate drinking no differently than immoderate talking or sleeping will come as no surprise to anyone who knows about his drinking habits.

Pollarites, I would not be surprised if the Conservatives had seized on confession as a point of distinction with the new "heresy" and thus been forced to emphasize it more in the decades to come.

The general proclamation that "all sins are forgiven" has been made to listeners in sermons since at least the 1930s (**4.6.2**). In the sermons of my youth, confession was emphasized through a caveat often added to that proclamation. One with "name matters" on the conscience was expected to confess them to some other individual believer and thus receive forgiveness, or at least personal and specific assurance of forgiveness. A sermon given by Havas many decades earlier in 1935 hinted at that understanding:

> † "Let no one leave from these services with bound consciences. In this temple there are hundreds of confessor fathers and mothers. Relate to them simply the burdens of your heart. They will bless you with a beautiful gospel of forgiveness" (Havas, 28).

Although Havas stops short of requiring confession, he certainly encourages it:

> † "We are not to say to any troubled soul: 'You must make a confession.' Rather we can instruct, in love, one whose sins still trouble his conscience, and who, due to them, falls into heavy doubts. We can tell them that it is grace that you can call unto yourself a father confessor, and also grace that you can experience the fruitful blessing of confession that brings assurance to your faith" (Havas [1935], 45).

> † "We have said that absolution is a condensed gospel; this gospel, the grace of God, is the only true power against sin. We can, in the word of absolution, be bold. To the penitent sinner we may preach forgiveness even before any act of confession is made, or even before the need to confess is fully realized by the one concerned" (Havas [1935], 47).

Later, the writings in my sample show a much stronger emphasis on confession, matching my recollections:

> † "General forgiveness is needed, but so is an individual and really personal forgiveness needed. When some named trespass has come upon the conscience, it does not leave otherwise, but one has to confess his sin to the priest like in the Old Testament,

and those royal priests are near. They are all of the believers. Use them for your benefit. Speak about that which is weighing on your conscience and listen and believe, when unto you is forgiven even the named trespasses and thus you preserve the peace of your conscience" (Taskila 1961, 44).

✝ "[I]f sin has come, which the Holy Spirit is preaching to you of, even as the Prophet Nathan, don't try to put away this sin and hide it. Sin doesn't spoil. It stays in real good shape. You cannot hide it on a closet shelf. It's always there on your conscience. If sin comes upon your conscience, put it away. Confess it as King David here confesses, 'I acknowledge my transgressions and my sin is ever before me.' Let us be reminded this morning hour that we make journey with a good conscience and with a clean heart in the Kingdom of God, for these fountains of grace and mercy are flowing yet even this morning in the Kingdom of God to wash you thoroughly as King David speaks" (Art Forstie, sermon given 1971).

This article, published in the midst of zealous caretaking meetings against false spirits (**4.4.7**), envisions the people in Jesus' Palestine going to somebody to confess their sins:

✝ "Confession is not a condition of salvation. Even the thief on the cross did not have time to correct his matters one bit, but was fully sanctified. Luke 23:43. If he had lived longer and had been given the opportunity, certainly he would have clarified the things on his conscience at an opportune time, bearing the humiliation of confession and correction of matters. We do not become children of God through confession, but confession does help us remain children of God. Confession is not imperative to death, but is essential to life" (VOZ, 7/1975).

Despite the disclaimer that confession is not a "condition of salvation," most sins beyond mere impure thoughts, doubts, etc. were considered to remain on the conscience until one had spoken of them "by name":

✝ "Certainly on the way of a Christian there have been sins which he has not had strength to bring to light. The Holy Spirit has reminded for years and perhaps decades. We the servants in the word have experienced this that perhaps even a graying elder may have brought to light sins of his youth, confessed them and had them forgiven. The questions, however, have often risen: oh, why didn't I release myself of those burdens before? Why carry these for years and years? . . . But I would advise you brothers and sisters as a servant of God in these admonishments, do not burden yourself with those nominal things, whether they are sins that have happened in youth, in middle age or old age. Here in the kingdom of God there is such freedom that one can speak of these to a confessor father or mother" (Lauri Hakso, sermon printed in VOZ, 6/1976).

† "It is never an easy matter to repent of sins for the flesh fights against the Spirit. But sin has a name, and those named sins will not go away without our speaking of them to a dear brother or sister. We are assured that we can freely go to a dear one and open our heart. But those sins that have affected the congregation of God are to be repented of before the congregation; otherwise we will not receive freedom" (VOZ, 10/1978).

I remember those difficult days all too well. One event that will always stand out in my mind is when I was coerced to confess to something that my peers had been engaged in, but that I had avoided. My denials were not believed, though, and I wound up confessing just so I would be left alone. (I suppose I should have then confessed the sin of lying.) Despite that high-pressure environment, the author of this April 1979 *Voice of Zion* article says that

† "much confusion and wrong understanding has come about amongst the Christians when from confession a merit unto salvation is made. The truth is still this that nothing comes before the righteousness of faith. Our only salvation is through Christ Jesus, for through faith we have become righteous. But also when confession is left out, then one has also gone astray in understanding. For it is through the Holy Spirit of God which has come to dwell in our hearts that we are instructed to put away sin. We can never underestimate the confession of sins, for in order to keep faith and good conscience and preserve Jesus as the only true reason of our salvation, we confess and put sin away. . . . Confession is a grace privilege for those of us in faith to remain in faith. It ensures unto us that those sins are forgiven in the blood of Jesus. It is not just that by confession we become saved, but rather confession is a fruit of living faith."

So, even though it was not a "merit unto salvation," it was a "fruit of living faith." In other words, you'd better be doing it regardless.

In my observation at least, confession is now much less practiced and expected, even though personal absolution remains a fundamental part of Conservative Laestadianism. I've heard several parents wonder about why their kids aren't bothering with confession. One friend on the board of an LLC congregation said that the lack of interest in confession has even been raised as a topic of discussion there. I asked some Finnish pastors about the matter, and their replies indicated to me that confession is on the wane in the SRK, too. One said that it is all too often the result of somebody being caught, and another that more and more people just ask for forgiveness generally or rely on the *yleinen saarna*, the proclamation to the congregation during the sermon.

The situation reminds me of how enthusiastically the people of Nürnberg abandoned the sacrament of penance when Luther came on the scene: "Laypeople quickly adapted to the new custom of relying on general confession and absolution to prepare them for the Lord's Supper" (Rittgers 2004, 94), to the point where "Luther argued that too many people had been abusing this new freedom: 'They take [it] to mean that they should or may no longer confess'" (p. 112). See **5.4.2** for further discussion of that historical background.

In a September 1979 *Voice of Zion* article, we see echoes of Laestadius's teaching that the "devil of honor" was what would stand in the way of someone making confession:

> † "If one has so much pride [that] one does not want to reveal to the other Christians the sinfulness inside, one is only deceiving ones' own self. In order to attain that heavenly home, it will be revealed eventually, so one should not hold back for how else can one be cleansed from all defilement."

If David's "conscience had accused him without Nathan's reminder," Laestadius said in his Fourth Rogation sermon of 1859, "then he could have made a secret repentance, although a secret repentance cannot succeed for the reason that the sins are covered, not with God's grace, but with the devil's honor. But when Nathan came to accuse him, he had to confess his sins, for by this accusation his honor was broken and then the spirit of God was able to effect true penitence" (*Fourth Postilla*, 230).

† "[I]t is a blessed fact that each one of us has been given guides who lovingly lead us and counsel us to put sin away even by name" (VOZ, 11/1979).

† "There have been accusations against the children of God that there are conditions of confession that must be made in order that one can be free from sin. This is not so. But there are also dangers in which the enemy of the soul wishes to attempt to bind a child of God in this, a doctrine of confession. That in order to be free of sin you must make a very careful and perfect confession. And even better yet, that you would bring those private matters before the congregation and that [in] a blessing from the congregation for private matters there is even a better forgiveness. In this doctrine rather than freeing a child of God, one becomes bound" (Dan Rintamaki, sermon given 1980).

Rintamaki was addressing (and perhaps trying to discourage, appropriately) the public confessions that had become a regular occurrence of the Sunday morning service. At least in some North American congregations, members would head up to the front of the church after the sermon and ask the entire congregation for forgiveness of various sins. That means of correcting infractions was much like that of the Amish, though of course the specific rules were different. The Laestadian equivalent of the *Ordnung* was not about modern conveniences but worldly entertainment. "[A]nybody who has been in violation of the Ordnung–and, theoretically, it could be anyone from somebody caught using a chainsaw to somebody seen driving a car to somebody committing adultery–has to confess his or her transgression in front of the entire congregation" (Mackall 2007, 117).

The mechanics of confession could get complicated:

† The "confessor father" to whom a person turns "proclaims all sins forgiven in Jesus' name and blood. The confessor father must not tell anyone about the forgiven matters. If two or more children of God have been overtaken in the same sin, they cannot become freed of it by absolving each other. Then another Christian–not involved in the matter–is needed to proclaim absolution. Sometimes, the sin may be of such nature that it should be confessed before the congregation. Then all the children of God know that the open and public offense has been openly mended" (*By Faith*, 91).

In the past 20 years, the official line has remained that confession is important, even to the point of the devil being the source of reluctance to use it:

> ☦ "When sin presses, the devil preaches that this is a most difficult matter to put away; no one has done such a great sin. Or, he wants to cheapen the grace of God by saying that this is such a small matter that it does not need to be cared for; it would sound foolish to confess such a small matter. I am sure that the psalm writer experienced these kinds of attacks by the devil, but holding faith precious, he emboldens to care for these matters. We also have permission to pray that strength and boldness would be given to us. We know and can be assured that the Heavenly Father hears these prayers and even provides those heavenly escorts, confessor fathers and mothers, so that we can drink from the fountain of grace and be cleansed in the name and blood of Jesus" (VOZ, 7/1990).

> ☦ Some "who are living in the permissiveness of sin on occasion defend themselves by claiming that they have no need to take care of the matters. It suffices their consciences to hear the general preaching of the gospel. This is, of course, possible, but it requires, as Luther says, a 'strong and firm faith.' Luther then asks, 'But how many have such a strong faith?' When the fruits of the flesh prevail in the lives of those that make these claims, their claims seem especially empty" (Jon Bloomquist, presentation given 1998).

> ☦ Regarding public confession, "matters are corrected as to the extent that offense has been caused. In private confession, matters may come out that we correct more broadly. The gospel preached by the confessor-father conveys the power of forgiveness to correct the matters. This takes place when, for example, one has caused an offense against another person or the government" (Uljas 2000, 90).

> ☦ One may attempt to believe that a sin that "especially weighs upon" the conscience has been forgiven "from the general preaching of the gospel" without confession. "From my own experience, I can say that one does not receive peace and freedom by this means. No matter how much I have tried to believe, that

known matter has always reminded me of its existence" (Uljas 2000, 92).

> † "While it is true that the general gospel [absolution proclaimed without confession, e.g., during services] promises the forgiveness of all sins, the common experience of God's children is that their faith is so weak that they have needed private confession and its absolution" (Markus Korpi, presentation given 2003).

Perhaps there is something self-perpetuating about the need that Korpi mentions? When people are told from childhood that "one does not receive peace and freedom" of particular sins without confession (as Uljas generalizes in the quote above, based solely on his own experience), is it any wonder that such winds up being "the common experience"? It seems a bit like Laestadius's observation that children arriving at confirmation school "are somewhat in a state of innocence; they do not know of any difference between good and evil. They must therefore be awakened to recognize their own corrupt nature; they must through their own experience become convinced that all people are naturally the children of wrath" (*VCW*, 72).

My youthful conscience spent altogether too much time being tormented by the non-scriptural Laestadian distinction of "name sins." Commensurate with the much-subdued practice of confession, it is not much emphasized anymore, this recent quote notwithstanding:

> † "The grace-privilege to confess even of 'name-sins' and the acknowledgment of our overall corrupt nature are part of our life as a child of God. Confession is a grace-gift that blunts the accusations of the enemy of souls. How fortunate we are that we can go to a fellow believer at any time and speak of the wounds of sin" (VOZ, 2/2009).

Luther had a much more extensive "hateful and wearisome catalogue of distinctions" to contend with in the theology of his day, the results of which were that, as he writes in his 1520 *Discussion of Confession*,

> the penitent makes so much of these trifles that he is not able really to give heed to the thing of chief importance, namely, the desire for a better life. He is compelled to tax his memory with such a mass of details, and so to fill his heart with the business of rightly expressing his cares and anxieties, while seeking out

forgotten sins or a way of confessing them, that he entirely loses the present pangs of conscience, and the whole profit and salutary effect of confession. When he is absolved, therefore, he rejoices not so much because he is absolved, as because he has freed himself once for all from the wretched worry of confession; for what he has been seeking has been not the absolution, but rather the end of the laborious nuisance of confessing. [PE 1, 91]

He certainly had mixed feelings about private confession. Luther said it was where "God's word and absolution are spoken privately and individually to each believer for the forgiveness of his sins." In his 1528 *Confession Concerning Christ's Supper*, he considered it "a precious, useful thing for souls," but added the caveat, "as long as no one is driven to it with laws and commandments but sinners are left free to make use of it, each according to his own need, when and where he wishes" (Lull 2005, 66; translation checked against WA 26, 507). And in his *Table Talk*, he looked back on the "many conflicts of the conscience" in which "we have been ensnared, confounded, and captivated under popedom, saying, "If we would but consider the tyranny of auricular confession, one of the least things we have escaped from, we could not show ourselves sufficiently thankful to God for loosing us out of that one snare" (§288).

The Laestadian concept of "name sins" is probably based on the "mortal sins" that in Catholic theology must be confessed by name: "All mortal sins of which penitents after a diligent self-examination are conscious must be recounted by them in confession, even if they are most secret . . ." (*Cathecism of the Catholic Church*, para. 1456). But Luther downplayed and criticized the distinction between mortal and venial sins, criticizing theologians who "strive zealously and perniciously to drag the consciences of men, by teaching that venial sins are to be distinguished from mortal sins, and that according to their own fashion" (*Discussion of Confession*, 89-90). Not all sins of either type "are to be confessed, but it should be known that after a man has used all diligence in confessing, he has yet confessed only the smaller part of his sins." Furthermore, he wrote,

> we are so far from being able to know or confess all the mortal sins that even our good works are damnable and mortal, if God were to judge with strictness, and not receive them with forgiving mercy. If, therefore, all mortal sins are to be confessed, it can be

done in a brief word, by saying at once, "Behold all that I am, my life, all that I do and say, is such that it is mortal and damnable." [p. 89]

4.6.4 Rebuke

> *Fundamentalism is not well-known for its claims to have imperfect knowledge and prophecies that will pass away. Nor are fundamentalists well-known for their openness, humility, or love toward those who disagree with them.*
>
> —Conrad Hyers, *The Comic Vision*

The Laestadian movement began as a rebuke of the lifestyle of drunken Lapps, and Laestadius's viewpoint about church displine was clear:

> † "When Prophet Nathan in God's name rebuked [David] of his ungodly life, he did not become offended as do many at the present time who become angry when they are rebuked but he received pangs of conscience when he allowed the Spirit of God to chastise him by the mouth of the prophet. Through this deep penitence, into which David fell because of this chastisement, his heart became ready to receive grace and the forgiveness of sins" (Laestadius, Fourth Rogation Day Morning sermon [1854]; *Fourth Postilla*, 223-24).

"Approximately 15 percent of evangelical churches practice church discipline," according to Joyce. "[H]undreds of congregants in fundamentalist Baptist and other evangelical churches have been excommunicated or shunned for misdeeds ranging from drunkenness, adultery, refusal to honor church elders, gossiping, and sowing disharmony" (2009, 212).

In the second half of the 1970s, after some decades of laxity, it "once again became a burning issue" to keep clear "the border between the Kingdom of God and the outside world":

> The leadership of the SRK-Laestadianism which consisted mostly of lay preachers began to see the unity and purity of the Kingdom increasingly threatened by harmful outside influences and lax discipline inside. It became a necessity to root out these influences and those who kept disseminating them. [Ketola 2010, 5]

Just a few decades after Heikki Jussila's 1948 criticism of the New Awakening, his words began to apply to his own Conservative Laestadianism: "There was no peace, but so many 'revelations of the spirit' that the Word of God could not be preached in peace" (p. 84).

During those decades, "caretaking meetings" were commonly held to discuss the spiritual state of individual congregation members. They were considered the third step in Jesus' instructions regarding the rebuke of a brother who has caused offense [Mt 18:15-16], not so much for individual actions against another member but as a result of his observed sins (e.g., acquiring a television) or erroneous doctrinal views.

> † In 1971, when the SRK made it clear that no "easing or moderation of position" had taken place in the issue of television, it instructed that those "who are disobedient in the television question must be spoken to once or twice in private or in meetings by SRK or the local association [congregation]. If the ones spoken to do not humble themselves to repentance, consider them pagans and publicans and refuse them membership in the association. The disobedient are not to be greeted with the greeting of God's children" (*Päivämies* No. 29, 1971). At its 1974 annual meeting, the AALC (now renamed LLC) took "precisely the same stand in America" (VOZ, 10/1974).

> † "Sin affects sore spots in the members of Christ's Body. Speedy care is always necessary, so that a member [of the congregation] doesn't need to be cut off. The instructions for care have been given by the Holy Spirit. Sickness is to be avoided but in care of sicknesses the help comes by way of individuals or at the center for care aided by the congregation of God. First the brother is to be reproved by one. Then with two or three witnesses present if the brother is not obedient to this reproof. Last of all the congregation decides the matter of the brother. The Church Law of Christ is particularly necessary at the end times" (VOZ, 5/1974).

Those accused of such spiritual sickness

> had to step in front of the whole congregation where they had to listen to the charges made against them. The whole congregation, not just those acting as chairmen, could join in making accusations. The accused then had the chance to repent and

receive forgiveness. If they did or could not do this in the right way, and this often meant using very specific words and phrases, they could be expelled from the congregation and thus from the Kingdom of God. [Ketola 2010, 5-6]

Understandably, these "events were traumatic for many accused. Many of them were old people who could not understand that they had done anything wrong. Many tried to repent immediately just to be spared further pain and humiliation but this was not possible because the leaders wanted to be certain that the accused really understood what they have done wrong" (p. 6). If they were unsuccessful, they were "bound." Then they were considered "pagans and publicans" and refused "membership in the association," as the 1971 *Päivämies* article instructs.

While some "bound" individuals were reconciled to the congregation, many became completely alienated and would never overcome their resentment toward the church. The following article refers to threats of "police action," probably those which disaffected individuals in Finland sometimes made against the church there on the grounds of pressure or emotional abuse. It is possible that the article also or instead refers to police action that might have been warranted against the disaffected individuals for their offenses:

> † "Even if some grounds have been sought to appeal to authorities, God does not take care of matters with the help of the police, but His manner of caretaking is different. Of home teachers, the most unerring one is the Holy Spirit, which always reveals God's own and uses as its support the Bible message. Always, when the condition of heart has been repaired from the faults of the fall, the 'sound of the bell has changed.' No longer would one frighten such with the police, but even to such is preached repentance and forgiveness of sins. When the vessel is cleansed from within, it becomes clean even from the outside! Surely we would not be like those who in temporal and especially in spiritual matters, would be zealous or anxious to give the matter to the police if something should happen. The possibility for correction is small, especially in that matter, which to us is the most important. Speaking in connection with one's own falls, accusations, use of authorities, are especially serious symptoms

and a first sign of a deep falling away and of hardening" (*Päivämies*, 1974).

Members were encouraged not to take offense, but to submit to the congregational meetings as acts of love:

> † "Sister or brother, if you have found yourself in that place that the congregation has had to rebuke you, do not be offended. Don't let the old Adam take hold of your heart, although it would hurt it. Your brothers and sisters have only one good intention, and it is that you would inherit eternal life. Although the words of instructions feel unloving and hard to you,, nevertheless, the intention is to bring you to repentance" (*Päivämies*, 1974).

But concern for the one being rebuked certainly was not the only motivation, as Peter Nevala makes clear in this article from the July 1974 *Voice of Zion*:

> † "When some serious defilement of flesh and spirit appears in the congregation which has 'moved stones from their place,' not many members of the congregation can be found who have not taken a stand in the matter. These sayings and opinions, which have not moved those concerned from the true foundation of faith and doctrine, are 'swept away.' First they cause only discord and dissension in the congregation, but if uncared for, they cause different spirit and heresy. Therefore the commandment was: first sweep the house, that is, let the loose litter be removed, so that on account of these the healthy would not be condemned as defiled."

The Amish use the same "preserve the community" rationale for excommunication and shunning wayward members: "A person who voluntarily or involuntarily leaves the fold after baptism is excommunicated and shunned. Shunning somebody who has been excommunicated strengthens the community, reinforcing to everybody the idea that the weakest link has been removed, and that the chain of community has been made even stronger" (Mackall 2007, 144). So do the Jehovah's Witnesses. If "persons willfully show disrespect for" rules about permissible sexual relations between husband and wife, for example, "it becomes necessary to remove them from the congregation as dangerous 'leaven' that could contaminate others" (from Wilson 2002, 249).

Sometimes the assembled congregation would simply refuse to grant forgiveness. I saw it done even in some cases where the individual expressed penitence for his actions but failed to recognize a "wrong spirit" that was the "root" of the matter:

> † "If we ask forgiveness for hard feelings and do not bring up the reasons, the root of bitterness is left untouched and is waiting for the next occasion to come up. It is necessary that we put our flesh to shame, and in so doing we receive power from the Holy Spirit to resist falling back into the same condition" (VOZ, 7/1974).

When the subject's request for forgiveness (often repeated desperately and tearfully) was not granted by the end of the meeting, the congregation would exercise the "binding key":

> † The third step in the Church Law of Christ, "which is given only to the Church of God or the kingdom of God, is then the highest tribunal upon this earth. Its decision is final. The church of God alone can use this binding key; and if man does not hear the Church of God, he has been bound in his sins because of his disobedience to the instructions of the Word and the Spirit of God that speaks in and through the congregation (church). Jesus has said, 'Whatsoever thou shalt bind on earth shall be bound in heaven.' Then such a one is no longer a child of God and is not greeted with God's Peace. But if after he has been bound by the congregation he should become penitent of his sins and wants to repent of them, then the children of God are always ready to forgive him his sins and use the key of loosening. Each individual Christian has the authority to use the key of loosening to forgive the penitent sinner his sins, but the fruits of his repentance will also lead him to make repentance before the congregation which has bound him" (VOZ, 8/1976).

> † "The congregation of God knowing how great a danger there is that the individual Christian may fall, has cared for her members with wholesome grace, using even the keys of binding as well as the keys of loosening. We are thankful to God even for this caretaking" (*Päivämies* No. 6, 1978).

That act of binding is something I personally witnessed several times as a youth. It is quite unforgettable to see people ask the congregation for forgiveness at a meeting held concerning their spiritual affairs and receive only cold silence as a response. Sometimes they would sit gamely at their table at the front of the church while the meeting continued to the bitter end, often late into the night. And sometimes they would reach their breaking point and storm out of the building, ending the meeting of their own accord. I saw it go either way. Both outcomes were heartbreaking to the subjects as well as the congregation members who sincerely believed that the soul of their brother or sister hung in the balance that night.

As one might expect, there could be a good deal of secret resentment even when one had jumped through the hoops set before him:

> † "True humility is known by this, that the faulty one does not pull concealment over himself, nor does he squirm before the truth of God, but upon falling into error acknowledges the fall as his own; without defensive speeches or seeking alleviating circumstances, submits himself to repentance of that which causes sorrow in the congregation of God. Having received the forgiveness of sins, he remains believing and enjoying the peace and freedom brought by the forgiveness as a child of God. When the heart is not right, the repentance made today is undone tomorrow and the situation is worse than before. One sign yet, that the heart did not thaw of its pride, is this, that a bitter heart remains toward the caretakers. If weaknesses are found in the caretakers, it does not help to grumble behind the back." One should approach them directly and "say where the 'shoe is pinching.'" (VOZ, 5/1979).

"*The Board!*," I recall a loved one intoning with exaggerated somberness in a discussion about all the "caretaking" that the church's local board of trustees was zealously carrying out. Grumbling behind the back of the church elders was the only possible relief. To approach them with concerns about their activities carried the very real danger of seeming unrepentant and becoming subject to yet another meeting. Instead, for a couple of years to come, the public face remained one of compliance and thankfulness for the opportunity of correction.

In many cases the corrected one was probably so beaten down by the experience as to feel a Stockholm-syndrome sense of gratitude. During Jack Worthy's time as a wayward Mormon missionary, he hated his "dirty worthless soul" and no longer cared for himself or about anything at all. His feelings about being called to account were not bitterness, but "a deep sense of humility before God." It causes "the sinner to gratefully soak up the bishop's, priest's, pastor's, or mission president's expressions of understanding, love, and concern. It turns God's mouthpieces into heavenly angels with remarkable healing powers, most notably the power to promise sinners that they will once again become whole and worthy of self-respect, even self-love" (2008, 137).

So it wouldn't be surprising if many of those subjected to the "care of the mother" in Conservative Laestadianism during the 1970s and early 1980s felt more relief and thankfulness than hurt pride:

> † "I have been able to sit at the meetings and have been able to see how this mother has taken care of even the children of God here. Allow yourself to be cared for, dear brothers and sisters; it does not matter one bit if your pride is scuffed" (Lenna Pellikka, sermon given 1979).

> † "Using the keys of the kingdom to bind one is important for it is love towards the faulty one to awaken and help him to see his own sins. Only the congregation of God has the power to use the keys of binding. But when the congregation of God does bind a sinner, we then no longer greet him [with God's Peace] nor do we go to him attempting to take care of his matters," because at that point "his place of repentance is in the congregation of God. One Christian can release a bound one from his sins if he with a penitent heart asks for forgiveness, but he is then instructed to also go before the congregation with his repentance. If two people have fallen into the same sin, a third party is needed on to whom they can make repentance" (VOZ, 9/1979).

> † "Here in America, and also in Canada and there in Finland, I have met many believers who in their hearts praise God, and even with their mouths say, 'The children of God came and corrected me. If God in His love would not have approached me through His Kingdom, I would have perished, deceived by the enemy'" (Voitto Savela, sermon given 1980).

By the early 1980s, the caretaking meetings had stopped, with one exception of which I'm aware, a meeting that I witnessed in the late 1980s. I am now ashamed to admit that, as a hot-headed and excessively devout youth, I helped instigate the proceedings. One happy outcome of the whole unpleasant affair was that I developed a strong rapport with one of the individuals who had been the subject of concern (misplaced, on my part). He was an intelligent, independent-minded individual who has now, to my sadness, passed away. And there's no doubt that his faith was of utmost importance to him until the very end of his life.

Though the practice of congregation-wide caretaking meetings ceased, the concept remained important, at least for a while:

> † "Generally, we find rebuking another person to be an unpleasant task and are often reluctant and timid to do so. A healthy timidity rises from the knowledge and understanding of our own poorness. But we must also acknowledge that there are other factors that may cause us to be timid and sometimes even negligent. For example, we may fear that we will start an argument, be rejected, lose a friend, or even make an enemy. Sometimes we may simply be lazy and indifferent. Such fears rise from our flesh and our darkened reason. God's Word, however, teaches us that when we ignore a brother's sin we both hate him and share in his guilt [Lev 19:17]. Proverbs teach that 'open rebuke is better than secret love' and that he that rebukes another will afterward be more favored than someone who has merely flattered him [Prov. 27:5; 28:23]. In the so-called 'church law of Christ' [Mt 18:15-17], Jesus teaches that when our brother sins against us, we should discuss the matter with him alone, one on one. If our brother does not hear us, Jesus says to take 'one or two more,' and if he still will not hear, Jesus says 'tell it unto the church.' If the offending brother refuses to hear the church, then he is no longer to be regarded a brother in faith. Then the keys of binding are used" (Don Lahti, presentation given 1997).

A healthy timidity finally took hold, which sometimes raised concerns that things were moving too far in the opposite direction:

> † "To be your brother's keeper means approaching the fallen one in a gentle, humble manner. We should not be harsh, yelling, or judging. We are being helpful, not nosy. It's good to speak of matters pertaining to faith life. Sometimes it is very difficult for the fallen one to talk about his sin, or even want to admit to it. As our brother's keeper, we need to remember this and approach them privately. A gentle reminder can be enough, you don't need

to reprimand. It's important to show concern; when a friend has strayed, help him" (VOZ, 1999).

† "The enemy of souls can cause one to not only neglect the role of being his/her brother's keeper but can influence one to even lie and deceive in an effort to cover up the faults of another, thinking it to be a display of friendship. That is anything but friendly. It is akin to putting a filthy, smelly, bacteria-laced and maggot-ridden rag on a wound instead of a clean, sterile dressing and bandage. Improper cleansing and covering up does not help but harms. The result is pain and sickness. The attempt to cover up sin with sin results in spiritual sickness, sorrow, and pain, the which, if uncared for, could lead to death. Don't cover up sins, yours or anyone else's" (Tomm Stewart, presentation given 2000).

† "I remember a time at haps [an informal name for youth gatherings] when one older friend invited us younger guys to come into the home and to join in the singing. He could have criticized or rebuked us in a harsh way; rather he lovingly invited us in. I remember another time when I was under heavy and difficult temptations and did not feel I could continue in faith when a friend came to me and asked how my matters were. I was able to speak openly to him and be freed from those matters that were troubling my conscience" (James Jurmu, presentation given 2003).

An article in the October 2005 *Voice of Zion* shows some tamping down of the "Church Law of Christ" (Mt 18:15-22). The idea, based on the KJV's "against thee" qualifier, is that the Church Law is applicable to personal offenses rather than for sin generally:

† "Jesus says, 'If thy brother shall trespass against thee.' First of all, the context is between brothers or sisters in faith. Secondly, the action in question is a trespass, a sin, or an offense. Thirdly, the sin has personally offended. The context is typically clear: we know who are believers and who are not. The second and third points may be ambiguous. It may not be quite clear to us whether the action is a sin or an offense, or whether it was personally against us. Nevertheless, if something disturbs us, and has [broken the] love between believers, go and initiate a discussion in which these two questions can be clarified" (VOZ, 10/2005).

However, the authentic text probably supported the earlier understanding that the "Church Law" was not just for offenses "between brothers or sisters in faith," but for sin generally. The earliest manuscripts do not include the words "against you" after "If your brother sins, ..." Ironically, the Conservative preachers of the 1970s who conducted hundreds of caretaking meetings about sins and "false spirits" rather than mere personal offenses were probably aware of only the (likely) inauthentic "against you" reading from the 1776 Finnish version and the KJV. But when there are witches to be hunted, textual nuances don't seem to be a major consideration.

Though the "Church Law" never makes it to the third stage of congregational action anymore, the idea of rebuke remains important:

> † "[A] characteristic of Christian love is to rebuke of sin when necessary. God's Word teaches that this is a correct love. A believer rebukes those whom he loves just as God corrects those whom he loves" (VOZ, 8/2006).

> † "Each child of God is a watchman on the walls of Zion. In our own places of watching, we have a duty to blow the trumpet when the enemy approaches. Part of that duty is to speak about matters that can trouble the journey, or claim the spiritual life of a believer. This can be difficult. Who has gone with joy to speak to a fellow traveler about spiritual concerns? . . . A lenient spirit often desires to not speak about wrongdoing but wants instead to cover up, or hope that the person alone could work things out. Dear friends, think of why God has given all of us this duty as watchmen. What would happen if, through the wiles of the enemy of souls, we became confused about matters and fell into sin and darkness?" (VOZ, 6/2009).

The last vestige I've seen of the false spirits is in that last quote, with a "lenient spirit" being the source of one's reluctance to "speak about wrongdoing." With all the history we have just seen, perhaps such reluctance is understandable. Even the SRK now admits, finally, that things went too far (**4.10.2**).

4.7 The Life of a Believer

> *The whole life of the new people, the faithful people, the spiritual people, is nothing else but prayer, seeking, and begging by the sighing of the heart, the voice of their works, and the labor of their bodies, always seeking and striving to be made righteous, even to the hour of death, never standing still, never possessing, never in any work putting an end to the achievement of righteousness, but always awaiting it as something which still dwells beyond them, and always as people who still live and exist in their sins.*
>
> —Martin Luther, from *Luther on Conversion*

4.7.1 Joys and Sorrows

> *In addition to the relief Evangelicals find from structure, they seem to have, as I came to appreciate, a kind of bottomless spring that keeps their happiness lush. I started to believe it was perfectly authentic, and I wanted some for myself.*
>
> —Gina Welch, *In the Land of Believers*

Laestadianism has its roots in 19th century Pietism, which had brought to Scandanavian Lutheranism an emphasis on an individual's personal awakening, sorrow, and repentance (Gritsch 2002, 185-86; Kulla 2004, 21-24; Kulla 2010, 126). The struggle does not end with the initial conversion. It continues until death. The "inner conflict" between the believer and sin

> † "and the victories that ensue of it, of which we knew nothing in our sorrowless condition, is a sure witness that such a traveler possesses Jesus by faith unto salvation. The world may rage, and the devil torment through our corruption, but Jesus increases peace and we have one victory after another in order that we may know the true God in Zion" (Matti Suo, *Siionin Lähetyslehti* [1917], from Kulla 1985, 202).

The theme of struggle against sin and personal unworthiness is evident in these quotes from the next several decades:

† "Battling in this world with sin, our own weaknesses and shortcomings[,] we often feel worried and realize that this world is not the place for our soul. The Children of God often feel like a lonely bird perched on the branch of a tree because this world can give them no pleasure or peace. But to live with Christ! That means to the Children of God the end of all sorrows, sighs, tears, relief from sin, full brightness, living with souls that are saved, meeting our Saviour face to face and praising Him forever and ever. Indeed, it would be much better!" (O.H. Jussila, *Siionin Lähetyslehti* [1919], from *Greetings of Peace*, 8/1949).

† "The feelings of poverty, coldness, and defileness cause one to look tremblingly to the author and finisher of our faith; the man of sorrows who carried all of our grief. Therefore, even you, who are burdened with your ailing body, try to learn to believe that the thorn in your flesh is a heaven sent gift and as precious as the most sweet feelings of revelations and openings of grace, and perhaps more wholesome. It detaches you from the earthly and attaches you to heavenly things" (Havas [1937], 65).

† "Come now, all you who are poor! All who feel that sin has deprived your soul of all its eternal treasures. You who feel that you have no merit before Almighty God to enjoy His favor and to hope for His Heaven as the eternal abode of your immortal soul. Come, you who find yourself lacking everything, you are poor in faith, poor in love, your repentance has been shallow, your walk as a Christian so faltering, the confession of your faith so timid. Your heart so cold and sinful. Your watching in prayer has been so sluggish. Often you have found yourself head over heels engrossed by the worldly temporal interests. Come, you ragged, miserable pauper to behold your Christmas Present. For He lies poor in the manger to make you rich" (Paul Heideman, *Greetings of Peace*, 12/1949).

We see some rays of sunlight breaking through the gloom in the next two quotes:

† "Oh how I have reason to praise Him that He has drawn me, a fallen sinner, into that fellowship of faith, love and hope with His blessed children and heirs. This christian love, my dear ones, is the most precious thing in all our life. And if it has been soul-happiness here on this sinful earth, how unspeakably great it will

be when at the end of our journey in this vale of tears, we tread on the shore of that new earth and heaven, where righteousness dwelleth, and where love reigns supreme" (Paul Heideman, *Greetings of Peace*, 9/1952).

† "God's kingdom is also a kingdom of joy, although many in the world may think it to be a house of sorrow, a convent, or a monastery. They may think that a person in faith cannot nor must he be joyous. If anyone should have a reason for joy it is the one whose name is recorded in the Book of Life in Heaven. Who else can be as cheerful as he whose conscience is not burdened!" (Taskila 1961, 2)

Peter Nevala talks about individual wretchedness, but also offers comfort to the discouraged in the March 1971 *Greetings of Peace*:

† "If there should be anyone who is wounded, sinful, hopeless and discouraged, be encouraged! You have the permission to believe even when sinful, even when walking with wounded conscience, for it is only through faith that you will or can receive power to put away those things from your life which can eventually separate you from God. Be therefore comforted, dear friend, through the grace of God."

The following quotes balance all the negativity with the joy of salvation:

† "Does it seem to us that we have been able to run with patience, or can we recall that there have been times when our patience has been short, when we may have at least in our innermost, grumbled–perhaps murmured–concerning this portion that the father has put before us. How good [this is], when we must recall that our running has not always been with patience, we can believe all those moments of impatience forgiven in the name and blood of Jesus" (John Waaraniemi, sermon given 1974).

† "[W]hen a man's sins are forgiven, the fruits of the Spirit are evident in his heart, and he is then free and happy. 'If the Son therefore shall make you free, ye shall be free indeed' (John 8:36). The marvelous grace of God is then blessing, teaching, guiding, and strengthening the traveler on the way, helping him to overcome all trials and temptations. ... This kingdom is dear and precious to us; here all our needs are fulfilled. ... Why would anyone want to forsake and leave such a wonderful grace

kingdom and go into the ways of the world and sin, there to lose Jesus?" (Alajoki [1975], 69)

✝ "In the trials of our journey we have even questioned the Lord that why do I have this heavy cross as my lot in life. We may even look at the lot in life of other Christians and see it to be much lighter. Sometimes we can even become envious of them. The Apostle Peter encourages the cross bearers; he wants to lead us to look at the inheritance which is reserved in heaven" for us (VOZ, 4/1978).

✝ "It is true happiness that we can be near God. God is in His kingdom and is cause for joy and happiness for us, and the difficulties we experience belong to Christianity and to the life of a Christian. Under these difficulties we battle and God will give strength to His children; we need not fight fearfully" (Voitto Savela, sermon given 1980).

✝ "We are thankful and praise God that we have been blessed so abundantly in this kingdom. We have received to our souls that life which is in Jesus. We have also been blessed with abundant goodness in life, both temporally and spiritually. The Heavenly Father has granted us power through His grace to follow the footsteps of our dear Savior Jesus. When these matters open to us, we realize what a great blessing it is that we can be children of God" (Alajoki [1989], 217).

✝ "Sorrows surround the endeavorer, but not one needs to remain under sorrows and be wearied to hopelessness. The exhortation belongs to a child of God to lift up one's eyes upward from this land of sorrow. One feeling sorrow because of sin can turn his gaze unto the Savior of sinners, the Lord Jesus. Through His suffering, death and resurrection we have access from death to life and from sorrow to joy. Even though we feel distress and pain here in time, our portion through living faith is the joy of the heart" (*Siionin Lähetyslehti*, 1989).

Elmer Alajoki expressed great emotion and gratitude concerning his life of faith, and that comes through in his 1989 sermon quoted above. But the first quote in my sample that really spells out some of the joys of life in the Conservative Laestadian fold is from a 1994 presentation by Matti Kontkanen:

> ✝ "[B]elieving itself is and brings righteousness, peace, and joy to one's heart. In this righteousness we are happy and rejoice of all the gifts which God grants us according to His will. There certainly are a lot of them: There is the home and parents, brothers and sisters, love and care of the home, unity and fellowship of the family members–don't let the [strife] for money destroy this source of joy in our Christian homes–There is the possibility of learning and going back to school, there is the beautiful nature, free and independent fatherland–we may pray for the good of our country. We may rejoice for being able to work for our country– there is daily bread–there is enough money even to give some of it to those who are in need. There is the fellowship of the Christians–I have seen many of you joyously meeting each other here in these days [during the national Summer Services]–There is the treasure of righteousness in Jesus in the kingdom of God. There is the joy of a good conscience. There is the joy of the hope of a better future. The Bible exhorts us to rejoice even in trials, in sorrow, and under ridicule. There is the work of the kingdom of God–we may do it willingly and with joy like the disciples of Jesus did–There will be the fulfillment of joy in Heaven."

Ultimately, the discussion keeps coming back to the forgiveness of sins:

> ✝ "God strengthens our faith with [trials] and teaches us patience. If we did not have patience, we would become discouraged encountering our first adversity and our endeavor would remain unfinished. Patience is especially necessary when we stumble and notice that we haven't become good and exemplary endeavorers. We continue to be weak, and corruption affects and lives in us. Patience is required when it becomes clear that our endeavor is not the reason and basis for our salvation. We must return again and again to the place where our journey of endeavor began. To the place where the Lord Jesus is the only reason for our salvation and that we, although unsuccessful, have the right to believe our sins forgiven in His name and blood" (Uljas 2000, 83).

> ✝ "Having joy and living hope are characteristic of a believer, and the basis for joy is in the manger of Bethlehem where our Savior was born.... Among many other reasons, we can be joyful for believing escorts to help us on our journey. Through them, we

hear the gospel of the forgiveness of sins preached to us when sin troubles the conscience. This gospel message restores freedom and joy to the heart of a child of God" (VOZ, 5/2000).

Patriotism is a part of life that is emphasized in youth camps and in July issues of the *Voice of Zion*, like this one from 2000:

> † "Living during a time of peace and prosperity, we too often forget to thank God. There are many reasons to thank; an important one among them is the God-gift of a free temporal homeland. We need to pause and consider this treasure and give credit to whom it is due. National holidays provide individuals the opportunity to mark their country's independence and also remember those who gave the ultimate sacrifice of their lives for the freedoms we enjoy."

For Americans at least, "their country's independence" is the result of military rebellion in contradiction to Paul's admonition for everyone to "be subject unto the higher powers" (**Rom 13:1**). I once mentioned that issue to a preacher in a coffee table discussion about patriotism and was dumbfounded by his facile explanation that "there were no believers in the American revolution."

The remaining quotes in the sample deal with a mix of trials, temptations, "believing" friends, and of course, the forgiveness of sins:

> † "Trials and tribulations teach patience, experience, and hope. When the believer encounters the fiery darts of temptations and trials he often begins to doubt, but then is able to rejoice and be comforted in the grace of Jesus as warm, living waters flow from heart to heart. . . . We are able to rejoice in our suffering because it is only temporary. Our hope is real and has a firm foundation" (VOZ, 6/2001).

> † "We live in a time when we see both the results of the work of the enemy of souls in this world and the great blessings of God in His kingdom. Today we are blessed with many sincerely believing young parents, youth and children. God's Kingdom has experienced growth from within. We have also experienced how the Good Shepherd yet seeks lost sheep in this world. It is truly a blessed time that we are living in God's kingdom" (Jim Frantti, presentation given 2001).

† "A believing friend is truly a gift from God. Being united by the same spirit believing friends are able to share their true joys and sorrows, and most importantly preach the gospel of the forgiveness of sins to each other" (James Jurmu, presentation given 2003).

† "There are many sorrows in life such as illness, loss of loved ones to death or unbelief, the trials and cares of rearing children, as well as the struggle each of us face with the threefold enemy. We are reminded through these experiences that we are yet on the journey of Faith" (VOZ, 7/2004).

† "David felt the joy and peace that one feels when a sin-burdened conscience is freed. Have you, dear brothers and sisters, also owned this feeling of joy when you have been able to be freed from the sins on your conscience? We all sin every day–in word, in thought, and in deed. But God has blessed us with an endless supply of forgiveness" (VOZ, 7/2008).

The quote from James Jurmu's 2003 presentation refers to a "believing friend" as a "gift from God." Unfortunately, that gift comes with a return receipt. When someone leaves or even questions faith, the phone stops ringing. What disturbs me most about the shunning (and what else is there to call it?) that I experienced–just from publicly voicing questions and concerns while still attending services regularly–is that it applied to my family as well. What did my wife and kids ever say to cause their supposed "friends" to drop them like hot potatoes? One young friend who left the church tells me that "no one calls anymore" and concludes sadly, "The social suicide is intense." The following are quotes from (presumably) different anonymous commenters on the **extoots site** <http://extoots.blogspot.com>:

- I left the LLC/SRK group (back in the day it was AALC) 17 years ago when I was 21. It was the most difficult, painful experience of my life. I guess I was a bit naive about the amount of time it would take to heal me. The most painful part for me was giving up everyone–all my friends, most of my family–and those that I still remained in communication with–our relationship was forever changed much for the worse because I was now an "unbeliever." I remember telling someone that when I saw church members it was like looking at photographs of dead people because they refused to see me as a full human being just like them with the same concerns and needs–there was just no way to relate with them.

- If a[n LLC] member leaves the church, other members badger them with a flurry of phone calls, letters, emails, visits, and so forth, and then, all contact just kind of dissipates, and suddenly one feels as though they have ceased to exist as far as the church members are concerned.

- When I left the LLC, I wouldn't say I was shunned, but I was treated like an outsider. My mother did not want my younger siblings going places with me. I guess I would have influenced them or something? And friends, well forget about it. They don't stick around. You['re] not one of them anymore, you['re] an unbeliever in their eyes. So you are not able to get close to them, the walls go up.

- There were things that happened when I left the LLC that I didn't expect. I had many young children, and until I was sure what I was going to do, I continued to bring them to Sunday school so their lives wouldn't be in too much of an uproar over a decision I had made. I hadn't expected it, but I heard that people were treating them disrespectfully there. I heard that someone told my oldest child that he was now responsible for making sure that all of the kids kept coming to church. What?? Says who? And yet, they were excluded and treated like outcasts. Hmmmmm . . . Yes, I think that will really make them want to keep going to church! Go figure.

- [In the LLC, l]oyalty to the church takes priority over loyalty to the family. I have a friend whose parent said to them, "I'd rather you were dead than out of the church." Some families act like the child that leaves the church is to be avoided because they might try to "corrupt" the other kids. It's really sad because family relationships can get damaged in the process. When my dad joined the church, he no longer associated with his own family, who was not in the church. When his own brother died, he told me, "Well, you lost an uncle today." I didn't even know I *had* an uncle! He did not go to the funeral, and it was never discussed again.

- Disagreeing with LLC teaching is equivalent to disagreeing with God himself. At that point, many LLC would discontinue feeling "comfortable" with someone they know disagrees with some LLC doctrine. They start to treat the person different than before, even if they haven't left the church, hence, the shunning. Of course, not everyone in the LLC church is like that, but in general I don't think I am wrong in saying that is the general atmosphere of the church.

- I have tried to be close to my family, tried to open up about faith. They close me out because I am not of their church.

- I left the LLC six years ago. And of course I have little to no contact with people I knew since childhood. The other night I dreamed about all my old friends. I dreamed I was yelling at them, telling them that even though I was no longer a Laestadian, I was still *me*. And they just blocked their ears to me. There's no way I could ever go back; they trust in their own behavior and attitude to save them and not in the grace of God. But I really miss the camaraderie, the ability to just hang out and laugh and be silly. I've found friends outside the church, but still my heart just hurts sometimes for those who now ignore me.

There are exceptions. One former member of the LLC wrote that he and his Laestadian roommate

> have a lot in common and we get along. I don't get shunned. And I am often treated like as a fellow believer, who just happens to not be a member of their denomination. I know this is impossible when compared to Laustadian [*sic*.] theology, but the fact is that when I'm around my friends and family, I feel so loved.

Unfortunately, there is plenty of support in the New Testament for inflicting the pain these people have experienced:

> I have written unto you not to keep company, if any man that is called a brother be a fornicator, or covetous, or an idolater, or a railer, or a drunkard, or an extortioner; with such an one no not to eat. For what have I to do to judge them also that are without? Do not ye judge them that are within? But them that are without God judgeth. Therefore put away from among yourselves that wicked person. [1 Cor 5:13]

If any man teach otherwise [than for slaves to honor their masters and masters not to despise their slaves], and consent not to wholesome words, even the words of our Lord Jesus Christ, and to the doctrine which is according to godliness; he is proud, knowing nothing, but doting about questions and strifes of words, whereof cometh envy, strife, railings, evil surmisings, perverse disputings of men of corrupt minds, and destitute of the truth, supposing that gain is godliness: from such withdraw thyself. [1 Tim 6:3-5]

[M]en shall be lovers of their own selves, covetous, boasters, proud, blasphemers, disobedient to parents, unthankful, unholy, without natural affection, trucebreakers, false accusers, incontinent, fierce, despisers of those that are good, traitors, heady, highminded, lovers of pleasures more than lovers of God; having a form of godliness, but denying the power thereof: from such turn away. [2 Tim 3:2-5]

Now we command you, brethren, in the name of our Lord Jesus Christ, that ye withdraw yourselves from every brother that walketh disorderly, and not after the tradition which he received of us. [2 Thess 3:7][41]

4.7.2 Prayer

> *Have you ever heard someone praying in church as if he or she were giving God a theology lesson? . . . After a while, you open your eyes and mutter, "Does he think God doesn't know this stuff? Why's he chewing God's ear with it?"*
>
> —Robert M. Price, *The Reason-Driven Life*

---

41. All of these four quoted passages except for 1 Cor 5:13 are from epistles considered by many scholars to be "pseudepigraphic," or, put less politely, forgeries written in Paul's name well after his time. There is a great deal of debate about whether Paul actually wrote various "Pauline" epistles. The only ones considered "undisputed" by most scholars are Romans, 1 & 2 Corinthians, Galatians, Philippians, 1 Thessalonians, and Philemon. By convention, I use the name "Paul" for all the Pauline epistles without implying that the writer was actually a person named "Paul."

Prayer has always been part of the believer's life, though its practice is more restrained (and, in my view, more sensible) than the frequent, overt, and long-winded praying of many modern evangelicals. Unlike the coworker I once had who would bow his head in prayer over a bag of candy in the break room, Conservative Laestadians take seriously Jesus' instruction to pray to the Father in secret (Mt 6:6) and don't make a show of prayer.

Public praying is mostly limited to the opening and closing of services and other solemn occasions such as baptisms, weddings, and funerals.[42] It's an ancient practice. Regarding the "love feast" (*agapè*, not *eros*) held by the early Christians as their worship service, Tertullian wrote: "As the feast commenced with prayer, so with prayer it is closed" (*Apologetic*, Apology, Ch. 39).

I suspect that a major function of such prayers is to consecrate the event and make it apparent to the assembled congregation that important words are about to be said. Ostensibly, though, the opening prayer of a Conservative Laestadian service offers thanksgiving to God along with requests for his continued blessings and the protection of believers not present. Usually a few cases are mentioned (for God or the audience?) where such absence might be expected, like military service.

An important part of the opening prayer is also the preacher's request that God would provide words to speak and "hearts to believe" that which is spoken. The preachers feel a genuine desire to have the Holy Spirit lead them in the sermon they are about to deliver extemporaneously (4.2.7). Augustine's admonition that the Christian orator "ought to pray for himself, and for those he is about to address, before he attempts to speak" is both fitting and beautiful: "And when the hour is come that he must speak, he ought, before he opens his mouth, to lift up his thirsty soul to God, to drink in what he is about to pour forth, and to be himself filled with what he is about to distribute" (*On Christian Doctrine*, Book 4, Ch. 15).

Often the opening prayer asks God to allow those have left the fold– sometimes also the unbelieving world in general–to see the light. I have

---

42. One jaded commentator on the Church of England's increasingly vacant pews referred to baptisms, weddings, and funerals as the only occasions for which the British subject turns to the church: to be "hatched, matched, and dispatched."

always puzzled over this entreaty, given the claims that God is both loving and omnipotent. Predestination means that God has already sorted out the sheep and the goats from the beginning of time. The preacher's solemn intonation of a few words about the lost is directed to the caring and concerned ears of the congregation, not an omnipotent and omniscient God. On the other hand, if God isn't happy about all the damnation that is going on despite his desire that all would be saved, is the public request of a preacher going to give God an extra boost of divine power to correct the situation? I can just picture him nodding his head with a thoughtful expression: "You know, that guy down there in the suit has a point–let's inspire a few converts today." Both cases are clearly nonsensical, and that is a direct reflection of the dilemma of predestination versus free will, discussed in **4.9.3**.

My sample of quotes on prayer begins with a 1940 sermon by Väino Havas:

> † "Heaven has heard supplications, which often have risen from lowly and small cabins. Though the enemy may lie, that your prayers will not reach Heaven, continue your supplications" (Havas, 77).

> † "Prayer is an appeal for assistance, in which we children of God can request the heavenly Father for both temporal and spiritual needs. We may also believe that if a request is right, and that which we ask is not dangerous for our soul's life, God shall give that which we have requested in Jesus' name" (Taskila 1961, 56).

> † "[W]e cannot and do not want to be without praying, for God through His spirit teaches us to pray trusting His word. . . . We have permission to pray from God for spiritual and temporal matters, as Jesus teaches us in the Lord's Prayer. Our own matters are always close to our heart, spiritual and temporal needs, also close relatives and friends, the Kingdom of God, dear brothers and sisters. We ask that God would bless and shield His purchased flock in these dangerous times in this world. We have reason to remember in prayer the servants of the Word of God, so that they would receive utterance. . . . God hears the prayers of His own in matters pertaining to kingdoms (or governments), as it is written in the Bible" (*Päivämies*, 1974).

✝ "We are told 'He spake a parable unto them to this end, that man ought always to pray and not to faint.' Many mistakenly use this statement of Jesus to justify the erroneous conception that prayer can justify! Not all prayers are even acceptable to God. Even the Pharisees quoted Scripture to indicate this truth, 'that the prayer and sacrifice of the ungodly is an abomination before God.' We know that God heareth not sinners, 'But if any man doeth His will, him He heareth.'" (VOZ, 6/1974).

✝ In prayer, the "child of God can speak to the Father about all of his lackings and needs. The all-knowing God gives gifts which are for the best of His children" (*By Faith*, 93).

✝ "We pray to God that we would always treasure in our hearts the great gift we have received from Him, and that we would, through His power and strength, make known this most precious gift to those on the outside of His kingdom" (VOZ, 7/1998).

✝ "Prayer is conversation between God and man. Man does not speak alone; God answers also." Sometimes it may seem that "our message does not reach its destination," but the lack of an answer "is not caused by God's poor hearing or our quiet or unclear speech. God truly hears and understands, and difficulties of language are not an obstacle. He is interested in us and our matters. He also answers, although it may be in a different way than we expected. Sometimes, we only later understand God's answer to our prayer" (Uljas 2000, 73).

✝ In prayer, the believer has a "secure and trusting discussion of a child with a Father who loves him" (Uljas 2000, 76).

✝ In Psalm 86, "David is confident in praying to God for he knows that God is good, forgiving and merciful. David had experienced that God hears the prayers of His own and cares for them. David says that the joy of a believing person is in the knowledge that God hears and answers his prayers" (VOZ, 9/2003).

✝ "Scripture does not teach us to present demands to God or command Him to act according to our desires. Jesus taught us to pray in humbleness, in spirit, and in truth. Prayer is not to emphasize outward matters, for praying does not require certain customs or rituals. Prayer is the simple speech of the heart to God" (VOZ, 5/2005).

Ingersoll noted in his *Lecture on Ghosts*, "The moment that it began to be apparent that prayer could do nothing for the body, the priest shifted his ground and began praying for the soul." That's pretty much the focus with Conservatives, who are too pragmatic to put much stock in any sort of faith healing. The "healing" is entirely spiritual:

> † "Even when one cannot understand why difficult things have to happen, or why things haven't gone as one would expect or hope they would go, it is still good and important to remember to pray. God listens and hears the prayers that rise from a sincere heart. He still works miracles of healing and grants living faith when one believes the proclaimed gospel message of salvation" (VOZ, 2/2008).

We are told that God has foreordained our salvation (according to some Bible passages at least), the bounds of our habitation, and the number of our days. So we can hardly expect that he will hear a message (typically self-centered) from a puny human and decide that, no, maybe he'd better do this or that a bit differently after all. The unavoidable fact is that "prayers are not truly answerable by an omniscient god because he would have already envisioned the concrete results of the future" (Long 2005, 198). In a 2009 presentation, Matti Kontkanen acknowledges that issue as well as God's omnipotence. But, for some reason, we are still asked to "let him know of our needs" even though he already knows them:

> † "Although God is high and holy, in Jesus' name we are allowed to approach Him. Although God knows what we need we are encouraged to let him know of our needs. Although God is almighty and decides what he does and what not, we are asked to pray for our matters, the matters of other people and those of the authorities in our country."

For me, the issue is not just an intellectual one. My outlook on prayer was dramatically diminished in one traumatic moment a few years ago, when I helplessly prayed out loud while a tragic death proceeded right before my eyes, unhindered by my pleas. There is just no evidence whatsoever that prayer has ever changed an outcome, even if it made any sense for the omniscient and omnipotent God to change his perfect will about the course of the universe by pleading our case to him.

4.7.3 Sacraments

> *There are only two sacraments in the church of God: baptism and the Lord's Supper. For only in these is there both a sign instituted by God and the promise of the forgiveness of sins.*
>
> —Paul Althaus, *The Theology of Martin Luther*

The Lord's Supper

Arguably the earliest record we have of Communion, or the Lord's Holy Supper as it is also called, is from 1 Cor 11:23-26. There Paul states how Jesus instituted that sacrament on the night of his betrayal. I say "arguably," because of Price's view that the passage looks out of place in a Pauline epistle and seems to descend, with alterations, from Mark. He is not persuaded by the Pauline writer's claim to have received this narrative material as a direct revelation from the risen Jesus:

> It appears to be an attempt by Paulinists to claim autonomous independent possession of the Eucharistic material, to deny their dependence on other quarters of Christianity for it, much in the vein of Gal 1:11-12. Just as Paul had insisted he derived his gospel from no man but directly from Jesus Christ, so is he depicted here as having received the [Markan] Last Supper material directly from Christ. [Price 2003b, 301]

At any rate, according to "Paul," Jesus gave thanks, broke the bread, and said, "Take, eat: this is my body, which is broken for you: this do in remembrance of me. After the same manner also he took the cup, when he had supped, saying, This cup is the new testament in my blood: this do ye, as oft as ye drink it, in remembrance of me."

The next (or first, depending on your point of view) record comes from Mark 14:22-24. As the disciples were eating the Passover meal with Jesus, "He took some bread, and after a blessing He broke it, and gave it to them, and said, 'Take it; this is My body.' And when He had taken a cup and given thanks, He gave it to them, and they all drank from it. And He said to them, 'This is My blood of the covenant, which is poured out for many'" (NASB). In copying this account, Matthew adds that the shedding of blood is "for the remission of sins" (Mt 26:28).

The familiar phrase "blood of the new testament" in the KJV comes from manuscripts where the word "new" was added. Without that embellishment, notice how much the original language seems to be taken from Moses' "pouring out" the blood of young bulls in Exodus 24:8: "So Moses took the blood and sprinkled it on the people, and said, 'Behold the blood of the covenant, which the LORD has made with you in accordance with all these words'" (NASB). "Jesus, in his coming death, will be doing the same thing Moses did, only with his own blood" (Price 2003b, 300).

John does not describe Jesus instituting the sacrament, but substitutes the story of Jesus washing the disciples' feet instead. His Gospel has Jesus saying that people have to "eat the flesh of the Son of man, and drink his blood" (Jn 6:53), not in the Last Supper but "as part of a synagogue sermon or debate in Capernaum" (Price 2003b, 302). Both Price and one of the pioneers of biblical "higher criticism," Rudolf Bultmann, believe those words were not written by the original author of John but by a later "Ecclesiastical Redactor." John's disinterest in describing Jesus breaking bread and offering wine at his last meal with the disciples leaves no place for the words there. So they are found in a narrative of an unrelated earlier event, having been "added to the gospel . . . to restore an implicit sacramentalism [the] earlier writer had omitted" (p. 302).

With all this borrowing and alteration in the biblical texts instituting Communion, it shouldn't be any surprise that the very nature of the sacrament has been the subject of much theological dispute. Is it a miraculous event wherein bread and wine are mysteriously converted into Jesus' body and blood? Or is it merely a "meal of remembrance" where the bread and wine provide a way to remind the participant of how Jesus sacrificed his body and shed his blood? Both viewpoints have had their proponents since early Christianity.

Ignatius [*c.* 100 A.D.] considered it heretical to "confess not the Eucharist to be the flesh of our Saviour Jesus Christ" (*Epistle to the Smyrnaeans*, Ch. 7). In his *First Apology* [*c.* 160 A.D.], Justin Martyr agrees, saying that the elements are received "not as common bread and common drink." Rather, "in like manner as Jesus Christ our Saviour, having been made flesh by the Word of God, had both flesh and blood for our salvation, so likewise have we been taught that the food which is blessed by the prayer of His word, and from which our blood and flesh by transmutation are nourished, is the flesh and blood of that Jesus who was made flesh" (Ch. 66).

But in his *Dialogue with Trypho,* Justin refers to "the bread which our Christ gave us to eat, in remembrance of His being made flesh for the sake of His believers, for whom also He suffered; and to the cup which He gave us to drink, in remembrance of His own blood, with giving of thanks" (Ch. 70). Here it is a meal of remembrance, with no hint of any transmutation of the bread and wine.

The transmutation belief gave rise to the charge of cannibalism against early Christians. Theophilus of Antioch [c. 180 A.D.] considered the accusation that the Christians "eat human flesh" to be the "most impious and barbarous of all" (*To Autolycus,* Book 3, Ch. 4). It seems clear that he did not want to be seen as munching on anyone's body, miraculously or otherwise.

Clement of Alexandria was definitely not taking it literally, either. In *The Instructor* [c. 200 A.D.], he treats Jesus' comment to eat his flesh and drink his blood as "preserving consistency in the use of figurative speech." We do not cannibalize Jesus' body any more than we obtain milk as a result of the statement, "I have given you milk to drink, and not given you food," which Clement associates with Jesus though it comes from 1 Cor 3:2:

> Elsewhere the Lord, in the Gospel according to John, brought this out *by symbols,* when He said: "Eat ye my flesh, and drink my blood"; describing distinctly *by metaphor* the drinkable properties of faith and the promise, by means of which the Church, like a human being consisting of many members, is refreshed and grows, is welded together and compacted of both,–of faith, which is the body, and of hope, which is the soul; as also the Lord of flesh and blood. [Book 1, Ch. 6, emphasis added]

Indeed, Clement defends moderate drinking with a reference to Jesus' "figurative" statement: "For rest assured, He Himself also partook of wine; for He, too, was man. And He blessed the wine, saying, 'Take, drink: this is my blood'–the blood of the vine. He figuratively calls the Word 'shed for many, for the remission of sins'–the holy stream of gladness" (*The Instructor,* Book 2, Ch. 2).

Isn't it glaringly obvious that this is metaphor and there is no actual cannibalism going on in Conservative Laestadian churches every month? Not with Luther, who firmly held to a literal view of Christ's statement of the bread he broke at the Last Supper, "This is my body."

As discussed in **5.3**, he vehemently condemned Huldrich Zwingli for viewing the bread and wine metaphorically, even though they had no other major grounds of disagreement. Luther's position would always remain "that the bread and wine in the Supper are Christ's true body and blood" (*The Smalcald Articles* [1537]; McCain 2005, 279).

Justin Martyr's *First Apology* provides a glimpse of how Communion was practiced in the mid-second century. The sacrament, at least in the case he describes, took place as a celebration of a new convert. After the believers "have thus washed him who has been convinced and has assented to our teaching," they

> bring him to the place where those who are called brethren are assembled, in order that we may offer hearty prayers in common for ourselves and for the baptized [illuminated] person, and for all others in every place, that we may be counted worthy, now that we have learned the truth, by our works also to be found good citizens and keepers of the commandments, so that we may be saved with an everlasting salvation. Having ended the prayers, we salute one another with a kiss. There is then brought to the president of the brethren bread and a cup of wine mixed with water; and he taking them, gives praise and glory to the Father of the universe, through the name of the Son and of the Holy Ghost, and offers thanks at considerable length for our being counted worthy to receive these things at His hands. And when he has concluded the prayers and thanksgivings, all the people present express their assent by saying Amen. [Ch. 65]

After the giving of thanks and expression of assent by all the people assembled, "those who are called by us deacons give to each of those present to partake of the bread and wine mixed with water over which the thanksgiving was pronounced, and to those who are absent they carry away a portion" (Ch. 65). As I discuss in **5.1.2**, the earliest extant Christian writings do not mention anything about absolution, and Justin's description is no exception.

There was simply no need for absolution when it was widely expected that one who had been washed in baptism would no longer sin. (If you did, too bad; there was dispute about whether even a second opportunity for repentance was possible.) The idea of absolution didn't appear, vaguely, until 50 years or so after Justin's writings. It took centuries to be refined into the private encounter between priest and penitent that many modern readers associate with confession.

Also gradually developing over the centuries was the idea that remission of sins could be obtained in Communion (Lea 1896, 84-86). But "when penitence was erected into a sacrament and the confessor held the keys of heaven," that idea "became a serious impediment to the enforcement of the new discipline and it had to be gotten rid of. This was accomplished by rendering confession and absolution a condition precedent to worthily partaking of the Eucharist . . . and declaring it a mortal sin to take communion when not in a state of grace" (pp. 85-86). Perhaps, but Cyprian wrote in the third century about the need for penitence and confession "made with investigation of the life of him who fulfils the penitence," and asserted that "no one can come to communion unless the hands of the bishop and clergy be first imposed upon him" (Epistle 9).

In any event, the year 1852 saw Laestadius still standing guard against the unworthy at the Communion rail:

> † "Some unworthy supper-guests say: 'I am not worthy to go to the Lord's supper, for I am a great sinner.' But when someone inquires as to what sin troubles their conscience, they answer: 'it's not necessary to confess.' Finally it becomes apparent that it is not unworthiness that hinders them from coming to the Lord's supper, but a secret pride. Partially it is hatred toward the pastor who does not admit them to the supper without an examination, partially a fear of the scourge of the Holy Spirit, for if they make promises of repentance at the Lord's Supper, a knot would come upon the conscience when they become bound by that promise" (Laestadius, Palm Sunday sermon; *Fourth Postilla*, 47-48).

Nowadays, attendees are encouraged to come to the Communion table "just as you are" and are only considered unworthy if they are not "believing," i.e., not in Conservative Laestadian Christianity. The question of whether forgiveness is received through the sacrament is made moot by a proclamation of the forgiveness of sins that almost always occurs in the sermon preceding the sacrament, and an additional proclamation that is read out during the Communion liturgy. (The roots for this "general absolution" actually go back even before Luther's time, as discussed in **5.4.2**.) In past decades, Communion was often a very emotional affair with young people going to each other and their parents for individual absolution, but now such takes place mostly just between spouses at the communion rail.

> ✝ "[L]ook in faith upon Jesus as such a Lamb of God who took away the sins of the world, even your sins! He approaches you in the word of reconciliation, in this sweet gospel of salvation, which echoes to your hungry soul from the table of the Kingdom of God today. You can believe that the body of the Son of God was once given for you and His holy blood was shed just for the forgiveness of your sins. The Lord Jesus approaches you also in the bread and wine of the communion table. Gather confidently here, even you most timid beggars of grace. This rich table is full of the manna of grace" (Väinö Havas [1898-1941], from *Greetings of Peace*, 10/1961).

> ✝ "Christian traveler, even you have a long journey. Go therefore often to the Lord's Supper. Eat and drink, so that from the holy bread and wine you receive new power to continue. Partake of it often, for Jesus says, 'As often as you do it, do it in remembrance of me.'. . .You may say that you love Jesus, but neither God nor His children can believe you, if a mile or ten are too long, so that your spiritual laziness will not permit you to go often to the Lord's Holy Supper" (O.H. Jussila, *Greetings of Peace*, 1/1953).

Contrary to some of Luther's teachings (**5.4.4**), Conservatives assert that there is no forgiveness of sins in Communion:

> ✝ "The lot of Judas Iscariot shows clearly that sins are not forgiven in Communion. . . . If sins were forgiven by partaking of Communion, then even the sins of Judas Iscariot would have been forgiven. But we know what happened to him, he departed. You know what his fate was, he hanged himself" (Kauko Mantyla, sermon given 1976).

> ✝ "Neither the unbeliever nor the believer receives forgiveness of his sins in Communion, for God has instituted in His kingdom the office of preaching, by which man is released from his sins through the Holy Spirit" (*By Faith*, 89).

> ✝ "In the sacrament of the holy supper, we can receive by faith the Passover lamb, the body and blood of the Lord Jesus, for the strengthening of our faith: [Mk 14:22-25 cited]. Jesus left this supper for His own. Communion is not a sacrament of

repentance, but a supper of the children of God, which Luther says requires a believing heart. . . . The Lord's Holy Supper is, by its basic nature, a holy meal in which one receives food for the soul and which is received by faith for a blessing" (Lepistö 1985, 40-41).

As we've seen many times already, "crazy" becomes "mystery" when religion is involved. This next quote makes clear that the Communion participant is actually eating the body of Christ and drinking His blood. That is the "mystery of the Lord's Supper," which, alas, "we do not fully understand":

† "Jesus deepened and clarified the meaning and substance of the Passover meal. He, himself, is the Paschal Lamb. The wine [he and the disciples] drank during the meal is His blood, which soon was to be shed for the remission of sins. The unleavened bread, which He broke to give each one his own portion, is His Body. He is the Bread of Life, which is owned by faith. The Passover meal changed into the Lord's Holy Supper. The Word of the Lord was joined to visible elements, bread and wine, and made them and the partaking of them a Sacrament. . . . As believers in the Lord's Supper, we can eat the body of Christ and drink His blood and thus enjoy the fruit of His work of atonement. Although we do not fully understand the mystery of the Lord's Supper, we still go" to it (Uljas 2000, 67-68).

That quote and Luther's fervent condemnation of Zwingli notwithstanding, not too much is made nowadays of the "real presence" of Christ in the Sacrament. When some wafers fell off one shaky server's tray some years ago, he and the rest of the servers just shuffled along in their work, trying to ignore it. None of them thought to do anything like Luther did when some consecrated wine spilled on the floor; he got on his hands and knees and licked it up lest it be trod underfoot. Despite the words they say each time they put one of those wafers in a person's mouth ("The body of Christ, given for you"), the servers seemed not to really believe that anything other than wafers had spilled, either.

Given that Jesus is the "Bread of Life," this next quote from the March 2007 *Voice of Zion* seems to disclaim the Real Presence:

† "Through faith we understand that the Bread of Life is not in our daily bread, nor is it in the sacrament of Holy Communion. Rather, it is in that perfect sacrifice which Jesus gave on Good Friday on the Middle Cross of Golgotha."

The LLC website says nothing about the role of Jesus' body and blood in Communion, merely calling it "a memorial meal established by Jesus. It is intended for believers for the strengthening of their faith" (**How We Believe** <http://www.llchurch.org/how-we-believe.cfm>). According to Althaus, Luther criticized such an understanding as not only despising the clear words of Christ, but also making the sacrament into man's own work of "genuine remembrance and love" (1963, 392). For Luther, he writes, "the meaning of the celebration of the Sacrament is not that we lift ourselves up to Christ by our own thoughts but that Christ lowers himself to us." Luther's idea of worship of God is not based on the fervor of one's own meditation on Christ's sufferings, but, in Althaus's words, "on the presence of Christ who bears and forgives our lack of devotion" (p. 393).

Luther makes some theological sense there, but I remain personally incapable of undergoing the mental gymnastics required for a sincere belief in the Real Presence. Nor does it seem required–despite Luther's reasoning–by the actual biblical text. Jesus sat there and broke pieces off a loaf of bread, handing them to his disciples. He referred to the bread as his body–which was very much in one piece at the time. *So what* if he did? As Dan Barker says, When Jesus refers to himself as a door (Jn 10:9), you don't look for hinges.

Look, if someone wants to maintain a belief that the church-supply store wafer he is chewing on is literally a piece of the (risen) corpse of Jesus, one of hundreds of tons' worth of such pieces parceled out over the last two millennia, that's fine. But no amount of condemnation by Luther or anyone else can force anyone into what I view as both a deluded and unnecessary interpretation of the text.

Baptism

Luther wrote, "Such power is given to Baptism by the Word that it is a washing of new birth, as St. Paul also calls it in Titus 3:5"; "[I]f you live in repentance, you walk in Baptism. For Baptism not only illustrates such a new life, but also produces, begins, and exercises it" (*Large*

Catechism, Part 4, from McCain 2005, 425-426 & 430). A January 2007 article in the *Voice of Zion* disagrees:

> † "Jesus has established His congregation here on earth where He offers the forgiveness of sins to all men. In his congregation, little children and those who receive the grace of repentance are able to enter into the covenant of Holy Baptism. 'Baptism does not signify new birth, but it is a covenant of a good conscience with God by the resurrection of Jesus Christ' (Manual of Sacred Acts)" (VOZ, 1/2007).

The Conservative position is foreign to not just Luther's teaching, but to the earliest Christian writings. For hundreds of years after Christ, those writings mention nothing about absolution but plenty about the washing of sins in baptism. (The awkward silence of the ancients about absolution will be discussed specifically in **5.1.2.**) Justin Martyr describes baptism as part of the process of conversion to Christianity:

> As many as are persuaded and believe that what we teach and say is true, and undertake to be able to live accordingly, are instructed to pray and to entreat God with fasting, for the remission of their sins that are past, we praying and fasting with them. Then they are *brought by us where there is water, and are regenerated in the same manner in which we were ourselves regenerated.* For, in the name of God, the Father and Lord of the universe, and of our Saviour Jesus Christ, and of the Holy Spirit, *they then receive the washing with water.* [*First Apology*, Ch. 61, emphasis added]

He notes that penitents "are instructed to pray and to entreat God with fasting," for the remission of their past sins, doing so along with those already in the faith. But the regeneration occurs where there is water, and Justin's next paragraph emphasizes the washing that occurs there: The sinner "may *obtain in the water* the remission of sins formerly committed" (Ch. 61, emphasis added). In his *Dialogue With Trypho*, he says the Christians "have believed, and testify that that very baptism which he announced is *alone* able to purify those who have repented; and this is the water of life" (Ch. 14, emphasis added).

The ritual cleansing was the *whole point* of baptism, going back to John the Baptist's "baptism for the remission of sins" (Mark 1:4). Irenaeus called it that as well, saying that "the baptism instituted by the visible

Jesus was for the remission of sins" (*Against Heresies*, Book 1, Ch. 21). In the "baptism of the Word," Clement of Alexandria writes, "our transgressions are taken away," and we "are washed from all our sins." The steps were "repenting of our sins, renouncing our iniquities," and being "purified by baptism" (*The Instructor*, Book 1, Ch. 6). Tertullian remarked, in a discourse on the simplicity of the baptismal rite, how wonderful it is "that death should be washed away by bathing" (*Ethical*, On Baptism, Ch. 2).

Augustine continues this clear teaching about the washing away of sin in baptism. He laments how he remained sitting "in the chair of lies" as a teacher of rhetoric for a few weeks after his spiritual awakening. "But hast not Thou, O most merciful Lord," he asks in the prayerful monologue of his *Confessions* [397 A.D.], "pardoned and remitted this sin also, with my other most horrible and deadly sins, in the holy water?" (Book 4). The significance of the singular baptism event is evident in his prayer for the sins of his beloved deceased mother, as he acknowledges that he dare "not say that from what time Thou regeneratedst her by baptism, no word issued from her mouth against Thy Commandment." And so, he asks God, "do Thou also forgive her debts, whatever she may have contracted in so many years, since the water of salvation. Forgive her, Lord, forgive, I beseech Thee; enter not into judgment with her" (Book 9). In *The City of God* [c. 410 A.D.], he continues to maintain the importance of baptism while also allowing for an alternative means of forgiveness: "For whatever unbaptized persons die confessing Christ, this confession is of the same efficacy for the remission of sins as if they were washed in the sacred font of baptism" (Book 13, Ch. 7).

Augustine's prayer for his mother and his allowance for confessing but as-yet unbaptized Christians shows how much emphasis there was on the baptismal washing away of sins, to the point that it was often viewed as the *sole* means of forgiveness. *The City of God* considers, in all seriousness, whether men should commit suicide "as soon as they have been washed in the laver [ceremonial basin] of regeneration, and have received the forgiveness of all sin." Then, it would seem, "is the time to escape all future sin, when all past sin is blotted out." But Augustine concludes that it would be foolish and mad to try persuading someone to kill himself in order to avoid sin. It would also remove the reason for "our consuming time in those exhortations by which we seek to animate the baptized, either to virginal chastity, or vidual continence, or matrimonial fidelity." If "there could be any just cause of suicide, this were so. And since not even this is so, there is none" (Book 1, Ch. 27).

Baptism was a one-time, life-changing conversion event, and there was a strong view that no more forgiveness was available for any further sins. Consider how Constantine [272-337 A.D.] put off his baptism until his deathbed, following "one custom at the time which postponed baptism until old age or death" in an effort "to be absolved from as much of his sin as possible" (**Wikipedia** <http://en.wikipedia.org/wiki/Constantine_the_Great#Sickness_and_death>).

Augustine himself was subject to this thought process when he fell ill as a boy. He writes that his Christian mother

> would in eager haste have provided for my consecration and cleansing by the health-giving sacraments, confessing Thee, Lord Jesus, for the remission of sins, unless I had suddenly recovered. And so, as if I must needs be again polluted should I live, my cleansing was deferred, because the defilements of sin would, after that washing, bring greater and more perilous guilt. [*Confessions*, Book 1]

For Conservative Laestadianism to go along with any of this would detract from the central role supposedly played by personal absolution, and that just won't do. The distinctiveness of the movement's whole doctrine depends on absolution being the sole means of grace (**4.6.2**). Conservatives cannot allow the sacraments or prayer to share the stage with absolution, no matter what the Bible, the early Church writings, or even Luther said to the contrary (**5.4.4**). So, to preserve a doctrinal tenet that *wasn't even established until after the Laestadian movement began* (**4.1.4**), the views of the ancients must be discarded. The movement needs Luther (what would the Laestadian *Lutheran* Church be without him, after all), so he was "believing" but "just a man" who made mistakes (**4.2.6**). Inconvenient parts of his *Small Catechism* that Conservative kids receive in Sunday School–like Part 4, §5, which tells them baptism "works forgiveness of sins"–must be disregarded or explained away.

And then, after eviscerating the sacrament of its original purpose, we are left wondering what to do with the corpse. These next quotes have baptism doing all sorts of ceremonial, non-biblical things. It "unites a child to be cared for" in the congregation's fellowship (whatever that means), gives the child a name, establishes a covenant (debatable), and has the uncomprehending infant promising to put sins away and serve God:

> † "In baptism, God unites a child to be cared for in the fellowship of His congregation. In connection with baptism a child is given a name. Then the endeavor begins as a child of God with that name. As the child grows, his personal battle against sin begins–baptism constrains him to this" (VOZ, 9/1998).
>
> † "God has made promises to people and made covenants with them," confirming the covenants "with visible signs" for weak man with his poor memory. He "made the first covenant with Noah and his sons," a second covenant with Abraham, placing "circumcision as a sign of this covenant," and a "third covenant in His Son the Lord Jesus. The Bible called it a new covenant. As a sign of this covenant Jesus established baptism. . . . This covenant is the fulfillment of God's plan of salvation" (VOZ, 9/1998).
>
> † "Baptism itself does not make a person acceptable to God. Man is acceptable only by faith–through believing on Jesus and His power to forgive sins. Baptism is a covenant of faith and a good conscience, a promise that is made to put sins away and to serve God. Parents desire to bring their children to be baptized in obedience of faith to God. Baptism also obligates parents and sponsors to feed and love the child or person with God's Word. If someone receives the grace of repentance and has not been baptized, the Holy Spirit, according to the instruction of God's Word, lovingly invites and exhorts him to be baptized after conversion" (VOZ, 6/2009).

Whatever reasons it gives for continuing to practice the sacraments, Conservative Laestadianism's exclusive focus on absolution leaves both baptism and Communion being treated as essentially ceremonial. Participation in the sacraments is expected, but more out of custom than for reasons that anyone can seem to articulate theologically. Conservatives consider neither baptism nor Communion to convey anything of significance to one's salvation. Communion is said to strengthen one's faith, but so is attending song services or being with other believers in most any other devotional context. The rites for either sacrament can be conducted by unbelievers as well as believers. Nobody's baptism is questioned for having been done in a "worldly" church, and military members are able to obtain Communion from their "worldly" chaplains.

4.7.4 Marriage

One area where I find Conservative Laestadianism to be in refreshing contrast with modern Christianity as a whole is its unwavering commitment to the sanctity of marriage. The rules are very simple, and biblical: you do not engage in sexual activity before or outside marriage, and you remain with the person you marry "in prosperity and adversity alike, until death do us part":

> † "If an unbelieving child from a Christian home leaves, to live common-law, his/her common-law partner will not be accepted into the child's home. If this type are accepted into the home it means the parents accept this type of life and become guilty of the same sin as those who live in it. Common-law is not a bond in any respect according to the Word of God and God's Word does not respect such a union" (*Päivämies*, 1977)

> † Marriage is "the only place for sexual union between a man and a woman," and is "lifelong and inseparable." Infidelity is "a sin unto death. One who is unfaithful in marriage won't inherit God's kingdom," though he can still experience the grace of repentance given to King David. Divorced people are "not to marry again" (VOZ, 9/2004).

After over two decades of marriage to a wonderful person with no end in sight, I am very thankful for the purity and strength of this teaching. Unfortunately for some, the simplicity and rigidity of the rules can lead to a lifetime of grief. When one person leaves both the church and the marriage, the remaining spouse is faced with essentially a lifetime of being alone.

Divorce

The November 1964 *Greetings of Peace* republished an article by Iver Lehtinen (who had died in 1946) that addressed marriage and divorce in some detail. Lehtinen quoted Mt 19:3-9 ("What therefore God hath joined together, let no man put asunder"), saying that "Jesus has strictly explained marriage to be inseparable before God." But he went on to write that "those who for the cause of fornication put away their spouse . . . are doing right," though "whether the spouse is divorced or rejected because of adultery, or even for other causes, they are still not separated before God." He then discusses the situation where

> ✝ the fallen one in penitence begs for grace and ceases from sin, to such a one sins are to be forgiven and this one cannot be rejected. . . . When Jesus says for the cause of adultery, he means a continuous life lived in sin; for such a one, who does not cease sinning, is one who is dead in life. Such a spouse Jesus permits one to put away, but not forever; for God does not forsake forever. The rejection is for the condemnation of the flesh and to shame. The rejecter can take him or her again for their spouse if the same repents and ceases from sin; that is acceptable to God.

Then, he addresses the situation where one has (impermissibly) remarried after divorce:

> Now, those who for adultery or other causes, have rejected their spouse, and have married another one while the former one is still living, if they do not undo their wrong deeds, refuse to part, they are living in adultery, and not one of adultery is saved. But now, if according to law, one cannot undo their evil deeds because they are confirmed by the earthly laws, even then one is to cease from sin and carry their bed and not to lay in it anymore; for no adulterer who commits adultery in the law, or without the law, shall inherit the Kingdom of God and Christ.

In recent decades, however, there have been a few instances in Conservative Laestadianism of divorcees remaining married to (and presumably sexually active with) their second spouses after (re)entering the church. When I first became aware of such a case around 1987, I shared the consternation of a friend who wondered what had happened to the plain words of Mt 19:9 ("Whosoever putteth away his wife, and marrieth another, committeth adultery: and whosoever marrieth her that is put away from her husband committeth adultery"). The prevailing explanation–the sin of remarriage was forgiven and thus a thing of the past–seems contrived, a way to deflect the irresistible force of supposedly inerrant scripture from the immovable object of established human relationships.

A few years after Lehtinen's death, Eino Rimpiläinen grappled with the fact that Matthew 5:31-32 provided an exception to the rule that otherwise prohibited divorce:

> † "[T]here is no other reason for separation then faithlessness[,] that is, fornication. One can claim, when the characters of husband and wife are so opposite, so that marriage becomes hell on earth, then it is better to separate. But is it any better before God, to exchange sin for sin? Impatience is exchanged for fornication. Would it not be better in such cases as well as all other cases, that we would remember first of all the holiness of marriage, and the vow which has been made before God and men . . ." (*Siionin Lähetyslehti* [1949], from *Greetings of Peace*, 2/1950).

The outcome of an eventual meeting of SRK preachers on the subject was that the exception really didn't count:

> † "According to Matthew, in Jesus' discussion with the Pharisees, He allowed divorce because of adultery," but when "divorce was discussed at length at a speakers' meeting . . . the speaker-brothers held to" the Gospel of Mark which has no adultery exception. "Marriage is lifelong: what God has joined, let not man put asunder. This does not lessen the seriousness of the sin of adultery, but provides an opportunity for a person to return, repent, and receive forgiveness for a grievous transgression" (Uljas 2000, 103-104).

Intermarriage

The biblical injunction to be "not unequally yoked together with unbelievers" (2 Cor 6:14) is considered applicable to marriage, and it is simply unthinkable for one to marry outside the church and still be considered a believer. When Arvi Hintsala wrote the following in the November 1949 *Greetings of Peace*, it was apparently not unheard of but certainly discouraged:

> † "In these days it is especially noticeable, that the boundary between the world and God's children does not remain clear. Those who profess Christianity enter bonds of matrimony with unbelievers. There are many sad results. Many, led by their unbelieving companion, become unbeliever[s]. . . . Many a man who during courtship, professed to favor Christianity, has after

marriage turned out to be an enemy of the Christians, a drunkard and cruel. Who knows all the suffering, that has come to those who have stepped on that road of disobedience!"

By 1976 marrying an outsider was considered sin:

> † "Remember, also, when you seek a life's companion, do not look outside of God's kingdom. This is sin" (VOZ, 3/1976).

> † Concerning "the young and marriage matters, . . . one need not be anxious and take these matters into his own hands. . . . Even here there should be that correct foundation so that we would, first of all, ask of God that He would direct and lead and would grant that life's companion whom He has foreseen. One should await God's time and if God has not foreseen a marriage partner, to be satisfied to remain single . . . Above all one should not unite with unbelievers" (Ruben Alajoki, sermon given 1979).

My sample does not include any quotes on the topic of intermarriage beyond this. That does not indicate any softening or looking the other way about the issue, however. Perhaps some issues like this are considered so settled and well understood within Conservative Laestadianism that little need is felt to devote extensive discussion to them in church publications and sermons, or perhaps this is just a case where my sampling of those discussions was flawed. In any event, there is no longer just a concern that one might be led by his or her "unbelieving companion" to become an unbeliever. Rather, it is now considered tantamount to giving up one's faith to marry someone outside the church.

Alajoki's comment shows how a form of predestination is present in the thinking about marriage. God is the one who directs and leads the single person to Mr. or Mrs. Right. It is a weighty matter, not only because the marriage is permanent "until death do us part" but because it forms the foundation of a new Conservative Laestadian family, most likely one of considerable size. Many life-altering decisions await the new couple after their commitment to eschew the use of contraception (**4.7.5**), and it is hard to see how they could build a home life that would be acceptable to one believing spouse with the other rejecting the doctrines and behavioral norms of the church.

Still, I suspect Price's criticism of "the universal fundamentalist ban on Christian teenagers dating non-Christians" has some relevance:

> Why the ban? The Christian getting emotionally close to the nonbeliever would be risking eroding the illusion that only one's co-sectarians are loving and noble. One would soon get the impression that morality and character are not the property of any one faith, and that they are not necessarily dependent on faith at all. No, the church wants her children to stay within the tribe, so as to keep the walls up high. [2006b, 109]

For Conservative Laestadian youth in the U.S. and Canada, the ban can pose a major challenge. Unless he or she travels to Finland or perhaps Africa, the single LLC member's marriage prospects must come from a group of about 7,000 people. There were 209 LLC confirmation students (9th grade) in 2011. It seems like a reasonable guess that a young person seeking a spouse within the LLC will have about 1,200 possible peers whose ages are within the few years of mismatch that are not exceeded between most husbands and wives. Half of those are of the opppsite sex and, for most young people in the LLC, many of the 600 remaining are cousins.

What kind of a social system limits its next generation's possibilities for marriage (or romance of any kind, for that matter) to a pool of **400** or so candidates in two countries with a combined population of 340,000,000 people, a dozen times more prospects who speak a foreign language in a country on the other side of the Atlantic, and a handful of others in a few third world countries?

Courtship

The term "dating" is avoided for its light-hearted connotations. Looking for the spouse of a lifetime is serious business, and it is treated as such, at least officially:

> † "It doesn't pay to extinguish the voice of reason in matters of courtship. It pays to be realistic and not superspiritual. One shouldn't think, for example, that two individuals who are mentally immature without a career or job will be 'taken care of' by God when they get married. This is a question of tempting God, similar to that with which Jesus was tempted. But on the other hand, fears about future financial needs do not need to become insurmountable so that one doesn't dare to get married" (John Lehtola, presentation given 1995).

† "Courtship is a serious matter, and yet a joyful one. Enter prayerfully not playfully. Share the gospel and God's word as a courting couple, pray for one another and for the blessing of God and of His congregation" (Tomm Stewart, presentation given 1996).

† "Courting is directed toward marriage, so light-minded 'flirting' is not appropriate for a believer. In such there is no question of love, or even of infatuation, but of selfish momentary pleasure, which causes sorrow and tears to the courting companion. The matter in consideration is serious enough, that a person who has fallen into this has reason to examine his heart and the foundations of his faith" (Uljas 2000, 101).

4.7.5 Children

> *To experience the knowledge of Jesus Christ, we didn't need to be born again; we simply needed to be born. Our parents, our teachers, and our favorite theologians took it from there, providing us with all the answers before we ever had time to really wrestle with the questions.*
>
> —Rachel Held Evans, *Evolving in Monkey Town*

Conservative Laestadians use the term "God's Children" for themselves, and demographically speaking the term is pretty accurate. With vanishingly few conversions from the outside (at least from my observation in the LLC), the membership is almost entirely sustained by "growth from within." Children by far outnumber the adults sitting in the pews on any given Sunday. The life of an average married couple is kept busy with their many children, the church camps and activities provided for those children, and a slew of cousins and friends coming and going.

Contraception

The reason for the many children is a firm rejection of contraception *in any form whatsoever*. It is not just artificial birth control that is considered sinful (as with the Catholic Church but few individual Catholics), but also natural family planning, *coitus interruptus*, or even abstinence except for limited cases of illness that are considered to fall under the "fasting and prayer" of 1 Cor 7:5.

There are other conservative religious groups that oppose birth control, though it is actually widely accepted in the two that most people think of, Mormonism and Catholicism, official pronouncements notwithstanding. In her book about the fundamentalist Christian "Quiverfull" movement, Kathryn Joyce writes about the "Protestant opposition to birth control" having

> three main scriptural bases: Psalm 127; the Genesis command to "be fruitful and multiply"; and the biblical story of Onan, slain by God for spilling his seed on the ground. This story is seen by Provan [1989, *The Bible and Birth Control*] and the Protestant forefathers–Martin Luther, John Calvin, and John Wesley–whose commentaries he drew on, as a form of birth control. (Castigating the "contraceptive mentality" among the elites of his own day, Luther called birth control an "inhuman attitude, which is worse than barbarous," and lamented, "How many girls there are who prevent conception and kill and expel tender fetuses, although procreation is the work of God!") [Joyce 2009, 146]

Conservative Laestadian attention to the topic appeared not long after the birth control pill did, and has never waned as new generations of married couples confront the challenge of welcoming double-digit numbers of children into their homes and marriages. (For my own part, I have eleven.) Besides the official writings and preachings, there is a great deal of private discussion going on. Comparing notes about the challenges of raising large families, dealing with rude comments by outsiders, etc. is a favorite topic between believing couples. It's a natural form of mutual support. The same kinds of discussions occur among outsiders (who, for all their Christian fundamentalism and rejection of birth control, are still considered "unbelievers" without any possible connection to those in "living faith"):

> There are . . . commonalities, traded among Quiverfull comrades as badges of honor: the frequency with which they're stopped in line at the grocery store by someone asking if "they're feeding an army," if they know "what causes that," if they know "there's a pill for that"? Are they Catholic? Are they Mormon? Do they know God gave us brains to use them? They're also frequently met with a host of assumptions about their beliefs, economic status, ethnicity, and possible welfare reliance. [Joyce 2009, 138]

But there is also private discussion among Conservatives that extends beyond mutual comfort and reinforcement of official teachings. From my reading of private and anonymous Internet forums and conversations with various Finnish friends and correspondents, it seems to me that a fair number–probably still only a minority–of couples in the SRK are now winding up with suspiciously small families. One correspondent tells me that, of the tens of relatives and friends he has in the SRK who have privately discussed the matter with him, almost all have admitted using some form of contraception to space out their children to some extent. The proof is in the small size of their families, he says, with significantly fewer children per family in the Helsinki capital area than in rural areas.

These are not just a few isolated observations. YLE News recently reported in Finland, "Some young Laestadians in Finland secretly use contraception":

> Laestadian women who use birth control keep it secret from their families because Conservative Laestadian teaching holds that contraception is a sin. Many Laestadians begin controlling their family size when they start to suffer from exhaustion or depression. Educated women were especially likely to use contraception, as large families and careers are difficult to combine. [2011 <http://yle.fi/uutiset/news/2011/11/laestadian_women_use_contraception_in_se cret_3024233.html>]

An informal poll posted <http://www.vauva.fi/keskustelut/alue/2/viestiketju/1204945/vlt_missa_pain_asut_mika_ on_sinun_kanta_ehkaisyyn> on the discussion forum for the Finnish mother's magazine *Vauva* reveals some of this private unorthodoxy about birth control among Conservative Laestadians. The options were

(a) Prevention (*ehkäisy*) is sin and wrong in all situations.

(b) Prevention is acceptable only if pregnancy threatens the woman's life.

(c) Prevention is acceptable as needed by exhaustion/health status of the woman/man.

(d) Prevention is a matter that is between each couple (*on jokaisen avioparin välinen asia*), without regard to exhaustion/sickness.

The survey wasn't even close to being statistically rigorous, and the small sample of people who responded probably isn't an accurate cross-section of Conservative Laestadianism in Finland. But the result is so much at variance with official doctrine that it cannot be dismissed. Indeed, a lot of the (more) Conservative commenters on the forum expressed shock at what they were seeing. Of the 48 responses that clearly expressed one of the four viewpoints, 31 (**65%**) of them went with (d), the most liberal of them all. The remaining responses were 10 (21%) for option (c), 4 (8%) for option (b), and just 3 (6%) for (a), the most conservative viewpoint that is asserted in at least the earliest of my sample's church statements.

The first is a remarkably nasty little one from a 1962 issue of *Päivämies* that has made the rounds on the Internet. (As with another one below from an unattributed Internet source, the translation is my own.)

> † "Contraception is a sin of filthiness and murder."

There isn't much room for discussion with a statement like that.

> † "Family planning, restricting the number of children, has become such an open and powerful movement. Young Christian mothers have been the objects of attack by unbelieving doctors and midwives. They are belittled and branded as foolish and ignorant" (Arvo Perala, *Greetings of Peace*, 8/1970).

The basic justification was and remains that "[b]irth and death are basic matters in the arrangement of God's work of creation":

> † "According to the Bible, God Himself, with His own words and without any mediators, gives this command to multiply and fill the earth. The importance of the matter is stressed by the fact that the command is given twice, both to the first human pair and to Noah. Believers receive perhaps the most ridicule for keeping this commandment of God, in a time when it would be, even in this matter, possible to live an easier life.... No matter how ridiculous it sounds in the ears of present-day unbelieving people, we believe that only the Almighty Living God shall set limits and numbers to mankind, He alone shall decide when the earth is full enough, and He has methods for keeping a balance when the Earth is 'full,' as nature as a whole is in an incomprehensibly complicated balanced system, at least in its natural state" (*Päivämies* No. 32, 1975).

In 2009, human rights concerns about mandatory motherhood spurred the SRK into providing more of a theological justification for its opposition to birth control. I discuss that in the next section (**4.7.6**) below.

There were no exceptions, no regard for the health of the mother. It was all in God's hands:

> † A "lenient mind sometimes puts pity for the mother before having love in the truth concerning family planning, especially then when humanly speaking, the birth could appear dangerous. We so easily forget that God has already before our birth ordained the number of our days and the form of our death" (VOZ, 8/1976).
>
> † "Never in any form does the prevention of human life come into question for God's children. As God's children, we know that life is a holy matter, and the possibility for life is hidden in the seed. Therefore, no form of contraception is acceptable. Even if it were to happen that a believing mother or child would die in childbirth, or during pregnancy, they would go to heaven" (*Päivämies*, Internet, 1979)

The uncompromising tone of these statements would soften somewhat in the years ahead, but the message remained. You just do not interfere with God's (pro)creation work:

> † "We know that one would not think of rejecting or destroying a gift at Christmas. Those who use birth control or abortion are rejecting the gifts God gives" (VOZ, 5/1990).
>
> † "Scripture does not teach family planning, but it guides us to regard children as God's gifts" (Uljas 2000, 106).
>
> † "The Bible teaches us to accept children as God's gifts. Each child is God's creation and is meant to be born, whether he is born to believing or unbelieving parents, within marriage or outside of marriage. Abortion and contraception are contrary to God's Word, and we cannot accept them. Accepting God's order of creation may sometimes seem overpowering in the midst of pressures and in the midst of a growing family. Reason battles against faith. All the same, we don't have to understand everything through reason. We don't even understand how a

large tree can grow from a small seed, let alone a living human being. Could a father or mother of a large family say that the youngest of the family wouldn't have the right to live and that he wouldn't be equally valuable and important as the other children in the family?" (VOZ, 9/2003).

† "The unbelieving world often uses the words of the Bible, 'Be fruitful, and multiply, and replenish the earth' (Gen. 1:28), as words of ridicule to shame believing families. God's blessing of children has become a curse to many modern people. In the name of a high standard of living and personal pleasure, people have started down a road that is contrary to God's Word. Birth control is now a common practice. Pressures against our Christianity and believing married couples have at times been very strong. Family planning is a temptation especially for young families perhaps also for the reason that modern youth have become used to going places freely. When a growing family suddenly stops this mobility, it can be difficult to adjust to this new lifestyle. Also the desire for comforts has increased pressure toward family planning. On the other hand, the fact that it is common in our surrounding society may cause the understanding that it is acceptable. Acceptance of family planning, however, means abandoning the main thought of the first article of the Creed, trust upon God the giver and maintainer of life. The birth of a child into a family is God's gift and blessing. In experiencing this, parents need encouragement and sharing of their joy, not pity. The Holy Bible does not instruct us to use birth control. It teaches to accept children with joy as God's gifts and instructs us to bring them up according to the Lord's will (Eph. 6:4)" (VOZ, 10/2003).

† "Believing fathers and mothers have comprehended as an unrelinquishable value the scriptural teaching that God is the Lord of life and death. He has the power to give life and the power to take it away. For this reason in our Christianity, we have considered children as gifts from God; they bring blessing, joy, meaning, and richness to our lives. That's why even the parents of large families have wanted to accept children, even though it has perhaps meant that they have had to give up certain things. The basis for Christian parents' decisions has been obedience to God's Word, faith upon God as the omnipotent Creator, and trust in His guidance and care. . . . The preservation

of the life of both the mother and child is important. A doctor, who has great professional ethics, helps humanity and respects a patient's wishes by preserving life and maintaining health. Surely parents do not relate belittlingly to their doctor's assessment given from a medical perspective. In difficult situations, faith guides us to make decisions based on preserving life according to God's Word" (*Päivämies* No. 5, 2009).

That last quote is from an article that was translated in the May 2009 *Voice of Zion*. There, the article is footnoted with the comment: "The Finnish media has erroneously reported that SRK has imposed an official contraception ban." The comment was no doubt prompted by concern voiced a few months earlier by the European Union's Human Rights Commission (4.7.6). In what way is the expected behavior of an individual believer different than if there *were* in fact "an official contraception ban"?

The reality that the article is dancing around with its obtuse references to doctors is that additional children are no longer always accepted when the mother's life is at stake. There have been many terminations of tubal pregnancies and even outright abortions in such cases. Women in their 40s are routinely advised by their doctors that their uteruses can't take any more abuse and undergo hysterectomies. However, that viewpoint is not universal. From numerous private discussions in recent years, I have learned (albeit second-hand) of cases in particular congregations and under the guidance of particular clergy where women are still being told to submit to the possibility of pregnancy at the risk of their lives. And I know of one case where such submission proved fatal.

Another consequence of the rigid rejection of contraception (whether you view it as a "ban" or a viewpoint held in miraculous unanimity by all believers) is the lack of accounting for the unique challenges of individual families. Although Conservative Laestadianism forms a remarkably cohesive social group, with large and intertwined families usually providing wonderful opportunities for mutual support and reliable friendships, there are cases where things aren't so rosy. Those parents unfortunate enough to have bad combinations of genes are faced with a seemingly endless sequence of children with physical or mental challenges. Parents (especially mothers) with fragile mental dispositions can have their lives and marriages clouded by the effects of repeated pregnancies and child-rearing stresses. In one case of which I have first-hand knowledge, a couple has been depriving their marriage of sexual relations for several years because they are no better equipped to deal with the mental health consequences of another pregnancy and child than with the guilt of using contraception.

Christian Upbringing

Paul Heideman lovingly described the act of Christian forgiveness between parent and child in a sermon he delivered sometime in the 1950s:

> † "[M]ay there always sound this blessing of Jesus' blood. Even for example when the Christian parents feel that, 'I have fallen into sin' and come to you Christian children and say, 'Will you forgive me, Child?' May God always fill your hearts and lips with the word of forgiveness in Jesus' precious blood. . . . Not only that the parents bless the children, but even that the children can in this way bless the parents with that heaven-sent good word, that in Jesus' blood all sins are forgiven."

My grandmother Sophia Suominen wrote a plaintive open letter in August 1962 to her 10 children, almost all of whom had left the faith of their childhood by that point. It appeared in the February 1968 *Greetings of Peace*:

> † "My dear children whom I have carried in my lap, and lulled to sleep, I have often prayed that the heavenly Father would preserve you from all evil. Even now you are on my heart. The ones who are believing are easy to carry, but you unbelievers are especially heavy, that it feels my heart will break. Mother even worries over the believing children, but I depend on God, that He will keep you together in the congregation of His saints, where there are many fathers and many mothers, brothers and sisters, many blessing hands, and where the blood of Jesus flows freely."

The worldly influences of secular education were of great concern in the 1970s. Here are some fairly hysterical warnings by Peter Nevala:

> † "Today we are faced with an ever worsening situation in our schools. . . . I am sure that most of you have believed, even as I believed until a few years ago, that our schools were places where our children were being educated and prepared for a wholesome,

useful life as future citizens in our country. Many of you have been shocked, even as I have, when we have discovered that our schools have been slowly changing for the worse. We have discovered that most of the *new* textbooks now being used in our schools contain objectionable language, revolutionary philosophies and immoral teachings. . . . [W]e are being subjected to a trend of thought in our country which believes that our children actually *belong to the state!* Our school system has been taken over by people who are known as 'humanists.'. . . Now we are witnessing psychological conditioning, drugs, sensitivity sessions, primitive religions, witchcraft, Satanism, death education, tribal moralities (Netsilik Eskimos in MACOS program) being forced on students. . . . We must warn our little ones about the godlessness they will be exposed to in school. They must be told the teachers are still to be respected but not believed in anything they say that is contrary to our Christian ethics and beliefs" (VOZ, 1/1977).

Luther warned about the consequences of a father not providing spiritual instruction to his children, a warning that Russell Roiko likewise made in a 1997 presentation:

> † "There are very serious consequences that result from neglecting the temporal needs of children. Such neglect is an indication of spiritual neglect. It is a much more serious issue. Spiritual responsibility is the duty given by God. If a parent falls into spiritual neglect it has eternal consequences."

It certainly seems odd to me that almighty God would allow such responsibility, with its "eternal consequences," to be the province of mere human parents. If he has predestined the children to heaven or hell before they are even born (4.9.3), it makes no difference what efforts are made to teach them anything of a spiritual nature. The saved ones will go on to accept "living Christianity," and the damned ones will not, no matter what. And if the contrary but also commonly asserted view is correct, that God wants everyone to be saved, then it's ridiculous to think that he needs parents to drag their kids to Sunday School and services in order to bring his divine will to fruition.

The disturbing third option that looms just below the surface is this: Children need to be indoctrinated into a religion when they are still too young to challenge the validity of its logically indefensible assertions:

> At the tender age this process usually begins ... children habitually give benefit of the doubt to their parents and role models. As time goes by, the vast Christian American environment consistently pounds the imperative system into their heads day after day, week after week, month after month, and year after year. By their teenage years, most Christians couldn't possibly consider the presence of an error in the Bible, much less a completely erroneous foundation, because it's unquestionably the perfect word of God to them. They believe this notion because they're lifelong members of a society that has continually reinforced the "special" nature of Christianity. [Long 2005, 14]

The ultimate goal of Mormon indoctrination, Jack Worthy writes, is "to ensure that children believe in Mormonism so strongly and so deeply that their belief can't be erased or replaced by other belief systems" (2008, 15). To do that, one must "start when children are very young," "frequently tell them you know the Church is true," and "get them to frequently say they know the Church is true" (pp. 15-16).

In this last quote from my sample, we read about the "precious task" of rooting the seed:

> ✝ "In God's kingdom the seed of the Word is sown with many different gifts. The sowing begins at home. Believing parents have the precious task of helping children and adolescents become rooted in God's kingdom. The main purpose of all activities in Zion is to proclaim God's Word" (*Siionin Lähetyslehti*, 9/2007).

Those "activities in Zion" are almost entirely focused inward, proclaiming God's Word over and over again to those who have grown up hearing it. There is quite a contrast between the limited amount of evangelizing (**4.2.4**) and the inordinate concern expressed about the behavior of people already within the fold (**4.6.4**). In one recent sermon, an LLC preacher recalled driving back and forth in front of the house of a "brother," working up the nerve to rebuke him about some violation of the rules. Yet that preacher would never dream of knocking on the doors of people on his block and telling them about his church.

To me it seems that there is a cynical, subconscious acknowledgment of a severe imbalance between effort and reward. It is relatively easy to cow an already-indoctrinated fellow believer into repentance and thus ensure his presence in the pew next Sunday. But it is difficult, embarrassing, and almost completely unproductive to try to convert people in the local society to abandon the Christianity they thought was just fine and join what to all external appearances is a weird little fundamentalist sect.

4.7.6 Women

> *If Eve had persisted in the truth, she would not only not have been subjected to the rule of her husband, but she herself would also have been a partner in the rule which is now entirely the concern of males.*
>
> —Martin Luther, *Lectures on Genesis*

Women's "God-given Lot"

A "core conviction of all fundamentalist movements is that women must be kept in their place" (Cox 2009, 223). In the view of this article from the January 1975 *Voice of Zion*, that place is women's "God-given lot as mothers and homemakers":

> † "Another thing that comes into our lives from the world is the so-called liberation of women. Women are made to feel discontent with their God-given lot as mothers and homemakers. It seems that our young women would need encouragement to submit themselves unto the will of God even in these matters" (VOZ, 1/1975).

But the reactionary efforts of fundamentalists "are attempting to stem an inexorable movement of the human spirit whose hour has come" (Cox 2009, 223). The women's liberation movement became uncomfortably prominent for American Conservatives in the 1970s, and their desire to stem it is apparent in this next quote from the July 1979 *Voice of Zion*:

> † "When we take notice of what kinds of results the modern-time upbringing has brought about, we surely cannot rejoice in it. . . . Even the struggle for the equality of both sexes is not affirmative. The women have achieved equality many times in sorrowful matters, as drunkenness, and smoking, obscenity, and even in brutality. When women, as mothers and as partakers in much of

> the upbringing, lose hold of their own lives and of the objectives of upbringing, the consequences are frightening."

The male author quoted in that article uses the word "we" like he expects his female readers to join in his lament. Conservative Laestadianism has toned down such rhetoric, but it is still surprisingly common for American fundamentalists to tout the "benefits" of submission in women and try to make it seem like the best arrangement for all concerned. Joyce cites the Reformed Baptist theologian John Piper for some extreme examples of such Orwellian doublethink. Piper argues "for the urgency of leading 'Christian women back to a joyous embrace of godly male leadership in the church'" (2009, 15). He asks women to exchange their freedom "to work, to vote, to drive, to control their bodies and sexual lives" (yes, he's talking about the U.S., not Saudi Arabia) for "a dubious freedom *from*, from the dangers and sexual threats of independent life in the world." He "suggests that women discover their true 'path of freedom' in God's good design of femininity" (p. 17). Another gem cited by Joyce is from two other authors who offer a "fresh vision" for women that "emphasizes gratitude to their husbands for helping relieve them of the burden of decision-making or the busywork that they would focus on if left to their own devices to prioritize their days: 'slaves' to their 'own whims and wishes'" (p. 97).

Statements touting the joys of repression may be especially effective when they come from the repressed themselves, as do these inspiring words of Mary Pride in her book *The Way Home: Beyond Feminism, Back to Reality*:

> Childbearing sums up all our special biological and domestic functions.... God intended women to spend their lives serving other people. Young women serve their children, their mothers, their husbands, and the community at large. Older women train and assist the younger women, and in some cases become church helpers.... We are responsible for keeping society healthy and human. And for this, we get respect. [from Joyce 2009, 135]

That sort of thing makes my skin crawl. Peter Nevala probably wouldn't have found it objectionable, though, given this quote of his from the April 1985 (*not* 1885) *Voice of Zion*:

> † "[T]he Scripture gives clear teaching about the role God has ordained for the Christian wife: 'Wives, submit yourselves unto your own husbands, as unto the Lord. For the husband is the head of the wife, even as Christ is the head of the church: and he is the savior of the body' (Eph 5:22-23). When this God-given order is violated, whether it be by an overbearing and shameless wife who disdains the Word of God, or results from the cowardice and lenience of the henpecked husband, it brings disorderliness and strife into the family and also into the church! This has never failed! We cannot violate any of God's clearly expressed wishes in these or other matters with impunity."

The sad thing is that Nevala is not incorrect in his appeal to the Bible for support of what most of us now recognize as knuckle-dragging sexism. There is such reverence for the Holy Book that "biblical patriarchy" can be the subject of a viable religious movement in 21st century America. And its leader, Doug Phillips, can get on stage and tell a group of women, without apparent risk of injury, "You are a helpmeet. The Bible says that man is not made for the woman but the woman is made for the man. If you have a problem with that, take it up with the Creator, not Phillips. I'm just quoting" (Joyce 2009, 8).

In **4.3.1**, we saw how Al Mohler, president of the Southern Baptist Theological Seminary, noted the dilemma of Biblical literalism regarding evolution. He articulates the same kind of "clear choice" for "biblical traditionalists" regarding women:

> We must choose between two unavoidable options: either the Bible is affirmed as the inerrant and infallible Word of God, and thus presents a comprehensive vision of true humanity in both unity and diversity, or we must claim that the Bible is, to one extent or another, compromised and warped by a patriarchal and male-dominated bias that must be overcome in the name of humanity. [from Joyce 2009, 16]

His choice is the former, but I'll go with the latter, thanks very much. I wish inerrantists like Mohler would stop to consider how their slavish devotion to the ancient text warps not just their view of humanity, but also their view of *divinity*. If the Bible is "inerrant and infallible," then God is a butcher of innocent children (**Numbers 31**) and Jesus is both a false prophet (**Mark 13**) and bald-faced liar (**John 18:20**). To paraphrase

Phillips: If you have a problem with that, take it up with the inerrantist, not me. I'm just observing.

Luther was just as much an inerrantist and literalist about the subject of women as he was about creationism. He was quite serious about the curse of Eve. Besides the "sorrows of gestation and birth," suffered by women,

> Eve has been placed under the power of her husband, she who previously was very free and, as the sharer of all the gifts of God, was in no respect inferior to her husband. This punishment, too, springs from original sin; and the woman bears it just as unwillingly as she bears those pains and inconveniences that have been placed upon her flesh. The rule remains with the husband, and the wife is compelled to obey him by God's command. He rules the home and the state, wages wars, defends his possessions, tills the soil, builds, plants, etc. The woman, on the other hand, is like a nail driven into the wall. She sits at home . . . [*Lectures on Genesis*, Ch. 3, §16]

I have to give Luther some credit, though, for the genuine respect and admiration he showed his wife Katherine in an unenlightened age. He encouraged her to read and understand the Bible, and refused to shoo her away from the dinner table when the men started talking about serious matters. He deferred completely to his *Kette* (an ironic and loving nickname, meaning *chain*) in practical matters of their large and busy household, and was a big fan of her home-brewed beer.

The following Conservative writer confidently expounds on biology and sociology:

> † "Men and women are inherently different" and "have their unique masculine and feminine drives. Men have a need to protect and provide and solve problems, whereas women have a need to nurture and 'nest.' These differences are God's blessings, and a reason for celebration. However, the post-feminist era wants to reverse these traditional roles, and devalue the roles played in the home" (VOZ, 11/2004).

I know a fair number of strong-willed, intelligent women in Conservative Laestadianism who don't hesitate to "protect and provide and solve problems" and snort in derision at sexist generalizations like those. To me, that quote is yet another example of how the preachers tend to put their foot in their mouth whenever they venture to say *anything* outside their bubble of theological abstraction. The next one is from a man who is a bit more circumspect:

> † "Spouses should carry the burdens, as well as the joys, together. [Eph 5:22-25 cited] . . . [T]he husband is the head of the household and that means that he is responsible for spiritual leadership and for sowing the seed of faith in the family. He does not function as a dictator" (VOZ, 8/2006).

In his literalism and 16th century mindset, Luther had a clear view of the gender roles. Woman "is needed not only to secure increase but also for companionship and for protection. The management of the household must have the ministration of the dear ladies. In addition—and this is lamentable—woman is also necessary as an antidote against sin." Alas, men are not satisfied to "copulate only once a year," but "are compelled to make use of intercourse with their wives in order to avoid sin" (*Lectures on Genesis*, Ch. 2, §18). Romantic, isn't it?

Role in the Church

There has been talk among the more liberal elements of the SRK about the ordination of women. One such ordination is set to take place in March 2012. The SRK historian Seppo Lohi is quoted in **Ijäs 2012** <http://www.kotimaa24.fi/uutiset/kotimaa/7090-tutkija-lestadiolaisesta-naispapista-tama-on-historiaa> as saying of this event, "It is history!" However, Lohi notes that female priesthood is not accepted in Conservative Laestadianism, and that the ordination of women is seen as heretical (*harhaopiksi*) in light of the Bible. An article from the April 2004 *Voice of Zion* states that position:

> † "Though God has not meant the office of preaching for women, he has nonetheless employed precious sisters in faith in other capacities in God's kingdom. An example of this is the sisters mentioned in our text [Mt 28:5-8]; they were the first to witness that Christ had risen from the dead."

In view of that, Lohi observes (being careful to couch his remarks as those of a researcher) that the prospective female pastor, Mari Leppänen, "loads quite a bit of pressure on herself concerning her relationship to Conservative Laestadianism. She shows that she has a different idea about the ordination of women than the Conservative Laestadian perception." Regarding the question of Leppänen's possible separation from the movement, Lohi declines to "use such drastic terms" as that, but says the ordination will undoubtedly lead to discussions and she must explain her action (Ijäs 2012).

Those "discussions" are already in the works for Risto Leppänen, Mari's husband, who is himself an ordained pastor in the SRK and the Turku congregation's theological secretary. A recently leaked **email** <http://keskustelu.suomi24.fi/node/10392508> from the Turku congregation's chairman to its board of trustees and Mr. Leppänen "prayerfully invites" them to a meeting to discuss the situation regarding speakers in the Turku RY [congregation]. "The subject of the discussion is the issue about releasing Risto and Heikki [Rainio] from their preaching duties temporarily in our home Zion."[43]

Leppänen is certainly not the only theologically educated woman in the SRK for whom this issue is relevant. Laura Kallio, a female Finnish theologian herself, says there are at least five such women, and thinks that the controversy is misplaced because Raattamaa was a proponent of allowing women to preach (Ahonen 2012). Indeed, it does seem that the early decades of Laestadianism saw some preaching by women. One aspiring female Laestadian pastor, a Masters-level theology student who wishes to remain anonymous,

> feels that this discussion about female pastors has many of the same characteristics that can be seen in the way the movement has handled its child abuse issues [4.10.1]. "For some reason it takes a long time for the movement to acknowledge the existence of victims and parties and even listen to what it is they have to say," [she] says ... [Ahonen 2012]

The SRK addressed the issue in an **editorial** <http://www.srk.fi/index.php?p=usko_ja_elama_22012> by Keijo Nissilä, observing that the discussion "about equality has continued to exist and has recently come up in Conservative Laestadian circles as well." The editorial begins by noting

---

43. According to a correspondent familiar with the Turku congregation and Heikki Rainio's relationship with it over the past decades, the concerns about Rainio are probably not in connection with Mari Leppänen's upcoming ordination, but his public criticism of the SRK's handling of the child sexual abuse issue (**4.10.1**) and singing in concerts at the state church, apparently still a concern for some. (See the discussion of the behavioral norms regarding entertainment in **4.6.1**.)

that "the priesthood is from Christ" and thus "isn't just anyone's subjective right." The universal priesthood of believers "engages all of the Spirit's grace gifts, without distinction." The Spirit is one and the same, and thus all of its "grace gifts are just as valuable and equal even if they are different."

The mention of difference, of course, leads to the heart of the matter:

> The Bible's teachings about the Holy Spirit's grace gifts include not only promises but also restrictions. The most well known of these restrictions is probably Apostle Paul's declaration to comply with the proper form of worship: Women are to keep silent in the churches (1 Cor. 14:34-35). This instruction stems from a lecture, or sermon, which gave this charge to the Congregation's shepherd, or priest, when implementing the framework of the worship process. Apostle Paul argues that he has "the Lord's command" on this particular directive concerning worship. Unfortunately, we do not feel any closer to understanding the meaning of "the Lord's command." The reasoning employed by Apostle Paul is most powerful and authoritative because it is the word of the Lord. [Nissilä 2012]

Well, sexism is rampant in the Bible, and the Pauline passages that are cited to oppose women taking on leadership roles in the church are no exception (7.4). But the Bible also mentions a number of women doing things that the quoted writer might not think "God has meant for women." Anna was a prophetess who served God with fastings and prayers in the the temple (Lk 2:36-37).[44] In Paul's own writings, Mercer finds some evidence in the earliest Christian period of a temporary and "slight rehabilitation of woman's role in that some women apparently took leadership positions in the new sect." He mentions "Phoebe and Priscilla in Romans 16:1-5; Euodia and Syntyche in Philippians 4:2-3; and possibly Chloe in 1 Corinthians 1:11 and Junia in Romans 16:7" (Mercer 2009, 122). In Phillipians 4:3, he asked an unnamed individual reader to "help those women which laboured with me in the gospel."

---

44. Origen was able to justify to himself and his patriarchal readers "a woman who was a prophetess" coming after Simeon because "it was necessary that women too should be saved." He consoled himself about it by pointing to how "beautiful the order is! The woman did not come before the man" (*Homilies on Luke*, No. 17, from Lienhard 1996, 70).

In many cases, translation and manuscript issues have obscured (perhaps deliberately) the role these women played. The KJV and NASB have Rom 16:1 describe Phoebe as a "servant," but Mercer says the correct translation is "deacon" (2009, 66). The masculine-sounding name *Junias* in Rom 16:7 apparently did not exist in Greek, but *Junia* was common and invariably feminine. A scribe may well have "corrected" what he saw as an aberration in Paul's listing of a woman as one of those "outstanding among the apostles." Cox believes "that women played a significantly larger leadership role than had previously been thought. But the power of false history to shape present perception goes even farther. Since the priestly elite insisted that women had always been subservient and marginal, people were unable to see clear evidence to the contrary" (2009, 179-80).

One grey area in recent Conservative Laestadian practice has been whether women should serve on the various congregations' boards of trustees. The minutes of the LLC's 2010 annual meeting reveal that the question was raised from one congregation whether "it is against God's teachings to have a woman on the local Board." The response from pastoral director Keith Waaraniemi was "that it is not contrary to Scriptures for women to serve in this way. It should be a question of God's calling and not equality. There are congregations in both North America and Finland that have women on the Church Boards."

I applaud that development, but let's not pretend that it's not contrary to any Scripture for women to be seated in the body that is the highest (practical) authority in each congregation. The writer of 1 Tim 2:11 wanted "women to learn in silence with all subjection," and would not permit "a woman to teach, nor to usurp authority over the man, but to be in silence." And referring to "God's calling" is an *ad hoc* justification that could just as well apply to the office of preaching. It seems ironic that there are women participating in solemn deliberations to select men (**4.2.7**) for an office they themselves are deemed unqualified to hold.

Obligatory Motherhood

This last quote defends the profession of motherhood:

> † "Motherhood, however, is not always honored in society. A career in the workplace can be seen as more honorable than being 'just a mother.' The believing mother is sometimes ridiculed,

especially those whom God has blessed with many children" (VOZ, 3/2008).

There is certainly some truth to that. Many modern women are postponing and even completely eschewing motherhood for the sake of their career interests. As we just saw in 4.7.5, however, the church does not think that such a decision should even be *available* to women.

Ultra-Orthodox Judaism in Israel is one society in which motherhood is definitely honored. There one finds mothers "who are raising not merely traditionally large families but families that eclipse even Hassidic tradition in size: well over twelve children and continuing to bear into their late forties in what one midwife called 'a social obsession to get pregnant'" (Joyce 2009, 185). Yet there is a dark side underneath the way such "mothers are highly honored" in that community:

> [T]he effects on the health of these mothers and on their families, often living in poverty, can be tragic–lives of quiet scarcity and unceasing labor, housework, and births. Elder daughters are required to pick up a great deal of household responsibilities early on in life while their mothers recover from pregnancies or ... die early. "They're workhorses," says Dr. Singer [a doctor working in a women's clinic]. "Their lives, looking from the outside, look like a form of slavery, never-ending. Sometimes I'm incredibly admiring of their stamina, what they're able to do day after day, after so many children." [p. 185]

The only thing that seems to separate them from Conservative Laestadian mothers is the "social obsession." Despite the quoted *Voice of Zion* language about believing mothers being "blessed," the fact is that Conservative women are not particularly hesitant to grumble about their repeated pregnancies–and the resulting stress and drudgery– among themselves.[45] Publicly, though, they are like the ultra-Orthodox, where

> the glorification of mothers of many children and the community's belief that women, while pregnant, are fulfilling their roles, leads to women scarcely able to articulate that they wish to stop having children. "They won't even let themselves

---

45. Please don't ask me how I know this, but I do. It's not an isolated phenomenon by any means. Ladies, carry on.

> say the words, 'I don't want any more children,' but will rather say, 'I'll bear as many children as God gives me,'" even as they tell Dr. Singer that they're exhausted. [Joyce 2009, 188]

One mother who was raised in the LLC but left after having seven children tells her own story of exhaustion and disillusionment in a posting on the **extoots site** <http://extoots.blogspot.com/2007/10/once_8148.html>. At first, she "noticed the unspoken competition" in her central Minnesota congregation

> over clothes, hair, and as they got older, houses and kids' clothes. Heck, I even played the wishful Keep Up With the [Joneses] game for a time. Can I have six kids and still clothe them all stylishly? If I buy their clothes at the second-hand store, perhaps. Or maybe if I sew their clothes, I can manage.
>
> Then it got to be, can we afford to feed them? And can we possibly make space in this little house for a seventh? And we are still expected to have more? God will provide? Let's see, my children are now wearing clothes from the free store and we almost qualify for food stamps (and let me tell you, that's not saying much).
>
> And when I am at the end of my rope with still another pregnancy, nauseated and vomiting all day long for several months (it was a very effective weight loss method, I must say), the only answer I hear is that God will never give me more than I can handle. He will provide.
>
> And then, when my gas is cut off because I can't afford to pay the bill, and there is no hot water with which to bathe my children, and I look forward to shopping at the food shelf so I can make it till payday, it becomes obvious that something is very wrong with this system.

It is "faith, pure and simple" that Joyce says the Quiverfull movement is all about: "Faith that God won't give a woman more children than she can handle, and faith that by opening themselves up to receive multiple 'blessings,' they will bring God's favor upon them in other areas of life as well: their husbands will get better jobs; God will send a neighbor with a sack of used children's clothes just when the soles on Johnny's shoes fall out" (Joyce 2009, 155).

When the system works, it seems to work well. There are many genuinely happy mothers of large families in Conservative Laestadianism who enjoy "God's favor upon them" both financially and with a great deal of social support from like-minded friends and extended family. Sometimes, though, it comes to seem that God has indeed given the believing mother "more children than she can handle." When and if that realization finally hits a desperate parent, it's too late to do anything about it but try to cope and keep from spiraling any further into pain or poverty, or both.

Human Rights Concerns

Some public pressure has been put on Conservative Laestadianism due to its well-known aversion to contraception. In March 2009, the European Union's Human Rights Commission expressed concerns <http://www.ihmisoikeusliitto.fi/images/pdf_files/ehkaisykielto.pdf> that the movement's teachings–whether a "ban" is said to be in place or not– effectively infringe on the individual right to freely make a determination about contraception. That right, it said, is a matter of human rights protection. It noted that the term "contraception ban" is not used. But it pointed out that Laestadians have experienced "very real social compulsion" about the issue, and "failure to comply will have serious spiritual and secular consequences."

The historian and SRK pastor Seppo Lohi responded with a detailed theological explanation in a document <http://freepathways.wordpress.com/2009/07/15/seppo-lohen-perustelut/> presented at the SRK's 2009 Summer Services. It begins with an appeal to tradition, saying that only two other such presentations had been needed to address the issue, the first in 1945 and the second in 1967. Thus Lohi infers "that contraception has not been any special problem to the members of the movement, at least not as a matter of principle."

Lohi's remarks quickly begin to show some tension about the human rights question. He uses some obscure terminology (*ehdonvallan kysymys*, "question where conditions may determine whether something is right or wrong," and *adiafora*, "not regarded as essential to faith") to say that there are no particular conditions or individual preferences where contraception is acceptable, while also claiming that it is up to the parents. Here's a not-quite literal but hopefully accurate translation:

> Even if the birth control issue should not be decided freely, the ultimate decision has always been made by two adults, mother and father. [Conservative Laestadian] Christians have made their choices as matters of faith, based on their God-directed conscience. This means that God's word has bound their conscience also in those decisions where the secular law would have allowed free decisions and own choices.

Conservative Laestadians, including the women who privately suffer and complain exactly like the Orthodox Jews we just encountered, are making these choices *from their consciences!* If your conscience tells you that enough is enough already, however, then it's not correct. In other words, there's no ban against contraception, but you still can't use it. The only people I know of who can say two opposite things in a single sentence are politicians, economists, and theologians.

Finally, Lohi gets to his actual theological arguments. He still has a hard time jumping off the dock of tradition and swimming in the cold biblical waters on his own, though:

> In Christendom, birth control was widely considered to stand against the Bible and the Christian tradition. In Christianity, the predominant view of humanity dictated that a new life was wholly God's act of Creation, which shall not be controlled by man. New life is a fundamental task of marriage, arising from God's command: "Be fruitful, and multiply, and replenish the earth (Genesis 1:28)." Also Luther, in his time, reinforced this conception and said: "Therefore, the word of God, 'Be fruitful, and multiply,' is not a command, but more than a mere command, namely a Divine Act, not being in our power to hinder or neglect."

So we now have one biblical reference, God's command following two events (biblical creation and Noah's flood) that *never actually occurred* (**4.3.1**, **4.3.2**). The next reference we see in Lohi's presentation is to Mark 10:6-9, Jesus' directive that God had made people male and female from the beginning of the creation: "For this cause shall a man leave his father and mother, and shall cleave to his wife; and the two shall become one flesh: so that they are no more two, but one flesh. What therefore God hath joined together, let not man put asunder." That is a fine bit of support for rejecting divorce (**4.7.4**), but what does it have to do with birth control?

Apparently, "the topic is not a question of any single issue, but of the whole marriage concept and of children's rights, first and foremost." The purpose of marriage, Lohi ventures without a single Bible quote for support,

> is not only personal pleasure and self-indulgence of the spouses, even if God himself said that it is not good for man to be alone. The actual purpose of marriage is reproduction. By means of marriage, God gives us children. For this act of Creation, God invites father and mother to work together with Him and grants them family and home. "Home is the power source of a society" and "child-rich marriages its best warranty." In preventing the birth of just one child, man takes unto himself a decision lasting even for generations.

Then he refers to the life of a child as holy and its value absolute, finally offering some biblical citations for that principle:

> "Whoso shall receive one such little child in my name receiveth me." A child is a member of God's Kingdom (Mark 10:14). "In heaven their angels do always behold the face of my Father who is in heaven." Children are examples of a right relationship with God, the Father. "Except ye turn, and become as little children, ye shall in no wise enter into the kingdom of heaven" (Matt. 18:3,5,10). When a life of a child is placed so high, there is nothing comparable in the world. From this child-appreciating view of humanity arises, as obvious, a child's right to life, existence, parents, home and upbringing, seamlessly connected with marriage. This does not only apply to an already fertilized ovum, which is considered to be the beginning of a new life in a womb.

The actual context of Mark 10:13-16 is Jesus' affection and tolerance for a bunch of kids who were initially shooed away by the disciples, and his use of them as an object lesson about childlike faith. Via the miracle of creative hermeneutics (**4.3.5**), Lohi transforms that into a command to "receive" speculative children not even conceived. The DNA defining a couple's next child exists only in the woman's ovaries and will not even be generated in her husband until a few days before their big night. If that encounter is postponed by an unexpected business trip, does a child lose its life? Of course not. It's just a different lucky one of a couple hundred million sperm and possibly a different egg that make their own wildly improbable combination.

Nobody wants to think they are the random outcome of a woman's ovulation, meiosis churning out cells by the billions in a man's testicles, and a race between millions of sperm whose microscopic tails furiously whip around in a quantum-level arena of fluid dynamics. But the alternative–claiming that conceptions are divinely ordained ahead of time–makes God into a puppet-master who stage-directs the universe down to its tiniest details. Then we are just puppets in an inane drama whose uncountable trillions of acts and final ending are all pre-ordained, our every movement reflecting a tug of the Deity's invisible strings. (This relates to the futility of spiritually "fighting the good fight" if predestination is true, **4.9.3**.)

Perhaps we should leave Lohi's speculations for a moment and look at a few Bible passages that *do* address the value of a child's life, both born and unborn. On the positive side, there is Jeremiah's claim that God told him, "Before I formed thee in the belly I knew thee; and before thou camest forth out of the womb I sanctified thee, and I ordained thee a prophet unto the nations" (Jer 1:5). The beautiful 139th Psalm includes a discourse about God weaving the writer's inward parts together in his mother's womb, and predestinating his life before his birth:

> Your eyes have seen my unformed substance;
> And in Your book were all written
> The days that were ordained for me,
> When as yet there was not one of them. [Psa 138:16, NASB]

Now let's consider the opposite view. (Despite the claims of its inerrancy and consistency, it seems that the Bible always provides opposing viewpoints when you look closely at it.) In Exodus 21:22, hurting a pregnant woman and causing her to miscarry incurred punishment "as the woman's husband will lay upon" the perpetrator and "as the judges determine." The next verses add, "And if any mischief follow, *then* thou shalt give life for life, eye for eye, tooth for tooth, hand for hand, foot for foot, burning for burning," etc. (emphasis added). Injuring a woman and causing the death of her unborn child was a matter for a civil penalty, but if the brawl continues and a *man* dies, *then* we are talking about "life for life."

Leviticus 27 places monetary valuations on human life. Boys from one month to five years of age were worth five shekels of silver, with the price going up to 20 shekels between the ages of 5-20 years. Men between the ages of 20 to 60 years had the highest price of all, 50 shekels, after which price the old duffers dropped to a mere 15 shekels in value. (Women, of course, had lower values at every age, usually 3/5 that of a comparable male.) *No value at all* was assigned to newborn infants.

When there is killing of women to be done, the Old Testament doesn't hesitate to inflict its cruelty on their children as well, both born and unborn. Hosea rants against Ephraim that he will "slay even the beloved fruit of their womb" (9:16). The people of Samaria had "rebelled against her God," according to Hosea, so "they shall fall by the sword: their infants shall be dashed in pieces, and their women with child shall be ripped up" (13:16). When Judah learned that his daughter-in-law was "with child by whoredom," his response was, "Bring her forth, and let her be burnt" (Gen 38:24). It was only when she produced some things that he had left during *his own* sexual encounter with her that he backed down.

Based on the 1945 presentation and the agreement voiced in the subsequent discussion, Lohi concludes that

> Conservative Laestadians' negative attitude to birth control can be summarized as follows: (1) According to God's order of Creation, marriage is a union between man and woman, and reproduction its principal task. God invites mother and father to collaborate with this act of Creation. (2) Because a child is an act of Creation, a gift from God, and its value absolute according to Jesus, the birth of a new life is from the very beginning a holy event, in which man must not intervene.

Nothing emerged after that to cause Conservatives to re-evalutate their attitude, Lohi said. He cited approvingly this statement from the SRK's annual meeting of 1974: "Birth control in all its forms requires abandonment of the Christian Church's First Article of Faith." And then we learn just what we're supposed to think about that scientific stuff I mentioned a few paragraphs ago:

> If I have faith, this means that Man has not appeared by chance. Unlike animals, a human is created in the image of God, as uniquely valuable. Therefore, the life of a human is sacred. At its deepest, the holiness of life opens perspectives for the core issue of the whole Christian Faith. God did not give His Son to die for beings evolved by a process of chance, but for uniquely valuable

humans created in the image of God. The message of the Cross is mindless, if the value of a human is not absolute. This should be acknowledged even now, in the 200th anniversary of Darwin's birth.

So much for science, including evolution. Once again we have arrived back in Eden, a place that Christian theology just cannot seem to leave.

4.8 Time

> *For the living know that they shall die: but the dead know not any thing, neither have they any more a reward; for the memory of them is forgotten. Also their love, and their hatred, and their envy, is now perished; neither have they any more a portion for ever in any thing that is done under the sun. Go thy way, eat thy bread with joy, and drink thy wine with a merry heart; for God now accepteth thy works.*
>
> —Ecclesiastes

4.8.1 Unchanging Faith

> *There are, of course, perfectly logical reasons for refusing to change one's religious beliefs. If they are part of a consistent world-view that one believes to have been revealed by God, then to change them implies that God is a liar, or that His truth is not eternal and changeless. The new evidence has to be assimilated to the story, rather than the story accommodated to the evidence. The story is in principle unfalsifiable.*
>
> —Peter Herriot, *Religious Fundamentalism*

For as long as I can remember, the church has claimed that its doctrine has never changed and need never do so, often citing the statement in Heb 13:8, "Jesus Christ the same yesterday, and to day, and for ever." The first two quotes in my sample make indirect reference to that passage:

> † "How good it is under the trials of the present moment of your journey, when you see how everything around you changes, to know from the assuring word of God, that Jesus has not changed

and does not change. He is the same today. And as you travel towards that day which is your last on this journey, how good to know and trust that He is still the same" (Paul Heideman, *Greetings of Peace*, 1/1944).

† "All other things in the world shall change but the word of the Lord shall remain forever. When God gives a promise–gives His Word–it shall never change. The Lord Jesus is the same yesterday, today, and forever. When we have based our faith upon this Lord Jesus Christ then it is such a rock which shall not be shaken, but shall remain forever" (Uno Makela, sermon given 1980).

An article originally published in Finnish in 1995 also refers to the Heb 13:8 passage. But note how it also casts "God's children" as being the unaltered successors of the "first congregation" and the apostles:

† "The members of Christ's congregation, God's children, have the same desire as they had in the time of the first congregation: to remain in the doctrine and common love of Christ and the apostles. The foundation hasn't changed, and it must not change, for the Bible warns us of going astray from the way marked by God's Son [2 John 1:9 cited]. The foundation of our faith must remain on the rock of Christ who is the same yesterday, today, and forever" (VOZ, 4/2007).

It is one thing for a first- or second-century text to say that the ascended Son of God is unchanging, or even to follow that with a warning not to be "carried about with divers and strange doctrines" (Heb 13:9). It is another thing entirely for a church that carries the burden of such later ecclesiastical innovations as the confessional rite (5.1.2), the near-worship of a collection of books (4.3.4) canonized hundreds of years after Christ and disputed for a thousand years to follow, and sectarianism whose exclusivity has become grotesque in a vast and populated world (4.2.1). Even the way that Christianity (Conservative Laestadianism being no exception) views the unchanging Christ has changed since the earliest statements of the Bible (7.1).

One change of recent years that nobody disputes is the presence of non-white Conservative Laestadians in faraway lands. The new phenomenon inspired some appropriate and thoughtful words of admonition that,

† "before God all men are the same and within the kingdom all believers are to be loved and accepted equally. Each of us is, however, a captive of the time in which we live and a product of the environment in which we were raised. The attitudes one carries regarding people of other races are, in large part, determined by the attitudes of those by whom one is taught, most commonly parents, immediate family, close friends and the prevailing societal norms at the time of one's youth. With the vast majority of the believers being of northern European extraction during this past 140-some years of God's visitation, dealing with race issues among believers has not always seemed pressing. It hasn't occurred to many believers to challenge and clarify their underlying attitudes towards people of other races, nationalities, or ethnic origin. Recent conversions in South America and Africa, however, have changed this scenario" (VOZ, 4/2001).

An article entitled "Faith Does Not Change with the Times" in *Päivämies* (No. 30, 2006) addressed the claim of people "[i]n our time" who

† "repeatedly claim that the foundation of Christian faith is crumbling. To the minds of many, the Bible is not God's Word, nor is it given fundamental value as a guide to faith and life. Jesus' death as the propitiation for our sins and His resurrection especially engender offense. Many demand change in the content of faith according to science and the majority opinions of people. In this way, human reason has risen as the yardstick for everything." Living faith "receives secure directional signs, in our time also, from the enduring Word of God."

Conflicts between faith and science are most certainly not limited to our time, as Petr Beckmann makes clear in *A History of Pi*. He writes that the "Christian Roman emperor Valens ordered the burning of non-Christian books in 373," lists other Christian book burnings in 1109, 1204, and the early 15th century, and tells how, in 1486, the Grand Inquisitor "sentenced the Spanish mathematician Valmes to be burned at the stake because Valmes had claimed to have found the solution of the quartic equation. It was the will of God, maintained the Grand Inquisitor of the Holy Office of the Inquisition Against Heretical Depravity, that such a solution was inaccessible to human understanding" (p. 80). In 1600, Giordano Bruno was burned alive for his claim that the earth moves around the sun. He preceded Galileo, who was forced to recant the same heretical idea, by some thirty years.

Every one of these battles has ended in victory for science. Today, missionary preachers of Christian faith fly around a world that wasn't supposed to be round, in jet aircraft burning fossil fuels from reservoirs that aren't supposed to be millions of years old, assured of their health by medicines engineered to resist microscopic species that aren't supposed to be evolving. With "faith" in full retreat from any position of authoritative teaching about the natural world, statements like those of Peter Nordstrom in 1973 (**4.3.1**) about six-day creation look quaint and the *Voice of Zion* now proclaims (in between regular discourses about Adam and Eve), "It is not the purpose of the Bible to answer questions about genetics, medicine, or natural sciences" (**4.3.4**).

Despite all that,

> † "The claim that God's word is bound to time and shackled to the culture of its time does not do justice to God's revelation. According to Jesus, the content and the message of the Word of God does not change along with changes in the world. God's Word is always timely. We cannot relinquish this principle" (VOZ, 4/2008).

At least there has been acknowledgment that enlightenment is possible in some areas:

> † "In the 1980s and '90s we experienced a time of enlightenment. I think it is safe to say, at least my experience is that we in American Zion have become more enlightened about music. We have learned much from our Finnish friends, brothers and sisters in faith, about music. . . . [T]here wasn't a lot of understanding about classical music and other forms of appropriate music" (Keith Waaraniemi, presentation given 2009).

Of course, acceptance of certain types of music other than church hymns isn't the only area where change has occurred. As we have seen in **4.7.5**, women are no longer expected to die rather than prevent life-threatening pregnancies; "false spirits" are nowhere to be found, congregational "caretaking meetings" are almost never conducted after having been almost a weekly occurrence at times decades earlier, and the expectation and practice of personal confession is greatly diminished.

4.8.2 Eschatology

> *The last times are come upon us.*
>
> —Ignatius, *Epistle to the Ephesians* [c. 100 A.D.]

There always have been Christians who thought that Jesus would come back in their own lifetimes, starting with Paul (Ehrman 2011, 106). He wrote to comfort his brethren who were concerned about the fate of their loved ones who died before Jesus' return, promising that

> *we which are alive and remain unto the coming of the Lord* shall not prevent them which are asleep. For the Lord himself shall descend from heaven with a shout, with the voice of the archangel, and with the trump of God: and the dead in Christ shall rise first: Then *we which are alive and remain* shall be caught up together with them in the clouds, to meet the Lord in the air: and so shall we ever be with the Lord. [1 Thess 4:15-17, emphasis added].

Some forty years later, the writer of *First Clement* wrote, "Of a truth, soon and suddenly shall His will be accomplished, as the Scripture also bears witness, saying, 'Speedily will He come, and will not tarry;' and, 'The Lord shall suddenly come to His temple, even the Holy One, for whom ye look'" (Ch. 23). His contemporary Ignatius also thought the "last times" were coming. A hundred years after that, Tertullian said the second coming "impends over the world, now near its close" (*Apologetic*, Apology, Ch. 21).

So it's no surprise to see Conservative Laestadians talking the same way throughout the decades, starting with Laestadius himself in 1852:

> † "Through this awakening, a great grace has taken place in these last times of the world through which God has permitted us to have a foretaste of heavenly blessedness. Do not become again fastened to the world, you few souls, who have become freed from the world. Strive, hasten and endeavor, that through love of the world, the enemy would not be able to extinguish the spark of faith and love that has been kindled in your hearts, when the Lord Jesus came to kindle fire upon the earth. If the spark of living faith should go out, sparks may soon shoot from hell and set the whole world afire" (Reading Examination sermon; *Fourth Postilla*, 109).

† "There has been false godliness throughout times, but in the last times the enemy of the soul is more cunning for he comes in under the cover of better Christianity and penetrates among the living children of God and there begins his hidden work of scattering through false doctrine and heresy. There are the most certain signs of the end of the world" (*Siionin Lähetyslehti*, 1920).

"Here on earth, all do not await the appearing of Jesus. Here are such that fear it, for their consciences are defiled" (Havas [1936], 1).

† "The shadow of the antichrist is falling over mankind. The light of truth dims. Night is coming. Therefore in the work of the Lord, there is reason for haste!" (Havas [1940], 9)

† "There are so many dangers in these last times. They are times which are written in the Bible. The enemy is set loose, and he knows he has but a little time. Now is such a time. We are living in the evening of the time of visitation" (Alajoki [1966], 125).

† "It seems the closer the end comes, the less men care about their souls' salvation. Things of the world are more important. When believers have no time to come to the services of Christians this is a sign that the world is falling away from God. Also, the fear of God is disappearing in the world today. All manner of sin enslaves man. Shame of sin is disappearing. Men live openly the life of sin. Immorality is rapidly rising. Marriages are broken, families are torn apart, children are rejected, and dishonesty grows. Greediness, selfishness, and all manner of disobediences are seen. Civil laws are forsaken. Drinking, fighting, murder, and other acts of violence are everyday news. The children of God look at all this and wonder how long God will endure this wickedness of man" (Alajoki [1968]).

† "The world is literally crowding with events and acts to fulfill the Scriptures; its predictions about the approaching end. No matter how one considers it, the future is not a happy prospect. How fortunate are those who now can finish the 'course' and go home! When I consider the future, the fear fills my heart, can I resist and fight the enemy until the end?" (*Greetings of Peace*, 1/1968).

In the 1980s, as the prospect of nuclear armageddon still loomed and the second millenium drew to a close, I remember hearing in many an apocalyptic sermon that we were living in the "Saturday evening" of God's work week. There was a strong impression conveyed that the end might well come at any moment. The following quote provides an example of this sentiment as well as the "Saturday evening" mentality:

> ✝ The statement, "Little children, it is the last time" in 1 John 2:18 "indicates that the last two-day period of God's week began with the birth of Jesus. Now this period has advanced so far towards evening that the signpost of the times is written on the calender as 1970. The entire period has been prophesied to be full of temptations, but especially the evening is so perilous, that if it were possible, even the elect would be deceived" (Arvo Perala, *Greetings of Peace*, 8/1970).

The quoted writer attempts to wedge his "last two-day period of God's week" symbolism into John's text without any appreciation that John (whoever he was)–like Jesus (see **Mark 13**), Paul, and the writer of 2 Peter–expected that he really was, literally, living in "the last time." Indeed, the full context of the passage Perala quotes makes that clear: "Little children, it is the last time: and as ye have heard that antichrist shall come, even now are there many antichrists; whereby we know that it is the last time."

Another writer whose imagination was better at spotting signs of the end times than anticipating the conversions of Africans and South Americans wrote,

> ✝ "We are living during very tumultuous times, but also very fascinating times, for we are privileged to witness the realization of God's prophecies of the return of His nation . . . As we dear Christians now consider these signs of the approach of the 'eternal spring,' let us be glad and watchful. We are the last of the Gentiles" (VOZ, 5/1975).

Then, it was still apparently believed among Conservative Laestadians that the world had only been around for some 6,000 years, because that timeframe was mapped into Creation-week symbolism, with the "1,000 years as one day" passage of 2 Pet 3:8 providing a handy scaling factor. It's actually not a new view of things. *The Epistle of Barnabus* asserts that "the Lord will finish all things in six thousand years, for a day is with

Him a thousand years" as part of an argument for the Christians' observance of the sabbath on Sunday rather than Saturday (Ch. 15).

For Ville Suutari, speaking here in 1976, the time from Adam until Noah occupied the first 2,000 years, from Noah until Christ the second 2,000 years, and from Christ until Judgment Day–well, it *had* almost been 2,000 years. At that point, on the end of the sixth day, the eternal Sabbath would begin:

> † "Here is a different mystery 'that one day is with the Lord as a thousand years and a thousand years as one day.' Peter [in 2 Pet. 3:8-16] speaks of two days. They are the days of the new covenant, those 2,000 years. The Old Testament had four days, nearly 4,000 years. Why does Peter speak of one day? Then had come the great time of peace when the kings came to govern! The laws of the lands were drawn up to protect freedom of living faith. It is for this reason that this one day has been separated and named. It has been predicted in the prophets: the swords will be made into plowshares, spears into scythes, no one will raise arms against another. The time of martyrs was to end this way. . . . We are now living the end of this 1,000 years. The Book of Revelations says of this that Satan was bound for 1,000 years. When 1,000 years have passed, Satan was released and then he will approach the nations of the world, to gather all the pagans into war whose numbers are as of the sands of the sea. This spiritual war is now on."

As the decades wore on, the drumbeat became quieter, although the last of the following quotes attests to the fact that eschatology remains part of the movement's worldview.

> † "This year, 1976 has been a year of many developments. We must say that the Scriptures are being rapidly fulfilled. The events of the world are achieving a feverish pitch of haste, the approach of the end is evident to many who would even favor ignoring this unpleasant prospect" (VOZ, 12/1976).

> † "Oh, how tiring it is to note that perilous times are at hand. . . . The predictions of the Bible are coming true in the so-called spiritual world. The wound that Luther struck in the beast during the Reformation appears to be healing. 'And I saw a beast. . .And I saw one of his heads as it were wounded to death; and his

deadly wound was healed...' Ecumenism and the religious disorder appear to be gathering strength. Now there is still external freedom to confess living faith in spite of this, but we do observe the signs of the time [Rev 20:7-9]" (*Päivämies* No. 6, 1978).

† "It is yet for a short moment that the Word of God will be preached upon this Earth. The sun of grace is now on the horizon; we laborers can hear the evening bells chime. Soon will come the final call beckoning us from the fields to begin the Sabbath rest. When the sun finally sets, no more will the gospel be preached unto mankind" (VOZ, 7/1990).

† "The signs [of the last times] are evident in both the outward and spiritual worlds. They are also in God's kingdom. Nevertheless, Christ will come unexpectedly. Ordinary workday life will continue until the end. . . . All of the Scriptural teachings regarding the last times are dominated by the admonition to watch and the warning against being led astray. We want to believe so that we will be ready to receive Christ. Ahead of us is a journey on which we will depart unexpectedly" (Uljas 2000, 121-22).

† "When a person in living faith is able to reflect on the present world around us, we know that the Second Coming of Christ must be at hand. In our time we see that the floodgates of sin have been opened wide, and we are–as was Lot–vexed by the life of sin around us. . . . We are living times like those of Noah" (VOZ, 11/2008).

Fundamentalism looks back to a "golden age" where man was in communion with God before man succumbed to Satan and ruined everything (Herriot 2009, 201). "However, the present age has plumbed new depths of depravity. The rot has really set in in modern times. True religion is threatened as never before by the Enemy, dressed up in a variety of garbs. Such a dire state of affairs indicates that the Almighty will surely soon intervene" (p. 201). Luther was saying that kind of thing 500 years ago: "The world cannot stand long, perhaps a hundred years at the outside" (*Table Talk* §759). The apocalyptic Conservative Laestadian preachers of past decades said it with great urgency. And I have no doubt that there will be fundamentalists saying it for generations to come.

4.8.3 Eternity

> *Take from the church itself the threat and fear of hell and it becomes an extinct volcano.*
>
> —Robert G. Ingersoll, *Ghosts*

Laestadius begins this sample of quotes about heaven and hell with the idea that there is a special place in hell reserved for those who should have known better:

> † "If hell is not a nice place for those who never have come to the knowledge of salvation, it surely is still hotter for those, who have once tasted the tribulations of hell and yet want to go there to eternal death. It must become still hotter for those who have had a foretaste of the kingdom of heaven and then return to the world from where the way leads to hell" (Laestadius, Twenty-second Sunday after Trinity sermon [1853]; *Fourth Postilla*, 172).

Justin Martyr leaves evidence of early Christian belief in a graded hell. In his *First Apology*, he says "we believe (or rather, indeed, are persuaded) that every man will suffer punishment in eternal fire according to the merit of his deed, and will render account according to the power he has received from God" (Ch. 17).

The promises of heaven were quite eloquent in the early days of Laestadianism. The Finns and Finnish immigrants to America had difficult and exhausting lives, which must have made the afterlife seem that much more appealing:

> † "Press onward, travelers! Do not tire of crying out so long as an edge of the sun is still visible! Soon you will arrive unto the Father in the Homeland where your weary bones may rest! Run yet to the end of this last quarter mile! Lift up your eyes and behold: already coming into view are the homes in the New Jerusalem! There the candles burn in crystal holders, the voices of the elect children begin to be heard and all God's children there await the new travelers, soon to arrive!" (Laestadius, First Rogation Day sermon [1859]; *Fourth Postilla*, 86).

> † "Blessed is he who gets into that grace-boat, where the bloody flag waves, before the signal to move to the home harbor is given. The eternal fiery sea of the wrath of God remains burning and all

who were not found written in the book of life, they were cast into the sea of fire. But the righteous can rejoice in the brightness of the new heaven and the new earth, where eternal righteousness and peace dwell. Where the tear-streams have dried up, all lackings and temptations ended. The notes of victory sound out from the lips of God's children. Glory-wreaths shine upon their heads. There is time to wonder, time to greet and to rejoice in the midst of the chosen. There they all leap for joy and endlessly praise their Bridegroom Holy, holy" (Matti Suo [1861-1927], from *Greetings of Peace*, 5/1964).

✝ "As you soon bow to this low supper table [for Communion], your eyes are tear stained because of the wickedness of the world and your own wretchedness; but once will begin such as supper where no one will weep. From this cold world's crust will rise a white robed throng; a glorified flock of supper guests. The Father will be there to receive them. He will wipe away the last tear from the eyes of the very last travelers" (Havas [1934], 33).

✝ "We know that death for a Christian is only a moment of calm sleep from which we awaken to heaven's joy. The grave is a warm bed which our Savior with tender hands has prepared for his own. In the graves, many beloved ones sleep, those who have departed as blessed. They are at rest. One day they will rise glorified to the wedding of the Lamb" (*Lasten Siioni* [1941], from VOZ, 4/1976).

✝ "Soon we shall be freed from this sin corrupted body, and sinless and perfect, like unto Christ, we shall be gathered with all the Saints at that great gathering where all poor feelings, doubts, and misgivings will be no more. But we shall completely comprehend the great love of our Saviour" (Paul Heideman, *Greetings of Peace*, 10/1942).

Then, probably as a coincidence of my sampling, we get a helping of fire and brimstone for the next several decades. I don't think there was any new emphasis on the damnation part of eternity–Laestadius certainly wasn't bashful about threatening it.

✝ "Modern children of the world do not tolerate the mention of judgment and the agony of hell. Such speech is considered old-fashioned and not enlightened. If someone dares to make known to a religiously minded person of our day the judgment of the wicked, according to the old folks' Word of God, jest is made of sermons that 'smell of brimstone.' Jesus is that 'old-fashioned' that He speaks of the furnace of fire into which people shall be cast and says 'There shall be wailing and gnashing of teeth'" (O.H. Jussila, *Greetings of Peace*, 4/1944).

✝ On Judgment Day "the righteous shall stand with great courage against those who have spurned them and rejected their labors. The days of lamentation shall end for the righteous and begin for the ungodly. Then you, a poor one of the Lord, may conclude your believing and begging, when you sit at your place at the communion table, where the Lord Jesus shall serve you forever" (Taskila 1961, 22).

✝ "Jesus admonishes His believers to watch in faith, love and unity of spirit also in the parable of the ten virgins and does not permit the door of the wedding-house to be closed from even one who strives to come in, not even from a heretic who has received the grace of repentance. He Himself closes it. And the people of God do not want to close it, for they know that the door is not closed day or night (Rev 21:25) as long as this world stands and Jesus is on His mercy-seat through the Holy Ghost in the kingdom of His children. But as soon as he moves from His mercy-seat to His judgment-seat, no one is pardoned nor taken in" (Eino Rimpiläinen, *Greetings of Peace*, 6/1963).

✝ "Woe to the ungodly on that moment when in a wink of an eye the Son of God comes to judge, when they shall have to sink to eternal distress. It is too late to repent. Hasten therefore, unbeliever, to the children of God to repent" (*Päivämies*, 1973).

The writer of this next quote fails to see the irony in his attempt to talk about God's love in the same sentence as eternal torment:

✝ The children of God "still rebuke people for their sins, through the insistence of God's love, and urge them to repent so that the human soul would not fall into eternal torment of hell" (VOZ, 6/1979).

God is the one who created this hell from which he "through the insistence of his love" is trying to save people. And he has chosen what has proved to be a highly ineffective mechanism for doing so, if the tiny number of conversions to Conservative Laestadianism is any indication.

I was 11 years old when Uno Makela said the following terrifying words, and I might well have been there in the audience to hear them:

> ☦ "Shall you experience eternal joy or shall you be cast into eternal damnation? These are great matters to consider. Eternity is long and if one must depart during this time of grace having sins upon the heart, that is, sins are not forgiven, he shall stand before the fiery-eyed judge and hear those terrible words: 'Depart from me ye cursed into that everlasting fire which has been prepared for the devil and his angels'" (Uno Makela, sermon given 1980).

Hearing all that during my childhood certainly had an impact on me. Whether by design or not, that sort of talk sets up a lifetime of coerced worship, or to reverse the order of words in 1 John 4:18, "perfect fear that casts out all love." Marlene Winell calls it the "most powerful technique of fundamentalism," a "terror tactic":

> Fundamentalism teaches the existence of hell, a place of eternal torment. If you do not believe in Jesus Christ as your personal savior, you are doomed.... Even other, non-fundamentalist Christians are considered lost. This appeal capitalizes on the natural fear people have of death, making it much worse with horrible images of everlasting torture. "Fire-and-brimstone" preachers have long known the power of such an approach. Especially for children, with their vivid imaginations and unclear notions of reality, the imagery of a fiery hell is intensely frightening. [1993, 64]

As a psychologist, Winell notes that it could easily be seen as abusive for a parent to threaten a child with such tortures *before* death. "But fundamentalist preachers have no shame about describing with relish the 'weeping and gnashing of teeth' that God will mete out to sinners," which, I would add, God will continue doing *forever*. "The fear of hell is frequently powerful enough to keep the person trying to conform" (p. 64). Even after leaving Christianity (with as much intellectual backing for his decision as anyone could really hope to have), Bart Ehrman was gripped by the fear of death for years and says "there are still moments when I wake up at night in a cold sweat," so deeply was the view of hell driven into him (2008, 127).

The book *By Faith* does its part to put this terror into the hearts of hundreds of confirmation students every year, citing the Bible as its source:

> † "A person is spiritually dead when his soul is in the state of unbelief.... When the spiritually dead person confronts temporal death he becomes forever separated from God. Eternal death is irrevocable: the fate of such a person is sealed eternally. According to the Bible, in hell or perdition begins anguish and torment that shall last forever" (p. 93).

But the idea of hell is actually only supported by a few passages in the New Testament. Even there, the reference is often to *Gehenna*, a garbage dump on the outskirts of Jerusalem where the bodies of those denied a proper burial were burned. The Old Testament has *absolutely nothing* to say about any place of eternal torment. Indeed, it is inconsistent even about the existence of any afterlife. Where it does discuss what if anything happens after death (well after the five books of Moses), it makes a pretty good case that there is no difference between the final destination of the righteous and the wicked. See my notes regarding **1 Sam 28:19, 2 Sam 12:23, 1 Kings 11:43, 2 Chron 9-14, Job 3:13-19, Ecclesiastes 9:2-3, Ezekiel 25:17.**

Ingersoll states the matter with his usual irreverent clarity. Despite the flaws of the Old Testament, "with all its stories of murder and massacre; with all its foolish and cruel fables; with all its infamous doctrines; with its spirit of caste; with its spirit of hatred," he said it was better than the New Testament in one important respect. In the Old Testament,

> when God got a man dead, He let him alone. When He saw him quietly in his grave He was satisfied. The muscles relaxed, and a smile broke over the Divine face. But in the new testament the trouble commences just at death. In the new testament God is to wreak His revenge forever and ever. It was reserved for one who said, "Love your enemies," to tear asunder the veil between time and eternity and fix the horrified gaze of men upon the gulfs of eternal fire. [*Lecture on Orthodoxy*]

So we are left with the threat whose import is so horrible as to seemingly remain impervious to any assault of evidence or logic:

> ✝ "This is a great question in the midst of man: Where will I spend eternity? Is it there where there is everlasting joy or is it there where there is everlasting suffering? This is a question that man himself must make. Where will I spend eternity which has no end?" (Uno Makela, sermon given 1985).
>
> ✝ "Soon will come the final call beckoning us from the fields to begin the Sabbath rest. When the Sun finally sets, no more will the gospel be preached unto mankind. Oh, how great will be the sorrow of those who reject this calling!" (VOZ, 7/1990).

And how great will be the confusion of those who never even heard that calling! The vast majority of mankind will supposedly wake up in hell wondering what hit them.

> ✝ "After this life, the loss of a soul is irrecoverable, and no compensation can be made for it any longer. Jesus points out the time when all this will become manifest, when the 'Son of Man' will appear with all of His angels to execute judgment. Christ will then reward every person according to his works. There is no way to escape the righteous judgment of God. The only work acceptable to God is faith upon His Son, Christ Jesus" (VOZ, 6/2001).
>
> ✝ "[E]ven those who sleep in the dust of the earth will awaken, some to everlasting life, and some to shame and everlasting contempt. On that day there will be only two groups. There will be those who have attempted to justify themselves through the carnal mind and the works of the flesh. Dear child of God, you will be found in that other group, where you have been able to wash your robes in the blood of the Lamb, and believe the gospel preached in God's kingdom" (VOZ, 11/2005).

The last quote once again resorts to caricature (**4.2.3**). Conservative Laestadianism condemns to eternal torment the billions of sincere, pious believers in other religions who have died and will die utterly ignorant of its doctrine. Is it necessary to also caricature them as making misguided attempts at their justification when they are simply attempting to achieve salvation via the spiritual framework they were taught from childhood?

4.9 The Problem of Evil

> *I form the light, and create darkness: I make peace, and create evil: I the LORD do all these things.*
>
> —The Book of Isaiah

4.9.1 An Ancient Dilemma

> *Is God willing to prevent evil but not able? Then he is impotent. Is he able but not willing? Then he is malevolent. Is he both able and willing? Whence, then, evil?*
>
> —Epicurus [c. 300 B.C.]

The problem of evil has troubled believers in an omnipotent God since antiquity. It has been discussed extensively enough to acquire its own name, *theodicy*. The epigraph above states the dilemma: An omnipotent God *could* prevent all evil, and an omnibenevolent (all-loving) God *would* prevent it. So it is a logical impossibility for God to have both properties in the world full of evil that undeniably surrounds us. It won't do to offer up the old platitude, "nothing is impossible with God," because the issue is *our conception* of God's nature. That result of human thinking is far from divine, and the combination of omnipotence and omnibenevolence is just one of its several impossibilities.

As I mention in **4.4.1** regarding God's nature, *no* entity can possess these conflicting properties, any more than a circle can have corners. If an object has corners, its shape is not a circle no matter how hard you squint at it. It may be a wonderful, precious, fine object. Perhaps it's made of gold, or extremely rare. But it still is not a circle, no matter what, because of the corners it possesses.

So, like it or not, we are left grappling with the problem of suffering, for which there is no easy answer. "It is an open sore that theology can never pretend to heal" (Haught 2000, 55). Ingersoll noted that "many eminent men" had endeavored to harmonize the existence of evil with the "infinite power and goodness of God," but concluded that they had "succeeded only in producing learned and ingenious failures" (*Lecture on Gods*). I think the discussion below will make it clear that no progress has been made in the hundred years since he said that.

4.9.2 Soteriology

> *If salvation is available only to Christians, then the gospel isn't good news at all. For most of the human race, it is terrible news.*
>
> —Rachel Held Evans, *Evolving in Monkey Town*

"Soteriology" is a fancy word referring to the study of religious doctrines of salvation. David Myers describes the "soteriological problem of evil" as a "special instance of the problem of evil":

> According to orthodox Christianity, there is no salvation apart from Christ. To put it more explicitly, apart from faith in Christ Jesus as saviour ... , one is condemned to hell. Orthodox Christianity is thus a form of exclusivism. From this perspective, it appears that all non-Christians are damned. [2003, 407]

Myers discusses three categories of non-Christians. First, there are those non-Christians who are simply "ignorant of Christ and never have an opportunity to accept or reject him." Second, some are "aware of the salvific role attributed to Jesus" but "reject Christ because they grow up in and uncritically accept another religious tradition." And, finally, there are "those who, after critical reflection, deliberately reject Christ" (p. 407). Myers asks why "members of any of these categories of non-believers deserve to be eternally punished":

> The eternal punishment of all non-Christians simply because they are non-believers, regardless of the reasons for their non-belief, seems arbitrary and ultimately unjust. This is called the soteriological problem of evil because it calls into question the justice of a doctrine of salvation. While the traditional problem of evil focuses on the suffering of the innocent in this world, the soteriological problem of evil focuses on the suffering of the innocent in the next world. If there are any inculpable non-believers in hell, there is eternal innocent suffering. [pp. 407-408]

The first category seems particularly troubling: "How can those who never have an opportunity to hear the Gospel message be justly condemned for not accepting Christ? In what sense can they be said to be guilty of disbelief if they never make a free decision to shut out God's mercy?" (p. 409). But the second category has problems, too:

> The power of early religious education seems undeniable. Schopenhauer points out that if religious education begins early enough, by adulthood a person will be, in effect, inoculated against other religions: she will tend to judge other religions against the standard of the home religion and find them wanting. [pp. 411-12]

Myers points to the example of how conventional Muslims (over a fifth of the world's population) reject the claim "that Jesus is the divine saviour." They may be aware of the claim, but "they have also been effectively conditioned to believe that the doctrine of the divinity of Jesus is blasphemous. Isn't it therefore unreasonable to hold that they can, in good conscience, freely choose Jesus as their saviour?" (p. 412).

Regarding the third category, seemingly the least troublesome, Myers says, "If someone really had convincing evidence that salvation comes through Christ alone and that failure to accept Christ's offer of salvation will result in eternal punishment, would she really be free to decline to believe?" Yet most of the few people who truly have the opportunity for "critical reflection" do in fact decline. That is true not just in Myers's framework of merely accepting *Christ*, but also in the far narrower one of accepting Conservative Laestadian *Christianity*. There are few conversions into the movement, and most of them seem to occur with little understanding of its doctrinal nuances. If the evidence were truly persuasive, that would not be the case: "Indeed, wouldn't this offer be difficult, if not impossible, to refuse?" (p. 416).

Suffering "in the next world is said to be endless," so the soteriological problem of evil is actually more serious "than the suffering of the innocent in this world" (p. 408), infinitely more serious, in fact. This quote from a 1974 issue of *Päivämies* touches ever so slightly on the issue, but quickly finds itself spinning into logical oblivion:

> † "Many have asked: 'Since God knew the plans of the enemy of the soul and besides this knew what would befall man, then why did God undertake to create man at all.' But if God would have canceled His plans, He would have confessed the enemy of the soul as Lord, but almighty God was not about to do this.... So God did not in the least permit the enemy of the soul to interfere with His plans or their fulfillment. On the other hand, God did not desire that man go to perdition through the deceit of the enemy of the soul. For that reason, the Father, Son and Holy

Spirit held a consultation in heaven before creation began. Then the Lord Jesus promised the heavenly Father that He would redeem fallen mankind with His own blood and the work of the Holy Spirit was to sanctify corrupted man to be acceptable for heaven."

God created uncounted billions of human beings with the full knowledge that he was going to damn almost all of them. It's like breeding puppies for the sole purpose of slowly torturing them, and making yourself feel better about it by sparing the one or two that manage to find a well-hidden squeak toy. And why? To save face in a grudge match with the enemy of the soul, whom an omnipotent God (4.4.1) could just squash underfoot like any other opponent if he really wanted to. If the issue weren't so serious, the *Päivämies* quote would be laughable. And it doesn't mention anything about Conservative Laestadian exclusivity (4.2.1), a nasty bit of doctrine that makes the problem all the more awful. It's not just most people who are damned for not "accepting Christ," but *almost all of them* for not being part of a tiny, almost unknown sect.

Please stop and ponder this for a moment: What possible justification could there be for blaming those who are innocently ignorant–all but a tiny fraction of the billions of people who live to the age of accountability–for *never even hearing about* the only possible way to be saved? And the consequence to them is an eternity of unimaginably horrible torture? It's not even punishment. There is no opportunity for rehabilitation, ever. It's not about deterrence, either, because almost all of those being tortured had no idea that such a fate was in store for them, much less how to avoid it. No, it is just the most unimaginably cruel and pointless sadism, from a God we are told is loving and gracious:

> † "Throughout time God has shown His unfathomable love toward mankind, the crown of His creation" (VOZ, 12/2008).
>
> † God "loved us so much that by His grace, He gave His only Son Jesus to save us from our sins" (VOZ, 9/2009).

If you can simply accept that by faith, then nothing else I've pointed out in this book could possibly be of the slightest impact. Luther says that God "conceals His eternal mercy and loving-kindness behind His eternal wrath: His righteousness, behind apparent iniquity" (*Bondage of the Will*, §24), but I think what's really happening is that unquestioning faith is being concealed behind meaningless platitudes about God's nature. If it works for you, congratulations: You have a bulletproof faith that is impregnable to any argument, any problem, any inconsistency whatsoever. I'm surprised you've read this far, but please continue long enough to consider Robert M. Price's impassioned wish

> to make fundamentalists see that they are defaming and blaspheming God by crowning him the Lord of Damnation. I urge them to stop spreading the slander that God is planning to torment most of his hapless creatures in an eternal hell. Don't get holier-than-thou with *me*, if *this* is what you are preaching. It is *you* who need to repent, Hellmonger, not me! It is you who are blaspheming the Spirit by calling all other religions false, not me, buster! Born-again Christians need to have the shoe placed on the other foot, where in fact it belongs. [2006b, 196]

4.9.3 Predestination

> *This is the highest degree of faith–to believe that He is merciful who saves so few and damns so many; to believe Him just, who according to His own will, makes us necessarily damnable . . .*
>
> —Martin Luther, *The Bondage of the Will*

Predestination is the view advanced by Luther and taken up by John Calvin [1509-1564] that God "chooses some to be saved and rejects the others without an apparent reason for either choice" (Althaus 1963, 274). Luther's hero Augustine had actually discussed and accepted the idea of "Divine foreknowledge" in both salvation and damnation a thousand years earlier (Kirk 1966, 340-41). But it was Calvin's unabashed articulation of predestination in all its horror that resulted in the label of *Calvinism*.[46]

Luther spent an entire tedious book arguing that God "foresees, purposes, and does all things according to His immutable, eternal, and infallible will" (*Bondage of the Will*, §9). That includes what Luther

---

46. It also resulted in Bill Watterson's choice of name for the lovable but incorrigible little brat in the comic strip *Calvin and Hobbes*. Calvin's stuffed tiger was named after Thomas Hobbes, a philosopher having what Watterson called "a dim view of human nature."

acknowledges to seem "iniquitous, cruel, intolerable," that God "should, of His mere will, leave men, harden them, and damn them, as though He delighted in the sins, and in the great and eternal torments of the miserable" (§94).

The whole repulsive idea "has given offence to so many and great men of so many ages," Luther says. "And who would not be offended?", he continues, "I myself have been offended more than once, even unto the deepest abyss of desperation; nay, so far, as even to wish that I had never been born a man." But then the Stockholm Syndrome takes over, and he says he "was brought to know how healthful that desperation was, and how near it was unto grace" (§94). Terrified by the monstrosity he has made God out to be, Luther spends page after page bowing before his tormentor and trying to rationalize its cruelty:

> [A] man cannot be thoroughly humbled, until he comes to know that his salvation is utterly beyond his own powers, counsel, endeavours, will, and works, and absolutely depending on the will, counsel, pleasure, and work of another, that is, of God only.
>
> If . . . I could by any means comprehend how that same God can be merciful and just, who carries the appearance of so much wrath and iniquity, there would be no need of faith. But now, since that cannot be comprehended, there is room for exercising faith, while such things are preached and openly proclaimed: in the same manner as, while God kills, the faith of life is exercised in death. [§24]

What Luther fails to realize is that "unconditional, eternal predestination both to salvation and to damnation" (Althaus 1963, 275) makes it *utterly pointless* to "be humbled" and "have faith." H.C. Lea noted the irony of predestination being taught "while men were earnestly urged to win God's favor by good works and repentance and amendment and to earn salvation through the sacraments, as though the freedom of the will had never been questioned and predestination had never been heard of." He considered the power to bind and loose from sins "a figment" if man "were predestined to bliss or to perdition" (Lea 1896, 98).

As Lea observes, the system relegates us to being mere predestinated puppets. Luther's cherished humility and faith are not means to any end, but just futile motions we go through at the hands of the divine puppet master, who has long since decided which of the two boxes he will be tossing us into at the end of his scripted show.

Which is it?

The following two quotes from sermons given two years apart by the same preacher illustrate how the opposite viewpoints of God's will about man's salvation have been taught:

> † "Our heavenly Father, according to the Scriptures, wishes that none would perish, but all would come unto repentance and receive eternal life. So this will of the Father is made known yet today through His kingdom here on this earth, and through this kingdom is that voice of the Good Shepherd which is calling sinners unto repentance" (Dan Rintamaki, sermon given 1978).

> † "So, we might ask, how does one receive living faith? We must say that it is a grace gift of God, who, according to His own will and purpose, according to His Word, calls whom He will call and hardens whom He will harden. So we can see that it is only of the pure grace of God that one has been called" (Dan Rintamaki, sermon given 1980).

In one viewpoint, God "wishes that none would perish, but all would come unto repentance and receive eternal life." In the other, just a few have "received living faith." They are the lucky beneficiaries of a "grace gift" according to the "will and purpose" of God who "calls whom He will call and hardens whom He will harden." There is an irreconcilable conflict here that is simply not acknowledged, perhaps because the conflict is also present in the Bible itself.

God's desire that all would come to repentance is expressed in the following passages:

- **Ezekiel 18:23-32 and 33:11** (No pleasure in death of the wicked);

- Luke 15:1 (Joy in heaven over one sinner who repents);

- John 3:16-17 ("For God sent not his Son into the world to condemn the world; but that the world through him might be saved");

- Acts 10:34-43 ("God is no respecter of persons: but in every nation he that feareth him, and worketh righteousness, is accepted with him");

- 1 Timothy 2:1-6 (God "will have all men to be saved, and to come unto the knowledge of the truth");

- 2 Peter 3:1 (The Lord is "not willing that any should perish, but that all should come to repentance");

- 1 John 2:1 (Jesus is the propitiation "for the sins of the whole world");

- Revelation 3:19 (Jesus knocks, "if any man hear my voice, and open the door, I will come in to him, and will sup with him, and he with me").

Contrast that with these passages:

- Isaiah 6:10-12 (Make people's ears heavy and eyes shut "lest they see with their eyes, and hear with their ears, and understand with their heart, and convert, and be healed");

- **Mark 4:11-12** (Mystery of the kingdom given to the disciples, but things done in parables to outsiders, that "seeing they may see, and not perceive; and hearing they may hear, and not understand; lest at any time they should be converted, and their sins should be forgiven them");

- Luke 10:21-24 (Jesus thanks God for hiding teachings from the wise and prudent, says "no man knoweth who the Son is, but the Father; and who the Father is, but the Son, and he to whom the Son will reveal him");

- John 6:64-65 (Jesus "knew from the beginning who they were that believed not," says "no man can come unto me, except it were given unto him of my Father");

- Acts 13:48 ("[A]s many as were ordained to eternal life believed");

- Romans 8:28-30 ("For whom he did foreknow, he also did predestinate to be conformed to the image of his Son . . . whom he did predestinate, them he also called");

- Romans 9:15-18 ("For he saith to Moses, I will have mercy on whom I will have mercy, and I will have compassion on whom I will have compassion. So then it is not of him that willeth, nor of him that runneth, but of God that sheweth mercy");

- Ephesians 1:3-6 (God "predestinated us unto the adoption of children by Jesus Christ to himself, according to the good pleasure of his will");

- 2 Thessalonians 2:11-12 ("God shall send them strong delusion, that they should believe a lie: That they all might be damned who believed not the truth, but had pleasure in unrighteousness")

- 1 Peter 1:1-2 ("Elect according to the foreknowledge of God the Father").

The Calvinist View

Predestination didn't start with Calvin or even Luther, though those two men are responsible for much of its continued prominence. Besides Augustine with his "Divine foreknowledge" mentioned above, we can see an early example from Justin Martyr, who referred to God's foreknowledge when attempting to explain Jesus' failure to return as expected: "For the reason why God has delayed to do this, is His regard for the human race. For He foreknows that some are to be saved by repentance, some even that are perhaps not yet born" (*First Apology*, Ch. 28).

Conservative Laestadianism eventually attempts to soften the blow with some talk from the other perspective, about God's desire for all to be saved. But for Laestadius, predestination of the "elect" was only one aspect of a harsh and unyielding theology:

> † "Our hope is that those few elect who remain in their most precious faith until the end, shall rejoice on Mt. Sion when the great Crossbearer holds the wedding with His bride. Then the bridesmaids leap as the hart and rejoice eternally. They sing a new hymn to God and the Lamb on Mt. Sion together with the hundred and forty-four thousand elect ones and eat fruit from the tree of life which refreshes their thirst now and eternally" (Laestadius, Mary's Day sermon [1851]; *Fourth Postilla*, 195).

> † "The apostles preached repentance and forgiveness of sins, but God made the Christians. In this thought even yet, it is encouraging to do the work of God's Kingdom. We weak travelers of the narrow way try to reveal to unbelievers their dangerous condition, but we cannot awaken one conscience. The Lord does it under the sermons of repentance. We proclaim the

ministry of reconciliation, the full redemption work of Christ according to the authority which we have received, but at the same time we have knowledge of this, that we cannot give faith to any penitent heart. Only the Lord does that through the gospel we preach" (Havas [1935], 23).

O.H. Jussila [1888-1955], the son of Heikki Jussila [1863-1955], addresses the question of why Jesus praised God that the news of redemption is hidden from some (see the discussion of Mark 4:11 in **7.1**):

> † "[W]hy did Doesn't God want to expose it to all? Does He purposely condemn some to remain lost? God truly desires that everyone should come to the knowledge of truth and be saved. If salvation could be obtained through learning and knowledge, then the babes would have neither chance nor part. They would have to remain hopeless in their own helplessness. Where could he find help who cannot trust to his own ability? Where would he turn in his distress who is dejected by his own imperfection? What would happen to the laboring and heavy laden, who find no rest by reason of their own pilgrimage? They would have no helper, the wise and learned would not bother to help them, rather, they trample the weak under their feet. Jesus rejoices over the good portion of these poor ones. God is on their side" (O.H. Jussila, *Greetings of Peace*, 11/1943).

He asks an excellent question but his attempt to answer it rings hollow. Almighty God would like to extend salvation to everyone but, alas, he is unable to do so because the "wise and learned" would, if included, "trample the weak under their feet"? Such trampling might be feared by people who suspect they aren't so wise or learned, but saying that God *must* condemn those who might do it because he lacks any better options is not only ridiculous, but insulting to the idea of God's omnipotence.

> † "God in His all-knowing wisdom still has elect ones to whom He wants to open His arms of grace. Since He has so richly blessed the candlesticks and throng of callers during this time of doctrinal winds, it shows that the time of this visitation will continue in our land and that the elect are being gathered with haste and the grain fields ripen and whiten for the harvest" (Jussila 1948, 105).

In a sermon published in the August 1956 *Greetings of Peace*, Lauri Taskila referred to Romans 8:30:

> † "It says here, 'Whom he did predestinate, them he called and whom he called, them he also justified.' God has called. God has sounded this call, as Jesus has said, 'many are called but few are chosen.' Here it mentions concerning those who have been called and those who have been chosen. But why is it not the called ones have been chosen [*sic.*]? It certainly is not that God does not want to save all people. The will of God is that all would turn to repentance and that all would be saved. But the reason why all have not been chosen is this: People have been disobedient to heaven's call." After a discourse on Jesus' parable of the wedding of the King's son, in which people gave various excuses for why they couldn't attend, Taskila asked, "What has been your excuse, you who still tonight listen to the Word of God with an unbelieving heart, you who have been called by God many times, but to this day you are not in the flock of the chosen ones? God has not been able to choose you through his gospel because you have not accepted the grace of election."

According to that viewpoint, the puny mortal who rejects the "grace of election" is more powerful than God, who "has not been able to choose" that person, notwithstanding that "the will of God is that all would turn to repentance."

Flirting with Free Will

Calvinism is sickening. The idea of God creating people with the intent to torture them forever violates the most basic of our own standards of decency, especially when you are forced to believe that he has created the vast majority of humankind with exactly that diabolical plan in mind. Ed Babinski said that he could not "conceive of any reasonably good person maintaining an eternal concentration camp, let alone God Himself" (2003, 214).

Neither could some of the biblical authors, nor some of the preachers who have expounded upon their writings. An early example is Ignatius, who wrote in his *Epistle to the Philadelphians* [*c.* 100 A.D.] that "our God is a lover of mankind, and 'will have all men to be saved, and to come to the knowledge of the truth.'" (Ch. 3). Despite its overt commitment to Luther's teachings, including those about predestination, Conservative

Laestadianism flirts with a version of "free will" that softens the rough edges of raw Calvinism:

> † "Paul said that God wants all men to be saved and that they would come to the knowledge of the truth. Therefore it is not the will of God that anyone be lost. He has not prepared hell for men, but for the devil and his angels. Of course, it is the will of many men to die blessed, but the world is dear and its vanishing course is pleasing where slavishness and scorn of men keep them from repentance" (Taskila 1961, 58-59).

God wants all men to be saved, and it's not his will that anyone would be lost! It sounds a lot nicer, doesn't it? So does this:

> † "It is grace of grace that yet in the kingdom of God flow living waters of life. To all who seek with sincere heart and truly desire to be obedient to the Will of the Father in Heaven, the doors of grace are still open day and night. Open your heart to ask: does grace still belong to me, and you will find that even the angels in Heaven are moved and will praise God that one more soul has received grace and peace through the forgiveness of sins in the name and blood of Christ" (VOZ, 1/1975).

The writer of the following quote doesn't try to dismiss the idea of God's elect, but says that God had not named his elect "by name," a vacuous idea if I ever heard one. Is there some sort of take-a-number system in place like at the auto licensing office? And the disturbing question of predestination he deflects by simply designating those fortunate enough to be reading his words as God's elect:

> † "What does God's Word say about His chosen or elect people? First of all, there are no 'ifs' or guesswork, as to who are God's elect according to the Word of God. Secondly, nowhere in the Bible can one find anyone's name printed boldly that he or she is God's elect. Had God named by name those who are His elect, then He would not have had to send His only begotten Son here to suffer and die on this Earth. . . . All we have to do is accept Him as our Savior; believe and be obedient to His will. In so doing, we will be found in the flock of God's chosen; whom Jesus calls His own. It is you, my dear brother and sister in faith, who is God's elect. Even though you may feel yourself unworthy to be called the elect of God. Be of good comfort for God looks at us

through the redemption work of Christ and sees us as perfect in Him" (VOZ, 3/1975).

Again, we read that God's will is for all to repent:

> ✝ "The message of God's kingdom is still heard in today's world. It is God's will that no man would perish, but all would repent. The Heavenly Father awakens a person to his condition. The awakened one can turn to God's kingdom and confess his sins and ask that they be forgiven in the name of Christ" (VOZ, 12/1999).

The following writer goes all the way into "free will" territory, referencing Deuteronomy 30:19:

> ✝ "Our destiny in eternity depends on our present choice. Whosoever will save his life, by denying Christ, shall lose it: and whosoever is content to lose his life, by owning Christ, shall find it. Here are life or death, good or evil, a blessing or a curse, set before us" (VOZ, 6/2001).

Man having a choice about his "destiny in eternity" is inconsistent with Luther's teaching, repeated *ad nauseum* over hundreds of pages in *The Bondage of the Will*, that it is all up to God and man has no free will. But then one would think that God's "will that no man would perish, but all would repent," as quoted a few lines earlier (from VOZ, 12/1999), would wind up being fulfilled in more than 0.002% or so of the world's present population.

Thus, in their efforts to play up omnibenevolence, the preachers often forget about that other critical property, omnipotence:

> ✝ "The Heavenly Father prepares men's hearts to receive the Word, and desires that all men would seek Him" (VOZ, 8/2003).

> ✝ "Even now Jesus is calling sinners to repentance" (VOZ, 6/2006).

> ✝ "God wishes that all people would seek and find the Kingdom of God while it is a time of grace" (VOZ, 4/2009).

If an omnipotent (i.e., all-powerful) God desires something to happen, then it *will* happen. But it clearly is *not* happening:

> ✝ "[W]hen someone is truly seeking, when someone with a penitent heart is realizing their own sinfulness and seeking a gracious God, then God leads them to find the Kingdom, or He leads the kingdom to find them" (Jim Frantti, sermon given 2010).

I would guess that not much more than a thousand of all of the Conservative Laestadians now living are converts (most of them being in the mission fields outside Finland and North America). Out of *seven billion people*! Those who presume to tell us about God's wishes and capabilities in the face of this have to decide that either God is not really omnipotent, or that he really doesn't want everyone to seek him. Of course, neither is an attractive option for the believer to consider.

Frantti uses the excuse that none of the billions of people who have failed "to find the kingdom" have been "truly seeking." It is an outrageous statement, but it is probably the only way he can reconcile a universal view of Jesus' statement "Seek and ye shall find" (Mt 7:7) with the Conservative Laestadian exclusivity he must preach.

Ultimately, the Conservative version of "free will" is an effort to burnish the image of a loving God while allowing him to remain omnipotent (**4.4.1**). But with an exclusivity doctrine that has God ultimately condemning almost all of his created humanity to eternal torture, you just can't have it both ways.

4.9.4 Human Suffering

> *During the time that it took for this Christmas Eve service to conclude, more than 700 children in the world would have died of hunger; 250 others from drinking unsafe water; and nearly 300 other people from malaria. Not to mention the ones who had been raped, mutilated, tortured, dismembered, and murdered. Nor the innocent victims caught up in the human trade industry, nor the suffering throughout the world from grinding poverty, the destitute migrant farm workers in our own country, those who are homeless and afflicted with mental disease . . . And where is God?*
>
> —Bart Ehrman, *God's Problem*

The dilemma of God damning most of humanity is one created by theology. Regardless of how sincerely people might believe in the horror of eternal torment, it is not something that they have had reported to them as an actual occurrence. People enter into the silence of death providing us with no more indication that they are crying out in vain for the opportunity to warn us ("I have five brethren; that he may testify unto them, lest they also come into this place of torment," Lk 16:28) than that their fate was to simply "go hence, and be no more" (Psa 39:13) and then "know not any thing" (Eccl 9:5). But the suffering we know about all too well, right here on this planet, cannot be denied.

Even though I've been sheltered from it in my comfortable, relatively trouble-free life, the misery experienced every day by much of humankind comes to mind for me during church services just as Ehrman describes in the epigraph above. The preachers begin their sermons by praising God for his goodness and thanking him for the many "temporal blessings" that they and their comparatively prosperous congregations have enjoyed. But they either do not think or do not dare to ask God why he hasn't spread things around just a bit more evenly. As Ehrman asks poignantly in his book about theodicy, "By thanking God for your good fortune, aren't you implicating him for the misfortunes of others?" (2008, 130).

The Old Testament God certainly wasn't interested in equal-opportunity blessings. "This is the God of the patriarchs who answered prayer and worked miracles for his people; this is the God of the exodus who saved his suffering people from the misery of slavery in Egypt" (p. 5). In saving "his people," God didn't seem to care much about the Egyptians on whom he inflicted so much pain, terror, and death. In the New Testament, through Jesus, he "healed the sick, gave sight to the blind, made the lame walk, and fed those who were hungry." But where

> is this God now? If he came into the darkness and made a difference, why is there still no difference? Why are the sick still wracked with unspeakable pain? Why are babies still born with birth defects? Why are young children kidnapped, raped, and murdered? Why are there droughts that leave millions of starving, suffering horrible and excruciating lives that lead to horrible and excruciating deaths? If God intervenes to deliver the armies of Israel from its enemies, why doesn't he intervene now when the armies of sadistic tyrants savagely attack and destroy entire villages, towns, and even countries? If God is at work in the darkness, feeding the hungry with the miraculous

multiplication of loaves, why is it that one child–a mere child!–dies every 5 seconds of hunger? [Ehrman 2008, 5-6]

A doubting Charles Templeton wondered the same thing while contemplating "a photo in *Life* magazine of an African woman with a dead baby in her arms." "As he saw the desperation in her eyes, he asked himself, 'Is it possible to believe that there is a loving or caring Creator when all this woman needed was *rain*?'" (Tucker 2002, 38).

One of the fascinating stories in Gina Welch's book *In the Land of Believers* is of a homeless man lecturing evangelicals about this problem of theodicy. She had infiltrated herself (an atheist) into a group of evangelicals who were undertaking a "street evangelism" effort. "Down alleyways and behind dumpsters," they sought out potential converts and delivered their pitch to one they encountered:

> Bristling visibly, the man said, "Dude, don't tell me about Jesus." He scoffed, staggered back, and released a peaty belch of whiskey. "Man, I'm out here every day. I could be hit by a goddamn train. If God loves everybody so much, why don't he stop people from getting kilt all the damn time? I could be run over by a goddamn car just minding my business, crossing this goddamn street." [Welch 2009, 247]

One of the proselytizers replied,

> "So could I. Anybody could. But when I die, I believe I'm going to be in heaven with Jesus." No tenderness. No flicker of opportunity. The man roared with laughter. The collar of his shirt shifted and I saw a white chain around his neck. "Yeah, yeah," he said, straps of bitterness suddenly cinching in his voice. "Anybody could die." In the placket of his shirt I saw that a crucifix dangled below his throat: a rosary. "You tell me where God is when people are dyin' in the streets. A dude got kilt the other day. How'm I supposed to believe in Him when He don't care about me?" Alice began to explain her beliefs about free will, but it was like explaining the electoral college to a music video on TV. The conversation was over. [pp. 247-48]

But of course the conversation is not over, at least not for those who feel obliged to praise God as loving and merciful while also maintaining that he is the omnipotent and omniscient ruler "over everything in heaven and on earth":

† "Always when sin has received some special form, the patience of God has ended. God by His judgment has prevented the power of sin and evil. In this way, God shows Himself to be a righteous God who hates sin. At the same time He rules over everything in heaven and on earth, so that His godly power and love will become manifest. The Bible speaks to us of God's works of deliverance and judgment. God is merciful even when He destroys nations. For if God in His righteous judgment did not destroy them and establish the limits of the power of evil, then everyone would have perished" (Saari 1968, 49).

Even Conservatives will now admit that Heikki Saari said some outrageous things. One of the worst I have encountered is that use of the word "merciful" to describe the destruction of nations. How many people have been saved (by conversion to Conservative Laestadianism, of course) due to God's wreaking such destruction in the past century or so, via earthquakes, tsunamis, two world wars, famine, and disease?

After listing some of "the ills, and pains, and agonies of this world" in his *Lecture on Gods*, Ingersoll concludes that it is impossible to harmonize them "with the idea that we were created by, and are watched over and protected by an infinitely wise, powerful and beneficent God, who is superior to and independent of nature. The clergy, however, balance all the real ills of this life with the expected joys of the next." And that is the focus of the next quote, from the July 1990 *Voice of Zion*:

† "In due time God speaks unto man. Many times the speaking happens through trials. These trials could be experienced by whole nations through wars and disasters but also by an individual person through sickness, dying of a dear one or an accident. . . . Trials are God's love towards man. Through them God draws a person unto Himself, undresses him of the self-righteous condition, and softens the soil of heart for the gospel seed to be sowed" (VOZ, 7/1990).

When God speaks to whole nations through wars and disasters, what does he say? For a critically burned and radiation-poisoned survivor of the Nagasaki bombing to somehow discern God saying "shape up" or "worship me" wouldn't do him much good, since it wouldn't begin to tell him that the only place he could be saved is on the other side of the world, much less put access to that place within his reach. It is all too easy to repeat old chestnuts like this without considering what if anything they really mean and whether there is any Scriptural basis for them.

This more recent statement addressing the December 2004 tsunami with its massive death toll, makes the claim of God "revealing himself" but at least offers some humility in the matter:

> † "Our human understanding is unable to understand" why God would allow such things to happen. "God is the Almighty Creator of the world. Our life–indeed that of the whole world–is in His hands. He reveals himself and calls people through both the fates of individuals and nations. Even in difficult situations we can trust in God's care" (VOZ, 2/2005).

It seems to me that God could reveal himself in ways that involve a lot less suffering and a lot more effectiveness. And Rachel Held Evans's disturbing question remains unanswered: "Why should I worship a God who shows mercy to me but not my neighbor? Why should we be outraged by things like the Holocaust or human trafficking when our own God is just as cruel to his creation as we are to each other?" (2010, 99-100).

Two popular attempts to explain this dilemma seem to be (1) blaming the devil for everything evil while praising God for everything good, and (2) saying that the suffering in the world arises from God's curse upon mankind for the Fall. Ehrman addresses the "blame Satan" viewpoint when discussing the book of Job. "God himself has caused the misery, pain, agony, and loss that Job experienced. You can't just blame the Adversary." The only reason for Job's loss of property, ravaging of his body, and the "savage murder" of his ten children was for God "to prove to the Satan that Job wouldn't curse God even if he had every right to do so." Job was innocent, and God himself acknowledges that fact. But he did it all to Job anyway,

> in order to win a bet with the Satan. This is obviously a God above, beyond, and not subject to human standards. Anyone else who destroyed all your property, physically mauled you, and murdered your children–simply on a whim or a bet–would be liable to the most severe punishment that justice could mete out. But God is evidently above justice and can do whatever he pleases if he wants to prove a point. [Erhman 2008, 168]

The second attempt at an explanation is that it's all Eve's fault. Luther believed the earth was cursed by the Fall, and that things got even worse after Noah's Flood (*Lectures on Genesis*, Ch. 3, §19). I heard this belief articulated to the point of absurdity in a sermon shortly after the March 2011 earthquake and tsunami that devastated Japan. The preacher expounded at length on the Adam and Eve story, explaining that such misery and death wouldn't have happened if only Eve hadn't eaten the fruit. When we got home from church, I said, "Kids, the earthquake in Japan was caused by tectonic plates rubbing up against each other, not by anybody eating the wrong thing in some garden." The response from my preteen daughters was telling: a rolling of the eyes and, "We *know* that, Dad." I had shared almost nothing with my children about the issues presented in this book, but these girls seem to know nonsense when they see it.

For those who don't, the earth was formed as molten rock some 4.5 billion years ago, and a very thin outer skin of that rock cooled into a number of tectonic plates. Those plates have been bumping up against each other for eons, causing earthquakes long before humans were present on this planet. Now, you say they were nicely fitted together for all that time, and only came loose when Eve ate the fruit? I don't think so. To assert that any earthquake is the result of some activity that took place only in the past few thousand (or, if you prefer the scientific consensus on human origins, several hundred thousand) years–a mere eyeblink of geologic time–is just ludicrous.[47] That's not even accounting for the fact that the whole Eden story is a myth (**4.3.1**).

Loftus discusses these and several other attempted explanations for the problem of evil at some length, dismantling them one by one (2008, loc. 4146-477). His conclusion about the logical options given the world we live in is unsettling but impossible to dispute: "Either God isn't smart enough to figure out how to create a good world, or he doesn't have the power to do it, or he just doesn't care. You pick" (loc. 4101-102).

4.10 Taking Responsibility

> *We know that not only the prophets like David and Nathan sinned and erred, but also often the Apostles like St. Peter sinned and erred. And the Holy Church itself must pray daily, "Forgive us our sins . . ."*
>
> —Martin Luther [1533]

For an organization to address problems with its doctrines or practices, it first needs to recognize that such problems can even exist. That's not

---

47. Two people who heard the sermon as well as my criticism of it protested that the preacher never said that earthquakes wouldn't have occurred without the Fall, but only human death and suffering. So people started occupying seismically active areas only because Eve ate the fruit? Not only is that ridiculous, but it's also unscriptural: God "made from one man every nation of mankind to live on all the face of the earth, having determined their appointed times and the boundaries of their habitation" (Acts 17:26, NASB). I suppose he made that determination after he saw what a mess the guy and his wife had made of things. Anything's possible with God, even a lack of divine foresight, right?

Let's look at the "human misery" claim just in the light of human anatomy. Humans along with all the other predators on Earth had their carnivorous teeth and digestive systems in place merely to eat vegetation before the Fall? What about the human immune system that fights disease but often with a great deal of misery in the process? There are many features of our bodies (e.g., decaying teeth, telomeres on chromosomes) that keep things going long enough until reproduction can take place (the *sine qua non* of evolution) but stop working or even limit the body's lifespan much beyond that point without modern medical intervention. It's uncanny how amazingly suitable those "designs" wound up being for the new suffering-and-death environment once the Fall took place.

possible if the organization views itself as inerrant and above reproach, which is the attitude we've seen expressed all too clearly in 4.2.6, 4.4.4, and 4.8.1. An authoritarian mindset (see "Authoritarianism" in 4.6.1) among leaders and followers alike helps maintain the attitude and keeps people from expressing concerns even within the confines of the group.

Taking such concerns outside, to raise the eyebrows of the scornful unbelieving world, is practically unthinkable. During the height of the "caretaking meetings," when word was getting out about the spiritual abuse going on in the SRK, these warnings made that clear:

> † "Let us not take one another's faults outside the kingdom of God to be trampled under the feet of unbelievers. Soon they will trample the entire kingdom of God, and trample every holy thing under their feet like swine, and even tear the bearer of tales like a dog" (Saari 1968, 14).

> † "The faults of the children of God should not be aired or talked about among unbelievers. It is the casting of pearls before swine, belittling of God's children within earshot of unbelievers. This is in effect a boomerang when consequently the unbelievers in turn berate the children of God. With this trampling, the one who spoke evil is trampled too" (*Päivämies*, 1974).

In the past couple of years, two major issues concerning the SRK have drawn the attention of Finnish society. One is child sexual abuse by persons having positions of trust within the SRK and the response to the problem by the SRK's leadership. The other is an increase in attention being paid to the spiritual abuse of the 1970s.

4.10.1 Child Sexual Abuse

> *The Christian's obedience to the church must . . . take the form of obedience to Christ. But these two can be different. It can happen that, for the sake of obeying Christ, we must refuse to obey the church.*
>
> —Paul Althaus, *The Theology of Martin Luther*

The Whistleblower

Dr. Johanna Hurtig is "an expert in child care issues" who learned about "child abuse hidden inside the Conservative Laestadian Movement" from a colleague at the University of Lapland. Her colleague had

> interviewed incest victims in the early part of the past decade. She asked me what it means that some of the victims said that they had achieved reconciliation with the perpetrator in the name of Jesus and through His blood. I recognized the words of atonement from the Gospel, and said that it required obedience to the law, and not turning a blind eye to crime. However, I did not think at the time that the problem would have been so extensive. [Vähäsarja 2011]

Hurtig began her approach to the SRK with a letter to Aimo Hautamäki, who was its secretary-general at the time, in August 2008. In the letter, she

> dealt with the base knowledge, awareness, and readiness in respect to child sexual abuse. As my hypothesis I said that readiness and understanding of the issue is not what it ought to be. I justified my view with examples. The letter was long, about 3-4 pages. I wrote it carefully, and my opinion is still that it was appropriate in style, even prophetic concerning the situation where we are now.[48]

She received no reply. In October, she found out about the rape of a girl who is a relative of hers. In that case, "the forgiveness of sins played a central role." The story of the girl outraged her all the more because it was a result of the problem she had tried to tell the SRK about, a warning she says they hadn't heeded. Hurtig told her father that if he couldn't get a meeting with the leaders arranged, she would go to the SRK offices and wait a week there until they would listen.

---

48. This quote about Hurtig's story is from a letter she sent to me in October 2011, based on a translation of the letter by Antti Kaunisto, as are other quotes not otherwise attributed in this section. I have been in touch with Dr. Hurtig for about a year, but she was reluctant to talk publicly about the SRK's reaction to her work for some time after it appeared in the Finnish media. Now, however, she says she is ready to tell the full story about her treatment by the SRK.

Her first meeting with the SRK came a month later, in November of 2008. She said it was conducted appropriately, and the issue was discussed. The chairman of the SRK's board of trustees, Olavi Voittonen, acted as the chairman of the meeting and behaved somewhat like an outsider, she said, not offering his own opinion about anything. Hurtig remained "very confident," thinking "that those men understand the seriousness of the matter and will act to tackle it in the future, when faced with this phenomenon."

In the beginning of 2009, a man from a family she knows was arrested for child sexual abuse and given an eight-year sentence. Tuomas Hänninen, who has since replaced Hautamäki as SRK secretary-general, gave a presentation in which he spoke about the issue in a way that she felt was neither accurate nor indicated at all that the leadership had any growing awareness of the issue. He pointed out "that although we are horrified by the idea that a devout father of a family would have abused his own child, it is a sin that is not any worse than what each of us are ready to commit in our own hearts." Dr. Hurtig felt such talk to be a "dangerous normalization" (Vähäsarja 2011) of abuse and contacted the leaders again with a letter telling of her disappointment about the lack of action. She included an action plan of "what should be taken into account at camps, in the local congregations, what should be told to and talked about with families."

They agreed on another meeting, which took place in May 2009. She spoke "very frankly" there, criticizing Hänninen's presentation and incorrect attitudes. She told the SRK board that she was "disappointed about their slow actions in the issue," but behaved professionally about it. The leadership rebuked her with strong words, however. She said they called her "an overgrown, fat sheep, unprofessional, in a false spirit," and said she didn't have their trust.[49]

Then Hurtig found out that several Conservative Laestadian men were receiving long prison sentences during 2009. She decided not to let the issue rest. Rather than take any further action through the SRK, she

---

49. "Otan johtoon yhteyttä uudestaan. Toukokuussa 2009 tapaamme uudestaan. Lähetän kirjeen, jossa kerron pettymykseni siihen, että asialle ei ole tehty mitään. Lähetän toimenpidesuunnitelman, mitä leireillä pitäisi ottaa huomioon, mitä rauhanyhdistyksissä, mistä puhua perheissä ja perheille. Sovimme palaverin, puhun siellä hyvin suoraan. Kritisoin Hännisen alustusta, vääriä asenteita.

contacted the leadership of the state-run Evangelical Lutheran Church of Finland, in which the SRK operates as a revival movement. She met with its highest official, the Archbishop of Turku, twice in the fall of 2009.

Bishops of the state Church issued a statement in January 2010, at which point the public became aware of the issue. Hurtig gave many interviews and was contacted by people telling her about their own experiences. She obtained more information very quickly, and decided to begin research.

She met with SRK leaders again in May 2010, and the atmosphere was tense. Voittonen and Hautamäki were angry, she says. "The men are just interested in why I don't trust them, and I'm accused of both the mistrust they feel I have against them and the mistrust they have in me."

Out in the Open

Then, in April 2011, the story broke wide open in the Finnish media. An article <http://www.hs.fi/english/article/Shedding+light+on+child+abuse+among+the+Laestadians/1135265532861> entitled "Shedding light on child abuse among the Laestadians" in the *Helsingin Sanomat* began as follows:

> As many as 100 abusers within the Conservative Laestadian revival movement are believed to have violated the sexual integrity of children over a period of about four decades. The figures came out a week ago when the Central Committee of Conservative Laestadian Congregations (SRK) reported on results of an internal investigation. The leadership expressed regret over the inability to recognize or to adequately deal with the cases within the movement. Instead of reporting cases to the police, the focus has been on forgiveness of sins, and keeping the victims quiet. [Vähäsarja 2011]

"Kerron pettyneeni heidän hitauteensa asiaan tarttumisessa. Olen silti kokouksessa kaiken aikaa asiallinen, en huuda, en ole vihainen, olen ammattilainen, toimin siten että ajattelen, että sen tilanteen olisi voinut vaikka televisiossa esittää.

"Johto moitti minua kovin sanoin. Sanon, että olen kasvanut lihava lammas, ammattitaidoton, väärässä hengessä, en nauti heidän luottamustaan jne."

The SRK held a press conference on April 7 to address the issue. Matti Taskila, the SRK's vice-chairman began by saying, "Everything that we have been accused of is true."[50] I had an opportunity to discuss the issue with Taskila on July 27, 2011, and asked him about that statement. He said he had been referring to the SRK's internal report, and the media tried to make his statement mean that everything *the media was saying* was true. I suspect that there had been pressure to do some backtracking and Taskila's original burst of candor was reeled in. It seems odd for an organization to begin a press conference by acknowledging the truth of its own findings, after all. But the fact remains that Taskila was honestly trying to admit fault in *some* fashion on behalf of the SRK, and I find that a refreshing change, however limited the admission may be.

I then asked Taskila how a member of the public could find out what was in the report, to know what exactly *was* being acknowledged as true. He said there were names of people and information about incidents that had been "confessed" or "cared for" (my recollection of his exact language is uncertain) in the report, and so the SRK had chosen not to make it public. The report did say that all of the incidents were in private homes and not at any official church events. Taskila added that there have been cases (or perhaps *a case*, singular) where the perpetrator asked forgiveness repeatedly and no report was made to authorities. This was a problem of individual congregations.

According to Dr. Hurtig, the SRK's leaders defend themselves and claim that the issue was a surprise for them. That's not far from what Taskila said to me himself: The SRK was so shocked at first by the pedophilia allegations that it was in denial about them. I was impressed by his candor in saying that, as well as his next statement that "we" were at fault for not recognizing the scope of the problem at first.

Given the doctrinal sensitivity about any acknowledgment of error on the part of the "mother" organization as a whole, I wasn't sure if the "we" to which Taskila referred meant the SRK or just the SRK board. But I replied by saying I found it refreshing that the SRK would admit fault. I added that I had witnessed the caretaking meetings in the U.S.

---

50. His exact words were, "Kaikki mistä meitä on syytetty, on totta." An audio recording of the statement is played in YLE.fi's video clip at areena.yle.fi/video/1302199271360.

and know what a failure to admit mistakes can lead to (**4.6.4**). Those meetings went on for a long time because the church would not admit to any error. While he didn't come out and say that, yes, the church can err, he was quite agreeable to my point. Perhaps he was already aware of or considering plans for the official apology that the SRK would finally wind up making about those days, discussed next in **4.10.2**.

Fallout

Though she has come across as somewhat indifferent in public statements since the news story broke, Hurtig made clear to me how upset she really is at her treatment by the SRK. Now she's ready to say so publicly. "In sermons, we that speak [in public] are rebuked, labeled with strong spiritual labels, grievous wolf among Zion, false prophet, spring storm, an angel of Satan, etc." In May 2011, she found herself in yet another meeting with the SRK board. The SRK elders had just seen their movement linked with pedophilia in news stories reprinted around the world, and tempers flared. She was yelled at across the table, and took it all pretty hard.

When I spoke with Taskila two months later, I told him about how upset Hurtig was at her treatment by the SRK. He was quite conciliatory, saying she has done important work. People were upset with her, he said, because of how the matter has gone to the media. He didn't come out and say she was at fault for doing so, seeming pretty neutral about that.

Hurtig appreciated Taskila's comments, and speaks highly of him personally. But at this point, she offers a pretty unflattering summary of the situation. The leaders in power aren't accustomed to such direct action from inside the movement, she says, especially by a woman.[51] They don't appreciate her attempts to advise them, her open criticism of the organizational culture, and her speaking out publicly about the community. And what she speaks about is "a shameful phenomenon that happens in a community that considers itself representing family values, decency, and respect for the law." She says, "I defy their great power as I act in the issue without asking their permission or opinion," having "shown in public many negative things about them: stalling,

---

51. My rule of thumb for women in the church: If you are intelligent, articulate, and female, you're in for trouble. Have just two of those characteristics–any two–and you'll probably be OK.

ignoring, and inconsistent public communications." They "have to admit their faults," and thus "a shadow is cast on the inerrant congregation," a doctrinal stance that had been maintained (not without dissent) since at least the stormy 1970s (4.2.6, 4.4.4).

What Dr. Hurtig wants unmistakably clear about her story is that the "essential point in the process was not to make public the cases or how many there were, but to create discussion about the movement's readiness to deal with child protection." She wanted to start thinking, with the leaders, about which issues could turn out risky or result in abuse being hidden, which we now see has happened in too many cases:

> The victims have suffered from abuse for years without getting help. And when they have sought it, they have been silenced on the grounds of the Gospel. That tells us that teaching, policies, and group culture have to be researched so that the positions of the problems faced and experienced by victims can be located. [Hurtig 2011]

Now dozens of victims in Conservative Laestadianism have taken part in her study by telling their experiences to her. Thus her research is helping the community to target the necessary changes. She has called for the movement's leaders to discuss the problems with her, but says they haven't co-operated. Any critical viewpoint about the church community has been considered a threat, she concludes, even when dealing with such a serious problem as the safety and rights of children and obeying the law.

LLC Editorial

In the June 2011 issue of the *Voice of Zion*, the LLC published an **editorial** <http://www.llchurch.org/articleWindow.cfm?aID=29> about the issue. It began with a lengthy preamble about "the depth of human corruption" and our "hyper-sexualized world":

> Popular culture, advertising, fashion, literature, everyday language and humor, news reports, and even academia, with its uninhibited course offerings, constantly bombard weak human beings with sexual imagery and notions that repeatedly stimulate the basest of fleshly impulses. Add to all that, the Internet, with its anything-goes forms of expression, including all sorts of easy-

access pornography, and it is not hard to believe that the occurrence of child sexual abuse has also increased.

Not so long ago the problem "was not dealt with so openly in society. Unfortunately, victims were often misunderstood, not believed, or even discredited or punished for bringing up shameful, family- or community-threatening "secrets." But progress has been made, the editorial said, and believers "have learned more about recognizing and dealing with the problem" along with the rest of society.

Finally, the church's involvement was gingerly introduced: "It can only be humbly acknowledged that believers, too, have been both perpetrators and victims." But the humility is not for the institution, only the individual believers who, like all human beings, "carry the inheritance of the Fall." And the world is never far from blame, for it is providing potential perpetrators with a "bombardment of titillating imagery and suggestion." Then we get to the heart of the matter:

> Recently cited cases of the sexual abuse of children among Finland's Laestadians, occurring over the last three decades, have been singled out for extensive media attention. Coverage has appeared in print, on television and radio programs, and on websites–news, blogs, chat pages, etc. Some of the focus has alleged that those entrusted with positions of leadership at the Central Organization of Finland's Associations of Peace (SRK) have mishandled or turned a blind eye to cases among the Conservative Laestadian membership.

The editorial added that some "news pieces or statements have *even opined* that there is something in the beliefs or culture of Laestadians that excuses or enables this behavior or shields the perpetrator" (emphasis added). Yes, they have, and with good reason: one of Conservative Laestadianism's core doctrines is that a sinner can go to another believer to have his sins forgiven as often as he falls into them. There are lots of nuances to this, and those are discussed under the next subheading below, **Doctrinal Issues**.

"The SRK engaged an attorney to conduct an internal inquiry into the matter," the editorial continues, leaving the impression that an objective third party got involved. However, the selected attorney is both an SRK member and a preacher. I guess that's what "internal" means. Anyhow, when the inquiry was completed, SRK called a news conference to present the inquiry's findings. The investigating attorney and SRK representatives, including several trusted brothers well known also to North American believers, attended the conference with journalists and other staff from approximately ten media outlets. The general societal problem of child sexual abuse was noted.

Well, actually, before *anything* was noted, Taskila made his opening remark, "Everything that we have been accused of is true." Perhaps that is what the editorial refers to as the "introductory statement about the inquiry," which "included acknowledgment that indeed sexual abuse of children has also occurred in Laestadian circles." But that's not the same thing. What seemed to hold such promise in Taskila's remark was that the *organization*–the inerrant Mother, the pillar and ground of truth–was finally telling those kneeling before it to get up and dust themselves off, like the angel in Revelation told John: "See thou do it not: for I am thy fellowservant, and of thy brethren the prophets, and of them which keep the sayings of this book: worship God" (Rev 22:9).

At least the editorial notes that "SRK expressed regret over failures to address the problem or adequately support victims, acknowledging that in its 'statements and communication, there has not been enough attention paid to the position of the victim, and victims have too often been forgotten.'" Good! I'll even take the third-person "mistakes were made" tone, as long as it gets said.

But "God's kingdom is unified on this matter. We do not deny or cover up falls of this nature," despite what has been reported above about the SRK's response. And "the incidents have not occurred in the sphere of congregational activity." The summary of the press conference minimizes the involvement of "living Christianity" by comparing the numbers of incidences in its "sphere" with cases overall, and by comparing the 10-15 alleged perpetrators who were preachers with the SRK's total number of preachers, which exceeds 950.

Then the editorial quickly whisks the reader back to where it began, peering out at the evil "world where a veritable war on children rages, from abortion to their exploitation, trafficking, neglect, and abuse—not to mention their exposure to poisonous popular culture." "God's kingdom remains an overwhelmingly secure place for children," "supports homes and families in wholesome living, speaks out against, and openly discusses the influences of today's sexualized society and the need to arm against its dangers."

The editorial then provides some commentary that reflects the genuine concern that I think does exist in the LLC about the issue. I now quote at some length what seems like useful material for troubled congregations and a watching outside world. It's important that this commendable content does not get lost amid my critique:

> [C]ongregation and central organization boards and pastors are open about the issue of sexual abuse, striving to educate themselves and families on prevention and how to properly deal with any past cases or ones that may occur. This means taking action in cases that come to light to stop any further abuse of the victim or potential victims, ensuring that spiritual and professional help are provided to victims and other suffering family members, and respecting a victim's privacy to the fullest extent possible. God's children also pray on behalf of all involved.
>
> The penitent perpetrator also needs to be approached with the mind of Christ. Here, too, the gospel is the power of God unto salvation for all who believe (Rom. 1:16). The fallen one needs a confessor who hears the confession, preaches the gospel, and supports and escorts the penitent one to make amends with all who have suffered and with the appropriate authorities. As a fruit of faith and having received strength from the gospel, the penitent one wants to follow through with making amends with the victim and others hurt by the abuse. He also is willing to accept society's punishment and to seek and cooperate with professional counseling.
>
> In no circumstance should a perpetrator attempt to blame the victim or divide near ones, including congregation members, by presenting the abuse as other than wrongdoing. The congregation and its servants must be clear that vigilant protection and support for innocent children and family members, the offender's forgiveness, and the legal ramifications the abuser faces are separate matters. The congregation is responsible for the former, God's grace and the gospel of Christ can begin restoration for the penitent, but society and its laws determine the latter.

Based on what friends on the boards of two LLC congregations have told me in years past, it seems that this guidance was followed very appropriately in a couple of prominent cases. Although I've heard reports of some disturbing situations on which I will not elaborate here, I do not know of anything comparable to what Hurtig has reported about in the SRK.

When I spoke with Taskila, I told him of my disappointment with the LLC editorial after having been somewhat encouraged by the SRK press conference. It seemed, I said, that the LLC was denying that the church was ever at fault and placing all the blame on media exaggerations. I don't recall any clear response to my point, but he did point out that "we" are learning about how to deal with these issues. Overall, it was an amiable discussion with an agreeable person about a topic that is disagreeable on many levels for all concerned.

Doctrinal Issues

As I mentioned above, one of Conservative Laestadianism's core doctrines is that a sinner can go to another believer to have his sins forgiven as often as he falls into them. Each time the absolution is preached, both the sinner and the one proclaiming absolution are expected to go on with life as if the sin had never been committed. When the sin is also a crime, things aren't quite so simple.

It is true that the need to "take care of the matter as far as it has gone" is also spoken of, including accepting any punishments meted out by society for the matter. The fact that the penitent thief on the cross still had to bear his punishment, despite being promised a place in paradise by the Son of God (Lk 23:43), has not escaped notice. The classic children's stories about stolen candy have the child go to his mother to have his sins forgiven, but the next stop is to the store to apologize and pay for what was taken.

When spiritual innocence can be obtained merely by believing the proclamation that "all sins are forgiven," though, a penitent one's feelings of relief and freedom can carry over into the secular realm. If God has forgotten about the sin (Heb 8:12 & 10:17), why shouldn't everyone else? The line between spiritual and legal innocence can be blurred all too easily, in the minds of perpetrator, victim, and religious community alike.

The expectation that the victim no longer should view the perpetrator as being guilty of the forgiven sin can be insidious, invalidating the victim's experience and making him or her feel guilty about natural feelings of resentment and the need for justice. It's especially true when, perhaps with good intentions and various biblical passages in mind, the perpetrator goes to the victim for absolution. There is no choice but to proclaim that all is forgiven "in the name and blood of Jesus."

Then there is the matter of the confessional seal. According to the LLC editorial, the SRK

> also explained that confession and the gospel of the forgiveness of sins preached in God's kingdom is not a cloak for sin and that, while a penitent one is assured that confessed sins are forgiven alone through Christ's redemption and merit, the confessor exhorts—and, if necessary, even accompanies—the confessed abuser to report the matter to the authorities.

What confessors have not always felt the need or even the ability to do, however, is to *compel* the perpetrator to report the matter or do so themselves. The following images show parts of one draft of a sexual misconduct policy reflecting that attitude. Thankfully, the underlined wording never made it into any final, official document that I know of.

Church Law of Christ
An offender may refuse to submit to law enforcement authorities. In such situations, we desire with prayerful hearts and minds to continue to speak to the condition of the heart of the offending one in Christian love and patience. The Church Law of Christ is a law of love and should not be used with urgency to compel one to submit to law enforcement authorities. However, it certainly can and should be used when one is unable to see their fault, does not admit to sin, or if fruits of repentance are not evident in their life.

Confession
In child abuse cases, the caretaker needs to ensure that temporal reporting laws are complied with, but should not violate the privacy of confession to do so. God's Word is a higher authority than the laws of our state and nation. When laws contradict faith, we follow God's Word and the instruction of the spirit rather than temporal laws. The confessor mother or father must be a sealed vessel, and not speak of the matters disclosed in confession (Prov. 11:13). This includes not disclosing information to spouses or others close to us even when we are confident they will not speak further of the matter. Ministers should not speak of specific soul care situations in sermons or presentations. The privacy of confession has long been held precious in God's kingdom so that a confessor can go boldly to the throne of grace to put sin away. The forgiveness of sins is the most important matter when sexual sins are committed, and private confession has been given as a grace privilege so that the sinner can be free from sin. If the penitent sinner cannot be confident that a confessor mother or father will be a sealed vessel, the enemy of the soul may successfully obstruct the way to the throne of Grace. If we are not a sealed vessel as a confessor mother or father, we are in error ourselves and endanger the grace gift of private confession.

According to the Conservative ordained pastor Johannes Alaranta, there was a problem distinguishing between confessions heard by ordained pastors and those heard by lay preachers. He told me, "The confidentiality of confession of ordained pastors is absolute according to the Church Act. There is no situation where a pastor could tell the name of a person who has been to confession. There are some crimes where the pastor should tell to the authorities the crime. But never the name of the penitent." In the media, however, Aimo Hautamäki and Olavi Voittonen

> said again and again that this confidentiality binds all "Christians." Many victims said that the confidentiality had made it difficult to stop sexual abusing or to get help. For example the abuser had said to the victim that if she told somebody about abuse, the sin would come onto her because it had been forgiven. [Alaranta 2011]

Alaranta has been an outspoken critic of the SRK leadership, with an **active blog** <http://gostaja.blogspot.com/>. Although I don't cite him as a named source everywhere in this book, he was willing to be quoted for this statement. Predictably enough, he is no longer asked to speak at SRK services, though he still retains his full duties within Finland's state church, including delivering sermons there. Other outspoken clergy in the SRK recently have found themselves in the same situation as well.

4.10.2 Rethinking the 1970s

> *A strong spirit of vehement legalism began to be apparent. Previous unanimous Christian love was swinging into quarreling, shouting and hollering one to another. Regular old fashion Christian services were changing to be so called "caretaking meetings," into which were summoned and brought Christians which supposedly were faulty with false spirit or doctrine, or some otherwise being faulty in their own personal walk of life. If they were not able to respond in repentance according to their examiners' requirements, they were excommunicated.*
>
> —Walter Torola, *Coming of the Lord Draweth Nigh*

The 1970s were a time of zealous dogmatism and authoritarianism whose main feature was a witch-hunt atmosphere of rebuke (**4.6.4**). But it had a widespread impact on the movement's doctrines, with its influence appearing in a hard-line stance about even thinking that people outside Conservative Laestadianism might be saved (**4.2.1**); a misplaced emphasis on a nearly divine congregation "Mother" (**4.4.4**); a pantheon of false spirits (**4.4.7**); endless, nit-picking rules, including some about instructional television and reading material that are now forgotten or ignored (4.6.1); and a militant approach to confession (4.6.3).

From what I can glean of the history (little of it from Conservative Laestadianism's own recollections), the blame initially rests at the feet of a few strident voices that started making themselves heard at the end of the 1960s. The judgment Irenaeus renders in his *Against Heresies* seems eerily applicable to those men who would come 18 centuries later,

> who give rise to schisms, who are destitute of the love of God, and who look to their own special advantage rather than to the unity of the Church; and who for trifling reasons, or any kind of reason which occurs to them, cut in pieces and divide the great and glorious body of Christ, and so far as in them lies, [positively] destroy it,–men who prate of peace while they give rise to war, and do in truth strain out a gnat, but swallow a camel. [Book 4, Ch. 33, §7]

Despite official silence for most of the decades since, the majority of Conservatives over the age of about forty can readily recall the spiritual abuse and overreaching of the period. The people traumatized by the hundreds of "caretaking meetings" certainly will never forget what happened to them. And in Finland where Conservative Laestadianism is well known as are the events of the 1970s, there are enough disgruntled voices to keep the matter fresh in mind even now.

When forced to discuss the matter, the SRK and LLC have offered two conflicting characterizations of the caretaking meetings and other excesses. One is that they were a "blessing," hard to understand now but necessary to address the unique issues of a difficult time. The other is that, yes, they were wrongheaded and excessive, but the mistakes were those of individual sinners in the Kingdom, not the organization itself.

This image from the "Omat polut" blog <http://freepathways.wordpress.com/2010/11/21/healing-meetings/> is worth a thousand words of reply to that latter point. It is of announcements from the SRK's *Päivämies* newspaper regarding 1978 caretaking meetings in two congregations:

PARKANO
Neuvottelukokous rauhanyhdistyksellä 11. 3. klo 19. Mukana SRK:n veljiä. Kaikkien jäsenten läsnäolo toivottavaa.
Parkanon
Rauhanyhdistys r.y.
Johtokunta

OIJÄRVI
Kuivaniemen alueen uskovaisten yhteinen neuvonpito Oijärven ry:llä 4. 9. 78 klo 19. Kaikkien uskovaisten läsnäolo välttämätön. Mukana veljiä työvaliokunnasta.
Oijärven
Rauhanyhdistys r.y.

There was never the slightest hint from the organizations themselves that anything abusive or excessive was happening in their congregations. Indeed, the SRK and LLC were actually promoting the caretaking meetings and other excesses at the very highest levels of both organizations. The SRK sent representatives to nearly 500 meetings (Ijäs 2011). As the above image shows, an announcement of one meeting promised that "SRK brothers" will be attending. Both organizations were making uncompromising statements about submission, obedience to the Mother, false spirits, and rebuke in their official publications (**4.2.6**, **4.4.4**, **4.4.7**, **4.6.4**).

If the inerrant "Mother" was opposed to what was going on, she certainly wasn't making her voice heard. It's really another version of the problem of God's hiddenness (**4.4.1**) and theodicy (**4.9.4**), applied to an organization that seems to consider itself divine. As noted by Antti Kaunisto and discussed in **4.4.4**, an inerrant Mother who is somehow hidden among fallible believers is *of no practical consequence*.

Finally, though, an objective look at history from *inside* the movement forced the SRK's official viewpoint to shift just a bit. Dr. Ari-Pekka Palola, a historian who is the SRK's publications manager, released a history of the SRK called "Expanding the Work of the Gospel" at an SRK board meeting on October 8, 2011. He had done a previous work, "Protected by Two Shells," that dealt with the years 1906-1946, and the new work went up to 1961. The next project would address the 1960s, when things were starting to get awkward, and move into the tumultuous 1970s.

As the October 13, 2011 issue of *Päivämies* tells it, "The SRK board had a preliminary discussion about the continuation of history work. The continuation demands a retrospect of the events of the 70s. To the board's way of thinking, it is reasonable to learn a lesson from the past." The next statement is remarkable, and I have gone so far as to borrow it as a theme for this book: "There must be the ability to encounter facts with openness and honesty, even when the facts are not pleasing to us." Well said!

To continue the story, I now turn to the Finnish news source *Kotimaa24*, which graciously granted me permission to publish a translation of its entire **article** <http://www.kotimaa24.fi/uutiset/kotimaa/6305-vanhoillislestadiolaiset-pyytavat-anteeksi-hoitokokousten-vaarinkaytoksia> covering the statement and its background (Ijäs 2011). Here it is, lightly edited from what was provided to me by Mikko Alasaarela:

Conservative Laestadians ask Forgiveness for Abuses of Caretaking Meetings

Johannes Ijäs

October 10, 2011

The Board of the SRK, which represents the conservative laestadians in Finland, asks forgiveness for the [revival] movement's doctrinal errors and misuse of power during so-called caretaking meetings in the 1970s. This is told to *Kotimaa24* by SRK's Executive Chairman Olavi Voittonen.

The SRK's Executive Board's statement given this weekend will be published in full in the coming week, appearing in the movement's *Päivämies* magazine.

According to Olavi Voittonen, the statement constitutes an apology.

However, Voittonen feels that the movement has already apologized for the doctrinal errors and abuse during the caretaking sessions. This apology took place in 1989, when the movement's then Secretary General Voitto Savela spoke at an Elders' Meeting during summer services at Ranua. Savela's speech was published in SRK's yearbook. According to Voittonen, the recent apology, however, is expressed more clearly and more forcefully than it was then, over twenty years ago.

In their statement, "doctrinal errors" refers to the internal undercurrents, which were called different spirits. According to Voittonen, these spirits caused actions that were not considered appropriate within the movement. These spirits were called, among others, the "dry," "gentle" [perhaps equivalent to *lenient*] and "kososlainen" spirit. According to Voittonen, the problem with these caretaking meetings, among others, was the fact that it was not enough to talk about an actual sin, but that the people that were taken care of each had to "dig a wrong spirit out of himself." This was an abusive practice, according to Voittonen.

Voittonen also points out as abuse the public and enforced confession of sins during caretaking meetings. Voittonen acknowledges that the caretaking meetings included spiritual abuse. However, he also points out that the vast majority of participants had a positive experience.

Caretaking Meetings "Went Beyond a Certain Point"

The reason why the movement is now asking for forgiveness for the caretaking meetings, according to Voittonen, is primarily the fact that the movement is in progress of writing its history, which will next move to the third part, covering the years 1962-2006. Voittonen says that society's values revolution that began in the early 1960s was the historical basis for the caretaking meetings in the late

1970s. The second part of the history covering years 1946-1961, written by Ari-Pekka Palola, has just been completed.

For the discussion this weekend, SRK had at its disposal a research report on the caretaking meetings. It was prepared from SRK's Executive Board and Executive Committee minutes from that period. There were 488 public caretaking meetings at local congregations where official SRK representatives attended.

Olavi Voittonen himself defines the caretaking meetings as "pastoral conversation, which examined doctrinal or ethical issues and deviations regarding the faith."

The history of the Church shows that such meetings have been held for ages, but then when the discussions went beyond a certain point, they took on some wrong features, Voittonen says.

Are the Caretaking Meetings Still Taking Place?

Three bishops of the Lutheran Church of Finland met SRK's representatives in August. From time to time, the bishops engage in discussions with various revivalist movements about current topics. The caretaking meetings were also discussed in the [August] meeting. Voittonen would not elaborate on the detailed questions, such as whether the bishops hoped for an official apology. He said that they agreed to share information on the discussions only on a general level.

Aini Linjakumpu, a researcher at University of Lapland who is working on a publication about the caretaking meetings, said in the summer that caretaking meetings still are being held within Conservative Laestadianism. For example, there is a desire to guard the members from critical views about the movement. Voittonen does not agree that Linjakumpu's outing would have had any influence on the public apology, but rather precisely the fact that the movement will now start writing the history of the period of the caretaking meetings.

Voittonen thinks the caretaking meetings declined in number and eventually ended in the early 1980s, but says the pastoral care "cannot end in the church of God." According to Voittonen, the movement cannot completely avoid the fact that some people will experience such pastoral care negatively also in the future.

SRK has prepared a press release about the caretaking meetings, which is due to be published on Wednesday, October 12. SRK's Secretary General Tuomas Hänninen handed the press release to *Kotimaa* already today at the request of Olavi Voittonen.

Press Release October 12, 2011

SRK Continues the Writing of History

The second part of the SRK's history, written by Ari-Pekka Palola and called "Expanding the Work of the Gospel," was published on October 8, 2011 at Siikatörmä. This current publication covers the history until 1961. The previous publication, "Protected by Two Shells," discussed the history of SRK's organization from 1906 to 1946.

After the publication, SRK's Executive Board held a preliminary discussion on the continuance of the history work, and concluded that continuing the work requires critical and open scrutiny of the events of the 1970s.

We Should Learn From Our Past

The Executive Board noted that we should learn from the past. We must be able to face the facts openly and honestly, even when they are not pleasing to us. This also applies to the so-called caretaking meetings, which were the result of the values revolution in society that took place in the 1960s and affected the faith community in a wide variety of ways. Beer was released to the grocery stores in 1969, television became a new phenomenon in rural areas, and in the early 1970s the municipalities began offering free counseling on contraception. The movement's positions towards TV, birth control, and beer drinking had to be thought through together.

The talks resulted in much-needed pastoral care. Unfortunately, since the mid-decade, the so-called caretaking meetings started including foreign elements, such as doctrinal errors and spiritual abuse that resulted from those.

The Executive Board regrets these doctrinal errors and abuses that have occurred, and says: "Any community consists of individuals, including a faith community. When individual Christians are wrong, the Church itself is not at fault."

People also experienced the caretaking meetings as blessings when the living gospel was able to release constricting internal bonds. What God has cleansed has produced good fruit.

Despite all the fanfare and the *Päivämies* article's acknowledgment that "it is reasonable to learn a lesson from the past," that it "is unfortunate and, in retrospect inconceivable that these errors were able to expand almost everywhere in our Christianity" (SRK 2011), we can still see the two standard responses in the press release: "The Church itself is not at fault," and there *were* blessings, the SRK insists in the end, with "good fruit" from what "God has cleansed." The ecclesiastical disclaimer goes on a bit longer in the *Päivämies* article directed at the SRK's membership:

> A community consists of individuals, and so does a faith community. We believe that the Holy Spirit gathers God's

congregation. When an individual person errs, the fault is not of the congregation. And so correction of the matters begins from the will of the individual wayfarer [*lit.* "striving one"] to travel with a good conscience before God and man. Even during the caretaking meetings, moments of blessing were always [*aina*, perhaps better read as "constantly"] experienced when the living gospel could release constricting internal bonds [of sin, *katkoa puristavat sisäiset siteet*]. What God purged, has produced good fruits. [SRK 2011]

Ultimately, the Church never allows itself to be blamed, no matter what. Not for the absurdities and contradictions we have seen throughout this book, not for the actions and inactions that Dr. Hurtig complains of in the previous section. Not even for what the SRK itself says were "the doctrinal fallacies and misconduct that took place" in the 1970s, for which "we" are sorry. It's hard to tell what is meant by the word "we," given that the organization says it cannot err and thus never can have anything to be genuinely sorry about.

Then, in the next breath, it is claimed that some good came of it after all. And for *that*, God, whose "Mother" congregation sat unseen and unheard as individuals went on a spree of error, is unhesitatingly given credit.

5 Martin Luther

How could I, a poor, stinking bag of maggots, have come to this, that people would refer to Christ's Children by my unholy name?

—Martin Luther

5.1 Predecessors

"Tom's Doubts," #14, by "Saji"

Where were the true Christians before Luther, from whom he must have personally received the Holy Spirit according to Church doctrine? The answer that I've heard among Conservatives is that the believers were hidden inside the Catholic Church, practicing the true religion with its person-to-person absolution in secret. That is a convenient theory, because it is unfalsifiable. But it seems inconsistent with the idea (**4.2.4**) that God has always called men unto repentance through his Kingdom.

I doubt if there is more than a handful of people in the LLC–preachers or anyone else–who have read anything from Christian writers earlier than Luther. There aren't many who even have read much of *his* writings. The Church Fathers from the first several centuries are completely ignored within the movement, even Augustine by whom Luther was so influenced as to have been called, in some ways, "Augustine's most faithful son" (Balge 1984, 9).

I cite Augustine in this book, along with several other writers of the first few Christian centuries. The following are my ancient sources, listed by date-order of their cited works (A.D., of course). Each list entry contains the author's name (if known), and title of each cited work. Most of the list entries also have one of the following codes indicating the authority I place on each source:

> **ENT** – Early New Testament. Writings considered by early Christians to be as authoritative as now-canonical New Testament works, as evidenced by citations or inclusion in early New Testament codices.
>
> **AF** – Apostolic Fathers. Writings by acknowledged leaders of the early church, cited approvingly since ancient times.
>
> **P** – Prominent. The author's works were extensive and well-known enough to give an indication of the prominent Christian ideas of his time.
>
> **L** – Luther. An author whom Luther considered authoritative, persuasive, or at least one of the saved.

Ancient Sources
Date : Author : Work(s) : Authority

> *c.* **95** : *Unknown* : *First Clement* : AF
>
> *c.* **100** : *Unknown* : *Epistle of Barnabus* : ENT
>
> *c.* **100** : Ignatius : *Epistle to the Ephesians, Epistle to the Philadelphians, Epistle to the Smyrnaeans, Epistle to the Trallians* : AF
>
> *c.* **140** : *Unknown* : *Shepherd* of Hermas : ENT
>
> *c.* **160** : Justin Martyr : *Dialogue with Trypho, First Apology* : P
>
> *c.* **170** : Tatian : *Address to the Greeks*
>
> *c.* **180** : Athenagoras : *Plea to the Christians*
>
> *c.* **180** : Theophilus of Antioch : *To Autolycus*
>
> *c.* **185** : Irenaeus : *Against Heresies* : P

197-200 : Tertullian : *Against Praxeas, Apologetic, Ethical, On Modesty* : P

c. **200** : Clement of Alexandria : *Stromata, The Instructor* : P

215 : *Unknown* : *Apostolic Tradition* : P

212-248 : Origen : *Homilies on Leviticus, Homilies on Luke, Against Celsus* : P

c. **384** : Ambrose : On Repentance : P

397-410 : Augustine : *Confessions, The City of God* : L

5.1.1 Luther's View

Luther wrote that the spirit is lost when it does not cause the Word to be preached and roused in the heart so that it is understood. That happened during the Papacy, he said, for "faith was stuck entirely under the bench and no man recognized Christ as his Lord, nor the Holy Ghost for that which would sanctify" (*Large Catechism*, Part 2, §43). He feared

> that since St. Peter's times there has been no Pope that has preached the Gospel. There has certainly been none who has written and left anything behind him in which the Gospel was contained. Saint Gregory, the Pope, was certainly a holy man, but his sermons are not worth a farthing; so that it would seem that the See of Rome has been under the special curse of God. It is very possible that some Popes may have endured martyrdom for the Gospel's sake; but nothing has been written of them to show that it was the Gospel. And yet they go on and preach that they must feed the flock; and yet they do nothing but bind and destroy the conscience, by laws of their own, while they preach not a word of Christ. [*Epistles of St. Peter and St. Jude Preached and Explained*, "The First Epistle General of St. Peter," Ch. 5]

Writing *The Papacy at Rome* in 1520, he asserted that "Christ's kingdom has been *at all times in all the world,* ... but never was it *entirely* under the pope, even for one hour, in spite of those who say otherwise" (*PE* 1, 375, emphasis added). He appeared to grant that "even if the papacy has been under Satan now and then, yet there have always been pious

Christians under it." But in the same breath he says that there are Christians under the rule of the Turk and in all the world (pp. 382-83). The first part of his statement may be consistent with the picture of a few true believers huddled together in some secret recesses of Catholicism, but the second isn't. Except perhaps in private admissions, Conservatives generally deny the possibility that there is any other saved group out there that is unknown to "the Kingdom." The true believers all know each other, it is commonly said.

Luther recognized a number of Church Fathers as having the Holy Spirit, including St. Bernard [923-1008], Jean Gerson [1363-1429], and John Hus [c. 1372-1415] (*Large Catechism*, Part 4, §50). Bernard, he wrote,

> was one of the best of the medieval saints. He lived a chaste and holy life. But when it came to dying he did not trust in his chaste life for salvation. He prayed: "I have lived a wicked life. But Thou, Lord Jesus, hast a heaven to give unto me. First, because Thou art the Son of God. Secondly, because Thou hast purchased heaven for me by Thy suffering and death. Thou givest heaven to me, not because I earned it, but because Thou hast earned it for me." [*Commentary on Galatians* (1535), from Graebner 1949, Ch. 4]

Luther left little doubt about his approval of John Hus, referring to him as "St. John" and asserting that all of his articles "condemned at Constance are altogether Christian" (*An Article in Defense of all the Articles of Dr. Martin Luther Wrongly Condemned in the Roman Bull* [1521]; *PE* 3, 97). Hus, along with Jerome of Prague [1379-1416], were "good Christians, [who] were burned by heretics and apostates and anti-christians,–the papists–for the sake of the holy Gospel" (p. 103).

He was heavily influenced by Augustine [354-430] and cited him throughout his writings. He considered it "intolerable nonsense not to consider St. Augustine one of the best [church] fathers, since throughout all Christendom he is esteemed the highest of them," though he also criticized "this endless trouble and labor of holding to the [church] councils and fathers, against the Scriptures, and judging ourselves by them" (*On the Councils and the Churches* [1539]; *PE* 5, 149). Luther "had praise, admiration and charitable words for Ambrose, Bernard and others. But it was Augustine he cited, to whom he appealed, from whom he learned" (Balge 1984, 9).

When Luther left the monastic order that had named itself after Augustine and his own theology developed, however, he found himself in disagreement with his ancient teacher on many important points. He was forced to acknowledge–as Conservatives do now about Luther himself due to disagreements with some of *his* teachings–that "St. Augustine was only a human being; we are not compelled to follow his interpretation" (from Balge 1984, 8). It was difficult for Luther

> to disassociate himself in many points of doctrine from the teacher to whom he owed so much: "No one will believe how great an ordeal it is and how severe a shock when a person first realizes that he must believe and teach contrary to the fathers. . . . When I read the books of St. Augustine and discover that he, too, did this and that, it thoroughly appalls me." [pp. 8-9]

Still, Balge concludes that Luther continued to

> speak appreciatively of the man whom he regarded as Paul's "most trustworthy interpreter." He believed that faith in the gospel had preserved Augustine's soul from the logical consequence of his errors. "Holy Christendom has, in my judgment, no better teacher after the apostles than St. Augustine." He opined that "Augustine is certainly a princely elector in heaven." He regarded him as "a teacher who shines in the church up to this day and teaches and instructs it." [p. 9]

5.1.2 Problems

I have pored over many Pre-Reformation church writings–most everything written by Christians of any type in the first couple of hundred years after Christ, some by Augustine, and some by John Hus– in search of teachings that would allow me to point to "believers" prior to Luther.[52] The Conservative Laestadian definition of a "believer" is extremely specific because the movement must differentiate itself from thousands of other Christian denominations and sects. That type of "us vs. them" differentiation is inherent to fundamentalism (**4.2.3**), but Conservative Laestadianism is even more prone to it because of the need to justify its extreme claim of exclusivity.

The single most significant point of distinction between Laestadians (not just Conservatives) and the rest of Christianity is the focus on personal absolution from one believer to another for day-to-day housekeeping of the conscience (**4.6.2**). So absolution (from lay believers or clergy) was what I focused on in my search for pre-Lutheran Laestadian equivalents. What I found–more precisely, what I did *not* find–shocked me as much as any of the many unsettling discoveries I have laid out in this book thus far: With only a few vaguely possible exceptions, the Christians prior to Luther have left a written record that makes them *nearly unrecognizable* as the "believers" of my childhood faith. In every case, they were clearly very different people of very different times, beliefs, and practices. They wrote about some strikingly non-Lutheran subjects such as asceticism, honoring ecclesiastical hierarchy, limited grace, numerology, and the veneration of martyrs.[53] There is almost nothing in their teachings or practices–certainly not about the most critical issue of personal absolution–that a Conservative Laestadian could point to and say, "He was one of us."

---

52. It's not that hard to cover the earliest writings: "With the exception of the Pastor of Hermas and the short tract called the Didache, we have nothing more than a dozen letters from the Fathers of the first hundred and fifty years of Christianity" (Casey 1899, 15). Keeping up with the century after that requires much more dedication, as it explodes with preserved works from such prodigious authors as Tertullian, Clement of Alexandria, and Origen. I've found those writings excellent bedtime reading, however, with just enough interesting material to keep me following along until the seemingly endless repetition finally puts me down for the night.

53. The asceticism often included celibacy, even in marriage. Indeed, there is a writing in the Pauline canon, 1 Cor 7:29-30, with instructions about that. Rev 14:4 appears to make celibacy a requirement for at least the inner circle of heaven. See the discussion of that passage in **7.9** to get an idea of how anti-sexual it and many other early Church writings were.

Absent Absolution

The *Apology of the Augsburg Confession* notes that all "good people of all situations, even the theological profession, undoubtedly confess that the teaching of repentance was very much confused before Luther's writings appeared" (Article 12a; McCain 2005, 158). It certainly was, beginning with two centuries of writings that not only fail to explicitly mention absolution, but provide many teachings incompatible with it. Even absolution as a sacramental, priestly function–the long-standing predecessor to Luther's "priesthood of all believers" (**5.4.5**)–was absent:

> Sometimes the power of discipline was assumed by the congregation, sometimes by the whole group of presbyters, but most frequently by the Bishop. It is significant however, that *the power to forgive sins was not claimed by these officials until the end of the second century*. The Johannine tradition that Christ had given such power to all the apostles was taken to mean that *everyone might approach God to ask for his own or another's forgiveness*; only the martyrs were recognized to have special privileges in according grace to those who had lapsed during the persecutions. [Burkhart 1942, 196, emphasis added]

Henry Charles Lea begins his monumental *History of Auricular Confession and Indulgences* (1896) with a brief summary of how "man dealt directly with God" in the primitive Christianity of the Gospels. The only requirements were "repentance, love, humility, [and] pardon of offenses or charity." Then he observes, "It required all the ingenuity of theologians for thirteen centuries to build up from this simplicity the complex structure of dogma and observance on which were based sacramental absolution and the theory of indulgences" (Lea 1896, 4).[54]

An equally significant work on the topic is K.E. Kirk's *Vision of God* (1966). He summarizes the occasions where "the New Testament and the Apostolic Fathers urge the confession of sins . . . from the pastoral

---

54. H.C. Lea's comprehensive and important book, *A History of Auricular Confession and Indulgences* (1896) is in the public domain. I got my copy of Vol. 1, *Confession and Absolution*, for free on Google's ebookstore <http://books.google.com/ebooks>. This long, ugly link <http://books.google.com/ebooks?as_brr=5&q=bibliogroup:22A+History+of+Auricular+Confession+and+Indulgences+in+the+Latin+Church%22&source=gbs_metadata_r> may at least get you in the neighborhood of it on Google's site. If you want to spend twenty bucks, you can also get a paperback reprint at Amazon.com <http://amzn.com/1402161107>.

point of view" in a half-page footnote. He concludes the summary by observing that "confession to God (which did not exclude the assistance of man and hearing the confession) was constantly urged upon the primitive Christian. It thus provided a permanent background of thought and practice from which sacramental 'confession' would emerge later when disciplinary penance broke down" (Kirk 1966, 172).

Lea does not mince words in expressing his dim view of the "transmission of power from the apostles to those who were assumed to be their successors," calling it "the most audacious *non sequitur* [Latin: 'it does not follow'] in history":

> That the primitive church knew nothing of this is plainly inferable from the silence of the early Fathers. It is proverbially difficult to prove a negative, and in this case the only evidence is negative. They could not discuss or oppose a non-existent doctrine and practice and their only eloquence on the subject must perforce be silence . . . [Lea 1896, 109]

Yet the Fathers did earnestly discuss "the methods of obtaining pardon for sins." Thus "their omission of all allusion to any power of remission lodged in priest or Church is *perfectly incompatible* with the existence of contemporaneous belief in it" (p. 109, emphasis added).

It's a mouthful, but Lea is making a critical point: The earliest Christian writers *never thought to mention* what became such an important aspect of Catholic (and, I might add, Conservative Laestadian) doctrine and practice, the absolution of sins by the proclamation of another human being. And the fact that they wrote about *other* means by which sins could be forgiven makes their silence about absolution all the more problematic.

It seems that the inattention to absolution continued into the early middle ages, at least when it came to the practice of everyday Christians. The Fourth Lateran Council of 1215 commanded all adults to undertake *annual* confession (Murray 1993, 52), which must seem astoundingly infrequent to Conservatives who hear the words of

---

It is well regarded, meticulously researched, and surprisingly readable. I highly recommend it. In the interest of objectivity, you may also wish to accompany your reading of the book with a short critique (also public domain) by Patrick H. Casey, a Catholic apologist: *Notes on a History of Auricular Confession and Indulgences* (1899).

absolution every Sunday and, between family members, often daily. Murray researched the practice of confession by laymen in the centuries leading up to the Lateran Council and concluded that, although "regular" lay confession had been urged for several hundred years, it "was a usage generally ignored, if often in favor of unofficial substitutes." (Amusingly to Conservative ears, he refers to "regular" practice as "once, twice or even three times per year," p. 58.) And where laymen did make such confessions, there was either "an active study of pastoral divinity" going on or "a body of clergy living under a common rule" (p. 79). In other words, it seems, those laymen who participated were doing what the people who surrounded and observed them expected them to do.

What They Said (and Didn't Say)

The *Shepherd of Hermas* was written in the early 2nd century, not many decades after the Gospels themselves, and was recognized and accepted up to the fourth century (McDonald and Porter 2000, 620). That acceptance is evidenced by its inclusion as part of the New Testament in *Codex Sinaiticus*. It is an early and authoritative Christian writing, but it clearly conflicts with the Conservative doctrine of forgiveness only by personal absolution. In the *Shepherd*, a narrator is "praying to the Lord and confessing my sins" (Vision 1,3; Ehrman 2005, 252) and being told to "pray to God, and he will heal your sins" (Vision 1:9).

Justin Martyr describes the weekly worship of the Christians around 160 A.D. There is a reading of scripture, common prayer, celebration of the Lord's Supper, and charity for the needy. But there's no hint whatsoever of absolution:

> [O]n the day called Sunday, all who live in cities or in the country gather together to one place, and the memoirs of the apostles or the writings of the prophets are read, as long as time permits; then, when the reader has ceased, the president verbally instructs, and exhorts to the imitation of these good things. Then we all rise together and pray, and, as we before said, when our prayer is ended, bread and wine and water are brought, and the president in like manner offers prayers and thanksgivings, according to his ability, and the people assent, saying Amen; and there is a distribution to each, and a participation of that over which thanks have been given, and to those who are absent a portion is sent by the deacons. And they who are well to do, and willing, give what

each thinks fit; and what is collected is deposited with the president, who succours the orphans and widows and those who, through sickness or any other cause, are in want, and those who are in bonds and the strangers sojourning among us, and in a word takes care of all who are in need. [*First Apology*, Ch. 67]

Justin's *Dialogue with Trypho* addresses the forgiveness of sins very briefly, telling the Jews that they should "hasten to know in what way forgiveness of sins, and a hope of inheriting the promised good things, shall be yours." But, he says, "there is no other way than this–to become acquainted with this Christ, to be washed in the fountain spoken of by Isaiah for the remission of sins; and for the rest to live sinless lives" (Ch. 64). That is hardly a clear indication of absolution. Indeed, it sounds a lot more like the one-time washing away of sins via baptism, a measure of grace that could not be repeated. (As we will see in the discussion below, there were absolute limits to God's grace in the first Christian centuries.)

Justin made clear his views on the atoning power of baptism when he wrote that "we have believed, and testify that that very baptism which he announced is alone able to purify those who have repented; and this is the water of life" (*Dialogue*, Ch. 14). The discussion of baptism in **4.7.6** quotes that and several other such statements from Justin, Irenaeus, Clement of Alexandria, Tertullian, and Augustine. These earliest Christian writers put so much emphasis on the ritual cleansing of baptism that they seemed not to have seriously entertained any other means of forgiveness.

Writing a few decades after Justin, Theophilus of Antioch presents repentance as manifesting God's constant desire "that the race of men turn from all their sins." He goes on to cite a number of Old Testament prophets as some of the "countless sayings in the Holy Scriptures regarding repentance" (*To Autolycus*, Book 3, Ch. 12). His loose paraphrase of Joel 2:16-17 seems to indicate a favorable view about forgiveness by prayer: "Gather the people, sanctify the congregation, assemble the elders, gather the children that are in arms; let the bridegroom go forth of his chamber, and the bride out of her closet, and *pray to the Lord thy God urgently that he may have mercy upon you, and blot out your sins*" (Book 3, Ch. 12, emphasis added).

With the passage of a few more decades, Clement of Alexandria also notes God's direct role in forgiveness. He acts seemingly to the exclusion of man, who has a different task: "The Lord ministers all good and all help, both as man and as God: as God, forgiving our sins; and as man, training us not to sin" (*The Instructor*, Book 1, Ch. 3)

Origen notes of Luke 3:3 that baptism "is also preached 'for the remission of sins.'" He encourages people in the process of conversion (which culminated in their baptism) to come and do "penance, so that Baptism for the remission of sins will follow. He who stops sinning receives Baptism 'for the remission of sins.'" He cautions them not to "come to Baptism without caution and careful consideration," because anyone who "comes sinning to the washing ... does not receive forgiveness of sins" (*Homilies on Luke*, No. 21; Lienhard 1996, 135). Two things are clear here about Origen's views: you receive forgiveness of your sins by coming to baptism, and you'd better have figured out how to quit sinning by that point. Both are in keeping with the viewpoints of early Christianity, and neither conforms in the slightest with the viewpoints of Conservative Laestadianism.

Ambrose [340-397] made a pretty clear reference to clerical forgiveness of sins: "If it be not lawful for sins to be forgiven by man, why do you baptize? For, assuredly, in baptism there is remission of all sins. What matters it whether priests claim this right as having been given them by means of baptism or penitence? One is the mystery in both" (*Concerning Repentance*, Book 1, Ch. 8, from Capel 1884, 13). But yet again, the forgiveness was not just through absolution (assuming that's what he means by "penitence"). Ambrose's point was that the forgiveness could occur equally through either baptism or penitence.

Despite the emphasis he and his predecessors put on baptism for the cleansing from sin, Augustine was of course aware of Jesus' gift of "the keys to His Church" so that "whatsoever it should bind on earth might be bound in heaven, and whatsoever it should loose on earth might be loosed in heaven" (*On Christian Doctrine*, Book 1, Ch. 18). He clarified the biblical statement as follows:

> [T]hat is to say, that whosoever in the Church should not believe that his sins are remitted, they should not be remitted to him; but that whosoever should believe and should repent, and turn from his sins, should be saved by the same faith and repentance on the ground of which he is received into the bosom of the Church. For he who does not believe that his sins can be pardoned, falls into despair, and becomes worse as if no greater good remained for

him than to be evil, when he has ceased to have faith in the results of his own repentance. [Ch. 18]

Still, there's no mention of any person–clergy or otherwise–proclaiming absolution. Rather, Augustine emphasized the individual's faith and repentance. Augustine's recollection of his own conversion, when "by a light as it were of serenity infused into my heart, all the darkness of doubt vanished away," is devoid of anything about absolution. It was a private spiritual experience, which he shared with a close friend and his mother only in retrospect (*Confessions*, Book 8).

Augustine must also have also known about the emerging practice of private confession, even though he didn't seem to write anything about it. He subscribed to a canon of 419 A.D. that prevented a bishop from using knowledge about a sin against a person if the bishop learned of the alleged sin in private confession and the sinner denied it (Lea 1896, 15). But he "seems to set little store on confession when he omits it entirely from his enumeration of what is requisite to obtain pardon for sin" (p. 180).

In addition to reading the Church Fathers, I have found it interesting to see what the less orthodox Christians were saying in the early centuries. After all, one way of attempting to explain the lack of pre-Lutheran "believers" that meet Conservative Laestadian doctrinal requirements in the historical record is that the true Christians were a disregarded minority back then, too. One early bit of Christian writing from the Gnostic "heresy" is *The Second Revelation of James*, dating from sometime in the first couple of centuries after Christ (Meyer 2007, 331-32). It contains a brief reference to the forgiveness of sins, but by direct prayer to God: James the Just prays on his deathbed for God to save him "from sin, and forgive me all the debts of my days" (from Meyer 2007, 341).

My reading of the Gnostics is pretty limited, but that is the most relevant passage about the forgiveness of sins I have come across in their writings. It just didn't seem to be much of a concern to them, which may be understandable given their views about the inner man being distinct from the flesh that carries him around. Price agrees, and also notes the Gnostics' claim of being superior to the law. "Judging from their own writings, they were radical ascetics. Also, 1 John condemns those who claimed to be sinlessly perfect, and that was very likely a reference to Gnostics who claimed perfect divine nature. Such folks are not going to be much concerned with gaining forgiveness!" (Price 2012).

Confession

Lea writes, "Evidently among the primitive Christians the practice of acknowledging sins was regarded as a wholesome exercise, contributory to their pardon and leading to self-restraint" (1896, 173). It was a direct confession to God, "with prostration and humiliation, whereby repentance was excited through which his wrath might be appeased. In the primitive Church this confession to God was the only form enjoined" (p. 174). Lea refers to one of the earliest Christian writings outside our present biblical canon, *First Clement* [*c*. 95 A.D.], in support of his point: The Lord "stands in need of nothing; and He desires nothing of any one, except that confession be made to Him" (Ch. 52).

No mention is made of any human mediator. Indeed, the direct confession to God is confirmed by the statement in *First Clement*'s Chapter 7 that the Ninevites repented "of their sins, propitiated God by prayer, and obtained salvation." Chapter 8 discusses repentance in the New Testament era, saying that to "all them that repent, the Lord grants forgiveness, if they turn in penitence to the unity of God, and to communion with the bishop." But again, even though the bishop is mentioned, there is no mention of confessing to the bishop or anyone else. Rather, the "*Didache* shows us that this confession was public, in church, and that each believer was expected to confess his transgressions on Sunday, before breaking bread in the Eucharistic feast, for no one was to come to prayer with an evil conscience" (Lea 1896, 174).

The next mention of confession of sins is in the *Epistle of Barnabas*, written sometime around 80-130 A.D. *Barnabas* was considered part of the New Testament early on in the church, as evidenced by its presence in both the *Codex Vaticanus* and *Codex Sinaiticus* of the 4th century. (It's an interesting book; you can find some pretty crazy stuff in *Barnabas* about numerology and the legend of the Phoenix rising from the ashes.) A lengthy paragraph of admonitions urges readers to "seek out every day the faces of the saints, either by word examining them, and going to exhort them, and meditating how to save a soul by the word," to not hesitate to give to every one that asks you, to hate the wicked, to not make a schism. Finally, readers are urged, in language that may well have been copied from the *Didache*, "Thou shalt confess thy sins. Thou shalt not go to prayer with an evil conscience. This is the way of light" (Ch. 19).

Presumably, the writer of *Barnabas* considered the act of confession to be a solution to an evil conscience, so some sort of absolution might be inferred as part of the act of confession. But it is impossible to know whether the clearing of the conscience took place, in his view, as a result of the act of confession, or whether it occured by an absolution that is not mentioned. A hint might be found in Chapter 16, which talks about the spiritual temple that is found in the mouth of a Christian:

> Before we came to believe in God, the dwelling of our hearts was rotten and weak like an actual structure built by human hands because it was a den of idolatry, a cave of demons, because of the things we did contrary to the will of God.... *When we received amnesty for sins and placed our hopes on the name, we were renewed, being created all over again from scratch*. This is why God truly lives inside us, in the dwelling that we constitute. How? By means of his message of faith, the summons of his promise, the wisdom of the commandments, the statutes of the teaching, his prophesying inside us and living inside us, *by his opening the door of the temple, that is, our lips, to speak his words, giving us a chance to repent* and in this way leading us, former slaves of death, into the unfading temple. For whoever wants to be saved focuses not on the individual who is preaching the news to him but on the one who lives in him and speaks through him. He is amazed at him, never having heard him speak thus with his mouth, nor has he himself ever wanted particularly to hear such speech. Both the speaking and the hearing attest the presence of the divine. The result is a spiritual temple being erected for the Lord. [from Price 2006a, 1129-30, emphasis added]

What are "his words"? Of absolution, or just the good news of Jesus Christ? The comparison one might make to the temple is that sins are forgiven via the mouth of the believer. But note how the "amnesty for sins" is viewed as a one-time event that the author and his readers are invited to look back on in retrospect.

When we get to Irenaeus, we finally see repentance being associated with confession, though there is still no mention of any corresponding act of absolution. Writing around 185 A.D. about a certain "Marcus" whom he considered a heretic (*Against Heresies*, Book I, Ch. 8), Irenaeus refers to a woman who "spent her whole time in the exercise of public confession, weeping over and lamenting the defilement which she had received from" Marcus after being converted "with no small difficulty" by "the brethren." He also discusses others who "have their consciences seared as with a hot iron," and some "of them, indeed, make a public confession of their sins; but others of them are ashamed to do this." Irenaeus also mentions a predecessor of Marcion who, "Coming frequently into the Church, and making public confession, ... thus remained, one time teaching in secret, and then again making public confession; but at last, having been denounced for corrupt teaching," was "excommunicated from the assembly of the brethren" (*Against Heresies*, Book III, Ch. 4).

Shortly after Irenaeus, the Christian priesthood appeared in Rome and Africa. The *Apostolic Tradition*–a document traditionally dated to around 215 A.D. but possibly written up to a century later–contains a prayer of consecration for a new bishop that refers to his authority "by the Spirit of high-priesthood ... to remit sins according to thy commandment, ... to loose every bond according to the authority which thou gavest to thy disciples ..." (from Burkhart 1942, 198). The "high-priestly bishop was recognized to have the power to forgive venial sins" in both Rome and North Africa (p. 199),

This was a bit beyond "the primitive period–in the days, for example, of Hermas, Clement, and Polycarp," when Kirk says "little stress was laid upon absolution, much upon the efficacy of true penitence" (1966, 287). Lea says it "is not until we reach the middle of the third century that we find any evidence of an occasional custom of sinners [unburdening] their souls to priests" (Lea 1896, 175), although what we just saw from Irenaeus and the *Apostolic Tradition* seem to push that date back just a bit. He continues, "The first allusion to it occurs in Origen, who, in the seven modes of pardon includes the remission of sins by repentance," which "is described as hard and painful," showing "that it was by no means a usual expedient" (p. 175). Origen's seven modes of pardon he summarizes as follows:

> I. Baptism, II. Martyrdom, III. Almsgiving, IV. Forgiveness of offenses [by others], V. Converting a sinner from the error of his ways, VI. Abundant loving charity, VII. and lastly, the hard and laborious way of repentance, when the sinner washes his couch

> with tears, when tears are his daily and nightly bread, and he does not blush to reveal his sin to the priest of God and ask for medicine. [Lea 1896, 81]

Ambrose's ambivalent statement quoted above about penitence vs. baptism indicates what Lea acknowledges was one of "three forms of voluntary confession in more or less frequent use" at the time: confession "to a priest or some other holy man" (p. 178). He claims, however, that "sacramental confession and absolution . . . was a practice permitted but not recognized by the Church" and that "Ambrose himself knows only of public penance for grave sins; the venials of daily occurrence were removed by repentance, and there is no class intermediate between them" (pp. 178-79). For his part, Kirk does not seem to believe that "a single case of private reconciliation (other than sick-bed cases) [can] be quoted from the first five centuries" (p. 540).

The doctrinal requirements of Conservative Laestadianism result in an assumption to the contrary. Apparently, it is more widespread than that, because Kirk (who probably never heard of Laestadianism) calls it an assumption, too, that "private penance *with private absolution*, running parallel to the public institution as a recognized alternative." But maintaining that "involves the hypothesis of a conspiracy of silence on the part of patristic authorities . . . and flies in the face of the vast bulk of contemporary evidence" (p. 540).

Lea says "it was perhaps necessary for the Council of Trent [held from 1545 to 1563] to declare that sacramental confession is of divine law." He then provides a scathing critique not just of those theologians who bore the "somewhat onerous task of proving from history" that the Council's declaration was correct, but also on the historicity of sacramental confession itself. To defend it,

> every shred of patristic literature has been searched with the result of finding a few scattered and irrelevant passages which at best are but indirect allusions or exhortations. This is in itself sufficient evidence of the fruitlessness of the effort. So infinitely important a priestly function, in a population so corrupt as that of the [Roman] empire, would necessarily have formed the subject of detailed treatises for both penitence and confessors. The Apostolic Constitutions embody the customs of the church towards the end of the third century, but they are silent as to this. A hundred years later St. Augustin, with untiring industry,

covered the whole ground of Christian ethics and duties, but he gives no counsel to confessors how to perform their most delicate and responsible functions. The councils, in a fragmentary manner, prescribed penances for the grosser sins, but they lay down no commands as to confession. [Lea 1896, 171]

No indications about confession appear until about the seventh century, Lea continues, and their nature shows "how rare as yet was confession" (p. 171). Some examples of what he may have in mind are a seventh-century council that declared "the penance of sinners" to be "medicine of the soul" and "useful to all men" and an eighth-century statement showing that the devout laity habitually received absolution before Christmas (Kirk 1966, 285). Lea is not impressed by the argument that literature about sacramental confession did in fact exist but is now lost: "To estimate the full force of this negative evidence it is only necessary to compare the silence of the early centuries with the clamor which arose as soon as confession was made habitual by the Lateran Council in 1216" (1896, 171). He cites the "increasing mass of literature which has swollen to vast proportions" since then, and says it "cannot be imagined that men like the Christian Fathers could have been blind to what has been so clearly seen since the thirteenth century, that the duties of the conscientious confessor are the most arduous and exacting, the most intricate and complex, that can be imposed on the fallibility of human nature" (p. 172).

Rigorism

The epistle to the Hebrews began a "rigorist practice of refusing reconciliation to grave sinners" (Kirk 1966, 161) that placed absolute limits on God's grace for five centuries (pp. 227, 275-81, 506-507) and associated it with severe public humiliation and punishment for centuries more (pp. 292-95). "Unfortunately for the Church, the rigorist view of the epistle to the Hebrews predominated for many generations, and poisoned the whole atmosphere of Christian ethics" (p. 165). The issue with Hebrews has been been long recognized; Luther's concern about the "hard knot" posed by its chapters 6 and 10 is discussed in **7.7**.

The first Church Father to leave us anything on the topic of rigorism is whoever wrote the *Shepherd* of Hermas around 140 A.D. Kirk says the book excludes grave sinners "from the Church without any hope of readmission" (p. 167). It does, however, offer to "the apostates and other excommunicates" what had been denied them, "one more chance, but one alone. Grave sinners within the Church he calls to open penance, with the threat that after this opportunity nothing awaits them except the penalty of permanent excommunication" (p. 168).

Justin's *Dialogue with Trypho* indicates an expectation that converts would stop sinning after baptism. He tells his Jewish reader to eradicate from his soul the hope that ancestry from God's chosen people would save him. Rather, he should "hasten to know in what way forgiveness of sins, and a hope of inheriting the promised good things, shall be yours. But there is no other [way] than this,–to become acquainted with this Christ, to be washed in the fountain spoken of by Isaiah for the remission of sins; and for the rest, to live sinless lives" (Ch. 44).

Irenaeus warned about a lack of second chances: "We ought not . . . be puffed up, nor be severe upon those of old time, but ought ourselves to fear, lest perchance, after [we have come to] the knowledge of Christ, if we do things displeasing to God, *we obtain no further forgiveness of sins*, but be shut out from His kingdom" (*Against Heresies*, Book 4, Ch. 27, emphasis added).

In the discussion of alternatives to absolution, we saw how Origen viewed baptism as an end to sinfulness. So did Tertullian, a few decades earlier: "That *baptismal* washing is a sealing of faith, which faith is begun and is commended by the faith of repentance. We are not washed *in order that* we *may* cease sinning, but *because* we *have* ceased, since *in heart* we have *been* bathed already" (*Ethical*, On Repentance, Ch. 6).

"Although the gate of forgiveness has been shut and fastened up with the bar of baptism," Tertullian thought God "has permitted it still to stand somewhat open. In the vestibule He has stationed" a second repentance that could be opened to those who knock (Ch. 7). He offers consoling words to those who have to do so: "Let none be ashamed. Repeated sickness must have repeated medicine. You will show your gratitude to the Lord by not refusing what the Lord offers you. You have offended, but can still be reconciled" (Ch. 7).

But don't push your luck–that's all the chance you'll get. It is the "second and only (remaining) repentance" (Ch. 9), and was for Clement of Alexandria, too. He advised that a person "who has received the forgiveness of sins ought to sin no more," because there would be only one more chance. God, "being very merciful," offers a second repentance to those "who, though in faith, fall into any transgression."

But that repentance was itself "not to be repented of," he warns, quoting the Hebrews 10 passage (*Stromata*, Book 2, Ch. 13). Even without the absolute limit imposed by the rigorism of his day, Clement would have little patience for the regular forgiveness of Conservative Laestadianism. Frequent repentance was itself sinful, and the "frequent asking of forgiveness ... for those things in which we often transgress, is the semblance of repentance, not repentance itself" (Ch. 13).

The rigorism was still in place when Origen did his writing in the early third century. "Among us," he noted "there is only one pardon of sins, which is given in the beginning through the grace of baptism. After this, no mercy nor any indulgence is granted to the sinner" (*Homilies on Leviticus*, No. 2; Barkley 1990, 66). And of "the sins which we commit in this life" he said, "some can now be healed but others cannot" (No. 8; p. 181).

Along with the epistle to the Hebrews, the *Shepherd* of Hermas established the strict limit of rigorism. But at least "Hermas proposed one post-baptismal reconciliation for *all* grave sins without exception" (Kirk 1966, 171). By the time Origen noted the distinction between sins that could and could not be healed, "the Church excluded even from this strictly limited amnesty the three mortal sins of apostasy, adultery and homicide." All that was available was submission "to life-long discipline in the hope that God would forgive after death that from which the church dared not absolve during life" (p. 171). Although there had been "[s]poradic instances of mitigation in one direction or another" since the mid-second century, "the rigour of the law was in general fully maintained. Adulterers, apostates and murderers ... were normally excluded from the Church without hope of readmission" (p. 224).

The absolute limits would soon loosen up a little bit, with the "rigorist attitude towards the remission of sins of the flesh" disappearing in Africa and Italy by the middle of the third century (Kirk 1966, 226). Forgiveness for murder only became available after a 314 A.D. council that allowed for reconciliation when the murderer's own death approached (p. 227).

The change does not imply a commensurate laxity about sin, however. Open penance was a requirement for forgiveness, and the severity increased to an almost unbelievable degree. Not only before, but even after his reconciliation, the penitent suffered every kind of temporal penalty–so much so that entry into a monastery came to be a recognized (and even preferable) alternative to penance, and evasion by suicide was not unknown. [p. 228]

Kirk summarizes the position of Western Christianity by the fifth century as follows:

> There are no longer any sins irremissible by the Church on earth, but the number of sins for which reconciliation will only be given [at the point of death] is considerable. Penance for grave sin after baptism, but one penance only, is still the invariable rule. So severe has the penitential discipline become, both in character and duration, that (with only the rarest possible exceptions) no one can be found to undergo it voluntarily–except indeed at the moment of death, when neither severity or publicity nor duration can be enforced. [p. 275]

During the period of penance, which could go on for years (Lea 1896, 25-26), the penitent man's head was kept shaved and the woman's veiled, sackcloth and ashes were worn, and bathing was forbidden (p. 28). In church, "the penitents were grouped apart in their hideous squalor" and publicly humiliated. A "complete separation between husband and wife was enforced," and even after the penance marriage or resumption of sex in marriage was a dicey question (pp. 29-30).

It was a hideous system that bears not the slightest resemblance to the grace and forgiveness of Christianity today, Laestadian or otherwise. And it went on for hundreds and hundreds of years.

Duplicating the Keys

It was during during the fifth and sixth centuries that "the rule of one penance" gradually disappeared, and "it is probably safe to associate this development with a growing ascendancy of the priesthood in the ministry of absolution" (Kirk 1966, 281). At first, sins could be forgiven only by the bishops, who stood apart from mere priests.

In the early Christianity Ignatius describes around 100 A.D., there was a single bishop, the leader of the entire church: "[T]here is but one altar for the whole Church, and one bishop, with the presbytery and deacons, my fellow-servants" (*Epistle to the Philadelphians*, Ch. 4). Ignatius urged his readers to "all follow the bishop, even as Jesus Christ does the Father, and the presbytery as ye would the apostles; and reverence the deacons, as being the institution of God. Let no man do anything connected with the Church without the bishop" (*Epistle to the Smyrnaeans*, Ch. 8). Decades later, the narrator of the *Shepherd* of Hermas was seeing a vision of *bishops* in the plural, rather than the singular (Ch. 27). Tertullian's writings from the end of the second century make it clear that there were a number of bishops at that point.

These bishops were the leaders of each regional body of a Church that, "although scattered throughout the whole world, yet, as if occupying but one house," preserved the preaching and faith that Irenaeus described around 185 A.D. in his *Against Heresies* (Book 1, Ch. 10). The men occupied the highest levels of the ecclesiastical hierarchy that had formed when the keys finally turned up around the turn of the second century. By "the middle of the 2nd century all the chief centres of Christianity were headed by bishops" (Wikipedia <http://en.wikipedia.org/wiki/Bishop>).

As soon as the ministry of reconciliation passed from the hands of the bishop "into the ordinary jurisdiction of the priest, repetition of penance–often secured, no doubt, by application to different priests at different times–became easy, and privacy easier still" (Kirk 1966, 280).

Origen offered an intriguing early reference to the forgiveness (and retaining) of sins by a person having divine authority:

> But consider the person inspired by Jesus as the apostles were and who can be known by his fruits as someone who has received the Holy Spirit and become spiritual by being led by the Spirit as a son of God to do everything according to the Word (or reason). This person forgives whatever God forgives and retains sins that cannot be healed, serving God like the prophets by speaking not his own words but those of the divine will. So he, too, serves God, who alone has authority to forgive. [*Treatise on Prayer*, 28:8-10, from Crouzel 1985, 229]

After providing us this quotation, Crouzel notes, "The priests of the Old Testament offered expiatory sacrifices only for sins that could be pardoned." He then quotes Origen again:

> Therefore, it is the same way that the Apostles and those like the Apostles, since they are priests according to the great High Priest, have received knowledge of God's healing and know, since they are taught by the Spirit, for what sins sacrifice must be offered and when and how; and they know for what sins it is wrong to do this ... I do not know how some arrogate to themselves powers that exceed the priestly dignity; perhaps they do not thoroughly understand priestly knowledge. These people boast that they are able to forgive adultery and fornication, supposing that through their prayers for those who have dared these things even on into death is loosed. For they do not read that "there is a sin which is unto death. I do not say that one is to pray for that." [from pp. 229-30]

Origen's words underscore the rigorism of his day: adultery and fornication could not be forgiven, by priests or otherwise. They also leave a tantalizing possibility that the "person inspired by Jesus," having "received the Holy Spirit and become spiritual" might be *any* believer, not just a bishop or priest. Crouzel, a Jesuit, dismisses that idea, saying such an interpretation "has little foundation." According to him, Origen is criticizing "priests or bishops who claim to forgive sins by their prayer alone, by a remission, *aphesis*, by grace alone, without expiation through public penance [by] which one displays repentance and makes the sinner fit to receive pardon, thus transforming a 'sin unto death' into one that is no longer unto death" (p. 230).

Crouzel notes that "the only person who exercises the power of the keys in accord with the divine intention is the priest who is a spiritual man and remits sin as God does and wills, and who has the knowledge required for this function" (p. 230). That conclusion may seem to be a presupposition of his Roman Catholicism, but it really isn't. The idea of laymen being able to forgive sins would have been utterly foreign to Origen or anyone else in Christianity. Even priests had only recently gained access to the keys from the bishops, and their authority was initially only delegated to them in the bishop's absence (Kirk 1966, 281). It "was very uncertain how far the priest, as distinct from the Bishop, had the power of the keys" (p. 281, n. 4). It would go no further until the monasticism that formalized in the centuries ahead brought with it the phenomenon of monks, even lay monks, proclaiming absolution to their brethren in the cloisters (p. 283-84). Luther's "system of lay confession"

(Lea 1896, 173) associated with his expansion of the priesthood to all believers would not appear for more than a thousand years.

The only case I've seen of ordinary lay Christians performing absolution before Luther was in the Bogomil heresy that began in the Balkans around 930 A.D.: "Bogomil's congregation had no priesthood or hierarchy; men and woman confessed their sins to one another and gave one another absolution" (Harris and Paich 1999). "[W]hile the Bogomils accept the necessity for Confession, it is of the non-auricular kind, i.e. they believe it enough to confess one's sins to another "Christian" (their name for each other). [A contemporary critic] Cosmas is particularly outraged that women are included among those to whom one may confess" (**bogomilism.eu** <http://www.bogomilism.eu/Other authors/Cosma.html>). It's an intriguing exception to the rule, but I have learned little else about it. The Bogomils were certainly no proto-Lutherans, being a "dualist and docetist sect" that talked about Satan being God's older son (**St. Pachomius Library** <http://www.voskrese.info/spl/Xbogomil.html>). Their founder was accused of teaching that "Christ our God was born of the Holy Mother of God and Ever-Virgin Mary as an illusion, and as an illusion he was crucified, but that he took this assumed flesh up with him, leaving it in the air" (**Synodicon** <http://www.bogomilism.eu/Other authors/Butler-synodicon.html>).

All in all, it was a tortuously slow expansion of those authorized to use the keys. At first the authority was neither claimed by nor given to anyone at all. Then the bishops appeared, keys in hand. Then the priests to whom they hesitantly delegated their authority got copies, and later monks did, too, within the walls of their closed communities. And finally, when Luther's system appeared, laymen got their chance to employ the keys, in theory if not so apparently in actual practice (**5.4.4, 5.4.5**).

Hiddenness Again

Conservative Laestadianism's focus on absolution "from faith to faith" and unchanging doctrine demands that there has been a special group of believers who make up an unbroken chain of people to whom the keys have been passed ever since Jesus conveyed them to the disciples. Those believers used the keys to absolve each other on a regular basis from sin that occurs at every turn. For most of the past two thousand years, these people have been completely hidden from any of the history we've just reviewed. To believe that, you must assume a "conspiracy of silence on the part of patristic authorities" about absolution in the earliest Christian centuries, as Kirk adeptly puts it.

You must also disregard how strictly limited the opportunity was for repentance from post-baptismal sin, and the corresponding assumption by the earliest Christians that they were immune to any further sinning. You must assume that free grace, by faith rather than works, was being offered to this select group of proto-Lutherans in secret, entirely removed from the suffering of harsh penances that was imposed on all known Christendom for many hundreds of years. You must assume that these hidden believers either had their own clergy to whom the keys had been authorized, or that Luther's revolutionary concept of lay absolution was accepted by them a thousand years before the Reformation, at a time when even *priests* were being denied access to the keys.

When absolution finally reaches laymen in the middle ages–certainly not preached by them, but received by them–there was such reluctance that annual participation had to be mandated. So you must make one final transition, from that somber, sacramental event to the weekly and even daily repetition of a verbal formula, largely disconnected from confession of anything. It's a big leap, after several impossibly huge ones, and the subject of this section's overall study, Martin Luther, is right in the middle of it.

5.2 The Church

> *No earthly power can draw the boundaries of the church and decide who belongs to it and who does not. Only Christ, who gives faith to the heart, knows this; and only he sees this faith.*
>
> —Paul Althaus, The Theology of Martin Luther

Luther's explanation of the Third Article of the Creed is widely quoted in writings of Conservative Laestadianism in support of its claim to be the one true church on this earth. My translation of the most popular quotes is as follows, after (i.e., based upon) the translation in McCain 2005:

> For first of all, [God] has his own particular congregation in the world, which is the mother. Thus each Christian is conceived and carried by the word of God, which He reveals and cultivates,

enlightens and enflames hearts, that they understand, take to themselves, hang onto, and remain in it. [*Large Catechism*, Part 4, §42; McCain 2005, 403-404]

I believe that there is a holy handful [little group] and congregation on Earth of pure saints, under one head, Christ, called together by the Holy Ghost in one faith, mind, and understanding, with many different gifts but united in love, without sects or schisms. Of the same I also am a part and member, of all goodness that it has, partaking and brought along by the Holy Ghost and incorporated into it by this, that I have heard and still hear God's word, which is the beginning of entrance. [Part 4, §51; McCain 2005, 404-405]

Another statement of Luther's that has been taken (at least by me, in years past) as supporting the Conservatives' doctrine of sectarian exclusivity is found in one of his sermons for the 17th Sunday after Trinity. There he quotes Eph 4:4-6 (a Laestadian favorite, see **4.2.1** for a couple of citations of it) and writes about the unity of the spirit, which "Christians should feel bound to maintain," since

they are all members of one body and partakers of the same spiritual blessings. They have the same priceless treasures–one God and Father in heaven, one Lord and Savior, one Word, baptism and faith; in short, one and the same salvation, a blessing common to all whereof one has as much as another, and cannot obtain more. What occasion, then, for divisions or for further seeking?

Here Paul teaches what the true Christian Church is and how it may be identified. There is not more than one Church, or people of God, [on] earth. This one Church has one faith, one baptism, one confession of God the Father and of Jesus Christ. Its members faithfully hold, and abide by, these common truths. Every one desiring to be saved and to come to God must be incorporated into this Church, outside of which no one will be saved [paras. 21-22, from *Luther's Epistle Sermons: Trinity Sunday to Advent*]

What Luther does not define in either of these quotes is the extent of the true Christian church. But he makes his view of that clear in other writings that most Conservative Laestadians have never heard of, nor will easily accept. I certainly understand that, since I somehow passed over these "other writings" until recently. That omission occurred despite my having studied Luther and his writings since the early 1990s, going to far as to learn German in order to access some of those writings without translations. The reason I missed these points is that my earlier study was mostly a search for support of my Conservative Laestadian presuppositions, which weren't open to an honest appraisal of facts that didn't fit those presuppositions.

Luther's writings about the extent of the Church were just one of many such inconvenient facts. Those writings were like the gorilla-suited participant in a famous psychological study, who walked into a crowd of people playing basketball and whose presence was completely missed by people instructed to count how many times the ball was passed:

> This gorilla study underscores how any choice of evidence depends on the mind-set of the observers. Each of us in the audience told our unconscious what to look for. To carry this out with maximal efficiency, an implicit second instruction was sent to the unconscious–to downplay or ignore irrelevant visual inputs. As we can't anticipate all inputs to be considered, this latter instruction is open-ended. The unconscious has free rein as to what should or should not be seen. [Burton 2008, 155]

So let's do an honest assessment and look for the gorilla, starting with Luther's 1520 tractate *The Papacy at Rome*. There he raises the question of "whether it is possible for Christians to say that all other Christians in the world are heretics and apostates, even if they agree with us in holding to the same baptism, Sacrament, Gospel, and all the articles of faith, but merely do not have their priests and bishops confirmed by Rome" or buy such confirmation with money. The "Muscovites, Russians, Greeks, Bohemians, and many other great peoples in the world" all "believe as we do, baptize as we do, preach as we do, live as we do, and also give due honor to the pope, only they will not pay for the confirmation of their bishops and priests." Thus, Luther held "that they are not heretics and apostates, but perhaps better Christians than we are, although not all, even as we are not all good Christians" (*PE* 1, 340-41).

Rejecting the papal position "that every community on Earth must have one visible head under Christ" (p. 348), Luther said that the Church or "Christianity" is called "the assembly of all the believers in Christ upon earth" and "consists of all those who live in true faith, hope and love; so that the essence, life and nature of the church is not a bodily assembly, but an assembly of hearts in one faith.... Thus, though they be a thousand miles apart in body, yet they are called an assembly in spirit because each one preaches, believes, hopes, loves, and lives like the other." The force of Luther's rhetoric may be lost to the modern reader here; a thousand German miles was a distance that few people would ever journey in his day, and "assemblies of hearts" so distant from each other would be essentially separate entities.

But, nonetheless, a spiritual "unity is of itself sufficient to make a church, and without it no unity, be it of place, of time, a person, of work, or of whatever else, makes a Church" (p. 349). In his view, such unity "does not consist in similarity of outward form of government, likeness of Law, tradition and ecclesiastical customs" (*Sermon for Seventeeth Sunday After Trinity*, para. 23, from *Luther's Epistle Sermons: Trinity Sunday to Advent*). But when "unity becomes division," he said in another sermon from the same volume, "certainly two sects cannot both be the true Church. If one is godly, the other must be the devil's own" (*Sermon for Fifth Sunday After Trinity*, para. 7).

Conservative Laestadians certainly have had, in my experience at least, a common spiritual understanding on most things during any one period of time, although one can see clear changes in teaching and practice over the decades just by reviewing the chronological listings of "†" excerpts earlier in this book. Modern travel and communications allow a close bond to remain between the multiple outward organizations of the SRK and LLC, and the various congregations outside Finland and North America where they do mission work.

But one must deal with Luther's assertion that, based on Jesus' identification of the Kingdom of God being "within you" (which is how Luke 17 appears in Luther's Bible translation), "it is clear to everyone that the kingdom of God ... is not at Rome, nor is it bound to Rome or any other place, but it is where there is faith in the heart, be a man at Rome, or here, or elsewhere" (pp. 349-50). Luther compares to the false prophets of Mt 24 those "preachers of dreams in material communities, which must of necessity be bound to localities and places. How is it possible, or whose reason can grasp it, that spiritual unity and material unity should be one and the same? ... Therefore, whosoever maintains that an external assembly or an outward unity makes a Church, sets forth arbitrarily what is merely his own opinion" (p. 350). There is not, he says, "one letter in the Holy Scriptures to show that such a purely external Church has been established by God." Rather, "the Christian assembly, according to the soul, is a communion [or congregation] of one accord in one faith, although according to the body it cannot be assembled at one place, and yet every group is assembled in its own place" (p. 355).

While it is true that Luther was dealing with a claim of exclusivity by the Pope and his outward institution at Rome, is it really much of a stretch to consider the similar way that Conservative Laestadianism views itself, a single "spiritual communion" consisting of the SRK, LLC, and SFC, and a handful of known others sustained by the mission efforts of those three interrelated groups? What would he say about how Conservatives disparage every other one of the tens of thousands of Christian denominations in the world–including several Laestadian ones–given that he could "neither endure nor keep silent" when the papists would "revile and slander and curse the Greeks, and all who are not under the pope, as though they were not Christians, as if Christianity were bound to the pope and to Rome, when St. Paul and Christ have bound it only to faith and to God's Word" (*An Article in Defense of all the Articles of Dr. Martin Luther Wrongly Condemned in the Roman Bull* [1521]; *PE* 3, 81-82). Read Luther's similar 1520 statement in *The Papacy at Rome* (*PE* 1, 391) with the contextual shelter of its final phrase "under the pope" stripped away to expose yourself to the general force of his viewpoints on the Church, and see if the answer isn't clear:

> I will not suffer any man to establish new articles of faith, and to abuse all other Christians in the world, and slander and brand them as heretics, apostates and unbelievers, simply because they are not . . .

The broad geographical reach of the Church as envisioned by Luther may come as a surprise, too:

> [I]t is clear that the Holy Church is not bound to Rome, but is as wide as the world, the assembly of those of one faith, a spiritual and not a bodily thing, for that which one believes is not bodily or visible. The external Roman Catholic Church we all see, therefore it cannot be the true Church, which is believed, and which is a community or assembly of the saints in faith, for no one can see

who is a saint or a believer. The external marks, whereby one can perceive where this church is on earth, are baptism, the Sacrament, and the Gospel; and not Rome, or this place, or that. For where baptism and the Gospel are, no one may doubt that there are saints, even if for only the babes in their cradles. [p. 361]

Under the rule of the Turk there are Christians, and likewise there are Christians in all the world, as there were aforetime under Nero and other tyrants. [pp. 382-83][55]

[T]he Greeks and Bohemians are not heretics or schismatics, but the most Christian people and the best followers of the gospel on earth. [*An Article in Defense of all the Articles of Dr. Martin Luther Wrongly Condemned in the Roman Bull* (1521); PE 3, 71]

I believe that there is one holy Christian Church on earth, i.e., the community and number or assembly of all Christians in all the world, the one bride of Christ, and his spiritual body of which he is the only head. . . . And this same Christianity is not only under the Roman Church or Pope, but in all the world, as the prophets foretold that the gospel of Christ should come into the entire world, Psa 2, 18. Thus also under the Pope, Turks, Persians, Tartars, and everywhere Christianity is scattered, but spiritually gathered in one gospel and faith, under one head, i.e., Jesus Christ. . . . In this Christianity, wherever it exists, is the forgiveness of sins, i.e., a kingdom of grace and of true pardon. [*Confession Concerning Christ's Supper*]

To an opponent who mocked his calling the Christian Church a "spiritual assembly," Luther demanded an answer to his proof texts:

"There is no respect of persons with God"; and, "The kingdom of God is within you"; also, "The kingdom of God cometh not with observation" . . . I dare say that you would call the Christian Church, or us, in whom God lives and reigns, the kingdom of God. How can I follow your reason and deny Christ, Who clearly

---

55. Luther's teaching on this topic, as with numerous other topics, is not without contradiction. In his *Table Talk*, he narrows the geographic window considerably, saying "we have the Gospel now only in a corner. Asia and Africa have it not, the Gospel is not preached in Europe, in Greece, Italy, Hungary, Spain, France, England, or in Poland." Rather, it was in "this little corner," Luther's Saxony (§759).

says here that there is no locality, place or anything external in the kingdom of God; it is not here or there, but the spirit within us. But you say, it is here and there. [*Answer to Emser of Leipzig* (1521); *PE* 3, 394-95]

[T]he Christian Church is not bound to any person, place, or time . . . firmly on my side are [the common people], also the little children in the streets, together with the great multitude of Christians in the world, and they stand with me against the painted and pretended Church of the pope and his papists. If you ask how that is possible, I answer briefly, all Christians in the world pray: I believe in the Holy Ghost, one holy Christian Church, the Communion of saints. If this article [of the Creed] is true, it follows that no one can see or feel the holy Christian Church, and no one can say it is here, or there. [pp. 396-97]

The *Apology of the Augsburg Confession* associates the Church with a "congregation of saints, who have with each other the fellowship of the same Gospel or doctrine" (Articles 7-8, *The Church*; McCain 2005, 144). But it also suggests an expansive Lutheran view of the Church:

[We should] not understand the Church to be an outward government of certain nations. Rather, the Church is people scattered throughout the whole world. They agree about the Gospel and have the same Christ, the same Holy Spirit, whether they have the same or different human traditions. [p. 144]

[W]e do say that this Church exists: truly believing and righteous people scattered throughout the whole world. We add the marks: the pure teaching of the Gospel and the Sacraments. [p. 146]

Luther taught that one could identify the presence of Christians by their possession and preaching of the Word of God. In his 1523 *Right and Power of a Christian Congregation*, he set forth "the certain mark of the Christian congregation" as "the preaching of the Gospel in its purity." One could be "certain that where the Gospel is preached, there must be Christians, no matter how few in number or how sinful and frail they be" (*PE* 4, 75). In his 1539 *On the Councils and the Churches*, Luther described the Church as "a Christian holy people that remains on earth and must remain until the end of the world," and explained how "a poor, erring man wants or is able to notice where such a Christian holy people is in the world" (WA 50, 628). Primarily, it is "recognized in that it has God's Holy Word," but that Word might be possessed unequally, with

> some having it completely pure, some not completely pure. Those who have it pure are called those who build a foundation of gold, silver, and precious stones. Those who have it impure are called those who build a foundation of hay, straw, and wood, but still are made holy by fire." [pp. 628-29]

The presence of the "external Word [being] orally preached by men like you and me," Luther wrote, is an outward sign whereby Christ's church is to be recognized:

> Wherever, therefore, you hear or see this Word preached, believed, confessed, and acted on, have no doubt that there must known be a true *Ecclesia sancta Catholica*, a Christian, holy people, even if you [plural, presumably referring to members] are very few . . . If there were no other mark than this one alone, it would still be enough to know that in that very place must be a Christian holy people. [p. 629]

Luther uses the indefinite article ("**ein** *Christlich heilig Volck*") here, but one can't read too much into that. At times he also refers to "*the* Christian holy people" when he goes on to discuss six other signs of the church.

Those additional signs are correct teaching and administration of the Sacraments of Baptism and Communion, a twofold "open and particular" use of the keys of loosing and binding, calling of pastors, "prayer and public thanksgiving and praise to God," and the "Holy Cross" in the form of hardship, persecution, and temptation. In discussing each of these additional signs, Luther writes that where you see it you can know that a (or, variously, "the") Christian Holy people are there (*WA* 50, 632; *PE* 5, 272-86).

The viewpoint of Conservative Laestadians is that the pure "gospel" or "external Word," Luther's primary mark of the Christians in both 1523 and 1539, is nothing more than the proclamation of the forgiveness of sins. Luther gave weight to that view by asking, "What is the difference between saying 'Thy sins are forgiven thee' and preaching the gospel?" (from Althaus 1963, 316). "For Luther, the greatest good which the [Christian] community possesses is that forgiveness of sins is to be found in it," Althaus notes, and goes on to quote Luther as saying, "I believe that the forgiveness of sins is to be found in this community and nowhere else" (p. 316).

But Conservatives are not the only Christians who proclaim the forgiveness of sins to each other. Members of other Laestadian groups even use much the same "believe sins forgiven" language, and it cannot be dismissed that they obtain comfort by hearing and accepting it. So where does that leave the seeker who is trying to be guided by Luther's teaching that where the Gospel or Word is preached, there must be Christians, even if the Word is present there with some impurity?

One area where Luther is in agreement with the Conservative view is that "the whole world is evil and that among thousands there is scarcely one true Christian," and that "the world and the masses are and always will be unchristian, although they are all baptized and are nominally Christian" (*Secular Authority* [1523]; *PE* 3, 236-37). The difference is that Conservative Laestadians view "true Christians" as few and clumped together in a few distinct places while Luther considered them to be "few and far between" (p. 237), "not many, but they are everywhere, though they are spread out thin and live far apart . . ." (*On War Against the Turk* [1529]; *PE* 5, 89). "[T]he number of upright and true Christians in every place is very small," he wrote in his *Table Talk* (§364), with the Christians being "invisible and unknown" to the world (§224).

5.3 Zwingli and the Real Presence

> *Credal athleticism: the boast that my faith is so strong that I can mentally embrace a bigger paradox than you can.*
>
> —Daniel Dennett, *Breaking the Spell*

Luther firmly held to a literal view of Christ's statement of the bread he broke at the Last Supper, "This is my body." His position would always remain "that the bread and wine in the Supper are Christ's true body and blood," though he did not care for "the sophistic cunning" of transubstantiation, which held that the elements are no longer also bread and wine after consecration but just look like bread and wine (*The Smalcald Articles* [1537]; McCain 2005, 279).

Luther was opposed in this view by Huldrich Zwingli, who viewed Communion as a "supper of thanksgiving" in which "the true body of Christ is present by the contemplation of faith." He called it an error to consider "that the body of Christ in essence and really, i.e., the natural body itself, is either present in the supper or masticated with our mouth and teeth" (Zwingli, An Account of the Faith, from Fosdick 1952, 189). In his 1528 *Confession Concerning Christ's Supper*, Luther rants against Zwingli for page after page, calling him "completely perverted" and having "entirely lost Christ" (p. 260).

Luther met Zwingli at the Marburg Colloquy in 1529, where Luther wrote "This is my body" in Latin on the tablecloth before him to leave no doubt about his position. The articles of the Colloquy express agreement on fourteen articles of faith, with the question of "whether the true body and blood of Christ are bodily in the bread and wine" remaining a point of disagreement. Although the articles state that, nonetheless, "each side is able to display Christian love to the other (as far as conscience allows)" (Lull 2005, 279), Luther made it known that he would not accept Zwingli as a brother in faith due to their disagreement on the matter. He said

> that "Zwingli begged with tears in his eyes before the Landgrave and all of them, saying 'There are no people on earth with whom I would rather be in harmony than with the Wittenbergers.'" He would not, however, surrender his position that the Lord's Supper, instead of being a repetition of Christ's sacrifice, was simply the grateful remembrance of it by faithful souls in the manner which Christ had appointed. On that point Luther was adamant–"impudent and obstinate," Zwingli called him–and, in the end, brushed his Swiss brethren off. "You have a different spirit from ours," Luther said. [Fosdick 1952, 159]

If you, like me, cannot make yourself believe that you are actually chewing on and swallowing the real, natural body and blood of the (risen) Jesus every month at Communion (**4.7.3**), you will no doubt find it sobering to realize that Luther would reject you as having a different spirit from his.

5.4 Conversion and The Forgiveness of Sins

> *Simon, Simon, behold, Satan has desired to have you, that he may sift you as wheat: But I have prayed for you, that your faith fail not: and when you have returned, strengthen your brethren.*
>
> –Jesus, in *The Gospel According to Luke*

5.4.1 *Voice of Zion* Article

Luther's experience and understanding of conversion and the forgiveness of sins is an area of study in which I have been engaged since the early 1990s. The following is an excerpt of an article I wrote on the topic as it appeared (with its original footnotes, here reproduced in a numbered list below the excerpted text) in the October 2003 *Voice of Zion*:

As believers, we can be comforted to see that God's Word remains the same today as He revealed it through Luther and the Reformation five centuries ago. First and most importantly, Luther was a partaker and preacher of the same forgiveness of sins that Jesus authorized to believers when he presented the Holy Ghost to that first congregation of disciples,[1] the same gospel we hear among ourselves today. "Forgiveness of sins," Luther preached in one sermon, "is nothing more than two words, in which the whole kingdom of Christ consists."[2] In another sermon, he called the forgiveness of sins "the great and important article of faith," the only article "by believing which we become and are called Christians, and which distinguishes us from all other saints on earth." He alone is a Christian, Luther preached, "who receives this article of faith and knows that he is in the kingdom of grace, in which Christ takes him under his wing and unceasingly forgives him his sins." But, Luther warns, "he who looks for something else or wishes to deal otherwise with God, must know that he is no Christian but is rejected and condemned by God."[3]

Thus Luther was given to understand that conversion, by the forgiveness of sins, is key to membership in the spiritual body of the Church[4] for one in unbelief. Luther's own conversion likely occurred when he had a meeting with an old priest that became a "living consolation to the disturbed young monk."[5] The old monk encouraged Luther to believe not just in the forgiveness of sins in general terms, but in the forgiveness of his own sins.[6] The identity of that priest, the brother from whom Luther received the "one Word" of absolution mentioned above, remains unknown. One possibility is Johann von Staupitz, whom Luther praised in the last year of his life for "first of all being my father in this doctrine, and having given birth [to me] in Christ."[7] Although Luther was saddened that Staupitz never joined him in public opposition to the Catholic Church's false teachings, he would always treasure the counsel of his erstwhile mentor on the topic of repentance. In one letter Luther told Staupitz that "I received your word as a voice from heaven [It] pierced me like a sharp arrow." When Luther afterward compared the portions of Scripture regarding repentance, that word, which had been the "bitterest in the Bible" to him "sounded dearer and sweeter than any other."[8]

No doubt those Scripture portions included Paul's Epistle to the Romans, from which Luther would so often write of man's justification by faith, without works. He considered the admonition of Romans 3:23 that "all have sinned, and come short of the glory of God" to be "the main portion and centerpiece of this epistle and the entire Scripture," interpreting it to mean that "everything that is not redeemed through the blood of Christ and become righteous in Faith is sin."[9] The righteousness of God was revealed to Luther as something that could not be earned or bought, but a gift for which Christ had paid the full price. Indeed, Luther held one who offers something for his sins to "deny the Lord Christ, yea, disgrace and slander him, as if Christ's blood did not count as much as our own repentance and making amends, or as if his blood were not enough to blot out all sin on earth."[10]

Luther rejected the ordained priests' claim of exclusive access to the confessional keys. He taught that all believers are members of a universal priesthood,[11] with confession being, in the words of one biographer, "an act Christians might perform in private conversation, even at a meal or on a walk."[12] Luther understood Jesus' giving of the Holy Spirit and the power to forgive sins the same way we do today: "This power is here given to all Christians, although some have appropriated it to themselves alone, like the pope, bishops, priests and monks have done: they declare publicly and arrogantly that this power was given to them alone and not to the laity. But Christ [in John 20:22] speaks neither of priests nor of monks, but says: 'Receive ye the Holy Spirit.' Whoever has the Holy Spirit, power is given to him, that is, to every one that is a Christian. But who is a Christian? He that believes. Whoever believes has the Holy Spirit. Therefore every Christian has the power . . . to forgive sins or to retain them."[13]

1. John 20:22-23.

2. Sermon for 19th Sunday after Trinity from *The Precious and Sacred Writings of Martin Luther*, John Nicholas Lenker, Trans. (Minneapolis: Lutherans in All Lands, 1906), vol. 14, p. 201.

3. Sermon for 19th Sunday after Trinity from *Lenker*, vol. 14, pp. 212, 216, author editing of translation based on original German sermon transcription.

4. Schwiebert, E. G. *Luther and his Times: the Reformation from a new perspective* (Saint Louis: Concordia, 1950), p. 292.

5. Schwiebert at p. 170.

6. D'Aubigné, J. H. Merle. *History of the Reformation of the Sixteenth Century* (New York: American Tract Society, 1848), 180-181.

7. As quoted in Oberman, Heiko A. *Luther: Man between God and the Devil* (Yale Univ. Press, 1989), p. 152.

8. *The Letters of Martin Luther*, Margaret A. Currie, Trans. & Ed. (London: MacMillan, 1908), p. 26.

9. Marginal note to Luther's 1546 translation of the New Testament, author trans.

10. Sermon for 19th Sunday after Trinity at p. 223, author trans. ed.

11. Grimm, Harold. *The Reformation Era 1500-1600*, (New York: MacMillan, 1973), p. 183.

12. Marius, Richard. *Martin Luther: the Christian between God and Death* (Cambridge, Mass.: Harvard University Press, 1999), p. 258.

13. Sermon for Sunday after Easter from Lenker, vol. 11, pp. 375-376.

The article presents certain of Luther's experiences and expressed views accurately, but the discussion is incomplete without exploring some important issues: the historical context of absolution around the time of the Reformation, Luther's own private experience of rebirth in the tower of the Wittenberg monastery, and his teachings about the forgiveness of sins in prayer and the sacraments. The article also leaves the incorrect impression that private, lay absolution was as significant and frequently discussed a topic in Luther's writings as it is in Conservative Laestadianism, where scarcely any devotional articles or sermons go without mentioning–often focusing on–the forgiveness of sins from believer to believer.

5.4.2 Historical Context

Ronald K. Rittgers has written an exhaustive and fascinating study, *The Reformation of the Keys: Confession, Conscience, and Authority in 16th-Century Germany*, of the theory and practice of absolution in the time leading up to, during, and immediately after Luther's Reformation ministry. It provides a great deal of insight about the historical context in which Luther's various quotes about absolution should be read. It focuses mostly on developments and attitudes in the imperial city of Nürnberg (some 300 km south of Luther's Wittenberg), which can probably be generalized with some accuracy to Luther's Germany as a whole. It is impossible to do justice to the depth of the book and its subject in a few pages, but here are a few points to at least paint a general picture.

On the eve of the Reformation, absolution was inextricably linked with both confession and penance. "Confessors were to assess penitents' debts and penalties and then mediate divine credit to them after being assured that they were sufficiently sorrowful for having plundered God. Penitents were to evidence regret for having sinned, acknowledge all their serious offenses, humbly receive God's undeserved mercy, and willingly pay the remainder of what they owed their Maker" (p. 33). There was no question of absolution being given without confession, or by anyone but a priest.

The confessional rite was both formal and infrequently administered (*e.g.*, an annual requirement), as compared to current-day Laestadian practice:

> Having fulfilled his obligation to elicit a full confession from the penitent, a confessor was then formally to exercise the power of the keys in absolving her of her guilt (that is, debt), using a form of the traditional "Ego te absolvo." According to the 1490-1491 Banberg synod [*i.e.*, church council], confessors were to absolve penitents with one of two formulas: "May our Lord Jesus Christ deign to absolve you," or, "I, by the authority I possess, absolve you from your sins in the name of the Father, Son, and Holy Spirit. Amen." Following the absolution, the priest was to assign the confessant some work of penance with which she could pay the penalty she had incurred for her sins. [p. 37]

Luther's teachings started making an impact in the late 1510s, with Nürnbergers coming "to reject the traditional faith, having been convinced in a matter of years that it was an elaborate hoax. Luther and his followers were able to persuade them that late medieval Christianity was a man-made religion, based on mere human teaching (*Menschenlehre*), whereas evangelical Christianity was a divinely revealed faith, grounded firmly on the Word" (p. 47). Luther's mentor Staupitz contributed to that, assailing "traditional piety for its reliance on human moral effort and the performance of religious rituals to merit divine forgiveness," and urging "trust in God's mercy and not in [one's] own good works to obtain absolution" (p. 49). But Staupitz never left Catholicism despite his fondness for and early influence on Luther, and "had no intention of dismantling traditional penitential Christianity" (p. 50).

In 1519, Luther wrote a *Sermon on the Sacrament of Penance* in which he "greatly elaborated his criticisms of the traditional practice of confession." He now "argued that forgiveness of guilt was far more important than remission of penances because it 'removes the fear and timidity of the heart toward God and makes the conscience inwardly light and happy.' This, for Luther, was true forgiveness because it reconciled one with God, whereas remission of sacramental penances only brought one back into fellowship with the visible Church. Forgiveness of guilt prevented sins from 'biting' one's conscience any longer and gave the penitent 'a joyful confidence' that his sins had been completely forgiven." But he still said that confession was valid and important, and that God "had given the sacrament of penance to be 'a consolation to all sinners'" (pp. 53-54).

There was plenty of popular opposition to the sacrament of penance because of its need for a person to search his conscience for all of his mortal sins, suffer the shame of telling them to the priest, and (more so in earlier years) perform some sort of penance in satisfaction for those sins. Thus, people were eager to embrace Luther's changes while tending to ignore his cautions. It should be said, too, that Luther wasn't entirely consistent; at one point early on he even stated "that the reception of private absolution should be a strictly voluntary matter" (p. 248).

Much of the tension at Nürnberg wound up centering around Andreas Osiander [1498-1552], a preacher appointed there in 1522 who became a leader of the city's evangelical movement. Early on, he preached "against the sacrament of penance, arguing it was a human creation," but "was also anxious to retain the power of the keys." While Osiander "likely envisioned [the] use of the keys taking place in a private encounter between penitent and priest free from the traditional interrogation of conscience and mandatory confession of all mortal sins," his "congregation interpreted his sermons to mean that they need not turn up in the confessional at all" (p. 67). Osiander's career would come to be defined by his objection to general absolution, a practice that, ironically, would be revived in the wake of his helping to dismantle the sacrament of penance and the private absolution it involved.

A pivotal event in that revival was in 1524, when a prior of the Nürnberg Augustinian order substituted a general confession in place of private confession for preparation of the celebrants of the mass. "This confession was quite evangelical in tone. It emphasized sins of unbelief and stressed that forgiveness came through placing one's faith in the divine promise of absolution." After the general confession, the cleric conducting the mass

> said to the congregation, "The Lord God says to us, 'according to your faith it will happen to you! Go forth in peace! Sin no more! Your sins are forgiven, pardoned, and remitted.'" He then pronounced a general absolution: "My dear brothers and sisters, God has had mercy on you and has forgiven us all our sins and will give us eternal life. Amen." [p. 84]

This new mass was revolutionary in its prominence and the importance it would have in the hearts and minds of a laity who were showing their disdain for private absolution and all that it had entailed. But it did not represent a wholly new invention of general absolution, which

> had long been part of the traditional mass in Germany, a rare inclusion of the vernacular in the Latin liturgy. The extant forms for general confession, or *Offene Schuld*, constitute some of the oldest remnants of the German language we possess, a few even dating back to the Carolingian era [i.e., before the tenth century]. General confession typically took place after the sermon and before the celebration of the Eucharist, providing laypeople with a final opportunity to prepare themselves for reception of the consecrated host. Though theologians debated its exact nature, by the beginning of the sixteenth century most held that general confession was not a sacrament and, at best, provided forgiveness for venial sins only. Evangelical reformers quickly adopted general confession as a way of confessing and absolving the laity without risking the alleged abuses of the sacrament of penance. By removing offensive elements from the traditional formulas (for example, references to the saints and the Virgin Mary, along with the optative wording of the absolution), early Protestants transformed general confession into an acceptable evangelical ritual [pp. 84-85].

Indeed, Luther's *Formula of Mass and Communion for the Church at Wittenberg* from a year earlier [1523] had specified the saying of

> The Peace of the Lord, etc, which is, so to speak, a public absolution of the sins of the communicants, truly the Gospel voice announcing remission of sins, the one and most worthy preparation for the Lord's Table, if it be apprehended by faith and not otherwise than though it came forth from the mouth of Christ Himself. [*PE* 6, 90-91]

Despite protests by Osiander and even the implicit disapproval of Luther, who had "instructed members of Wittenberg's clergy to resurrect private confession in their churches" (p. 82), the laity embraced general confession as their "preferred way of preparing for the Lord's Supper" (p. 92).

Conflict continued, with Osiander opposing general absolution as "a source of 'cheap grace' that made a mockery of true forgiveness of sins" (p. 140) and Luther finding value in it, but only alongside private absolution. Writing jointly to the Nürnberger city authorities, Luther and Melanchthon affirmed

> the value of private absolution [and] repeated their previous position that forgiveness could be obtained by believing hearts through either private absolution or a sermon. Both owed their authority to God's promise to be present with his Word, and both required faith [p. 164].

A colleague of Osiander, Johannes Brenz, took a nuanced view

> that pronouncing general absolution after the sermon–its usual place in the liturgy–was an abuse of the clerical authority to bind and loose sins because it suggested to the laity that the sermon itself was not a valid form of forgiveness. Such a practice would inevitably lead to a de-emphasis on the sermon as a means of absolution. [p. 142]

This, then, is the context for Luther's teachings about absolution and the *Augsburg Confession*'s 1530 statement that "private Absolution should be retained in the churches" (Article 11; McCain 2005, 35).

5.4.3 Shared Doctrine and Significance

The single most compelling aspect of Conservative Laestadianism to me is how remarkably its doctrine and practice conforms with the teachings of Luther about absolution and the Keys of the Kingdom. The importance of absolution is shared by both. Even in 1519, a year before excluding penance from the list of sacraments, Luther wrote that the "true way and the right method, for which there is no other," of attaining "forgiveness of guilt and for calming the heart in the face of sins" is

> that most worthy, gracious, and holy sacrament of penance, which God gave for the comfort of all sinners when he gave the keys to St. Peter in behalf of the whole Christian Church and, in Matthew 16[:19], said "Whatever you bind on earth shall be bound in heaven, and whatever you loose on earth shall be loosed in heaven." This holy, comforting, and gracious word of God must enter deeply into the heart of every Christian, where he may with great gratitude let it become part of him [*The Sacrament of Penance*, from Bachmann 1970, 10-11].

Luther then described the "holy sacrament of penance" as having three parts, absolution being the first: "These are the words of the priests which show, tell, and proclaim to you that you are free and that your sins are forgiven you by God according to them by virtue of the above-quoted words of Christ to St. Peter." The second part "is grace, the forgiveness of sins, the peace and comfort of the conscience, as the words declare." The third part "is faith, which firmly believes that the absolution and words of the priests are true" (p. 11). In this formulation, Luther discarded "the traditional division of the sacrament into contrition, confession, and satisfaction" (Rittgers 2004, 54).

Luther's 1525 sermon for the Nineteenth Sunday after Trinity, quoted above in this author's *Voice of Zion* article, is for Conservatives another treasure trove of doctrinally consistent teaching. He concludes the sermon with a rousing summary of the "power on earth to forgive sins," which he, like Conservatives, connects with Christ's giving of the Holy Ghost in John 20:22-23:

> All men who are Christians and have been baptised have this power. For with this they praise Christ, and the word is put into their mouth, so that they may and are able to say, if they wish, and as often as it is necessary: Behold O Man! God offers thee his grace, forgives thee all thy sins; be comforted, thy sins are forgiven; only believe and thou wilt surely have forgiveness. This word of consolation shall not cease among Christians until the last day: "Thy sins are forgiven, be of good cheer." Such language

a Christian always uses and openly declares the forgiveness of sins. For this reason and in this manner a Christian has power to forgive sins. [from *The Precious and Sacred Writings of Martin Luther*, John Nicholas Lenker, trans., Vol. 14, 208-209]

Luther preached another sermon for the Nineteenth Sunday after Trinity in 1529 with the same text (Mt 9:1-8) and emphasis on absolution and the oral word. He criticizes those who "imagine that God will deal separately with each one by some special internal light and mysterious revelation, and give him the Holy Ghost, as though there was no need of the written Word or the external sermon." To the contrary, Luther said, "we are to know that God has ordained that no one shall come to the knowledge of Christ, nor obtain the forgiveness acquired by him, nor receive the Holy Ghost, without the use of external and public means; but God has embraced this treasure in the oral word or public ministry, and will not perform his work in a corner or mysteriously in the heart, but will have it heralded and distributed openly among the people" (p. 224). In words quite supportive of Conservative Laestadians' view of conversion as something obtained from the proclamation of a believer, Luther said he had "always taught that the oral word must precede everything else, must be comprehended with the ears, if the Holy Ghost is to enter the heart, who through the Word enlightens it and works faith. Consequently faith does not come except through the hearing and oral preaching of the Gospel, in which it has its beginning, growth and strength" (p. 225).

In 1530, Luther wrote *The Keys*, a seminal work in which he sought to correct "[t]he horrible abuse and misunderstanding of the precious keys" that he called "one of the greatest plagues which God's wrath has spread over the ungrateful world" (*LW* 40, 325). The "real basis and true nature" of those keys, he wrote, is Christ's statement in Mt 18:18: "'Truly, I say to you, whatever you bind on earth shall be bound in heaven and whatever you loose on earth shall be loosed in heaven.' Notice that assuredly, yes assuredly, it shall be bound and loosed what we bind and loose on earth" (p. 364). Christ does not expect us to know what he binds and looses in heaven: "Who would and could know that? But he speaks in this fashion, If you bind and loose on earth, I will also bind and loose right along with you in heaven" (pp. 364-65). Those with a mistaken notion about the keys think of God as 'way up there in heaven, very, very far removed from his Word here below. So we stand there and with open mouth stare heavenward and invent still other keys. Yet Christ says very clearly in Matt. 16:19 that he will give the keys to Peter. He does not say he has two kinds of keys, but he gives to Peter the keys he himself has and no others. It is as if he were saying: Why are you staring heavenward in search of my keys? Do you not understand I gave them to Peter? They are indeed the keys of heaven, but they are not found in heaven. I left them on earth. Don't look for them in heaven or anywhere else except in Peter's mouth where I have placed them. Peter's mouth is my mouth, and his tongue is my key case. His office is my office, his binding and loosing are my binding and loosing. His keys are my keys, and I have no others, nor do I know of any others. [pp. 365-66]

The significance of the keys, then, is that they "are an office, a power or command given by God through Christ to all of Christendom for the retaining and remitting of the sins of men." Luther urged his readers not to be led astray by "Pharisaic babbling by which some deceive themselves, saying, 'How can a man forgive sins when he can bestow neither grace nor the Holy Spirit?' Rely on the words of Christ and be assured that God has no other way to forgives sins than through the spoken Word, as he has commanded us. If you do not look for forgiveness through the Word, you will gape toward heaven in vain for grace, or (as they say), for a sense of inner forgiveness" (p. 366).

This is, as with the 1529 *Nineteenth Sunday after Trinity* sermon quoted above, a powerful refutation of the attitude of many present-day protestants who indeed seek "a sense of inner forgiveness" through the Sinner's Prayer and private, direct communion with Jesus as their "personal Savior." It is a passage from which Conservative Laestadians can rightly take much comfort, who continue to place such value and emphasis on the "loosing key"–more so than all other Christian groups of which I'm aware except the OALC and FALC–that it still "carries forward the work of the gospel. It invites to grace and mercy. It comforts and promises life and salvation through the forgiveness of sins" (p. 373).

The year 1530 also saw the publication of the *Augsburg Confession*, which indicates that the first Lutherans were "taught that they should highly prize the Absolution as being God's voice and pronounced by God's command. The Power of the Keys is set forth in its beauty. [The people] are reminded what great consolation it brings to anxious consciences and that God requires faith to believe such Absolution as a voice sounding from heaven" (Article 25; McCain 2005, 50). A year later, the *Apology of the Augsburg Confession* went on to state:

> Many troubled consciences have derived comfort from our teaching. They have been comforted after they heard that it is God's command, no, rather the very voice of the Gospel, that we should believe the Absolution and regard it as certain that the forgiveness of sins is freely granted to us for Christ's sake. We should believe that through this faith we are truly reconciled to God. [Article 11; McCain 2005, 156]

> [T]he Power of the Keys administers and presents the Gospel through Absolution, which is the true voice of the Gospel. We also it include Absolution when we speak of faith, because "faith comes from hearing," as Paul says in Romans 10:17. When the Gospel is heard and the Absolution is heard, the conscience is encouraged and receives comfort. Because God truly brings a person to life through the Word, the Keys truly forgive sins before God. According to Luke 10:16, "the one who hears you hears Me." Therefore, the voice of the one absolving must be believed no differently than we would believe a voice from heaven. [Article 12a; p. 162]

> Absolution is God's Word which, by divine authority, the Power of the Keys pronounces upon individuals. Therefore, it would be wicked to remove private Absolution from the Church. If anyone despises private Absolution, he does not understand what the forgiveness of sins or the Power of the Keys is. [Article 12b; p. 172]

In 1539, Luther criticized the pope for misinterpreting Christ's statement to Peter about binding and loosing as applying to his own power, and said "one finds that Christ is speaking of the binding and loosing of sin. The keys are keys to the kingdom of heaven, into which no one enters except through forgiveness of sin, and from which no one is excluded except those who are bound because of an impenitent life. Thus the words do not concern Saint Peter's power, but the need of miserable sinners, or of proud sinners . . . " (*On the Councils and the Churches*, from *PE* 5, 174-75).

5.4.4 Thorns in the Rose Bed

For all this, it is important to remember that, although Luther "clearly regarded absolution as a means of grace, he was still very reluctant to refer to the keys as a sacrament." In *The Keys*, "[a]bsolution was still a pseudo-sacrament in his mind. He would not place it on the same level with baptism and the Lord's Supper" (Rittgers 2004, 156). He had done so in the 1519 *The Sacrament of Penance*, but changed that view just a year later, in *The Babylonian Captivity of the Church*. There he said that "there are, strictly speaking, but two sacraments in the Church of God–baptism and bread [i.e., Communion]; for only in these two do we find both the divinely instituted sign and the promise of forgiveness of sins. The sacrament of penance, which I added to these two, lacks the divinely instituted visible sign, and is, as I have said, nothing but a return to baptism" (*PE* 2, 291-92).

Absolution seems to have been elevated back to sacramental status in *The Apology of the Augsburg Confession* [1531], however. Its Article 11 says that "most people in our churches frequently use the Sacraments (Absolution and the Lord's Supper) during the year" (McCain 2005, 156). Article 13 states explicitly that "Baptism, the Lord's Supper, and Absolution (which is the Sacrament of Repentance) are truly Sacraments. For these rites have God's command and the promise of grace" (p. 184).

Whether or not Luther ultimately viewed absolution as one of the sacraments, it is hard to reconcile the importance he places on baptism and Communion with Conservative Laestadian belief and practice. The proclamation of absolution is, for Conservatives, the exclusive means by which those few who possess the Holy Spirit are able to proclaim the forgiveness of sins and personally convey God's grace to mankind.

Despite Luther's various comments about how highly prized and indispensible absolution is, he did *not* view it as the only means of grace. Summarizing Luther's view of the matter, Althaus writes, "In baptism we are immediately given complete forgiveness of sins and purity in God's judgment" (1963, 356). And, regarding Communion, "the forgiveness of sins stands in the center of Luther's thinking as the special gift of the sacrament" (p. 381). That may be unthinkable for Conservatives who equate "the forgiveness of sins" with absolution itself, conveyed by nothing else but the *proclamation* of forgiveness. But consider the following quotations from various of Luther's writings:

The significance of baptism is a blessed dying unto sin and a resurrection in the grace of God, so that the old man, which is conceived and born in sin, is there drowned, and a new man, born in grace, comes forth and rises.... For just as a child is drawn out of its mother's womb and born, and through this fleshly birth is a sinful man and a child of wrath, so man is drawn out of baptism and spiritually born, and through this spiritual birth is a child of grace and a justified man. Therefore sins are drowned in baptism, and in place of sin, righteousness comes forth. [*A Treatise on Baptism* (1519); PE 1, 57]

[W]hen a man comes forth out of baptism, he is pure and without sin, wholly guiltless. [p. 59][56]

[W]e must have a care that no false security creeps in and says to itself: "Baptism is so gracious and so great a thing that God will not count our sins against us, and as soon as we turn again from sin, everything is right, by virtue of baptism; meanwhile, therefore, I will live and do my own will, and afterwards, or when about to die, will remember my baptism and remind God of His covenant, and then fulfill the work and purpose of my baptism." *Baptism is, indeed, so great a thing that if you turn again from sins and appeal to the covenant of baptism, your sins are forgiven.* Only see to it, if you thus wickedly and wantonly sin, presuming on God's grace, that the judgment does not lay hold upon you and anticipate your turning back; and beware lest, even if you then desire to believe or to trust in your baptism, your trial be, by God's decree, so great that your faith is not able to stand. [p. 71, emphasis added][57]

---

56. One who would argue that Luther's asserted benefit of baptism is quickly lost to sin (that only can be remitted through absolution) should consider the thousands of adult baptisms performed in other churches and missionary encounters every day around the world. Conservatives would not contest the efficacy of those baptisms for having been done by "unbelieving" officiants (nor would Luther himself), but also would not consider the baptized person to be "heaven acceptable" even if he died moments after receiving the rite.

57. Luther's reply to the sinner completely misses the point of Conservative Laestadian doctrine, which would instead warn the sinner that baptism does nothing for his committed, unforgiven sins even if he "turns again from" them.

[I]f you are present at mass [i.e., Communion] and do not consider nor believe that here Christ through His testament has bequeathed and given you forgiveness of all your sins, what else is it, then as if you said: "I do not know or do not believe that it is true that forgiveness of my sins is here bequeathed and given me"? Oh, how many masses there are in the world at present! But how few who hear them with such faith and benefit! Most grievously is God provoked to anger thereby. [*A Treatise on Good Works* (1520); *PE* 1, 223-24]

Lo, how rich therefore is a Christian, or one who is baptised! Even if he would, he cannot lose his salvation, however much he sin, unless he will not believe. For no sin can condemn him save unbelief alone. All other sins,–if faith in God's promise made in baptism return or remain,–all other sins, I say, are immediately blotted out through that same faith, or rather through the truth of God, because He cannot deny Himself if you but confess Him and cling believing to Him that promises. But as for contrition, confession of sins, and satisfaction [the three parts of penance],–if you turn your attention to them and neglect this truth of God, they will suddenly fail you and leave you more wretched than before. [*The Babylonian Captivity of the Church* (1520); *PE* 2, 222]

[W]e cannot confess our secret sins, for God alone knows them, and we are to obtain remission by prayer. ["An Article in Defense of all the Articles of Dr. Martin Luther Wrongly Condemned in the Roman Bull" (1521); *PE* 3, 52]

We believe that we have the forgiveness of sins in Christianity, which takes place through the holy Sacraments and absolution, as well as all kinds of comforting sayings of the entire Gospel. [*Large Catechism* (1529), Part 2, §54]

Look at . . . the power and benefit that is ultimately instituted in the Sacrament, in which also the most necessary thing is, and what we should seek and go there for. Now that is clear and easy to understand, even from the words of Jesus, "This is My body and blood, given and shed for you for the forgiveness of sins." Briefly, that is like saying, "For this reason we go to the Sacrament, that we there receive such a treasure through this, and in this, that we have the forgiveness of sins handed to us. [*Large Catechism*, Part 5, §§21-22]

> [W]hen we pray, we remember the promise and thus think: "Dear Father, for this reason I come and ask you, that you would forgive me, not that I could make satisfaction for or earn it, but rather because you have promised it and have attached the seal to it, that it should so be known, as if I had an absolution proclaimed from you yourself." [*Large Catechism*, Part 3, §§97-98]
>
> [Baptism] works forgiveness of sins, releases from death and the devil and gives eternal salvation to all who believe it, as the word and promises of God declare. [*Small Catechism* (1529), Part 4, §§5-6]
>
> What then is the benefit of such eating and drinking [of the Sacrament]? That is indicated to us by these words: "Given and shed for you [*plural*] for the forgiveness of sins," that is, the forgiveness of sins, life, and salvation are given to us through these words, for where forgiveness of sins is, there is also life and salvation. [*Small Catechism*, Part 6, §§5-6]
>
> To the Anabaptists it appears to be great wisdom when they come with their big talk and rant that water cannot touch the spirit or the soul, but only the naked skin, and that for this reason Baptism contributes nothing to the remission of sins. [*Lectures on Genesis* (1535), Ch. 3, §6]

In a 1522 sermon, Luther asked what harm there is if a man "humbles himself a little before his neighbor, puts himself to shame, looks for a word of comfort from him, and takes it to himself and believes it, as if he heard it from God himself" (*PE* 2, 424). We must, he said,

> have many absolutions, so that we may strengthen our timid consciences and despairing hearts against the devil and against God. Therefore no man shall forbid the confession nor keep or drive any one away from it. And if any one wrestles with his sins, is eager to be rid of them and looks for some assurance from the Scriptures, let him go and confess to another in secret, and receive what is said to him there as if it came directly from God's own lips. Whoever has the strong and firm faith that his sins are forgiven, may ignore this confession and confess to God alone. But how many have such a strong faith? Therefore, as I have said, I will not let this private confession be taken from me. Yet I

> would force no one to it, but leave the matter to everyone's free will. [p. 424]

But Luther's "we must have many absolutions" can be taken two ways. The one that matches Conservative Laestadian doctrine is that we would resort often to obtaining absolution from our neighbor. The other, which seems like a more likely reading based on the paragraph immediately following in Luther's sermon, is that such personal contact is just one of many types of "absolutions":

> For our God is not so miserly that He has left us with only one comfort or strengthening for our conscience, or one absolution, but we have many absolutions in the Gospel, and are showered richly with them. For instance, we have this in the Gospel: "If ye forgive men their trespasses, your heavenly Father will also forgive you." Another comfort we have in the Lord's Prayer: "Forgive us our trespasses," etc. A third is our baptism, when I reason thus: See my Lord, I am baptized in Thy name so that I may be assured of Thy grace and mercy. After that we have the private confession, when I go and receive a sure absolution as if God Himself spake it, so that I may be assured that my sins are forgiven. Finally I take to myself the blessed sacrament, when I eat His body and drink His blood as a sign that I am rid of my sins and God has freed me from all my frailties; and in order to make me sure of this, He gives me His body to eat and His blood to drink, so that I shall not and cannot despair: I cannot doubt I have a gracious God. [pp. 424-25]

5.4.5 Lay Absolution

Many of these quotes, and those in the last paragraph of my *Voice of Zion* article reproduced above, make it clear that Luther included the possibility of lay absolution from believer to believer. Conservatives who have grown up receiving absolution on an everyday basis from their friends and family–and preaching it back to them in return–should appreciate what a revolutionary idea this was after over a thousand years of complete clerical monopoly over the keys.

For Luther, "all brothers and sisters" were to be permitted "freely to hear the confession of hidden sins, so that the sinner may make his sins known to whomever he will and seek pardon and comfort, that is, the word of Christ, by the mouth of his neighbor" (*The Babylonian Captivity of the Church* [1520]; *PE* 2, 252). In *The Sacrament of Penance* (1519), he expressed no doubt that "every one is absolved from his hidden sins when he has made confession, ... sought pardon and amended his ways, privately before any brother, however much the violence of the pontiffs may rage against it; for Christ has given to every one of His believers the power to absolve even open sins." He would "permit all brothers and sisters freely to hear the confession of hidden sins, so that the sinner may make his sins known to whomever he will and seek pardon and comfort, that is, the word of Christ, by the mouth of his neighbor" (*PE* 2, 252). And when Luther asked in 1522 what harm there is if a man "humbles himself a little before his neighbor, puts himself to shame, looks for a word of comfort from him, and takes it to himself and believes it, as if he heard it from God himself," as quoted above (*PE* 2, 424), he continued to support the idea of lay absolution.

Rittgers is quite restrained about the impact of lay absolution, though. While it was "still valid in theory," it "was soon overshadowed by confession to a pastor" (Rittgers 2004, 113), and there is certainly evidence for that view. For example, even in 1520, Luther's *Open Letter to the Christian Nobility* relegated lay baptism and absolution to "cases of necessity":

> If a little group of pious Christian layman were taken captive and set down in a wilderness, and had among them no priest consecrated by a bishop, and if there in the wilderness they were to agree to choosing one of themselves, married or unmarried, and were to charge him with the office of baptizing, saying mass, absolving and preaching, such a man would be as truly a priest as though all bishops and popes had consecrated him. [*PE* 2, 67]

Another example of a case of necessity is also found in the *Open Letter*, when Luther's "brethren and sisters" still in the Catholic convents were unable to get their superiors "to grant you permission to confess your secret sins to whomever you wish, then take them to whatever brother or sister you will and confess them, receive absolution, and then go and do whatever you wish and ought to do; only believe firmly that you are absolved, and nothing more is needed" (p. 124).

Still, I think the importance of Luther's support for the idea of the priesthood of all believers should not be understated. Luther "constantly emphasizes the Christian's evangelical authority to come before God on behalf of the brethren and also of the world" (Althaus

1963, 314). He certainly "limits the public preaching of the word within the church to those who have been called through the community." But within those limitations, "all have been called to proclaim God's word to one another" (p. 315). And a "special form of such preaching of God's word to each other is speaking the forgiveness of sins" (p. 316), which became possible outside the priestly confessional *only* as a result of Luther's reforms.

5.4.6 Luther's Conversion

As with the early figures of Laestadianism (see 4.1.4), Luther's own experiences don't exactly fit in with the Conservative view of conversion by the proclamation of the forgiveness of sins. There were a couple of moments in his early life that Luther considered pivotal in his conversion. The one that most closely comports with Conservative doctrine is what I referenced in my 2003 *Voice of Zion* article by stating that Luther had "'received comfort from a brother through this one word' of absolution during his years in the Erfurt monastery of Augustinians." D'Aubigné, in a passage within the citation for that statement, places the event in "the second year of [Luther's] abode in the convent" (around 1507) and describes it as follows:

> One day, as he lay overwhelmed with despair, an aged monk entered his cell, and addressed a few words of comfort to him. Luther opened his heart to him, and made known the fears by which he was tormented. The venerable old man was incapable of following up that soul in all its doubts, as Staupitz had done; but he knew his *Credo*, and had found in it much consolation to his heart. He will therefore apply the same remedy to his young brother. Leading him back to that Apostles' Creed which Luther had learnt in early childhood at the school of Mansfeldt, the aged monk repeated this article with kind good-nature: *I believe in the forgiveness of sins.* The simple words, which the pious brother pronounced with sincerity in this decisive moment, diffused great consolation in Luther's heart. "I believe," he repeated to himself erelong on his bed of sickness, "I believe in the forgiveness of sins!"–"Ah!" said the monk, "you must believe not only in the forgiveness of David's and of Peter's sins, for this even the devils believe. It is God's command that we believe our own sins are forgiven to us." How delightful did this commandment seem to poor Luther! "Hear what St. Bernard says in his discourse on the

Annunciation," added the aged brother: "The testimony of the Holy Ghost in my heart is this: Thy sins are forgiven thee." From this moment light sprung up in the heart of the young monk of Erfurth. The word of grace had been pronounced: he had believed in it" [pp. 180-81]

There is certainly much in this that compares with the current Laestadian experience of conversion. Luther had to believe in that forgiveness, not just as some abstract concept, but for himself personally.

But why did Luther refer to two other epiphanies in later correspondence and writings? As discussed in my *Voice of Zion* article, Staupitz's words about repentance "pierced him like a sharp arrow" and he took on an entirely new viewpoint about Paul's writings on repentance. That was undoubtedly a separate occasion from his encounter with the anonymous "aged monk," who was (contrary to my article) probably *not* Staupitz, the latter being around 47 years old at the time. And the other epiphany, his *Turmelebnis* in the Wittenberg monastery, is problematic in its lack of human contact, the touchstone of Laestadian conversion today.

The *Turmelebnis*, or tower experience, undoubtedly took place after his encounters with the "aged monk" and Staupitz, but the exact date is still the subject of scholarly debate. Luther's own recollection in the last year of his life was that it occurred in 1519, but such a date seems unlikely, being after some important early works including his *95 Theses*. Gritsch says the search for the date of Luther's "'conversion' or spiritual 'breakthrough'" has "created a literary jungle. Recent scholarship tends to date the breakthrough late, about 1517 or 1518" (Gritsch 2002, 10 & 273). Gritsch co-authored another book with Robert W. Jenson, *Lutheranism: the Theological Movement and its Confessional Writings*, which places the tower experience "sometime between 1508 and 1518" (p. 45).

In any event, Luther recalls it as being a pivotal experience in his life: "The Holy Spirit unveiled the Scriptures for me in this tower" (from Gritsch 2002, 12). And, strikingly to the Conservative Laestadian reader, it was a very private one:

> Though I lived as a monk without reproach, I felt that I was a sinner before God with an extremely disturbed conscience. I could not believe that he was placated by my satisfaction. I did

not love, yes, I hated the righteous God who punishes sinners, and secretly, if not blasphemously, certainly murmuring greatly, I was angry with God, and said, "As if, indeed, it is not enough, that miserable sinners, eternally lost through original sin, are crushed by every kind of calamity by the law of the Decalogue [*i.e.*, Ten Commandments], without having God add pain to pain by the gospel and also by the gospel threatening us with his righteousness and wrath!" Thus I raged with a fierce and troubled conscience. Nevertheless, I beat importunately upon Paul at that place, most ardently desiring to know what St. Paul wanted.

At last, by the mercy of God, meditating day and night, I gave heed to the context of the words, namely, "In it the righteousness of God is revealed, as it is written, 'He who through faith is righteous shall live.'" There I began to understand that the righteousness of God is that by which the righteous lives by a gift of God, namely by faith. And this is the meaning: the righteousness of God is revealed by the gospel, namely, the passive righteousness with which merciful God justifies us by faith, as it is written, "He who through faith is righteous shall live." Here I felt that I was altogether born again and had entered paradise itself through open gates. There a totally other face of the entire Scripture showed itself to me. . . .

And I extolled my sweetest word with a love as great as the hatred with which I had before hated the word "righteousness of God." Thus that place in Paul was for me truly the gate to paradise . . . [*Preface to the Complete Edition of Luther's Latin Writings*, from Lull 2005, 8-9].

6 The Old Testament

Now therefore kill every male among the little ones, and kill every woman that hath known man by lying with him. But all the women children, that have not known a man by lying with him, keep alive for yourselves.

—Moses, *The Book of Numbers*

6.1 Genesis

• Chapters 1 and 2 contain two different creation narratives that conflict with each other. Arch Taylor, after acknowledging that while claiming to "believe the Bible" he "had not really paid attention to what the Bible actually said" (2003, 159), provides a concise summary of the two different accounts (p. 160):

Genesis 1

> God separates dry land out of watery chaos.
>
> God causes vegetation to grow out of the earth.
>
> God creates fish in the sea and birds on dry land and in the air.
>
> God causes the earth to bring forth wild and domestic animals.
>
> God creates humankind, male and female, in the divine image.

Genesis 2

> Dry land, no vegetation or rain, only mist.
>
> God forms a male human out of the dust of the earth.
>
> God plants a garden and causes vegetation to grow.
>
> God forms animals from the ground.
>
> God makes a female human from a rib taken from the male.

Taylor says he

> had conveniently ignored the details of the two accounts that were mutually inconsistent: the difference in the numbering of the days and the order in which God was said to have created

> various things. In keeping with the children's story Bible on which I had been brought up before having my own Bible, I had unquestioningly assumed that the story about Adam and Eve was just a more detailed description of what had taken place when, as chapter 1 had said, God created them in the divine image on the sixth day. The Bible doesn't say that; it obviously says something different. [p. 160]

- One reason why the evolutionary origin of life has been rejected in Conservative Laestadianism is that it conflicts with a literal reading of these creation narratives. In Reinikainen's 1986 view (4.3.1), even interpreting "the biblical account of creation to mean that God's creation work occurred through evolution" is considered "an outrage to the word of God."

In the decades since Reinikainen attempted to slam the door shut on evolution, the evidence for it has continued to pile up and much of Christianity has come to view Genesis in an allegorical fashion. (Though not Conservative Laestadianism, at least not judging by any of the statements quoted in 4.3.1.) But even that doesn't remove all the difficulties. Besides some major issues with Paul's teachings of original sin (7.3), there is the dimished and confused role that evolution by random mutations and natural selection leaves for God the Creator.

This was brought out eloquently by John Haught, a Catholic theologian and "evolutionary creationist," in a panel discussion broadcasted on Internet video by FORA.tv <http://fora.tv/2009/11/17/Great_Issues_Forum_What_Is_Religion>. Haught was asked why and how religions exist after Darwin. Saying he had spent a lot of time thinking about that question (he certainly has, with several books on the topic), Haught replied with a frank explanation of the "biggest reason why people have problems religiously and theologically with the Darwinian picture of things." There are three ingredients,

> which are problematic to those who think of God primarily as a designer. And those ingredients are: there have to be lots of accidents, plus natural selection, plus lots and lots of time. And to people who believe in divine providence, the Darwinian recipe at least at first seems to be very, very problematic. Because there are accidents not only in the origin of life but accidents in variations and mutations that provide the raw material for evolution, accidents in natural history such as the asteroid that impacted the

Yucatan Peninsula, wiping out the dinosaurs, apparently making room for mammalian development and primates and eventually us. Why if there is a providential deity in charge of things is there so much *undirected* happening in the cosmos? Why isn't there more evidence, would be the question that science would ask, of a designer as it were. And then there is natural selection, which operates so impersonally and mechanistically, and apparently unjustly and unfairly. Very difficult to reconcile, for a lot of people, with a benign providence. Certainly it's true of Darwin himself, and it's been true of countless people since then. And the vast amount of time that it takes for evolution to unfold. If God were truly interested in bringing about life and consciousness, why fool around and fool around for all these billions of years before this happens? [38:50-40:40]

Schimmel criticizes a small number of scientists from his former Orthodox Judaism who interpret the Bible literally and are hostile to evolution (2008, 68). But he also has little patience for the many more who defend theistic evolution. They "claim that the divine purpose and goal of evolution–cosmic and biological–was the creation of humans, and from humans, the designation of Israel as a chosen people," which he finds "myopic, parochial, species-arrogant, and irrational":

What they are claiming, in effect, is that God triggered the Big Bang event 14 billion years ago, which subsequently produced a universe of immense vastness filled with innumerable galaxies, stars, and planets *in order to* bring into existence the planet Earth *so that* organic life should evolve on it, *for the purpose of* the evolution of human beings (who are but a small fraction of all living species), *with the goal* of selecting for a special relationship with him a specific group, consisting of a fraction of a percent of the entire human population. But if God is all-powerful, why would he have used such an inefficient and wasteful process to achieve his ultimate goal? [p. 69]

• If Adam and Eve were the first human pair and Cain was their oldest child, why was Cain afraid of being killed? God put a mark on him so that he wouldn't be harmed, and then Cain found himself a wife and built a city (Genesis 4:15-17), both of which imply that other people were around somewhere.

- As discussed in **4.3.2**, the story of the Flood is impossible to reconcile with reality. Is it to be understood as historical fact? If the story is just metaphorical or allegorical, why all the detail, e.g., exact dimensions of the ark, number of months, depth of water over the high mountains? If it was just a local flood, why does it refer to "every beast," the entire world, all mankind, etc. (7:21-23)? And why would Jesus and the writers of Hebrews, 1 Peter, and 2 Peter refer to the story in a factual and historical sense (Mt 24:38, Lk 17:27, Heb 11:7, 1 Pet 3:20, 2 Pet 2:5), long afterward in the New Testament?

- Why do many aspects of the flood story have so much in common with the ancient *Epic of Gilgamesh*, c. 2500-1500 B.C.? The main character rides out a deluge on a large, multi-decked boat covered with pitch (Gen 6:14-16; Tablet 11:58-68), which is loaded with animals (Gen 7:14-16; Tablet 11:86). After a while the deluge ends and the boat runs aground on a mountain (Gen 8:2-5; Tablet 11:142). The main character sends out a dove, which returns because it had no place to land (Gen 8:8-9; Tablet 11:148-150). He sends out a raven, which flies around (Gen 8:7; Tablet 11:153-156). He leaves the ark and makes a burnt offering, the aroma of which God smells, or the gods smell (Gen 20-21; Tablet 11:157-162).

The only way this level of coincidence seems plausible is for one narrative to have adapted the other. An unconnected Babylonian observer of the worldwide flood wouldn't have picked up on all the details, and of course the idea of any survivors outside of Noah's clan is contrary to the Genesis account (7:21-23). If the Genesis story is the original, the author of the *Epic of Gilgamesh* must have been a descendant of Noah. If so, why does the *Epic* appear to be much older than the Genesis account, and with the more primitive religious ideas, e.g., multiple gods?

- Were there rainbows before the flood receded? If so, why does God say that "it shall come to pass, when I bring a cloud over the earth, that the bow shall be seen in the cloud" (9:14)? If not, how did water fail to refract light up to that point? Human eyes wouldn't have worked, for one thing.

- When God smells the sweet savor of Noah's burnt offerings, he promises, "I will not again curse the ground any more for man's sake; for the imagination of man's heart is evil from his youth; neither will I again smite any more every thing living, as I have done" (8:21). Is the "as I have done" a caveat that he won't use a flood again, or a reference to the fact that he just killed every living thing (except Noah et al.)? If he acknowledged that man's heart is evil and that's just the way it is, why is he planning to destroy humanity again?

• Why was Noah told that every moving thing that is alive shall be food for him (9:3) when there were many dietary laws about what critters not to eat later, but still in the Old Testament? The reason is that the text is not from a single author. It relates to the contradiction between the two pairs or seven pairs of clean animals. Those numbers arise from different authors, an original "Yahwist" or "J" author and a much later "priestly" or "P" author who was aware of distinctions between kosher and non-kosher. It was the later "P" writer who portrays Noah as ignorant of kosher and able to eat everything because this later writer wants the kosher parts of the law to have been given by Moses (Price 2011).

• Why did Noah, who was found to be the only righteous head of a household in the whole world, get drunk (9:21)? And why was it Ham who was punished for not ignoring the whole situation, rather than Noah for causing the scene in the first place?

• If Noah's grandsons were separated, every one according to his language (10:1-5), how was it that the whole earth used the same language in the later narrative about the tower of Babel?

• Imagine a father who finds his house surrounded by a rampaging, lustful mob of men. To settle things down, he offers the guys his two daughters to do with what they will. What kind of father would that seem like to you? Later, he lets his daughters get him stone cold drunk, to the point where he is insensible when they have sex with him. That man, of course, is Lot (19:4-8, 19:30-35). Why is he considered "righteous," and his the only household to be spared God's wrath that destroys an entire city?

• In the story of Lot and Sodom, we are told that God would have been willing to withhold the fire and brimstone if just ten "righteous" had been found in the city (18:32). He didn't, though. Apparently innocent children did not count as "righteous," as there must have been at least hundreds of them there. That of course contradicts the belief that all children are born into faith and lose it to sin as they grow up.

- Why all the deceit in Jacob and his sons when he was favored by God? Jacob stole Esau's birthright (27:18-29). Later, Jacob's sons persuaded some foreigners who wanted to live peaceably with them to be circumcised, then killed them all when they were recovering from the painful procedure (34:13-29).

6.2 Exodus

- If Egypt became filled with Israelites, and they became more numerous and mightier than the Egyptians (1:7-9), why is there almost no record of the Israelites in Egypt's many historical records? The only known records are a stele claiming that "Israel is laid waste, its seed is not," and a drawing of some Semitic nomads meeting some Egyptian soldiers. Egypt's ancient records include mundane details about everyday commerce as well as religious texts and narratives about kings. In all of that, there is nothing about a slave population that swelled to become a majority and rebelled, about plagues, or even a one-sided battle narrative that would favorably record Egypt expelling the rebellious slaves in their millions.

- God announces that he will harden Pharaoh's heart so that he won't let the people go (4:21, 7:3-5). He tells Pharaoh (through Moses) that he is allowing him to remain in order to show God's power and to proclaim his name through all the earth (9:16). By the 15th century B.C., when the Bible asserts that the Exodus took place (1 Kings 6:1) the entire earth was populated; the last human colonizations had brought people from Southeast Asia into Polynesia around 1,500 years before (Wells 2006, 189). Pagan chiefdoms were found across Europe, the Shang dynasty was well underway in China, and domesticated crops were being farmed in South America. However, at the time of the Exodus and for hundreds and even thousands of years thereafter, this vast and populous world outside the Mideast remained completely unaware of the God of Israel.

- Why didn't the Egyptians, with all their detailed record keeping, not make any mention of the firstborn of every one of their homes dying in one night, including Pharaoh's own firstborn (12:29-30)?

- If all the livestock of Egypt died in Plague #4 (9:6), how did one servant of Pharaoh later have livestock to send into the houses to avoid Plague #6, and another to have livestock to leave in the field (9:20-21)?

- Why is there no archaeological evidence of the 600,000 Israelite men (plus children, and presumably, women) on the forty-year Exodus (12:37)? Despite fervent attempts to find such evidence during Israel's occupation of the Sinai peninsula, despite specific place names being provided in the biblical account, absolutely nothing has been found that would indicate anything like such a mass migration. The Sinai Peninsula's "climate has preserved the tiniest traces of ancient Bedouin encampments and the sparse 5000-year old villages of mine workers," but "there is not a single trace of Moses or the Israelites; and they would have been by far the largest body of ancient people ever to have lived in this great wilderness" (Romer 1988, 58).

We are told that the people gathered manna from heaven, but how did the livestock eat? Light bread is not a suitable diet for ruminants, and there was no grazing to be had in the desert of Sinai. And even with miraculous food supplies, what about the logistical problems involved with moving, supporting, and coordinating around two million people in a desert over a forty-year span, without modern communication, sanitation, sources of replacement clothing, etc.?

Just getting everybody through the gap in the sea in time would have been an incredible feat. (The literal term used for the body of water they crossed was "Sea of Reeds," which is widely mistranslated as the "Red Sea," e.g., at Exodus 13:18.) They had just a few hours for the crossing, starting their march at their place of captivity in the "morning watch," and getting everybody on the other side of the sea by daybreak (14:24-27). Assuming a sustained march at 3 mph (with children and livestock) and a procession 20 miles long, there would have been about 15,000 rows of some 150 people abreast slogging feverishly over soggy sea bottom in sandals and hooves for five hours straight, and that's just to complete the crossing.

- The famous Ten Commandments are listed in Exodus 20. One of them is routinely violated by Christians who don't really know what the Commandments actually say:

"Thou shalt not make unto thee any graven image, or any likeness of any thing that is in heaven above, or that is in the earth beneath, or that is in the water under the earth" (20:4). Guess what? That fish symbol is a "likeness of [a] thing" that "is in the water under the earth," at least as far as ancient cosmology was concerned.

• Various rules on slavery are provided. The master can give a Hebrew slave a wife, but she and any children they have remain the master's property even after the Hebrew slave goes free (21:2-5). A man may sell his daughter as a slave, under various conditions (21:7-11).

• God's edicts start getting pretty harsh during the Exodus. You could be put to death for cursing your mother or father (21:17), owning a habitual person-goring ox (21:29), being a witch (22:18), bestiality (22:19), or sacrificing to any god other than the Lord (22:20). But striking a slave (male or female) to the point of near-death was not a problem, as long as the slave survived a day or two, because the person was considered your property (21:20-21).

• When Moses saw that Aaron had let the people get out of control with the golden calf, he had the sons of Levi go back and forth in the camp and kill their brothers, friends, and neighbors (32:25-28). This wanton massacre of about 3,000 randomly picked members of God's chosen people got no comment from God when Moses next spoke to him, but he then "smote the people" in some unspecified additional way (32:30-35).

• In chapter 33, God says that no man can see him and live. (Likewise, 1 John 4:12 says that no man has seen God at any time.) How was Moses able to speak to God "face to face just as a man speaks to his friend," as recorded earlier in that same chapter? How was Abraham able to converse with the Lord when he appeared at his tent by the oaks of Mamre, as recorded in Genesis 17:20?

• How did Moses remember all of the painstaking details God gave him on Mount Sinai about the construction of the ark of the covenant and the tabernacle (chapters 25-31)? Why did God care about specific floral designs, the number of branches on lampstands, exact lengths of curtains, linen hangings, and screens, the number of loops on the curtains, etc.?

• Why does God say he is "visiting the iniquity of the fathers upon the children, and upon the children's children, unto the third and to the fourth generation" (24:7)? Why should someone suffer for what his great-grandfather did before he was even born? And why then are we told elsewhere that "[t]he fathers shall not be put to death for the children, neither shall the children be put to death for the fathers: every man shall be put to death for his own sin" (Deuteronomy 24:16) and "[t]he son shall not bear the iniquity of the father, neither shall the father bear the iniquity of the son" (Ezekiel 18:20)?

6.3 Leviticus

• Two sons of Aaron offered "strange fire before the Lord, which he had not commanded them" (10:1). The response was fire that consumed them, "they died before the Lord." Aaron and two of his other sons were warned not to mourn the loss or they might die and incur God's wrath toward the whole congregation (10:6-7).

Jason Long writes, "No matter how many times I read passages like this, I'm always amazed how God kills people because they do something silly like build a displeasing campfire, but as we will soon see, he allows them to rape female prisoners of war" (2005, 88).

• Rabbits don't chew cud (11:6, see also Deut 14:7), though it might look like they do, given the motions of their mouths. This is just one of many cases where the Old Testament describes the world in ways that one would expect from the limited perspective of an ancient human observer, a perspective that is uninformed by and clearly in conflict with what we all now readily acknowledge:

> • There is no "firmament" in which one might set stars or the moon or the sun (Genesis 1:14-17), though it might appear that something must be holding up those heavenly bodies. Isaiah certainly thought so, predicting that God would someday roll the sky up like a scroll (Isaiah 34:4).
>
> • Putting cattle in view of a speckled rod does not influence the coloring of their offspring (Genesis 30:37-41), though it was

common to believe in such environmental influencing even into the nineteenth century.

• In Leviticus 11:19, bats are listed as birds; an easy assumption to make, but not what they are any more than flying fish would be.

If all of this was divinely inspired, why couldn't the writers show any evidence of knowledge beyond what we would expect of them as mere mortals? I will dare to yet again quote Robert G. Ingersoll:

> Man has no ideas, and can have none, except those suggested by his surroundings. He cannot conceive of anything utterly unlike what he has seen or felt. He can exaggerate, diminish, combine, separate, deform, beautify, improve, multiply and compare what he sees, what he feels, what he hears, and all of which he takes cognizance through the medium of the senses; but he cannot create. Having seen exhibitions of power, he can say, omnipotent. Having lived, he can say, immortality. Knowing something of time, he can say, eternity. Conceiving something of intelligence, he can say God. Having seen exhibitions of malice, he can say, devil. A few gleams of happiness having fallen athwart the gloom of his life, he can say, heaven. Pain, in its numberless forms, having been experienced, he can say, hell. [*Lectures on Gods*]

• Sins punishable by death expanded to taking the life of a person (except, apparently, in the many cases where killing is commanded by God), blasphemy, adultery, incest, homosexual sex, being or consulting a medium or spiritist. In a special case, marrying both a woman and her mother results in all three being "burned with fire" (20:14). However, if a man has sex with someone else's female slave, they won't be put to death because she wasn't free (19:20)

A host of other sins would get you "cut off from among the people," which seems like it could well be a death sentence out in the desert of the Sinai peninsula. They include having sex during menstruation (both parties), touching any unclean thing (the uncleanness of man or unclean beasts), and eating flesh of sacrificial animals or any manner of blood.

• Why is God so particular about the physical attributes of the priest? He can't be blind, lame, disfigured in the face, have any deformed limbs, broken feet or broken hands, have a hunchback or be a dwarf, or have any eye defect, excema, scabs, or crushed testicles (21:18-20).

- Why is God so hostile and cruel in his threats to punish his people for disobedience? He will inflict sudden terror, consumption and fever that will waste away their eyes. He will cause their enemies to rule over them. If that doesn't make the people obey, he will punish them seven times more, rendering the land barren. If that doesn't work, he will increase the plague seven times again, letting loose the beasts of the field to kill their children and cattle, and reduce their number until their roads lie deserted. If that doesn't do the trick, he will send pestilence among them. Finally, as a last resort, he will act with "wrathful hostility" against them, whereupon they will eat the flesh of their sons and daughters, he will heap their remains on the remains of their idols and lay waste their cities. Understandably, any that may be left after all this will "have weakness in their hearts; the sound of a driven leaf will chase them and even when no one is pursuing they will flee and fall" (26:36).

It is interesting to note the one threat that God does *not* include in the many he makes against his chosen people, neither here nor anywhere else in the five books of Moses. That is the threat of hell, of any unpleasantness in any afterlife. There is no hint of any place of eternal torment until at least the Psalms, and even at that point it is unclear and contradictory.

Indeed, there is no Hebrew word for hell at all. The word *Sheol* is translated as "hell" in the King James Version, but refers to a shadowy nether world beneath the earth, neutral of any judgment, where *all* men go upon death. For example, King Hezekiah, who had no obvious issues with God, lamented what he thought would be his early entry there in Isaiah 38:10.

- Why are human beings assigned monetary values, with different figures for males and females, for young and old (27:1-7)? A male aged 20-60 years was worth 50 shekels of silver, versus 30 shekels for a female. Males aged 5-20 years were worth 20 shekels, twice that of female of that age. Males 60 years and up were worth 15 shekels, versus 10 shekels for females of that age. In Acts 10:34, Peter says that God is not one to show partiality, but that certainly was not true in the Old Testament.

6.4 Numbers

• Another capital offense, for a stranger to approach the tabernacle ("dwelling place") in which the ten commandment tablets were placed (3:10).

• We recall with horror and disgust the trials "by ordeal" during the Salem witch madness. Consider, though, how a woman suspected of adultery without witnesses to prove anything is tried (5:11-28). The priest puts dirt in some water and has the woman drink of the "water of bitterness." If her abdomen swells and her thigh rots, she did it. (There is no mention of anything a woman can do if she suspects her husband of adultery.)

• In chapter 11, Moses has finally had enough and talks back pretty forcefully to God, who takes it surprisingly well. His response is ultimately to blow in quail from the sea, covering the ground 3 feet deep, which the people gathered to the tune of at least 120 bushels apiece. When they're eating the meat, God's anger is kindled against the people and he strikes them with a "very severe plague."

• In chapter 12, we again see God getting angry with his people, threatening them, but being calmed down and talked out of the worst of it by Moses. Isn't it disturbing to see a mere mortal leading an all-wise God through these anger management sessions?

• In chapter 13, why does God have Moses send spies into the land of Canaan when he could just tell Moses what was going on there himself?

• A man is found gathering wood on the sabbath and is stoned to death for it (15:32-36).

• Korah and his followers question the authority of Moses and Aaron, though they say nothing against God himself (16:3). Nonetheless, God's retribution is dramatic and violent; some of them are swallowed up into a crack in the Earth, and the rest are consumed by flame (16:30-35). The next day "all the congregation" grumble against Moses and Aaron. In response, God kills nearly 15,000 more of his chosen people with a plague (16:41-49). Contrast this story with the current-day church congregation having authority over its leaders.

• God gets angry at the Israelites because they joined themselves to Baal of Peor. He tells Moses to "[t]ake all the heads [NASB, *leaders*] of the people, and hang them up before the Lord against the sun, that the fierce anger of the Lord may be turned away from Israel" (25:3-4).

• In the midst of this unpleasantness, an Israelite brings a Midianite woman home to his relatives. In our day, this would likely be met with a resigned politeness and mixed emotions between joy at the loved one finding his soul mate and sadness at him leaving the faith. Not so in the Old Testament! When one of Aaron's grandsons saw the couple, he ran a spear through them both, killing them then and there. Pleased with this action, God stops his latest plague, capping the body count of his chosen people at 24,000, and gives the grandson his "covenant of peace" (25:12). He then tells Moses to "be hostile to the Midianites and strike them," something that will happen in the most horrific terms a bit later.

Why does God hate the Midianites so much? Yes, they apparently worship false gods, though there isn't much specific detail on that. But at this point in history, the world was populated with people who had been developing widely varied religions, from the multiple gods of the Shang dynasty in China to a mature pagan cult centered around Stonehenge (it had been in use for at least a thousand years). None of them got any of the sort of abuse that the Israelites' neighbors suffered.

• God changes his mind on something again in chapter 27, this time after some women point out that they stand to lose their father's inheritance because they have no brothers. He acknowledges that they have a point and makes some new rules on the matter. It's nice that he listens to reason, but why would an all-seeing, all-wise God have to do this?

• The slaughter of the Midianites recounted in chapter 31 is easily one of the most troubling portions of the Bible. The bloodshed begins with God telling Moses to take full vengeance for the sons of Israel on the Midianites. Moses sends out the troops to make war on Midian; they kill every male, capture the women and children, plunder all their cattle, flocks, and goods, and burn their cities and camps. The Israelites bring the captives, prey, and spoil to Moses, who is angry at them. Why? Not because of their brutality, but because they spared the women! He commands the killing of all the boys and the women who aren't virgins, but "all the women children, that have not known a man by lying with him, keep alive for yourselves." Stop and read the words again; they are horrific.

God then commands Moses to divide up the booty that was captured, both of man and of animal. The various participants divide up nearly a million head of livestock and 32,000 humans (the virgin girls), as recounted in precise mathematical detail for the remainder of the chapter.

Massacre, plunder, and rape of virgin girls, all from God's chosen people and their leader operating under God's direct command?

6.5 Deuteronomy

• The Israelites are warned not to lift up their eyes to heaven and see the sun, moon, and stars, lest they be drawn away and worship them (4:19).

• As the forty years draws to a close and they arrive in Jordan, Moses tells the Israelites that theirs is a compassionate God who will not fail them or destroy them (4:31). What about the tens of thousands of Israelites that God killed in various massacres and plagues, never mind the killing of Egyptians, Midianites, etc.?

• The Israelites are told to "consume all the people which the Lord thy God shall deliver thee; thine eye shall have no pity upon them" (7:16). We are often told that the Old Testament is ultimately all about Jesus. In fact, Jesus said that Moses spoke of him (John 5:46). But how is this instruction, along with all the other violence discussed above, anything like Jesus' commands to love our neighbors as ourselves, turn the other cheek, have compassion, etc.?

• How did Moses go without food *and* water for forty days in the desert (9:18)? The only explanation is a miracle, but Moses was recounting actions he took as his own demonstration of fear and prayer before God, not as something God was directing or supporting.

• Toward the end of Revelation is a warning about changing any words of the "prophecy of this book," which is often extended to the entire Bible. But Moses makes his own such statement: "What thing soever I command you, observe to do it: thou shalt not add thereto, nor diminish from it" (12:32). Why do we then only observe parts of what Moses taught (e.g., the ten commandments) but not others (e.g., stoning sabbath-breakers to death)? Yes, it's the Old Testament, but Jesus said that not even the smallest part would pass from the law until all be fulfilled (Matthew 5:18). And even in the Old Testament, Moses' commands were diminished. How else can one explain why David was not executed for murder and adultery?

• If a family member or your wife or a dear friend secretly asks you to go worship other gods, it's not enough to say no and rebuke him or her for the apostasy. You have to kill him or her: "thine hand shall be first upon him to put him to death, and afterwards the hand of all the people. And thou shalt stone him with stones, that he die" (13:9-10).

The same goes for an entire city. If its inhabitants have gone off to serve other gods, you will utterly destroy it and all that is in it, burning the city and all its booty as a burnt offering for God (13:12-16).

• A list of things the Israelites are told they can buy with some tithe money includes "wine or strong drink," or whatever their hearts desire, and to eat in the presence of God and rejoice (14:26). Why so when the Old Testament elsewhere says that wine is a mocker and strong drink is raging, and whosoever is deceived thereby is not wise (Proverbs 20:1)?

• Moses says that there will be no poor among the Israelites (15:4), but then says what to do if one of your brothers is a poor man (15:7) and warns that the poor will never cease to be in the land (15:11).

• More capital offenses: not listening to a Levitical priest or judge (17:12), prophesying something that doesn't happen (18:20-22), and being a stubborn and rebellious son (21:18-21).

• An Israelite soldier who finds a beautiful woman among his captives can bring her home to be his wife. He just needs to let her mourn for a month (21:10-13).

• New brides had reason to be a bit nervous on their wedding night because the husband might charge her with not being a virgin, another capital offense. Chapter 22 goes into some detail about how the girl's parents might present a bloody garment to the elders of the city as a defense against the husband's charge.

• No one with his testicles crushed or his penis cut off was allowed to enter God's assembly (23:1). Why? Was this checked on a regular basis?

No bastard, Ammonite, or Moabite, nor up to ten generations of their descendants could enter, either (23:2-3). Why should someone be denied entry because a distant ancestor from a couple of hundred years ago had parents who weren't married or were of the wrong tribe? It is hard to recognize any similarity between this and Peter saying that God is no respecter of persons (Acts 10:34), or Paul writing that there is neither Jew nor Greek (Galatians 3:28).

• Specific instructions on defecating are provided in 23:12-14. You had to go outside the camp with a peg and dig a hole, and then cover everything up when you finished. The reason given was not to avoid the spread of disease but concern that God might see something indecent when he walks in the midst of the camp.

• A wife had to be careful how to defend her husband if he got in a fight with another Israelite. If she grabbed the other guy's privates, she'd have her hand cut off (25:11-12).

• In chapter 28, Moses makes a litany of threats against the Israelites should they disobey any of God's commands (few of which are reported in later accounts of Israel's numerous strayings). God will smite them with consumption, fever, inflammation, blight, mildew, boils, tumors, scabs, itch, madness, blindness, and bewilderment. It will rain powder and dust until they are destroyed. They will be oppressed and robbed continually. Their wives will be raped. They will be driven mad by what they see. They will eat their offspring; women will eat their afterbirth for lack of anything else. God will delight over them to make them perish and destroy them. The curses will pursue and overtake them until they are destroyed, and will become a sign and wonder because they did not serve God with "joyfulness and with gladness of heart."

6.6 Joshua

• Why was Joshua (like Moses) exalted by God in the sight of all Israel, so that they revered him (4:14)? We don't revere our church leaders, but consider them fellow sinners. God says that he will not give his glory to another (Isaiah 42:8).

• More slaughter and pillage by God's people, this time against Jericho. Except for Rahab and her family, they destroyed everything in the city, both man and woman, young and old. They burned the city and all that was in it, except for the precious metals that they "put into the treasury of the house of the Lord" (6:24). What had the people of Jericho done to deserve this except be in the way and have some valuables?

- One of the Israelites, Achan, takes some of the Jericho booty for himself. Joshua implores him to give glory and praise to God and tell Joshua what he has done. Achan confesses that he has sinned and tells how he coveted the stuff and took it (7:19-21). At this point, given how Joshua approached Achan and Achan's penitence, we would expect forgiveness of some sort. Aren't these the Old Covenant believers, who believed in the promise of a savior and forgave sins through the ritual sacrifices?

But that's not what happened; the Israelites stoned Achen *and* his sons and daughters to death and burned them (7:24-25). No mercy, no forgiveness. And so much for sons not being put to death for the sins of their fathers (Deuteronomy 24:16).

- The next city on God's hit list was Ai. He tells Joshua that he has given into his hand the king of Ai, his people, his city, and his land. The Israelites destroyed the city and killed everyone but the king, as recorded chillingly in 8:24-26:

> And it came to pass, when Israel had made an end of slaying all the inhabitants of Ai in the field, in the wilderness wherein they chased them, and when they were all fallen on the edge of the sword, until they were consumed, that all the Israelites returned unto Ai, and smote it with the edge of the sword. And so it was, that all that fell that day, both of men and women, were twelve thousand, even all the men of Ai. For Joshua drew not his hand back, wherewith he stretched out the spear, until he had utterly destroyed all the inhabitants of Ai.

The king of Ai got special treatment; he was hanged on a tree until evening (8:29). Again, what had this people done to deserve this? How does the initiator of all this remotely resemble the God of love and grace that we hear of today?

- During the next battle, we are told that "the sun stood still in the midst of heaven, and hasted not to go down about a whole day" (10:13). Such a miraculous event might seem plausible in a time when God carried out conversations with people and the earth was viewed as a disk of fairly limited size, with the sun going up and down around it. In view of what we now know about the conservation of momentum and energy and the earth being a rotating sphere illuminated by a distant sun, it is hard to know where to begin in accounting for the necessary miracles.

The entire spinning mass would have had to suddenly stop in place, the thin crust of the earth staying exactly in place atop the liquid mantle as an unimaginable amount of kinetic energy just disappeared into nothing. Then, when the fighting had finished, all that kinetic energy was miraculously inserted back into everything in and on earth again, in perfect timing and quantity, and the earth resumed spinning. And all this happened without any of the other peoples dispersed across the entire earth making any note of it, including the neighboring Egyptians who made detailed astronomical records and worshiped the sun as a god.

This event gets only a few verses in the Bible; it probably just didn't seem that significant for the bright little dot of the sun to stop moving across the sky for a while. But the science-bending that in truth would have been involved makes it apparent that it is really the most incredible miracle of the entire bible. And for what? So that Joshua could continue a bloodthirsty campaign of conquest against some neighboring tribes in a tiny corner of the Mideast.

- After the next batch of enemies (apparently the Amorites) had been conquered, when Joshua and the sons of Israel had "made an end of slaying them with a very great slaughter" (10:20), Joshua told the chiefs of the men of war to put their feet on the necks of the five kings of the Amorites. After the kings were amply humiliated, Joshua struck the five kings dead and hanged them on five trees. Then he resumed his day's work by capturing Makkedah and utterly destroying it, leaving no survivors.

- The bloodshed continued with Joshua and the Israelites killing everybody in the cities of Libnah, Lachish, Eglon, Hebron, and Debir. We are given a summary at 10:40 as follows:

> So Joshua smote all the country of the hills, and of the south, and of the vale, and of the springs, and all their kings: he left none remaining, but utterly destroyed all that breathed, as the Lord God of Israel commanded.

Some more conquests are then recounted, with the Israelites leaving no one who breathed. The conquered peoples were not going to have peace or surrender even come up as an option, because "it was of the Lord to harden their hearts, that they should come against Israel in battle, that he might destroy them utterly, and that they might have no favour, but that he might destroy them, as the Lord commanded Moses" (11:20).

This is the loving and merciful God who we teach about in Sunday School, who we hear about in sermons, who will welcome everyone to him with open arms if they will only humble themselves and come unto him? The God who came down in the form of man to teach that we should turn the other cheek and love our neighbor as ourself?

- Joshua informs the people that God will not forgive their transgressions or their sins (24:19). Weren't these the people of the promise? What about the animal sacrifices?

6.7 Judges

- "And the Lord was with Judah; and he drave out the inhabitants of the mountain; but could not drive out the inhabitants of the valley, because they had chariots of iron" (1:19). So much for God's omnipotence (see **4.4.1**).

- Earlier, Moses had completely wiped out Midian, leaving only virgin girls alive as captives (Numbers 31). So how could God give the sons of Israel into the hands of Midian for seven years, and how did the "hand of Midian prevail against Israel" (6:2)? How was it that there were any Midianites left to do that?

- With the spirit of God coming upon him, Jephthah passes over a bunch of places and reaches the sons of Ammon, whom he wants to kill. He makes a vow to God that he will make a human sacrifice of whoever walks out of his house upon his return if God allows him to do the killing he wants (11:30-31). God does so, but when he returns home from his slaughter-and-conquer adventure, it is his daughter who walks out of the house. (Who did he think it would be, the postman?) Poor Jephthah explains his dilemma to his daughter, who takes it all in stride, mourning for two months before submitting to her fiery fate.

- Samson's parents are told by the angel of God that their son-to-be would have no razor come upon his head (13:5). One would, though, by Deliah (16:19). Why does Paul teach that long hair is a shame to a man (1 Cor 11:14) if this special man of God was never to have his hair cut?

- How did the pre-haircut Samson manage to kill a thousand men with the jawbone of a donkey (15:15)? Even assuming miraculous assistance, the men would have had to get their throats slashed one at a time by this amazingly sharpened mandible, a process that would take two hours at a rate of seven seconds per throat, all the while failing to somehow get a spear or sword into Samson.

- A certain Levite (one of God's holy priests) goes off to fetch his concubine, who has run off to her father's house. During their return trip, they stay at an old man's house in Gibeah. A bunch of men surround the house and demand to have sex with the Levite. He sends his concubine out to the men instead, and they gang-rape her all night long (19:25). The next day, as she is lying on the doorstep, he tells her to get up. When she doesn't get up and he finally realizes that she's dead, he brings her body home, cuts it into twelve pieces, and sends them throughout Israel (19:29). Upon receipt of these grisly obituary notices, the anger of the Israelites is stirred up against the perpetrators, and they go into battle against Gibeah, with the usual slaughter of thousands.

There is a bit of a plot twist this time, though. Gibeah is a city of the sons of Benjamin, one of the tribes of Israel, and so the warfare was between fellow Israelites. After they had smote the sons of Benjamin "with the edge of the sword, as well the men of every city, as the beast, and all that came to hand" and "set on fire all the cities that they came to" (20:48), the remaining eleven tribes swore that they would never give their daughters to Benjamin in marriage. This created a problem for the remaining men of Benjamin.

The solution, it turned out, was that some other fellow Israelites in Jabesh-Gilead had not helped in the fighting. The congregation of Israel was able to teach these guys a lesson and get virgins for the lonely Benjaminite men with one simple act: slaughter all the men, and their non-virgin women and children. The 400 young virgins that were left were brought back to the camp, and given to the Benjaminite men.

6.8 First Samuel

- The sons of Eli sinned very greatly. The explanation given is in 2:13-16:

> [T]he priests' custom with the people was, that, when any man offered sacrifice, the priest's servant came, while the flesh was in

seething, with a fleshhook of three teeth in his hand; And he struck it into the pan, or kettle, or cauldron, or pot; all that the fleshhook brought up the priest took for himself. So they did in Shiloh unto all the Israelites that came thither. Also before they burnt the fat, the priest's servant came, and said to the man that sacrificed, Give flesh to roast for the priest; for he will not have sodden flesh of thee, but raw. And if any man said unto him, Let them not fail to burn the fat presently, and then take as much as thy soul desireth; then he would answer him, Nay; but thou shalt give it me now: and if not, I will take it by force.

Got that? So Eli went and rebuked his sons, asking "If one man sin against another, the judge shall judge him: but if a man sin against the Lord, who shall intreat for him" (2:25)? We are told that these were people of the promise, the Old Covenant believers who looked forward to the coming Messiah and sacrificed animals for their sins in the meantime. So we would expect some answer to the question (e.g., "the priests sacrifice for their own sins, too, go and sacrifice," "one will come who will intreat for us"). But no such answer is given, and the question was asked in a way that implies that there is no answer. It doesn't matter, though, because God wanted to put them to death (2:25), and thus they would not listen to Eli.

Later (3:13), God tells Samuel that he is going to judge Eli's house forever because his sons had brought a curse on themselves and Eli did not rebuke them. Huh? How did Eli not rebuke his sons when we are told all about it in 2:23-25? God further tells Samuel that the iniquity of Eli's house "shall not be purged with sacrifice nor offering for ever" (3:14). Not much of a forgiving God here.

• God kills all of the people of Beth-shemite, 50,070 men to be exact, because some of their men had looked into the ark of the covenant (6:19).

• After Samuel hears the people's demands for a king, he repeats the words of the people in God's hearing (8:21). Why couldn't God hear what they were saying without Samuel having to repeat it?

• Samuel tells Saul that God wants the Amelekites dead. Saul is to utterly destroy all that Amelek has, put to death both man and woman, child and infant, plus livestock (15:3). Saul went and fought the Amelekites utterly destroyed all the people, except that he captured their king alive. He also spared the best of the sheep, oxen, fatlings, lambs, and all that was good. This disobedience made God regret that he had made Saul king (15:10-11).

Here we have another example of God regretting something he had done. How is that possible with an all-seeing, all-wise God? We also have yet another example of how bloodthirsty God is, at least as depicted in the Old Testament. Again, stop and think about the horror of it all. God commanded a massacre of this entire people, including women, children, and infants. The only thing that he appears to find evil about the whole episode is the fact that Saul failed to completely obey him and left the king and some animals alive (15:19).

- Saul confesses his sin to Samuel and asks him to "pardon my sin, and turn again with me, that I may worship the Lord" (15:24-25). This would appear to be an ideal moment for the Old Testament to show that one could indeed turn to another for forgiveness, for these people believed on the promise. But Samuel declines to offer any forgiveness, saying that God will not "will not lie nor repent: for he is not a man, that he should repent" (or "change his mind," 15:29). And God did in fact change his mind before this time, e.g., when "it repented the Lord that he had made man on the earth, and it grieved him at his heart" (Genesis 6:6) and when "the Lord repented of the evil which he thought to do unto his people" (Exodus 32:14).

Saul persists and Samuel goes with him to where the captured Amelekite king was held. Samuel tells the king, "As thy sword hath made women childless, so shall thy mother be childless among women." Then he cuts "Agag in pieces before the Lord in Gilgal" (15:33). Samuel apparently misses the irony in the statement he makes to the king before he butchers him, in that Samuel is the one who ordered the attack on the Amelekites, children and infants and all.

- The search for a new king is on, and God tells Samuel not to look at the appearance or height of one rejected candidate's stature, "for the Lord seeth not as man seeth; for man looketh on the outward appearance, but the Lord looketh on the heart" (16:7). If that's the case, why did God specify a bunch of "outward appearance" disqualifications for his Levitical priests, including having a disfigured face, a hunchback, or any deformed limb, or being a dwarf (Leviticus 21:18, 20). And why does the story then bother to describe the ultimately successful candidate, David, as being "of a beautiful countenance, and goodly to look to" (16:12)?

• An "evil spirit from God came upon Saul" (18:10) that made Saul want to kill David. How can evil come from God? Why would God send an evil spirit that could result in the death of his chosen candidate for king?

• David brought a hundred foreskins of the Philistines to Saul as a dowry for his daughter (18:27).

• If this is all nonfiction, why does Nabal (i.e., "fool" in Hebrew) just happen to have an unflattering name that fits his role in the story narrated in chapter 25?

• How could an evil medium at Endor have power to "bring up" Samuel, one of God's holy men, in a vision from the dead (28:13-19)?

In that story, Samuel tells Saul that he will be given into the hands of the Philistines, and therefore Saul and his sons will be with Samuel tomorrow (28:19). Samuel was righteous and indeed had talked with God on a regular basis, so how is it that he and Saul, the wicked king who ended his own life in the sin of suicide, wind up in the same place after death? As will be evident below, the simple reason appears to be that the concept of hell didn't develop until late in the Old Testament.

6.9 Second Samuel

• Saul had given David's first wife Michal (1 Samuel 18:27) to Phalti the Son of Laish (1 Samuel 25:44) after David's escape. Fair enough–Saul does lots of bad things and is not to be considered an example for us. But what are we to make of David's behavior when he takes Michal from Phalti, not to get his first wife back, but to use her as a bargaining chip (3:13-15)? The text, by the way, talks about Phalti following her crying but doesn't bother to note anything about her own reaction to being forced yet again into a new marriage not of her choice.

• Some guys decide to kill one of Saul's sons as a way of avenging for Saul's attempts to kill David, but David is not pleased. He has them killed, has their hands and feet cut off, and has them hanged up (4:12).

• David gathers "all the chosen men of Israel, thirty thousand" (6:1) to move the ark of the covenant on an oxcart. (What happened to the nearly two million Israelites of the Exodus?) One of the drivers of the cart, Uzzah, puts his hand to the ark and takes hold of it when it starts to shake (the cart had reached a threshing floor, apparently bumpy). For some reason, God does not look favorably on this instinctive attempt to steady his precious object. Rather, "the anger of the Lord was kindled against Uzzah; and God smote him there for his error" (6:7). God's behavior here is not baffling only to a modern-day reader; even at the time "David was displeased, because the Lord had made a breach upon Uzzah" (6:8).

• David dances around in a way and in a garment that apparently leaves little to the imagination. His ex-wife (not by her choice, of course) Michal sarcastically says to him, "How glorious was the king of Israel to day, who uncovered himself to day in the eyes of the handmaids of his servants, as one of the vain fellows shamelessly uncovereth himself" (6:20)! David replies that God chose him a ruler over Israel and so he will play before God. Furthermore, he says, "I will yet be more vile than thus, and will be base in mine own sight: and of the maidservants which thou hast spoken of, of them shall I be had in honour" (6:22). What is David's behavior and arrogant reaction to her criticism supposed to teach us?

• David smites the Moabites and measures them with a line, "casting them down to the ground; even with two lines measured he to put to death, and with one full line to keep alive" (8:2). Sound familiar? It should; these sorts of capricious live-or-die choices were made by the Nazis in the concentration camps.

• Did David kill the men of 700 chariots of Syria (10:18) or 7,000 (1 Chronicles 19:18)?

• In the story of David and Bathsheba, we are told that David had Uriah (Bathsheba's husband) eat and drink before him and got him drunk (11:13). Was drunkenness considered a routine part of the life of an Israelite? Why is it not mentioned again in the story, even where Nathan chastises David for his sins in chapter 12?

• There seems to be a reference to the afterlife in David's lament about the son who was was killed as punishment for his sin (*David's* sin, I might add, not any of the innocent child). He says, "I shall go to him, but he shall not return to me" (12:23). If all David had in mind for himself after death were non-existence, it seems that he would not have talked about *going to* his son.

In any event, his vague statement is one of just a few we will encounter in the Old Testament that *even arguably* refer to an afterlife. The lack of attention given to one's fate after death may come as a surprise to the Christian reader whose primary religious motivations are the carrot and stick of eternal bliss versus eternal torture. So too with the bland, neutral nature of the only place the ancient Jews did think about as their final destination, *Sheol*:

> All the dead go down to Sheol, and there they lie in sleep together–whether good or evil, rich or poor, slave or free (Job 3:11-19). It is described as a region "dark and deep," "the Pit," and "the land of forgetfulness," cut off from both God and human life above (Pss. 6:5; 88:3-12). Though in some texts Yahweh's power can reach down to Sheol (Ps. 139:8), the dominant idea is that the dead are abandoned forever. This idea of Sheol is negative in contrast to the world of life and light above, but there is no idea of judgment or of reward and punishment. If one faces extreme circumstances of suffering in the realm of the living above, as did Job, it can even be seen as a welcome relief from pain–see the third chapter of Job. But basically it is a kind of "nothingness," an existence that is barely existence at all, in which a "shadow" or "shade" of the former self survives (Ps. 88:10). [Tabor]

- The anger of God burns against Israel (24:1), which incited David to command a census of Israel and Judah. God is angry at his chosen people yet again, but no reason for the anger is given. And why that anger would prompt David to count everybody is also unclear.

- After the census, David feels himself to have sinned greatly by wanting to know the number of people in his kingdom (24:10). One wonders why that action would be so sinful; as the name implies, the book of Numbers is full of descriptions of how the people were numbered. For example, "Moses numbered, as the Lord commanded him, all the firstborn among the children of Israel" (3:42). But God apparently agrees with David's guilt, because he punishes his census by sending a pestilence that kills 70,000 innocent Israelites (other than David), the unfairness of which was apparent even to David (24:17).

Although it seems foreign to the modern reader, the criticism of David's actions may be explainable in the context of an ancient Israelite who was to have trust in God as his secret weapon in holy war. For David to take the census implied a lack of trust in that area (Price 2011).

6.10 First Kings

• Did Solomon have 40,000 stalls of horses for his chariots (4:26) or 4,000 stalls for horses and chariots (2 Chronicles 9:25)? Did the molten sea in the temple hold 2,000 baths (7:26) or 3,000 baths (2 Chronicles 4:5)?

• Why is the circular sea of cast metal reported as measuring 10 cubits from brim to brim and 30 cubits in circumference? The ratio would be pi (3.141 and change), and wouldn't it have been easy enough to report the circumference as 31, or even rounding up to 32 given that the walls were about a handbreadth thick? Sure, it seems like a minor point and we can easily accept that the ancient reporter might have been sloppy with his measuring. But if we acknowledge an error in this passage, why are we certain there are no errors in more significant portions nearby, e.g., where we are told that a cloud filled the temple (8:10)?

• Solomon's prayer of dedication talks about God forgiving sins through prayer, both inside the temple (8:33-34) and outside, but directed toward it (8:35-50).

• How did Solomon manage to sacrifice 22,000 oxen and 120,000 sheep in one day (8:63-64)? That works out to more than three head per second over the course of 12-hour day! A different sacrifice recounted much later in 2 Chronicles 29:32-34 posed logistical problems with a small fraction of that number of animals. Even if Solomon pulled off the feat somehow, what was the point of such a large slaughter?

• In one year Solomon took in 666 talents of gold, or about 50,000 pounds (10:14).

• Solomon let his wives turn his heart away after other gods when he grew old, and his "heart was not perfect with the Lord his God, as was the heart of David his father" (11:4-5). Why would he do such a thing, with all the great wisdom and very great discernment God had given him, making him wiser than all men (4:29-31)? Remember this wasn't just "man's wisdom"; it was provided directly by God.

- God was angry with Solomon for turning his heart from God and failing to keep God's covenant and statutes. He punished Solomon by taking the kingdom from his son. As in the rest of the Old Testament, however, there is no sign of any everlasting punishment. Indeed, we are told that "Solomon slept with his fathers, and was buried in the city of David his father" (11:43). That is the exact same end that came to Asa (15:24), one of his successors whose "heart was perfect with the Lord all his days" (15:14). On the other hand, chapters 14-16 list a bunch of other successor kings who were evil but, like Solomon, wound up "sleeping with their fathers," including Omri who "wrought evil in the eyes of the Lord, and did worse than all that were before him" (16:25).

This is eternal life versus eternal damnation we are talking about, certainly no trifling matter! So why does this book of Scripture make it appear that there is no distinction between the fate of the evildoer and the faithful?

Luther was persuaded that all of all those who "slept with their fathers" are all in heaven (*Table Talk* §540). That retrojects the post-Exilic idea of a place of eternal reward into this early biblical text, whose authors more probably meant what they said when they referred to the unconscious "sleep" of death.

6.11 Second Kings

- Why are we told that Elijah was taken up into heaven in a whirlwind (2:11) when John 3:13 says that "no man hath ascended up to heaven, but he that came down from heaven, even the Son of man which is in heaven"?

- One of the first things that Elijah's replacement Elisha does is to get back at a bunch of young boys who mocked him saying "go up, you baldhead, go up you baldhead!" He curses them in the name of God, whereupon two female bears come out of the woods and tear up 42 of the boys (2:23-24). That'll teach those brats not to disrespect God's prophet!

- Did Ahaziah begin to reign in the twelfth year of Jorab at age 22 (8:25-26) or in the eleventh year of Jorab (9:29) at age 42 (2 Chronicles 22:2)?

- Elisha informs Jehu that God has anointed him as king over Israel (9:6) and that "the dogs shall eat Jezebel in the portion of Jezreel, and there shall be none to bury her" (9:10). Later Jehu has Jezebel thrown down from a window and he rides his horse over her bloodied body (9:33). Miraculously, when they go to bury her, there is nothing left but her skull, feet, and the palms of her hands (9:35). Sure, Jezebel had done some bad things, but why does God's punishment (he commended Jehu later) always have to be so vicious and disgusting?

• Imagine that a modern-day leader wants to kill all the adherents of a religion he believes to be false. He pretends to have a worship gathering for this false religion and invites all the adherents to assemble for it at their service hall. When they are all gathered together and the leader is certain that none of the members of his own religion in the hall, he massacres all the false-religionists and vandalizes their worship hall.

This is basically what Jehu did to the worshipers of Baal (10:19-27). And God commended Jehu for all his actions (10:30), including that, the killing of seventy people and laying their heads in heaps by the city gate (10:7-8), and taking 42 other captives alive and slaughtering them in a pit (10:14).

• In 18:3, we are told that Hezekiah "did that which was right in the sight of the Lord," and in the next verse that Hezekiah "removed the high places, and brake the images, and cut down the groves, and brake in pieces the brasen serpent that Moses had made: for unto those days the children of Israel did burn incense to it." God had specifically told Moses to make that brazen serpent back in Numbers 21:8.

• God says that he will wipe Jerusalem as one wipes a dish, wiping it, and turning it upside down (21:13). Are people just like so much scum on a dirty dish to him?

6.12 First Chronicles

• David says to Solomon that he has prepared for the temple 100,000 talents of gold and 1,000,000 talents of silver. That's over *seven million pounds* of gold, nearly as much as is currently held in Fort Knox. And this was accumulated by a kingdom of a million or so people in the Bronze Age Mideast?

• Satan is finally mentioned, for the first time since the Fall of Man back in Genesis 3, assuming the serpent of Genesis and Satan are one and the same. And it is only a very brief mention: "Satan stood up against Israel, and provoked David to number Israel" (21:1). The Chronicler attributes David's actions as being motivated by Satan, though the original story, written centuries earlier, says that "the anger of the Lord was kindled against Israel, and he [God!] moved David against them to say, Go, number Israel and Judah" (2 Samuel 24:1).

Price explains the apparent discrepancy by noting that Satan was actually viewed as an agent of God at that point in Old Testament theology. In both versions of the story, God wanted to test David (mustn't say "tempt") to see if he would rest on God's assurances about being ruler over Israel, or if he would decide to do a census to get some earthly assurance as well. But that leaves us with Satan playing the remarkable role of acting in God's stead, which seems even harder to reconcile with our current theology than the presence of a drastic discrepancy between the two versions.

6.13 Second Chronicles

- Chronicles is a much later retelling of the stories of the kings, dating from around the fifth century B.C. Still there is still no mention of any reward or punishment after death. Good and evil kings alike all "slept with their fathers," Solomon (9:31), Rehoboam (12:16) who "did evil, because he prepared not his heart to seek the Lord" (12:14), and Asa (16:13) who "did that which was good and right in the eyes of the Lord his God" (14:2).

- God has a conference with the "host of heaven" with various spirits chattering away around his throne. He asks who among the spirits will entice King Ahab to take a fall, and one of the spirits volunteers for the job. God sends the volunteer to be a "lying spirit in the mouth of all his prophets" (19:18-22). This picture of God as a cunning king who uses spirits as courtiers and resorts to subterfuge to achieve his ends is hardly the stuff of current Christian theology.

- Was Jehoiachin eight years old when he began to reign (36:9) or eighteen (2 Kings 24:8)? If the former, how did an 8-year old boy manage to do evil in the sight of God during his three-month reign (36:9)?

- The sons of Judah capture 10,000 people and throw them from the top of a cliff so that they are "broken in pieces" (25:12).

6.14 Ezra

• Some of the Israelites had intermarried with Canaanites, Hittites, etc. "so that the holy seed have mingled themselves with the people of those lands" (9:2), which gets Ezra very upset. Isn't this all about tribalism ("the holy seed"), rather than about marrying unbelievers? Anyhow, Ezra weeps and casts himself down before the house of God and persuades the transgressors to "put away all the wives and such as are born of them" (10:3). What happened to these wives and children that they "put away"? Assuming that we are just talking about divorce, it was not grudgingly allowed due to the hardness of hearts, as Jesus said Moses had permitted, but was commanded by one of God's prophets.

Stark calls Ezra a "xenophobic nationalist" who was commissioned by a Persian Emperor to finish restoring the Jerusalem Temple. He returned "home to discover that Judeans had begun to intermarry with 'the people of the land,' i.e., non-Jewish inhabitants of the region." To purify God's people from these undesirables, "despite the fact that many of these marriages had already produced numerous children, Ezra decreed that every Jewish man married to a non-Jewish woman and her offspring were to be expelled from the land, abandoned to fend for themselves" (2011, 1-2).

6.15 Nehemiah

• Reading the book of Moses and finding it to command that "the Ammonite and the Moabite should not come into the congregation of God for ever" prompts the Israelites to exclude all foreigners (13:1-3). Apparently the centuries-old misdeeds of the foreigners' ancestors now prevented them from being in the one place where they could worship the true God.

• Nehemiah seems pretty proud of himself. The book is written in the first person, and talks at length about his own works. He concludes one account of his doings with a request that God think upon him for good, "according to all that I have done for this people" (5:19). After another account, he asks God to remember him "concerning this, and wipe not out my good deeds that I have done for the house of my God, and for the offices thereof" (13:14).

6.16 Esther

• King Ahasuerus made a feast and gave drink to the people in his palace, and "royal wine in abundance" (1:7) "And the drinking was according to the Law" (1:8). On the seventh day, "the heart of the king was merry with wine" (1:10).

• What are we supposed to learn from the story of Esther's continued demands for the Jews' vengeance, culminating in the killing of 75,000 of those who hated them (9:16)?

6.17 Job

• Job offers burnt offerings for his sons, saying "It may be that my sons have sinned, and cursed God in their hearts" (1:5). But we can't believe for our children, can we?

• Who are the "sons of God" who "came to present themselves before the Lord" (2:1)?

• The book of Job speaks much of the sufferings of this life, of God's justice, of Job's yearning for an end to it all. In 19:23-27, Job does look forward to some sort of afterlife:

> For I know that my redeemer [literally, *kinsman*] liveth, and that he shall stand at the latter day upon the earth [lit., *dust*]: And though after my skin worms destroy this body, yet in my flesh shall I see God: Whom I shall see for myself, and mine eyes shall behold, and not another; though my reins be consumed within me.

Elihu mentions the prospect of a righteous man seeing God's face with joy, of God delivering such a man's "soul from going into the pit," and his life seeing the light (33:26-28).

But why does the rest of the book make it seem as though death is the end of everything, for good and evil alike? Note the following:

> 1. Job laments that he did not die at birth or in infancy, for he should "have lain still and been quiet, I should have slept: then had I been at rest, with kings and counsellors of the earth, which built desolate places for themselves; or with princes that had gold, who filled their houses with silver: or as an hidden

untimely birth [NASB: *miscarriage*] I had not been; as infants which never saw light. There the wicked cease from troubling; and there the weary be at rest. There the prisoners rest together; they hear not the voice of the oppressor. The small and great are there; and the servant is free from his master" (3:13-19).

There the wicked cease from troubling? And they are in the same place as innocent infants?

2. Job says that, as a cloud is gone when it vanishes, "he that goeth down to the grave shall come up no more. He shall return no more to his house, neither shall his place know him any more" (7:9).

3. He says that he will "go whence I shall not return, even to the land of darkness and the shadow of death; a land of darkness, as darkness itself; and of the shadow of death, without any order, and where the light is as darkness" (10:21).

4. Unlike a tree that may sprout again after being cut down, "man dieth, and wasteth away: yea, man giveth up the ghost, and where is he? As the waters fail from the sea, and the flood decayeth and drieth up: so man lieth down, and riseth not: till the heavens be no more, they shall not awake, nor be raised out of their sleep" (14:10-12). The "till the heavens be no more" clause looks interesting to us because it looks like what we view as the end of the world, but there was no such apocalyptic expectation in Job's Old Testament worldview. Still, intriguingly, he laments to God, "O that thou wouldest hide me in the grave, that thou wouldest keep me secret, until thy wrath be past, that thou wouldest appoint me a set time, and remember me! If a man die, shall he live again? all the days of my appointed time will I wait, till my change come" (14:13-14).

5. Job says that, when a few years are come, then he shall go the way of no return" (16:22).

6. In Chapter 18, Bildad the Shuhite goes on at some length about the fate of the wicked. He mentions nothing about any eternal punishment (nor is there any such mention in the entire book of Job), but says that the memory of the wicked perishes from the earth, he is driven from light into darkness and chased from the inhabited world.

7. Job compares the fate of one who dies in his full strength, and one who dies with a bitter soul, never tasting anything good. "They shall lie down alike in the dust, and the worms shall cover them" (21:26). He asks who will confront the wicked with his actions, who will repay him for what he has done? "While he is carried to the grave, men will keep watch over his tomb. The clods of the valley will gently cover him; moreover, all men will follow after him, while countless ones go before him" (NASB, 21:32-33). God's justice thus seems to be cold comfort for Job; he then asks his companions how will they vainly comfort him, for their answers remain full of falsehood.

8. He complains about the lack of justice for the wicked: "Drought and heat consume the snow waters: so doth the grave those which have sinned. The womb shall forget him; the worm shall feed sweetly on him; he shall be no more remembered; and wickedness shall be broken as a tree" (24:19-20).

9. Job knows that God will bring him to death, "and to the house appointed for all living" (30:23; NASB: *house of meeting for all living*).

• The book of Job describes a micromanaging God who fits ancient perceptions. Elihu describes God telling the snow and rain to fall (37:6), and of frost being given by God's breath (37:10). God himself asks Job if he has perceived the breadth of the earth (38:18), or if he has entered "the storehouses of the snow," or of the hail? (NASB, 38:22-23) He asks from whose womb the ice has come, and who has given birth to the "frost of heaven" (38:29). He asks if Job can "tip the water jars of the heavens" (38:37).

• God goes on at some length about a fearsome "Leviathan," whose sneezes flash forth light (41:18) and out of whose mouth go burning torches and sparks of fire (41:19).

• Ehrman isn't particularly impressed with the book of Job, citing it as part of "God's Problem" of human suffering (**4.9.4**). He finds the end of the book most offensive,

> when God restores all that Job had lost–including additional children. Job lost seven sons and three daughters and, as a reward for his faithfulness, God gives him an additional seven sons and three daughters. What was this author thinking? That

the pain of a child's death will be removed by the birth of another? That children are expendable and replaceable like a faulty computer or DVD player? What kind of God is this? [Ehrman 2008, 172]

To Ehrman, the book is "supremely dissatisfying. If God tortures, maims, and murders people just to see how they will react–to see if they will not blame him, when in fact he is to blame–then this does not seem to me to be a God worthy of worship. Worthy of fear, yes. Of praise, no" (p. 172).

6.18 Psalms

- "David" laments to God that "in death there is no remembrance of thee: in the grave who shall give thee thanks?" (6:5).[58] He also says that he will depart and will "be no more" (39:13). This sure doesn't sound like a belief in an afterlife.

On the other hand, David states in Psalm 16 that God will not abandon his soul to *Sheol*, nor allow his "holy one" (or "godly one" per NASB; from the context, presumably David himself) to undergo decay. He says that God will make know to him the path of life; in God's presence is fullness of joy and in his right hand there are pleasures forever (16:10-11).

Elsewhere David mentions being given "length of days for ever and ever" (21:4). He also says that "all they that go down to the dust shall bow before him" (22:29). In the familiar Psalm 23, he says will dwell in the house of the Lord forever (lit. "for length of days" per NASB) and he says he will praise the Lord "forever" in 30:12. The writer of Psalm 71 says that God will revive him again and will bring him "up again from the depths of the earth" (71:20).

The writer of Psalm 49 says that man will not endure, that he is like the beasts that perish (49:12). Death will feed on the foolish, that "their beauty shall consume in the grave from their dwelling" (49:14). He describes no further punishment for the foolish, but the writer says that

---

58. I use the traditional attribution as it appears at the beginning of each Psalm, without regard to any evidence for David actually being the writer. For most of the discussion here, it doesn't really matter.

God will redeem his own soul from the power of the grave and will receive him.

The first hints of anything that is arguably like the hell of the New Testament are in Psalms 11 and 140:

> Upon the wicked He will rain snares; Fire and brimstone and burning wind will be the portion of their cup. For the Lord is righteous, He loves righteousness; The upright will behold His face. [NASB, 11:6-7]

> As for the head of those that compass me about, let the mischief of their own lips cover them. Let burning coals fall upon them: let them be cast into the fire; into deep pits, that they rise not up again. [140:9-10]

Hell as we understand it is the ultimate threat of punishment, where God is going to allow the wicked to suffer unimaginably cruel tortures for all eternity. (Had your skin peeled off and your limbs slowly hacked away for trillions of years? You're just getting started!) But the above references, a full two thirds of the way through the Old Testament and written thousands of years after the dawn of civilization, are the first that could be construed as providing any warning of the horrors of hell.

Given the magnitude of what's at stake, why does God completely ignore the topic for most of the history of his chosen people? It's not that God is uninterested in details; he specified what people could eat, when they could have sex, what body parts wives shouldn't grab when defending their husbands, and how many hins and ephahs of flour and oil to sacrifice with this or that animal. And it's not just a lack of warnings; God allows it to appear that there really is no hell at all, providing scripture that tells of the good and evil kings all going to sleep with their fathers and the story of Samuel and Saul winding up in the same place after death.

• David brags about being rewarded according to his own righteousness:

> The Lord rewarded me according to my righteousness; according to the cleanness of my hands hath he recompensed me. For I have kept the ways of the Lord, and have not wickedly departed from my God. For all his judgments were before me, and I did not put away his statutes from me. I was also upright before him, and I

kept myself from mine iniquity. Therefore hath the Lord recompensed me according to my righteousness, according to the cleanness of my hands in his eyesight. [18:20-24]

• In Psalm 18, David glories in his violent adventures, noting how he has pursued and overtaken his enemies and did not turn back "until they were consumed" (18:37). He praises God who has given him the necks of his enemies,

that I might destroy them that hate me. They cried, but there was none to save them: even unto the Lord, but he answered them not. Then did I beat them small as the dust before the wind: I did cast them out as the dirt in the streets [18:40-42].

It is God, David continues, that executes vengeance for and subdues people under David, who delivers David from his enemies and lifts him up above those that rise up against him. Then, without apparent irony, David notes that God has rescued him "from the violent man" (18:47-48).

• David asks God to have mercy on him and to blot out his transgressions, probably those involving Bathsheba, "according unto the multitude of thy tender mercies" (51:1). In a significant departure from the teachings of Moses, he asserts that God does not desire sacrifice or burnt offering. Instead, David says, "the sacrifices of God are a broken spirit" (51:16-17).

How was David authorized to change the "statutes and judgments" that Moses had taught under God's command, which he said that the Israelites should do in the land where they were to go to possess (Deuteronomy 4:5)? And wasn't the substitute for the animal sacrifices to be the sacrifice of God's own son? David alludes nothing to that. Indeed, he says that, at that point, God does not desire sacrifice.

• David considers the reward of the righteous as seeing God's vengeance and having the opportunity to "wash his feet in the blood of the wicked" (58:10-11). Again, though, no eternal punishment is envisioned. Instead, the wicked will pass away like a melting snail or a woman's miscarriage, "that they may not see the sun" (58:8).

• David says, "unto thee, O Lord, belongeth mercy: for thou renderest to every man according to his work" (62:12). What about the tens of thousands of people that God had killed via Joshua, for no apparent reason except that they were in the way of the land that had been promised to his chosen people? What about the tens of thousands of children whom he had killed along with their fathers? What about the grandchildren of the Ammonites and the Moabites, who were cast out of the congregation because of what their great-grandfathers did? And that doesn't consider our current understanding of hell, to which untold millions of people have been been condemned, starting thousands of years before the Psalms were written, for not knowing anything of God's chosen nation or having access to the sacrifices that pleased him.

• Various New Testament writers present parts of Psalm 69 as foreshadowings of Jesus' work and his suffering on the cross. John 2:17 writes of Jesus' cleansing of the temple as being prophesied by the statement that "the zeal of thine house hath eaten me up" (69:9). Paul tells the Romans (15:3) that Jesus did not please himself, but that "the reproaches of them that reproached thee are fallen upon me" (69:9). John 19:28-30 tells us that Jesus drank sour wine to fulfill the Scripture, apparently referring to the Psalmist's statement, "They gave me also gall for my meat; and in my thirst they gave me vinegar to drink" (69:21). But why does the Psalmist sound so unlike Jesus outside the verses that have a familiar ring, e.g., where he asks that his oppressors have

> their table become a snare before them: and that which should have been for their welfare, let it become a trap. Let their eyes be darkened, that they see not; and make their loins continually to shake. Pour out thine indignation upon them, and let thy wrathful anger take hold of them. Let their habitation be desolate; and let none dwell in their tents [69:22-26].

Jesus, in sharp contrast to the Psalmist, asked God to "forgive them, for they know not what they do" (Luke 23:34).

• The Psalmist laments "the prosperity of the wicked, for there are no pains in their death" (73:3-4). He consoles himself with what he finally understood to be their end: "Surely thou didst set them in slippery places: thou castedst them down into destruction. How are they brought into desolation, as in a moment! [NASB: *destroyed in a moment*] They are utterly consumed with terrors [NASB: *swept away by sudden terrors*]" (73:18-19). It would be easy for someone steeped in the New Testament's theology of eternal damnation to see this as a vision of hell, but look at the words and consider the viewpoint of the Israelites at the time of the Psalmist's writing: God has destroyed and swept away the wicked in sudden moments of terror, and continues to do so.

The Psalmist, naturally, does not see any such unpleasantness in his own future. It seems that he may even look forward to something after death, because he says to God that "Thou shall guide me with thy counsel, and afterward receive me to glory" (73:24).

- The writer of Psalm 83 asks God to deal with some unnamed enemies who are making an uproar as he did with Midian and other recipients of God's wrath. He asks that God pursue them with his tempest like a fire burns wood, fill their faces with shame ("that they may seek thy name"), let them be ashamed and dismayed forever, and let them be humiliated and perish (83:14-17).

- "For the Lord God is a sun and shield: the Lord will give grace and glory: no good thing will he withhold from them that walk uprightly" (84:11). What does this mean, given that believers in the Old and New Testaments alike have suffered violence, hunger, and poverty at various times in history? Of course, the verse can be made immune to criticism simply by defining a "good thing" as whatever God has decided, in his inscrutable wisdom, to be good. An example of this is the well-meaning explanation I heard about a child's tragic death I witnessed: The child made it to heaven without having to undergo a normal lifetime of temptation and peril.

- Psalm 88 is a lament about the writer's imminent death and lack of any conviction about any life thereafter. He considers the dead to be remembered by God no more, cut off from his hand (88:5). He asks, skeptically it seems,

> Wilt thou shew wonders to the dead? shall the dead arise and praise thee? Selah. Shall thy lovingkindness be declared in the grave? or thy faithfulness in destruction? Shall thy wonders be known in the dark? and thy righteousness in the land of forgetfulness? [88:10-12]

- Contrary to Psalm 98:3, which states that "all the ends of the earth have seen the salvation of our God," only a tiny fraction of the world's population at the time had heard of the God of Abraham.

- Psalm 104 shows an ancient view of cosmology that probably seemed reasonable enough when it was written but no longer can be considered anything but devotional. It is also interesting to consider the possible influence of Egyptian sun worship, as evidenced in the "Great Hymn to Aten," written in the 14th century B.C. The following passages are excerpted from the NASB:

God covers himself with light as with a garment, stretches out the heavens like a curtain, lays the beams of his chambers in the waters, and makes the clouds his chariot (104:2-3). He walks on the wings of the wind, making the winds his messengers and flaming fire his ministers (104:3-4). He established the earth on its foundations so that it will not totter forever and ever (104:5), covered it with the deep as a garment; the waters were standing above the mountains but fled at his rebuke and the sound of his thunder (104:6-7). He waters the mountains from his upper chambers (104:13), the sun knows the place of its setting (104:19), he looks at the earth and it trembles, he touches the mountains and they smoke (104:32-33).

It is interesting to see one parallel with modern geology, though. "The mountains rose, the valleys sank down" (NASB, 104:8), which indeed they did over billions of years, contrary to the pre-scientific thought that the world is exactly as God made it a few thousands of years ago.

- The Psalmist praises God for causing vegetation to grow for food and "wine that maketh glad the heart of man" (104:15).

- Psalm 127 is one of the few parts of Scripture cited against the use of birth control: "Lo, children are an heritage of the Lord: and the fruit of the womb is his reward" (127:3). But the NASB translates this as "Behold, children are a gift [or *heritage*] of the Lord, the fruit of the womb is *a* reward." Luther translates it as "See, children are a gift [*Gabe*] of the Lord and the fruit of the womb is a present [*Geschenk*]."

- The Psalmist is angry at the "daughter of Babylon," and pronounces blessings on the one who "taketh and dasheth thy little ones against the stones" (137:9).

Departing from his usual disdain for wild allegory, Luther attempted to whitewash this disgusting statement by associating it with "prayer and the Word of God," a fleeing to prayer "when evil lust stirs":

> Thus says Psalm 137: "Happy shall he be, that taketh and dasheth the little ones of Babylon against the rock," that is, if the heart runs to the Lord Christ with its evil thoughts while they are yet

young and just beginning; for Christ is a Rock, on which they are ground to powder and come to naught. [*Treatise on Good Works* (1520); *PE* 1, 276]

• Many authors who attempt to make God fit into the framework of 21st century scientific knowledge treat him as a hands-off deity who started things off at the Big Bang, set things up with laws and chemical reactions that would result in us evolving as humans eventually, and then stepped away to watch the fun. But that's certainly not the kind of God David writes about in Psalm 139:

> O Lord, thou hast searched me, and known me. Thou knowest my downsitting and mine uprising, thou understandest my thought afar off. Thou compassest my path and my lying down, and art acquainted with all my ways. For there is not a word in my tongue, but, lo, O Lord, thou knowest it altogether. Thou hast beset me behind and before, and laid thine hand upon me. Such knowledge is too wonderful for me; it is high, I cannot attain unto it. Whither shall I go from thy spirit? or whither shall I flee from thy presence? If I ascend up into heaven, thou art there: if I make my bed in hell [*Sheol*], behold, thou art there. If I take the wings of the morning, and dwell in the uttermost parts of the sea; Even there shall thy hand lead me, and thy right hand shall hold me. If I say, Surely the darkness shall cover me; even the night shall be light about me. Yea, the darkness hideth not from thee; but the night shineth as the day: the darkness and the light are both alike to thee. For thou hast possessed my reins: thou hast covered me in my mother's womb. I will praise thee; for I am fearfully and wonderfully made: marvellous are thy works; and that my soul knoweth right well. My substance was not hid from thee, when I was made in secret, and curiously wrought in the lowest parts of the earth. Thine eyes did see my substance, yet being unperfect; and in thy book all my members were written, which in continuance were fashioned, when as yet there was none of them.

It is also not the kind of God we read about earlier in the five books of Moses, who apparently didn't forsee how evil man would be (Genesis 6:6) and changed his mind numerous times. And how about the God of Job, who had Satan test him repeatedly to see what he would do?

• David clearly didn't agree with his descendant Jesus that we should love our enemies (Matthew 5:43-44, Luke 6:27). He says, "Do not I hate them, O Lord, that hate thee? and am not I grieved with those that rise up against thee? I hate them with perfect [NASB: *the utmost*] hatred: I count them mine enemies" (139:21-22). Why did God change such a fundamental thing as loving versus hating from the Old Testament to the New Testament if he didn't change things like working on the Sabbath, being fruitful and multiplying, coveting stuff, and honoring one's father and mother?

• David proclaims God to be "gracious, and full of compassion; slow to anger, and of great mercy. The Lord is good to all: and his tender mercies are over all his works" (145:8-9). How can this possibly be a description of the same deity who commanded the genocide, conquest, plague, deception, and misogyny that we have already seen, and will continue to see, through the entire length of the Old Testament? Does being "good to all" include subjecting the Egyptians to horrible plagues, or authorizing Joshua's conquest of the Canaanites for their land and valuables, and the slaughter of all their people, men, women, and children alike?

• Psalm 145:18-20 assures us that God is

> nigh unto all them that call upon him, to all that call upon him in truth. He will fulfil the desire of them that fear him: he also will hear their cry, and will save them. The Lord preserveth all them that love him: but all the wicked will he destroy.

In our time, millions and perhaps billions of people fear and love God in complete sincerity. They agonize over their sins, and write eloquently of their struggles with doubt over their beliefs. Many of them are driven to read the Bible, pray, sing praises, and evangelize. Quite a few of them draw comfort from personal forgiveness of their sins in the name of Jesus. But in the Conservative Laestadian viewpoint they are excluded, and the phrase "all them" means "almost none of them."

6.19 Proverbs

• Contrary to the assertions of Proverbs 12:21 ("There shall no evil happen to the just") and 19:23 ("The fear of the Lord tendeth to life: and he that hath it shall abide satisfied; he shall not be visited with evil"), the just and those who fear the Lord have experienced plenty of evil. Nero's persecutions of the Christians come to mind. Jesus acknowledged the equal-opportunity nature of things by noting that

God "maketh his sun to rise on the evil and on the good, and sendeth rain on the just and on the unjust" (Matthew 5:45).

• "The simple believeth every word: but the prudent man looketh well to his going. A wise man feareth, and departeth from evil: but the fool rageth, and is confident" (14:15-16). Does that advice apply to words of doctrine that have been handed down for generations?

• There may be an oblique reference to *Sheol* being more than just the shadowy "nether world" in the admonition to discipline one's child: "You shall strike him with the rod and rescue his soul from Sheol" (23:14).

• We are told to "[r]ejoice not when thine enemy falleth, and let not thine heart be glad when he stumbleth: Lest the Lord see it, and it displease him, and he turn away his wrath from him" (24:17-18). But the Psalms are full of such vindictive thoughts. For example, David praises God, saying "I will be glad and rejoice in thee: I will sing praise to thy name, O thou most High. When mine enemies are turned back, they shall fall and perish at thy presence" (Psalms 9:2-3).

6.20 Ecclesiastes

• The Preacher writes that "the earth abideth for ever" (1:4), which contradicts the New Testament's apocalyptic teachings and our current understanding that the world will end. Nowhere in the Old Testament thus far (except in the story of Noah and the destruction of the "first world") has there been any mention of an end of the world.

• The Preacher writes at some length about a man's ultimate fate, and it is definitely not what a typical Christian reader would expect to see written in Scripture. The Preacher says he knows that one fate befalls both the wise man and the fool who walks in darkness (2:14). He looks back on his life and wisdom, saying "there is no remembrance of the wise more than of the fool for ever; seeing that which now is in the days to come shall all be forgotten. And how dieth the wise man? as the fool" (2:16). He concludes that "[t]here is nothing better for a man, than that he should eat and drink, and that he should make his soul enjoy good in his labour. This also I saw, that it was from the hand of God" (2:24).

He wishes that the sons of men would realize that they themselves are beasts (3:18), a conclusion that puts him in agreement with modern evolutionary biologists. And the fate of *Homo sapiens* and beasts is the same:

> [A]s the one dieth, so dieth the other; yea, they have all one breath; so that a man hath no preeminence above a beast: for all is vanity. All go unto one place; all are of the dust, and all turn to dust again. Who knoweth the spirit of man that goeth upward, and the spirit of the beast that goeth downward to the earth? [3:19-21]

Again, the Preacher concludes that "there is nothing better, than that a man should rejoice in his own works." That is man's portion, he says, "for who shall bring him to see what shall be after him?" (3:22)

He certainly doesn't look forward to any eternal correction of injustice for the oppressed. Rather, he says he congratulated the dead more than the living, who had no comforter in their oppression. But better than both of them is the one who has never existed, who has never seen the evil that is done under the sun (4:1-3). This is quite a contrast to how we often comfort ourselves about one who has "gone to his reward!" The reward of a man, the Preacher contends, is "to eat, to drink, and enjoy oneself in all one's labor in which he toils during the few years of his life which God has given him" (NASB, 5:18).

Just as he sees no difference between the fates of man and beasts, the Preacher sees one fate for the righteous and the wicked, for the good and clean and for the unclean, for the man who offers sacrifice and the one who does not, for the good man and the sinner (9:2). It is, he laments, "an evil among all things that are done under the sun, that there is one event unto all." The hearts of the sons of men are full of evil, and full of madness while they live, and afterwards? They go to the dead (9:3).

And the dead, according to the preacher,

> know not any thing, neither have they any more a reward; for the memory of them is forgotten. Also their love, and their hatred, and their envy, is now perished; neither have they any more a portion for ever in any thing that is done under the sun. [9:5-6]

His conclusion then? It is a very pragmatic, cheerful one, with none of the agonizing over sinfulness and its eternal consequences that would torture fearful souls in the thousands of years to come:

Go thy way, eat thy bread with joy, and drink thy wine with a merry heart; for God now accepteth thy works. Let thy garments be always white; and let thy head lack no ointment. Live joyfully with the wife whom thou lovest all the days of the life of thy vanity [NASB: *your fleeting life*], which he hath given thee under the sun, all the days of thy vanity: for that is thy portion in this life [NASB: *your reward in life*], and in thy labour which thou takest under the sun.Whatsoever thy hand findeth to do, do it with thy might; for there is no work, nor device, nor knowledge, nor wisdom, in the grave, whither thou goest. [9:7-10]

6.21 Isaiah

• Why does God change his mind about sacrifices, new moon festivals, and Sabbaths (1:11-14)? He went into a lot of detail establishing all that stuff through Moses, who had warned the Israelites, "What thing soever I command you, observe to do it: thou shalt not add thereto, nor diminish from it" (Deut 12:32). And the transition from Old Testament to New Testament won't happen for centuries.

• God sends Isaiah to prophesy to the people with a divine guarantee of failure: "Make the heart of this people fat, and make their ears heavy, and shut their eyes; lest they see with their eyes, and hear with their ears, and understand with their heart, and convert, and be healed" (6:10). Why does God deliberately prevent people from converting and being healed?

• In a familiar passage, Isaiah says that the Lord will give the house of David a sign:

> Behold, a virgin shall conceive, and bear a son, and shall call his name Immanuel. Butter and honey shall he eat, that he may know to refuse the evil, and choose the good. For before the child shall know to refuse the evil, and choose the good, the land that thou abhorrest shall be forsaken of both her kings. [7:14-16]

The word "virgin" was translated from the Hebrew word *almah* which has a rather generic meaning of "young woman" or "maiden." (Elsewhere Isaiah uses the specific word for a virgin, *betulah*, but not here.) That translation was questioned already in antiquity. Around 200 A.D., Irenaeus defended the "virgin" translation based on the presupposition that

> God in truth became man, and the Lord himself saved us, giving the sign of the virgin; but not as some say, who now venture to translate the Scripture, "Behold, a young woman shall conceive and bring forth a son," as Theodotion of Ephesus and Aquila of Pontus, both of them Jewish proselytes, interpreted; following whom, the Ebionites say that he was begotten by Joseph. [from Eusebius, *Church History*, Chapter 8]

However, we no longer are dependent on the Septuagint translation into Greek. *The Dead Sea Scrolls Bible* translates the passage as follows, based on the ancient scrolls found at Qumran, including the complete record provided by the Great Isaiah scroll:

> Look, the young woman has conceived and is bearing a son, and his name will be Immanuel. He will eat curds and honey by the time he knows to refuse evil and choose good. For before the child knows to refuse evil and choose good, the land whose two kings you dread will be deserted.

The passage is familiar because Matthew, probably relying on the Septuagint, quotes it as a prophecy of Jesus:

> When as his mother Mary was espoused to Joseph, before they came together, she was found with child of the Holy Ghost. Then Joseph her husband, being a just man, and not willing to make her a publick example, was minded to put her away privily. But while he thought on these things, behold, the angel of the Lord appeared unto him in a dream, saying, Joseph, thou son of David, fear not to take unto thee Mary thy wife: for that which is conceived in her is of the Holy Ghost. And she shall bring forth a son, and thou shalt call his name JESUS: for he shall save his people from their sins. Now all this was done, that it might be fulfilled which was spoken of the Lord by the prophet, saying, Behold, a virgin shall be with child, and shall bring forth a son, and they shall call his name Emmanuel, which being interpreted is, God with us. [Matthew 1:18-23]

If we look afresh at the words of the original passage, though, without trying to make it fit, the prophecy seems a lot less clear. Obviously, lots of young women bore sons, and Isaiah states that this particular young woman had already conceived. We know nothing about Jesus eating curds and honey, or any land of two dreaded kings that became deserted during his youth.

- Finally we see what may be the first real prophecy of the Messiah in the Old Testament, not counting the vague stuff about the seed of the woman in Genesis 3:

> For a child is born to us, a son is given to us. The government will be on his shoulders. He is called Wonderful Counselor, Mighty God, Everlasting Father, the Prince of Peace. His government will expand, and peace will be endless for the throne of David and his kingdom, to establish it and to sustain it with justice and righteousness from now on and forevermore. [*Dead Sea Scrolls Bible*, 9:6-7]

A child is born, a son given, bearing the title of Mighty God himself, along with that of Wonderful Counselor!

Still, parts of the passage don't entirely add up. Nowhere in the New Testament is Jesus referred to as the "Prince of Peace." Isaiah looks forward to the Prince of Peace expanding his government, and peace without end for the throne of David. However, Jesus did not have any role in the government of Israel (which was Roman, not Jewish, in his day), and said that he did not come to send peace on earth but a sword (Matthew 10:34). And what do we make of the text right after the quoted passage, which is full of God's typical Old Testament threats and anger? The Lord will set up adversaries who will devour Israel, but his anger will not be turned away. Therefore he will

> cut off from Israel head and tail, branch and rush, in one day. The ancient and honourable, he is the head; and the prophet that teacheth lies, he is the tail. For the leaders of this people cause them to err; and they that are led of them are destroyed. Therefore the Lord shall have no joy in their young men, neither shall have mercy on their fatherless and widows: for every one is an hypocrite and an evildoer, and every mouth speaketh folly. For all this his anger is not turned away, but his hand is stretched out still. For wickedness burneth as the fire: it shall devour the briers and thorns, and shall kindle in the thickets of the forest, and they shall mount up like the lifting up of smoke. Through the wrath of the Lord of hosts is the land darkened, and the people shall be as the fuel of the fire: no man shall spare his brother. And

he shall snatch on the right hand, and be hungry; and he shall eat on the left hand, and they shall not be satisfied: they shall eat every man the flesh of his own arm: Manasseh, Ephraim; and Ephraim, Manasseh: and they together shall be against Judah. For all this his anger is not turned away, but his hand is stretched out still.

All that is certainly a jarring contrast with a promise to send a wonderful counselor and Prince of Peace.

- Another Messiah prophecy concerns a shoot who "will come forth from the stump of Jesse," a branch from his roots who will bear fruit. "The spirit of the Lord will rest upon him, the spirit of wisdom and understanding, the spirit of counsel and might, the spirit of knowledge and fear of the Lord. His delight will be in the fear of the Lord" (*Dead Sea Scrolls Bible*, 10:1-2).

Sounds good, but what's with all the talk about the Messiah judging and ruling, and not in a particularly Jesus-like manner? "He will not judge by appearance, nor decide by what he hears, but with righteousness he will obtain justice for the poor and decide with equity for the meek of the land. He will strike the land with the rod of his mouth, and with the breath of his lips the wicked will be killed" (*Dead Sea Scrolls Bible*, 10:3-4).

- Isaiah prophesies bad things for Egypt. Among other things,

> [t]he waters of the Nile will dry up, and the riverbed will become parched and dry. And the canals will become foul, and the streams of Egypt will dwindle and dry up, reeds and rushes, and they will wither away. The reeds along the Nile, on the brink of the Nile, and all the sown fields of the Nile, will dry up and be driven away, and there will be nothing in it. [*Dead Sea Scrolls Bible*, 19:5-7]

Also, the land of Judah is prophesied to become a terror to the Egyptians, and there will be five cities in Egypt that speak the language of Canaan and swear allegiance to the Lord of Hosts. There will be an altar to the Lord in the midst of Egypt and a pillar to the Lord at its border (19:17-19). The Egyptians will cry unto the Lord, and

> he will send them a savior and he will go down and will rescue them. So the Lord will make himself known to Egypt, and the

> Egyptians will acknowledge the Lord on that day. They will even worship with sacrifices and burnt offerings . . . [*Dead Sea Scrolls Bible*, 19:20-21]

None of this has ever happened, and we are well past the times when God was in the practice of smelling burnt offerings. The prophecy has nothing to do with anything about the Second Coming, either. According to the New Testament, Jesus will be in no mood to rescue people at that point.

• God tells Isaiah to walk around naked and barefoot for three years "for a sign and wonder upon Egypt and upon Ethiopia; So shall the king of Assyria lead away the Egyptians prisoners, and the Ethiopians captives, young and old, naked and barefoot, even with their buttocks uncovered, to the shame of Egypt" (20:2-4).

• We finally see a real, worldwide apocalypse in chapter 24. The earth is to be completely laid waste and devoured by a curse. Its inhabitants are to be burned, and few men left (24:6). There is more apocalypse in chapter 30.

• Other lords have had dominion over Judah, but "[t]hey are dead, they shall not live; they are deceased, they shall not rise: therefore hast thou visited and destroyed them, and made all their memory to perish" (26:14). It doesn't seem like there is anything after death for these lords; they will not rise. But just a few verses later, it says "Thy dead men shall live, together with my dead body shall they arise. Awake and sing, ye that dwell in dust: for thy dew is as the dew of herbs, and the earth shall cast out the dead" (26:19).

• God will slay Leviathan, the dragon that is in the sea (27:1).

• We come upon a clear mention of a resurrection of the dead, arguably for the first time in the Old Testament:

> [T]he dead will live, their dead bodies will rise. The dwellers in the dust will awake and shout for joy! For your dew is like the dew of the dawn, and the earth will give birth to the dead. [*Dead Sea Scrolls Bible*, 26:19]

• We are told that the guilt of Jacob will be forgiven by its contending with an enemy by banishment and exile (27:8-9). There's no hint that the forgiveness comes by anything other than the people's work; nothing about any sacrificial offering, either the Old Testament animal sacrifices or the coming sacrifice of Christ.

• God says he is "laying in Zion a foundation stone, a tried stone, a precious cornerstone of sure foundation; whoever believes will not be in panic" (*Dead Sea Scrolls Bible*, 28:16). Paul quotes the passage in his letter to the Romans, but erroneously:

> Israel, which followed after the law of righteousness, hath not attained to the law of righteousness. Wherefore? [i.e., *Why?*] Because they sought it not by faith, but as it were by the works of the law. For they stumbled at that stumblingstone; As it is written, Behold, I lay in Sion a stumblingstone and rock of offence: and whosoever believeth on him shall not be ashamed. [Romans 9:31-33]

In the original passage of Isaiah, though, God doesn't say anything about the stone being something to cause offence or stumble over. It's a cornerstone, not an obstacle. It's also not clear that he refers to anyone believing in the stone (or Jesus, which Paul supposes it represents) as opposed to one who merely "believes."

• The beasts of the Negev included the lion, viper, donkey, camel, . . . and the "fiery flying serpent" (30:6).

• Isaiah prophesies a day of God's indignation and slaughter against all the nations, where the mountains will be drenched with blood, the host of heaven will wear away, and the sky will be rolled up like a scroll (34:1-4). That sounds a lot like the Last Day, until you read further about pelicans, hedgehogs, owls, ravens, jackals, ostriches, desert creatures, wolves, hairy goats, night monsters, tree snakes, and hawks dwelling in the desolate land thereafter (34:10-15). So either our understanding of the Last Day has changed to fit a more global and eternal judgment theme (requiring us to disregard parts of the original text), or Isaiah just got this one wrong and prophesied something that never has and never will happen.

• In contrast to the idea that God would like everyone to be saved, e.g., in 1 Tim 2:3-4, God here states that his sword will come down upon Edom, upon the people he has "doomed for judgment" (*Dead Sea Scrolls Bible*, 34:5) or, as the NASB translates it, the people he has "devoted to destruction." And he certainly didn't want Pharaoh to believe, having hardened Pharaoh's heart throughout a bunch of plagues.

- The angel of the Lord goes out and strikes dead 185,000 Assyrians (37:36). It's just a single verse, and we've read about so much killing by God at this point that it's easy to just gloss over it. But think about it; God snuffs the life out of more souls (unbelieving Assyrians) in *a single day*, for reasons not particularly clear, than the number he has preserved in the last *hundred years* via services, Sunday School, etc. in Conservative Laestadian Christianity.

- As a sign to Hezekiah, God makes a shadow to go back ten steps on a stairway (38:8). Apparently no other shadows were so disturbed, at least not that anyone has ever recorded. Isaiah treats this as a run-of-the-mill "sign," devoting just a few lines to it, but it has the same incredible scientific ramifications as the fixing of the sun during Joshua's battle, discussed in 6.6.

Theologians typically deal with the gaping conflict between modern science and what is asserted in these difficult passages by retreating behind Dennett's "pious fog of modest incomprehension" (2006, 10). Often, as we saw in 4.3.5, they redirect our attention to some supposed spiritual meaning. Thus, we can throw up our hands and say that we just don't understand how the entire population of the earth avoided noticing and recording that sun not only stopped, but suddenly went backwards. Surely the Chinese astronomers who were studying the skies at the time would have noticed? In many parts of the populated world, the dusk skies would have suddenly brightened, and in other parts the evening would have ended into abrupt darkness. But in the spiritual realm, we can dismiss the fact that the mass of the earth's crust and everything resting on it instantly lost all its momentum and violated the physical laws holding that energy can never be destroyed.

- In chapter 40, widely quoted as prophesying John the Baptist and Jesus, we finally see a compassionate God, who comforts his people and pardons their iniquity (40:1), who promises to

> come with strong hand, and his arm shall rule for him: behold, his reward is with him, and his work before him. He shall feed his flock like a shepherd: he shall gather the lambs with his arm, and carry them in his bosom, and shall gently lead those that are with young. [40:10-11]

This is a kind, loving God, more characteristic of the New Testament than the Old. It's easy to see Jesus in the prophecy of God's arm who will rule for him and act as a shepherd. God shows a compassionate side in other parts of Isaiah, for example where he says he longs to be gracious and waits on high to have compassion (30:18).

It is a bit jarring, though, to come upon these passages after reading about a cruel, angry, unforgiving, killing God for more than half of the Bible. The Psalms speak much of God's lovingkindness, but that is mixed heavily with praise for how God destroys his enemies and with calls for him to do more of it. Even elsewhere in Isaiah, we see abundant examples of God's anger and cruelty (3:24-26, 5:25, 6:11, 9:17-21, 10:23-26, 13:6-18, 14:21-13, 14:30, 15:9, 24:1-6, 29:5-6, 30:27, 34:1-9, 37:36, 47:1-5, 63:3-6, 66:24).

- God put water in the wilderness and rivers in the desert for his people, his chosen, to drink, the people which he formed for himself (43:20-21). God has not "formed for himself" the tens of millions of other people who were spread out around the globe at the time Isaiah wrote? Similarly, Moses had said that God has chosen the Israelites to be a special people unto himself, above all people that are upon the face of the earth (Deuteronomy 7:6). Doesn't it seem a bit coincidental that the people who recorded these words were themselves members of the chosen people? Where is there any record of any of the millions of "unchosen" people outside the Mideast agreeing with or even recognizing this categorization? How about the fact that the definition of "the chosen people" had morphed from one based on Jewish ethnicity to one based on Christian belief by the time 1 Peter 2:9 was written on the topic, for a partly or even predominantly Gentiles readership?

- "Verily thou art a God that hidest thyself, O God of Israel, the Saviour" (45:15). That is certainly the way things seem today, but earlier in the Old Testament, God was not hidden at all. He appeared in cloud and fire, and spoke directly to Noah, Moses, Joshua, et al. What happened?

- Sexual assault as metaphor for God's judgment?

> Come down, and sit in the dust, O virgin daughter of Babylon, sit on the ground: there is no throne, O daughter of the Chaldeans: for thou shalt no more be called tender and delicate. Take the millstones, and grind meal: uncover thy locks, make bare the leg, uncover the thigh, pass over the rivers. Thy nakedness shall be

uncovered, yea, thy shame shall be seen: I will take vengeance, and I will not meet thee as a man. [47:1-3]

- Isaiah's amazingly prophetic description of the "suffering servant" in chapter 53 is one of the bright spots in the Old Testament, assuming that it does is fact portray the fate of Jesus the Messiah. Other uplifting and "easy" passages are chapters 55, 56, and 61. It is too bad that nothing like them really appears (with the exception of some psalms, as discussed above) until we are most of the way through the book of Isaiah, and indeed through the Old Testament itself.

And guess what? There are problems with even this centerpiece of the supposed prophecies. Jews and some scholars assert that the Messiah was supposed to be a powerful king-like figure, nothing like the "suffering servant" of chapter 53. That servant doesn't entirely match up with Jesus, either. Two significant issues are posed by verse 10: He "shall see his seed [NASB: *offspring*]," and "he shall prolong his days." The website "Jews for Judaism" has a **collection*** of short articles that (as might be expected) attempt to explain away any connection. **One**** of the articles has this to say about verse 10:

> Christian commentators would like us to believe that the term "seed" is used metaphorically, meaning ... "disciples." Generally, the Hebrew word *bayn* ("son") may be employed metaphorically with the meaning "disciples," but never is the term *zer'a* ("seed") used in this sense.... Hence, *zer'a* must be taken literally, which rules out the possibility that it refers to Jesus since he had no children of his own.
>
> The second part of the promise, "... he shall prolong days," also cannot be applied to Jesus, who died at a young age. To apply these words, as Christian commentators do, is not only evasive but also meaningless. How can such a promise have any meaning for Jesus, who is viewed as being of divine substance and whose existence is believed by Christianity to be eternal? There would be no need for God to assure a fellow member of the Trinity eternal life.

---

*<http://jewsforjudaism.org/index.php?option=com_content&view=category&id=48:suffering-servant&layout=blog&Itemid=500&layout=default>

**<http://jewsforjudaism.org/index.php?option=com_content&view=article&id=130:does-qhe-shall-see-see-prolong-daysq-appy-to-jesus&catid=48:suffering-servant&Itemid=500>

The impact of Isaiah 53 is how *literally* it seems to apply to Jesus in many ways. So attempting to explain these issues with allegory looks an awful lot like trying to have it both ways–literal prophecy where it suits one's doctrinal purposes, and allegorical to patch up everything else.

6.22 Jeremiah

• God threatens his chosen people yet again in chapter 5. He will bring a nation (apparently Babylon) against them from afar, and they will devour their harvest, sons and daughters, flocks and herds, etc. God will avenge himself against his people in this violent way because, among other things, they did not plead the cause of the orphan or defend the rights of the poor (5:28-29).

• God says that he did not speak to or command the Israelites concerning burnt offerings or sacrifices, but commanded them to obey his voice and they would be his people (7:22-23). But that's simply not true. God gave many instructions on the subject; Exodus and Leviticus are full of them. As one of many examples, he commanded:

> An altar of earth thou shalt make unto me, and shalt sacrifice thereon thy burnt offerings, and thy peace offerings, thy sheep, and thine oxen: in all places where I record my name I will come unto thee, and I will bless thee. [Exodus 20:24]

• God will fill the inhabitants of Jerusalem with drunkenness and will dash them against each other, the fathers and the sons together. He will not show pity or compassion (13:13-14).

• God says that he will relent concerning the calamity he planned against a nation if it turns from its evil, and might think better of the good with which he had planned to bless a nation if it does evil (18:8-10). Thus he makes it clear that he doesn't know the future, and it is up to man to decide to do good versus evil. Contrast this with our contemporary view (and David's, as expressed in Psalm 139) of God as all-knowing and all-seeing.

• Jeremiah is a real drag, going on for chapter after chapter about the destruction that God will bring to the people for their sins. He seems to positively delight in the details he provides of God's forthcoming cruelty. And he tops off one litany by asking God *not* to forgive the iniquity of his opponents, or blot out their sin from his sight (18:23).

Like David in his more vengeful psalms, Jeremiah has an attitude that is completely opposite to that of Jesus and the martyred Stephen of the New Testament.

- In 20:14-18, Jeremiah sounds a lot like Job cursing his birth, before his repentance (Job 3:1-19). Who borrowed from whom? Why does Jeremiah apparently get away with his curse?

- Jeremiah 23:5-6 says,

> Behold, the days come, saith the Lord, that I will raise unto David a righteous Branch, and a King shall reign and prosper, and shall execute judgment and justice in the earth. In his days Judah shall be saved, and Israel shall dwell safely: and this is his name whereby he shall be called, the Lord our righteousness. Therefore, behold, the days come, saith the Lord, that they shall no more say, The Lord liveth, which brought up the children of Israel out of the land of Egypt; But, The Lord liveth, which brought up and which led the seed of the house of Israel out of the north country, and from all countries whither I had driven them; and they shall dwell in their own land.

That passage is widely viewed as a prophecy of Jesus. But when you read it objectively, without the hindsight provided by the Gospel writers, what really matches up? Judah and Israel weren't even a divided kingdom when Jesus arrived on the scene, and the Jews of the Roman-ruled Israel that he dwelled in suffered great oppression, culminating in the awful destruction of Jerusalem a few decades after his death. They certainly didn't "dwell in their own land," nor did they "dwell safely." And Jesus said his kingdom was not of this world (John 18:36); he certainly didn't execute "judgment and justice in the earth."

- God tells Jeremiah about his upcoming wrath against the gentiles:

> For this is the day of the Lord GOD of hosts, a day of vengeance, that he may avenge him of his adversaries: and the sword shall devour, and it shall be satiate and made drunk with their blood: for the Lord GOD of hosts hath a sacrifice in the north country by the river Euphrates. [46:10]

God also promises destruction to the Philistines (chapter 47); Moab (chapter 48); Edom, Damascus, Kedar, and Elam (chapter 49); Babylon and the land of the Chaldeans (chapter 50). At this point in the Old

Testament, God relies on his faithful soldiers to do his killing for him. We no longer hear about God striking down with fire, sending plagues, and opening up crevasses in the earth. Lest anyone doubt how serious God is about getting his killing done, however, he curses any of his soldiers who "keepeth back his sword from blood" (48:10).

• In the New Testament, John tells us of a loving God in whom there is no darkness at all (1 John 1:5). But here and elsewhere thus far in the Old Testament, we have seen a very different God who promises to "bring evil" with the sword in his "fierce anger" against entire cities (49:37), who will send soldiers who "shall hold the bow and the lance . . . are cruel, and will not shew mercy" (50:42). He promises to the people of Babylon that he will

> break in pieces man and woman; and with thee will I break in pieces old and young; and with thee will I break in pieces the young man and the maid; I will also break in pieces with thee the shepherd and his flock; and with thee will I break in pieces the husbandman and his yoke of oxen; and with thee will I break in pieces captains and rulers. [51:22-23]

6.23 Lamentations

• The writer of Lamentations, Jeremiah (at least per ancient tradition), tells of a famine so bad that women cannibalized their children (2:20). In chapter 3, he tells of affliction that he personally suffered because of the rod of God's wrath, where God turned his hand against him repeatedly all the day, causing his flesh to waste away, breaking his bones and teeth. Despite all that he asserts that God's "lovingkindnesses never cease, for his compassions never fail" (NASB, 3:22-23). How can such brutal treatment constitute "lovingkindness" or "compassion"? Do the plain meanings of words simply fade away in the face of pious rationalization?

6.24 Ezekiel

• God introduced himself to Ezekiel by showing him four weird creatures, each of which had four faces, four wings, and feet like calves' hooves, yet somehow had human form (1:5). The things ran to and fro like lightning bolts around a bright fire, without turning as they went (1:12-14). They each had a wheel on the earth beside them, with the wheels having rims that were "lofty and awesome . . . full of eyes round about" (NASB, 1:18).

• Ezekiel was instructed to play pretend war using a portrayal of Jerusalem on a brick. He was to lay siege against it and build a fort against it, etc. This child's sandbox activity was to be a "sign to the house of Israel" (4:1-3).

• Then Ezekiel was told to lie on his left side for 390 days, by which action he somehow was to "bear the iniquity of the house of Israel" (NASB, 4:4-5). Wasn't bearing the iniquity of sinners supposed to be the task of Christ alone?

After over a year of lying on his left side, Ezekiel was to turn over and lie on his right side for 40 more days. To keep him from turning from one side to another, God put ropes on him (4:8). Ezekiel's bedsores must have been pretty bad, but his diet wasn't too great, either. God proposed that he live on water and barley cake baked over human dung. Ezekiel objected that he had never eaten anything unclean, sounding a lot like Peter during his dream of the sheet full of beasts (Acts 10:14). God relented and allowed Ezekiel to cook his barley cakes over cow dung instead.

• God is still in the business of tormenting his chosen people. Because of their failure to keep his judgments, he says,

> the fathers shall eat the sons in the midst of thee, and the sons shall eat their fathers; and I will execute judgments in thee, and the whole remnant of thee will I scatter into all the winds. Wherefore, as I live, saith the Lord God; Surely, because thou hast defiled my sanctuary with all thy detestable things, and with all thine abominations, therefore will I also diminish thee; neither shall mine eye spare, neither will I have any pity. A third part of thee shall die with the pestilence, and with famine shall they be consumed in the midst of thee: and a third part shall fall by the sword round about thee; and I will scatter a third part into all the winds, and I will draw out a sword after them. [5:10-12]

In behavior that would be labeled psychopathic if exhibited by a person, God kills in anger and fury, and takes comfort in the suffering he inflicts:

Thus shall mine anger be accomplished, and I will cause my fury to rest upon them, and I will be comforted: and they shall know that I the Lord have spoken it in my zeal, when I have accomplished my fury in them. Moreover I will make thee waste, and a reproach among the nations that are round about thee, in the sight of all that pass by. So it shall be a reproach and a taunt, an instruction and an astonishment unto the nations that are round about thee, when I shall execute judgments in thee in anger and in fury and in furious rebukes. I the Lord have spoken it. When I shall send upon them the evil arrows of famine, which shall be for their destruction, and which I will send to destroy you: and I will increase the famine upon you, and will break your staff of bread: So will I send upon you famine and evil beasts, and they shall bereave thee; and pestilence and blood shall pass through thee; and I will bring the sword upon thee. I the Lord have spoken it. [5:13-17]

• God promises death and destruction in various forms so that the victims, his chosen people, will know that he is the Lord (6:14, 7:27, 12:16, 12:20, 13:14, 13:21, 20:26). He will pour out his wrath on them and spend his anger against them; his eye will show no pity nor will he spare. Then his people will know that he, the Lord, does the smiting (7:8-9). Why does he have to reveal himself through cruelty? When we look at the abundant death and destruction still afflicting humanity across the globe today, we don't point to it and say, "Aha, there's evidence that the God of Abraham is indeed the Lord." We tend to credit God for our own personal health and well-being and ignore the horrors going on in the world, or vaguely blame them on Satan.

• God indignantly shows Ezekiel the "abominations" being committed against him. They consisted of 70 "men of the ancients of the house of Israel" burning incense and surrounded by carvings on the walls of his sanctuary of "creeping things, and abominable beasts, and all the idols of the house of Israel" (8:10-11), some women weeping for a Babylonian fertility god (8:14), and 25 men prostrating themselves toward the sun and "putting the branch to their nose" (8:16-17). These activities, misguided pagan worship though they were, caused no harm to anyone. But God's wrathful, grossly disproportionate retribution certainly did.

He called for the executioners of the city to draw near, each "with his destroying weapon in his hand" (9:1). He commanded that the men of Jerusalem who disapproved of the aforementioned abominations be marked on their foreheads. Then, he directed,

> Go ye after him through the city, and smite: let not your eye spare, neither have ye pity: Slay utterly old and young, both maids, and little children, and women: but come not near any man upon whom is the mark; and begin at my sanctuary. Then they began at the ancient men which were before the house. And he said unto them, Defile the house, and fill the courts with the slain: go ye forth. [9:5-7]

It's bad enough to see God engaging in yet another vengeful, pitiless massacre. But what possible justification is there for the slaughter of women and innocent children who, unlike the men, had no way to take sides and avoid God's wrath?

• After inflicting all this bloodshed, God has the temerity to complain about the house of Israel having "multiplied your slain in this city, and . . . fill[ing] the streets thereof with the slain" (11:6).

• In chapter 16, Ezekiel seems to have sex on his mind a great deal as he portrays God as the jealous husband of Jerusalem. Like chapter 23, it is not a text you will find read anywhere on church property.

God found the metaphorical Jerusalem as an abandoned infant and watched her grow to the point where her breasts had formed and her pubic hair had grown, yet she was naked and bare (16:7). He passed by her and saw that her "time was the time of love," so he spread his skirt over her and covered her nakedness, and entered into a covenant with her so that she became his (16:8). He bathed her, washed away her menstrual blood, and anointed her with oil (16:9). He dressed her in fine clothes and sandals (16:10), and adorned her with bracelets, a necklace, a nose ring and earrings (not making very Laestadian fashion choices there), and a crown on her head (16:11-12).

Unfortunately, Jerusalem turned out to be quite a gal. She "poured out her harlotries on every passer-by who might be willing" (16:15). She took the fair jewels that had been made of God's gold and silver and made for herself "images of men, and didst commit whoredom with them" (16:17). She "spread [her] legs to every passer-by to multiply [her] harlotry" and "played the harlot with the Egyptians, [her] lustful neighbors" (NASB, 16:25-26). Still unsatisfied, she went on to play the harlot with the Assyrians and the Chaldeans (16:28-29).

God of course didn't put up with this forever. He said to her,

> Because thy filthiness was poured out, and thy nakedness discovered through thy whoredoms with thy lovers, and with all the idols of thy abominations, and by the blood of thy children, which thou didst give unto them; Behold, therefore I will gather all thy lovers, with whom thou hast taken pleasure, and all them that thou hast loved, with all them that thou hast hated; I will even gather them round about against thee, and will discover thy nakedness unto them, that they may see all thy nakedness. And I will judge thee, as women that break wedlock and shed blood are judged; and I will give thee blood in fury and jealousy. And I will also give thee into their hand, and they shall throw down thine eminent place, and shall break down thy high places: they shall strip thee also of thy clothes, and shall take thy fair jewels, and leave thee naked and bare. [16:36-39]

After subjecting his Jerusalem to violent sexual assault, God has her stoned and thrust through (16:40). Then, finally satisfied, he says, "will I make my fury toward thee to rest, and my jealousy shall depart from thee, and I will be quiet, and will be no more angry" (16:42).

• Does God want everyone to be saved from condemnation by their sins or not? This would seem to be the most important question of all religion, and yet *no clear answer* is provided by the Bible! In the Old Testament, the question is limited to an earthly condemnation of (early) death, because the vast majority of Old Testament writings do not even hint at any afterlife or eternal consequences, only God's killing of sinners. For those who try to fit the New Testament Hell onto the Old Testament writings, however, this discussion will apply to the question discussed later regarding God's wishing for everyone to avoid eternal damnation, or not.

In chapter 18, Ezekiel has God expressing the wish for all to be saved from condemnation. God asks rhetorically, "Have I any pleasure at all that the wicked should die? . . . and not that he should return from his ways, and live?" (18:23-24) He goes on to say that his ways are equal and a wicked man can turn "away from his wickedness that he hath committed, and doeth that which is lawful and right, he shall save his soul alive" (18:27, *save his life* per NASB). He urges the house of Israel to repent, "and turn yourselves from all your transgressions; so iniquity shall not be your ruin" (18:30). For, God says, "I have no pleasure in the death of him that dieth ... wherefore turn yourselves, and live ye" (18:32).

Chapter 33 has near-duplicates of these statements. God declares,

> I have no pleasure in the death of the wicked; but that the wicked turn from his way and live: turn ye, turn ye from your evil ways; for why will ye die, O house of Israel? Therefore, thou son of man, say unto the children of thy people, The righteousness of the righteous shall not deliver him in the day of his transgression: as for the wickedness of the wicked, he shall not fall thereby in the day that he turneth from his wickedness; neither shall the righteous be able to live for his righteousness in the day that he sinneth. When I shall say to the righteous, that he shall surely live; if he trust to his own righteousness, and commit iniquity, all his righteousnesses shall not be remembered; but for his iniquity that he hath committed, he shall die for it. Again, when I say unto the wicked, Thou shalt surely die; if he turn from his sin, and do that which is lawful and right; If the wicked restore the pledge, give again that he had robbed, walk in the statutes of life, without committing iniquity; he shall surely live, he shall not die. None of his sins that he hath committed shall be mentioned unto him: he hath done that which is lawful and right; he shall surely live. [33:11-16]

In contrast, consider just a few examples we've already seen of God's merciless killing of sinners:

- In Exodus, God hardens Pharaoh's heart so that God can inflict plagues that include a lot of killing of Egyptians, none of whom had the option to side with the Israelites.

- God orders the massacre of the Midianites (Numbers 31) and Amelekites (1 Samuel 15), citing their wickedness, and had Joshua go on a reign of terror and conquest to make room for his chosen people in the promised land. But he sent no missionaries to call repentant sinners beforehand, nor did he offer any mercy to innocent children. He just ordered his troops in with the sword, got angry when they left anyone alive against his orders, and had the booty divided up amongst his people.

- God kills off thousands of his chosen people as punishment for the sins of one or a few (1 Samuel 6:19, 2 Samuel 24:17).

- God says that his sword will come down upon Edom, upon the people he has "doomed for judgment" (*Dead Sea Scrolls Bible*, Isaiah 34:5) or, as the NASB translates it, the people he has "devoted to destruction."

- The following are excerpts from chapter 20. Do they seem like the pronouncements of the all-wise, all-powerful creator of the huge and magnificent world we have occupied on all its continents (except Antarctica) for many tens of thousands of years as *Homo sapiens*, evolving in all of our *hundreds* of different cultures with our varied physical characteristics, beliefs, and modes of living?

> In the day when I chose Israel, and lifted up mine hand unto the seed of the house of Jacob, and made myself known unto them in the land of Egypt, when I lifted up mine hand unto them, saying, I am the Lord your God; In the day that I lifted up mine hand unto them, to bring them forth of the land of Egypt into a land that I had espied for them . . . [vv. 5-6]

> But I wrought for my name's sake, that it should not be polluted before the heathen, in whose sight I brought them out. Yet also I lifted up my hand unto them in the wilderness, that I would not bring them into the land which I had given them, flowing with milk and honey, which is the glory of all lands. [vv. 14-15]

> I will bring you out from the people, and will gather you out of the countries wherein ye are scattered, with a mighty hand, and with a stretched out arm, and with fury poured out. [v. 34]

> For in mine holy mountain, in the mountain of the height of Israel, saith the Lord GOD, there shall all the house of Israel, all of them in the land, serve me: there will I accept them, and there will I require your offerings, and the firstfruits of your oblations, with all your holy things. I will accept you with your sweet savour, when I bring you out from the people, and gather you out of the countries wherein ye have been scattered; and I will be sanctified in you before the heathen. [vv. 40-41]

Well, that was written by holy men of the one isolated tribe of nomadic warriors and herdsmen, eking out a tenuous and fearful existence in a small, harsh region of the Middle East, the very same people who seem to be so favored by the God that their writings describe. Now we know that the world is made up not just of the Israelites and its surrounding enemies, but has been fully populated by humanity–since the days of Ezekiel–from Africa to Asia and Europe to the Pacific Islands and Americas. Human skeletons have been found in Australia that date from at least 45,000 years ago (Wells 2006, 120). Yet theologians still venerate these xenophobic words and claim that the God of Abraham who speaks through them is indeed the creator of all mankind, despite the fact that he completely ignores, or at most dismiss as "heathens" and "countries wherein ye are scattered," *everyone else*. Those "others" are all part of God's miraculous creation, we are told, but he expresses nothing but contempt for them.

- Because his children had rebelled against him, failed to execute his judgments, despised his statutes, and polluted his sabbaths, God "gave them also statutes that were not good, and judgments whereby they should not live" (20:25). This is remarkable–the same deity that is praised as having in him no darkness at all (1 John 1:5), the father of lights with whom there is no variableness nor shadow of turning (James 1:17), gave his children bad statutes and unlivable judgments! not only that, but God himself has claimed *to create evil*, saying in Isaiah 45:7, "I form the light, and create darkness: I make peace, and create evil: I the Lord do all these things."

It gets worse when you read in Ezekiel's next verse that God "polluted them in their own gifts, in that they caused to pass through the fire all that openeth the womb" (20:26) and realize that he is probably talking about human sacrifice of the firstborn child. It's not far-fetched at all to think so when you consider that God commands in Exodus 22:29, "Thou shalt not delay to offer the first of thy ripe fruits, and of thy liquors: the firstborn of thy sons shalt thou give unto me" (Stark 2011, 66), comparing it in the next verse to the sacrifice he also requires of oxen and sheep. Such cases of sacrifice were not unprecedented: recall from Judges 11 (**6.7**) that Jepthah sacrificed his daughter to satisfy a vow he had made to God, and that Abraham was fully prepared to sacrifice his firstborn son in obedience to a command he had heard from God (Gen 22).

Stark asks "inerrantists who are committed to Reformed [i.e., Calvinist] conceptions of divine sovereignty" the following poignant question:

> If Yahweh's sovereignty entails the use of evil means to accomplish his undisclosed objectives, if Yahweh sent lying spirits in order to deceive [see **6.13**], if Yahweh intentionally commanded the Israelites to sacrifice their children in order to punish them, if he intentionally gave them bad commands ... then what is to prevent God from intentionally giving us *other* bad scriptures, intentionally obfuscating revelation as a form of punishment, or as some sort of examination, to test our mettle? [p. 66]

- Ezekiel devotes chapter 23 to a vivid description given by God of the sexual habits of two sisters, who played the harlot in Egypt in their youth, "there their breasts were pressed and there their virgin bosom was handled" (NASB, 23:2-3). The older one, a metaphor for Samaria, lusted after her lovers, after the Assyrians,

> desirable young men, horsemen riding on horses. She bestowed her harlotries on them, all of whom were the choicest men of Assyria; and with all whom she lusted after, with all their idols she defiled herself. She did not forsake her harlotries from the time in Egypt; for in her youth men had lain with her, and they handled her virgin bosom and poured out their lust on her. Therefore, I gave her into the hand of her lovers, into the hand of the Assyrians, after whom she lusted. They uncovered her nakedness; they took her sons and her daughters, but they slew her with the sword. [23:6-10, NASB]

Her younger sister, a metaphor for Jerusalem, saw this and became even more corrupt in her lust. She lusted after the Assyrians as well,

> desirable young men. [God] saw that she had defiled herself; they both took the same way. So she increased her harlotries. And she saw men portrayed on the wall, images of the Chaldeans portrayed with vermilion, girded with belts on their loins, with flowing turbans on their heads, all of them looking like officers, like the Babylonians in Chaldea, the land of their birth. When she saw them she lusted after them and sent messengers to them in Chaldea. The Babylonians came to her to the bed of love and defiled her with their harlotry. And when she had been defiled by

> them, she became disgusted with them. She uncovered her harlotries and uncovered her nakedness; then [God] became disgusted with her, as [he] had become disgusted with her sister. [23:12-19, NASB]

Size mattered indeed for this younger sister, for she lusted after the sisters' paramours, whose genitals were like that of donkeys and whose seminal issue was like that of horses (23:20). She became wistful about the lewdness of her youth, when the Egyptians handled her bosom because of the breasts of her youth (23:21).

Upset at all this untoward behavior, God told her that he would

> arouse your lovers against you, from whom you were alienated, and I will bring them against you from every side: the Babylonians and all the Chaldeans, Pekod and Shoa and Koa, and all the Assyrians with them; desirable young men, governors and officials all of them, officers and men of renown, all of them riding on horses. . . . I will set my jealousy against you, that they may deal with you in wrath. They will remove your nose and your ears; and your survivors will fall by the sword They will take your sons and your daughters; and your survivors will be consumed by the fire. They will also strip you of your clothes and take away your beautiful jewels. Thus I will make your lewdness and your harlotry brought from the land of Egypt to cease from you, so that you will not lift up your eyes to them or remember Egypt anymore. . . . They will deal with you in hatred, take all your property, and leave you naked and bare. And the nakedness of your harlotries will be uncovered, both your lewdness and your harlotries. [23:22-29, NASB]

- God takes Ezekiel's wife from him and tells him not to mourn or weep (24:16), thus making him a sign to the house of Israel (24:24). Too bad for the wife and any human emotions Ezekiel may have had.

- God continues his threats and cruelty: "I will destroy thee" (25:7); "I will execute great vengeance" (25:17); "I will bring terrors on you" (26:21, NASB). But there's a silver lining in this cloud; God says that those with whom he has such displeasure "shalt be no more . . . never be found again" (26:21); "never shalt be any more" (27:36); "never shalt thou be any more" (28:19). (The NASB uses the phrase "cease to be forever" in 27:36, 28:19.) At least the Old Testament God is still satisfied with inflicting a bit of terror and a painful, humiliating death, followed by simple annihilation. There's no resurrection unto eternal damnation in these passages.

- God tells Ezekiel that he will bring Nebuchadnezzar the king of Babylon upon the city of Tyre (26:7). Nebuchadnezzar would slay the daughters of Tyre with the sword, to make siege walls against it, and raise up a large shield against it (26:8). He would break down the walls and towers and pillars, a multitude of horses and wagons and chariots would enter and he would slaughter the people with the sword (26:9-11). Tyre would be made into a bare rock, never to be built any more (26:14), a desolate city (26:19).

Well, Nebuchadnezzar attacked Tyre, but what he got after some fifteen years of siege was a negotiated settlement. He never broke down any walls or towers and his horses never set foot into the city. Later, Ezekiel himself admits that Nebuchadnezzar's army had no wages from Tyre for the labor he had performed against it (29:18). But take heart, Neb, for God will give you Egypt as a consolation prize! You "shall take her multitude, and take her spoil, and take her prey; and it shall be the wages for [your] army" (29:19). The land of Egypt was to become

> utterly waste and desolate, from the tower of Syene even unto the border of Ethiopia. No foot of man shall pass through it, nor foot of beast shall pass through it, neither shall it be inhabited forty years. And I will make the land of Egypt desolate in the midst of the countries that are desolate, and her cities among the cities that are laid waste shall be desolate forty years: and I will scatter the Egyptians among the nations, and will disperse them through the countries. [29:10-12]

But that has never happened, either.

- After expressing his disgust at "the shepherds of Israel," God promises,

> I, even I, will both search my sheep, and seek them out. As a shepherd seeketh out his flock in the day that he is among his sheep that are scattered; so will I seek out my sheep, and will deliver them out of all places where they have been scattered in the cloudy and dark day. And I will bring them out from the people, and gather them from the countries, and will bring them to their own land, and feed them upon the mountains of Israel by

the rivers, and in all the inhabited places of the country. I will feed them in a good pasture, and upon the high mountains of Israel shall their fold be: there shall they lie in a good fold, and in a fat pasture shall they feed upon the mountains of Israel. I will feed my flock, and I will cause them to lie down, saith the Lord God. I will seek that which was lost, and bring again that which was driven away, and will bind up that which was broken, and will strengthen that which was sick: but I will destroy the fat and the strong; I will feed them with judgment. [34:11-16]

That seems like a prophecy of Jesus, and indeed Luke reports Jesus as saying he had "come to seek and to save that which was lost" (Luke 19:10). But then, a few verses later, we read that God's servant **David** is to be the "one shepherd over them," who will feed them and be a prince among them (34:23-24). So much for that, unless you construe God's servant David to somehow actually be Jesus through his (adoptive) genealogy.

• Because the cities of Mount Seir did not hate bloodshed, God will make bloodshed pursue them (35:6).

• God as jealous landowner: "Surely in the fire of my jealousy have I spoken against the residue of the heathen, and against all Idumea, which have appointed my land into their possession with the joy of all their heart . . ." (36:5).

• In what is widely held as another messianic prophecy, God says,

> David my servant shall be king over them; and they all shall have one shepherd: they shall also walk in my judgments, and observe my statutes, and do them. And they shall dwell in the land that I have given unto Jacob my servant, wherein your fathers have dwelt; and they shall dwell therein, even they, and their children, and their children's children for ever: and my servant David shall be their prince for ever. Moreover I will make a covenant of peace with them; it shall be an everlasting covenant with them: and I will place them, and multiply them, and will set my sanctuary in the midst of them for evermore. My tabernacle also shall be with them: yea, I will be their God, and they shall be my people. [37:24-27]

There are a couple of problems with this, though. God is speaking not about some group of people to come who will believe in any Messiah, but only about two divided peoples of Judah and Joseph, respectively (37:16), whom he will join together (37:17-19). The reunited people were to walk in God's judgments (NASB, *ordinances*), and observe his statutes, whereas the Christians jettisoned much of those ordinances and statutes right away.

• Ezekiel talks to mountains (35:2, 36:1), the land of Israel (21:3), skeletons (37:12), and birds and beasts (39:17). In the latter instance, Ezekiel informs the critters that God will be giving the flesh and blood of mighty men to them to eat as a sacrifice for them (39:17-19). Why is offering a sacrifice (of humans, no less) to mere birds and beasts? It is certainly an ironic reversal of the early ritual killing of animals as sacrifices for humans!

• Why did God give to Ezekiel a painstakingly detailed vision, with precise specifications of layout, measurements, materials, and customs of use taking up five chapters (40-44), of a temple *that would never be built*? In the vision, chapters 43-45, God explains exactly how the priests are to operate in the temple, clearly assuming that it would in fact be built. Either God failed to accurately forsee the future, or Ezekiel was, at least in this instance, a false prophet.

An easily dismissed alternative is that God really meant that this temple would be of some nebulous "spiritual" form, all the detailed physical plans notwithstanding. The only other option would be that the temple is yet to be built. Nobody, certainly not any but the most marginalized Jews and Christians, would now be in any way inclined to construct an edifice of Bronze-Age worship. And the reinstatement of animal sacrifice after Jesus made his ultimate sacrifice would seem to be a blatant contradiction and repudiation of the New Testament. One possible "way out" would be for such new temple sacrifices to be somehow considered a commemoration of Jesus' sacrifice rather than precursors to it (Price 2010).

6.25 Daniel

• In 3:25, Nebuchadnezzar sees four men loose, walking unhurt in the midst of the fire. The KJV has him saying that "the form of the fourth is like *the Son of God*." Many expositors have of course latched onto this as being a prophecy of Jesus. In the NASB, the fourth man is reported as having an appearance "like a son of the gods."

- Nebuchadnezzar, who died in 562 B.C., is asserted to be Belshazzar's father in chapter 5, verses 2, 11, 18, and 22. But Belshazzar was actually the son of Nabonidus, who was the last king of Babylon (555-538 B.C.). There is no evidence that Belshazzar was even a descendant of Nebuchadnezzar.

- We are told that "Darius the Mede" received the kingdom of Babylon at about 62 years of age (5:31), and that this "King Darius" cast Daniel and his friends into the Lions' den. But there is no historical record of any "Darius the Mede," and there was never any "King Darius" of Babylon.

- Daniel has what seems like a remarkable prophecy of the Messiah:

> I saw in the night visions, and, behold, one like the Son of man came with the clouds of heaven, and came to the Ancient of days, and they brought him near before him. And there was given him dominion, and glory, and a kingdom, that all people, nations, and languages, should serve him: his dominion is an everlasting dominion, which shall not pass away, and his kingdom that which shall not be destroyed. [7:13-14]

As always, though, there are some issues with the details of the prophecy. The NASB translation states it as "one like **a** Son of man was coming," with no implication that there is just one "Son of man." Why did this Son of man have to be brought before the "Ancient of days" if he was one with the Father (John 10:30), being in the Father and having the Father in him (John 14:10)?

- Most scholars now believe that Daniel was written around 165 B.C. rather than the traditional 530 B.C. date. One reason is that the alleged prophecies of the book (see chapter 11) become increasingly accurate as the date of their occurrence gets closer to 165 B.C., and then get very cloudy after that point. There's no historical record of the events predicted in 11:40-45. At the end of the book, Daniel is finally told to go on his way, for the words of prophecy at that point "are closed up and sealed till the time of the end" (12:9).

It is possible that Daniel was a prophet whose vision was divinely limited. But the more mundane possibility that historians do and must consider more realistic is that the book was the product of a second-century B.C. writer who presented history as prophecy (much more accurately about events of his recent past), made some vague guesses about what would happen after his times, and dealt with his inability to even guess about the distant future by having the prophecy "close up" on him at that point.

• According to a footnote to Daniel 12:2 in Zondervan's NASB Study Bible, the verse offers "the first clear reference to a resurrection of both the righteous and the wicked." Well, it's about time! Even assuming the traditional 530 B.C. date of authorship, there's been a lot of muddy water about the afterlife under the Old Testament bridge at this point. As mentioned way back in the discussion on 1 Kings, there would seem to be no more important topic for God to address than the eternal fate of the righteous versus that of the wicked. Yet the righteous and wicked alike have lived and died over scores of generations, from the earliest days of God's chosen people through the Exile, the Mosaic law, the judges and kings of Israel, without having any "clear reference to a resurrection of both the righteous and the wicked."

And, actually, this supposedly "clear reference" has a very large patch of mud smack in the middle, the word "many." It does not specify a fate for every last soul, but says rather that "*many* of them that sleep in the dust of the earth shall awake, some to everlasting life, and some to shame and everlasting contempt." What happens to the others? And "shame and everlasting contempt" sounds more like a bad legacy than the pitiless, unabated torture of the New Testament hell.

6.26 Hosea

• Why does God order the prophet Hosea to take "a wife of whoredoms and children of whoredoms" (1:2)? When Hosea complies, God gives the resulting children names that reflect his lack of compassion (1:4,6,9).

• What is it with these guys and their fixation on misogynist cruelty and sexual imagery? According to Hosea, God says that a certain woman (no doubt metaphorical) is to "put away her whoredoms out of her sight, and her adulteries from between her breasts; Lest [God] strip her naked, and set her as in the day that she was born" (2:2-3). God "will not have mercy upon her children; for they be the children of whoredoms. For their mother hath played the harlot: she that conceived them hath done shamefully" (2:4-5). He will take away his wool and flax that were "given to cover her nakedness. And now will [he] discover her lewdness in the sight of her lovers, and none shall deliver her out of

[his] hand" (2:9-10). Somehow it seems doubtful that battered wives of cruel, dominating husbands turn much to this passage for comfort, or to the ones discussed earlier that are so much like it (Isaiah 47, Ezekiel 16,23,33).

- Why does God tell Hosea, "Go yet, love a woman beloved of her friend (lit. *companion*), yet an adulteress" (3:1)?

- God says, "My people are destroyed for lack of knowledge: because thou hast rejected knowledge, I will also reject thee, that thou shalt be no priest to me: seeing thou hast forgotten the law of thy God, I will also forget thy children" (4:6). It is ironic to see a condemnation of someone "rejecting knowledge," because that is exactly what we are told to do when that knowledge doesn't support our doctrinal presuppositions.

- God says he will not punish his people's daughters when they play the harlot, or their brides when they commit adultery, for the men go with harlots and the people are without understanding (4:14). It seems like some small progress towards fairness and civility, but it is a change to the supposedly never-changing Mosaic laws nonetheless (Deut 12:32).

- Hosea asks God to give Ephraim "a miscarrying womb and dry breasts" (9:14). There are no "love your enemy" or "pro-life" sentiments in his angry rant that he

> hated them: for the wickedness of their doings I will drive them out of mine house, I will love them no more: all their princes are revolters. Ephraim is smitten, their root is dried up, they shall bear no fruit: yea, though they bring forth, yet will I slay even the beloved fruit of their womb. My God will cast them away, because they did not hearken unto him: and they shall be wanderers among the nations. [9:15-17]

- Ephraim will return to Egypt (8:13). Wait, no, they won't (11:5).

- "Samaria shall become desolate; for she hath rebelled against her God: they shall fall by the sword: their infants shall be dashed in pieces, and their women with child shall be ripped up" (13:16).

6.27 Joel

• After descriptions of the day of the Lord coming as destruction from the Almighty, with food cut off, seeds shriveling, beasts groaning, fire devouring pastures, etc. (1:15-19), we are told that God "is gracious and merciful, slow to anger, and of great kindness" (2:13). Does that description make any sense, do those words have any meaning, in view of what we've seen thus far?

• God promises that his people will never be put to shame (2:26-7). Later, Israel would come under Roman rule and ultimately have its temple and holy city destroyed. The Jews would be scattered into countries where they would be persecuted for millennia, and a large proportion of them would perish horribly in the Holocaust. If we are to speak of the Christians instead, under the assumption that they and not the Jews would be God's people once the New Testament commenced, we need only refer to the cruel and humiliating persecutions they suffered under Nero.

6.28 Amos

• As we near the last books of the Old Testament, God is still very much in the killing business. In chapters 1-2, he promises to send fire to numerous places, devouring their palaces. To people he calls "cows of Bashan," he says he has "sworn by his holiness, that, lo, the days shall come upon you, that he will take you away with hooks, and your posterity with fishhooks" (4:1-2). He has smitten with scorching wind and mildew, caterpillars, plagues, and slaughter by the sword (4:9-10).

• Those who "desire the day of the Lord" are not given any comforting words about a resurrection unto eternal glory, as one might expect to hear when "believing on the promise." No, woe unto you, Amos says, for

> to what end is it for you? The day of the Lord is darkness, and not light. As if a man did flee from a lion, and a bear met him; or went into the house, and leaned his hand on the wall, and a serpent bit him. Shall not the day of the Lord be darkness, and not light? even very dark, and no brightness in it? [5:18-20]

That sounds like a sad, nihilistic end for people who are waiting longingly for the last day. Presumably the godless evil ones were too busy living it up to even think about it.

6.29 *Jonah*

- We are told that Jonah spent three full days alive in the stomach of a large fish (1:17), where he prayed to God (2:1-9) and from which he was vomited onto dry land (2:10). He apparently made his way down the esophagus and back again, had a continuous supply of breathable air, and avoided being crushed or digested.

This story has been the subject of discussion at LLC gatherings as an example of how we need to put our "carnal mind" aside and believe "God's Word." It's certainly a good test case. Luther mused at his dinner table that the "history of the prophet Jonah is almost incredible, sounding more strange than any poet's fable; if it were not in the Bible, I should take it for a lie; for consider, how for the space of three days he was in the great belly of the whale, whereas in three hours he might have been digested and changed into the nature, flesh and blood of that monster" (*Table Talk* §547).

But if we set aside that slavish devotion to the Bible's inerrancy for a moment, does this really seem like a historical event, a miraculous way for God to transport Jonah to his destination? Or does it seem more like an ancient myth, an explanation for how Jonah made his journey without God having to do something that a reader of the ancient world would have *really* found impossible, like teleporting him there in a puff of smoke? The answer seems painfully obvious to me, but the stakes are higher than just shrugging our shoulders at some wild tales of the Old Testament. Matthew 12:40 has Jesus referring to the Jonah story as a factual event when making a metaphor about his upcoming death. (It's not just Jonah. Jesus gives historical treatment to Noah and the Ark in Matthew 24:37-39.) Thom Stark isn't too concerned about that, saying that it

> hardly amounts to a claim on Jesus' part that Jonah should be taken to be historical. Jesus regularly used parables to make theological points that pertained to the real world, and he was not duplicitous in doing so. The genre of the fictional short story was very common in Jewish literature of the second temple period,

and Jesus no doubt would have been astute enough to recognize it when he saw it. [2011, 4]

• God sees the repentance of Nineveh and relents about the calamity he had declared he would bring upon them (3:10). That's nice, but it shows that God cannot be omniscient and have everyone's fate predestined.

• For some reason, Jonah is angry that God decides not to destroy Nineveh. God asks him,

> Should I not have compassion on [*spare*, KJV] Nineveh, the great city in which there are more than 120,000 persons who do not know the difference between their right and left hand, as well as many animals? [NASB, 4:11]

It's great to see this sort of compassion, but take a look again at where we've been in the Old Testament. This is not a picture of God that is consistent with the anger, cruelty, and violence we've seen earlier, where God wiped out cities at least as big as Nineveh without giving them any opportunity for repentance. And how compassionate is it to send *billions* of people who have never even heard of the correct means of repentance to an eternity in hell?

6.30 Micah

• A favorite passage of Micah that is widely held to be a messianic prophecy, and referenced as such in Matthew 2:6, is the following:

> But thou, Bethlehem Ephratah, though thou be little among the thousands of Judah, yet out of thee shall he come forth unto me that is to be ruler in Israel; whose goings forth have been from of old, from everlasting. [5:2]

When viewed in isolation through our Christian lenses, this seems remarkably clear. But how does it look when read objectively in its full context?

> Now gather thyself in troops, O daughter of troops: he hath laid siege against us: they shall smite the judge of Israel with a rod upon the cheek. But thou, Bethlehem Ephratah, though thou be little among the thousands [NASB, *clans*] of Judah, yet out of thee shall he come forth unto me that is to be ruler in Israel; whose goings forth have been from of old, from everlasting. Therefore

> will he give them up, until the time that she which travaileth hath brought forth: then the remnant of his brethren shall return unto the children of Israel. And he shall stand and feed [NASB, *will arise and shepherd his flock*] in the strength of the Lord, in the majesty of the name of the Lord his God; and they shall abide: for now shall he be great unto the ends of the earth. And this man shall be the peace, when the Assyrian shall come into our land: and when he shall tread in our palaces, then shall we raise against him seven shepherds, and eight principal men. And they shall waste the land of Assyria with the sword, and the land of Nimrod in the entrances thereof: thus shall he deliver us from the Assyrian, when he cometh into our land, and when he treadeth within our borders. [5:1-6]

Israel was bracing itself against a siege by the Assyrians, and looked forward to being rescued by a mighty king from the clan of Bethlehem Ephrata, who would draw strength from "the Lord his God." Under his reign, the land of the Assyrians would be wasted with the sword. How does this speak about a gentle, meek prince of peace who would in fact be God himself in the flesh, and would be humiliated and executed by hated occupiers of Israel as an offering for the sins of the people?

• Remarkably, Micah comes to question the whole business of offering sacrifices for sins:

> Wherewith [*With what*] shall I come before the Lord, and bow myself before the high God? shall I come before him with burnt offerings, with calves of a year old? Will the Lord be pleased with thousands of rams, or with ten thousands of rivers of oil? shall I give my firstborn for my transgression, the fruit of my body for the sin of my soul? [6:1-7]

God has told us what is good and what he requires of us, Micah says, and apparently has concluded that sacrifice isn't it. Rather it is "to do justly, and to love mercy, and to walk humbly with thy God" (6:8). It's a beautiful thought, but it is hard to see how the person writing it was a "believer in the promise" that God would someday torture his son to death as a final, perfect sacrifice for sins.

6.31 Nahum

- This book consists of an angry rant by God against Nineveh. That city, we may recall, was the one to whom God relented concerning the calamity he had declared he would bring upon them, to Jonah's chagrin (Jonah 3:10-4:1). Now God has changed his mind again, in a big way; he is jealous, avenging and wrathful (1:2), there are many slain, a mass of corpses, countless dead bodies, "[b]ecause of the multitude of the whoredoms of the wellfavoured harlot, the mistress of witchcrafts, that selleth nations through her whoredoms, and families through her witchcrafts" (3:4). In sexual imagery that is now all too familiar, Nahum has God saying to Nineveh that he will "lift up your skirts over your face, and show to the nations your nakedness, and to the kingdoms your disgrace" (NASB, 3:5). He will throw filth on her and make her vile, and set her up as a spectacle (3:6).

6.32 Habakkuk

- Habakkuk begins by lamenting God's failure to right the wrongs of an unjust world. To anyone who has struggled with doubt about God's existence, about the one-way connection that prayer seems to be, the words are poignant:

> O Lord, how long shall I cry, and thou wilt not hear! even cry out unto thee of violence, and thou wilt not save! Does God help in time of need? Why dost thou shew me iniquity, and cause me to behold grievance? for spoiling and violence are before me: and there are that raise up strife and contention. Therefore the law is slacked, and judgment doth never go forth: for the wicked doth compass about the righteous; therefore wrong judgment proceedeth. [1:2-4]

- God pronounces woe "to him who builds a city with bloodshed and founds a town with violence" (2:12). Does that include Joshua, who undertook a ruthless and bloody conquest of the cities of Jericho, Ai, and Gibeon (to name a few) under God's direct command?

6.33 Zephaniah

- Zephaniah predicts that the "great day of the Lord is near, it is near, and hasteth greatly," (1:14) "near and coming very quickly" as the

NASB puts it. God will "utterly consume all things from off the land," including man and beast, birds, and fish (1:2-3). The mighty man will cry bitterly, in that

> day of wrath, a day of trouble and distress, a day of wasteness and desolation, a day of darkness and gloominess, a day of clouds and thick darkness, A day of the trumpet and alarm against the fenced cities, and against the high towers. And [God] will bring distress upon men, that they shall walk like blind men, because they have sinned against the Lord: and their blood shall be poured out as dust, and their flesh as the dung. Neither their silver nor their gold shall be able to deliver them in the day of the Lord's wrath; but the whole land shall be devoured by the fire of his jealousy: for he shall make even a speedy riddance [NASB: *a complete end, indeed a terrifying one*] of all them that dwell in the land. [1:14-18]

This is the clearest indication yet of a Revelation-style "End of the World." But there is still no hint of any eternal punishment; to the contrary, there will be a "speedy riddance" (or "complete end, indeed a terrifying one" per NASB). And Zephaniah's statement that the great day is near and coming very quickly puts him in the distinguished company of Jesus, Paul, Luther, and many Laestadian preachers who each made it seem that the end was imminent in *their* time.

6.34 Zechariah

• Zechariah makes a prophecy that does seem impressive; Jerusalem's king would be just, endowed with salvation, and humble (9:9), in contrast to the expectations we've seen thus far that the Messiah would be a powerful warrior king. Zechariah's king would arrive mounted on a donkey, a triumphal entry scene with the ironic contrast of a lowly beast of burden that is vividly portrayed in the New Testament and subsequent Christian teachings. Less attention is paid to the inconvenient fact that Zechariah mentions two mounts: the donkey and a colt, the foal of a donkey. Of the four gospels, Matthew follows the prophecy most faithfully, portraying Jesus as somehow riding on both (Mt 21:2-7).

• Zechariah provides his own bit of the now-familiar divine threats of gory destruction that we have found scattered throughout the Old

Testament. God will no longer have pity on the inhabitants of Lebanon. While Zechariah had "pastured the flock doomed to slaughter" (NASB, 11:7) per God's command, he is no longer to do so. Instead, he says he will break his covenant that he had made with all the peoples (11:10). "What is to die, let it die, and what is to be annihilated, let it be annihilated; and let those who are left eat one another's flesh" (NASB, 11:9).

- God promises to raise up a shepherd in the land who "will *not* care for the perishing, seek the scattered, heal the broken, or sustain the one standing, but will devour the flesh of the fat sheep and tear off their hoofs" (NASB, 11:16, emphasis added). This is not the "Good Shepherd," but someone quite the opposite. And we can't dismiss this uncaring, indifferent "bad shepherd" as some dark force in a fight of good versus evil; he was to be raised up by God himself.

- Zechariah predicts that Jerusalem will kick butt someday. God will make Jerusalem "a cup of trembling unto all the people round about" and "a burdensome stone for all people: all that burden themselves with it shall be cut in pieces, though all the people of the earth be gathered together against it" (12:2-3). In that day, God says,

> I will smite every horse with astonishment, and his rider with madness: and I will open mine eyes upon the house of Judah, and will smite every horse of the people with blindness. And the governors of Judah shall say in their heart, The inhabitants of Jerusalem shall be my strength in the Lord of hosts their God. In that day will I make the governors of Judah like an hearth of fire among the wood, and like a torch of fire in a sheaf; and they shall devour all the people round about, on the right hand and on the left: and Jerusalem shall be inhabited again in her own place, even in Jerusalem. [12:4-6]

He goes on about God saving the tents of Judah, defending the inhabitants of Jerusalem, making him that is feeble among them as strong as David, and seeking "to destroy all the nations that come against Jerusalem" (12:7-9). And, God says,

> I will pour upon the house of David, and upon the inhabitants of Jerusalem, the spirit of grace and of supplications: and they shall look upon me whom they have pierced, and they shall mourn for him, as one mourneth for his only son, and shall be in bitterness

for him, as one that is in bitterness for his firstborn. In that day shall there be a great mourning in Jerusalem, as the mourning of Hadadrimmon in the valley of Megiddon. [12:10-11]

Buried in all this is a passage that has been plucked out as a messianic prophecy: "They shall look on him whom they pierced" (John 19:37). Never mind the parts about Jerusalem's vengeful military conquest, which was not exactly in the cards around 33 A.D. when Jerusalem was a powerless occupied territory entirely under the control of the Roman empire.

• God will strike a plague against all the people who have fought against Jerusalem. "Their flesh shall consume away while they stand upon their feet, and their eyes shall consume away in their holes, and their tongue shall consume away in their mouth" (14:12).

6.35 Malachi

• God says he hated Esau (1:3). He's not expressing disappointment, sadness, or even dislike here, just simple hatred.

• Penitent sinners are turned aside: "This is another thing you do: you cover the altar of the Lord with tears, with weeping and with groaning, because he no longer regards the offering or accepts it with favor from your hand" (NASB, 2:13). There's nothing to indicate that Malachi is speaking of any future event, e.g., at the Judgment Day described in the New Testament. No, it seems that Malachi envisions God denying grace to the penitent right in the here and now, which is utterly inconsistent with the "seven times seventy" endless grace of Conservative Laestadianism and Lutheranism.

It is not that inconsistent with the rigorism of Christianity in its first couple of centuries, however, which allowed for at most a single post-baptismal repentance (5.1.2). The epistle to the Hebrews clearly asserts "that, if those who have tasted of the heavenly gift fall away, it is impossible to renew them again unto repentance" (Kirk 1966, 160). "Unfortunately for the Church, the rigorist view of the epistle to the Hebrews predominated for many generations, and poisoned the whole atmosphere of Christian ethics" (p. 165).

• God will send his messenger, who "shall prepare the way before me: and the Lord, whom ye seek, shall suddenly come to his temple, even the messenger of the covenant, whom ye delight in: behold, he shall come, saith the Lord of hosts. But who may abide [NASB, *endure*] the day of his coming? And who shall stand when he appeareth? For he is like a refiner's fire, and like fullers' soap: And he shall sit as a refiner and purifier of silver: and he shall purify the sons of Levi, and purge them as gold and silver, that they may offer unto the Lord an offering in righteousness" (3:1-3).

Malachi clearly views the arrival of this messenger as a fearsome thing, asking rhetorically who will be able to endure the day when he comes, and who will be able to stand when he approaches. Then God will draw near to the people for judgment (3:5), and will consult a "book of remembrance" to identify and spare those who fear him and esteem his name (3:16-17). At that point, the people will once again "discern between the righteous and the wicked, between him that serveth God and him that serveth him not" (3:18).

Matthew 11:10-11 has Jesus referring to the messenger as John the Baptist, a connection also made in Mark 1:2-4. But John the Baptist was an ascetic preacher who emerged from the desert to preach "a baptism of repentance for the forgiveness of sins" (Mark 1:4). No fire and brimstone accompanied his arrival; nobody was struck down with his judgment. Indeed, the Baptist's only recorded rebuke ended in his beheading, hardly a testament to any divine power of judgment (Mark 6:18-28).

7 The New Testament

> *When he was gone forth into the way, there came one running, and kneeled to him, and asked him, Good Master, what shall I do that I may inherit eternal life? And Jesus said unto him, Why callest thou me good? There is none good but one, that is, God.*
>
> *–The Gospel of Mark*

7.1 The Gospels

• Matthew (1:2-17) and Luke (3:23-38) list genealogies of Jesus that are completely different. They diverge shortly after David and only sporadically name the same men until they reach Joseph, whose father and grandfather were "Jacob" and "Matthan," respectively, according to Matthew. According to Luke, Joseph's father was "Heli," his grandfather was "Matthat," and the only mention of "Jacob" is the patriarch son of Isaac.

The genealogies certainly go to a lot of trouble to establish Davidic lineage of a man from whom Jesus took no actual ancestry. The KJV has Luke saying that "Jesus himself began to be about thirty years of age, being (as was supposed) the son of Joseph" (3:23), and Matthew saying that Joseph was "the husband of Mary, of whom was born Jesus, who is called Christ" (1:16). Interestingly, the *Syriac Sinaitic*, a 4th century manuscript, renders Matthew's statement as follows: "Joseph, to whom was betrothed Mary the Virgin, *begat* Jesus, who is called the Christ" (*Old Syriac Gospels*, Agnes Smith Lewis, ed., 1910, emphasis added).

• Luke has Joseph and Mary going to Bethlehem because of a census ordered by Caesar Augustus when Quirinius was governor of Syria. No such census ordered by Augustus appears in any of the meticulous historical records of that time. MacDonald and Porter ask why Augustus would even do so, given that Herod the Great was king and had his own taxes and tax collectors (2000, 120). And it is inconceivable that a man would be required to register not at the city of his birth but at that of his ancient ancestor David from many centuries earlier (Price 2003b, 60). "Why should everyone have had to register for a census in the town of one of his ancestors forty-two generations earlier? There would be millions of ancestors by that time, and the whole empire would have been uprooted" (Loftus 2008, loc. 5478-79).

Then there is the well-documented fact that Quirinius didn't become governor of Syria until 6 A.D., about a decade after the death of Herod the Great, during whose reign both Matthew and Luke say Jesus was born. These are not trivial issues.

• With his Jewish emphasis, Matthew goes to some trouble to establish Jesus as the fulfillment of various Old Testament prophecies. Only in his gospel are we told that Jesus' virgin birth was based on Isaiah ("a virgin shall be with child," 1:23); that Joseph took Mary and Jesus to Egypt, "that it might be fulfilled which was spoken of the Lord by the prophet [Hosea], saying, Out of Egypt have I called my son" (2:15); and that the reason they returned to a city called Nazareth was "that it might be fulfilled which was spoken by the prophets, He shall be called a Nazarene" (2:23).

Problems with the Isaiah reference are discussed in **6.21**. The closest thing the Old Testament has to Matthew's statement about Jesus being a Nazarene is Judges 13:7, but that refers to Samson as a "Nazorean" or "Nazarite," someone who has taken an ascetic vow described in Numbers 6. There is no reference to any town of Nazareth in the Old Testament, nor indeed in *any* Jewish or historical writings until centuries after Christ. Indeed, as Rene Salm **points out** <http://www.nazarethmyth.info/>, there is considerable evidence that Nazareth *did not even exist* until after Jesus' time!

• In Mark 2:25-26, Jesus asks the Pharisees if they had never read about David eating the consecrated bread in the house of God "in the days of Abiathar the high priest," but the part of Scripture to which Jesus referred (1 Sam. 21:1-6) tells of this occurring when Ahimelech was high priest, not Abiathar, who was his father (1 Sam. 23:6, 30:7). Either Mark put the wrong words in Jesus' mouth or Jesus himself got his Bible history wrong. (When Matthew and Luke reproduce this passage in their own gospels, they wisely leave out the identification of the high priest.)

• Contradictions and errors within the Bible are often of a somewhat trivial nature, involving passages that have no spiritual impact. See, for example, the discrepant accounts of how many horse stalls Solomon had (1 Ki 4:26 vs. 2 Chron 9:25) and how many baths the Solomonic temple's molten sea held (1 Ki 7:26 vs. 2 Chron 4:5), discussed in **6.10**. They are useful, though, as a simple way of refuting the bald claim that the Bible is an entirely inerrant and divinely inspired book (**4.3.4**), a claim that has caused me to suffer a great deal of cognitive dissonance over the years because I know it's just not true.

Apologists often protest that it is only the translations and extant manuscripts that could be in error, not the original "word of God" dictated to the Gospel writers themselves. This viewpoint is unfalsifiable, just like the assertion of believers hidden away in the pre-Reformation Catholic church (**5.1**). But it also trivializes God's power, relegating him to the role of a helpless bystander as ancient scribes corrupted his now-inaccessible "pure word," accidentally or otherwise.

One example of a provable error in the New Testament is Jesus' statement that the mustard seed is "less than all the seeds that be in the earth" (Mk 4:31, "smaller than all the seeds that are upon the soil" per NASB); "the least of all seeds" (Mt 13:32, "smaller than all other seeds" per NASB). If your faith rests on the proposition that the Bible is utterly without error, then it will take nothing more than the following image to destroy it:

Another somewhat trivial example is in a contradiction between the Gospels in their narratives about Jesus sending the twelve disciples out two by two. In Mark 6:7-9, he "commanded them that they should take nothing for their journey, save a staff only (NASB, *except a mere staff*); no scrip, no bread, no money in their purse: But be shod with sandals; and not put on two coats." But Matthew 10:9-10 has Jesus telling them to provide "neither gold, nor silver, nor brass in your purses, nor scrip for your journey, neither two coats, neither shoes, nor yet staves (NASB, *not . . . even two coats, or sandals, or a staff*): for the workman is worthy of his meat." In Luke 9:1, Jesus' instruction to them is to take "nothing for your journey, neither staves, nor scrip (NASB, *neither a staff, nor a bag*), neither bread, neither money; neither have two coats apiece."

- As anyone who has ever attended a Sunday School Christmas program knows, Jesus' birth was heralded by angels calling for peace on earth and good will toward men (Luke 2:14). The supposed messianic prophecy in Isaiah 9:6 called him a "Prince of Peace." Yet Jesus says in Mt 10:34, "Think not that I am come to send peace on earth: I came not to send peace, but a sword." Even Luke–the guy who told us about the angels–has Jesus asking, "Suppose ye that I am come to give peace on earth? I tell you, Nay; but rather division" (Lk 12:51).

Origen's solution to this was in the phrase "peace among men of good will," which is how he reads Luke 2:14. (The NASB acknowledges that as the literal translation.) "Origen distinguishes earthly peace, which is not the Lord's, from heavenly peace, which the Lord gives to men of good will" (Lienhardt 1996, 100, n. 11).

- The story of the "thief on the cross" is a regular feature of sermons. God's mercy is so great that even at the very last moment of his life, that most unlikely candidate for salvation was repentant and told he would be joining Jesus in paradise! What is not mentioned is that only Luke tells this story, and in doing so he contradicts what Mark and Matthew both say: "[T]hey that were crucified with him reviled him" (Mk 15:32); "The thieves also, which were crucified with him, cast the same [ridicule] in his teeth" (Mt 27:44).

Another contradiction is Jesus' promise to the repentant criminal that he would be with him in paradise "today" (Lk 23:43). Jesus would actually wind up being detained in the tomb until his recurrection on "the third day" (Lk 24:46). (Actually, it was 1.5 days later, but who's counting?) In Luke 24:51, after appearing to his disciples for the first and only time,

Jesus was carried up into heaven. According to Acts 1:1-12, the resurrected Jesus hung around appearing to the disciples for another forty days before finally ascending to heaven. Whoops–we seem to have just come across yet another contradiction.

At least we can agree that Jesus ascended from Jerusalem, because he told the disciples not to leave the place before being baptized with the Holy Spirit (Acts 1:4-5). It was "when they had come together" that he made a final promise of the Holy Spirit and was then lifted up out of their sight (Acts 1:6-9). Right? No, wait a minute . . . Matthew 28:16 tells us that the "disciples proceeded to Galilee, to the mountain which Jesus had designated" for his last pre-ascension words. Galilee is about 60 miles north of Jerusalem. What about Luke 24:50-51, which says Jesus led them out (from Jerusalem) as far as Bethany (two miles away) and was carried up into heaven from there?

These discrepancies are well known to biblical scholars. "Only Matthew has the account of guards being placed around the tomb. Mark and Matthew have the post-resurrection appearances occur only in Galilee. Luke has the appearances occur only in and around Jerusalem. John has some of both. Luke also adds that Jesus was present for forty more days after the resurrection before he ascended" (White 2005, 105). McDonald and Porter acknowledge the lack of cohesion in the Gospels regarding the resurrection appearances, as well as "the seriousness of the matter" of differences "or the still significant problems in the narratives" (2000, 197). They devote several pages to a sympathetic discussion of the various solutions that have been proposed, but conclude that there "is no indication in the Gospels that harmonization is possible" (p. 201).

After following this rabbit trail of contradictions–just one of hundreds in the Bible–it's easy to understand why preachers dare not venture far from the same few familiar passages. Their memories preserve those passages in splendid isolation from all of these complications, which most of them probably don't even know about. What they *do* know from hundreds of hours of sitting through sermons themselves are the standard doctrinal interpretations that have been passed on from one generation of preachers to the next.[59] Even those preachers who have

---

59. Consider the criticism that the *Apology of the Augsburg Confession* levels against "later writers" who "did not create their own writings, but only, by compiling from the writers before them, transferred these opinions from some books into others. They have exercised no judgment. Just like petty judges they

managed to develop some awareness of the difficulties are probably not overly burdened by thoughts of them when warming the hearts of their audiences with–returning to our original story–a repentant thief's last-minute experience of grace. Sermons are not places for verbal footnotes about biblical particulars, certainly not ones that the faithful are deemed better off not knowing about.

- Mark 5:39-42 and Luke 6:29-30 have Jesus instructing to accept evil treatment unresistingly, "turn the other cheek," give the coat and shirt off your back to one who sues you, and give to everyone who begs. Who actually does this, Conservative Laestadian or otherwise? Certainly none of the Christians Ken Daniels knew as an Evangelical:

> The Bible is silent or ambiguous concerning some of the most vexing moral issues of the day, leading sometimes to bitter disagreement among Christians. There are earnest believers who consider warfare immoral, while others deem it a necessary evil. In a recent nontraditional Sunday school meeting, I asserted that most Christians I know simply do not believe Jesus' teachings on violence and wealth. One responded by claiming he believed Jesus' teachings but that he fell short of practicing them. I countered that no, if he didn't practice them, he probably did not believe them. [Daniels 2010, 178]

He does not criticize the Christian's decision to defend oneself in spite of Jesus' instruction. But we must acknowledge that when we do so, as we inevitably will, we are "cherry picking":

> We decide it's unreasonable to interpret it according to its apparent meaning, so we search for other possible texts to mitigate its implications and settle on an alternative ethic we consider to be both biblical and reasonable. But in so doing, we have violated the unambiguous teachings of Jesus; we have cherry picked the texts we prefer, and we might as well have based our decision in the first place on common sense and reason like an unbeliever, since the text bears so little real weight for us in any case. [p. 179]

---

have silently approved the errors of their superiors, which they have not understood" (Article 12a; McCain 2005, 167).

- Mark, which is now widely accepted as being the earliest of the four gospels, portrays Jesus in considerably more human terms than do the others. According to Mark 6:5, Jesus is unable to do any mighty works in Nazareth except for healing a few sick people, but Matthew 13:58 merely says that Jesus did not do many mighty works there, without leaving any implication that Jesus' power had limits. Mark 3:5 says Jesus "looked round about on" those seeking to accuse him "with anger, being grieved for the hardness of their hearts" before healing a man's withered hand, but Matthew and Luke omit any mention of Jesus' emotions when describing the incident. Only Mark (1:45) says that "Jesus could no more openly enter into" a city after one of his first miracles of cleansing a leper. Only Mark tells us about Jesus restoring sight to a blind man using what was a well-known magical technique of the time (Price 2003b, 136), and not even being fully successful until he had repeated the technique a second time (Mk 8:23-25).

The other synoptics do reproduce Mark's account of Jesus' agonized prayer in Gethsemane, "Abba Father, all things are possible unto thee; take away this cup from me: nevertheless not what I will, but what thou wilt" (Mk 14:36).[60] The latest of the gospels, John, will have none of that human frailty, however. Instead, Jesus asks rhetorically, "What shall I say, 'Father, save me from this hour'? But for this purpose I came to this hour" (Jn 12:27, NASB).

- Matthew 5:18-20, showing an emphasis on the importance of Jewish law not shared by the other gospels, has Jesus warning,

> Till heaven and earth pass, one jot or one tittle shall in no wise pass from the law, till all be fulfilled. Whosoever therefore shall break one of these least commandments, and shall teach men so, he shall be called the least in the kingdom of heaven: but whosoever shall do and teach them, the same shall be called great in the kingdom of heaven. For I say unto you, That except your

---

60. Just how did Mark or anybody else know that, by the way? Perhaps Jesus called the club-wielding mob to a halt after they captured him: "Wait a minute, guys . . . I have to tell my eyewitnesses what just went on back there." I suppose he did have the chance to mention it to the groggy disciples after shaking them awake between prayers. Certainly not the last time, because Judas and the crowd came to Jesus while he was still griping at the disciples about sleeping through his last prayer (Mk 14:43).

righteousness shall exceed the righteousness of the scribes and Pharisees, ye shall in no case enter into the kingdom of heaven.

If you've been going around doing stuff like wearing clothes with mixed fibers or buying them for your kids (Deut 22:11), having sex with your spouse within seven days of menstruation (Lev 15:19-24), or letting your son or someone else's lip off to his parents without being stoned (Deut 21:18-21), watch out!

- Consider Jesus' criticisms in Mt 5:46-47: "[I]f ye love them which love you, what reward have ye? Do not even the publicans the same? And if ye salute (NASB, *greet*) your brethren only, what do ye more than others? Do not even the publicans so" (Mt 5:46-47)? Sadly, the "us versus them" behavior Jesus criticizes, with its conditional and selective love and friendship, seems to be more the norm rather than the exception in Conservative Laestadianism. See **4.2.3** and **4.7.1**.

- In Matthew 7:7-8 (similarly in Lk 11:9-10), Jesus says, "Ask, and it shall be given you; seek, and ye shall find; knock, and it shall be opened unto you: for every one that asketh receiveth; and he that seeketh findeth; and to him that knocketh it shall be opened." But apparently that doesn't apply everywhere: just a couple of verses later in Matthew 7:14, Jesus says of the way that leads unto life, "few there be that find it." And some chapters later, Jesus will say to the disciples that "many prophets and righteous men have desired to see those things which ye see, and have not seen them; and to hear those things which ye hear, and have not heard them" (Mt 13:17; similarly in Lk 10:24).

Many millions of people in this world have sincerely and even painfully sought after God, yet the number of conversions (not births) into Conservative Laestadianism over the past century is probably not more than a few thousand. Over the past few decades in the United States, there have been perhaps a few dozen outsiders who have entered and remained in fellowship. If Jesus' words are taken as applying to everyone, the only way to deal with that reality is to say that those millions are not "truly seeking," as Jim Frantti does in **4.9.3**.

Exposing oneself to information about the spiritual experiences of "unbelievers" is considered unhelpful at best, but this author has done so nonetheless and come across many heartfelt writings of people seeking peace with God. In many cases (see, e.g., the conversion testimonials in **4.2.5**), they found solace in what Conservative

Laestadianism dismisses as "dead faith," and in other cases their search ended in nothing but unanswered prayers for revelation and utter disbelief. Here, for example, are excerpts of some prayers by a "worldly" evangelical who found himself an atheist some years later:

> Father God, take me in your arms just as I would take [our children] in my arms in a time of trouble, and comfort me with words of assurance and love and healing. I know you are my creator. I know beyond a shadow of a doubt that you made me and love me. I ask you to have compassion on me and lead me to the truth. I ask you to search my heart and reveal to me anything that displeases you and that stands in the way of my finding the truth about the Bible. Open up my eyes so I can see my sin as you see it, and give me the courage and strength to put it away. [Daniels 2010, 33]

> Father God, Creator of all things, lover of my soul, have mercy on me, a sinner. How I learn more and more each day of my inadequacy to discern truth by myself! I don't know whether it's because of pride or because for some other reason you've chosen not to reveal yourself to me, at least to the extent I would like. All I know is that I do not have full assurance of the truth, and I submit myself before you now, asking that you will somehow reveal the truth to me and give me confidence that it is indeed the truth. [p. 36]

But remember that, according to Conservative Laestadianism, the hurdle he would need to overcome is inconceivably higher than he could have realized. Even if his anguished prayers had been answered in the manner he had expected, restoring him to his evangelical social circle in Texas, he would be no closer to salvation. Instead, he would need to find someone from a handful of congregations in the United States (the closest organized ones being in Florida and Arizona) who are in a particular branch of the Laestadian revival of the Lutheran version of Protestant Christianity.

• Matthew 11:2 and Luke 7:19-20 have John the Baptist questioning (from prison, where he died) whether Jesus is the one who is to come, or whether John's disciples should look for another. But John himself had baptized Jesus, finding himself unworthy of the task according to Matthew 3:14. According to John 1:29-34, he had introduced Jesus as "the Lamb of God, which taketh away the sin of the world. This is he of whom I said, after me cometh a man which is preferred before me: for he was before me," having seen "the Spirit descending from heaven like a dove, and it abode upon him" and bearing record "that this is the Son of God."

In the June 2010 edition of this book, my conclusion about this was that John would needed to have been either "an amnesiac or an idiot." But that was one of the few points to which I heard a reasonable objection. John simply had doubts, as do most all believers, and in his time of distress wanted assurance about his belief in Jesus. Viewed in that light, John is no different than any believer who attends church on a regular basis to hear the same message of faith assuring him again and again.

- In both Matthew 12:30 and Luke 11:23, Jesus makes the exclusivist statement, "He that is not with me is against me; and he that gathereth not with me scattereth." But in Mark 9:38-40, when John reports that the disciples had forbidden a non-follower from casting out devils in Jesus' name, Jesus rebukes them, saying "Forbid him not: for there is no man which shall do a miracle in my name, that can lightly speak evil of me. For he that is not against us is on our part." Luke 9:49-50 tells the same story, with Jesus saying of the non-follower, "Forbid him not: for he that is not against us is for us."

- In Matthew 12:40, Jesus makes a comparison between his upcoming brief encounter with death and Jonah's time in the fish's belly (see **6.29** for a discussion of that whale of a tale). He says that he, the Son of Man, will be "three days and three nights in the heart of the earth." Well, Good Friday is one night and Holy Saturday is another. Arising Easter Sunday morning, Jesus would have been in the "heart of the earth" two nights, not three, and two days from Friday to Sunday, not three. As with some other issues, this may seem like nit-picking, but the point is directed at those who confidently assert that the Bible is inerrant and who look askance at anyone who dares to question that assertion.

- Mark 7:6-7, copied in Mt 15:7-9, has Jesus calling the Pharisees hypocrites and quoting Isaiah 29:13 as prophesying of them: "This people honoureth me with their lips, but their heart is far from me. Howbeit in vain do they worship me, teaching for doctrines the commandments of men." But that quote is from the Greek Septuagint. Here is how the original Hebrew text reads, as provided by the *Dead Sea Scrolls Bible*:

> Inasmuch as this people draw near to honor me with their mouth and with their lips, but have removed their hearts far from me, and fear of me has been like a human commandment that has been taught them; therefore, see, as for me I am about to do a marvelous work among this people, even a marvelous work and a wonder; and the wisdom of their wise men will perish, and the insights of their prudent men will be hidden. [p. 313]

The original text says nothing about worship, and it does not criticize any teaching of Pharisaic commandments as doctrine. Rather, the people had been taught as a human commandment to have a fear of God. Of course, God himself taught to them to fear him in many other places, with both his direct command (Lev 19:14, "Thou shalt ... fear thy God: I am the Lord") as well as many plagues and massacres.

Besides quoting the text inaccurately, what was the Aramaic-speaking Jesus doing referring to a Greek translation when in discourse with Pharisees in Palestine, who rejected everything about Hellenistic culture including, no doubt, use of its language?

• One of Conservative Laestadianism's favorite passages is Matthew 16:18-20, where Jesus says:

> That thou art Peter, and upon this rock I will build my church; and the gates of hell shall not prevail against it. And I will give unto thee the keys of the kingdom of heaven: and whatsoever thou shalt bind on earth shall be bound in heaven: and whatsoever thou shalt loose on earth shall be loosed in heaven.

Jesus' reference to "this rock" is clearly a pun, and the implications are not funny at all for Protestant Christians who disagree with Catholicism's claim that Peter was the first Pope, alone entrusted with the keys of the kingdom. "'Peter' was not a personal name before Peter was given it as a nickname by Jesus himself. According to the Gospels, this disciple's real name was Simon. But Jesus indicated that he would be the 'rock' (Greek *petros*) on whom the church would be founded" (Ehrman 2011, 66).

Also noteworthy is that the Greek has both a singular and plural form of the personal pronoun, which the KJV's archaic English preserves. When Jesus talked about giving "*thee* the keys," and "whatsoever *thou* shalt" bind or loose, he was addressing Peter alone, not the others who were in hearing of his statement.

For Tertullian, having become a **Montanist** <http://en.wikipedia.org/wiki/Montanism> by the time he wrote *On Modesty*, the keys were a gift that Jesus conferred "personally upon Peter," and even the Church should not "presume that the power of binding and loosing has derived to" it. Doing so would be "subverting and wholly changing the manifest intention of the Lord." He rejected the claim that the bishops of the newly institutionalized Christianity had made on Peter's keys. I'm frankly not sure who Tertullian had in mind as the "spiritual men that this power will correspondently appertain, either to an apostle or else to a prophet," but it was clear who he thought did *not* have the power of the keys: "not the Church which consists of a number of bishops. For the right and arbitrament is the Lord's, not the servant's; God's Himself, not the priest's" (Ch. 21).

Further along in Matthew, the power of binding and loosing is given to the entire body of the twelve disciples (Mt 18:18). It would look awkward to have Jesus explicitly passing out keys after having done so once, but the "binding" and "loosing" language leaves a strong implication that each of the disciples was now getting his own copy. Higher critics believe an unknown author has inserted the second story to diminish Peter's primacy in the first. Following Arlow J. Nau and his book *Peter in Matthew*, Price says it appears that "Mark underwent at least two stages of expansion on its way to becoming canonical Matthew. In the first, Peter is exalted with a view to his successors' authority. In the second, Petrine primacy is undermined, and the authority democratized" (Price 2011). Kirk writes that it "is difficult to say which of the two versions–the apostolic or the Petrine commission– is the more original," and discusses arguments for primacy of each (1966, 152-53).

And what about Mark? *Neither* version appears in that earliest of the Gospels! The source from which Matthew (and Luke) cribbed much of their material *declines to mention* what is the most important of all the New Testament events to the uniqueness of Laestadian doctrine.

• In Mark 9:17-29, we read about Jesus healing casting out "a dumb spirit" whose effects look an awful lot like those of epilepsy. The victim's father says, "[W]heresoever [the spirit] taketh him, he teareth him: and he foameth, and gnasheth with his teeth, and pineth away," and then, right in front of Jesus and the disciples, "the spirit tare him; and he fell on the ground, and wallowed foaming." The problem, like epilepsy, was from childhood. Mark could of course envision no anticonvulsants for Jesus to prescribe or operating rooms to wheel the sufferer into. Instead, Jesus "rebuked the foul spirit, saying unto him, Thou dumb and deaf spirit, I charge thee, come out of him, and enter no more into him," and explained to the disciples afterward, "This kind can come forth by nothing, but by prayer and fasting."

It is never really acknowledged among Conservative Laestadians that this and the other exorcism narratives in the Gospels might not be descriptions of historical facts. The closest I've seen to such an acknowledgment is the statement in the October 2002 *Voice of Zion* (4.3.5) that it "was a *common understanding* at that time that physical sicknesses were caused by sin or evil spirits" (emphasis added). Of course, that is exactly what we do in practice; who gives the slightest thought to their loved one's illness being the result of sin or evil spirits?

And where have all the demons gone? If the Bible is literally true, they should not have disappeared from our modern world merely because we have acquired an understanding of the naturalistic causes of disease. But the demons were very much part of Jesus' world, and he gives no indication that they aren't real. To the contrary, he converses with them, casts them out, and discusses them with his disciples.

People have been trying to recast the exorcisms as something more practical for over a hundred years now. When Ingersoll gave his 1884 *Lecture on Orthodoxy*, it seemed that "the church is now trying to parry, and when they come to the little miracles of the new testament all they say is: 'Christ didn't cast out devils; these men had [epileptic] fits.' He cured fits." Ingersoll was having none of it: "Then I read in another place about the fits talking. Christ held a dialogue with the fits, and the fits told Him his name, and the fits at that time were in a crazy man. And the fits made a contract that they would go out of the man provided they would be permitted to go into swine. How can fits that attack a man take up a residence in swine?"

• Jesus promised the disciples that "if two of you shall agree on earth as touching any thing that they shall ask, it shall be done for them of my Father which is in heaven" (Mt 18:19). After serving on the building committee of my local congregation, I can attest to the fact that this is no longer true. Perhaps only the disciples had the awesome ability to get God to grant their every request by such modestly agreeable petitions, though the text doesn't offer any such disclaimer. And why did Jesus' instruction to those same disciples in the immediately preceding verses get enshrined as the "Church Law of Christ," applicable to believers in the present day?

• In the "little apocalypse" of Mark 13 (copied almost verbatim in Matthew 24), Jesus answers the disciples' question about the destruction of the temple and "what shall be the sign when all these things shall be fulfilled" with a prediction of wars and rumors of wars, earthquakes, famines, persecution, a flight to safety, the sun and moon being darkened, stars falling to earth (It would be entirely plausible to a 1st century author that "the stars shall fall from heaven," Mt 24:29, being just a bunch of little dots in the firmament hovering over the earth) and, finally,

> the Son of man coming in the clouds with great power and glory. And then shall he send his angels, and shall gather together his elect from the four winds, from the uttermost part of the earth to the uttermost part of heaven. [Mk 13:26, copied in Mt 24:30-31]

Of the exact day and hour no man when this will take place, Jesus says no man knows, "no, not the angels which are in heaven, neither the Son, but the Father" (Mk 13:32, copied in Mt 24:36). But, he assures the disciples, "this generation shall not pass, till all these things be done" (Mk 13:30, be fulfilled in Mt 24:34). Apologists have attempted to deal with these verses by redefining the word "generation" (used in both the KJV and NASB) to actually mean have something other than its plain meaning. Once they have squinted piously at the text long enough, the word somehow comes to "mean 'race,' as in 'this race of people will certainly not pass away until all these things have happened.' But that is not the obvious meaning, given the context" (Loftus 2008, loc. 5144). In *The Stars will Fall from Heaven*, Edward Adams says, "It is virtually certain that 'this generation' means the generation living at the time of utterance. The time frame in [Mk 13:30] is thus the lifetime of Jesus' own contemporaries" (from Loftus 2008, loc. 5145-46).

Similarly, Matthew 16:28 has Jesus saying to his disciples, "Verily I say unto you, There be some standing here, which shall not taste of death, till they see the Son of man coming in his kingdom." In Mark 9:1 he says, "till they have seen the kingdom of God come with power," with the phrase, "come in power" being "an apocalyptic code word for the end times" (Stark 2011, 207). In Matthew 10, Jesus sends his twelve apostles disciples out to "the lost sheep of the house of Israel," with instructions not to go to the Gentiles or into any city of the Samaritans, and says to them, "Ye shall not have gone over the cities of Israel, till the Son of man be come."

Well, as we read this nearly a hundred generations later, with everyone who ever stood around Jesus long dead and Christianity almost exclusively residing with Gentiles far beyond the cities of Israel, what are we to make of his words? Deut 18:22 says, "When a prophet speaketh in the name of the Lord, if the thing follow not, nor come to pass, that is the thing which the Lord hath not spoken, but the prophet hath spoken it presumptuously: thou shalt not be afraid of him." Ken Daniels says a "skeptic could hardly ask for a more objective falsification of any religion: the religion's leader prophesies a globally identifiable series of events within a specified time period, but the events do not take place within that time period" (2010, 224).

• Mark 13 is an example of the dependence of Matthew on Mark, which is well known by biblical scholars. Lacking a knowledge of Greek, I came to appreciate just how extensively Matthew copied blocks of Mark's text from a detailed study of Matthew's sources kindly provided by Robert M. Price, *Correcting Matthew* (2007, unpublished).

There's nothing wrong with relying on the work of others, of course, if it's done appropriately. This book is full of quotes from many writers who know a great deal more than I do about various matters I discuss. But where I describe things I've witnessed first-hand, like my experiences attending OALC services (**4.1.6**), I use my own words. It wouldn't make any sense to do otherwise, and that is the problem with how Matthew (and Luke) make use of Mark's words: *They are not giving their own independent testimony as eyewitnesses.*

• Slavishly trying to follow what he thinks the Old Testament was prophesying, Matthew has Jesus simultaneously riding two animals into Jerusalem. Jesus tells the disciples to go "into the village over against you, and straightway ye shall find an ass tied, and a colt with her: loose them, and bring them unto me" (21:2). This took place, Matthew says, to fulfill what was spoken through the prophet: "Rejoice greatly, O daughter of Zion; shout, O daughter of Jerusalem: behold, thy King cometh unto thee: he is just, and having salvation; lowly, and riding upon an ass, and upon a colt the foal of an ass" (Zech 9:9). From modern scholarship about rabbinic reading of Scripture, we now understand that the repeated "ass and colt" language in the Old

Testament text was probably understood as being a poetic form. It meant something along the lines of "mounted on a donkey, yes, a purebred donkey" (Price 2006a, 157). But Matthew interprets that language in the wooden manner of a scribe, preserving everything about the literal text. He has the disciples dutifully do as Jesus commanded, and they "brought the ass, and the colt, and put on them their clothes, and they set him thereon" (21:7).

Luke 30-31 sticks with the language he has gotten from Mark 11:2-3, with a single colt on which no man has ever sat, and no attempt to refer back to any words of prophecy.

- John presents Jesus very differently than the synoptic Gospels, with much more emphasis on his relationship with God the Father and less on details about his life and miracles. It was written decades–some scholars say up to a century–after Jesus' time. That late dating causes scholars to question it more than the synoptics, given the tendency for memories and recollections to grow and become more doctrinally driven with time, and the propensity of ancient scribes to impart what they viewed as pious improvements to the sacred works they copied.

One of the most hauntingly beautiful passages in the book is its seventeenth chapter, in which Jesus speaks his "high priestly prayer" to God immediately before his torment began in Gethsemane. He begins as follows:

> Father, the hour is come; glorify thy Son, that thy Son also may glorify thee: As thou hast given him power over all flesh, that he should give eternal life to as many as thou hast given him. And this is life eternal, that they might know thee the only true God, and Jesus Christ, whom thou hast sent. I have glorified thee on the earth: I have finished the work which thou gavest me to do. And now, O Father, glorify thou me with thine own self with the glory which I had with thee before the world was. I have manifested thy name unto the men which thou gavest me out of the world: thine they were, and thou gavest them me; and they have kept thy word. Now they have known that all things whatsoever thou hast given me are of thee. For I have given unto them the words which thou gavest me; and they have received them, and have known surely that I came out from thee, and they have believed that thou didst send me. I pray for them: I pray not for the world, but for them which thou hast given me; for they are

thine. And all mine are thine, and thine are mine; and I am glorified in them. And now I am no more in the world, but these are in the world, and I come to thee. Holy Father, keep through thine own name those whom thou hast given me, that they may be one, as we are. [Jn 17:1-11]

Many devotional readers and preachers of these words have spent a lifetime being inspired by them without appreciating the doctrinal disputes from which they likely arose, and which would follow in their wake. Conservative Laestadians, for example, almost never read or preach from the Bible in anything other than a devotional sense. "Childlike faith" and a reverence for the text as God's inerrant word make it unseemly to view the books in the way that Bible scholars do–as the products of individual human authors or theological communities immersed in the doctrines and disputes of their time.

And when we "get the bandage of reverence" from our eyes (Ingersoll, *Lecture on Gods*) and read John's words, they come to sound a lot like someone's attempts to correct various viewpoints of God and Jesus that had arisen by the late 1st century. Those lofty words that are attributed to Jesus in John 17:1-11 somehow escaped the attention of the synoptic Gospel writers of decades earlier. He addresses "the only true God" and refers to himself in the third person by name and mode of origin, "Jesus Christ, whom thou hast sent," having "come out from" the Father but having shared his glory "before the world was." In doing so, He asserts himself to be one with the Father in a way that he never did in the Synoptic Gospels. In the whole chapter, the "Johannine idiom and theology is thick enough to cut with a knife" (Price 2003b, 236).

• In the Synoptic Gospels, Jesus celebrates the Passover with his disciples. But in John, the Passover hadn't yet occurred when Jesus is tried before Pilate, who asks the crowd if they want him to release Jesus "at the passover" (18:39) and then hands down his judgment on "the day of Preparation of the Passover" (19:14).

• Matthew 27:5 says Judas became contrite, cast down his blood money in the Temple, and hanged himself. But the account of his death in Acts says nothing about contrition. To the contrary, Judas bought a field "with the reward of iniquity," where "falling headlong, he burst asunder in the midst, and all his bowels gushed out" (1:18). Price considers the phrase "falling headlong" (used by both the KJV and NASB) an attempt to harmonize the version in Acts with Matthew's, "as if Judas had hanged himself with a length of old, rotting kite string that snapped under his weight, and the impact of the fall caused the body to split open." Not only is that far-fetched, he says, "but it will not work even as a harmonization, since the priests buy the field in Matthew, and Judas buys it in Acts" (2003b, 309-10).

- In John 18:20, Jesus says to the high priest, "I spake openly to the world; I ever taught in the synagogue, and in the temple, whither the Jews always resort; and *in secret have I said nothing*" (emphasis added). According to Mark 4:34, however, Jesus expounded on the meaning of his parables "when they were alone." All three Synoptics tell of one case in point, after Jesus told the crowd the parable of the sower, which Mark 4:10 specifies again was "when he was alone" with the disciples. They asked him about the parable. Did Jesus say, "What's wrong with you guys? Can't you understand plain Aramaic?" Nope. He told them they were being let in on the mysteries (*mystery*, singular, in Mark) of the Kingdom that were being kept hidden from the unwashed masses (Mk 4:11; Mt 13:11; Lk 8:10).[61] He then proceeded to explain the parable to them.

This is a pretty bad situation for those who believe the 66 books of the Bible make up the inerrant Word of God with "one completeness" (*By Faith*, 11) and no contradictions (**4.3.4**). If both John and the Synoptics are telling the truth about what happened, *then Jesus did not*. Personally, I would rather call the the Bible a flawed, discrepant collection of competing narratives (which it is) than the alternative, calling Jesus a bald-faced liar, even a violator of the Eight Commandment.

Price believes this is a case of an *intentional* contradiction between John and the Synoptics. The writer of John "rejects the esotericism of Mark and changes the story," which he also did to avoid the "unseemly" stories of Jesus not carrying his own cross and not wanting to go through with his suffering. "For John, there was no private teaching in the Markan, Gnostic sense." (*Gnosis* was secret spiritual knowledge not shared with everybody else.) "Everything is public, though some do not hear because they are not of his flock. Thus within John's retold narrative Jesus is telling the truth" (Price 2011).

---

61. The Revised Standard Version translates the word as "secrets" (*secret*, singular, in Mark), which makes the problem even more apparent. Both the KJV and NASB use the term "mysteries" (and "mystery").

Apart from the issue of an undeniable Bible contradiction, Jesus' words letting the disciples in on the real story sound pretty horrendous to anyone holding out for the idea of a loving God: "Unto you it is given to know the mystery of the kingdom of God: but unto them that are without, all these things are done in parables: That seeing they may see, and not perceive; and hearing they may hear, and not understand; lest at any time they should be converted, and their sins should be forgiven them" (Mk 4:11-12). Jesus *doesn't want* those other people to be converted and have their sins forgiven them? Wasn't that the whole point of his existence? And it sure doesn't sound like the actions of a God (or a redeemer sent by God, if you prefer) who wants everybody to be saved, which the hand-wringing quotes in the "Flirting With Free Will" subsection of **4.9.3** tell us about.

• There's another case where Jesus seems to be at least stretching the truth, and this story is fully contained within a single continuous portion of Scripture, the seventh chapter of John:

> Now the feast of the Jews, the Feast of Booths, was near. Therefore His brothers said to Him, "Leave here and go into Judea, so that Your disciples also may see Your works which You are doing. For no one does anything in secret when he himself seeks to be known publicly. If You do these things, show Yourself to the world." For not even His brothers were believing in Him. So Jesus said to them, "My time is not yet here, but your time is always opportune. The world cannot hate you, but it hates Me because I testify of it, that its deeds are evil. Go up to the feast yourselves; I do not go up to this feast because My time has not yet fully come." Having said these things to them, He stayed in Galilee. But when His brothers had gone up to the feast, then He Himself also went up, not publicly, but as if, in secret. [Jn 7:2-10, NASB]

The KJV translates Jesus' statement in verse 8 as, "Go ye up unto this feast: I go not up *yet* unto this feast: for my time is not yet full come" (emphasis added). Neither option is without merit. Some of the oldest manuscripts include an equivalent to the word "yet" (e.g., *Codex Vaticanus*) but some do not (e.g., *Codex Sinaiticus*). But even with the word "yet" there to soften the blow, it seems clear that Jesus wanted to mislead his brothers.

- This story will be familiar to believers having even a casual acquaintance with the Bible even if its words are different:

> [H]e happened to meet some fishermen engaged in drawing up from the deep their heavily-laden fish-nets. He told them he knew the exact number of the fish they had caught. The surprised fishermen declared that if he was right they would do anything he said. He then ordered them, after counting the fish accurately, to return them alive to the sea, and what is more wonderful, while he stood on the shore, not one of them died, though they had remained out of their natural element quite a little while. [He] then paid the fisher-men the price of their fish, and departed . . .

It is not the account of the resurrected Jesus with the disciples from John 21:4-13, however. It's one of many exploits of Pythagoras, the 6th century B.C. hero of Greece and bane of elementary school geometry students to this day (Iamblichus *Life of Pythagoras* 8). Price cites it as one of many example of the Gospel writers being influenced by the legends of their place and time: "John's version retains unassimilated marks of the Pythagorean original, namely, the fact that the fishermen counted the fish as well as the specific number of them, 153," which turns out to be one of the "triangular" numbers that the followers of Pythagoras deemed sacred (2003b, 158). Price asks,

> Can one really picture these men carrying on inventory as usual if they now realized their crucified master had risen from the dead? "The rest of you fellows go have breakfast with the resurrected Son of God. I'll count the fish." Not likely. The elements of counting the fish makes sense only in the Pythagorean original, where the vegetarian sage's supernormal wisdom enabled him to intuit the exact number. [p. 158]

Sounds pretty fishy to me.

- What is the single most significant event in sacred history for Christians? Undoubtedly the resurrection of Jesus from the dead. And yet this event is only attested to in the Bible, by a few contradictory and problematic passages. As McDonald and Porter write, "It seems fair to say that if Christians wish to affirm faith in the resurrection of Jesus today, they must either do so in opposition to the conclusions of modern historical science or find some other way to confess their faith in the risen Lord, one that will speak responsibly both historically and kerygmatically [as preaching of the Christian gospel]" (2000, 15). Once again, we encounter the faith versus reason dilemma: "If the historian could prove the unique actions of God in history, there would indeed be no need for faith at all (2 Cor 5:7). Yet even though one cannot prove it historically, to deny the resurrection of Jesus is to deny the very heart of the Christian proclamation (1 Cor 15:17)" (p. 16).

Historically, the question can be dismissed by the fact that there are no independent attestations of this event that would be the most astounding occurrence of all time. But there are problems even with reference to the Bible's accounts.

The first of those is by Paul. His references to the recurrection are sparse enough that they can all be listed here:

> For I delivered unto you first of all that which I also received, how that Christ died for our sins according to the scriptures; And that he was buried, and that he rose again the third day according to the scriptures: And that he was seen of Cephas, then of the twelve: After that, he was seen of above five hundred brethren at once; of whom the greater part remain unto this present, but some are fallen asleep. After that, he was seen of James; then of all the apostles. And last of all he was seen of me also, as of one born out of due time. [1 Cor 15:3-8]

> Jesus Christ our Lord ... was made of the seed of David according to the flesh; and declared to be the Son of God with power, according to the spirit of holiness, by the resurrection from the dead ... [Rom 1:3-4]

> [W]e are buried with him by baptism into death: that like as Christ was raised up from the dead by the glory of the Father, even so we also should walk in newness of life. For if we have been planted together in the likeness of his death, we shall be also in the likeness of his resurrection: Knowing this, that our old man is crucified with him, that the body of sin might be destroyed, that henceforth we should not serve sin. For he that is dead is freed from sin. Now if we be dead with Christ, we believe that we shall also live with him: Knowing that Christ being raised from the dead dieth no more; death hath no more dominion over him. [Rom 6:4-9]

> That I may know him, and the power of his resurrection, and the fellowship of his sufferings, being made conformable unto his death; If by any means I might attain unto the resurrection of the dead. [Phil 3:10-11]
>
> Remember that Jesus Christ of the seed of David was raised from the dead according to my gospel . . . [2 Tim 2:8]

There isn't much detail in any of this, and the last of the five references wasn't even written by Paul, in all likelihood. Paul is "the most crucial preacher of Christ's resurrection" but didn't even consider the empty tomb worth mentioning (Loftus 2008, 6273-74).

The first Gospel, Mark, didn't mention *anything* about the resurrection until later scribes saw the glaring omission and added its "**longer ending** <http://en.wikipedia.org/wiki/Mark_16>," Mk 16:9-20.[62] None of the Gospels, even with such scribal additions, actually narrates the resurrection itself! "They do say that Jesus was buried and indicate that on the third day his tomb was empty, but *they do not narrate the account of his actually emerging from the tomb*" (Ehrman 2011, 17, emphasis added). And, as we saw **above**, when the Gospels pick up the story post-resurrection, they differ significantly in what they say.

In addition, the Gospels' statements about the crucifixion and resurrection seem to have been cobbled together from the Old Testament. Price notes that almost all of the narrative of Jesus on the cross, brief as it is, "seems to have come not from eyewitness memory, even indirectly, but rather from Scripture exegesis" (2003b, 321). He then outlines the crucifixion step by step alongside the Old Testament sources, mostly Psalm 22, and asks pointedly what we are to "make of this very strange circumstance, that no memory of the central saving event of the Christian religion survived" from any original eyewitness testimony? As a result, "when someone first ventured to tell the story of the crucifixion of the Savior, the only building blocks available for the

---

62. The earliest manuscripts end at Mark 16:8 with the jarring conclusion that the women did not say "any thing to any man; for they were afraid," despite having been commanded by the angelic young man at the tomb to tell the disciples about the resurrected Jesus. Most New Testament scholars now "recognize that Mark 16:9-20 is a late addition to the Gospel," though "not all agree that 16:8 was the original ending of Mark" (McDonald and Porter 2000, 290).

task were various Scripture texts" that were rewritten to fit the occasion (p. 322).

7.2 Acts

• Paul's encounter with Ananias is a key biblical event for Conservative Laestadians. A 2009 *Voice of Zion* article quoted in **4.2.5** asserts the doctrinal position that the encounter represented Paul's conversion by a personal proclamation of the Gospel: "Ananias laid his hands on Saul and preached the gospel, and Saul was immediately filled with the Holy Ghost and received his sight. Not only did Saul receive his physical sight, but he also received spiritual sight." But none of the accounts of the event in Acts say that Ananias "preached the gospel." Instead, they state:

> [Ananias] putting his hands on him said, Brother Saul, the Lord, even Jesus, that appeared unto thee in the way as thou camest, hath sent me, that thou mightest receive thy sight, and be filled with the Holy Ghost. And immediately there fell from his eyes as it had been scales: and he received sight forthwith, and arose, and was baptized. [9:17]

> [Paul recalled, Ananias c]ame unto me, and stood, and said unto me, Brother Saul, receive thy sight. And the same hour I looked up upon him. And he said, The God of our fathers hath chosen thee, that thou shouldest know his will, and see that Just One, and shouldest hear the voice of his mouth. For thou shalt be his witness unto all men of what thou hast seen and heard. And now why tarriest thou? Arise, and be baptized, and wash away thy sins, calling on the name of the Lord. [22:13-16]

Why didn't the writer of Acts go ahead and state that Paul received the forgiveness of his sins by the proclamation of Ananias? It is not, after all, an insignificant issue. Instead, Paul experienced a physical "laying on of hands" that is practiced not so much in Conservative Laestadianism, but in charismatic churches "of this world." And note that Ananias instructed him, "be baptized, and wash away thy sins," tying the actual forgiveness of Paul's sins to baptism and implying that it had not yet occurred when Ananias laid hands on him and proclaimed the restoration of his sight.

Paul doesn't even mention any meeting with Ananias at all in his cursory recollections of his conversion. Indeed, in Gal 1:11-12, he *denies* that the gospel he has preached *is something he received from man or was taught*, but rather he received it by the revelation of Jesus Christ. As important as personal absolution was to Luther for caretaking of the conscience, he makes no apology for the plain meaning of this text in his 1535 *Commentary on the Epistle to the Galatians*:

> Paul received his Gospel on the way to Damascus when Christ appeared to him. "Arise," said Christ to Paul, "and go into the city, and it shall be told thee what thou must do." Christ did not send Paul into the city to learn the Gospel from Ananias. Ananias was only to baptize Paul, to lay his hands on Paul, to commit the ministry of the Word unto Paul, and to recommend him to the Church. Ananias recognized his limited assignment when he said to Paul: "Brother Saul, the Lord, even Jesus, that appeared unto thee in the way as thou camest, hath sent me, that thou mightest receive thy sight, and be filled with the Holy Ghost." Paul did not receive instruction from Ananias. Paul had already been called, enlightened, and taught by Christ in the road. His contact with Ananias was merely a testimonial to the fact that Paul had been called by Christ to preach the Gospel. [from Graebner, Ch. 1]

- Ehrman discusses a number of differences between how Acts describes Paul's post-conversion activities and Paul's own writings about them in Galatians. "Acts is quite clear that Peter realized, even before Paul did, that it was a good and right thing to share meals with Gentiles who did not keep kosher." But "in Galatians 2 *this is precisely what Peter refuses to do* when Jewish 'brothers' show up in town" (2011, 204, emphasis added).

Paul stresses in Gal 1:15-19 that, "after the vision of Christ that converted him, he did not even go to Jerusalem to talk with the apostles. He went away into Arabia, then back to Damascus, and did not go to Jerusalem for another three years." Did Paul stay away from Jerusalem, as he himself says in Galatians, "or did he go there first thing, as Acts says?" (p. 205).

The discrepancies between how Acts portrays Paul and Paul's own writings "involve just about every aspect of the historical Paul." There are discrepancies at "just about every point where it is possible to check what Acts says about Paul with what Paul says about himself in his authentic letters." Ehrman thus concludes that "Acts was probably not written by one of Paul's traveling companions" (p. 208).

7.3 Romans

- One of the foundational ideas of Christianity is set forth in Romans 5:12-19:

> Wherefore, as by one man sin entered into the world, and death by sin; and so death passed upon all men, for that all have sinned: (For until the law sin was in the world: but sin is not imputed when there is no law. Nevertheless death reigned from Adam to Moses, even over them that had not sinned after the similitude of Adam's transgression, who is the figure of him that was to come. But not as the offence, so also is the free gift. For if through the offence of one many be dead, much more the grace of God, and the gift by grace, which is by one man, Jesus Christ, hath abounded unto many.... For if by one man's offence death reigned by one; much more they which receive abundance of grace and of the gift of righteousness shall reign in life by one, Jesus Christ.) Therefore as by the offence of one judgment came upon all men to condemnation; even so by the righteousness of one the free gift came upon all men unto justification of life. For as by one man's disobedience many were made sinners, so by the obedience of one shall many be made righteous.

Paul makes the same basic point in 1 Corinthians 15:21: "For since by man came death, by man came also the resurrection of the dead. For as in Adam all die, even so in Christ shall all be made alive."

As discussed in **4.3.1** (Creation and the Fall of Man) and **4.3.2** (Noah and the Ark), I no longer attempt to disregard the overwhelming evidence against a first pair of humans popping into a paradisaical existence and playing out the drama of the Fall of Mankind. Conservative Laestadian preachers and authors are largely oblivious to or in denial about that evidence, at least in the LLC. Until very recently, there seemed to be references to Adam and Eve and the Fall in nearly every new issue of the *Voice of Zion* and every sermon in my local LLC congregation.

Yes, I understand that the very purpose of Christianity is to justify "sin-fallen mankind." But the evidence is overwhelming that there was no first pair of humans who could have popped into a paradisaical existence and played out the drama of the Fall of Mankind. Sorry, but *it just didn't happen.* It is not a question of faith being the evidence of things not seen (Heb 11:1). It is a question of willfully discarding a mountain of evidence–from anthropology, paleontology, zoology, archeology, and now molecular biology–that is right before our eyes if we choose to look.

- When Paul wrote, "The word is nigh thee, even in thy mouth, and in thy heart: that is, the word of faith, which we preach," he assured his reader that "if thou shalt confess with thy mouth the Lord Jesus, and shalt believe in thine heart that God hath raised him from the dead, thou shalt be saved" (10:8-9). Nothing other than these two conditions is mentioned.

At times Luther presented the matter with equal simplicity. "[W]hoever hears the Gospel, and believes thereon, and is baptized, he is called and saved," he wrote in *The Epistles of St. Peter and St. Jude Preached and Explained* (The Second Epistle General of St. Peter, Ch. 1). Later in the same chapter, he wrote that "the Gospel is nothing else than the preaching of Christ," and said, "This is God's word–even the Gospel– that we are ransomed by Christ from death, sin and hell: whoever hears that, he has this light and has kindled this lamp in his heart, even that by which we may see the one that enlightens us, and teaches us whatever we should know."[63]

Why, then, are the millions of "worldly" Christians, who both confess Jesus with their mouths and fervently believe in their hearts that God raised him from the dead, headed for eternal torture? The answer might be that "the word of faith" that Paul preached included the Laestadian-style proclamation of the forgiveness of sins, and the hearers could be saved from confessing and believing in the risen Jesus only after receiving that "gospel." So, why didn't Paul bother to explain such a significant caveat, instead of allowing readers for thousands of years to remain blissfully ignorant that their Christian confession and belief isn't really going to be enough to save them?

One might also try to explain away this passage (and others like it, e.g., Psalms 145:18-20) as being directed to a specific place and time. But then

---

63. It must be noted that Luther was not immune to adding his own conditions for salvation, as when he condemned Zwingli for disagreeing with him about the Real Presence (see **5.3**).

we would be making the very same kind of statement that Uljas criticizes as being unacceptable if we hold the Bible to be the Word of God, namely "that the Bible does not need to be interpreted so literally, nor do its teachings hold any longer" (**4.3.4**).

• Paul continues his discourse in Rom 10 about belief in and confession of Jesus by saying that

> with the heart man believeth unto righteousness; and with the mouth confession is made unto salvation. For the scripture saith, Whosoever believeth on him shall not be ashamed. For there is no difference between the Jew and the Greek: for the same Lord over all is rich unto all that call upon him. For whosoever shall call upon the name of the Lord shall be saved. How then shall they call on him in whom they have not believed? and how shall they believe in him of whom they have not heard? and how shall they hear without a preacher? And how shall they preach, except they be sent? as it is written, How beautiful are the feet of them that preach the gospel of peace, and bring glad tidings of good things! But they have not all obeyed the gospel. For Esaias saith, Lord, who hath believed our report? So then faith cometh by hearing, and hearing by the word of God. [10:10-17]

Conservatives often quote verses 14 ("how shall they believe in him of whom they have not heard" and 17 ("faith cometh by hearing") in support of the doctrine that one can only enter "living faith" by hearing the proclamation of the forgiveness of sins. But Paul mentions nothing about any special proclamation to be heard nor of any special group of people from whom it is to be heard. Read the passage again in its context and plain meaning. Paul is discussing Jews and the new Greek believers to whom God is equally rich in salvation. His statement is just the self-evident observation that people can't have been expected to believe in something or someone they've never heard of.

• When Paul admonishes everyone to "be subject unto the higher powers," he asserts that "there is no power but of God: the powers that be are ordained of God. Whosoever therefore resisteth the power, resisteth the ordinance of God: and they that resist shall receive to themselves damnation" (13:1-3). What about the American Revolution? The resistance against Nazi occupation and deportation of Jews to death camps? The marches and civil disobedience against racial injustice in the South? Even based on the behavior of the Roman Empire in his own time, Paul is pretty unrealistic in concluding that "rulers are not a terror to good works, but to the evil" (13:3).

It is not just an academic question for me. I have great pride in the memory (alas, only as a figure and not firsthand) of an uncle who refused to serve in the Nazi army and was shot for it. His courageous actions were in sharp contrast to those many Germans whose lack of resistance to Hitler was based in part on what they were taught about Romans 13 by their pastors and the Nazis alike.

7.4 First Epistle to the Corinthians

• Philip A. Harland (2010) says that the earliest information about the historical Jesus is found in Paul's letters, and those references are very scant. (By most accounts, Paul's letters date from *c.* 50 A.D.) Paul makes a brief mention of Jesus' death in 1 Thess 2:15 (blaming the Jews for killing him), but that is widely regarded as something that scribes later added to Paul's words (Long 2005, 184). He mentions Jesus' death and resurrection in 1 Thess 4:14, but as second-hand information to be accepted on faith: "For *if we believe that Jesus died and rose again*, even so them also which sleep in Jesus will God bring with him" (emphasis added).

According to Harland (whom I quote from Harland 2010), Paul makes three main references to something that Jesus said, all of them in 1 Corinthians. The first is in Chapter 7, concerning the issue of marriage. Paul mostly agrees with the Corinthians who believe that one should not be married in order to follow Jesus, "but he goes into some qualifications. He happens to mention what Jesus taught about divorce, that you shouldn't divorce." Here's the passage in question:

> "And unto the married I command, yet not I, but the Lord, Let not the wife depart from her husband: But and if she depart, let her remain unmarried, or be reconciled to her husband: and let not the husband put away his wife" (1 Cor 7:10).

Harland says the second reference concerns how Paul works with his hands and engages in an occupation to financially support his travels to spread the good news. "Other followers of Jesus who travel around get supported by the people who are joining. What does Paul do? He actually refers to a teaching of Jesus, and that is, that a worker is worthy of pay. He paraphrases something Jesus said. Namely, that Jesus taught that you should be supported financially by the people who you're teaching. And what does Paul say? 'Well, I don't follow that.' So one of the few times when Paul refers to a saying of Jesus," Paul actually does something different than what Jesus said:

> "Do ye not know that they which minister about holy things live of the things of the temple? And they which wait at the altar are partakers with the altar? Even so hath the Lord ordained that they which preach the gospel should live of the gospel. But I have used none of these things: neither have I written these things, that it should be so done unto me: for it were better for me to die, than that any man should make my glorying void" (1 Cor 9:13-15).

The "final reference Paul makes to Jesus is concerning the Eucharist," Harland concludes, is 1 Cor 11:23-26:

> "For I have received of the Lord that which also I delivered unto you, That the Lord Jesus the same night in which he was betrayed took bread: And when he had given thanks, he brake it, and said, Take, eat: this is my body, which is broken for you: this do in remembrance of me. After the same manner also he took the cup, when he had supped, saying, This cup is the new testament in my blood: this do ye, as oft as ye drink it, in remembrance of me. For as often as ye eat this bread, and drink this cup, ye do shew the Lord's death till he come."

Paul's writings, including his description in Gal 2 about a meeting with Peter and James who were supposedly Jesus' disciples and close friends, tell us almost nothing about Jesus. Surely Paul would have known how much his audience would have wanted to hear about "Jesus' divine birth, teachings, miracles, exorcisms, crucifixion, and resurrection," and "we should consequently question why he exercises this stunning silence" (Long 2005, 185).

• A note to all married men who believe the Bible is inerrant and not limited to any particular place or time: Hands off your wives! Paul says "the time is short: it remaineth, that both *they that have wives be as though they had none*; and they that weep, as though they wept not" (7:29-30, emphasis added).

• Paul says every woman who prays or prophesies with her head uncovered disgraces her head (11:5), and asks rhetorically, "is it comely that a woman pray unto God uncovered?" (11:13). This is almost completely ignored now.

• Contrary to Jesus' statement that one must become as a little child and the emphasis on "childlike faith," Paul writes, "When I was a child, I spake as a child, I understood as a child, I thought as a child: but when I became a man, I put away childish things" (13:11). He urges his brethren to "be not children in understanding: howbeit in malice be ye children, but in understanding be men" (14:20). Similarly, the writer of Ephesians said he and his readers should "henceforth be no more children, tossed to and fro, and carried about with every wind of doctrine" (4:14).

• Another passage about women that is almost completely ignored is the admonition for them to

> keep silence in the churches: for it is not permitted unto them to speak; but they are commanded to be under obedience, as also saith the law. And if they will learn any thing, let them ask their husbands at home: for it is a shame for women to speak in the church. [14:34-35]

These sentiments are echoed in 1 Tim 2:11:

> Let the woman learn in silence with all subjection. But I suffer not a woman to teach, nor to usurp authority over the man, but to be in silence. For Adam was first formed, then Eve. And Adam was not deceived, but the woman being deceived was in the transgression. Notwithstanding she shall be saved in childbearing, if they continue in faith and charity and holiness with sobriety.

In modern-day Conservative Laestadianism, women do not serve as preachers, but they are used as Bible class leaders in some congregations, Sunday School teachers, and are not inhibited anywhere from speaking freely in church discussions. Apparently, the same sort of thing happens in the fundamentalist Churches of Christ where, at a

> Wednesday night Bible study service, you might have a problem getting a word in edgewise between all the questions and comments typically made by women. However, Bible study on Wednesday night is not really an official worship service; therefore, women are permitted to speak. The same argument is

used for Sunday school classes, which women frequently teach. Wouldn't we all like to see the verses that make that distinction? [Simpson 2009, 222]

Personally, I find the statement of 1 Tim 2 distasteful and ill-founded, being based on an ancient myth that subjugates women as secondary creations. It also should be remembered that neither epistle to "Timothy" (nor the one to "Titus") was the writing of Paul. Those epistles were, to put it bluntly, later forgeries written in Paul's name to correct "pastoral" issues encountered as the primitive "house church" matured. Women of the ancient world had considerable authority over what happened in their own homes, presumably including the holding of church services there (White 2005, 184). Their voices were not welcome as men jockeyed for positions of leadership in an increasingly hierarchical institution.

It seems silly and unjust to treat half the population as second-class citizens, and the activities of women in the church today (especially in the SRK) indicates a widespread unspoken agreement on that point. But those who consider the Bible inerrant and not bound to place or time are themselves in a bind about how to treat women as equals if they are inclined to do so. How do they go about disregarding certain parts of Scripture that have become socially uncomfortable?

• Speaking rhetorically of one who would doubt the resurrection, Paul says "Thou fool, that which thou sowest is not quickened, except it die" (15:36). Oops. In Matthew 5:22, Jesus warns that "whosoever shall say, Thou fool, shall be in danger of hell fire" (5:22). Well, Paul is in good company, at least. Jesus himself called the scribes and Pharisees "Ye fools and blind" in Matthew 23:17 and 23:19, the same book in which he made that warning.

7.5 Galatians

• Paul lists "works of the flesh" that include not just clearly unchristian behavior of sexual immorality, drunkenness, and murder, but also emnities (i.e., making enemies), strife, jealousy, outbursts of anger, disputes, and dissensions, warning that those who practice such things will not inherit the kingdom of God (5:19-21). Then he describes the "fruit of the Spirit" as "love, joy, peace, longsuffering, gentleness, goodness, faith, meekness, and temperance" (5:22-23). Thus he draws a sharp distinction between those governed by the spirit and those by the flesh.

When Jesus promised his listeners that they would recognize false prophets by their fruits, he offered an analogy of fruitful and unfruitful plants that seems to make a similar distinction:

> Do men gather grapes of thorns, or figs of thistles? Even so every good tree bringeth forth good fruit; but a corrupt tree bringeth forth evil fruit. A good tree cannot bring forth evil fruit, neither can a corrupt tree bring forth good fruit. Every tree that bringeth not forth good fruit is hewn down, and cast into the fire. Wherefore by their fruits ye shall know them. [Mt 7:16-20]

It is painfully obvious that there is no such clear distinction in real life today, nor has there appeared to be one at any point in the long existence of Christianity. You don't need to read much history to realize that many of Paul's "works of the flesh" were all too evident in the Church from very early on. It almost seems like making enemies, causing strife, and engaging in disputes was the everyday business of clerics and theologians. Luther and Laestadius and their claimed successors were certainly no exceptions.

As discussed in **4.2.3** and **4.5.2**, the private behavior of "believers" versus "unbelievers" hasn't exactly been a clear beacon of distinction, either. Luther's own conduct is a source of considerable embarrassment. In 1536, he signed "a document demanding the death penalty for denial of any article in the Apostles' Creed" (Babinski 2003, 43). Early on, he came to the defense of the Jews ("Jesus was himself a Jew") and was pretty understanding of them. But he finally lost patience with their failure to convert and became a vicious anti-semite. I will understand if you decide to pass on reading the awful stuff in his tractate *On the Jews and Their Lies*, but the title ought to give you a pretty good sense of it. After the peasants' rebellion in 1525, he wrote another tellingly titled work, *Against the Robbing and Murdering Hordes of Peasants*. There he asserted that it was not murder to kill a peasant ("Crush them! Cut their throats!"). Many Anabaptists were beheaded with his official approval (Babinski 2003, 57).

The distinction hasn't gotten any clearer. Winell writes about finding that out after being "disappointed with sexist and hypocritical Christians." (Let's disregard for a moment the claim that everybody with whom she ever had contact is equally lost and depraved.) But she found that two new friends involved in an Eastern religion "were just as enthusiastic about their religion as I was about mine. They were happy and loving and delighted with their marriage and I saw more 'fruits of the Spirit' in them than I saw in most Christians" (1993, 37). Harpur "could no longer believe in only one right and true faith" after "seeing the grace and glory of God at work in saintly men and women of other faiths" (2003, 99).

While I do not go so far as Ken Daniels as to deny the existence of the Holy Spirit, I sadly and reluctantly share his

> conviction that every moral unbeliever and every immoral believer is a strike against the notion that the Holy Spirit exists and enables us to lead a life defined by the "fruits of the Spirit" in Galatians 5. If we believe in the role of the Holy Spirit, how do we explain the existence of millions of kind, loving, moral unbelievers in the world, many of whom are better people than the average evangelical Christian who seeks the indwelling of the Spirit? [2010, 190]

- Here are two blatantly contradictory statements:

  1. Bear ye one another's burdens, and so fulfil the law of Christ. For if a man think himself to be something, when he is nothing, he deceiveth himself.

  2. But let every man prove his own work, and then shall he have rejoicing in himself alone, and not in another. For every man shall bear his own burden.

At this point, after seeing all of the contradictions we have encountered so far, you might reluctantly concede that they are both found in the Bible. But in the *very same chapter* of the *very same book*? In fact, the second passage (Gal 6:4-5) immediately follows the first (Gal 6:2-3).

7.6 Colossians

- Paul is supposed to have written to the Colossians, "I rejoice in my sufferings for your sake, and in my flesh I do my share on behalf of His body, which is the church, *in filling up what is lacking in Christ's afflictions*" (1:24, NASB, emphasis added). This is incredible.

The guy is claiming that he, Paul, is suffering in order to complete what Jesus himself did not! It is perhaps the most astounding single passage in the entire Bible. The Old Testament atrocities are plenty shocking, but this statement upends the entire idea of Jesus being the perfect Son of God who obtained the salvation for mankind that man could not.

This, like **John 18:20**, is a case where Conservatives ought to be *glad* the Bible is not inerrant and entirely authentic. With this outrageous assertion being attributed to the leading voice of Protestant Christianity, it might actually be a relief to know that Colossians probably wasn't an authentic Pauline epistle (Ehrman 2011, 112-14).

7.7 *Hebrews*

- Conservative Laestadians are encouraged to always remain in "childlike faith," with the focal point of spiritual life being the regular forgiveness of sins by the proclamation that is equated to the "laying on of hands" (see, e.g., Lauri Hakso's 1965 sermon in **4.6.2**). But the writer of this epistle advocates "leaving the elementary teaching about the Christ." Instead, he says, "let us press on to maturity, not laying again a foundation of repentance from dead works and of faith toward God, of instruction about washings and laying on of hands, and the resurrection of the dead and eternal judgment" (NASB, 6:1-2).

The point is easily missed in a casual reading of the KJV's archaic language, but still evident: "Therefore leaving the principles of the doctrine of Christ, let us go on unto perfection; not laying again the foundation of repentance from dead works, and of faith toward God, of the doctrine of baptisms, and of laying on of hands, and of resurrection of the dead, and of eternal judgment." The "baptisms" ("washings" per NASB) are probably acts of "daily baptism, typical of Judean baptizing sects" (Price 2006a, 937).

- Having arguably disparaged the laying on of hands as being part of an elementary foundation from which we are to mature, the writer goes on to *reject as impossible* the Lutheran idea of forgiveness for repeated sinfulness:

> [I]t is impossible for those who were once enlightened, and have tasted of the heavenly gift, and were made partakers of the Holy Ghost, and have tasted the good word of God, and the powers of the world to come, if they shall fall away, to renew them again

unto repentance; seeing they crucify to themselves the Son of God afresh, and put him to an open shame. [6:4-6]

Constantine apparently took this passage quite seriously, waiting until his deathbed to be baptized so as to avoid "falling away." Luther recognized the difficulties posed by the passage and a similar one in Heb 10:26, which warned that "if we sin wilfully after that we have received the knowledge of the truth, there remaineth no more sacrifice for sins." In his 1522 preface, he wrote that

> there is a hard knot in the fact that in chapters 6 and 10 [Hebrews] flatly denies and forbids to sinners repentance after baptism, and in chapter 12, it says that Esau sought repentance and did not find it. This seems, as it stands, to be against all the Gospels and St. Paul's epistles; and although one might make a gloss on it, the words are so clear that I do not know whether that would be sufficient. [from *PE* 6, 476-77]

7.8 First Epistle of John

• As long as you were a Christian not of the docetic variety,[64] you were fine: "Every spirit that confesseth that Jesus Christ is come in the flesh is of God" (4:2); " Whosoever shall confess that Jesus is the Son of God, God dwelleth in him, and he in God" (4:15); "Whosoever believeth that Jesus is the Christ is born of God" (5:1). How does the exclusivity of Conservative Laestadianism not make a lie of these statements?

• In the KJV, the *Johannine Comma* (5:7) says "there are three that bear record in heaven, the Father, the Word, and the Holy Ghost: and these three are one." But, as discussed in **4.3.5**, that passage is almost certainly inauthentic.

7.9 Revelation

• This is another book that Luther didn't like. In his 1522 preface to it, he said "My spirit cannot abide this book, and for me it is reason enough not to hold it in high regard that Christ is neither taught nor recognized in it" (from Krey 2007, 46).

---

64. Docetism was an early Christian belief that Jesus' brief physical presence on earth was merely an illusion and that he never did "come in the flesh."

- John beheld "a great multitude, which no man could number, of all nations, and kindreds, and people, and tongues" standing before the throne and the Lamb (7:9), or as the NASB puts it, the multitude includes people "from every nation and all tribes and peoples and tongues." These people are "they which came out of great tribulation, and have washed their robes, and made them white in the blood of the Lamb" (7:14).

One would presume from a plain reading of that text that *no* nations or peoples are excluded from having saved individuals in this great multitude, from the highlands of New Guinea to the aborigines of Australia to the Chinese of three thousand years ago. One might try to read a qualification into the text, saying that all those from non-Christian or non-Laestadian countries are just children. But then why does the text refer to them having their own tongues (language groups), coming out of great tribulation, and washing their robes in the blood of the Lamb?

- Standing with the Lamb John saw 144,000 redeemed ones, who are described among other things as virgins who had not defiled themselves with women (14:4). This description was likely written in the midst of, and perhaps even in sympathy with, an anti-sexual viewpoint pervading the early church. Even intercourse between man and wife was discouraged because it and any resultant children would distract from the work to be done before Christ's imminent return to earth.

Various non-canonical but ancient Christian writings attest to this anti-sexual outlook. The *Acts of Thecla*, which was circulating by the 2nd century, has Paul described as "depriving young men of their wives and virgins of their husbands, by saying that 'You will not be raised from the dead unless you remain chaste, abstain from polluting the flesh, and guard your chastity.'" It tells a lurid story of Thecla, a woman who became smitten by Paul, abandoned her fiance, and miraculously survived several unsuccessful attempts to make her a martyr" (Ehrman 2005, 116-21). The *Acts of John*, probably written in the late 2nd century, has John praising "one which refused to be inflamed by filthy lust, to succumb to levity, to be ensnared by thirst after money, or to be betrayed by the strength of the body and anger," and tells a macabre story about a woman named Drusiana who had "separated even from her husband out of piety" and whose body is lusted after even in death (pp. 97 & 99).

The 3rd century *Acts of Thomas* tells the bizarre story of Jesus paying a visit to a newlywed couple who are just about to consummate their marriage and persuading them to "refrain from this filthy intercourse." By doing so, he assures them, they will "become temples holy and pure, being released from afflictions and troubles," and "will not be involved in the cares of life and of children, whose end is destruction." Happily, the young couple "gave themselves over to him and refrained from filthy lust" (pp. 126-27).

Even in the 5th century, the letter of *Pseudo-Titus* opposed sexuality, making a clear reference to the Rev 14:4 passage: "Those then who are not defiled with women [the Lord] calls an angelic host." The letter continues, with a reference to 1 Cor 7:34, "Those who have not abandoned themselves to men, he calls virgins, as the apostle of Christ says: 'The unmarried think day and night on godly things,' i.e., to act properly and to please Him alone, and not to deny by their doings what they have promised in words. Why should a virgin who is already betrothed to Christ be united with a carnal man?" (p. 240).

• The wall of New Jerusalem "had twelve foundations, and in them the names of the twelve apostles of the Lamb" (21:14). What about the Apostle Paul? Apparently he wasn't viewed too highly by the author of Revelation, since "one cannot help but notice the conspicuous absence of Paul's name from the list of apostles" (Price 2006a, 750).

8 Epilogue

> *Our little systems have their day;*
> *They have their day and cease to be:*
> *They are but broken lights of thee,*
> *And thou, O Lord, art more than they.*
>
> —Alfred Lord Tennyson, *In Memoriam A.H.H.*

No Cheating

If you have skipped or been directed to this section of the book without having read the hundreds of pages that precede it, I ask you to stop right now. Please head back to wherever you left off–all the way to the **Introduction** if you haven't been through even that, or at least to **Section 4** where the substantive discussion begins. This Epilogue is as close as I will come to offering summary conclusions about what I have tried to objectively examine in the other 99% of this book. Coming to such conclusions is not something I take lightly, nor should you. Accepting or rejecting any religion, in whole or in part, is a very important personal decision of each individual human being, and it is not something you can delegate to anyone else. Not to preachers of *any* sect or creed, not to family or friends, and certainly not to me.

Of course you will probably decide not to spend thousands of hours researching seemingly every aspect of Conservative Laestadian history, doctrine, and practice, plus Christianity in general, plus the Bible and the very nature of God. To do so and write about it in over 500 pages of painstakingly referenced text required both a good deal of time and a level of interest bordering on obsession. For me it has been a labor driven by love, but also by the mental anguish of being unable to avoid questioning a doctrinal system that demands firm confession of belief, on pain of eternal damnation. When I found little basis for the required convictions beyond the unsupported assertions of others, I looked ever closer, and the project went on and on. Examining this pearl of Conservative Laestadianism was in some sense to cherish and value it. But I also had a very personal need to confront it, to stare down its threats and dismantle–to my own satisfaction at least–its most outrageous claims.

Can you do the same by reading this book? I will dare to claim that in some sense you can. Certainly, you can learn more about Conservative Laestadianism–or Christianity–than it cares to tell you itself. By all means doubt what you read in it. Unlike the God portrayed in Christian sermons, honest authors are not offended by anyone's doubts about what they say, so long as it has actually been *read* and honestly considered.

So read carefully. Click around and evaluate the related material that I link throughout the book. Use the extensive **index** as a way to survey particular topics of interest. Check out some of the 180 or so cited **references**. Read the Bible–entire books of it and not just isolated passages–for yourself, preferably in a faithful but also readable translation like the NASB or RSV that won't put you to sleep after the first page. Get to know some of the people you may have heard caricatured as "blind," "deceived," or "worldly," and see for yourself what they believe and how they live.

I won't presume to tell you what to think. But I will suggest that you *do* think, for yourself, with all the tools that are now available to the inquisitive mind.

Pre-Publication Correspondence

Before publication, I sent a draft of this book to the most prominent representatives of the LLC and the SRK. I enclosed the draft with my wishes that they would seriously review it and correct any factual errors or mischaracterizations that it might contain. I recognized that I would be accused of many things, but didn't want inaccuracy or unfairness to be among them if at all possible.

In an effort to head off what I felt was an inevitable part of any response, I noted up front that it is almost impossible for anyone in this faith to undertake a critical review of it without himself being subject to personal scrutiny. My request was this, if they chose to address my spiritual condition in addition to offering substantive comments about the book: "Please read this book and tell me which of its observations are incompatible with *your* faith. Then tell me how those observations are wrong." I also borrowed a line from the SRK's recent *Päivämies* article apologizing for the excesses of the 1970s: "There must be the ability to encounter facts with openness and honesty, even when the facts are not pleasing to us" (**4.10.2**).

There was a polite initial response that expressed concern about the book's content but also appreciation for my "offering the opportunity for us to review it prior to publication." It also indicated a need to visit with me in person about the book's "general message" and my own struggles in faith. I declined in view of the experience I had already undergone with such a "visit," described in the Introduction (**1.2**). Unfortunately, the church's preferred forum of a face-to-face meeting with elders–wrapped in all the somber sanctity of opening and closing songs and prayer–seems to me like more of a coercive tool for dealing with troublemakers than an opportunity for the objective evaluation of issues.

I asked again that the focus stay on specifics, even though I didn't expect that the LLC and SRK would feel the need to question anything about their doctrine that has been pointed out by some ordinary person, believer or not: "That's not how things are supposed to work, is it? The organization is 'God's Kingdom,' and it is the one that does the instructing, from a position of inerrancy and divine inspiration." But those specifics were

> the whole point of this pre-publication review I am offering. Do I unfairly characterize the LLC or SRK's position about some issue? Does my admittedly imperfect effort to sample the sermons and writings leave out some important aspect of the teachings? Is my comment about some specific statement unnecessarily harsh, where I might make the same point in a more respectful tone?

Conclusion

Two weeks later, I received a response that was thoughtfully written and conveys a deep sense of concern and patient Christian love. It also seems like the end of the road for dialogue with the church about this book, and so I quote it in full with my thoughts interspersed:

> Dear Ed,
>
> On Thursday, January 5, several of us had the opportunity to discuss your e-mail messages and the manuscript of your book. I don't think that anyone has had the opportunity to read the entire manuscript, but all of us did at least read portions of it. [Various brothers] have also seen your e-mails and the manuscript and were involved in the discussion. I am writing to try to convey our thoughts to you.

> As I mentioned in my earlier message, the contents of your book are very troubling to us. You have asked for feedback with regard to inaccuracies and unfair characterizations. We have found such, even with just a partial reading. However, we feel that we are in a situation where we do not have a common ground from which to begin. It seems pointless to address your request given the lack of common ground. It feels a bit like chewing at gnats and swallowing camels.

The contents of this book were troubling to me, too, as they will be to anyone professing a "simple, childlike faith" that turns out to have so many complications. Is part of the problem the way I identify and discuss those complications? If so, I'm left with only the vaguest of assertions and a protest about a lack of "common ground," which is used as an excuse not to provide any details. Yes, even in just the "partial reading" (all that they could manage collectively over the course of *three weeks*), they found inaccuracies and unfair characterizations. But it "seems pointless" to tell me what they are.

One of the claims that we have encountered time and again throughout this book is that some Very Important Thing is hidden, but you'd better believe it's really there. God's stamp of workmanship in creation is so well hidden that completely naturalistic explanations for everything from the Big Bang onward are no longer in serious dispute. God himself went into hiding shortly after he retired from directly conducting the Israelites' military campaigns, thereafter making himself heard only through the voices of those who claimed to speak on his behalf. The Egyptian plagues and the subsequent Exodus, impossibly, left no trace in either the records of the Egyptian scribes or the sands of Sinai. The supposed "believers in the promise" left no trace of proto-Christianity in the pages of the Old Testament, either, with problems plaguing each and every one of the supposed messianic prophecies. Jesus was well hidden, too, with no historical evidence whatsoever of his existence, no records of the astounding miracles that are claimed to have occurred during his life. All we have are a few mutually dependent yet often inconsistent accounts written by devotees decades after the fact.

As we move beyond the Bible, the hide-and-seek game of faith "in things not seen" continues unabated. Christians teaching or practicing absolution? Not until the third century, and then in a sacramental, penitential form that Conservatives would find utterly alien until Luther came along more than a thousand years later. "God's Kingdom" as a distinct sectarian entity? That was something Luther explicitly argued *against*. No such entity that would meet Conservative Laestadian requirements–with its keys to the kingdom busily opening and re-opening the locks of consciences at every turn–materialized until *after* the conversion of the Laestadian founders.

How about the present day? "God's Kingdom" is still almost entirely hidden, with only the tiniest sliver of the humanity that God supposedly wants saved having the slightest awareness of it. Even within the Kingdom, the infallible "Mother" Congregation failed to materialize and stop the 1970s activities that even the SRK now recognizes as having been a mistake. She didn't seem to show up at the initial meetings about child sexual abuse in recent years, either.

Now my alleged errors that were the *very purpose* of offering a pre-publication review have joined this extensive list of hidden things known only to the theologians. I'm not impressed.

> To us, God's Word is our foundation and highest authority, and we examine everything in its light. As Apostle Peter wrote, "We have also a more sure word of prophecy; whereunto ye do well that ye take heed, as unto a light that shineth in a dark place, until the day dawn, and the day star arise in your hearts: knowing this first, that no prophecy of the scripture is of any private interpretation. For the prophecy came not in old time by the will of man: but holy men of God spake as they were moved by the Holy Ghost." (2 Pet. 1:19-21) Apostle Paul wrote to the believers in Ephesus that they "are built upon the foundation of the apostles and prophets, Jesus Christ himself being the chief corner stone." (Eph. 2:20) You would like to examine "the pearl" with the light of reason. We must examine it by the light of God's Word.

The foundation and authority is "God's Word," presumably referring to the King James (or Finnish 1776) Bible, which goes largely unread except for familiar passages that serve as a latticework on which sectarian doctrine has grown and grown. And the church demands to be examined, not "with the light of reason" but by the light of *what it has claimed as its foundation and authority*! The only thing that such an examination could possibly accomplish is demonstrate how closely the chosen authority is being adhered to.

But when your foundation and authority has as many contradictions as the Bible, such adherence is impossible. To follow one passage, you must deviate from its contradictory counterpart. And as this book has amply demonstrated, Conservative Laestadianism encounters doctrinal landmines with even straightforward, uncontroversial passages like

Paul's assertion that you will be saved if you merely confess the Lord Jesus and believe in your heart that God has raised him from the dead (Rom 10:8-9).

The quotation of 2 Peter as the work of the "Apostle Peter" showcases a lack of regard for biblical scholarship at the movement's highest levels: "There is less debate among scholars of the New Testament about the authorship of 2 Peter than for any of the other books sometimes considered forgeries. Whoever wrote 2 Peter, it was not Simon Peter" (Ehrman 2011, 68). It is quite ironic to see a *forged* portion of the Holy Book cited to show the importance of it as an unquestionable authority.

> It feels that the overriding message in your book brings into question the accuracy and validity of God's Word. Some of the issues you raise may be answered or refuted by reason. Others cannot be, and they cannot be understood by reason. They require faith, because in the end we cannot know or understand God or the things of God without faith. It seems to us that if we begin down this path, there is no end. Reason cannot be satisfied. So we do not know where to begin. For that reason, we humbly ask that you relieve us from the task of reviewing your book or offering commentary on it. We also respect your time and feel that this would not work.

Yes, I certainly do question the sixty-six flawed, discrepant books that Christianity has imperfectly translated, creatively edited, bound together in a somber leather cover after centuries of argument about what should be included in it, and labeled as the Word of God. How anyone could read the Bible, or even the summaries of its Old and New Testaments I have provided here, and *not* question it, is entirely beyond my capability to understand. Perhaps the real meaning of its outrages, inaccuracies, and contradictions is yet another Very Important Thing that, alas, must remain hidden from my questioning mind.

Or perhaps, to follow the–ahem–reasoning of the response, that real meaning is something we cannot understand by reason. It is the basis for almost every other issue we ever consider, but in deciding *the most important matter of our lives*, reason is expected to remain silent. I've addressed this in the book (see **4.5.4**), and will not repeat the discussion here except to respond to the next point: Yes, reason *can* be satisfied. It is satisfied in every case where there is sufficient evidence to back up assertions of belief. To claim otherwise seems like an excuse not to shine the light of reason on that which would, embarrassingly, seem all too unreasonable.

> Yet, we carry you as a brother in faith and do not want to leave the matter there. We also feel that you do not want to sever this connection.

No, I do not want to sever this connection with most of the closest friends I have ever known, with the promises of heaven that I have heard repeated Sunday after Sunday since my earliest childhood. I do not want to sit alone with my thoughts in the darkness of sleepless nights, wondering how things could have come to this. An unpopular truth is a cold companion. But it cannot be anything other than truth, no matter how hard we try to persuade it otherwise.

> We sincerely think that the best avenue is an in-person visit. It seems to us that it would allow us to visit openly and freely and to find common ground to approach this matter. In God's Kingdom, we need each other. The love of Christ constrains us to help one another. We all want to be enclosed in the unity and love of God's children. I hope that you, dear brother, could consider this request and that we could work together to find an opportunity for such a visit.

Visiting openly and freely is, unfortunately, the exact opposite of what would occur. I would be sat down in a room full of somber piety with the only two exits being submission and damnation. The unity and love is enclosing, all right, thick enough to squeeze the last gasp of intellectual integrity right out of your mind. Been there, done that. Not doing it again.

> We understand that you felt the need to examine some of the things that were weighing on your mind and heart. However, once this manuscript is distributed, it cannot be recalled. Are you really sure that is what you want to do?

Yes, with the same sense of grim conviction that motivated the Gnostic monks of Nag Hammadi to bury their library of irreplacable works out of reach from the heresy hunters' torches. Knowledge for its own sake, come what may. Yes.

> One other thought that I offer for your consideration is in regard to the use in your manuscript of quotations from sermons. Many of these quotations are lifted out of context from extemporaneous speeches and are then analyzed or characterized in a way that seems unfair. Our speakers recognize and feel the truth of Apostle Paul's words when he wrote to the Corinthians that he did not come to them "with excellency of speech or of wisdom" and that he was with them "in weakness, and in fear, and in much trembling." (1 Cor. 2:1,3) Our words are often weak, especially then when we are speaking extemporaneously. We all must

confess that we understand only in part and see things as if through a dark glass. (1 Cor 13:9,12) We rely on the love and grace and care of God's children when we must serve the congregation in this way.

Wait a minute. Wasn't 2 Peter just quoted as reserving biblical interpretation for "holy men of God" who are moved by the Holy Ghost? (A viewpoint contrary to Luther's, by the way.) And now extemporaneous sermons–the very occasions where the Holy Ghost is appealed to directly, without the editing and reconsidering hand of man–are deemed unworthy of quotation and analysis? The church itself saw fit to transcribe most of the sermons from which I quoted, publishing them alongside its regular articles and as collections in the back of *Voice of Zion* annual editions from the 1970s through the 1990s.

The charge of quoting out of context I simply reject. If the painstaking care and scrutiny I devoted to making this book accurate (with no help from the church's response, I might add) is not self-evident to the reader, then nothing I say will persuade otherwise. And if preachers don't like having certain things quoted, then they should just stop saying them.

> Dear brother, I find it difficult to convey the thoughts of those of us involved in the discussion of your request. All of the brothers expressed their hope that we could convey to you that we carry you in brotherly love and hope for the opportunity to visit with you in the near future.
>
> "Now the God of peace, that brought again from the dead our Lord Jesus, that great shepherd of the sheep, through the blood of the everlasting covenant, make you perfect in every good work to do his will, working in you that which is wellpleasing in his sight, through Jesus Christ; to whom be glory for ever and ever. Amen" (Heb. 13:20,21).
>
> God's Peace.

Thus the LLC graciously concludes, offering carefully chosen words about extending brotherly love while still hoping for the opportunity for that pastoral "visit," a Bible passage that gently hints at the importance of doing the right thing, and–generously–the Laestadian "spiritual acceptance" greeting of "God's Peace." I certainly appreciate the patience and love that these men have shown in the face of what has to be a difficult and perplexing matter for them and the institution they must defend at all costs.

I have a Bible passage of my own to quote in closing, too, from Phillipians 4:8: "Finally, brethren, whatsoever things are true, whatsoever things are honest, whatsoever things are just, whatsoever things are pure, whatsoever things are lovely, whatsoever things are of good report; if there be any virtue, and if there be any praise, think on these things."

These are things on which I have thought for a long time indeed. I've pondered what is *true*–disturbingly but irrefutably true–about the origins of humankind and the flawed nature of the Bible. I've agonized about *honesty* when coming across a seemingly unending parade of doctrinal and scriptural contradictions, of distortions in biblical passages, history, and the beliefs of others. I've searched for a sense of *justice* in the outrages carried out by the cruel, vindictive tribal God of the Old Testament and the eternal torturer God of the New. I've wondered what is *pure* about a doctrine whose single-minded focus on absolution disregards the Laestadian founders who converted without it, Luther who placed it merely alongside the sacraments, his fellow believers who seemed to require it but a few times a year, and the earliest Christians who ignored it entirely. I've found little that is *lovely* in an exclusivism that condemns all but the tiniest sliver of the earth's thoughtful, sincere people of faith to the horrors of damnation, no matter what their creed or the impossibility of their finding the One True alternative. I've seen the *report* on slow and confused responses to child sexual abuse and the 1970s witch hunts, and the grade seems not a good one at all. I've seen more *virtue* and reason for *praise* in individuals who have dared to question the institution–sometimes to the point of personal attack or walking away from a once-cherished faith, or both– than in those who drone on with mindless and endless defenses.

It is impossible to "think on these things" freely and objectively without seeing a crack in the pearl that Conservative Laestadianism proffers as "God's Kingdom." I have dithered at the market stall long enough, stared at the pearl in the eager seller's hand closely enough, listened to his fervent entreaties tolerantly enough. His explanations for the crack are unsatisfactory and, deep down, he knows it. The whole market is littered with pearls of allegedly incomparable value whose flaws are evident to everyone but the equally persuasive sellers of each. What choice is there, finally, but to shake one's head, decline the flawed merchandise with an apologetic smile, and move on? And when one does move on–away from the indignant seller whose offering was declined, past the other stalls and their assembled hawkers and gawkers who haggle and cajole oblivious to everyone else in the market except with sneers and slander, out into the open spaces of one's honest, unforced conclusions–the shouting still rings out in the distance for miles and miles.

References

Sources Cited by Abbreviation

LW: *Luther's Works* ("American Edition"). Edited by Jaroslav Pelikan and Helmut T. Lehmann. 55 vols. St. Louis: Concordia; Philadelphia: Fortress Press, 1955-86.

NASB: New American Standard Bible. 1960-1995. La Habra, CA: The Lockman Foundation.

PE: *Works of Martin Luther* ("Philadelphia Edition"). 6 vols. Philadelphia: Muhlenberg, 1915-43. Reprinted 1982 by Baker Book House Company.

VCW: Laestadius, Lars Levi. *The Voice of One Crying in the Wilderness*, periodical published 1852-1854, book compilation and translation by OALC, 1988.

VOZ: *The Voice of Zion*. Monthly newspaper of the LLC.

WA: *D. Martin Luthers Werke.* Kritische Gesamtausgabe ("Weimarer Ausgabe"). Weimar, 1883-. Author translation after *PE* unless indicated otherwise.

Images

Cover: Used with permission of Carol Selby Price.

Ecuadorian youth: Scanned from a portion of the front page of the March 2011 *Voice of Zion* for purposes of review.

Human races: Downloaded under a Creative Commons license from the Flickr page of "perpetualplum,"
flickr.com/photos/perpetualplum/3864724077.

Chimp family: Downloaded under a Creative Commons license from the Flickr page of "Shiny Things,"
http://www.flickr.com/photos/33389938@N00/2609711377

Laestadianism timeline: Reprinted with permission from Foltz and Yliniemi 2005.

"Tom's Doubts" history lesson: Reprinted with permission from "Pastor Saji" of "St. Thomas the Doubter Church, PCA," thomasthedoubter.com.

Mustard seed and poppy seed jars: Author photo taken 2011.

Fish symbol: Wikipedia, public domain.

Sources for Conservative Laestadian Statements

Alajoki, Elmer. Collected writings and sermons in: Jim Frantti, ed. 1995. *God is Love*. Plymouth, MN: AALC.

Alaranta, Juhani. Presentation given at December 2006 preacher's meeting in Oulu, Finland. Author translation from copy posted at p2.foorumi.info/keskusteluavanhoillislestadiolaisuudesta.

By Faith. 1982. Plymouth, MN: AALC. Originally published as: *Uskon Kautta*. Oulu, Finland: SRK, 1980.

Greetings of Peace. Monthly newspaper of North American Conservative Laestadianism until 1973.

Havas, Väinö. Collected sermons from 1933-1940. Published in *He Entrusted Us with the Word of Reconciliation*. Elmer H. Alajoki and Felix E. Ruomavaara, trans. Minneapolis: Finnish Apostolic Lutheran Congregation of Minneapolis, Minnesota, 1964.

Hepokoski, Warren. 2000. *Lars Levi Laestadius and the Revival in Lapland*. http://users.erols.com/ewheaton/lars/lars.pdf (accessed October 2011).

———. 2002. *The Laestadian Movement: Background Writings and Testimonies*. http://users.erols.com/ewheaton/background/background.pdf (accessed October 2011).

———. 2002. *The Laestadian Movement: Disputes and Divisions 1861-2000*. http://users.erols.com/ewheaton/disputes/disputes.pdf (accessed October 2011).

Hintikka, Matti. 2012. New Year's Eve. *Päivämies*. Oulu, Finland: SRK, January.

Junes, Leena. 2008. God's Creation Work was Pondered in Vantaa. *Päivämies*. Oulu, Finland: SRK, October. Translated by Emerson Beishline.

Jussila, Heikki. 1948. *Kutsujan Armo*. Oulu, Finland: Kirjapaino-OY Kannan Kirjapainossa. English edition: *The Grace of the Caller*. Peter Nevala and John Waaraniemi, trans. Plymouth, MN: AALC, 1989.

Kiviranta, Jorma. 2008. Alussa Jumala loi taivaan ja maan. *Siionin Lähetyslehti*. Oulu, Finland: SRK. No. 1, 12-13.

Korteniemi, Pauli. Historical sermon originally published in *Greetings of Peace* in 1963, transcribed from audio presentation in 1971.

Kulla, Carl A., ed. 1985. *The Streams of Life*. Brush Prairie, WA: Streams of Life Publishers.

———, ed. 1993. *The Continuing Streams of Life*. Brush Prairie, WA: Streams of Life Publishers.

———, ed. 2010. *The New Awakened Laestadians*. Brush Prairie, WA: Streams of Life Publishers.

Laestadian Lutheran Church. 2009. *Christmas in Zion*.

———. *About Us*. llchurch.org/about-us.cfm (accessed Oct. 2011).

———. *How We Believe*. llchurch.org/how-we-believe.cfm (accessed Dec. 2011).

———. Position Statement, 2006.

———. Website, www.llchurch.org (accessed 2011-2012).

———. Christ, the Ransom for Our Sins. laestadianlutheran.org/wounded.html (accessed November 2011).

———. The Bible, God's Word–Christian Faith's Highest Authority. laestadianlutheran.org/rightwrong/bible_gods_word.html (accessed November 2011).

———. Presentations given 1994-2009, available in PDF format at llchurch.org/timely-topics.cfm.

Laestadius, Lars Levi. Sermons, from *www.laestadiustexter.se* unless indicated otherwise.

———. *The Fourth Postilla*. Hancock, MI: Book Concern Printers (OALC), 1985.

Laitinen, Aatu. 1980. English edition: *Memoirs of Early Christianity in Northern Lapland*. Translated by Helmar Peterson. New York Mills: Apostolic Lutheran Church Federation, 1973.

Lampi, Walt. God's Word is Unchanging and Eternal. LLC. llchurch.org/gods-word-unchanging-eternal.cfm (accessed Jan. 2012).

Lepistö, Einari. 1985. *Lammasten askelissa*. Oulu, Finland: SRK. English edition: *In the Footsteps of the Sheep*. Paul Sorvo, trans. Plymouth, MN: LLC, 2002.

Nissilä, Keijo. 2012. Usko ja elämä: Pappeudesta – yhteisestä pappeudesta erityisesti. Päivämies, No. 2. srk.fi/index.php?p=usko_ja_elama_22012 (accessed Jan. 2012). Quotes translated by Emerson Beishline.

Päivämies, Weekly newspaper of the SRK, from translations published in the *Voice of Zion* unless indicated otherwise.

Reinikainen, Erkki. 1969. *Lisää meille uskoa*. Translated as: Nevala, Paul. 1990. *The Storms Will Cease*. Plymouth, MN: AALC.

———. 1986. *Näin on kirjoitettu* (Thus it is Written), SRK, after an anonymous translation.

Saari, Heikki. 1968. *The Measure Is Being Filled*. Apostolic Lutheran Church.

SRK. *History*. srk.fi/index.php?p=history (accessed October 2011).

———. 2006 Summer Services Presentation.

———. 2011. SRK:n historiatyön jatko edellyttää keskustelua. *Päivämies*, Oct. 13, p. 13. Quotes edited from a translation provided by an anonymous correspondent.

Taskila, Lauri. 1961. *Journey of Fiery Trials*. Apostolic Lutheran Church.

Siionin Kevät, Monthly children's newspaper of the SRK, from translations published in the *Voice of Zion* unless indicated otherwise.

Siionin Lähetyslehti, Devotional monthly newspaper of the SRK, from translations published in the *Voice of Zion* unless indicated otherwise.

Uljas, Juhani. 2000. *The Treasure Hidden in a Field*. Translated by LLC.

Waaraniemi, Ray. 2011. The Triune God. Presentation to LLC Ministers and Board Members Meeting, July 2. **llchurch.org/topics/The %20Triune%20God.pdf** (accessed Dec. 2011).

Quoted portions of sermons by Gust Wisuri (1950s), Paul Heideman (1950s), Art Forstie (1971), Peter Nordstrom (1972-1973), Peter Nevala (1981), Jim Frantti (2010), and George Koivukangas (2010) were transcribed by the author from audio recordings. The others were from transcriptions published with annual collections of the *Voice of Zion* unless indicated otherwise.

Other Sources

Abegg, Martin, Jr., Peter Flint, and Eugene Ulrich. 1999. *The Dead Sea Scrolls Bible: The Oldest Known Bible Translated for the First Time into English*. New York: HarperCollins.

Ahonen, Jan. 2012. Lestadiolaisia naispappeja tulossa lisää. *Kotimaa24*, Jan. 16. **kotimaa24.fi/uutiset/kotimaa/7164-lestadiolaisia-naispappeja-tulossa-lisaa**.

Alaranta, Johannes. 2011. Personal communication.

Almquist, Alan. J. and John E. Cronin. 1988. Fact, Fancy, and Myth on Human Evolution. *Current Anthropology* 29, No. 3 (June), 520-22.

Altemeyer, Bob. 2006. *The Authoritarians*. University of Manitoba. Self-published, PDF available at **members.shaw.ca/jeanaltemeyer/drbob/TheAuthoritarians.pdf**.

Althaus, Paul. 1963. *The Theology of Martin Luther*. Translated by Robert C. Schultz. Philadelphia: Fortress Press, 1966.

Armstrong, Karen. 2007. *The Spiral Staircase: My Climb Out of Darkness*. Anchor Books.

Augustine. 2008. *Works of Augustine of Hippo: On Christian Doctrine, The Confessions of Saint Augustine* and *The City of God*. MobileReference (Kindle edition).

Babinski, Edward T. 2003. *Leaving the Fold: Testimonies of Former Fundamentalists*. Amherst, NY: Prometheus Books.

Bachmann, Theodore, E., ed. and trans. 1970. *Word and Sacrament I*, Minneapolis: Fortress Press.

Bagely, William. Reflections on a Christian Experience. In Babinski 2003, 185-92.

Balge, Richard D. 1983. Martin Luther, Augustinian. In Edward C. Fredrich et al., eds. 1983. *Luther Lives: Essays in Commemoration of the 500th Anniversary of Martin Luther's Birth*. Milwaukee, WI: Northwestern Publishing House. Reprint at wlsessays.net/files/BalgeAugustinian.PDF (accessed Jan. 2012).

Barkley, Gary Wayne, trans. 1990. *Origen: Homilies on Leviticus*. Vol. 83 of *The Fathers of the Church: A New Translation*. Washington D.C.: Catholic University of America Press.

Barnhart, Joe. 2003. Fundamentalism as Stage One. In Babinski 2003, 103-7.

Beckmann, Petr. 1976. *A History of Pi*. New York: St. Martin's Press.

BioLogos Foundation. Paul's Adam (Part I). biologos.org/blog/pauls-adam-part-i (accessed November 2011).

Burkhart, B. Le Roy. 1942. The Rise of the Christian Priesthood. *Journal of Religion* 22, No. 2 (Apr.), 187-204.

Burton, Robert. 2008. *On Being Certain: Believing You Are Right Even When You're Not*. New York: St. Martin's Press (Kindle edition).

Capel, Thomas J. 1884. *Confession and Absolution*. Philadelphia: Cunningham & Son.

Coffin, David. 2003. Fundamentalism: A blessing and a Curse. In Babinski 2003, 83-88.

Colenso, John William. 1862. *The Pentateuch and Book of Joshua Critically Examined*. In Babinski 2003, 367-71.

Coyne, Jerry. 2011. How big was the human population bottleneck? Another staple of theology refuted. whyevolutionistrue.wordpress.com/2011/09/18/how-big-was-the-human-population-bottleneck-not-anything-close-to-2 (accessed November 2011).

Cox, Harvey. 2009. *The Future of Faith*. New York: HarperCollins Publishers.

Crouzel, Henri. 1989. *Origen*. Translated by A.S. Worall. New York: Harper and Row (originally published 1985).

Daniels, Ken. 2010. *Why I Believed: Reflections of a Former Missionary*. Self-published.

Darwin, Charles. 1859. *On the Origin of Species by Means of Natural Selection*. London: Murray.

Dennett, Daniel C. 2006. *Breaking the Spell: Religion as a Natural Phenomenon*. New York: Penguin Group.

Domning, Daryl P. 2001. Evolution, Evil and Original Sin. *America: The National Catholic Weekly*. November 12. americamagazine.org/content/article.cfm?article_id=1205 (accessed Nov. 2011).

Ehrman, Bart. 2005. *Lost Scriptures: Books that Did Not Make It into the New Testament*. New York: Oxford University Press.

———. 2008. *God's Problem*. New York: HarperCollins Publishers.

———. 2010. *Jesus, Interrupted*. New York: HarperCollins Publishers.

———. 2011. *Forged: Writing in the Name of God–Why the Bible's Authors Are Not Who We Think They Are*. New York: HarperCollins Publishers.

Evans, Rachel Held. 2010. *Evolving in Monkey Town*. Grand Rapids, MI: Zondervan.

Everett, Daniel L. 2008. *Don't Sleep, There Are Snakes: Life and Language in the Amazonian Jungle*. New York: Pantheon Books.

Foltz, Aila and Miriam Yliniemi, eds. 2005. *A Godly Heritage*. Wolf Lake, MN: Spruce Grove Apostolic Lutheran Church.

FORA.tv. 2009. Great Issues Forum: What Is Religion? fora.tv/2009/11/17/Great_Issues_Forum_What_Is_Religion (accessed Nov. 2011).

Fosdick, Harry E., ed. 1952. *Great Voices of the Reformation*. New York: Random House.

George, Andrew, trans. and ed. 1999. *The Epic of Gilgamesh*. London: Penguin Books.

Graebner, Theodore, trans. 1949. *Commentary on the Epistle to the Galatians by Martin Luther*. Grand Rapids, MI: Zondervan. Accessed at Project Wittenberg website, iclnet.org/pub/resources/text/wittenberg/wittenberg-home.html.

Gritsch, Eric W. 2002. *A History of Lutheranism*. Minneapolis: Fortress Press.

Hallamaa, Hannu and Matthew Parry. 2009. Urbanisation a challenge to conservative Christian group. *Helsinki Times*, Feb. 19. helsinkitimes.fi/htimes/domestic-news/general/5404.html (accessed Dec. 2011).

Harland, Philip. 2010. Podcast series: *The Historical Jesus in Context*. Episode 5.2. philipharland.com.

Harpur, Tom. 2003. Heaven and Hell. In Babinski 2003, 97-100.

Harran, Marilyn J. 1983. *Luther on Conversion: The Early Years*. Ithaca, NY: Cornell University Press.

Harris, Daniel Y. and Slobodan Dan Paich. 1999. Strangers and Friends–Cultural Identity and Community. In *Papers: The Vienna Peace Summit*. Vienna: The Society of Founders of The International Peace University, 4th Annual Conference. Available at danielyharris.com/pdfs/Strangers-Friends-Cultural-Identity-and-Community.pdf (accessed Dec. 2011).

Harris, Sam. 2005. *The End of Faith*. New York: W.W. Norton and Co.

Haught, John F. 2000. God After Darwin: A Theology of Evolution. Boulder, CO: Westview Press.

———. 2010. *Making Sense of Evolution: Darwin, God, and the Drama of Life*. Louisville, KY: Westminster John Knox Press.

Herriot, Peter. 2009. *Religious Fundamentalism: Global, Local and Personal*. London: Psychology Press.

Hemke, Kevin R. 2003. A Little Horse Sense Is Worth a Thousand Inerrant Doctrines. In Babinski 2003, 241-252.

History of Living Christianity in America. 1974. OALC.

Hughes, Rupert. 1924. *Why I Quit Going to Church*. New York: Freethought Press Association. Available at infidels.org/library/historical/rupert_hughes/why_i_quit_going_to_chur ch.html (accessed Nov. 2011).

Hurtig, Johanna. 2011. Personal communication.

Hyers, Conrad. 2003. The Comic Vision. In Babinski 2003, 103-107.

Ijäs, Johannes. 2010. Hautamäki: Nimetön keskustelu on arvotonta. *Kotimaa24*, Oct. 31. kotimaa24.fi/uutiset/kotimaa/679-hautamaki-nimeton-keskustelu-on-arvotonta. Quotes translated by Antti Kaunisto.

———. 2011. Vanhoillislestadiolaiset pyytävät anteeksi hoitokokousten väärinkäytöksiä. *Kotimaa24*, Oct. 10. kotimaa24.fi/uutiset/kotimaa/6305-vanhoillislestadiolaiset-pyytavat-anteeksi-hoitokokousten-vaarinkaytoksia. Translated by Mikko Alasaarela and reprinted by permission.

———. 2012. Tutkija lestadiolaisesta naispapista: Tämä on historiaa! *Kotimaa24*, Jan. 5. kotimaa24.fi/uutiset/kotimaa/7090-tutkija-lestadiolaisesta-naispapista-tama-on-historiaa.

Ingersoll, Robert G. [1833-1899]. All cited lectures and interviews are from *The Complete Lectures and Interviews of Robert G. Ingersoll*. Kindle edition.

James, William. 1902. *The Varieties of Religious Experience*.

Joyce, Katheryn. 2009. *Quiverfull: Inside the Christian Patriarchy Movement*. Boston: Beacon Press.

Kaunisto, Antti. 2011. Personal communication.

Ketola, Mikko. 2010. Apologising for Past Errors: Two Finnish Religious Revival Movements and Their Different Strategies. University of Helsinki / University of London, Institute of Historical Research. The International Historical Congress, Amsterdam (August), 22-28.

Kinnunen, Mauri. 2012. Personal communication.

Kirk, Kenneth E. 1966. *The Vision of God: The Christian Doctrine of the Summum Bonum*. New York: Harper & Row. (Orig. pub. 1931.)

Krey, Philip. 2007. *Luther's Spirituality*. Mahwah, NJ: Paulist Press.

Kulla, Carl A. 2004. *The Journey of an Immigrant Awakening Movement in America*. Self-published.

Lea, Henry Charles. 1896. *A History of Auricular Confession and Indulgences in the Latin Church*. Philadelphia: Lea Brothers & Co., Vol. 1.

Lehtola, John. 2007. A Look at the Schisms in Laestadian History. Master's Thesis, Luther Seminary.

———. 2010. Personal communication.

Leivo, Seppo. 2005. Absolution Introduced "In Jesus' Name and Blood." In Foltz and Yliniemi, 125-34.

Lewis, Kathleen. 2004. *The Church Without a Name*. Self-published.

Lienhard, Joseph T., trans. 1996. *Origen: Homilies on Luke, Fragments on Luke*. Vol. 94 of *The Fathers of the Church: A New Translation*. Washington D.C.: Catholic University of America Press.

Loftus, John W. 2008. *Why I Became an Atheist: A Former Preacher Rejects Christianity*. Amherst, NY: Prometheus Books (Kindle edition).

Lohi, Seppo. 2009. Minä uskon Jumalaan, Isään (I Believe in God the Father). Oripää Summer Services: SRK. Reproduced at freepathways.wordpress.com/2009/07/15/seppo-lohen-perustelut/ (accessed Dec. 2011). Translation provided to the author Dec. 2011 by Antti Samuli Kinnunen.

Long, Jason. 2005. *Biblical Nonsense: A Review of the Bible for Doubting Christians*. iUniverse.

Lull, Timothy F., ed. 2005. *Martin Luther's Basic Theological Writings*. Minneapolis: Fortress Press.

Luther, Martin. 1528. *Confession Concerning Christ's Supper*. In WA, 26, 506. Author translation after Lull 2005, 66.

———. 1529. *Large Catechism* and *Small Catechism*. Author translations from *Triglot Concordia: The Symbolical Books of the Evangelical Lutheran Church*, 1917, after McCain 2005.

———. *Lectures on Genesis*, Vol 1. George V. Schick, trans., 1958. Saint Louis, MO: Concordia Publishing House.

———. *Table Talk*. New Century Books.

———. 1523-1524. *The Epistles of St. Peter and St. Jude Preached and Explained*. Translated by E.H. Gillett, 1859.

———. Translated as: John Lenker. 1909. *Luther's Epistle Sermons: Epiphany, Easter and Pentecost*.

———. Translated as: John Lenker. 1909. *Luther's Epistle Sermons: Trinity Sunday to Advent*.

———. *The Bondage of The Will*. Translated by Henry Cole, 1823.

———. *The Sermons of Martin Luther*. Baker Book House (from e-text scanned and edited by Shane Rosenthal).

Mackall, Joe. 2007. *Plain Secrets: An Outsider Among the Amish*. Boston: Beacon Press.

MacDonald, Dennis Ronald. 2003. From Faith to Faith. In Babinsksi 2003, 109-116.

Marcin, Raymond B. 2008. The Kingdom of God is Within (Among) (in the Midst of) You. American Journal of Biblical Theology, Vol. 9, No. 32. biblicaltheology.com/Research/MarcinR01.pdf (accessed Jan. 2012).

McCain, Paul T. 2005. *Concordia: The Lutheran Confessions*, St. Louis, MO: Concordia Publishing House.

McDonald, Lee M. and Stanley E. Porter. 2000. *Early Christianity and its Sacred Literature*. Peadbody, MA: Hendrickson Publishers.

Mercer, Calvin. 2009. *Slaves to Faith: A Therapist Looks Inside the Fundamentalist Mind*. Westport, CT: Praeger Publishers.

Meyer, Marvin, ed. 2007. *The Nag Hammadi Scriptures*. New York: HarperCollins.

Miller, Kenneth R. 2007. *Finding Darwin's God*. New York: HarperCollins. (Orig. pub. 1999.)

Mohler, Albert, Jr. 2011. False Start? The Controversy Over Adam and Eve Heats Up. albertmohler.com/2011/08/22/false-start-the-controversy-over-adam-and-eve-heats-up (accessed Nov. 2011).

Murray, Alexander. 1993. Confession before 1215. *Transactions of the Royal Historical Society*, Sixth Series, Vol. 3, pp. 51-81.

Myers, David B. 2003. Exclusivism, Eternal Damnation, and the Problem of Evil: A Critique of Craig's Molinist Soteriological Theodicy. *Religious Studies*, Vol. 39, No. 4 (Dec.), 407-19.

Nature. 1998. Vol. 394, No. 6691:313.

Palola, Tuomas. 2000. From a Difficult Peace to Open Battle–American Apostolic Lutheranism from 1884 to 1908. Master's Thesis, Helsinki University. Unpublished English translation by Paul Sorvo (File: *englanniksi.doc*, modified Aug. 26, 2006, 132 pages).

———. 2010. Personal communication.

———. 2011. Personal communication.

Pieti, Bob. *Reconciliation between the First Apostolic Lutheran Church (FALC) and Grace Apostles Lutheran Congregation*. PDF copy obtained in 2009, apparently no longer accessible online.

Potter, Charles Francis. 1951. The Preacher and I. In Babinski 2003, 383-400.

Pulkkinen, Saara-Maria. 2011. SRK:n vuosikokous: Ei naisia johtokuntaan. *Kotimaa24*, Jul. 2. **kotimaa24.fi/uutiset/kotimaa/5586-srkn-vuosikokous-ei-naisia-johtokuntaan**. Translated by Antti Kaunisto.

Price, Robert M. 2003. Beyond Born Again. In Babinski 2003, 145-150.

———. 2003. *The Incredible Shrinking Son of Man: How Reliable Is the Gospel Tradition?* Amherst, NY: Prometheus Books.

———. 2006. *The Pre-Nicene New Testament*. Salt Lake City: Signature Books.

———. 2006. *The Reason-Driven Life*. Amherst, NY: Prometheus Books.

———. 2010. Personal communication.

———. 2011. Personal communication.

———. 2012. Personal communication.

Reed, Robert R. 2001. The Iglesia ni Cristo, 1914-2000. From obscure Phillippine faith to global belief system. Bijdragen tot de Taal-, Land- en Volkenkunde, The Philippines Historical and Social studies 157, No. 3, 561-608. PDF copy from kitlv-journals.nl.

Rittgers, Ronald K. 2004. *The Reformation of the Keys: Confession, Conscience, and Authority in 16th-Century Germany*. Cambridge: Harvard University Press.

Romer, John. 1988. *Testament: The Bible and History*. New York: Henry Holt and Company.

Ruse, Michael. 2010. *Science and Spirituality: Making Room for Faith in the Age of Science*. New York: Cambridge University Press.

Schaff, Philip. 1885. *Ante-Nicene Fathers*. Kindle version: Christian Classics Ethereal Library. Unless otherwise indicated, source for *First Clement*, Ignatius, Barnabus, Justin Martyr, and Irenaeus (Vol. 1); *Shepherd of Hermas*, Tatian, Athenagoras, and Clement of Alexandria (Vol. 2); and Tertullian (Vols. 3 & 4).

Schimmel, Solomon. 2008. *The Tenacity of Unreasonable Beliefs: Fundamentalism and the Fear of Truth*. New York: Oxford University Press.

Simpson, Charles. 2009. *Inside the Churches of Christ*. Bloomington, IN: AuthorHouse.

Sin. Wikia Scratchpad page: scratchpad.wikia.com/wiki/Synnit (accessed Dec. 2011).

Stark, Thom. 2011. *The Human Faces of God*. Eugene, OR: Wipf & Stock.

Stamos, David N. 2003. Why I Am Not a New Apostolic. In Babinski 2003, 337-345.

Tabor, James D. What the Bible Says About Death, Afterlife, and the Future. religiousstudies.uncc.edu/people/jtabor/future.html (accessed Jan. 2012).

Talonen, Jouko. 2005. Laestadianism/Apostolic Lutheranism in North America Today. In Foltz and Yliniemi, 195-210.

Taylor, Arch B. Jr. 2003. The Bible, and What It Means to Me. In Babinski 2003, 153-168.

Taylor, Matthew T., Sr. 2005. *Tent Revival for Agnostics*. Chesapeake, VA: Maximilian Press.

Tavris, Caroll and Elliot Aronson. 2008. *Mistakes Were Made (But Not by Me): Why We Justify Foolish Beliefs, Bad Decisions, and Hurtful Acts*. Orlando, FL: Houghton Mifflin Harcourt.

Teeple, Howard M. 2003. I Started to Be a Minister. In Babinski 2003, 347-57.

The Father's Voice II, OALC.

Till, Farrell. 2003. From Preacher to Skeptic. In Babinski 2003, 293-295.

Torola, Walter. 1987. *Coming of the Lord Draweth Nigh*.

Tucker, Ruth A. 2002. *Walking Away from Faith: Unraveling the Mystery of Belief and Unbelief*. Downers Grove, IL: InterVarsity Press.

Vähäsarja, Irina. 2011. Shedding light on child abuse among the Laestadians. *Helsingin Sanomat* International Edition, April 17. hs.fi/english/article/Shedding+light+on+child+abuse+among+the+Laestadians/1135265532861 (accessed Nov. 2011).

Vauva Discussion Forum. 2010. "Vl:t! Missä päin asut? Mikä on sinun kanta ehkäisyyn?" Posted July 23. vauva.fi/keskustelut/alue/2/viestiketju/1204945/vlt_missa_pain_asut_mika_on_sinun_kanta_ehkaisyyn (accessed Nov. 2011).

Wangberg, Andrew. 1928. *Bible Pioneer Work in Norwegian Lapland*. Hulbert Publishing Co.

Welch, Gina. 2009. *In the Land of Believers: An Outsider's Extraordinary Journey into the Heart of the Evangelical Church*. New York: Henry Holt and Company.

Wells, Spencer. 2006. *Deep Ancestry: The Landmark DNA Quest to Decipher our Distant Past*. Washington D.C.: National Geographic Society.

White, L. Michael. 2005. *From Jesus to Christianity*. New York: HarperCollins.

Wikipedia. See context for embedded hyperlinks, accessed Nov.-Dec. 2011.

Winell, Marlene. 1993. *Leaving the Fold: A Guide for Former Fundamentalists*. Berkeley, CA: Apocryphile Press.

Wilson, Diane. 2002. *Awakening of a Jehovah's Witness: Escape from the Watchtower Society*. Amherst, NY: Prometheus Books.

Worthy, Jack B. 2008. *The Mormon Cult: A Former Missionary Reveals the Secrets of Mormon Mind Control*. Tucson, AZ: See Sharp Press.

Wright, Robert. 2009. *The Evolution of God*. New York: Little, Brown and Company.

YLE News. 2011. Laestadian Women Use Contraception in Secret, Nov. 14. **yle.fi/uutiset/news/2011/11/laestadian_women_use_contraception_in_secret_3024233.html** (accessed Nov. 2011).

Index

abortion 333
   in God's name 606
absolution
   confession and 352, 495, 523
   conversion by 132, 134
   emphasis on 40, 88, 376
      in conversion 129
      Luther and 518, 522
      public proclamations 351
      re numerous behavioral norms 299
      regular usage and 340, 350, 490
      sacraments and 396
   from faith to faith 342
      apostolic succession and 345
   historical basis
      Bible 129, 185, 339, 341, 350, 627
      early Christianity 389, 489
      Laestadianism 336
      Reformation era 185, 351, 357, 518, 519
   Luther on
      from faith to faith 343
      importance 341
      shared teachings 40
   preached by congregation 347
   preached by laymen 148, 341, 488, 502, 503, 531
   problems with 345, 473
   public 295, 344, 346, 350
      from congregation 358
      to unbelievers 348
   sole means of forgiveness 339
      early Christianity and 491
      Laestadian founders and 46, 48, 50, 51, 131
   written 74, 351
absolutism 91, 407
Adam & Eve 154, 255, 288

    as source of human suffering 461
    biblical conflict about 537
    generations from 166
    original sin and 201, 641
    required belief in 15
    Satan and 257
    subjugation of women and 646
    supposed promise of savior to 188
afterlife
    absence in Old Testament 574
    argued against 578
    carrot & stick 441, 560
    promised 437
    Sheol 547, 560, 570
apostolic succession 39, 345, 429, 490
arrogance 229, 414, 468
    of analyzing God 220
    of infallibility claims 142, 471, 481
    of uninformed criticism 70, 144
asceticism 306
atheism 23, 168, 171, 265, 284, 285, 290, 293
authoritarianism 138, 143, 246, 303, 325, 462, 468, 475, 643
baptism 393
    forgiveness of sins by 527, 531, 639
        sole means of 395
    full immersion 99
    reduced to ceremony 396
Bible
    as closed book 214
    as object of worship 199, 201
    authenticity 199, 276, 381, 638, 650, 651, 660
    contradictions 197, 618
        between Old and New Testaments 555, 563, 614, 620
        in Jesus' statements 618, 626, 634
        regarding predestination 449, 595
        regarding unborn children 426
        within New Testament 238, 620, 633, 640, 647, 649
        within Old Testament 537, 544, 551, 560, 565, 580

        distortions of 207, 575
            regarding absolution 212, 272, 340
            regarding divorce 400
            regarding Laestadianism 190
            regarding Satan 254
            regarding sectarianism 90, 643
        failed prophecies in 583, 585, 601, 603, 607, 630
        historical issues 200, 201, 236, 542, 543, 617, 631, 636
        inerrancy 173, 183, 195, 203, 209, 268, 286, 415, 634
            asserted against science 166, 200
            Luther on 160, 197, 650, 651
        literalism 172, 173, 178, 192, 211, 286, 608, 628
            Luther on 165, 169, 416, 417, 514
        oddities 550, 551, 584, 591, 600, 603
        outrages 224, 559, 563, 565, 607, 614
            against chosen people 547, 552, 589, 592
            capital punishment 544, 546, 548, 551
            Conservative Laestadian discussion of 181
            genocide 549, 550, 552, 554, 557, 586, 590, 593, 596, 611
            incest 183
            Paul's claim 649
            sexual assault 549, 587, 594, 599, 605, 611
            slaughter of innocents 427, 594, 606
            slavery 182, 544, 546
        pagan influences on 540, 574, 636
        translation 26, 244, 580, 603, 651
            ambiguities 204, 241
            KJV 13, 627, 650
            manuscript issues 206, 370, 386, 420, 635
            NASB 13
    blasphemy 110, 142, 328, 445, 447, 546
    Bogomils 505
    caricature 70, 101, 109, 271, 442
    change
        acknowledgment of 20, 144, 431
        denial of 224, 268, 428, 430
        imposed from outside 173
        in Conservative lifestyle 314, 317, 357, 405

in racial attitudes 429
regarding evolution 171
regarding false spirits 261
regarding remarriage 399
regarding the real presence 392
regarding women 646
resistance to 125, 168, 427, 464, 480

Church Council 486
Banberg synod 519
Fourth Lateran 490, 499
of Trent 498

Church Fathers 483
citation of 26, 484
Ambrose 493, 498
Apostolic Tradition 497
Athenagoras 333
Augustine 382, 395, 493
Clement of Alexandria 18, 94, 221, 263, 283, 307, 309, 323, 327, 330, 388, 395, 492, 500
Cyprian 390
Epistle of Barnabus 235, 434, 495
First Clement 89, 145, 241, 309, 432, 495
Ignatius 225, 332, 387, 432, 453, 502
Irenaeus 274, 394, 476, 496, 500
Justin Martyr 387, 389, 394, 437, 491, 492, 500
Origen 207, 291, 493, 497, 503, 620
Shepherd of Hermas 491, 499
Tatian 241
Tertullian 312, 333, 382, 395, 432, 500, 628
Theophilus of Antioch 311, 388, 492
conflicts with 489
Luther and 485
Augustine 486

Church Law of Christ 363, 370
coercion 15, 117, 142, 356, 362, 440
cognitive dissonance 180
as doubt 291
mental cost 161, 296

Communion 386
    confession before 352, 390
    forgiveness of sins by 390, 391, 527, 531
    real presence of Christ in 387, 392, 514
confession 352
    of faith 103, 332
    of sins
        by name 355, 360
        complications with 358
        in OALC 62
        Laestadius and 47, 352, 357
        public 358, 496
        Raattamaa and 353
        reduced emphasis on 357
        rejected by IALC 77
        to laity vs. clergy 474, 519, 531
    psychological need for 359
    secrecy of 474
conscience 268, 423
Constantine 650
contraception
    rejection of
        basis for 334, 404, 406, 575
        complications 409, 421
        in all forms 403
    usage among Conservatives 405
cult 11, 25
dating 402
demons
    absence today 251, 629
    in 1970s 258
    Jesus interacting with 628
dissent 116, 145
doctrine
    as object of worship 277, 284
    contradictions 89, 223
    dealing with pedophiles and 473
    deviations from 3

actual practice 264, 622
Church Fathers 394, 489
Laestadian founders 52, 64
Luther 165, 197, 391, 393, 507, 527, 533
New Testament 212, 624, 639, 645, 650
Old Testament 543, 558, 578
previous understandings 63, 128, 431, 474, 475
divisive issues
  law and Christians 263, 266
  Peter's denial of Christ 72, 329
vs. history 39
doubt 149, 255, 291, 611, 625
  acknowledgment of 113
  commonality of 112
  forgiveness of 284, 295, 342, 351
  hidden 15, 296, 325
  personal struggle with 8, 34
  sanitized 295
Ecuador 79, 83, 119, 122, 273, 310
emphasis on
  absolution
    regular usage and 519
end times 432, 611
Estonia 122
evil
  God as source of 559, 589, 598, 613
  problem of 220, 228, 443
    eternal suffering 444
    human suffering 456
evolution 151
  computerized 9
  Ecclesiastes and 578
  Noah story and 178
  theological implications 152
    Adam & Eve 154, 641
    Apostle Paul 155
    omniscience 223
    personal realization of 10, 151

    sin 170, 227
    undeniability of 157, 161, 167
exclusivity 94
    Bible passages against 642, 643, 651, 652
    Luther and 71, 80, 114, 506, 515, 642
    of Conservative Laestadianism 79, 94, 274, 446
        arguments for 87, 177, 204
        Bible passages against 577
        circular argument 71
        cruelty of 83, 127, 442, 446, 642
        diminishment of Holy Spirit 241
        proposed origins of 81
        Raattamaa's viewpoint 82
    of other sects
        FALC 75
        IALC 76
        Iglesia ni Cristo 5
        More Than Conquerors Faith Church 99
        OALC 63
faith
    against evidence 203, 289, 291, 298, 641
    appropriate emphasis of 18, 278
    as devotional luggage cart 282
    as gift 274, 279
        issues with 280
    as mystery 85, 283, 297
    childlike 138, 163, 291, 422, 646, 650
    criticism of 291
    feelings and 55, 279, 295
    living vs. dead 55, 111, 279, 624
    resilience of 292, 297, 446
    vs. reason 86, 288, 407, 608
fatalism 90, 407
fear
    of contrary ideas 14
    of hell 34, 440
    of institutional scrutiny 116, 463
forgiveness

    by absolution only 339
    Conservative Laestadian emphasis on 299
    denial of
        in 1970s 142, 366
        in Bible 558, 614
        in early Christianity 499
    joy of 134, 138, 374
    of false spirits 258
fundamentalism
    and education 286
    Bible reading and 217
    connection to authoritarianism 303
    Conservative Laestadianism as 23, 167, 172
    distinctive features of 214, 225
    education and 290
    eschatology and 436
    intolerance of dissent 73, 468
    outreach and 114, 271
    relations with out-groups 101, 108, 112
    women and 413
Ghana 79, 83, 119, 273
Gnosticism 284, 494, 634
God
    contradictory properties of 220, 443
    cruelty of 456, 460, 592, 595, 596, 600
    cruelty of
        in damnation 444, 448
    deceitfulness of 220, 565, 571
        breaking covenant 612
        if evolution false 154, 157
    human projections of 546
        as jealous husband 594, 599, 605
        by theologians 170, 223, 226, 452, 456
        in Old Testament 218, 221, 224, 540, 548, 549, 557
    omnibenevolence of 225
        issues with 242, 446, 607
        vs. omnipotence 455
    omnipotence of 220, 452, 455

    omniscience of 222, 589, 609
    timelessness of 194, 218, 224
    tribalism and 183, 219, 587, 597
  greeting 69, 662
    denial of 300, 363, 368
    of "heretics" 68, 71, 92
  groupthink 142, 325
  hatred 576, 614
  heaven 437
    in Old Testament 584
  Heideman, A.L. 23, 59, 65
    son Paul and 244, 305, 340
  Heideman, Paul 73, 75, 124, 270, 410
  hell
    absence in Old Testament 3, 229, 441, 547, 560, 605
      examples of 559, 563, 565, 567, 570, 573, 574, 578
      possible counter-example of 571
    Conservative statements about 438
    cruelty of 571
    incompatibility with loving God 116, 228, 230, 242, 439, 453
    levels of 437
    psychological impact of 34, 440, 448
  hiddenness 658
    of absolution
      in Bible 639
      in early Christianity 489, 498, 505
    of archeological evidence 192
    of God 172, 220, 457, 587, 611
      contrary to stated goals 542
    of God's Kingdom 126, 127, 266, 624, 642
    of God's Kingdom
      God and 109, 230, 446, 452, 456, 459
      law and 266
    of miracles 239, 542, 553
    of Mother congregation 249, 477
    of pre-Lutheran believers 483, 487, 505
    of proto-Christianity 184, 189
Holy Spirit 3

honesty 28, 206, 273
hypocrisy 15, 30, 80, 93, 126, 324, 327, 594, 648
indoctrination 24
    avoidance of contrary views 104, 118, 331
    of children 133, 411
    reinforcement of 326, 412
inequality 413, 426, 429, 547
intolerance
    in Old Testament 549, 551, 564, 593
    inherent to religion 114
isolation 3
Jesus
    as advocate 231
    conflicting genealogies of 617
    crucifixion of 232, 638
    deification of 233, 623, 632
    devotional elaboration of 234
    historicity of 200, 236, 644
    Paul and 233, 644
    possible shortcomings of 626, 630, 634, 635, 648
    resurrection of 202
    supposed prophecies of 189, 590
        assertions of 187, 201, 235, 618, 631
        disappointment about 189
        in Daniel 603, 604
        in Ezekiel 601, 602
        in Genesis 160, 188
        in Isaiah 580, 582, 583, 586, 588
        in Micah 609
        in Psalms 573
        in Zechariah 612, 613
joy 105, 138, 373
Judaism 199, 297, 421, 539
    Christianity and 262, 588
    Matthew and 272, 618, 623
keys
    Jesus' gift of 337, 342, 345, 493, 627
        Luther and 523, 524

proclamation of forgiveness 335, 513
Raattamaa and 51
late discovery of 51
Kulla, Carl 63, 69, 74, 93, 267
Laestadius, Lars Levi
as doctrinal father 41
conversion of 46
graphic sermons of 42
mysticism and 53
reluctance about absolution 44, 346
Lapp Mary 46
law 3, 262
ineffectiveness of 265
irrelevance of 268
Laestadius and 42, 335
purpose of 264, 267
secular, obedience to 306, 468, 472, 474
selective appeal to 301
vs. grace as teacher 266
laying on of hands 350
Lot 183, 320, 321, 541
love 34
as fruit of the spirit 69
between believers 105, 244
equated with unity 143, 172
God's 3
asserted 158, 176, 217, 232, 236, 586
issues with 193, 242, 554, 591, 592
Jesus' 231, 234
of enemies 576
of outsiders 77, 380
of the world 193
spiritual concern and 117, 142, 370, 410
Luther, Martin
95 Theses 27
alcohol and 322, 353, 416
as doctrinal father 39
as source 27, 39

conflicts with 39, 144
conversion of 533
on confession 353, 360, 520, 522
on contraception 404, 424
on faith 283
on predestination 447
on reason 287, 288
on women 416
personal shortcomings of 648
Lutheran confessions 27, 60
Melanchthon, Philipp 27, 344
mission work 119
mockery 108, 222
Mother congregation
    1970s emphasis on 246, 368
    infallibility of 246, 480
        refuted 249
    Luther on 80, 249
    resurgence of 249
    veneration of 244
        deification 246
        vs OALC veneration of elders 62
mysticism 3
    disparaged 57
    Laestadius and 53
Noah 15, 173, 286, 540
    contraception and 406, 424
objectivity
    church historians, difficulties 26
    difficulty of 507
    illusion of 470
    in Bible reading 13, 196, 633
    outsider test 7
    sectarian resistance to 94
    vs. devotion 301, 633
omnibenevolence of
    God
        issues with 577

Osiander, Andreas 344, 520
penance 501
Peter's denial of Christ 3
Pietism 62, 67, 128, 266, 372
Pirahã Indians 121, 265
politics 274, 313, 319
polytheism 184, 218
pornography
    in Bible 556, 594, 599
    in books 253, 318
    in Laestadius 42
prayer
    for salvation 128
    forgiveness of sins by 339, 384, 529, 531, 562
    of unbelievers 384, 624
    problems with 230, 382, 385
    public 150, 251, 382
preachers
    ambition discouraged in 147
    compensation for 208, 644
    extemporaneous delivery 146, 382
    humility of 143, 294, 382
    Luther and 148
    selection of 148
    women as 417, 646
predestination 447
    Conservative Laestadianism and 126, 451
        inconsistency regarding 449
    cruelty of 116, 453
    futility and 222, 411, 426, 448
    in marriage 401
    prayer and 127, 385
    unto damnation 580, 585, 635
pride
    as impediment to confession 357
    of biblical characters 566, 571
    rebuke and 368
Raattamaa, Juhani

as doctrinal father 45
   conversion of 48
   differences with Laestadius 336
   discovery of keys 51
   mysticism and 56
   OALC and 64
   on absolution 48, 336
   on confession 353
reason
   Celsus on 291
   disparaged 144, 176, 285
   indispensability of 288
   Luther on 298
   Paul's use of 289
rebuke 142, 362, 475
rejoicing 52, 55, 132
      attributed to false spirit 260
      in IALC 77
      in OALC 62
repentance 3
resentment 364, 367
resurrection
      of humans
            in Old Testament 560, 567, 578, 584
      of Jesus 620, 636, 644
Russia 83, 122, 310, 508
Saari, Heikki 72, 175, 183, 185, 208, 322, 459, 463
sacrifice
      forgiveness of sins by 186
      human 555, 598
      in Old Testament
            pagan basis for 540
            practiced 556, 567
            questioned 589, 610
      Jesus as 225, 234
   Satan 252
      absence in Old Testament 564
      as serpent 159, 257

    deification of 254
    suffering and 460
    trinitarianism of 257
    vs. God 222
  science
    biblical conflicts with 169, 562, 569
      defensiveness and 161
      examples of 176, 179, 545, 586, 608, 619
      God's nature and 576
      inerrancy and 538, 608
      modernism and 628
    miracles and 210, 553
    theological retreat in the face of 165, 171, 201, 430
  sects 23, 198
    Amish 147, 150, 358, 365
    Christian Convention Church 70, 93, 95, 214, 331
    Churches of Christ 96, 110, 125, 281, 331, 646
    Iglesia ni Cristo 3
    Jehovah's Witnesses 90, 104, 141, 206, 247, 296, 331
    Laestadian 58
      awareness of 38
      FALC 71, 241, 329
      Federation (ALC) 68, 266
      IALC 75, 353
      New Awakening 67
      OALC 60, 108, 147, 241, 247, 266
    More Than Conquerors Faith Church 99
    Mormonism 92, 289, 296, 331, 412
    New Apostolic Church 97, 198
Sheol 3
shunning 325, 378
sins
  abortion 333
  alcohol 307, 308, 328, 330, 388
    Bible and 175, 322, 551, 575
    Laestadius and 321
  apostasy 280, 329
  card games 308, 327

contraception 334, 403, 421, 423
cosmetics and jewelry 308, 310
dancing 307, 321, 560
divorce 398
doubts 295
dress 309
drugs 323, 328
entertainment 308, 311
enumerated 299
envy 327, 329
euthenasia 334
gambling 327
hypocrisy 324
idolatry 319
intermarriage 400
labor unions 305
music 306-308, 314, 326
questioning 92, 330
reading material 317
sex 227, 320, 328, 465, 469, 652
    after divorce 399
    homosexuality 320
    masturbation 320
spiritual neglect 411
sports 319, 332
video games 308
vulgarity 330
worldy friends 332
sins unto death 322, 328, 398
    name sins and 361
    theological nuances 268, 329
social aspects
    fellowship 17, 375
    friendship 104, 378
    isolation 101
    marriage 398
        limited possibilities 401
        sanctity of 398

motivation to conform 30, 150, 296, 325
  obligatory motherhood 420
  persecution complex 107
  sin vs. crime 473
  sins as behavioral norms 301
 sources
  Church Fathers 26
  Conservative Laestadian 11, 21
  Luther 27
 Stockholm Syndrome 281, 367, 447
 temptation 104, 139, 370, 377
  as sign of true church 513
  by reason 286
  by Satan 87, 254
  by television 306
  forgiveness of 234
  of Adam & Eve 159
  of contraception 408
  of the last times 434
  sexual 320
  vs. trial 223, 565
 times of visitation 120, 127
 Togo 79, 83, 119, 122, 273, 310
 Trinity 206, 228, 240
 truth 10, 89, 168, 662
  Bible as ultimate 200
  commitment to 18, 27, 298, 661
  disregard for 16, 163
  pillar and ground of 91, 206, 247, 471
  suppression of 203
  vs. theological imperative 73, 157
unity
  1970s emphasis on 141, 209, 246
  altar of 143
  aspirations of 139
  claims of 80, 144, 423, 471
  illusion of 301, 325
  limits to 19, 89, 248

Luther and 509
works 269
   absence of 115, 241, 271, 648
   following faith 270

Manufactured by Amazon.ca
Bolton, ON